The Christ of Cynewulf

A poem in three parts, The advent, The
ascension, and The last judgment

Albert S. Cook

Alpha Editions

This edition published in 2019

ISBN : 9789389450491

Design and Setting By
Alpha Editions
email - alphaedis@gmail.com

THE ALBION SERIES

OF

Anglo-Saxon and Middle English Poetry

J. W. BRIGHT AND G. L. KITTREDGE

GENERAL EDITORS

The Albion Series.

This series will comprise the most important Anglo-Saxon and Middle English poems in editions designed to meet the wants of both the scholar and the student. Each volume will ordinarily contain a single poem, critically edited, and provided with an introduction, notes, and a full glossary.

Ecce lingua Britanniae, quae nil aliud noverat quam barbarum frendere, jamdudum in divinis laudibus Hebraeum coepit Alleluia resonare. Ecce quondam tumidus, jam substratus sanctorum pedibus servit Oceanus, ejusque barbaros motus, quos terreni principes edomare ferro nequiverant, hos pro divina formidine sacerdotum ora simplicibus verbis ligant; et qui catervas pugnantium infidelis nequaquam metuerat, jam nunc fidelis humilium linguas timet. Quia enim perceptis caelestibus verbis, clarescentibus quoque miraculis, virtus ei divinae cognitionis infunditur, ejusdem divinitatis terrore refrenatur, ut prave agere metuat, ac totis desideriis ad aeternitatis gratiam venire concupiscat.

GREGORY THE GREAT, *Moral.* 27. II.

Translation in C. & T. Select
Trans. from OE Prose, p. 28

THE

CHRIST OF CYNEWULF

A Poem in Three Parts

THE ADVENT, THE ASCENSION, AND THE LAST JUDGMENT

EDITED
WITH INTRODUCTION, NOTES, AND GLOSSARY

BY

ALBERT S. COOK

PROFESSOR OF THE ENGLISH LANGUAGE AND LITERATURE
IN YALE UNIVERSITY

GINN AND COMPANY
BOSTON · NEW YORK · CHICAGO · LONDON

TO THE MEMORY OF

Francis James Child

PROFESSOR IN HARVARD COLLEGE FROM 1851 TO 1896

WHOSE MODESTY AND KINDNESS

NO LESS THAN HIS FRUITFUL LABORS IN ENGLISH SCHOLARSHIP

HAVE MADE HIM AN INSPIRATION AND A MODEL

TO HIS YOUNGER COMRADES

THROUGHOUT AMERICA

PREFACE.

My especial interest in the *Christ* dates from the year 1889, when I published in *Modern Language Notes* the discovery that a hymn quoted by Bede constitutes an important source for the Third Part. A little earlier in the same year I had commented on the word *synrust*, occurring in line 1320. In 1896 I published some notes on the *Christ* in the *Festgabe für Eduard Sievers*. Besides, I had interested myself in Cynewulf to the extent of publishing, in the first number of *Anglia* for 1892, an article on the date of the Old English *Elene*. It was not unnatural, therefore, that when the editors of the present series requested a contribution from me, I should designate the *Christ* as my choice. At that time I had made no collections toward an edition, and everything not mentioned above, including my notes in the *Journal of Germanic Philology*, has accordingly been done since the invitation was extended. The discovery of the sources of the First Part was made on March 8 and 9, 1897.

So far as the existing state of English scholarship would allow, I have sought to edit an ancient English classic with some approach to the care which has been bestowed upon certain of the Greek and Roman masterpieces. This has required not only an acquaintance with the labors of my predecessors in the same field, but also some reading in the Fathers, the liturgies, and the hymns of the Church. Where I have been baffled, I have not hesitated to say so frankly, that the future inquirer may the more readily discover the problems that stand in pressing need of solution. Some, I doubt not, are insoluble; but I cannot flatter myself that I have left nothing for my successors to do.

For the readings of the manuscript I have chiefly depended upon Assmann, in the Grein-Wülker *Bibliothek*, upon Gollancz, and upon Schipper. In capitalization and punctuation I have followed my own

judgment.   The Variants make no account of the employment of þ
and ð according to the views of the different editors.   Where an
emendation seemed reasonably certain, I have not hesitated to incor-
porate it into the text, whether it originated with another or with
myself. ' I regret that Cosijn's notes in Vol. 23 of Paul and Braune's
Beiträge reached me too late to enable me to make a consistent use
of them throughout; but in one way or another I have endeavored
to turn them to full account.   A number of changes required, according to Sievers, on metrical grounds, have been recorded in the
Variants, but I have not been courageous enough, in most cases, to
embody them in the text.   The subdivisions of the poem recognized
by previous editors, as well as those which I approve, have been
indicated by breaks in the printing ; the object in preserving the
former is to indicate the progress made in the understanding of the
text.

The arrangement of the Glossary on the principle that *æ* is
alphabetically equivalent to *a* has been adopted in deference to the
demand of the general editors, and it should be understood that
I personally regard it as wholly indefensible ; students had at length
obtained some measure of relief from the perplexing arrangements
adopted in Ettmüller's *Lexicon* and Grein's *Sprachschatz*, and henceforth we should, I believe, have adhered to the strictly alphabetic
order, which, so far as relates to *a* and *æ*, ought to cause no more
difficulty in Old English than in Latin lexicons.

One or the other of the general editors has read most of the
proof.   My chief obligations to Professor Bright are mentioned in the
Notes ; but it should also be said that he is responsible for the indicated quantities in proper names.

The assistance of others than the general editors has in all cases,
I believe, been recorded in the Notes.   I have particularly to record
my gratitude to Professor T. Bouquillon, of the Catholic University
of America, for information concerning the Greater Antiphons, duly
quoted in its proper place.   With respect to the latter, the fact
that Cynewulf is now known to have used them may be of interest
to liturgiologists.

It has frequently been urged as a reproach against Old English
that it had no literature worthy of the name, and was itself not
literary.   Even Lowell somewhere says : ' Hasty generalizers are apt
to overlook the fact that the Saxon was never, to any great extent,

a literary language. Accordingly it held its own very well in the names of common things, but failed to answer the demands of complex ideas derived from them.' If this book, by elucidating somewhat more perfectly the meaning of a noble piece of Old English poetry, should do something to remove this unfounded and unfortunate prejudice, I shall not regret a labor which, after all, has been its own abundant reward.

GREENSBORO, VERMONT,
August 15, 1899.

ADDITIONAL NOTE.

For this second impression, I have corrected some misprints in the text, and have added a few supplementary notes, and a select list of books and articles which have appeared since the above was written.

NEW HAVEN, CONN.,
April 3, 1909.

TABLE OF CONTENTS.

INTRODUCTION.

xi

CHRIST.

INTRODUCTION.

I. THE CHRIST.

THE EXETER BOOK. — Since the *Christ* is contained in the *Codex Exoniensis*, or *Exeter Book*, in which it forms the first poem, a general account of this volume and of Leofric, its donor, is here presented.

Leofric,[1] a priest whose education had been acquired in Lotharingia, and who had been the chaplain of Edward the Confessor during some part of the latter's residence on the Continent, which terminated in 1042, was in 1046 or thereabouts made Bishop of Devon and Cornwall, and Chancellor to King Edward. His see was first at Crediton, but being dissatisfied with this place as a residence, on account of the depredations practised by pirates, he removed to Exeter, and was enthroned in the old cathedral in 1050.

Leofric found the cathedral despoiled of lands, books, and ornaments ; King Athelstan (925–940), who had provided Exeter with the first stone fortifications mentioned in Anglo-Saxon history, had endowed the church with twenty-six estates, but of these only one of the poorest remained, consisting of two hides, on which there were but seven head of cattle. For some time Leofric fed the congregation from his own means ; he recovered much, if not the whole, of the alienated land, and bestowed on the cathedral much real estate of his own. At his accession the cathedral possessed but five books — a Capitulary (*Capitulare*), a worn-out Vesperale (*Nihtsang*), an Epistolary, and two worn-out Lectionaries. Besides these, its sole treasures were one old mass-vestment and one reliquary.[2] Leofric gave to it, among other things, crosiers and vestments, silver chalices and ivory candlesticks, bells and banners, an ivory altar, two copies

---

[1] The best account of his life is by Warren, *The Leofric Missal*, pp. xix–xxvi; see also the article in the *Dict. Nat. Biog.*, and the authorities quoted there, among whom, however, Warren does not appear.

[2] Kemble, *Cod. Dipl.* 4. 276; Warren, p. 2.

of the Gospels bound in ivory, more than thirty other service-books, Boethius' *Consolations* in Latin and in Old English, Gregory's *Pastoral* and *Dialogues*, portions of the Bible, and various works by Porphyry, Prosper, Prudentius, Isidore, Bede, Orosius, Persius, Sedulius, Arator, and Amalarius, all in Latin, besides the work which we have still to mention.[1]   This, the only one now remaining in the possession of the cathedral, is described as I MYCEL ENGLISC BOC BE GEHWILCUM ÞINGUM ON LEOÐWISAN GEWORHT, that is, *One great English book on various topics, composed in verse*, known now as the *Codex Exoniensis*, or *Exeter Book*.   The other existing volumes of Leofric's donation are the following : —

Brit. Mus.: Harl. 2961.

Corp. Chr. Coll. Camb.: S. 12 ; D. 5 ; L. 12.

Camb. Univ. Lib.: Gg. 3. 28 ; Ii. 2. 11.[2]

Oxford: Bodl. 579 ;[3] 708 ; Auct. F. 1. 15 ; Auct. F. 3. 6.[4]

The manuscript is 14 centimetres in height and 18½ in breadth — approximately 5½ by 7½ inches.[5]   It is written on vellum, apparently by a single hand[6] of the early eleventh century.[7]   Schipper explains any difference in the writing as probably due to the varying consistency of the parchment.   Thorpe calls the writing 'fair and rather fine,' and Conybeare speaks of 'the clearness and beauty of its characters.'[8]

At present the volume proper consists of 123 leaves, or 246 pages, from 8ª to 130ᵇ.   Only one leaf is wanting in the interior of the volume, that between fol. 37 and fol. 38.[9]   On the other hand, several leaves are missing at the beginning and end.[10]   Probably because

[1] The document recording these gifts is extant in MS. Bodl. Auct. D. 2. 16.fol. 1ª–2ᵇ, and MS. Harl. 258. fol. 125ᵇ.   Some librarian has also transcribed it on fol. 1–2ª of certain comparatively modern leaves bound in at the beginning of the *Exeter Book*.   It is printed in Kemble, *Cod. Dipl.* 4. 274–6 (No. 940), and in Dugdale, *Monasticon* 2. 527, with a translation ; see also the abstracts, with translation, in Conybeare, *Illustrations*, pp. 199–200, in Warren, pp. xxi–xxiv, and in Wright, *Biog. Brit. Lit., Anglo-Saxon Period*, pp. 38–39.

[2] This is a copy of the Old English Gospels; see Skeat, *Gospel of Saint Mark*, p. vii.   [3] *The Leofric Missal.*

[4] For the contents of these MSS. in general, see Warren, pp. xxiii, xxiv.

[5] Schipper, in *Germania* 19. 327.   [6] Schipper, p. 328.

[7] Thorpe says, of the tenth ; but cf. Conybeare, *Illustrations*, p. 10 ; Schipper ; Wülker, p. 223.   [8] P. 198.   [9] Schipper, p. 327.

[10] A copy of the MS., made by Robert Chambers in 1831, now constitutes Addit. MS. 9067 of the British Museum (Wülker, *Grundriss*, p. 222).

of the book's remaining unbound for a considerable period, the first
page shows signs of wear and is marred by ink-blots, so that in
several places it is practically undecipherable. The last page 'has
sustained serious damage by the action of a fluid on the ink, whereby
much of the writing is rendered wholly illegible.'[1] The last twelve
leaves have been burned through, apparently by a bit of ignited
wood or other substance; only slight traces of the injury appear on
foll. 116, 118.[2]

Only the commonest abbreviations are found. The whole manuscript must have been corrected by another hand after writing, the
corrections being in a paler ink. Thorpe's transcript is in general
accurate, but he has overlooked fragments of six riddles toward the
end.[3] The hemistichs are but seldom divided by a point. Vowels
marked long in the MS. are noted by Wülker, *Bibl.* 3[1]. 239–243.

The first account of our volume was given by Wanley, pp. 279–281.
He describes the book in general, then notes in order the legal docu-
ments contained in the first seven leaves, and finally catalogues the
poems of the manuscript proper, as he understood them, dividing the
whole into ten books. His list of the poems is reproduced with substantial correctness by Wülker, *Grundriss*, pp. 219–221 ; an excerpt
relating to the *Christ* is to be found on p. 67, *infra*. Referring to
Leofric's designation of the volume as large ('mycel'), Wanley says
that it is now of only medium thickness, but ascribes this to the loss
of leaves at the beginning and end.[4]

In 1812, Conybeare published in *Archaeologia*, Vol. 17, his 'Account
of a Saxon Manuscript,' etc.[5] This was followed by his *Illustrations*,
edited by his brother in 1826. In the latter the volume is designated
as the *Exeter Manuscript*.[6]

Thorpe's description, contained in the preface to his edition
(1842), is very brief and vague, consisting of only a single paragraph.

The collation by Schipper,[7] in 1874, was made with much care,
and is the basis of the chief statements here made concerning the
manuscript.

[1] Thorpe, *Cod. Exon.*, p. v.   [5] See Wülker, p. 221.

[2] Schipper, p. 327 ; cf. Trautmann, in *Anglia* 16. 207.

[3] Schipper, p. 328 ; Wülker allows only five in his *Grundriss* (p. 224), but cf.
Bibl. 3[1]. 237.   [6] P. 8.

[4] P. 279; Wülker, p. 218.   [7] *Germania* 19. 327–338.

From the date ascribed to the volume by the most competent experts, it seems not unlikely that it may have been executed and carefully revised under Leofric's own directions, in which case we are tempted to assume that the selection and compilation of the poems was also due to the good bishop. It is clear that he was a man of taste as well as of judgment, a lover of art as well as an excellent administrator. At present, the *Christ* is the longest and most important poem in the collection, being at least one-fifth longer than the *Guthlac*, and nearly two and a half times as long as the *Phoenix* or the *Juliana*. If the book were put together by a man as judicious, learned, and artistic as Leofric, it would seem fitting that he should begin it with a poem of such great beauty and significance.

The *Christ* is contained on folios 8ª–32ᵇ, the very beginning of the manuscript proper. Part I ends in the middle of 14ª, and Part II near the foot of 19ª. For details see the Variants.

UNITY OF THE CHRIST. — The unity of the *Christ* was apparently never suspected until Dietrich undertook his investigation.[1] Wanley had prepared the way for the recognition of the three Parts, as indicated in the present edition, by dividing the whole into three books at 440 and 867,[2] but this division was ignored until after the time of Dietrich. This scholar divided at 440 and 779, a division which is manifestly untenable in view of the fact that there is a two-line space at 440 and 867, while there is only a half-line space at 779; that there is a 'long flourish of capital letters' at the beginning of each Part;[3] and that an inspection of the sources confirms the indications of the manuscript.[4]

Dietrich connects I and II in the following manner. Rightly regarding lines 378–439 as the conclusion of I, he assumes that the *hē* of 436, 438 refers to Christ, and that the *ēþel* where Christ is represented as dwelling points forward to II, which relates how he ascended to his home in the skies[5] (cf. 630, 741). This view is to some extent invalidated by the strong probability that *hē* does not refer to Christ.[6] Further, Dietrich remarks that 445–453 unmistakably points back to the Nativity, and that *Nū*, 440, has an illative significance.[7]

---

[1] *Haupt's Zs.* 9. 193–214.
[2] See *infra*, p. 67.
[3] Gollancz¹, p. xviii.
[4] See notes on 782ᵇ–796, 850–866, and pp. 171–2.
[5] Cf. *infra*, p. 114.
[6] See note on 436.
[7] P. 208.

Dietrich's III begins at 779, evidently because 779–866 contains allusions to the Last Judgment (782–814, 824–849).[1] Having assumed this, it is easy to prove that 779–866 is closely related to the remainder of the poem, which is all occupied with the Last Judgment. The remarkable fact is that Dietrich, who discovered the dependence of Part II upon Gregory's homily, should have overlooked the dependence of 779–866 upon that part of the homily which is really its basis. Moreover, as a proof of the close connection of all three Parts, Dietrich would call every Part a 'coming.' For I and III this is evident, but it verges on the absurd when he declines to call the Ascension a departure from earth, or a return to heaven, and designates it as an arrival — a coming — into glory. Not less strained is it to designate the Ascension as the middle point of the life of Christ, the Nativity and the Last Judgment marking the beginning and the end. More acute is Dietrich's suggestion that the unity of the poem is indicated by the fact that on all three occasions Christ is represented as accompanied by angels.[2] Its force is weakened, it is true, by the consideration that this attendance of angels is mentioned only in II and III. On the other hand, since I does not describe the Nativity, as Dietrich assumed, but expresses the sentiments proper to the season of Advent, it is not surprising that this omission should occur. Dietrich adds that, should linguistic differences between the three Parts be urged, the answer is that such must occur between the different works of every good poet, along with resemblances; so, for example, between the *Elene* and the *Juliana*. He reserves for eventual future publication the coincidences between I and II, taken together, and III, and the resemblances between all three and the *Elene* and *Juliana*, as well as the *Andreas*. He thereupon adduces the internal rime of 591–6, as compared with *El.* 114–5, 1237–1246, 1248–1251, and five instances in the *Andreas*.

Sievers appears to have been the first to question the unity of the *Christ*. In 1887, in an article on expanded lines in Old English, he argued as follows.[3] There is only one expanded line in I and II (v. 621). Part III (assumed by him to begin at 779[4] and end at

---

[1] Cf. *infra*, paragraph at foot of p. 175.
[2] Cf. 449–461, 941, 1013, etc.
[3] *PBB.* 12. 455–6.
[4] He admits, however, the possibility that 779–866 end II.

1693) has, on the other hand, many expanded lines, distributed pretty uniformly.[1] Accordingly, in this respect I and II resemble the *Juliana*, while III is rather akin to the *Elene*. Furthermore, an author is much more likely to name himself at the beginning or end of a work than in the middle of it. He accordingly concludes that I and II at all events belong to a different period from III, and that, if Cynewulf is the author of all three, each must be regarded as an independent work.

In 1888, Cremer[2] came to a different conclusion. 1–778 was called A, while B was 779–1693. Utilizing his own results and Frucht's, Cremer maintained that B differs neither linguistically nor metrically from *Elene* and *Juliana*, while, in respect to metre, A is more remote. A is to be subdivided into I and II; B is by Cynewulf, as further proved by the runes. Conceding the justness of Dietrich's view with respect to the unity of the thought underlying the whole, and allowing that there are passages markedly transitional from I to II, and from II to III, Cremer still contended that, in at least one case,[3] A differs linguistically from B[1], and that when I and II were completed, it was easy for a later poet to perceive the drift, and determine the subject of the poem which should logically follow. Moreover, III being well organized, while I and II, according to Cremer, are not organized at all, III must be by a better poet (Cynewulf), who has thus completed an unfinished poem. He then repeats Sievers' argument about the position of the runic passage. Cynewulf introduces III with his name, as if to say, 'Here my part begins.'

In 1892 Mather,[4] from 'independent work and a careful consideration of Cremer's dissertation,' came to the result, after applying several new metrical and alliterative tests, that 'there is no good reason for doubting that the three Parts of the *Christ* are by Cynewulf.'

In 1894, Trautmann expressed his belief that, on metrical grounds, II was not by the author of I and III,[5] and in 1896 presented his

---

[1] These are: 888–9, 921, 1049, 1162–3, 1208, 1304, 1359, 1377, 1381–5, 1409 1422–7, 1460, 1487–8, 1495–6, 1513–4, 1546, 1561, [1665–7, 1669, 1689].

[2] *Metr. und Sprachl. Untersuchung*, pp. 47–8.

[3] The dat. *hăm, hăme*.

[4] *M. L. N.* 7. 97–107.

[5] *Anglia, Beiblatt* 5. 93, note. Cramer agrees with Trautmann.

views on the subject in full.¹ He adduces several considerations
tending to invalidate Dietrich's opinion:

1. The three Parts, divided as in our text, are without transitional
passages, and are therefore independent poems.

2. The styles are different: I is chiefly invocation and praise,
II homiletic and doctrinal, III descriptive.

3. The divisions, capitals, points, and 'Amen' of the manuscript
are to the same effect.

4. The argument from the position of the runes.

5. II is based upon Gregory's homily, while the source of I remains
undiscovered, that of III is only partially known.

6. In II there is 'a not wholly incomplete description of the Last
Judgment.' This is out of place, if III is by the same author.

7. 'The threefold coming of Christ' has not been found in any
other author. With such a conception of 'coming,' we might go
further, and add the harrowing of hell, the resurrection, and the
Pentecostal descent of the Holy Ghost.

8. I and III have many expressions not found in Cynewulf's other
works. Extensive lists of these are presented.

9. The metre, especially that of III, is not in Cynewulf's manner.

Trautmann concludes that we know nothing of the author, either
of I or of III, but that II is, according to the concordant testimony
of language, metre, and runes, by Cynewulf.

In 1897, Blackburn published a paper² written in 1895, before
he had seen Trautmann's views, in which he presents the following
opinions:

1. An argument identical with No. 3 of Trautmann. He adds
that a line of capitals is used to mark the beginnings of other poems
that he names.

2. Part I should be called The Immaculate Conception. It is
strange, on Dietrich's hypothesis, that the poet treats only of what
precedes Christ's birth or follows his death. Poems on such single
topics are found elsewhere, e.g. the Last Judgment, and the Harrowing of Hell.

3. This resembles Trautmann's No. 2. I is almost purely lyric;
II is a poetical homily; III is descriptive, or descriptive-lyrical.
Each part has a distinct plan, and seems complete and perfect in

¹ *Angl.* 18. 382-8.   ² *Angl.* 19. 89-98.

itself. [Blackburn does not realize that 779–866 has a source in Gregory.] Lines 1665–1693 do not belong to III.

4. Identical with Trautmann's No. 4.

He concludes that II is by Cynewulf, but that as yet we have no proof concerning the other Parts. Dietrich's only argument for the connection of I and II is from *Nū*, but this is inconclusive. Dietrich argues that differences of style do not prove difference of authorship; true, but neither do resemblances in style prove identity of authorship. Blackburn adds names and epithets of the Deity peculiar to each of the three Parts, and states that I averages one kenning to 6½ lines; II, one to each 5⅓; and III, one to each 13⅓. In respect to style, he says that the differences between I and II are but slight, not enough, unsupported by others, to prove difference of authorship, but that III differs from the other two to an extent which suggests such difference.

In 1896, Wülker[1] believed that the manner of II and III is quite different from that of I, and that a considerable interval may have elapsed between the composition of I and of II, whereas II and III are closely connected.

In 1899, Brandl[2] subscribed to Trautmann's opinion.

Resuming what precedes, we have this result :

Sievers separates 1–778 (perhaps 1–866) from 779 (867)–end.

Cremer assigns 779–end to Cynewulf, while I and II are by an undiscovered poet.

Mather believes that all these parts (following Dietrich's division) are by Cynewulf.

Trautmann and Blackburn assign 440–866 to Cynewulf, but deny him the authorship of I and III.

Moreover, while Sievers unites I and II, and opposes them to III, in which respect he is followed by Cremer and Blackburn, Trautmann regards all three as independent, though he groups I and III in contradistinction to II. All agree, of course, in ascribing to Cynewulf the Part which contains the runes, though Cremer assigns the runic passage to III, Trautmann and Blackburn to II, while Sievers is undecided. The variety of results with respect to which two Parts, if any, are to be associated together, leads one to look with suspicion, at the outset, on the attempts to overthrow Dietrich's conclusion.

[1] *Gesch. der Engl. Litt.*, p. 41.

[2] Ten Brink's *Gesch. der Engl. Litt.*, I². 64.

There are manifest difficulties in the way of determining the common authorship, or even the coherence, in a particular order, of various poems whose association in a given manuscript *may* be purely accidental. If any one doubts this, let him assume that the various poems, or even the various groups of poems, comprised in Tennyson's *Maud*, had come down to us from a remote age, undated and *adespota*, perhaps wholly disarranged from their present order, and it may be with their number incomplete. Let him then assume that he is required to determine, by tests of vocabulary, metre, rime, tone, and subject-matter alone, whether these poems were written by a single author, and in what order they originally stood, and he may readily convince himself that he would have no slight task. Now the task is evidently harder where the metre is uniform through numerous poems, and the poetical vocabulary is partly conventional, and includes many stock formulas, as is the case in Old English. Differences in vocabulary, etc., between different poems by the same author are to be expected, as Dietrich has said, even when the poems are on kindred themes, or form members of a poetical cycle ; witness, for example, the sonnet-cycles of the Elizabethans, or Spenser's *Shepherd's Calendar*. Similarities, on the other hand, while they may indicate common authorship, might quite as well, in a period when there was a strongly marked poetical tradition, or when the influence of an individual was powerful, denote deliberate or unconscious imitation. On the whole it is easier, as one can readily see, to make out a plausible argument for diversity of authorship than for identity, especially in a literature in which transitions between one member of a poem and another were not, in general, very definitely marked.

Taking for granted, then, that the task is one of extreme difficulty and delicacy, let us endeavor to ascertain what are the probabilities concerning the coherence of the three Parts, as we may provisionally agree to call them, and the existence of the poem which Dietrich called *Christ*.

1. The argument that each has a distinct plan and style is not conclusive against the unity. This may be tested by *Maud*, or *In Memoriam*, or even by the *Idylls of the King*.

2. So long as we have no other OE. example of a long poem divided into several members, the capitals, points, etc., which occur at 440, 867, and 1665, while they are pretty conclusive with respect to the intended unity of each of the Parts, by no means demonstrate

that the several poems do not constitute members of a larger unity.

3. The argument from the position of the runes seems to favor Sievers' theory that some time elapsed between the composition of II and of III, and Cremer's view that II may originally have been intended to complete the poem. I can not regard it, however, as conclusive against the assumption that III forms part of the whole. The same may be said of the references to the Last Judgment toward the close of II.

4. The sources of I are from the Breviary[1]; so, too, is Gregory's homily, the most important source of II,[2] and perhaps also the Ascension hymn, or at least part of it, since, as it is found in the *Surtees Hymns*, it may have existed in the Breviary of the period.

5. The secondary source of II is a hymn ascribed to Bede; the chief source of III is a hymn first quoted by Bede.[8]

6. Not only is Gregory the author of the principal source of II, but he furnishes important subsidiary sources for III.[4]

7. Part II contains allusions to the Nativity: 444 ff., 587, 628, 720 ff., 786 ff.; and to the Judgment: 520 ff., 782 ff.; III refers to the Nativity: 1418 ff.

8. Several of the features of the Judgment are common to II and III: thus, the great numbers assembled, and their dread of the coming sentence: (II) 795–6, 801–4, 833–847: (III) 889–892, 1015–1026, 1040–1042, 1229b–1230a; the destruction of beauteous and precious things: (II) 804b–805a, 807b–808a, 812–14; (III) 995–6; the progress of the destroying flame: (II) 808b–811: (III) 964–1004; the destruction of buildings: (II) 811: (III) 973–4, 976b–977a; the shaking of the heavens: (II) 825: (III) 932; and the requital of the wicked: (II) 827–831: (III) 1265, 1269–1271, 1538–1543 (cf. *leahtrum fā*, 529: 1538).

9. The motive of the Harrowing of Hell is found in every Part: I (25 ff., 145 ff.); II (558 ff., 730 ff.); III (1159 ff.). Elsewhere in OE. poetry it is found only in the poem of that name, and in *Gu.* 1076, *El.* 181, *Rid.* 565. Surely this circumstance is not purely fortuitous.

10. Dietrich's argument from *Nū*, 440, seems to be borne out by several instances in the *Christ;* see especially (I) 326, (II) 512, 850.

---

[1] Cf. *infra*, pp. 71 ff.   [2] Cf. *infra*, pp. 115–6.   [8] Cf. *infra*, p. 171.
[4] See notes on 1127b–1198, 1247–1259, 1280 ff., 1305, 1327–1333, 1649–1664.

11. Rime is found in II and III: 591–6, 757: 1320, 1481–2, 1496, 1570–1, 1646. So is etymological or identical alliteration: 592ˣ: 980, 1121, 1395ᵃ.

12. Abstract nouns preceded by *tō* occur pretty uniformly through the three Parts.[1]

13. There are traces of pleonasm in both I and II: 41, 118: 592.

14. The Trinity is glorified in both I and II: 378 ff.: 598ᵃ–599, 773–4.

15. The co-eternity of Christ with the Father is emphasized in both I and II: 122, 216 ff., 236 ff., 350 ff.: 465.

16. There are verbal and material resemblances between the several Parts, ranging from the occurrence of a rare word, or of a word in an unusual sense, through that of groups of two, three, or four words, to the partial identity of two or more lines. I give illustrations and tolerably full references under each of the following heads:

I : II : III.

61–2.   . . . hū þec heofones Cyning
                          sīðe gesēceð, ond *sylf* cymeð.

143–6.   *Sylfa* wolde
                    gefælsian *foldan mǣgðe*,
                    swylce grundas ēac . . .
                    sīþe gesēcan.

523–4.   *Wilc* eft swā-þēah *eorðan mǣgðe*
              sylfa gesēcan.

945–7.   . . . þonne folca Weard
                          . . . *eorðan mǣgðe*
              sylfa gesēceð.

Again : —

418.   *Onfēng* æt *fǣmnan* flǣsc unwemme.

720–2ᵃ.   . . . þā hē on *fǣmnan āstāg*
              mægeð unmǣle, ond þǣr mennisc hīw
              onfēng būtan firenum.

1418ᵇ–1420ᵃ.   þā ic sylf *gestāg*,
              māga in mōdor, þēah wæs hyre mægdenhād
              æghwæs onwālg.

Other instances are (*a*) 15, 27 : 504, 656 : 1042 ; (*b*) 59, 239, 356: 672: 1087 ; (*c*) 65 : 722, 758 : 1421 ; (*d*) 124, 427 · 632 : 1421 ; (*e*) 296 : 488, 653 : 1383, 1401 ; (*f*) 387 : 661 : 1467–8.

---

[1] See *infra*, note on 28.

I : II.

106 : 696, sōðfæsta sunnan lēoma.

142 (cf. 250), 367 : 587, hidercyme ('Advent').

Again : —

298.   *þurh clǣne* gebyrd *cennan* sceolde.

444.   *ācenned* wearð *þurh clǣnne* hād.

Other instances : —

(*a*) 22, 82, 337 : 613, 789 ; (*b*) 83 : 740 ; (*c*) 102, 209 : 601, 612 ; (*d*) 122 : 465 ; (*e*) 150, 374 : 586, 754 ; (*f*) 159 : 743 ; (*g*) 201 ff., 335 ff. : 823 ; (*h*) 207 : 728 ; (*i*) 223 : 788 ; (*j*) 226 : 588 ; (*k*) 251 : 559, 821 ; (*l*) 255 : 786^b–787^a ; (*m*) 273 : 755 ; (*n*) 316 : 463 ; (*o*) 316 : 474, 714 ; (*p*) 407 · 631 ; (*q*) 420 : 513.

I : III.

230, 277 : 1343, 1543, tō wīdan fēore.

Other instances : —

(*a*) 7 : 1113 ; (*b*) 92, 113, 359 : 1442 ; (*c*) 102 : 1342, 1520 ; (*d*) 103 : 1228 ; (*e*) 117 : 1542, 1631 ; (*f*) 128 : 1219, 1367 ; (*g*) 171 : 1120 ; (*h*) 181 : 1263, 1268 ; (*i*) 207^a, 211^a : 1419–1420^a ; (*j*) 227 : 1198 ; (*k*) 235, (107) : 968 ; (*l*) 266, (112) : 1414 ; (*m*) 278, 381 : 1024, 1368, 1599 ; (*n*) 284 : 1189 ; (*o*) 359 : 1442.

II : III.

492 : 927, heofonengla þrēat.

Again : —

548–9.   þæt him *ælbeorhte* englas tōgēanes
                          . . . *hēapum* cwōman.

928–9.   ymbūtan faraðð, *ælbeorhtra* scolu,
                          . . . *hēapum* geneahhe.

Again : —

604^b–605^a.   . . *ǣhta spēd,*
                          welan ofer wīdlond.

1383^b–4^a.   . . . meahta *spēd,*
                          welan ofer wīdlonda gehwylc.

Again : —

832–3^a þonne *magna Cyning on gemōt cymeð*
                          þrymma mǣste.

941–2.   Wile Ælmihtig mid his engla gedryht,
                          mægencyninga Meotod, *on gemōt cuman.*

Other instances : —

(*a*) 470 : 1129, 1179 ; (*b*) 479 : 1645; (*c*) 489 : 1360; (*d*) 515ᵇ: 941ᵇ; (*e*) 518 : 904; (*f*) 563 : 1407–8 ; (*g*) 610 : 1596 ; (*h*) 618: 1515 ; (*i*) 621ᵃ: 1379–80ᵃ ; (*j*) 621ᵇ–626 : 1409ᵇ–13 ; (*k*) 623, (414): 1196 ; (*l*) 632, 739, 841, 849 : 971, 1080, 1148, (1333), 1558, 1570, 1585, 1588 (see note on 1588) ; (*m*) 632, (427) : 1471, (1173) ; (*n*) 681 : 1529 ; (*o*) 707, 816 : 1057 ; (*p*) 729 : 1467 ; (*q*) 768 : 1504 ; (*r*) 785 : 947 ; (*s*) 795, 832 : 942 ; (*t*) 800: 1283 ; (*u*) 819 : 1326, 1579–80 ; (*v*) 820 : 1480 ; (*w*) 824–5ᵃ: 1527–8ᵃ ; (*x*) 825ᵇ: 932ᵇ ; (*y*) 829 : 1538 ; (*z*) 830 : 985 ; (*aa*) 831 : 965, (931), 1006 ; (*bb*) 832 : 916, 942 ; (*cc*) 834 : 998 ; (*dd*) 835 : 1229 ; (*ee*) 848–9 : 1580–1 ; (*ff*) 865 : 1220.

Whatever may be said of individual parallels, I cannot think that such a series of correspondences is without significance.

17. There are no clearly marked dialectal differences between the three Parts.[1]

18. The Advent implies the Second Advent, and the two notions were constantly associated in the liturgies ;[2] the Ascension, too, suggests the Last Judgment.[3]

I conclude, therefore, that there is a strong presumption, amounting in my judgment to certainty, that the three divisions are by the same author, Cynewulf; that they stand in an organic relation to one another; and that they may thus be fairly regarded as forming, in combination, a single poem. This of course does not exclude the possibility that the three Parts may have been written at different times.

✠ PART I. THE ADVENT.[4] *The celebration of Advent by the mediæval church.* — The beginnings of the observance of the Advent season are lost in the obscurity of the early Christian ages. About the middle of the fifth century the indications begin to be unmis-

---

[1] See pp. xlvi–li.   [2] See pp. xxvii, xxix ff.

[3] See Acts I. 11 ; *infra*, p. 117, vv. 67–8; p. 118, vv. 113–6; note on 782ᵇ–796; and p. xliv. It is significant that in Otfrid the treatment of the Last Judgment follows immediately upon that of the Ascension.

[4] The section on the Advent has been developed at such length because this part of Cynewulf's poem can be fully understood only through a comprehension of its historic basis, and through participation in the spirit of the season which it celebrates. The nature of the Ascension and of the Last Judgment is presented with sufficient clearness by Cynewulf himself.

takable. Maximus of Turin (fl. 465) has left us two homilies [1] and a sermon [2] in which he exhorts the faithful to clothe themselves with the garments of righteousness, and thus to make ready for the celebration of their Lord's nativity. Similarly, Caesarius of Arles [3] (d. 542) delivered two sermons [4] on the subject of the Advent, in which he urges Christians to abstain from avarice, hatred, pride, anger, drunkenness, and lasciviousness, and to be sober, merciful, pure, humble, and rich in alms-deeds. In one of these he draws a vivid picture of the preparations in some great man's household for his birthday, in order to illustrate how the soul should be made ready for Christ's coming. 'Abstain,' he exhorts, 'even from conjugal endearments; invite the poor frequently to your banquets; rise early for vigils; stand in church at prayers and singing; utter no idle or worldly speeches yourself, and reprove those who do; keep peace with all men, and bring back to concord those whom you perceive to be at variance.'

The general observance of Advent in the Western world is probably due to the Franks. About the year 480, Perpetuus of Tours recommends the faithful to fast three times a week from Martinmas (Nov. 11) to Christmas, [5] a period of forty-three days. In 524, the Council of Lerida interdicts marriage during the Advent season, a precept which is still observed. In 567, the Second Council of Tours enjoins monks to fast from the beginning of December till Christmas. [6] In 582, the Council of Macon ordains that from Martinmas to Christmas the Mondays, Wednesdays, and Fridays shall be days of fasting, and that mass shall be celebrated according to the Lenten rite. [7]

The practice of observing an Advent fast must have been introduced into England as early as the seventh century, even if it was not already in use among the Irish. Bede tells us of Eadbert, Bishop of Lindisfarne (d. 698), that he used to spend the forty days before Christmas in a place remote from the church, and encompassed by the sea, continuing in abstinence, prayer, and tears. [8]

---

[1] Migne 57. 221–8.
[2] Migne 57. 531–4.
[3] Cf. infra, p. 210.
[4] Migne 39. 1973–7.
[5] Gregory of Tours, Hist. Franc. 10. 31.
[6] Guéranger, The Liturgical Year, Advent, p. 25.
[7] Ib.
[8] Eccl. Hist. 4. 30.

Three-quarters of a century earlier, St. Egbert (d. 729), we are told on the same authority,[1] used to subsist on one meal a day of bread and skimmed milk during the three fasts of forty days — Lent, Advent, and the period immediately following Whitsunday. The same three quadragesimal fasts are recognized in the Penitential ' drawn up under the eye, and published with the authority ' of Archbishop Theodore [2] (d. 690), who may have been influenced by the Greek practice.[3] In the *Dialogue* [4] of Egbert, Archbishop of York (d. 766), there is the appointment, in addition to the Ember Feasts, of a period of twelve days before the Nativity, to be spent in fastings, watchings, prayers, and alms ; on which twelve days not only were the clergy, but the laity also, with their wives and households, exhorted to resort to their confessors.[5]

The fast of forty days, or six weeks, was observed in France throughout the reign of Charlemagne, as well as in Spain, and is to this day practised in the Cathedral of Milan. In the oldest manuscripts of the Sacramentary of Gregory the Great, the number of Sundays is five, but by the ninth or tenth century they were reduced to four,[6] as in the present Roman Breviary and Anglican Prayer Book. In 867, as we know from a letter of Pope Nicholas I to the Bulgarians, four weeks was the period recognized at Rome.[7]

The Church recognized a threefold, or even fourfold, advent of Christ, which should form the theme of meditation at this season :

1. Christ's coming in the flesh.
2. His coming to the soul of the believer through faith.
3. [His coming to the individual Christian at death.]
4. His coming to judgment.[8]

---

[1] 3. 27.

[2] Haddan and Stubbs, *Councils* 3. 173–204, esp. p. 202 ; for other references cf. Mayor and Lumby's *Bede*, p. 283. The Irish also recognized the three fasts ; cf. Plummer's *Bede* 2. 197. The Christmas fast was known to them as Winter Lent, Moses' Lent, St. Martin's Lent.

[3] Alban Butler, *Feasts and Fasts*, p. 75 ; Guéranger, p. 27.

[4] Haddan and Stubbs, *Councils* 3. 412–3.

[5] *Dict. Chr. Ant.* 1. 662.

[6] Guéranger, p. 29.

[7] Butler, p. 74.

[8] Thus St. Bernard in his third Advent Sermon (Migne 183. 45) : ' Triplicem enim ejus adventum novimus : ad homines, in homines, contra homines.' For the second he refers to Jn. 14. 23. In the fifth Sermon he says : ' In the first he

It is disputed whether the tone of Advent is on the whole one of joy or sorrow, whether penitence or joyful anticipation gives it its prevailing character. ' The people are forcibly reminded of the sadness which fills the heart of the Church by the sombre color of the vestments. Excepting on the feasts of the saints, purple is the only color she uses ; the deacon does not wear the dalmatic, nor the subdeacon the tunic. Formerly it was the custom, in some places, to wear black vestments. . . . The Church also, during Advent, excepting on the feasts of saints, suppresses the Angelic Canticle, *Gloria in excelsis Deo, et in terra pax hominibus bonae voluntatis ;* for this glorious song was only sung at Bethlehem over the crib of the Divine Babe — the tongue of the angels is not loosened yet. . . . Again, at the end of mass, the deacon does not dismiss the assembly of the faithful by the words *Ite, missa est.* He substitutes the ordinary greeting, *Benedicamus Domino,* as though the Church feared to interrupt the prayers of the people, which could scarce be too long during these days of expectation. In the Night Office the Holy Church also suspends on these same days the hymn of jubilation, *Te Deum laudamus.* It is in deep humility that she awaits the supreme blessing which is to come to her ; and in the interval she presumes only to ask, and entreat, and hope. . . . On the ferial days, the rubrics of Advent prescribe that certain prayers should be said kneeling at the end of each canonical Hour, and that the choir should also kneel during a considerable portion of the mass.'[1] To these it may be added that the organ, under the same circumstances, is silent.

But there is also a joyful aspect to the season. ' The word of gladness, the joyful Alleluia, is not interrupted during Advent, except once or twice during the ferial office. It is sung in the masses of the four Sundays, and vividly contrasts with the sombre color of the vestments. On one of these Sundays — the third — the prohibition of using the organ is removed, and all are gladdened

---

comes in flesh and weakness ; in the second, in spirit and power ; in the last, in glory and majesty ; and the second coming is the means whereby we pass from the first to the third.' To a similar effect Honorius of Autun, *Gemma Animae* 3. 1 (Migne 172. 641), who says that we put ourselves back into the days of his saints of old who looked forward to his coming ; we anticipate his coming to us at death ; and we remember that he is to be our judge. Cf. Guéranger, pp. 81 ff.

[1] Guéranger, pp. 35–7.

by its grand notes, and rose-colored vestments may be used instead of the purple.'[1] Honorius of Autun[2] explains that the *Gloria in excelsis* and *Te Deum* are not sung, because the righteous before Christ's Advent were kept in the sadness of hell. So the dalmatic was not worn, because the garments of innocence and immortality were restored to us by Christ. Usage, however, must have differed under different circumstances. Tl e laity were least strenuous in observing the rigors of the season, the clergy more so, and the monks most of all.[3] Then, north of the Alps the tone seems always to have been a sadder one. 'The four Sundays of Advent, which, under the influence of Frankish monastic customs, were soon to be regarded as so many stages in a penitential season, marked at Rome, on the contrary, in the eighth century, and even in the twelfth, the progress of a season of gladness, in which everything took its tone from the joyful expectation of the coming of the Redeemer; and the third, the Sunday *Gaudete*, with all the pomp of its " station " at S. Peter's, was the culminating point of this joyous going up to Bethlehem. The six days before the 24th of December garnished their ferial Psalms at Vespers and Lauds with Antiphons which already reflected the sparkle of the Savior's star. . . . And so at last the 24th was reached, when the Benedictus at the ferial Lauds had for its Antiphon that which is now transferred to the first Vespers of Christmas : "*Dum ortus fuerit sol, videbitis Regem regum procedentem a matre*[4] [*sic*], *tanquam sponsus de thalamo suo.*" Yet but one more night, and the King of kings would come forth from His tabernacle.'[5]

The spirit of Advent.—The spirit of Advent is one of impatience with the present, and of longing for the future. The believer, like the prophets under the Old Dispensation, looks forward to the manifestation of Christ upon the earth; as the hart pants for the waterbrooks, so he desires that Christ shall fill his soul, and that the Kingdom of God shall indeed come among men ; and he looks forward to the Last Day with a dread not unmixed with exultation, when he thinks that his Judge is also his Redeemer, and that the

---

[1] Guéranger, p. 37.

[2] *Gemma Animae* 3. 3 (Migne 172. 642).

[3] Cf., for example, Butler, p. 95.   [4] In the present Breviary, *Patre*. — ED.

[5] Batiffol, *Hist. Rom. Brev.*, pp. 117-8 ; the mixed character of the Advent celebration is recognized by Ralph of Tongres (d. 1403): *De Canon. Obs.*, Proprietat. 16. .

terrors of that scene shall usher in a joy that for him, if he be found faithful, shall know no end. It is in this sense that the office for Advent must be conceived, if it is to be comprehended and deeply enjoyed. In particular, the relation between the First and the Second Advent must be kept in mind, if we would fully enter into the anticipatory Christmas joy, and yet feel the solemnity with which the Middle Ages contemplated the coming of Christ as Judge, with its tremendous consequences for every man.[1] In this connection it is significant that the first preparation for the approaching Advent season is, in the Roman Breviary, indicated by the Text (Capitulum) recited at the Vespers of the Saturday preceding the First Sunday :

> Brethren, now is it high time to awake out of sleep, for now is our salvation nearer than when we believed.

The verse immediately following this in the Bible (Rom. 13. 12), is the one on which the first part of the Collect is based.

Ælfric has two sermons on the Advent,[2] which are very instructive with reference to the Church's attitude in his time. In the first of them he says : 'The holy prophets foretold both the First Advent at the birth, and also the Second at the Great Judgment. We also, God's servants, confirm our faith with the services of this tide, because we in our hymns confess our redemption through his First Advent, and we admonish ourselves to be ready on his Second Advent, that we may from the Judgment follow him to everlasting life, as he has promised us.' In another place he says:[3] 'We should honor Christ's generation and nativity with spiritual gladness, and adorn ourselves with good works, and occupy ourselves with hymns to God, and shun those things which Christ forbids, which are sins and works of the devil; and love those things which God has enjoined, that is, lowliness and mercy, righteousness and truth,

---

[1] The Prayer Book Collect for the First Sunday in Advent, though it does not directly represent any ancient one, yet beautifully reflects this sentiment :

'Almighty God, give us grace that we may cast away the works of darkness, and put upon us the armor of light, now in the time of this mortal life, in which thy Son Jesus Christ came to visit us in great humility; that in the last day, when he shall come again in his glorious Majesty to judge both the quick and dead, we may rise to the life immortal, through him who liveth and reigneth with thee and the Holy Ghost, now and ever. Amen.'

[2] *Hom.* 1. 600–619.

[3] *Hom.* 2. 22.

alms-deeds and temperance, patience and chastity. . . . . Guard yourselves against surfeiting and drunkenness, as Christ said in his Gospel.'

We may now turn to a brief consideration of the Roman office for Advent, selecting those points which may best illustrate its beauty and meaning, though selection is most difficult, and the choice may not always be the happiest one.

At the Vespers of the Saturday preceding the first Sunday in Advent we have the following verse, the appropriateness of which will readily be seen, as the Antiphon to the Magnificat:

> Behold, the name of the Lord cometh from far, and his glory filleth the world.

The Collect for this service, which recurs ever and anon throughout the season, is the following:[1]

> O Lord, we beseech thee, stir up thy strength and come, that through thy protection we may be delivered from the dangers which hang over us by reason of our sins, and through thy making us free we may be saved, who livest and reignest with God the Father in the unity of the Holy Ghost, [one] God, world without end. Amen.

We now come to the first Advent service proper, that for Matins on the First Sunday. The first words of the Church, in the still midnight, are these:[2]

> Come let us adore the King our Lord, who is to come.

As this Sunday is often called the *Aspiciens a longe*, its character may be illustrated from that Respond. I borrow the language of Batiffol:[3]

'Take, for example, that admirable Respond for Advent Sunday, the *Aspiciens a longe*, where, assigning to Isaiah a part which recalls a celebrated scene in the *Persae* of Æschylus, the liturgy causes the precentor to address to the listening choir these enigmatic words:[4]

> I look afar off, and behold, I see the power of God coming, and a cloud covering the whole earth. Go ye forth to meet him, and say: Tell us whether thou be he who shall rule over the people Israel.

[1] The beginning from Ps. 80, which may well be read here for its bearing on the service.
[2] Guéranger, p. 128.
[3] Pp. 115-17.
[4] I translate the Latin. — ED.

'And the whole choir, blending in one wave of song the deep voices of the monks and the clear notes of its boy readers, repeats like a reverberating echo of the prophet's voice :

I look afar off, and behold, I see the power of God coming, and a cloud covering the whole earth.

PRECENTOR.

All ye children of the earth and sons of men, the rich and the poor together, —

CHOIR.

Go ye forth to meet him, and say:[1] Tell us whether thou be he that shall rule over the people Israel.

PRECENTOR.

Hear, O thou Shepherd of Israel, thou that leadest Joseph like a sheep, [thou that sittest upon the Cherubim].[2]

CHOIR.

Tell us whether thou be he who shall rule over the people Israel.

'But what need thus to scan the horizon in doubt ? He whose coming is known, he is the Blessed One, and no triumph can be fair enough to welcome his Advent :

PRECENTOR.

Lift up your heads, O ye gates, and be ye lift up, ye everlasting doors, and the King of glory shall come in —[3]

CHOIR.

Who shall rule over the people Israel.

PRECENTOR.

Glory be to the Father, and to the Son, and to the Holy Ghost.

'And then the whole of the opening text is repeated in chorus :

I look afar off, etc.'[4]

---

[1] This sentence is omitted in Batiffol, probably through inadvertence.
[2] So in Batiffol.   [3] Cf. below, pp. 132–3.
[4] The variations in the Sarum Use are interesting. Cf. Procter and Words-worth, col. xxi. — ED.

The four Sundays of Advent have each a distinct character. The first is sufficiently designated by the Respond quoted above. According to Honorius of Autun, the second relates to the prophecy of Christ's coming to Jerusalem, the third to the Second Advent, and the fourth to the calling of the Gentiles. However, usage and interpretation varied at different times. To some extent the Gospel for the day is an index to the thought for which the day stands. In the Roman Missal the Lessons are : (I) Lk. 21. 25–33 ; (II) Mt. 11. 2–10; (III) Jn. 1. 19–28 ; (IV) Lk. 3. 1–9.[1] According to this, the First Sunday would have reference to the Second Advent. In Ælfric's time, Lk. 21 is the Gospel for the Second Sunday. According to Guéranger,[2] the sentiment of the Second Sunday is one of hope and joy, and the coming designated is that to the soul of the believer. The Third Sunday is still more joyful. 'This Sunday has had the name of *Gaudete*[3] given to it, from the first word of the Introit ; it also is honored with those impressive exceptions which belong to the fourth Sunday of Lent, called *Laetare*. The organ is played at the mass ; the vestments are rose-color ; the deacon resumes the dalmatic, and the subdeacon the tunic ; and in cathedral churches the bishop assists with the precious mitre.'[4] Finally, the Fourth Sunday ' is called *Rorate*, from the Introit, but more frequently *Canite tuba*, which are the first words of the first Responsory of Matins, and of the first Antiphon of Lauds and Vespers.'[5] The thought is that of the desert, which needs the refreshment of the dew, and the personage in view is, besides the Savior, John the Baptist. The Introit is :

> Drop down dew, ye heavens, from above, and let the clouds rain the Righteous One ; let the earth open and send forth a Savior.[6]

For the Third and Fourth Sundays the Invitatory is :[7]

> O come, let us worship ; the Lord is now at hand.

Out of the series of offices for the season I select, as sufficiently exhibiting the character attributed to the four Sundays by the Roman Breviary, the Antiphons for Lauds and Vespers :

[1] In the Anglican Prayer Book as follows: (I) Mt. 21. 1–9; (II) Lk. 21. 25–33 (as in Ælfric); (III) Mt. 11. 2–10; (IV) Jn. 1. 19–28.
[2] P. 165.
[3] Cf. the Anglican Introit for this day.
[4] Guéranger, p. 206.
[5] Guéranger, p. 243, note.
[6] Cf. Isa. 45. 8.
[7] Cf. p. xxxv. 1.

First Sunday.

1. In that day the mountains shall drop down new wine, and the hills shall flow with milk and honey. Alleluia.

2. Rejoice greatly, O· daughter of Zion ; shout, O daughter of Jerusalem. Alleluia.

3. *Behold, the Lord shall come, and all his saints with him ; and the light in that day shall be great.*[1] Alleluia.

4. Ho, every one that thirsteth, come ye to the waters ; seek ye the Lord while he may be found. Alleluia.

5. Behold, the great Prophet shall come, and he shall rebuild Jerusalem. Alleluia.

Second Sunday.

1. *Behold, the Lord shall come in the clouds of heaven with great power.* Alleluia.

2. Zion is our strong city ; salvation will God appoint for walls and bulwarks ; open ye the gates, for God is with us. Alleluia.

3. Behold, the Lord shall appear, and shall not lie ; though he tarry, wait for him, because he will come, he will not tarry. Alleluia.

4. The mountains and the hills shall break forth before God into singing, and all the trees of the field shall clap their hands, for the Lord, the King, shall come unto his everlasting kingdom. Alleluia, Alleluia.

5. Behold, our Lord shall come with power, and shall enlighten the eyes of his servants. Alleluia.

Third Sunday.

1. The Lord will come and will not tarry, *and will bring to light the hidden things of darkness, and manifest himself to all nations.* Alleluia.

2. Rejoice, O Jerusalem, with great joy, because thy Savior shall come unto thee. Alleluia.

3. I will place salvation in Zion, and my glory in Israel. Alleluia.

4. Every mountain and hill shall be made low ; and the crooked shall be made straight, and the rough places plain ; come, O Lord, and tarry not. Alleluia.

5. Let us live righteously and godly, looking for that blessed hope and the appearance of the Lord. Alleluia.

[1] Italics indicate the explicit allusions to the Second Advent.

FOURTH SUNDAY.

1. Blow ye the trumpet in Zion, for the day of the Lord is at hand ; behold, he shall come and save us. Alleluia.

2. Behold, the Desire of all nations shall come, and the house of the Lord shall be filled with glory. Alleluia.

3. The crooked shall be made straight, and the rough places plain ; come, O Lord, and tarry not. Alleluia.

4. The Lord shall come ; go out to meet him and say : Great is his beginning, and of his kingdom there shall be no end ; the mighty God, the Lord, the Prince of Peace. Alleluia.

5. Thy almighty Word, O Lord, shall come from thy royal throne. Alleluia.

The Greater Antiphons. — Before proceeding to the special consideration of the Greater Antiphons, we must first examine the Antiphon in general and fix its meaning and use. On this subject Cardinal Newman[1] says : ʻThe Antiphons or Anthems are sentences preceding and succeeding the separate Psalms and Songs, and are ordinarily verses taken from the particular compositions to which they are attached. They seem to answer the purpose of calling attention to what is coming, of interpreting it, or of pointing out the particular part of it which is intended to bear on the service of the day; in all respects answering the purpose of what is called by musicians a key-note. They are repeated at the end, as if to fix the impression or the lesson intended.ʼ See also Neale and Littledale, *Comm. on the Psalms* 1. 34–5, and cf. 35–45, 51–62.[2]

The importance attached to the Antiphons by the ministrants in divine service is attested by a story told of Ceolfrith and (probably) Bede in the anonymous *History of the Abbots* :[3] ʻIn the monastery over which Ceolfrith presided, all who could read, or preach, or recite

---

[1] *Tracts for the Times*, No. 75 (Vol. III), p. 22.

[2] It is to the city of Rome itself, and not to any of the provincial churches, that the systematic use of Antiphons is due. So Batiffol, p. 1. The *Dialogue* of Egbert, Archbishop (735–766) of York (Haddan and Stubbs, *Councils* 3. 412) mentions the Antiphonaries attributed to Gregory, which were extant, and those which Egbert had seen at Rome (*apud apostolorum Petri et Pauli limina*). Bäumer (p. 280) thinks the Antiphonaries used by Egbert at York were identical in content with those which Amalarius found in use at Metz. Pope Hadrian caused a revision to be made in 783 or 784.

[3] Cited in Plummer's ed. of Bede 1. xii.

the Antiphons and Responds were swept away, except the abbot himself and one little lad nourished and taught by him, who is now a priest of the same monastery, and both by word of mouth and by writing commends to all who wish to know them the abbot's worthy deeds. And the abbot, sad at heart because of this visitation, ordained that, contrary to their former rite, they should, except at Vespers and Matins, recite their Psalms without Antiphons. And when this had been done with many tears and lamentations on his part for the space of a week, he could not bear it any longer, but decreed that the Psalms, with their Antiphons, should be restored according to the order of the regular course; and all assisting, by means of himself and the aforesaid boy he carried out with no little labor that which he had decreed, until he could either train himself, or procure from elsewhere, men able to take part in the divine service.'[1]

The following passage from Guéranger[2] will explain the particular use made of the Greater Antiphons, which underlie so much of the First Part of the *Christ:* 'The Church enters to-day [Dec. 17][3] on the seven days which precede the Vigil of Christmas, and which are known in the liturgy under the name of the Greater Ferias. The ordinary of the Advent office becomes more solemn; the Antiphons of the Psalms, both for Lauds and the Hours of the day, are proper, and allude expressly to the great Coming. Every day, at Vespers, is sung a solemn Antiphon, which consists of a fervent prayer to the Messiah, whom it addresses by one of the titles given him by the sacred Scriptures.

'In the Roman Church there are seven of these Antiphons, one for each of the Greater Ferias. They are commonly called the O's of Advent, because they all begin with that interjection. In other churches, during the Middle Ages, two more were added to these seven:[4] one to our Blessed Lady, *O Virgo Virginum;* and the other to the angel Gabriel, *O Gabriel;* or to St. Thomas the Apostle, whose

---

[1] On the speed with which certain unworthy priests hurried through the service, omitting the Antiphons, cf. Tommasi 4. xxxiii, where he quotes an anonymous author of *De Benedictione Dei*, in the preface to Batheric, Bishop of Ratisbon, who was consecrated A.D. 814.

[2] *The Liturgical Year*, Advent, pp. 508–9.

[3] According to Blunt, p. 249, the Antiphons were sung from Dec. 16 to Dec. 23, St. Thomas' day having its own proper Antiphon; but this must be an error. — ED.

[4] Martène says (lib. 4. cap. 10): 'Et revera novem designat ordinarium Namnetense'; so, he adds, does the Antiphonary of St. Martin of Tours. — ED.

feast [Dec. 21] comes during the Greater Ferias; it began *O Thoma Didyme.*[1] There were even churches where twelve Great Antiphons were sung; that is, besides the nine we have just mentioned, there was *O Rex pacifice* to our Lord, *O Mundi Domina* to our Lady, and *O Hierusalem* to the city of the people of God.

' The canonical Hour of Vespers has been selected as the most appropriate time for this solemn supplication to our Savior, because, as the Church sings in one of her hymns,[2] it was in the evening of the world (*vergente mundi vespere*) that the Messiah came amongst us. These Antiphons are sung at the Magnificat, to show us that the Savior whom we expect is to come to us by Mary. They are sung twice, once before and once after the Canticle, as on Double Feasts, and this to show their great solemnity. In some churches it was formerly the practice to sing them thrice : that is, before the Canticle, before the *Gloria Patri*, and after the *Sicut erat*. Lastly, these admirable Antiphons, which contain the whole pith of the Advent liturgy, are accompanied by a chant replete with melodious gravity, and by ceremonies of great expressiveness, though, in these latter, there is no uniform practice followed.'

[1] ' It is more modern than the *O Gabriel ;* but, dating from the 13th century, it was almost universally used in its stead.' See p. xxxix, note 1.

[2] The *Conditor alme siderum.* The line is thus introduced :

Qui condolens interitu
Mortis perire saeculum,
Salvasti mundum languidum,
Donans reis remedium,
Vergente mundi vespere.

Cf. the reason for the use of the Magnificat at vespers given by Bede (*Works* 5. 306) : ' It comes to pass by the bounty of the Lord that if we at all times meditate upon the acts and sayings of the Blessed Mary, the observance of chastity and the works of virtue will always continue in us. For the excellent and salutary custom has grown up in Holy Church that all shall sing her hymn [the Magnificat] every day with the Vesper Psalms, in order that the recalling of the Lord's incarnation by this means may the oftener incite the souls of the faithful to devotion, and that the consideration of the example set by his mother may confirm them in the stability of virtue. And it is meet that this should be done at Vespers, so that the mind, wearied in the course of the day, and distracted by various opinions, may, at the approach of the season of quiet, collect itself in the oneness of meditation, and through this wholesome reminder may hasten to cleanse itself by the prayers and tears of the night from everything useless or harmful which it had contracted by the business of the day.'

These Greater Antiphons [1] are usually designated by their opening words, as follows : [2]

1. O Sapientia.
2. O Adonai.
3. O Radix Jesse.
4. O Clavis David.
5. O Oriens.
6. O Rex gentium.
7. O Emmanuel.

This is the order observed in the Roman Breviary and the Sarum Use.[3] Durandus [4] mystically interprets many circumstances relative to the first seven Antiphons. Thus they express the longing of the ancient fathers for the coming of Christ ; there are seven of them, because Christ possessed the seven gifts of the Spirit,[5] and bestowed them on the world, but also because these seven gifts enlightened the prophets. In these Antiphons the Church reveals the diversity of her ills. We are ignorant (cf. Ant. 1), subject to eternal pains (2), servants of the devil (3), bound by habitual sin (4), enveloped with darkness (5), and exiles from our fatherland (6 and 7) ; 6 refers to the salvation of the Gentiles, and 7 of the Jews. When two more are added, the *O Virgo*, or the *O Gabriel*, and the *O Thoma*,[6] the nine orders of angels are signified. Certain churches sing twelve Antiphons, which then signify the twelve prophets, apostles, tribes, and the number of thousands saved from each tribe. The O is a note of admiration rather than a call.[7] It is proper that there shall be special Antiphons, Responds, etc., for this season, that they may, like heralds coming thicker and faster, arouse us to make ready for our Lord, and to prepare a fit dwelling-place for him. This is the significance of the quotation from Rom. 13, with which Advent begins :[8] 'Let us cast away the works of darkness, and put on the armor of light.' [9]

---

[1] See pp. 71 ff. They are translated by Blunt, pp. 249–250.

[2] Cf. *infra*, pp. 101, 72, 107, 76, 88, 73, 94.

[3] As noted below (p. 85), the order in Amalarius is 1, 4, 7, 3, 5, 2, 6 (Migne 105. 1266–9).

[4] *Rationale* 4. 11.   [6] Cf. p. xxxix, note 1.

[5] Cf. *infra*, p. 72.   [7] Cf. *infra*, p. 72.

[8] Rather from the Capitulum for Sext of the First Sunday in Advent.

[9] Note the appropriateness of this to the season of the year.

For the feast of the Expectation of the Virgin (Dec. 18), which has been kept since the Tenth Council of Toledo (A.D. 656), there is another : [1]

8. O Virgo virginum.[2]

In the Vatican MS., 8 is substituted for 7 ; in the St. Gallen Antiphonary [3] 8 follows 7, and is in turn followed by these : [4]

9. O Gabriel.
10. O Rex pacifice.[5]
11. O mundi Domina.
12. O Hierusalem.[6]

[1] This feast is observed with special devotion in Spain (Batiffol, p. 514). The first sentence is more grammatical in the Vatican MS. B. 79, the Responsorial and Antiphonary printed by Tommasi, Vol. 4. It there reads (p. 28): 'O Virgo virginum, quomodo fiet istud? quia nec primum tui similis visa est, nec habebis sequentem.' This Antiphon occurs also in the Sarum, York, and Hereford Breviaries (cf. *infra*, pp. 84, 85). A part of the usual form is found among the Antiphons for Lauds on Christmas Day. The Antiphon for St. Thomas' Day, Dec. 21, is as follows (Batiffol, p. 522): 'O Thoma Didyme, qui Christum meruisti cernere : te precibus rogamus altisonis, succurre nobis miseris, ne damnemur cum impiis in Adventu Judicis.' This does not, however, come into question as one of our sources. [2] Cf. *infra*, p. 84.

[3] *Antiphonarium Hartkeri*, MS. St. Gallen 390, 391, pp. 40, 41. This is described on p. 133 of the *Verzeichniss der Handschriften der Stiftsbibliothek von St. Gallen*, Halle, 1875, as a small parchment quarto of the tenth or eleventh century ; the date is confirmed by Tommasi 4. XXXIII. According to my measurement on Aug. 3, 1898, it is 16 centimetres wide by 22 high, the writing occupying about 12 by 16½, though a marginal *e* extends to 15 centimetres. The Antiphons are provided with neumes ; the spelling is not exactly reproduced by Tommasi, pp. 182-3. Vezzosi says (Tommasi 4. XXXIV) : 'Romanis ritibus admiscentur passim illi monachorum, quorum usui olim inserviebat. . . . Exhibet porro X saeculi ritus in cursu diurno atque nocturno usitatos ; exhibet discrimen inter Romani cleri et monachorum in Galliis Antiphonarios libros.'

[4] Cf. *infra*, pp. 73, 100, 103, 81.

[5] The First Antiphon for the Vespers of Christmas Eve begins : 'Rex pacificus magnificatus est.'

[6] Tommasi says of them : 'I know not whether they are additions made by monks,' and adds that they certainly seem older than Honorius of Autun (see quotation on p. 72). The St. Gallen MS. adds another Antiphon, which cannot, however, be classed with the O's : [13]. 'Qui venturus est veniet, et non tardabit; jam non erit timor in finibus nostris.'

The best authorities seem to be of opinion that these occasional Antiphons are of monastic origin. This is quite in consonance with the historic fact that the

The following information with respect to the O's has been kindly communicated to me in a letter from Professor T. Bouquillon, of the Catholic University of America:

'Those Antiphons were generally sung at Vespers at the Magnificat, sometimes at Lauds at the Benedictus. Sometimes the Antiphon was recited before and after the Magnificat (as is done to-day) ; sometimes repeated three times in succession ;[1] sometimes recited after each verse of the Benedictus, beginning with the verse, *In sanctitate et justitia*.[2] They were and are intoned by a dignitary — bishop, archdeacon, etc.

' The Antiphons were and are sung in churches where the divine office is sung publicly and solemnly, as in cathedrals (of Europe), churches to which chapters are attached, and churches connected with monasteries. Even where part of the office is only recited, Vespers and Lauds are sung. The melodies of which Guéranger speaks are undoubtedly the Gregorian or plain-chant. You may find them complete in the publications of the Benedictines of Solesmes ; in the Vesperale[3] of our churches they are abbreviated. The Antiphons are not divided ; a member of the choir intones, and all follow with him.[4]

development of the liturgy was in large measure due to monks (see Batiffol, chaps. I and II). The arch-cantor John, whom Benedict Biscop brought into England, was, it will be remembered, abbot of St. Martin's monastery at Rome (Bede 4. 18). We shall not be far astray, I believe, if we suppose these four Antiphons to be of Benedictine origin.

[1] So at Tours, according to Martène, *De Antiquis Ecclesiae Ritibus*, lib. 4. cap. 10. — ED.

[2] The Vatican MS. printed by Tommasi assigns them (p. 27) to the Benedictus, and hence to Lauds. Tommasi notes: 'Consentit . . . Rituale M. S. Benedicti Canonici,' but refers to Amalarius and Alcuin (and so p. 182) as if testifying in favor of Vespers. The St. Gallen MS. assigns them to Vespers (p. 182). The Vatican MS. adds : 'Ad has omnes Antiphonas versus *Ostende nobis*,' which Tommasi interprets as meaning that the verse *Ostende nobis, Domine, misericordiam tuam*, etc., is to precede the Canticle. — ED.

[3] Note that Exeter cathedral possessed a well-worn Vesperale when Leofric succeeded to the bishopric; cf. *supra*, p. vii. In the Vesperale published by H. Dessain at Mechlin, the music of the Greater Antiphons is on pp. 17–20. — ED.

[4] On the whole question of how the Antiphons were sung, see especially Tommasi 4. XXI–XXXVII. The subject is too large to discuss here. I give but one quotation, from the Vatican Antiphonary (Tommasi 4. 37) : 'In nocte Natalis Domini, ad omnes Antiphonas Vigiliae chorus choro respondet, et sic omnes Antiphonas cantamus ante Psalmos et infra Psalmos ubi inveniuntur, et in fine

'They were begun Dec. 17, St. Nicholas' Day, and finished on St. Lucia.[1] When eight were sung, they were begun a day earlier, and so on.'

It is scarcely necessary to dwell at length on the Antiphons for Trinity Sunday; the important facts are presented at the appropriate place in the Notes.[2]

The character of the Antiphons and their influence upon Cynewulf. — The Antiphons which underlie Part I are prose, but rhythmic prose. In their general frame they are not unlike a brief Collect. The better to illustrate this statement, let us see what a typical Collect contains. According to Goulburn,[3] the constituent parts of a Collect are : ' 1st, the invocation; 2dly, the recital of some doctrine or fact, which is made the basis of the petition ; 3dly, the petition itself, which rises upon this basis ; 4thly, the aspiration, which is the feather or wing to the petition ; 5thly, in all Collects addressed to the Father, the alleging of the Mediator's work on our behalf, and the pleading of his name.'[4] Of course many Collects are deficient

Psalmorum, et post *Gloria Patri,* et post *Sicut erat.* Sed chorus cujus est versus infra Psalmum qui est Antiphona incipit Antiphonam, alter respondet, et qui incipit finit eam.' To this Tommasi subjoins: ' Hoc est, ab uno choro prima Antiphonae parte cantata, chorus alter alteram perficit partem.' This is borne out by Amalarius, *De Eccl. Officiis* 4. 7 (Migne 105. 1180) : ' Antiphona dicitur vox reciproca. Antiphona inchoatur ab uno unius chori, et ad ejus symphoniam. Psalmus cantatur per duos choros. Ipsa enim, id est Antiphona, conjunguntur simul duo chori. . . . Duobus choris alternatur Antiphona.' Tommasi observes (4. XXXVI) that the men were on the right of the officiating priest, and the women (of course not in the choir) on the left ; with this cf. *Exod.* 576–7 :

> Weras wuldres sang, wíf on ŏŏrum,
> folcswēota mæst fyrdlēoŏ gōlon.

See also Bäumer, p. 122; Batiffol, pp. 94–6. — ED.

[1] This is of course an error : St. Nicholas' day is Dec. 6, and St. Lucy's Dec. 13. Professor Bouquillon is evidently referring to the Vatican Antiphonary, which, as already mentioned, assigns the O's to the Benedictus, and also inserts them between St. Nicholas' day and St. Lucy's. — ED.

[2] Cf. *infra,* pp. 108 ff.

[3] *The Collects of the Day,* i. 22.

[4] This is beautifully illustrated by the Collect for the Burial of the Dead. The divisions begin as follows: (1) ' O most merciful God '; (2) ' who is the resurrection '; (3) ' we meekly beseech thee '; (4) ' that, when we shall '; (5) ' grant this '; (5) ' through Jesus Christ.'

in some respect, or reduced to the barest essentials.[1] In these cases
the resemblance to one of the O's is more evident, as may be seen
by a comparison, for example, with the *O Sapientia*.[2] It is significant that the English Collect for the Sunday after Ascension has
been modeled upon the *Antiphon* for Ascension quoted in the
Notes.[3] The structure of Collect and Antiphon is here so far one
that we have the parallelism of invocation and recital on one hand,
and of petition on the other.[4] This parallelism, and the resulting
rhythm, and in some cases rime, tend to approximate prose to verse.
The mediæval sermons are full of it,[5] and this circumstançe may
account for the relation between our poem and the sermons of
Gregory and Caesarius.

From all that has been said, it is apparent that we must conceive
of Cynewulf as so thrilled by the sweet and solemn chanting of the
Greater Antiphons of Advent, and so imbued with their spirit through
reflection upon their rich devotional and doctrinal contents, that he
gladly yielded to the impulse to reproduce them in English under
the form of variation. In so doing he employed the peculiarly
monastic Antiphons side by side with those sanctioned by the
Church universal; he abridged, expanded, suppressed, or trans-
posed, as his genius dictated; freely interpolated matter from other
sources, when it suited his purpose so to do; and welded the whole
together by closing with a magnificent doxology to the triune God,

---

[1] Thus in the Collect for Whitsunday: 'Deus, qui hodierna die corda fidelium
Sancti Spiritus illustratione docuisti : da nobis in eodem Spiritu recta sapere, et
de ejus semper consolatione gaudere. Per . . . in unitate ejusdem. . . .' Except
for the 5th division, this much resembles one of our Antiphons.

[2] *Infra*, p. 101.   [3] P. 118.

[4] So in the first seven of the O's, the *O Rex pacifice*, and the *O Hierusalem* (?),
but not in the others (*infra*, pp. 73, 84, 103, 108).

[5] Norden goes so far as to say (*Die Antike Kunstprosa* 2. 844): 'Die rhetor-
ischen an den hohen Festtagen gehaltenen Predigten der Christen waren nichts
anderes als *Hymnen in Prosa*,' adducing as early examples Gregory Nazianzen
(*Patr. Gr.* 35. 537 ; 36. 72) and Sophronios (*Patr. Gr.* 87 III. 3321). Not less
significant are the remarks of Bäumer (*Gesch. des Breviers*, p. 2): 'Da das Gebet
der Ausdruck der tiefsten und innersten das Menschenherz bewegenden Gefühle
und Empfindungen ist, so haben auch diese Gebete der Kirche, gleich denen des
Alten Bundes, naturgemäss einen vorherrschend lyrischen Charakter. . . Diese
wunderbare Vereinigung von lyrischer Poesie und gottgegebenem Inhalt ist auch
dem officiellen Gebete der Kirche eigen geblieben.' Cf. my Notes, pp. 195, 209,
210, 222, 223, etc.

followed by a few resumptive lines in which, returning to the theme of Advent, he alludes to the reward which Christ will bestow upon the righteous at his second appearing.[1] Throughout the whole he alternates between joy and exultation over the approaching fulness of Christ's manifestation,[2] and intense desire that he will liberate the individual sinner from the thraldom of sin and build up his own Church in its most holy faith, while interspersed are rejoicings over the manifest fulfilment of prophecy, tributes to the mother of the Divine Son, and vivid realization of the historic circumstances connected with the Nativity. ⚚

PART II. THE ASCENSION.[3] — As the source of Part I is found in the Breviary, so also is the principal source of Part II, the Ascension sermon of Pope Gregory the Great. The fact that Gregory was the father of English Christianity, or at least of Roman Christianity in England, together with the circumstance that to him was attributed the constitution of the liturgy, the compilation of the musical service-books employed by the Church, and the institution of the school for chanters from which England had received its training in sacred song,[4] imparts a singular interest to this poetic amplification of one of his most eloquent homilies.[5] The Venerable Bede, too, as in the Third Part, is represented among the originals by a hymn full of spirited movement and dialogue, and thus two of the glories of the English Church are associated in the substance of this Ascension poem. If now we consider the highly dramatic character of the angelic addresses in the opening portion,[6] the vivid allusions to contemporary activity in the most varied walks of life,[7] the touches of personal senti-

---

[1] Cf. 434 with 846, 1361, 1587.
[2] As, for example, 45 ff.
[3] See p. xxv, note 4.
[4] Joan. Diac. 2. 6.
[5] Ozanam (*Dante et la Philosophie Catholique*, p. 32; cf. p. 27) is tempted to call him the last of the Romans. If this be true, he in whom ancient Rome died was he from whom the civilization of England began to live. As to its truth, cf. Gregory's own words (Migne 76. 1010): 'Ipsa autem quae aliquando mundi domina esse videbatur qualis remanserit Roma conspicimus? Immensis doloribus multipliciter attrita, desolatione civium, impressione hostium, frequentia ruinarum. . . . Ubi enim senatus? Ubi jam populus? . . . Quia enim senatus deest, populus interiit, et tamen in paucis qui sunt dolores et gemitus quotidie multiplicantur, jam vacua ardet Roma.' Cf. Lanciani, *The Destruction of Ancient Rome*, p. 88.
[6] E.g. 517–526, 558–585; cf. the dramatic lines, 164–214.
[7] 664–681.

ment,[1] and the introduction of the poet's name in the puzzling runic passage,[2] we shall be able to understand the peculiar fascination exerted by this Part. A conspicuous link with Part I is provided by a section in which the Advent is definitely named,[3] while Part III is as evidently preluded by the references to the Last Judgment in the passage which includes the runes, no less than by the circumstance that the Ascension is the express pledge of the Second Coming. Moreover, the Trinity is here glorified,[4] as in I,[5] and two hymns transmitted by Bede furnish sources respectively for II and III.[6]

It is an artistic flaw that certain sequences are insufficiently motived here, as throughout the *Christ*. Especially is this true of the fine address on the Harrowing of Hell,[7] and of the reference to the Advent.[8] These may be compared with the lack of art in portions of Part III.[9]

On the whole this Part compares favorably, allowance being made for the character of its theme, with the two others, and Cynewulf has escaped the censure visited upon religious painters by Ruskin :[10] 'I can not understand why this subject was so seldom treated by religious painters, for the harmony of Christian creed depends as much upon it as on the Resurrection itself, while the circumstances of the Ascension, in their brightness, promise, miraculousness, and direct appeal to all the assembled Apostles, seem more

---

[1] 789–796. We are not bound, I think, to attach very great importance to the use of the first personal pronoun in this passage. Why, for example, should we lay any more weight upon

Hūru ic wēne mē
ond ēac ondrǣde dōm ðȳ rēþran, etc.,

than upon the following lines in the *Doomsday* translated from the Latin of Bede (15–20 ; *Bibl. z.* 251) ?

Ic ondrǣde mē ēac dōm þone miclan
for māndǣdum mīnum on eorðan,
ond þæt ēce ic ēac yrre ondrǣde mē
ond synfulra gehwām æt sylfum Gode,
ond hū mihtig Frēa eall manna cynn
tōdǣleð ond tōdēmeð þurh his dīhlan miht.

The 'I' may very easily be used as frequently in hymns and homilies, or as in the Book of Psalms.

[2] 797–807.
[3] 586–599.
[4] 599.
[5] 378 ff.; cf. 357-8.
[6] *Infra*, pp. 116, 171.
[7] 558–585; cf. *infra*, pp. 129 ff.
[8] 586–599.
[9] See pp. xci ff.
[10] *Giotto and his Works in Padua.*

fitted to attract the joyful contemplation of all who received the faith. How morbid and how deeply to be mourned was the temper of the Church which could not be satisfied without perpetual representation of the tortures of Christ, but rarely dwelt upon his triumph !'

PART III. DOOMSDAY. — For the general organism of this Part Cynewulf is dependent upon the hymn quoted by Bede; [1] for the suggestion of the Sign of the Son of Man to the vision of Constantine, a passage in Ephraem Syrus,[2] or one doubtfully attributed to Augustine ; [3] for the mourning of the universe at Christ's death, to Gregory ; [4] for the bloody sap of the trees, to the Apocrypha; [5] for Christ's address to the sinner, to Caesarius of Arles,[6] or, more ultimately, Ephraem Syrus; for the sword of victory in the hand of the Judge, to Prudentius; [7] and for the account of the joys of the blessed, to Gregory and Augustine.[8] Yet such is Cynewulf's imaginative power and command of language that sutures are nowhere visible; the whole is molded, or rather fused, into a poem of the greatest moral fervor, intensity, and vividness. Though there is somewhat too much pausing for reflection, and though the poet occasionally retraces his steps, there is much vigor, and almost continual progress. The scenes described are realized with startling clearness ; the speeches are majestic and yet tender, pathetic but awful.; the poet's personal appeals are by no means conventional, and the fates of the damned and the blessed are depicted according to the dictates of an unwavering faith.

As the organism of this Part is less transparent than those of the other two, it may not be superfluous to attempt an analysis.[9] The great lines are apparently these :

1. The trumpet call to judgment, and the resurrection of the dead.

2. The coming of the Judge.

3. The destruction of the universe.

4. Men's deeds and thoughts shall be manifest.

5. The good and the evil are irresistibly urged and drawn before the throne of judgment.

6. The celestial Rood, the Sign of the Son of Man, shall be advanced in the sight of all.

[1] *Infra*, pp. 171 ff.   [3] Pp. 193–4.   [5] P. 200.   [7] P. 216.
[2] Pp. 189 ff.   [4] P. 195.   [6] P. 210.   [8] P. 222.
[9] A more detailed analysis will be found on pp. 170–171 ; cf. pp. 175–7. Artistic flaws are noted on pp. xci ff.

7. The reminiscences and reflections aroused by the sight of the Rood. (Dumb creatures sympathized with the death of Christ, while sinners remained hard of heart.)

8. The redeemed are gathered on the right, and the wicked on the left.

9. Three causes of the happiness of the just and the misery of the unrighteous.

10. The good are welcomed to heaven.

11. The wicked are first reminded of Christ's love, and then cast down to hell.

12. Exhortation to be wise in time.

13. The horrors of hell.

14. The joys of heaven.

GRAMMATICAL NOTES.—Only the more significant facts are noticed, especially those that bear on the question of dialect and on the mutual relations of the three Parts.

Stressed vowels. — Here may be noted :

Short *a* : usually *ǫ* before *m* and *n*. Isolated exceptions are (once each, unless otherwise stated) : Latin words like ancrum (II), sancta (I); then anginn (I), āscamode (III), forhwan (III), fram (III, twice), lange (I, III), manna (I, II), onfangen (I), scandum (III).

Short *a* in inflection : blacra (III), wrace (III).

Breaking, and *u*- and *o*- umlaut, occur regularly in all usual positions, the latter sometimes going beyond the strict WS. limits, as in beofian, cearu, cleopian, freoðian, heafela, lioðu-, meotud, teala (but fela, wela) ; in inflection : -cleofu, freoða, -hleodu (III ; also -hlidu, II), -hleoðu, leomo ; but brego (not breogo), gemetu, gesetu. Giofu (I), geofum (II), occur side by side with the obl. cases giefe, gife.

Gedreag (999) is not clear to me.

Before *l* + cons. occurs exceptionally *ā* (*Gram.* 158. 2) : alwālda, ālwihta(?); cāld (II, III); hāls (II, but mundheals II); wāldan, -end always except wealdan (1388), onwāld (I); onwālg (III). Umlaut of this *ā* in ælde (I, II, III, MS. once elda, 311 ; but yldu, 'age,' III), wǣlm (II, III). Umlaut of *a* before *r* + cons. (*Gram.* 158. 1) gives *æ* in wærgðu (I, III). Meaht is constant, but meahtig (II, III; once ælmeahtigne, 759), mihtig (I, II, III); the vb. has meahte. Niht is constant (II, III), but sinneahtes (I), sinnehte (III). *W* affects a following *eo, io* only in woruld, wudu, utan ; so sweopu, sweotul-, weorud (once weredum, III), etc.; but witon (1243), not wioton ; wiht, not wuht.

I-umlaut of *a* varies in mænigo (I), męngu (II).

For swǣr, swǣse occur swār (III), swāse (III, but swǣs, II, III). Gǣst is constant (no gāst). Ēngan (237) seems to represent ǣngan.

Short *i* is usually retained, but becomes *y* in crybb (III), drync (III), fyrwet (I), hyder (II, but hider-, I), sygor (II, but sigor, I, II, III), wynster(III, but winster,III), yrmen(II). Gehwylc, swylc are constant. Long *i* is regularly retained, but scȳnan (III).

Short *y* is regularly retained. Rare exceptions are : cinn (III), flihte (399), hingrendum (III), riht (18), simle (I, II, but symle, I, II, III), ðrim (I, 423).

Long *ȳ* is regularly retained. Exception : fir (III).

Confusion of *ea* and *eo*, *ēa* and *ēo*, pointing to Anglian influence, in pret. 3 sg. beorn (II) ; geondsprēot. Besides geoguð (III) occurs gioguð (III) ; nēod (I, III), nīod (I) ; gēo (II), īu (I, III) ; cf. sioh ; īowa.

WS. *ie, īe* are usually represented by *y, ȳ* : byldo, dyrne, fyllan, hwyrfan, scyppend, scyrian, āwyrged, yrre, etc.; gebȳgan, dȳre, hȳhsta, strȳnan, etc. But scild- (II ; sceldun, III). Occasional forms are fier (I) ; giedd (II); -giell (II) ; gietan (II, III) ; gīet (I) ; hīenþu (II) ; dēgol (I, II) ; lēg (II, III, līg, III) ; tōlēseð (III). Alternative are gief-, gif, gyf- ; yrmðu (I, II, III), ermðu (I); gild (I) gield (III), gyld (III); gielp (II), gylp (II) ; styll (II), styllan (II), stiell (II) ; syleð (III), sęleð (II) ; gīeman (II, III), gīman (III); īecan (II), ȳcan (III) ; nīed (I), nȳd (III) ; nȳhst (II), nēhst (I) ; onsīen (II, III), onsȳn (II, III) ; scȳne (II, III), scīenne (III) ; yldu, 'age,' may be compared with ǣlde, 'men' ; with and without umlaut are beornan (II), byrnan (II, III) ; ēowan (I, II, also īowan, I), ēawan (I, III), ȳwan (I, II, III) ; lȳhtan (I, III), lēohtan (I) ; ðēostor (I, III), ðȳstro (I, III).

With regular sylf (I, II, III) occurs once self (III).

Influence of palatals on following vowels. Here occur with *g* : gēo (II), īu (I, III); gioguð (III), -geoguð (III); geatu (I, II); gatu (I); giefan (but gifen, III, gyfen, III), giefe (but gife, II), geaf, gēfon ; gietan, -geat, ǫndgiet ; gield (III), gyld (III); gielp (II), gylp (II); giedd (II); wīdgiell (II) ; gīet (?).

With *c* : ceafl ; cear- ; ceaster ; cyle ; cyrran.

With *sc* : scēaden ; gesceaft ; sceal ; gesceap, gesceapen ; scearp ;

sceaða; sceolde, sceolon (II, III, but sculon I, II, III); scild (II); scēop (III, but scōp, I, II), scyppend; scyrian (I, III); but scæcen (II), sceldun (III), scōd (III); scǫmu, scǫmian, scǫnd; scūa. *Unstressed and slightly stressed vowels.* — Variation between orgete (III; cf. ǫndgete) and orgeate (III). Weakening of middle vowel in inlocast (I; cf. *Gram.* 43. 3). Exceptional change of middle vowel in firina (56). Weakening of swā-þēah to se-ðēah (I). Mānsworan for -swaran (1611). Wīdeferh (I, II) side by side with -feorh (II). With ōwiht (I, III) occurs ōht (I), and with āwo (II, III) occur ā (I, II), ō (I, II; cf. nō, I, III). Dædhwæte and dōmhwate both occur in I.

Nouns regularly ending in -*u* generally have -*o*: byldo, hælo, word-gerȳno, etc.; less frequently -*u*: hælu, etc. Once (MS.) wærgða (98).

Be- and *bi-* occur as follows in the three Parts: I has *be-*, 9; *bi-*, 6; II has *be-*, 5; *bi-*, 15; III has *be-*, 2; *bi-*, 36. In 1000 lines this would be expressed by saying that *be-* occurs in I, 20.5 times; in II, 11.7; in III, 2.5; *bi-* occurs in I, 13.7 times; in II, 35.1; in III, 45. Expressed in ratios this would give for *be-*:

$$II : I : : 57 : 100$$
$$III : I : : 12 : 100$$

For *bi-*:

$$II : I : : 256 : 100$$
$$III : I : : 329 : 100$$

For   I : *be-* = 1½ *bi-*.
For II : *be-* = ⅓ *bi-*.
For III : *be-* = $\frac{1}{18}$ *bi-*.

This is striking, yet can hardly invalidate the conclusion, derived from an examination of the other grammatical phenomena, that the three Parts do not greatly differ. The preposition, it may be added, occurs as *bi* in I (4), II (5), III (6); as *be* in III (2) — a result which does not seem compatible with that above.

After long syllables the syncopation of the vowel of a short syllable takes place regularly, and the same is true after the short syllables of fæger(?), hefig, micel, and yfel. MS. exceptions occur in the case of certain adjectives in -*ig*, such as ælmihtig, ænig, blōdig, gesælig, wērig. For these, which have been usually normalized in the text, see the Variants. Synnig has oblique syngum, etc. No syncopation in ēowerum, 1503; fēowerum, 878. On the other hand

MS. syncopation irregularly occurs after short syllables (see Variants): bitrum (I, III), dysge (III), mọnge (III), etc. Ẹgsa is uniform, not ẹgesa; mægne (I, II, III), but mægene (I, 382). *Consonants.* — *C* regularly changes to *h* in pp. dreahte, ðeahte, rẹht, slæht, but not in ðrycton (III). *D* interchanges with ð in ēad- (II), ēaðmōd (I), ēaðmēdu (I, III), and in Dāuīdes (I), Dāuīþes (II). *G* final is not changed to *h*: dēag, drēag, stāg; *g* before *d*, ð, and *n* is retained, except in ongēan (III), tōgēanes (II), -hȳdig (II, III). *H* is usually retained in compounds of hēah, but hēagẹngel (I, III; also hēahẹngel, I, II), hēadūne (II); ns. hēa; asm. hēanne; assimilation of *h* also in hēannissum (I); loss before cons. ending in hrēone; fāh, pl. fā; feorh, fēores, etc.; loss initially in raþe (III, but hraðe, III). *L* is irregularly geminated in ællbeorhte (III), ẹllþēodum (III); spātl occurs as in WS. (*Gram.* 196. 2). Metathesis of *r* is not constant in bearhtm (III), brehtm (III). *S* is assimilated in blis (I, II, III), liss (I, III), but not in blēts- (I), milts (I, III). *Đ* is retained in cȳðde (I, II, III). *W* occasionally becomes *u* in sāul (I, II), is lost in fēa (III), hrā (I), and fluctuates in ā (I, II), āwo (II, III); for ọndlata see note on 1435.

Nouns. — Dæg has gp. dagena (II, III), daga (III). Sunu has np. sunu (I). Dohtor has np. dohtor (I). Tungol has np. tungol (II, III), tunglas (I). Sǣ has np. sǣs. Short monosyllabic and polysyllabic neuter nouns end np. in -*o*, -*u*.

Weak adjectives. — Besides sylfa, for which see Glossary, adjectives are declined weak where prose would require strong in the following lines: nom. 932, 983; gen. 21, 58, 94, 110, 165, 396, 711, 867; dat. (tō wīdan fēore, ealdre) 230, 277, 1343, 1514, 1543; acc. 183 (gen.?), 439 (ealne wīdan feorh); inst. 309, 371, 389, 510, 1086; nom. pl. 363, 364.

Comparison of adjectives. — Comp. ǣrra; sēlla, sēllra; strẹngra; wyrsa. Sup. ǣrẹst; æðelast (III), bẹtast (III), bẹtst (III); hȳhsta; sēlest. Adverbs: comp. fier, lẹng.

Pronouns. — Personal: mē (I, II), mec (III); ðē (I, III), ðec (I, II, III); ūre (I, II); ūs (I, II), ūsic (I, III); ēowic (II); hyre (III); hire (III); hȳ (I, II, III), hī (II, III), hīe (I, II), hīo (I, 322); hyra (I, II, III), hira (III, 1171). Possessive: his, but sīn (III, five times). Ūser (but gen. ūre above) has ūsses, ūssum, etc. (I, II, III). Demonstrative: sēo (I, II, III), sīo (I, III); inst. ðȳ (II, III), ðī (I, II), ðon (I, II); ðǣm (once ðǣn, III); ðāra. Đēs has ðisse, -es, -um. Indefinite: gehwone (I, II, III), gehwane (I).

Numerals. — Ānne occurs twice (III), ænne once (III).

Verbs. — The ind. pres. 2 and 3 sg. of strong verbs take no umlaut, except cymeð (I, II, III) and færeð (III). Neither do they contract the ending, with the exception of regular contract verbs and two in ð: biwrīðan, cweðan; these have bewrīð (II), cwið (II, III). Verbs in *e* of Ablaut Classes III and V regularly take *i* in the ind. pres. 2 and 3 sg.: spriceð (I), wigeð (III).

Ind. pres. 2 sg. of both strong and weak verbs ends in *-st*: bemurnest (I), spricest (I); cleopast (I). Exception: inlīhtes (I).

Ind. pret. pl. ends in *-on, -an, -un.*

Ind. pret. 2 sg. of weak verbs, preterite presents, and willan ends in *-es*: brōhtes (I), gebohtes (I), gehogdes (III), hȳrdes (III), sealdes (I), þolades (III), worhtes (I); sceoldes (III), wisses (III), nysses (III), noldes (III). Exception: gefyldest (I, 408).

Many weak verbs of Class II form the pret. in *-ade.*

Certain past participles of Ablaut Classes III, V, and VI vary the root vowel between *a, æ,* and *e* (*Gram.* 368, N. 4; 378, N. 1, 2): (*a*) bigrafan, hafen (II), but āhæfen (II); (*b*) gefrægen (II), scæcen (II); (*c*) ofslegen (III). That of cuman is cymen (I), cumen (II); that of dōn is -dēn (III), -dōn (III); that of fōn is -fēn (III), -fǫngen, -fangen (I, II, III).

Bisēon, 'moisten,' has pp. bisēon (*Gram.* 383, N. 4).

Onwrēon has the pret. 3 sg. onwrāh, not onwrēah (*Gram.* 383).

Cuman has 3 sg. cymeð; pret. 3 sg. cwōm; pl. cwōman, -un; opt. 3 sg. cume (I), cyme (I); imp. sg. cum (I), cym (I); pp. cymen (I), cumen (II).

Niman has 3 sg. nimeð; pret. 3 sg. nōm.

Giefan has pret. 3 pl. gēfon (III); pp. giefen (III), gifen (III), gyfen (III).

Sēon takes the pret. pl. in Angl. sēgun (II, III, but sāwan II, 740); gesewen (I). Imp. sg. sioh (I).

Licgan has 3 sg. ligeð; pret. 3 sg. læg; pl. lǣgon, -un (I, III), lāgun (III).

Hātan has pret. 3 sg. heht.

Scildan has pret. sceldun (III, 979; MS. scehdun).

The three forms, ēawan, ēowan (īowan), ȳwan are used side by side; imp. sg. īowa (I), ȳwe (I).

The imp. sg. of gesēcan is gesēce (I), though that of sēcan is sēc (II).

The irregular weak verbs in *cc* of the First Class have breaking in the pret. and pp.: āreahtum (III), beþeaht (I, III), gedreaht (III); but also geręht (I); geslæht (I). Ȳcan has pp. geȳced; biðryccan the pret. pl. biþrycton.

Uninflected past participles of weak verbs in *d* do not contract the ending: sended (I). Inflected past participles from long stems regularly syncopate the *e* of *-ed*, *-en*: bibyrgde, gedȳrde, gecȳpte, geswencte, etc.; biwundne, gebundne, etc. Short stems retain the *e*: gecorene.

Sorgian has ptc. sorgende (*Gram.* 412, N. 11). Hæbbe has 2 and 3 sg.: hafast, hafað. Lifgan has 3 sg. leofað; imp. sg. leofa; ptc. lifgende. Sęcgan has 3 sg. sagað (III), -sęgð (III); imp. sg. saga. Hycgan has pret. pl. hogdun. Ðrēan has 3 sg. ðrēað; pp. ðrēad. Frēogan has 3 pl. frēogað. Sculan has pl. sculon (I, II, III), sceolon (II, III); pret. sceolde, etc.; opt. scyle.

Magon has 2 sg. meaht, pl. magon (I, II, III), mægon (I); pret. pl. meahtan; opt. pl. mægen (III), magon (III).

Of the verb wesan the following are the more interesting forms: eam (I), bēom (III); eart (I), bist (I); is (I, II, III), bið (II, III); sind (I, II, III), sindon, -an (II, III), bēoð (II, III); sīe (I, III), sī (II), sȳ (III); wesan (II, III), bēon (I). Negative contract: nis (I, III.)

Willan has sg. wille (II, III), wile (I, II, III); neg. nyle (II, III), nele (III); pl. nellað (III).

II. POEMS ATTRIBUTED TO CYNEWULF.

THE RIDDLES AND CYNEWULF. — Many of the accounts of Cynewulf, popular and even scholarly, are based upon the assumption that he wrote the collection of riddles in the Exeter Book, or at least the largest part of them. This assumption dates from 1857, when Leo published his famous interpretation of the First Riddle. As soon as Cynewulf was credited with the authorship of this riddle, it was easy to assign others to him, then the whole series, and then, by subtle combinations of inferences from this hypothesis with known facts or other hypotheses, to weave an extensive web of more or less credible supposition concerning the poet. In the last analysis, this romantic fable depends wholly upon the assumed discovery of the name Cynewulf in the First Riddle (so-called), conceived as a charade. Hence it is necessary first to examine this poem, or poetic fragment, which is accordingly presented here.

> Lēodum is mīnum swylce him mon lāc gife;
> willað hȳ hine āþecgan gif hē on þrēat cymeð.
>   Ungelīc is ūs.
> Wulf is on īege, ic on ōþerre;
> fæst is þæt ēglond, fenne biworpen;
> sindon wælrēowe weras þær on īge;
> willað hȳ hine āþecgan gif hē on þrēat cymeð.
>   Ungelīce is ūs.
> Wulfes ic mīnes wīdlāstum wēnum dogode.
> þonne hit wæs rēnig weder ond ic rēotugu sæt,
> þonne mec se beaducāfa bōgum bilegde;
> wæs mē wyn tō þon, wæs mē hwæþre ēac lāð.
>   Wulf, mīn wulf, wēna mē þīne
> sēoce gedydon, þīne seldcymas,
> murnende mōd, nāles metelīste.
> Gehȳrest þū Ēadwacer, uncerne earne hwelp?
> bireð wulf tō wuda.
> þæt mon ēaþe tōslīteð, þætte næfre gesomnad wæs,
> uncer giedd geador.

To this I append a literal translation, with alternative renderings where such are necessary, it being premised that the poem is, at best, decidedly obscure.

To my people it is as if one give to them a gift (*or*, gifts) ;
They will *áþecgan* him if he comes into [the] throng (*or*, into a calamity).
Different is it with us.
Wolf (*or*, Wulf) is on an island, I on another ;
Firm is the island, surrounded with bog;
There on the island are fierce men ;
They will *áþecgan* him if he comes into the throng (*or*, calamity).
Different is it with us.
I *dogode* with (*or*, to) the far-wandering hopes of my wolf (*or*, Wulf).
(*Or*, I *dogode* in hopes with the long journeys of my wolf (*or*, Wulf)).
(*Or*, I *dogode* my Wulf with (*or*, to) far-wandering hopes)
When it was rainy weather and I sat tearful,
Then the warlike one covered me with boughs (*or*, arms);
It was joy to me to that extent, yet it was also sorrow.
Wolf (*or*, Wulf), my wolf (*or*, Wulf), me thy hopes
Have made sick, thy infrequent comings,
Anxious heart, not at all needs of food.
Dost thou hear Eadwacer, our *earne* cub?
(*Or*, Dost thou hear, Eadwacer? Our *earne* cub)
(*Or*, Dost thou hear Eadwacer? Our *earne* cub)
(He) beareth a wolf (*or*, Wulf) to the wood.
(*Or*, A wolf (*or*, Wulf) beareth to the wood.)
One easily separates that which never was united,
    Our song together.

It will be seen that there are three words whose meaning is
unknown, *áþecgan*, *dogode*, and *earne;* four whose meaning is
ambiguous, *þréat*, *wulf* (*Wulf*), *wídlāstum*, *bōgum;* one whose
usual sense does not seem quite to fit the context, *wēnum* (*wēna*).
Besides, the construction is ambiguous in vv. 3 and 4 from the end,
ambiguous or unintelligible in v. 4 from the end.

On this precarious basis, fabrics of ingenious interpretation have
been reared. The most famous of these has had a deleterious effect
upon Old English scholarship, especially as regards Cynewulf. I
refer to that of Leo,[1] which was published in 1857. By arbitrarily
changing words, significations, and syntax,[2] Leo succeeds in rendering as follows :[3]

[1] *Quae de se ipso Cynewulfus Poeta Anglosaxonicus tradiderit.*

[2] *Léodum* to *leoðum*, *dogode* to *dō gōde* (with *gōde* as adv. (!) and the phrase
rendered as 'enjoy,' 'yield to '), *áþecgan* as 'reveal,' 'as if' to 'as' (*swylce*), 'gift'
to 'meaning' (*lāc*), 'there' to 'here' (*þǣr*), 'thy' (third indented line) to 'after
thee' (i.e. subjective to objective genitive), *uncerne earne* to 'of us two,' *hine* and
hē to stand for the neut. *lāc*, and *geador* from adv. to adj.

[3] A fairly accurate translation of Leo's version may be found in Morley, 2. 218-9.

[1]

Meine Glieder verhalten sich wie man ihnen Bedeutung zutheilt;
Sie werden dieselbe offenbaren, wenn die Bedeutung sich zusammenschaart.

[2]

Ungleich verhält sich's mit uns.
Ein Wolf ist auf einer Insel, ich auf der andern;
Vollkommen ist die Insel mit Sumpfland umgeben.
Wilde Männer sind hier auf dem Eilande.
Sie werden dieselbe offenbaren, wenn er mit (ihrer) Schaar zusammenkömmt.

[3]

Ungleich verhält sich's mit uns.
Ich gebe mich den weitgehenden Sehnsuchten nach meinem Wolf hin.
Wenn es regniges Wetter war und ich weinend sass,
Dann umfasste mich der Kampfschnelle mit seinen Armen.
Das ward mir Wonne, ward mir doch auch Leid.
Wolf! mein Wolf! die Sehnsuchten nach dir
Haben mich krank gemacht, deine seltenen Besuche;
Das trauernde Gemüth (that's), nicht durch Nahrungsmangel.
Hörst du? Eadwaccer, unserer beider Jungen, trägt ein Wolf zum Holze.

[4]

Das sondert man leicht aus einander, was nie Zusammenhang hatte,
Unserer beider gemeinschaftliches Lied.

This becomes a charade, embodying the name of Cynewulf, by a
resort to the following expedients. In the first place, we must
assume that *cyne* may be represented indifferently by *cēne*, *cǣn*, and
cēn, but never by itself. Secondly, *cǣn*, regarded as a Northumbrian
word, must represent *cwēn*. Thirdly, *Ēadwacer*, a noun represented
in Continental history by Odoacer, and found in the later period of
Old English history, must here stand for the vowel *e*, and besides
must be represented as the child of the 'queen' and Wulf. Fourthly,
'island' must = 'syllable,' and *bōg* must = 'anything that parts one
syllable from another.' Fifthly, *wælhrēowe*, 'fierce,' must = *cēne*,
'bold,' and *wuda*, 'wood,' must = *cēn*, 'pine-torch,' assumed to be =
'split wood.'

With these presuppositions, everything follows logically. No. 1
(of course in Leo's translation) shows that the relation between
the two elements (according to Leo, syllables) of the name varies
according to the meaning attributed to each, but that the sense will
be clear the moment you put the two words together. No. 2 declares

that _cēne_ = _wælhrēowe_ is in one syllable, and _wulf_ in another, but that you will understand them when they meet, because when they meet they will be sure to fight, and the difference between them will thus become evident ('Sensus revelabitur, si congrediuntur — scilicet _cēne_ et _wulf_, quia pugna necessario inter eos sequitur, et diversitas eorum luce clarius apparet'). The reader must overlook, in his acceptance of this, that, the cruel ones have all the time been on the island of the wolf (_þær on īge_). No. 3 makes known that the person in whose mouth it is put is a queen, or at least a woman, and that therefore she is to be called _cwēn_, which we may easily represent as _cǣn_, since we are dealing with the Northumbrian dialect. It is true that in North. we once find _coen_ (L. 11. 31), as we have an occasional _coeðanne_ (Mk. 2. 9), etc., but side by side with it six _cwoen_, _cuoen_, and two _cuen;_ accordingly, we must assume that there is a mere graphic loss of one or the other of the two vowels, or else that _coen_ was pronounced not essentially otherwise than _cwǣn_. But No. 3 also reveals to us that _e_ joins _wulf_ to _cēn_, since a wolf carries something to the wood, and this something is apparently Eadwacer, who, as we have seen, stands for _e_. It might be objected that _hwelp_ is perhaps the object of _gehȳrest_, and that _wulf_ may be the object of _bireð_, instead of the subject. Finally, in No. 4 we are reminded that since _cēne_ and _cǣn_ are, after all, diverse in sound, it cannot be difficult to sever them.[1]

And now that the solution of the first riddle is evidently _Cynewulf_, we may go on, as Dietrich[2] (1859) did, and interpret the last riddle, No. 89 (95), as 'the wandering minstrel' — who but Cynewulf? — and 86 (90), which is written in Latin and introduces the word _lupus_, as referring to the same poet.[3]

Only one step remained, to attribute to Cynewulf the whole collection of riddles, which was virtually done by Dietrich.[4] As he had now become a wandering minstrel, it was easy to see the application of _Elene_ 1259–1260 :

> þeah hē in medohealle māðmas þēge,
> æplede gold.

[1] 'Facile fit ud id, quod nunquam inter se cohaeserit, separetur, scilicet communis duarum syllabarum, sive potius membrorum nominis, _cēne_ et _coen_, cantus.'

[2] _Die Räthsel des Exeterbuches_, in _Haupt's Zs._ 11. 448–490; see esp. pp. 487–9; cf. Dietrich in _Lit. Centrbl._ for March 28, 1858, p. 191. and _Jahrb. f. Rom. und Eng. Lit._ 1. 241.   [4] P. 251.

[3] Dietrich, p. 489; cf. _Haupt's Zs._ 12. 232–252, esp. 249–250.

For the romance that grew out of these assumptions, cf. Wülker, *Angl.* 1. 483–5; Grein, *Kurzgefasste Angelsächsische Grammatik,*[1] pp. 11–15.

As the question whether the First Riddle is to be interpreted as 'Cynewulf' is one on which a whole train of assumptions concerning the poet has depended, and still continues to depend, it is important to see how other scholars have dealt with the problem presented by these perplexing lines.

Rieger[2] (1868, pub. 1869) was the first to formulate weighty objections to Leo's solution, though he had no other rendering to propose.[3]

[1] The solution of the First Riddle as 'Cynewulf' was accepted not only by Dietrich (see above, p. lv; also, 1860, in *Kynewulfi Poetae Aetas,* p. 1), but by Eduard Müller, 1861 (*Ueber das Ags. Rätsel des Exeterbuches,* p. 5); Grein (*Germ.* 10. 307; so still in his *Kurzgef. Ags. Gram.,* 1880, p. 13); Rieger, 1868, pub. 1869 (*Zs. f. D. Phil.* 1. 215–219); Sweet, 1871 (Warton's *Hist. Eng. Poet.* 2. 16, and so still in *Anglo-Saxon Reader,* 7th éd., 1894, p. 164); Hammerich, 1873 (*Aelteste Christliche Epik,* p. 96, tr. Michelsen); Ten Brink, 1877 (*Hist. Early Eng. Lit.,* pp. 51–3); Wülker, 1878 (*Angl.* 1. 483–507), 1885 (*Grundriss,* pp. 165–6), and 1888 (*Ber. der K. Sächs. Ges. der Wiss., Philos.-Hist. Klasse,* p. 211); Th. Müller, 1883 (*Ags. Gram.,* p. 29); Lefèvre (*Angl.* 6. 182, 185); D'Ham, 1883 (*Der Gegenwärtige Stand der Cynewulffrage,* p. 12); Prehn, 1883 (*Komposition und Quellen der Rätsel des Exeterbuches,* p. 11; *Neuphil. Studien,* 3. 155); Robinson, 1885 (*Our Early Eng. Lit.,* pp. 60–61); Sarrazin, 1886 (*Angl.* 9. 517); Hicketier, 1888 (*Angl.* 10. 564 ff.); Brooke, 1892 (*Hist. Early Eng. Lit.,* pp. 7, 8, 134 ff.), 1898 (*Eng. Lit. from the Beginning to the Norm. Conq.,* pp. 160–162, somewhat doubtfully).   [2] *Zs. f. D. Phil.* 1. 215–9.

[3] He is inclined to find the word *cynn* signified by the *lēodum mīnum* of v. 1, yet is obliged to confess that *dryht* would be a better rendering, and that in any case, *cynn,* or even *cynne,* is not *cyne.* In No. 3 he would read *cœne = cwene,* instead of *coen = cwēn,* referring to *Rid.* 73[1]. The last two lines of No. 3 he translates: 'Hörst du Eadwacer, unsern zornigen Welf? Er trägt den Wolf zum Holze (das zerlegt man leicht was nie vereinigt war) unser Rätselwort zusammen.' After suggesting various emendations and new renderings, he gives his restored text of the Riddle, as follows :

Lēodum is mīnum swylce him mon lāc gife.
Wulf is on īege, ic on ōðerre.
Fæst is þæt ēglond, fenne biworpen.
Sindon wælrēowe weras þær on īge:
willað hȳ hine āþecgan gif hē on þrēat cymeð.
    Ungelīce is ūs.
Wulfes ic mīnes wīdlāstum, wēnum dōgode,
þonne hit wæs rēnig weder and ic rēotugu sæt.

In 1883, Trautmann [1] attempted to overthrow Leo's supposed proof, and provide a wholly new solution. In the former attempt he was entirely successful; in the latter he remains on the same plane of ingenious, but impossible, conjecture as his predecessor.[2] His answer to the charade is 'The riddle.' Trautmann will not allow that Riddle 86 has any reference to Cynewulf, and solves Riddle 89 again as 'The riddle,' and not as 'The wandering minstrel.' [3]

> þonne mec se beaducāfa bōgum bilegde,
> wæs mē wyn tō þon, wæs mē hwæþre ēac lāð.
> Wulf, mīn Wulf, wēna mē þīne
> sēoce gedydon, þīne seldcymas,
> murnende mōd, nāles metelīste.
> Ungelīce is ūs.
> Gehȳrest þū Ēadwacer, uncerne earne hwelp?
> Bireð wulf tō wuda,
> (þæt mon ēaðe tōslīteð, þætte næfre gesomnad wæs)
> uncer giedd geador.

[1] *Anglia*, Anz. 6. 158–169.

[2] Thus he proceeds. The first two lines mean: 'We riddles like to be guessed,' or, more circuitously expressed: 'It is to us riddles as agreeable (i.e. to be guessed) as if somebody made us a present; we will receive him (i.e. the guesser) if he comes to us' ('es ist meinen Leuten (d.i. uns Rätseln), als ob ihnen jemand Gaben bringe; sie wollen ihn aufnehmen wenn er zu ihnen kommt'). Passing on to No. 2, we may easily see that the guesser is on one island, the riddle on another; that this island is encompassed with difficulties (*fenne*); that the wolf is accompanied by other fierce guessers. In No. 3, it is clear that the riddle is saddened by the wild (wandering) conjectures of Wulf, but that when she is guessed (embraced) she is at once happy and sad. Why? Simply for this reason: As a maiden likes to be won and not to be won, so a riddle likes to be guessed and yet not to be guessed. But further: Wulf's bad guesses, his infrequent hitting of the mark, make the riddle ill. At length, Eureka! the wolf drags the whelp to the forest — the riddle is guessed. No. 4 enounces: Riddle and solution may easily be disjoined, since they were never united; but the answer brings riddle and guesser together.

[3] Cf. also *Anglia*, Anz. 7. 210. Trautmann's views were accepted by Holthaus, 1884 (*Anglia* 7, Anz. 120 ff.) and Ramhorst, 1885 (*Das Altengl. Gedicht vom Heiligen Andreas*, pp. 2, 23). They were opposed, so far as his own solution is concerned, by Nuck, 1888 (*Angl.* 10. 390–394), and by Hicketier, 1888 (*Angl.* 10. 564 ff.), the latter of whom argues at length in favor of Leo's identification of Riddle 1, and Dietrich's of 86 and 89. Morley, 1888 (*Eng. Writers* 2. 217 ff.) follows Trautmann in rejecting Leo's explanation, but also rejects Trautmann's, which he attributes, by the way, to Dietrich, though he translates faithfully from the former. Morley would render Riddle 1 by 'The Christian preacher' (P. 225),

We now come to Henry Bradley's (1888) view[1] concerning the
First Riddle, so-called. To him 'the so-called riddle is not a riddle
at all, but a fragment of a dramatic soliloquy, like *Deor* and *The
Banished Wife's Complaint*, to the latter of which it bears, both in
motive and in treatment, a strong resemblance.' He adds: 'The
poem is certainly "enigmatical" enough; but its obscurity may be
due to the absence of context, and in part also to the monodramatic
form. . . . The speaker, it should be premised, is shown by the
grammar to be a woman. Apparently she is a captive in a foreign
land. Wulf is her lover and an outlaw, and Eadwacer (I suspect,
though it is not certain) is her tyrant husband. Whether the subject of the poem be drawn from history or Teutonic legend, or
whether it be purely the invention of the poet, there seems to be no
evidence to determine.' Bradley then translates:

> [.   .   .   .   .   .   .]

> Is to my people as though one gave them a present.
> Will they give him food if he should come to want?
>   It is otherwise with us.

> Wulf is on an island, I on another.
> The island is closely surrounded by fen.
> On yonder isle are fierce and cruel men;
> Will they give him food if he should come to want?
>   It is otherwise with us !

> I waited for my Wulf with far-wondering longings
> When it was rainy weather, and I sat tearful.

> When the brave warrior encircled me with his arms
> It was joy to me, yet was it also pain.

> O Wulf, my Wulf! it was my longings after thee
> That made me sick — it was thy seldom coming —
> It was a sorrowful heart, not the want of food !

> Dost thou hear, Eadwacer? The cowardly (?) whelp of us two
> Shall Wulf carry off to the wood.
> Easily can that be broken asunder which never was united,
> The song of us two together.

> [.   .   .   .   .]

sees in 86 a series of allusions to the Bible, and recognizes no ground for asso-
ciating 89 with Cynewulf, even if it be granted that it means 'The wandering
minstrel.'

[1] *Academy*, No. 829, March 24, 1888, pp. 197–8.

Bradley subjoins :[1] 'Some points in this translation are open to
dispute.   The rendering of *on ðréat cuman* as "to come to want" is
suggested by the Icelandic phrase *at þrotum koma* in the same sense
[but Cleasby-Vigfusson does not so render it]. . . . *Āþecgan*, which
occurs only in this passage, I take as the causative of *þicgan*, and as
meaning "to give food to, to entertain." The adjective *earne*, which
I regard as the accusative of *earh*, "cowardly" [Holthausen, *Angl.*
15. 188, proposes *earmne*], is commonly explained as "swift," from
earu [but against this would be *Gram.* § 300, though see Anm.]. . . .'
  Finally, Sievers (1891)[2] calls Leo's interpretation impossible, and
approves of its overthrow by Trautmann.   That Leo in 1857 could
suppose that the poet would reveal the first two syllables of his name
by means of the adj. *cǣne, cēne*, and the nouns *cēn* and *cǣn*, is compre-
hensible in view of the knowledge of OE., and especially of Early
Northumbrian, then current, but nowadays this ought to be impossible.   Sievers then adduces these points :

  1. *Cynewulf* must have the first syllable short.
  2. *Cǣnewulf* is inadmissible ; the first syllable being long, the form
must be *Cānwulf*.
  3. In Early Northumbrian there could be no possible interchange
of *cyne, cǣne, cēn*, and *cwǣn ;* besides, in Early Northumbrian there
is no such loss of *w* as occasionally takes place in Late Northumbrian.   Sievers' date for the Riddles, it should be said, is earlier
than the time of Cynewulf.   How, concludes Sievers, could a hearer
of the riddle be expected to guess *Cyni*, when there were set before
him *cǣni, cwǣn*, and *cēn ?*   Even the Norse scalds never reached
such a point as this.
  The conclusion of the whole matter is accordingly this.   Cynewulf's name is not found in the First Riddle, which in all probability
is not a riddle at all.   Hence there is no ground for assuming that
either Riddle 86 or Riddle 89 is intended to denote Cynewulf.
There is therefore nothing in any of the Riddles to indicate that
Cynewulf was a wandering minstrel.   Finally; the Riddles, on the
best authority, probably antedate Cynewulf.

[1] Bradley's explanation is approved by Herzfeld, 1890 (*Die Rätsel des Exeterbuches*, p. 67), who adduces further considerations in its favor, and thinks that
Wulf drags away the child of Eadwacer and the lady as a hostage, while she is
kept in custody by her husband.   Bülbring, 1891 (*Literaturbl.* 1891, No. 5, 157)
discusses Bradley's theory; so Gollancz, *Acad.* 44. 572.   [2] *Angl.* 13. 19–21.

THE ANDREAS AND CYNEWULF. — Grimm[1] assumed that the *Andreas* might be by Cynewulf, though he seemed rather to incline to Aldhelm.[2] Kemble[3] says that Cynewulf was probably the author of all the poems in the Vercelli Book, 'and those likewise which occur in the other collection ' [the Exeter Book]. Thorpe subscribes to Kemble's opinion.[4] Ettmüller says of *Andreas*:[5] 'Eodem fortasse auctore, nam, quod dictionem attinet, cum priore [*Elene*] bene convenit.' Dietrich[6] weakened the force of the disparities alleged by Grimm, and adduced correspondences between *Andreas* and both *Juliana* and *Christ*, the more notable being such as *Jul.* 242–3 : *An.* 1464ᵇ–5 ; *Jul.* 245–6ª : *An.* 1343–4ª ; *Jul.* 629 : *An.* 1344 ; *Jul.* 481 : *An.* 1328; *Chr.* 861 : *An.* 555, 602 ; *Chr.* 998–9ª : *An.* 1556–7ª ; *Jul.* 233ᵇ–4 : *An.* 57ᵇ–8 ; *Jul.* 236–7 ; *An.* 1077, 1079 ; *Jul.* 590 : *An.* 1473 ; *Jul.* 307–311 ; *An.* 1700 ff. Grein[7] followed Dietrich, without adducing any reason, and so do Rieger[8] and Sweet,[9] the latter assuming it as probable that the *Andreas* originally contained an acrostic, and that it and the *Elene* are by the same author, 'from their marked resemblance of language and style.' Ten Brink[10] likewise assigns the *Andreas* to Cynewulf. Hammerich[11] leaves the question undecided. Wülker[12] denies *Andreas* to Cynewulf, though he gives no reason. Fritzsche[13] follows Wülker, his arguments being drawn from the treatment of the sources, the verse, the vocabulary, and the absence of runes ; on the other hand, he conceives *Andreas* to be by an imitator of Cynewulf, perhaps a pupil. Müller[14] follows Fritzsche, while Ten Brink[15] and Ebert[16] are half inclined to agree, as is also Lefèvre.[17]

[1] *Andreas und Elene*, pp. L, LI.

[2] He adduced such correspondences between *Andreas* and *Elene*, not found in other poems, as *on herefelda, wōpes hring, brecan ofer bæð·weg, ǣht besittan, byrlas (secgas) gǣldon, hrēopon friccan ; gehð·u, ūð·weota, sewte, earhfær, unslāw.* On the other hand, he recognized the disparity of (*An.. El.*): *siŏ·nesa : brimnesen ; ǣrgeblond : earhgeblond ; ferhð·loca : ferhð·sefa ; siŏ gesettan ; siŏ āsittan.*

[3] *Arch.* 28. 363; *Cod. Verc.*, p. viii.   [10] *Early Eng. Lit.*, p. 58.
[4] *Hom.* I. 622.   [11] P. 97.
[5] *Scopas*, p. XI, and previously (1847) in his *Handbuch* I. 132 ff.
[6] *Kynewulfi Poetae Aetas*, 2–5; cf. *Haupt's Zs.*   [13] *Angl.* 2. 441.
9. 210, 213.   [14] *Ags. Gram.*, p. 26.
[7] *Germ.* 10. 365 ; *Ags. Gram.*, p. 11.   [15] *Early Eng. Lit.*, p. 389.
[8] At least by implication ; *Zacher's Zs.* I. 319. [16] P. 69.
[9] Warton's *Hist. Eng. Poet.* 2. 16.   [17] *Angl.* 6. 184.
[12] *Angl.* I. 506 ; later, in his *Gesch. der Engl. Litt.*, p. 45 (so already in 1888, cf. p. lvi, note 1), he ascribes it to an imitator, as does Fritzsche.

Holtbuer took the same side.[1] Ramhorst[2] came to an opposite conclusion from Fritzsche. Sievers[3] assumes non-Cynewulfian authorship, on account of the dat. *fæder, An.* 1412, and is followed by
Cremer[4] and Mather.[5] Sievers reiterated his opinion in much more
emphatic terms in his later article,[6] regarding the conclusion that
Andreas is not by Cynewulf as one of the few certainties established
by the researches into the questions of authorship in Old English.
Brooke hesitates between the view of Fritzsche and that of Gollancz.[7]
Sarrazin[8] sought once more to vindicate the *Andreas* for Cynewulf, on the ground that the runic passage discovered by Napier is
the conclusion of the *Fates of the Apostles*, and that, in turn, of
the *Andreas;* the same opinion is enunciated by Gollancz[9] and Trautmann.[10] Arnold is persuaded that the writer of the *Andreas* was not
Cynewulf.[11] Brandl[12] characterizes the *Andreas* as ' eher die Arbeit
eines begabten Nachahmers in anderer englischer Mundart.' Fräu-
lein Buttenwieser is convinced that the *Andreas* is not by Cynewulf,[13]
while Kölbing is as certain of the opposite view.[14]

Finally, it should be mentioned that Dr. Arthur W. Colton, in an
unpublished investigation undertaken while he was a graduate student
at Yale, discovered some striking correspondences between *Andreas*
and the undoubted poems of Cynewulf. Words and phrases were
listed separately, and these were divided into four main categories,
according as the expression occurred in one, two, three or four poems
besides the *Christ*, the plan being that formulated in my edition of
the *Judith*. The ratio of correspondences between the *Christ* and
the *Elene* was .085, this ratio being the result of dividing the total
number of correspondences by the number of lines in the poem ; in
the *Juliana*, .084 ; in the *Andreas*, .075 ; in the *Guthlac* and *Phoenix*,
.09 each. Other results were : *Hymns*, .055 ; *Satan*, .043 ; *Salomon*,
.04 ; *Daniel*, .039 ; *Beowulf*, .032 ; *Genesis, Riddles*, .03 each ; *Metres*,

---

[1] *Angl.* 8. 40.   [3] *PBB.* 10. 483.   [5] *M. L. N.* 7. 106.
[2] Cf. p. lvii, note 3.   [4] P. 49.   [6] *Angl.* 13. 25.
[7] *Early Eng. Lit.*, pp. 413, 485 ; *Eng. Lit. from the Beginning*, p. 187.
[8] *Angl.* 12. 383 ; cf. *Beibl.* 6. 205 ff.   [9] *Cynewulf's Christ*, p. 173.
[10] *Angl., Beibl.* 6. 21 (recanting 5. 93) ; *Kynewulf*, p. 9. Cramer agrees with
Trautmann.   [11] *Notes on Beowulf*, p. 123.
[12] Ten Brink's *Gesch. der Engl. Litt.*, 1². 68. In *Herrig's Archiv*, 100. 330–334,
Brandl argues that the beginning of the *Andreas* is imitated from the *Fates of the
Apostles*, the latter being an independent poem, a traveler's charm or prayer.
[13] *Studien über die Verfasserschaft des Andreas.*   [14] *Engl. Stud.* 26. 100.

.027; *Exodus*, .025; *Psalms*, .011. Poems under 500 lines were included in the inquiry, but their ratios were not calculated. Many of the more striking correspondences with the *Andreas* will be found in my *Notes*, as, e.g. 404–5, 481, 488, 856, 888^b–889^a, 999, 1111, 1196, 1343, 1373, 1437–8, 1564, etc.

As for myself, I am strongly inclined to assign the *Andreas* to Cynewulf, though I hesitate to express a positive opinion, in the present state of our knowledge, especially against Fritzsche's hypothesis of a close imitation. If the view of Sarrazin, Gollancz, and Trautmann were quite convincing, one need not hesitate; but of this I do not feel certain.

THE GUTHLAC AND CYNEWULF. — The *Guthlac* is perhaps the dullest of Old English poems, or at least of the longer ones, so that it cannot even sustain a comparison with *Juliana*. For this reason, one would be tempted to affirm that Cynewulf could have had nothing to do with it. Yet Kemble, Thorpe, Dietrich, Grein, Rieger, Sweet, Ten Brink, Lefèvre, D'Ham, and Brooke all assign it to him.[1] Thomas Arnold can see no reason for assigning it to him.[2] That the second part, or *Guthlac B* (791–1353), alone belongs to Cynewulf, is the opinion of Charitius,[3] Cremer, Mather, Wülker, Trautmann, Cramer, and Brandl. According to Dr. Colton,[4] not only is the ratio of correspondences of the *Guthlac* with the *Christ* .09, surpassing that of either the *Elene* or the *Juliana*, but, while the ratio with *Guthlac A* is .078, that with *Guthlac B* mounts to .113, while if only the first 500 lines of *Guthlac A* be taken into consideration, it falls to .058. Sievers merely says that *Guthlac A* contains two instances of *fēondas* (189^a, 392^a), while Cynewulf employs *frýnd* for the corresponding plural (*El.* 360^a). The ascription of at least *Guthlac B* to Cynewulf is therefore practically universal,[5] and the best authorities assume that in this case it must have preceded *Juliana*. Recently Mr. Gollancz has prefixed the lines printed at the end of the *Christ* in the present edition to the *Guthlac*, as the beginning of that poem;[6] but this procedure is likely to meet with scant approval.

The passages of *Guthlac B* which seem to me to be most nearly

---

[1] References on p. lx; Rieger in *Zacher's Zs.* 1. 325; D'Ham, in *Der Gegenwärtige Stand der Cynewulf-Frage*, 1883.

[2] *Notes on Beowulf*, p. 123. [4] See p. lxi.

[3] *Angl.* 2. 265–308. [5] It is denied by Holtbuer (*Angl.* 8. 1 ff.).

[6] *The Exeter Book*; cf. *Cynewulf's Christ*, p. xix; *infra*, pp. 63–4.

Cynewulfian in thought and tone are lines 791–843[a], 1067–1077, 1252[b]–1317, though it must be admitted that these contain phraseology which is non-Cynewulfian, if judged by the standard of the undoubted poems; that they cannot well be torn from their context; and that my designation of them as Cynewulfian signifies scarcely more than that I consider them the finest passages in this Part. If either *Guthlac B* or the whole was written by Cynewulf, a good deal of it must be prentice-work, touched up when he had attained the fulness of his power and art. A strong argument against the ascription to him of *Guthlac A* (and perhaps of the whole poem) is that not only is mention made in the poem of persons still living who remembered the temptations of the hermit,[1] but apparently also of their occurrence within the lifetime of the poet himself.[2] Now, as Guthlac died in A.D. 714, Cynewulf, who wrote neither the *Juliana* nor the *Elene* before 750, nor the *Christ* and the Vercelli fragment before 800,[3] cannot have known him personally, though he may have been acquainted with men who had known him. Either, then, we must refrain from pressing the assumption that the words

Hwæt! wē þissa wundra gewitan sindon;
eall þās geēodon in ūssera
tīda tīman.

refer to Cynewulf himself, or we must be prepared to accept the conclusion that he did not write *Guthlac A*, whether or not, with Ten Brink, we admit the possibility that both parts may proceed from the same author.

THE PHOENIX AND CYNEWULF. — The *Phoenix* is ascribed to Cynewulf by Kemble, Thorpe, Dietrich, Grein, Sweet, Hammerich, Ten Brink, Gäbler, Holtbuer, Brooke, and, though hesitatingly, by Trautmann.[4] Those who would deny Cynewulf's authorship are Wülker, Sievers, Cremer, Ebert,[5] Mather, Cramer, and Brandl.[6] Dietrich calls

[1] 124–8.
[2] 724–7; cf. 372–3. On the other hand, in *Guthlac B* the poet appeals to the testimony of books (850[b] ff.).   [3] See p. lxviii.
[4] References in general as on p. lx; Gäbler's views in *Angl.* 3. 488 ff.; Holtbuer's in *Angl.* 8. 1 ff.; Trautmann's in his *Kynewulf* (cf. *Angl. Beibl.* 5. 93).
[5] *Gesch. der Litt. des Mittelalters* 3. 75. Ebert says of the arguments employed by Gäbler, ' On such grounds all the works of Schiller could be ascribed to Goethe, and all of Goethe's to Schiller.'
[6] Wülker in the *Anglia, Grundriss, Berichte,* and *Geschichte;* Sievers in *PBB.* 10. 501; Brandl in Ten Brink's *Gesch.* 1². 63.

attention [1] to the fact that the real theme of the poem is similar to that of the Third Part of *Christ*. He alleges the similarity of words, phrases, and ideas between the *Phoenix* and the *Christ*,[2] and, though less important, between it and the *Elene*, as well as the *Guthlac* and the *Andreas*, which Dietrich assigns to Cynewulf. The stylistic method was employed at much greater length by Gäbler, who came to the same result as Dietrich. The counterproof is based upon metrical considerations. Trautmann gives a list of correspondences in phrase between the *Phoenix* and the other Cynewulfian poems, reckoning the *Andreas* among them, sums up the discussion, and announces his own opinion,[3] for which reason it is unnecessary here to enter into the matter at length.

The theme of the *Phoenix* would have been congenial to Cynewulf, and his reading may well have included Lactantius.[4] The verbal parallels and similarities of thought are striking, and the percentage of correspondences in Dr. Colton's table [5] agrees remarkably with that of the *Juliana* and the *Elene*. In respect to the prominence of color, flowers, fragrance, and music, of brooks, trees, groves, and plains, the *Phoenix* excels the undoubted poems; but against this must be set Cynewulf's impressibility, the fact that his vocabulary and imagery change to some extent with his mood and with the original upon which he is working. From no three of his undoubted poems could one, on stylistic grounds, and in the absence of the runic testimony, have ascertained his fourth. When he is paraphrasing long, didactic speeches he is another man than when he is telling a stirring tale, or reproducing the spirit of a poem full of sublime sentiment and magnificent appeals to the imagination. There is therefore no *a priori* ground for assuming that the *Phoenix* cannot be by Cynewulf. Much of the sentiment is demonstrably his; the correspondences in phraseology indicate the hand of a master, so inwoven are they into the tissue of the style; and a doxology like that of lines 615–629 would of itself almost persuade the critic to believe in

---

[1] *Kynewulfi Poetae Aetas*, p. 8.

[2] Thus *Ph.* 420 : *Chr.* 142, 250–253, 367, 587 ; *Ph.* 50–70, 589, 611–617 : *Chr.* 1634–1664 (esp. *Ph.* 56, 613 : *Chr.* 1660–1661) ; *Ph.* 329, 493 : *Chr.* 1228 ; *Ph.* 516 : *Chr.* 1079 ; *Ph.* 525 : *Chr.* 811 ; *Ph.* 584 : *Chr.* 820 ; *Ph.* 604 : *Chr.* 505 ; *Ph.* 628 : *Chr.* 726.

[3] *Kynewulf*, pp. 1–30, 42.

[4] Lactantius was among the authors included in the York Library, according to Alcuin. [5] See p lxi.

Cynewulf's authorship, so similar is it in tone and setting to those of the *Elene*[1] and the *Christ*.[2] It cannot be said that the question is decided; but I believe that scholars will end by assigning the *Phoenix*, like the *Andreas*, to Cynewulf.

OTHER POEMS ATTRIBUTED TO CYNEWULF. — Among other poems which have been ascribed to Cynewulf, perhaps the most important are the *Dream of the Rood*,[3] the *Harrowing of Hell*,[4] and the *Physiologus* (*Panther, Whale, Partridge*).[5] In no case has cogent proof in favor of the affirmative view been offered. The *Dream of the Rood* is worthy of Cynewulf, and in certain respects is strikingly suggestive of the *Elene* and of parts of the *Christ;* there are, too, certain correspondences of phraseology; but nothing has yet been alleged which forces us to conclude that Cynewulf was its author. Under these circumstances a certain scepticism is almost obligatory upon the student ; for with every poem assigned to an author upon insufficient grounds, the possibility of new combinations favorable to the admission of still another poem is increased, until one might end by imputing practically the whole of Old English poetry to a single author — a danger by no means imaginary, as the history of Old English scholarship is sufficient to prove.[6]

[1] 744-754.   [2] 385-415.

[3] Kemble, Thorpe, Dietrich (*De Cruce Ruthwellensi*), Grein (*Grammatik*), Rieger, Sweet, Ten Brink (esp. in *Haupt's Zs.* 24. 61–70), Zupitza, Müller ; opposed by Wülker, Ebert (*Sitzungsberichte der K. Sächs. Ges. der Wissenschaften, Phil.-Hist. Klasse*, 1884, pp. 81–93), Sievers (*Angl.* 13. 21), Holtbuer, Trautmann (*Kynewulf*, p. 40), Brandl.

[4] Kemble, Thorpe, Dietrich (*Haupt's Zs.* 9. 213), Grein, Ten Brink, Lefèvre, Kirkland ; opposed by Wülker, Holtbuer, Cramer, Trautmann, Brooke, Brandl.

[5] Kemble, Thorpe, Dietrich (*Kynewulfi Poetae Aetas*), Trautmann.

[6] Cf. p. lxiii, note 5.

III. FACT AND OPINION CONCERNING CYNEWULF.

CYNEWULF AND THE EPILOGUE TO THE ELENE. — Certain lines[1] at the close of the *Elene* are so important with reference to the biography of Cynewulf that a new translation is here presented :

'Thus I, old and ready to depart by reason of the treacherous (*or*, dying[2]) house[8] (*or*, tabernacle), have woven wordcraft and wondrously gathered, have now and again pondered and sifted my thought in the prison of the night. I knew not at all the truth concerning it (*or*, concerning the cross[4]) before wisdom, through its (*lit.* the) noble power, inspired (*lit.* revealed) a larger view into the cogitation of my heart. I was guilty of misdeeds, fettered by sins, tormented with anxieties, bound with bitternesses (*or*, bitter ones), beset with tribulations, before he bestowed inspiration through the bright order[9] (i.e. the clerical office, *or*, those in holy orders) as a help to the aged man. The mighty King granted [me his] pure (*lit.* blameless) grace and poured it into my mind, revealed it [as] glorious, and in the course of time dilated it ; he set my body free, unlocked my heart (*lit.* the enclosure of the breast), and released (*or*, revealed) the power of song, which I have since joyfully made use of in the world. Not once alone, but many times, I reflected on the tree of glory, before I had the miracle disclosed concerning the glorious tree, as in the course of events I found related in books, in writings, concerning the sign of victory. Until that the man[6] had always been buffeted by billows of sorrow, [was] an expiring TORCH,[7] though in the mead-hall he had received treasures, appled gold.[8]

---

[1] 1238-1277. [2] Reading *fǣge ;* cf. *El.* 881.
[8] I.e. his body ; cf. *Chr.* 14, 820, 1480.
[4] Supplying *rōde*, with Grein ; cf. 601.
[5] Cf. *þurh hāligne hād, Gu.* 65; see p. lxxxii, note 1.
[8] MS. 'strife.'
[7] These words represent the runes.
[8] Cf. Jul. 683 ff. :

> Ne þorftan þā þegnas . . .
> . . . wēnan þæt hȳ in winsele
> ofer bēorsetle bēagas þēgon,
> æpplede gold.

Cf. *Ph.* 506.

Y (?) lamented ; the companion in MISERY (*or*, FORCED companion) . suffered affliction, an oppressive secret, where (*or*, though[1]) before him the STEED measured the mile-paths and proudly ran, decked with wires (i.e. metal ornaments). JOY has waned, pleasure has decreased with the years ; youth has fled, the former pride. U (?) was of old the splendor of youth ; now, after the allotted time, are the days of [his] years departed, the joys of [his] life have vanished, as WATER glides away, the hurrying floods.   Every one's WEALTH is transitory under the sky ; the ornaments of the field pass away under the clouds like the wind when it ris⬤loud before men, roams among the clouds, rushes along in rage, and again on a sudden grows still, close locked within its prison, held down by force.'

In order that the essential points shall be more evident, the passage may be thus condensed :

'I, now old and failing, have practised the art of authorship, reflecting on my themes in the watches of the night.   While I was still an unregenerate sinner I had no real conception of the significance of the cross and its story.   Then God's ministers instructed me (*or*, *perhaps*, I took orders) when I was no longer young, and God himself has inspired me by the gift of his grace.   Only since that time have I been able to compose poetry, and this I have done with joy.   I had already meditated much upon the cross before I was enabled to discover (*or*, reveal) the miracle concerning it which I found recorded in books.   Until then (i.e. the time of his conversion) Cynewulf was unhappy, though he received gifts in hall, and though his horse, in trappings of gold, raced proudly along the highways.   For him the joys of youth are now fled ; and even thus the riches and the beauty of the world, nay, the world itself, vanishes away.'

Still more briefly, Cynewulf's autobiography, as contained in the *Elene*, may be thus formulated .

1. When I was young I received gifts in hall, and was present when my horse careered across the plain in gorgeous trappings (*or*, *perhaps*, when horses were raced) ; yet I was not happy, for I was still a sinner.

2. In later years I was converted, and life acquired a new meaning.   I began to reflect, practised the poetic art, thought deeply and

---

[1] Emending *þǣr* to *þēah* ; cf. 1259.

read widely about the cross of Christ, and finally have been enabled
to write this account of its Invention by St. Helena.

3. The joys of sense, the pride of life, have departed with my
youth. I am now an old man; yet I realize that I am not only ransomed from the power of sin, but have received special grace from
on high, and by divine assistance have brought to a close this poem
on a subject very near to my heart.

THE DATE OF CYNEWULF. — The name which our poet bore is found
in three forms — *Cyniwulf, Cynewulf, Cynwulf (Cynulf)*. Of these,
the oldest is *Cyniwulf*, and ● latest *Cynwulf*, — *Cynewulf* being
intermediate in date between the two.[1]

The loss of the vowel, as in *Cynwulf*, takes place only before *l, r,
w,* and *h* (at a late period also before *s*), sounds which are especially
favorable to such elision. In the South and the Midland, and pre-
sumably also in the North, the change of *i* to *e*, and hence of *Cyni-*
to *Cyne-*, took place about 750, and at all events not earlier than
740.[2] The *i* continues to persist sporadically, but it is clear that
such use is archaic, since by 750 the use of *e* is perfectly well established. *Cyn-* is at least fifty years later, apparently, and except
in one word, *Cynric*, is not found in Saxon territory. With a single
exception, *Cynuise* (Bede, *Eccl. Hist.* 3. 24), *Cyn-* appears to belong
to the ninth century. It occurs in the *Liber Vitae*, which Sweet
says is 'of the beginning of the ninth century, or end of the preceding
one ';[3] in the *Northumbrian Genealogies*, 'written between the years
811 and 814';[4] and in the charters dated 799–802.[5] The *e* continues
traditionally, like the *i*, side by side with the syncopated form.

The application of what precedes to the dating of the Cynewulfian
poems will at once be evident. The *Juliana* and the *Elene* have
Cynewulf; the *Christ* without question, and the *Fates of the Apostles*
almost certainly, have *Cynwulf;* and there is no *Cyniwulf.* Hence
the *Juliana* and the *Elene* were not written down before 750,[6] nor the

---

[1] These statements all repose upon the demonstration by Sievers, *Angl.* 13.
11–15 (written in 1890, pub. 1891).

[2] Sievers notes an exception, p. 11, in the case of a single charter, but evidently
does not consider this as invalidating the general principle.

[3] *OET.*, p. 153.   [4] *OET.*, p. 167.   [5] *OET.*, pp. 430 ff.

[6] Sievers, p. 15: 'Also vor 750 können *Juliane* und *Elene* auch aus sprach-
lichen Gründen nicht wol fallen.' He adds (p. 19) that the *Riddles* belong to the
period of the *i*, and still earlier.

Christ and the *Fates of the Apostles* (or, at all events, the Vercelli runic fragment) before 800. This is quite in accord with the results of my own study. In a paper published in 1892, entitled *The Date of the Old English Elene*,[1] I showed that vv. 1277–1321 of that poem correspond to a portion of Bk. 3, chap. 21 of Alcuin's treatise on the Trinity, which was dedicated to Charlemagne as Emperor, and, therefore, after the year 800, probably in 802, or between this date and 804, the year of Alcuin's death. There is no need to repeat the arguments employed in my article. The thought of Alcuin is not dissimilar to that of Caesarius of Arles, in a sermon printed among Augustine's works,[2] but, on the whole, the resemblances between the passage of the *Elene* and that in Alcuin are much closer. One indication that Cynewulf is drawing from Alcuin, and not from Caesarius, is the fact that the latter, in speaking of purgatorial torment, allows that it may be inflicted in this life;[3] Alcuin, on the other hand, knows nothing of the alternative.[4]

If it be admitted that the resemblances between the two passages point to a relation of dependence between Cynewulf and Alcuin, it can hardly be doubted which is to be regarded as dependent, the famous Alcuin, in the judgment of all enlightened persons in Europe undoubtedly the first man at Charlemagne's court, or the clerical poet, of whom no record outside his own poems remains. Alcuin was a theologian of repute; Cynewulf, though conversant with doctrine, would hardly have ventured, if we may judge from his procedure throughout the *Christ*, to speak so confidently on a tenet of vital importance, without being supported by an authority whom all his associates would regard as a champion, or at least a prominent representative, of orthodox belief. Alcuin had vigorously combated the Adoptian heresy and the worship of images. Moreover, with the possible exception of the Pope and Charlemagne himself, no man on

---

[1] *Angl.* 15. 9-20. [2] Migne 39. 1946-9.

[3] 'Sed prius aut in hoc saeculo . . . amarissimis tribulationibus sunt excoquendi . . . aut certo illo igne . . . longo tempore cruciandi.'

[4] 'Sunt ergo quidam justi minutis quibusdam peccatis obnoxii, . . . quae illius, ignis ardore purgantur. . . . Illoque transitorio igne et toto extremi diei judicio completo, dividentur,' etc. Cf. *El.* 1312-4:

> Swā biŏ ļāra manna ǣlc
> āscyred ond āscēaden scylda gehwylcre,
> dēopra firena, þurh þæs dōmes fȳr.

the Continent had so much influence in England as he. What more natural, then, than that his views on a subject like the Last Judgment should be promulgated and eagerly accepted in the region where he was educated, where he had won his first distinction as a teacher and scholar, and where his friends and correspondents were the highest in the land?

But if Cynewulf obtained his conception of the fire of the Judgment Day from Alcuin, then the *Elene* must have been written subsequent to 802. From this conclusion we can only escape by assuming that Alcuin's views were divulged to friends before the *De Fide Trinitatis* was published; but even on this supposition the date could hardly be set back more than a very few years. The *Elene*, then, it would appear, was written at least as late as 800, and probably later. This is not inconsistent with the retention of the *e* in *Cynewulf*, for, as we have seen, the later form never quite supplanted the earlier. If, however, our poet continues to write *Cynewulf* subsequently to 800, and in two poems writes *Cynwulf*, the latter poems must probably, in accordance with the facts adduced above, be assigned to a still later date. It would be hard to disprove an assumption that they were produced as late as 820 or 825, though, as we have seen, it is not impossible that they may have been written in the first decade of the ninth century. The order of the poems may have been: *Juliana, Elene, Fates of the Apostles* (?), *Christ*, though all that can well be affirmed with confidence is that the first three preceded the last one. Since the poet speaks of himself as old in the *Elene*,[1] the interval between this and the *Christ* can hardly have been very long. As to Cynewulf's date,[2] we may assume that he was born about the year 750, or perhaps somewhat earlier, and died not very far from 825, though these dates are mere inferences from those respecting the composition of his poems.[3]

---

[1] *El.* 1237.   [2] See the table of Significant Dates, p. xcix.

[3] The views of others may be briefly presented. Kemble thought that Cynewulf flourished at the beginning of the eleventh century (*Arch.* 28. 362). He was followed by Thorpe (*Ælfric's Homilies*, 1. 622), Ettmüller (*Scopas und Boceras*, p. x), and Earle (*Anglo-Saxon Lit.*, p. 228); in 1865 (*Two of the Sax. Chron.*, p. xxi), he had assigned Cynewulf to the tenth century. Grimm believed him to have been a contemporary, and perhaps a pupil, of Aldhelm, who died in 709 (*Andreas und Elene*, pp. LI–LII, 169). Dietrich rejected Thorpe's view, and assigned the poet to the latter part of the eighth century (*Ebert's Jahrb.* 1. 242 ff., 246; *Kynewulfi Poetae Aetas*, p. 16; cf. *Haupt's Zs.* 9. 212), identifying him with the bishop who

THE HOME OF CYNEWULF. — Upon this point we are restricted to
inference. Grimm seems to intimate [1] that he considers Cynewulf to
have been a West Saxon. He was at first followed by Dietrich, and
the same opinion was also held by Th. Müller. Leo was the first to
assume that he was a Northumbrian,[2] though on grounds that were
largely untenable. Not till 1865 did Dietrich change his opinion,
and concede that Cynewulf was a Northumbrian.[3] Rieger assented
to this,[4] as did Grein and Ten Brink.[5] Wülker, who at first regarded
Cynewulf as a West Saxon,[6] in 1895 endeavored to prove that he was
a Mercian.[7] Sievers, in his articles on rime[8] and metre,[9] brought
forward new arguments to show that the poet was a Northumbrian.[10]
Ramhorst[11] and Leiding[12] were of the same opinion. Trautmann
says :[13] 'Ich stehe nicht an, den Satz, "Cynewulf war ein Nordhum-
bre," für einen der best bewiesenen zu halten die es gibt.' This
seems to him so certain that he deems it unnecessary to attempt a
refutation of Wülker's opinion.

There seems to be no reason to doubt that Cynewulf was an
Anglian,[14] whether or not a Northumbrian in the narrower sense.
We know too little about the Mercian dialect, as distinguished from
Northumbrian proper, to make any very positive affirmations respect-
ing the possibility of assigning a given poem of Cynewulf's to the
one region rather than the other.[15]

died in 782 or 783 (*De Cruce Ruthw.*, pp. 11 ff., 14). Dietrich is followed by
Grein (*Ags. Gram.*, p. 11). Ten Brink thinks of the period 720-730 to not later
than 800 (*Early Eng. Lit.*, p. 51); in substantial agreement are Wülker (*Angl.*
1. 483 ff.), Heinzel (*Ueber den Stil der Altgerm. Poesie*, p. 43), Müller (*Ags. Gram.*,
p. 26), Ebert (*Lit. des Mittelalters*, 3. 40), Gollancz (*Cynewulf's Christ*, p. xxii),
and Brooke (*Hist. Early Eng. Lit.*, p. 375 ; *Eng. Lit. from the Beginning*, p. 165).
Trautmann (*Kynewulf*, pp. 93 ff.) has recently revived and championed Dietrich's
identification of the poet with the bishop who died in 783.

[1] See p. lx, note 1.   [5] The proofs in *Haupt's Zs.* 23. 68 ff.
[2] *Op. cit.*, p. 21.   [6] *Angl.* 1. 507.
[3] *De Cruce Ruthw.*, pp. 13, 14.   [7] *Angl.* 17. 106-9.
[4] *Zacher's Zs.* 1. 219.   [8] *PBB.* 9. 235, note.
[9] *PBB.* 10. 209 ff., and esp. 464-475.
[10] Cf. also *Angl.* 13. 10 ff.
[11] *Das Altengl. Gedicht vom Heiligen Andreas*, pp. 26, 27.
[12] *Die Sprache der Cynewulfischen Dichtungen*, 1888, p. 77.
[13] *Kynewulf*, p. 91.
[14] For indications of Anglian dialect in the *Christ*, see pp. xlvi-li.
[15] See the conjecture on p. lxxiv.

CYNEWULF'S IDENTITY. — Attempts have been made to identify the poet with (1) Cēnwulf, or Kenulph, abbot of Peterborough and bishop of Winchester (d. 1006), to whom Ælfric dedicated his life of St. Æthelwold;[1] (2) with Cynewulf, bishop of Lindisfarne from 737–8 to 779–780, who died 781–3. Kemble was the first to suggest Cēnwulf,[2] and was followed by Thorpe, Ettmüller, and Earle.[3] Dietrich proposed the bishop of Lindisfarne,[4] and was followed by Grein; this theory has been revived by Trautmann.

The former conjecture is impossible, because the poet unmistakably spells his name Cynewulf or Cynwulf, while the bishop's name is as certainly Cēnwulf (Kēnulf).

The latter conjecture is inadmissible for two reasons. First, what we know of the bishop is not consistent with what we infer concerning the poet. The former lived as bishop in continual trouble. He was confined for a time in Bamborough by order of King Eadbert,[5] because he had allowed a relative of the king, named Offa, who had taken refuge from his enemies at the shrine of St. Cuthbert, to remain without food until he nearly perished with hunger, and then to be taken from the Sanctuary and put to death. After a time he was restored to his office, but not before the king had ordered that Lindisfarne should be besieged. In 779 or 780 he retired, worn out with age and labors, and spent the last three years of his life in retirement and prayer.[6] Nothing is said of his being a monk, which the poet probably was;[7] nothing of any love for literature; while it is evident that his life from 738 to 790 was quite unfavorable either to study or to the composition of poetry, and that it was too late to begin, when more than seventy years of age,[8] the pursuits from which he had been debarred by anxiety and toil. This is the first reason, and it is perhaps sufficient, though Wülker[9] adduces still others.[10]

---

[1] White, Ælfric, p. 65.

[2] Arch. 28. 362.

[3] See the references above, p. lxx, note 3.

[4] De Cruce Ruthw., p. 14.

[5] In 750, according to Simeon of Durham.

[6] Simeon of Durham, Hist. Dun. 2. 2, 4.

[7] See p. xcv.

[8] Bishops must at least be thirty years old, the canonical age for a priest.

[9] Angl. 1. 496–8.

[10] He assumes, for example, from the lines in Elene, that Cynewulf must have been at least fifty years old before he renounced the secular life. He would

But the second principal reason is quite as conclusive. The poet had not ceased his writing by 783, and perhaps had not even begun it.[1]

It is evident that the two attempts to identify the poet with ecclesiastics of the same name have been failures. There is one possibility, however, which has been overlooked, but which I am tempted to bring forward as a hypothesis which has some considerations in its favor. Before doing this, however, it will be desirable to summarize Wülker's reasons for believing Cynewulf to have been a Mercian.[2] They are these:

1. Literature is not brought forth amid continual tumult and strife, but under the reign of peace. Now Northumbria was anarchic in this period, and the devastations of the Danes had begun; the better condition of Mercia is indicated by the fact that while Northumbria had fifteen rulers from 685–809, Mercia had but seven from 675 to 819.

2. If Cynewulf was a Mercian, we can more readily understand why his poems have reached us in a West Saxon transcription. Wessex had no direct relation with Northumbria, while, on the other hand, Egbert conquered Mercia (825), and may thus have brought the poems into Wessex.

3. The poem of *Guthlac* was no doubt written by Cynewulf; and Guthlac was a Mercian. A Northumbrian would have preferred to write about an Aidan, a Cuthbert, or an Oswald.

4. If Cynewulf was a Northumbrian, it is strange that Alcuin nowhere mentions him.

So far Wülker. It may be added that the Mercian reigns particularly in question are those of Offa, 758–796; Ecgfrith, 796–7; and Cænwulf, 797–820.

There was a certain Cynulf at the synod of Clovesho in 803. This

hardly have been made bishop in less than five years from that time. He would accordingly have been ninety years old at his death. Again, the *Elene* is interpreted as meaning that he left the world to devote himself to quiet contemplation, which the bishop of Lindisfarne certainly did not do.

[1] See the arguments on pp. lxviii ff. No one now believes, with Grimm (see p. lxx, note 3), that Cynewulf was a contemporary of Aldhelm, nor with Earle in 1865 (*ib.*), that Cynewulf was the father of Cyneweard, the bishop of Wells who died or was exiled in 975, as recorded in the poem on the death of Edgar in the OE. Chronicle.

[2] *Angl.* 17. 106–9 ; see p. lxxi.

is attested by his signature to a decree executed at Clovesho on October 12 of that year. The synod was a notable one, in that the primacy of the see of Canterbury, which had for several years been contested in favor of the newly created archiepiscopate of Lichfield, was here solemnly recognized, according to the tenor of a letter received from Pope Leo III, and the archbishopric of Lichfield was abolished. This involved the full reinstatement in his rights of Æthelheard, archbishop of Canterbury from 793 to 805. The same day, by a synodal act, Æthelheard and the clergy, assembled in obedience to the papal orders, forbade the election of laymen to the lordship of monasteries, and it is this decree[1] that was signed by Cynulf, in common with all the other members of the synod. Cynulf is one of the subscribers following Tidfrith, bishop of Dunwich, and was no doubt a priest of that diocese.[2] The whole episode which engrossed the attention of the synod is said by an eminent authority to be 'perhaps the most important piece of English church history between the death of Bede and the age of Dunstan.'[3]

Now it would seem to be possible that this Cynulf might be the poet. Briefly stated, the arguments are these : —

1. The date agrees with what we should expect.[4]

2. The form of the name is such as the poet was using at this time (-ulf for -wulf may be disregarded).[5]

3. Cynewulf was almost certainly an ecclesiastic ; if not a monk, then a priest, or perhaps both.

4. Dunwich was the seat of a school established by its first bishop, Felix, from which school, in later times, the University of Cambridge was asserted to have sprung ; so that the traditions of learning may well have persisted there.

5. Through Æthelheard, the archbishop of Canterbury, and Tidfrith, his own bishop (798 ?–823 ?), Cynewulf could have kept in touch with Alcuin, from whom he derived his notions concerning the fire of Doomsday.[6] Æthelheard was in favor at once with Offa and with Charlemagne, and Alcuin constantly corresponded with

---

[1] In Kemble, *Cod. Dipl.* 5. 64 (No. 1024); *OET.*, p. 441; Birch, *Cart. Sax.*, No. 323 ; *Palaeogr. Soc.*, No. 23.　　　　[4] See pp. lxviii ff.

[2] The subscriptions are as follows : 'Ego tidfri∂, dammucae (Kemble, 'dummucae') ciuitatis episc' sig' crucis subscripsi' ; then two abbots, and then, as one of four priests, 'cynulf p̃r.'　　　　[5] See p. lxviii.

[3] Stubbs, in *Dict. Chr. Biog.*, s.v. *Ethelhard (3)*.　　　　[6] See p. lxix.

him.[1] About the time of the Council of Clovesho, Tidfrith received a letter of advice from Alcuin, who had heard of his exemplary life from an East Anglian abbot named Lull, one of the two abbots that subscribed the charter of 803, as related above.[2] Possibly Tidfrith, Æthelheard, or, more likely, Alcuin, may have been the 'eminent man' whom Cynewulf apostrophizes at the beginning of Part II. Cf. pp. lxix, lxx.

6. At Dunwich, Cynewulf would have had ample opportunity to become acquainted with the sea.

A few facts about Dunwich may here be of interest. About 631, Felix, who had been born and ordained in Burgundy, came to Honorius, archbishop of Canterbury, and desired to preach to the Angles. He succeeded in his mission, was made bishop of Dunwich, and held his see for seventeen years, until his death.[3] Soon after his accession, he assisted King Sigebert in founding a school. Bede's account is:[4] 'Patriam reversus, ubi regno potitus est, mox ea quae in Galliis bene disposita vidit imitari cupiens, instituit scolam in qua pueri litteris erudirentur, juvante se episcopo Felice, quem de Cantia acceperat, eisque pedagogos ac magistros juxta morem Cantuariorum praebente.' A couple of years after this, the Irish monk Fursey came to the King, and built a monastery at Burgh Castle, near Yarmouth ; it was here that he had the visions of the other world, which have been called anticipations of the sterner parts of the *Divina Commedia*,[5] and which might have been in Cynewulf's mind when he wrote the Third Part of the *Christ*. Of Dunwich the antiquary Spelman heard that it was reported at one time to have had fifty churches, but its ancient site is now swallowed up by the ocean. In the time of Felix, it was the chief seaport on the East Anglian coast, and the most central place for communications inland.[6] Finally, it is of interest to remember that East Anglia fell under the rule of Offa in 794,[7] that Egbert came to the throne of Wessex in 802, and that Mercia and East Anglia virtually passed under his sway at the battle of Ellandune in 825.

Objections may no doubt be brought against this theory, but to me there seems nothing intrinsically improbable in it. If it be urged

---

[1] *Dict. Nat. Biog.* 18. 24.

[2] *Dict. Nat. Biog.* 56. 384 ; *Mon. Alcuin*, ed. Dümmler, p. 739.

[3] Bede, *Eccl. Hist.* 2. 15.

[4] 3. 18.

[5] Bright, *Early Eng. Ch. Hist.*, p. 126.

[6] *Dict. Nat. Biog.* 18. 291.

[7] Green, *Making of England*, p. 416.

that we know nothing about the dialect of East Anglia, one might reply that at all events it was Anglian; if that the Dunwich school may by this time have become extinct, it is yet possible, nay, very likely, that Cynewulf may have attended the still more famous one of York, and by no means certain that he was not a Northumbrian or Mercian by birth. If the influence of Offa was sufficient to raise the Mercian Æthelheard to the see of Canterbury,[1] it was sufficient to induct a priest from another province into his East Anglian office. It is thus possible that the court which Cynewulf knew was the court of Offa, and that it was there that he received the 'appled gold' mentioned in the *Elene*.[2]

THE THEOLOGY OF CYNEWULF. — In general, Cynewulf is an orthodox believer, after the standard of the Western Church in his time, and, except for his doctrine of Purgatory, is no doubt in substantial agreement with Gregory the Great, the father of Roman Christianity in England.[3]

Not only does he frequently extol the Trinity,[4] but he specifies the three Persons,[5] even explicitly identifying the Father with the Son,[6] and with the Spirit.[7] The Father is thought of especially as the Creator,[8] though this function is sometimes attributed to the Son,[9] and sometimes exercised by him in conjunction with the Father.[10] Christ, though God's Son,[11] and conceived by the Holy Ghost,[12] is God of God,[13] without beginning,[14] co-eternal and co-abiding with the Father,[15] and eternally generated by him.[16] He is called Emmanuel,[17] and designated a priest after the order of Melchisedec.[18] Of his life on earth, we have mention of his birth,[19] his miracles,[20] his trial and

---

[1] *Dict. Nat. Biog.* 18. 23.   [2] See p. lxvi.

[3] Only the more important points are touched on in this sketch. In general, no attempt is made to give exhaustive references, though they may be complete in particular cases.

[4] *Jul.* 726; *El.* 177; *Chr.* 379, 599.

[5] *Chr.* 357, 773.   [13] *Chr.* 109.

[6] *El.* 1084–6; *Chr.* 470 ff., 727–8.   [14] *Chr.* 111.

[7] *Jul.* 724; *El.* 1106.   [15] *Chr.* 122, 236 ff., 350 ff., 465.

[8] *Jul.* 111 ff.: *Chr.* 224 ff., 472; and often in kennings.

[9] *El.* 726 ff.; *Chr.* 14 ff.   [16] *Chr.* 216 ff.

[10] *Chr.* 239–240.   [17] *Chr.* 132.

[11] *El.* 179, 770, 813; *Chr.* 205.   [18] *Chr.* 137 ff.

[12] *Chr.* 207–8.   [20] *El.* 298 ff., 779.

[19] *El.* 392, 776; *Chr.* 65, and *passim* in Part I; 724 ff., 786 ff., 1418 ff.

crucifixion,[1] harrowing of hell,[2] resurrection,[3] and ascension.[4] He sitteth at the right hand of the Father,[5] throned among the angels,[6] and thence shall come in glory to judge the world.[7] He is eternally forgiving men,[8] visits their souls in response to prayer,[9] grants them abundant and manifold gifts,[10] and even exhibits his kindness to the impenitent wicked whom he is about to condemn.[11] The Holy Ghost, frequently designated as the Comforter,[12] proceeds, according to the Western doctrine, from both the Father and the Son ;[13] his agency is manifested in various ways,[14] but especially as the Giver of Grace.[15]

Angels are represented as communicating with men,[16] but chiefly as in attendance upon Christ.[17] The rebellion and overthrow of Satan and his attendant angels are recorded ;[18] he and his are ever the instigators of evil,[19] and hurl their darts,[20] sometimes represented as poisoned,[21] at the believer.

Mary, the mother of Christ, is regarded as ever virgin.[22]

The redemption of the world was effected by the death of Christ,[23] and on this account the Cross is extolled.[24] The sinner may obtain

[1] *Jul.* 289 ff., 304, 447; *El.* 180, 205 ff., 424, 480, 671, 774, 855; *Chr.* 727, 1428 ff.

[2] *Chr.* 30 ff., 145 ff., 558 ff., 730 ff., 1150 ff.

[3] *El.* 185 ff., 486, 780 ff.

[4] *El.* 188; *Chr.*, Part II, *passim.*

[5] *Chr.* 531–2.

[6] *El.* 732 ff.

[7] *El.* 726; *Chr.* 782 ff., and Part III, *passim.*

[8] *Chr.* 426 ff.

[9] *Chr.* Part I, *passim.*

[10] *Chr.* 600 ff., 659 ff., 776 ff.; 860 ff.

[11] *Chr.* 1379 ff.; cf. *Chr.* 1116–7, 1200–1203, 1208–1212.

[12] *Jul.* 724; *El.* 1037, 1106; *Chr.* 207, 728.

[13] *Chr.* 357–8.

[14] *Jul.* 241; *El.* 1037–9, 1058, 1144 ff., 1157 ; *Chr.* 207–8.

[15] *El.* 199 ; *Chr.* 649, 710.

[16] *Jul.* 563; *El.* 72 ff.; *Chr.* 315 ff., 506 ff., 558 ff.

[17] *El.* 733 ff.; *Chr.* 385 ff., 440 ff., 492 ff., 548 ff., 941 ff., 1008 ff., 1649, etc.; the Cherubim and Seraphim are mentioned, *El.* 750, 755, the Seraphim *Chr.* 386.

[18] *Jul.* 420 ff.; *El.* 761 ff., 942 ff.

[19] *Jul.* 242 ff., 396 ff.; *El.* 940 ff.; *Chr.* 256 ff., 363 ff.

[20] *Jul.* 382 ff., 404 ff.; *Chr.* 761 ff.

[21] *Jul.* 471; *Chr.* 768.

[22] *El.* 340; *Chr.* 37 ff., 77 ff., 207, 211, 298, 300, 333, 419, 1420.

[23] *El.* 181; *Chr.* 616 ff., 1093 ff., 1449 ff.

[24] *El.*, *passim ;* *Chr.* 1084 ff.

pardon if he repents and turns from his evil ways ; [1] confession is to be practised,[2] and the believer to be baptized.[3] Every one is to be judged according to the deeds done in the body ;[4] according to these he is assigned to hell,[5] a brief purgatorial fire [6] (especially clear in the *Elene*), or heaven;[7] but the purgatorial fire ceases on the Day of Judgment, and thereafter there is only the twofold division into sinners and the righteous.[8]

Cynewulf deplores the blindness of error,[9] believes in the intercession of saints,[10] and desires the prayers of his readers.[11]

CYNEWULF AS MAN AND AS POET. — Cynewulf, the one Old English poet who has left us at once his name and a body of poetic work distinctly recognizable as his own, was born not far from the year 750.[12] Bede had then been dead several years, Boniface was terminating his apostolate in Germany, and Egbert of York was in the midst of his flourishing and beneficent archiepiscopate. Alcuin, who was to exert so important an influence upon education in Western Europe, who was to inaugurate, under the patronage of Charlemagne, the first Renaissance of ancient letters, and who was to leave his impress on Cynewulf's writings, was a youth of fifteen years or thereabouts. Pepin had just ascended the Frankish throne, and Charlemagne was a mere lad of eight. Egbert, who was to bring England under a single sceptre, was not for many years to be born, but Offa, whose name has become so celebrated in history and legend, must have been nearly, if not quite, a man grown.

For more than a century the great rival powers in England had been Northumbria and Mercia. Northumbria began a long contest for supremacy in the closing years of the seventh century. Penda,

---

[1] *El.* 513-6.

[2] *Chr.* 1301 ff.

[3] *El.* 172, 192, 490, 1034-6, 1044 ; *Chr.* 484.

[4] *Jul.* 702, 707, 728; *El.* 527, 623, 825, 1301; *Ap.* 81; *Chr.* 128, 434, 473, 783, 803, 827 ff., 846, 891, 1219, 1240, 1361, 1367, 1575-7, 1589, 1629.

[5] *Chr.* 1269-1271, 1531 ff., 1593 ff.

[6] *El.* 1295-8; 1396 ff.; (?) *Chr.* 956-9, 999-1006; (*Ph.* 520-526 ff.).

[7] *El.* 825, 1315 ff.; *Chr.* 434 ff., 1639 ff.

[8] Cf. my article in *Angl.* 15. 9 ff.

[9] *Jul.* 13, 61, 138, 301, 368, 460; *El.* 306 ff., 311, 371, 1041, 1119; *Ap.* 46; *Chr.* 344, 1126-7, 1187.

[10] *Jul.* 695 ff., 716 ff. ; *Ap.* 90 ff.; *Chr.* 335 ff.

[11] *Jul.* 718 ff.; *Ap.* 88.   [12] See p. lxx.

the powerful king of Mercia, who for years had fought valiantly in the waning cause of heathenism, was slain in 655, and the people of this middle province at last turned to Christianity. From 670, on the death of that Oswy who had been victorious over Penda, the glory of the Northumbrian kingdom began to decline. Mercia, which almost immediately had begun to recover, under Wulfhere (659–675), from the blow inflicted by Oswy, continued to be a formidable rival of Northumbria. The genuineness of its conversion was attested by the foundation of the abbeys of Ely, Peterborough, and Crowland, and the arts of peace came in the train of the new religion. But it was Northumbria which, while beginning to decline as a military state, distinguished itself by application to learning and culture.

From the death of King Egfrith, in 685, to that of Alcuin in 804, York was the national centre of education. Among its archbishops were two such men as Egbert (732–766) and Æthelbert (766–780). Egbert was not only a patron of learning, but himself a writer of authoritative books, some of which are still extant. He had splendid tastes. ' He acquired many sacred vessels for his churches, made of silver and ornamented with jewels and gold, together with figured curtains of silk, apparently of foreign manufacture. He was also a reformer of church music, and seems to have introduced the observance of the hours.' But his ' chief claim to the gratitude of posterity was his establishment of the school or university of York, and his commencement of the library in connection with it. . . . Scholars flocked to York from all parts of Europe, and among the pupils was the illustrious Alcuin, who speaks affectionately of the piety and goodness of Egbert, telling us what an excellent instructor he was, how just and yet how gentle. . . . The children of the school of York taught the schools or universities of Italy, Germany, and France.'[1] Æthelbert, or Albert, his successor, really had the principal direct share, while Egbert still lived, in the formation of the library, and the conduct of the school. 'He sought for MSS. everywhere. More than once did he go abroad, with Alcuin as his companion, not only to gain hints for his educational work, but to acquire books for his collection at home. Alcuin speaks of Albert's visit to Rome and of his honorable reception by kings and great

[1] *Dict. Chr. Biog.* s.v.

men, who tempted him in vain to take up his abode with them. The same writer in a well-known passage [1] enumerates many of the works which the library contained. He mentions forty-one authors, a few out of many, whose works were in the collection at York. Among these are some of the fathers, Christian poets, and grammarians. The classical writers are only Cicero, Pompeius, Pliny, Virgil, Statius, Lucan, and Boetius, in Latin, and Aristotle in Greek. Alcuin speaks of treatises in Greek and Hebrew without telling us what they are. In the western world there was probably no library out of Rome itself so large and important as this.' [2] As archbishop he rebuilt York minster, which had been wholly or partially destroyed by fire in 741, and set up in its chapel an altar decorated with silver, jewels, and gold, and over it a tall crucifix, also made of precious metals. [3] Unfortunately, in the archiepiscopate of his successor, Eanbald I (780–796), a state approaching anarchy supervened. 'King after king was murdered or dethroned, and all the foundations of society were so violently shaken that it would be impossible for the church and school of York to make their influence properly felt. Alcuin did his best to restore peace and order. He had gone to France soon after Albert's death to assist Charlemagne in his educational work, but he came home to Northumbria in A.D. 790 to lend the king and Eanbald a helping hand. It was all in vain. The disorder was so great that after a short sojourn the great scholar left Eanbald and York and went back to France, where the rest of his life was passed.' [4] In 793 Lindisfarne was devastated by the Danes, who followed it up with an attempt upon Jarrow in 794.

While the ascendency of Northumbria, military, religious, and educational, was thus passing away, Mercia had more than regained the ground temporarily lost. For twenty years it was the head of all England south of the Humber, and, though this supremacy was successfully contested by Wessex in the battle of Burford in 754, the remaining years of the century were marked by a steady advance. As Freeman says, 'During the greater part of the eighth century everything looked as if the chief place in the island was destined for

---

[1] This passage is frequently quoted. A translation may be found in West, *Alcuin*, pp. 34–35.

[2] *Dict. Chr. Biog.* s.v. *Ethelbert* (6).

[3] This fact is interesting in relation to the *Elene* and the *Dream of the Rood*.

[4] *Dict. Chr. Biog.* s.v.

Mercia. Æthelbald (716–757), Offa (757–796), and Cenwulf (797–819), through three long reigns, taking in more than a century, kept up the might and glory of their kingdom. . . . Though none of these Mercian kings are enrolled on the list of Bretwaldas, yet the position of Offa was as great as that of any English king before the final union of the kingdoms. In one way it was higher than that of any of them. Offa held, not only a British, but a European position. . . With the great king of the Mercians Charles [Charlemagne] corresponded as an equal.'[1]

Thus Mercia had succeeded to the position forfeited by Northumbria, and was ready in turn to resign its sway to Wessex. In 802 Egbert, who had learned the art of empire at the court of Charlemagne, ascended the throne of that kingdom. In 821 Cenwulf of Mercia died, and his kingdom was immediately involved in civil war. Egbert profited by the advantage thus offered, and in 825 was fought the battle of Ellandune, which decided the fate of Mercia. By 829 Egbert was overlord of all England, and the crown was on its way to Alfred.

Thus Northumbria, Mercia, and Wessex successively played the leading parts in the struggle for the primacy in England ; and literature and learning came southward as the preponderance of dominion shifted. Cynewulf's life may well have witnessed both transfers of power. In his youth the school of York was at the acme of its usefulness and reputation, and it is no idle conjecture that he may have attended it under the mastership of Æthelbert, and that both the latter and Alcuin,[2] and perhaps Egbert himself, may have personally instructed the future poet. If it is he who witnessed the decree at Clovesho in 803,[3] he was present at the final abandonment of the attempt made by Offa in 787 to rival the ecclesiastical claims of Canterbury by the creation of an archbishopric at Lichfield, this retreat being significant of the decline of the Mercian power since the death of Offa in 796, and perhaps as well during the closing years of that king's life. Finally, Cynewulf may well have lived to see the sceptre depart from Mercia with the overthrow at Ellandune in 825. If these inferences be correct, his maturity would have corresponded with the prominence of Mercia in English affairs, and he would stand, not only as the sole representative of the literature of that

---

[1] *Encyc. Brit.* 8. 282.   [2] See pp. lxix, lxxix.   [3] See p. lxxiv.

province and period, but as the chief representative of its learning
and culture. He would have received the torch from Northumbria,
and have been the means of its reaching Wessex, if he did not
actually deliver it with his own hands.

Whether or not Cynewulf received instruction at the Minster
School of York, he must have acquired at least the rudiments of
Latin at some school during childhood or adolescence, since on no
other hypothesis can we account for the ripeness of scholarship
which he displays in his poetry. His reading was so extensive, and,
what is more to the purpose, so perfectly assimilated, that it is incon-
ceivable that he should have been ignorant of letters until late in
life, if we press the *gamelum tō gēoce*[1] of *Elene* 1247, and assume that
he was an old man when his conversion took place. On this assumption we still have no little difficulty in accounting for his mastery of
patristic, hymnic, and liturgical literature, his clearness and certainty
as a theologian, his command of poetical form, and his perfect
subordination of a considerable variety of material to the demands
of a noble and delicate art. Even if he was a comparatively young
man at the time of his conversion, or calling, or awakening — however we choose to name it — it is still almost necessary to assume that

---

[1] It is true that in *El.* 1237 Cynewulf represents himself as old at the time of
writing this epilogue; it is also true that he represents the bestowal of divine
grace or inspiration through clerical influence as a comfort to him in his age, or
perhaps even as designed to be such a comfort. Yet we are not absolutely bound
to conclude that because he was old at the time of writing the epilogue he was old
at the time of this bestowal, nor even that because such bestowal was a comfort
to him in his age he was therefore old at the bestowal; formulas like *gamelum tō
gēoce* do usually, it is true, denote purpose, but occasionally, as in *Falsehood of
Men* 46, *Chr.* 124, seem to denote mere result. Having already called himself
old in line 1237, and being, at least in his own view, old when he wrote, he may
have confused the present comfort derived from the earlier grace with a comfort
instantaneously derived from the divine gift; in other words, he may have confused his age at the time of the bestowal with his present age.

The translation of *lāre* by 'grace' or 'inspiration' perhaps calls for a word of
explanation. The word frequently means 'precept,' occasionally 'prophecy,' in
Gen. 771 apparently 'grace,' 'favor' (being synonymous with *hyldo*). Here it is
explained by *rūmran gepeaht* (1241), which certainly does not mean mere instruction, by *gife unscynde*, where '*gife*' may, as often, mean 'grace' (cf. *Jul.*
516-7), and by *lēoðucræft onlēac*, etc., which certainly points to something else
than mere learning. Cf. p. lxvi.

he had received instruction in letters as a youth. The facilities for
a grown man to acquire, from a state of perfect illiteracy, such knowledge as he came to possess, were, we may be sure, practically
unknown in that age, for they are not precisely common even now.
The case of Alfred is not in point, for Alfred was a king, and could
command instruction not accessible to meaner men ; yet, with all
the help afforded him by scholars, he by no means surpassed our
author in the quality of his scholarship.

Cynewulf was almost certainly, for at least a part of his younger
manhood, a thane or retainer of some king or great lord, and possibly, though by no means certainly, of noble birth. If noble birth
be denied him, then his valor must have been proportionately greater,
since he was the recipient of gold in the mead-hall,[1] and possessed
a beautifully caparisoned charger.[2] That he was neither a king's
minstrel nor a wandering gleeman is evident from two considerations.
First, though horses were often bestowed as gifts upon warriors, we
have no mention of their bestowal upon minstrels. Secondly,
though Cynewulf speaks of the minstrel who can loudly play the
harp in the presence of warriors,[3] it is in quite other terms that he
refers to himself[4]— in terms that suggest, not the dashing improvisator, but the reflective student, drawing his materials from many
sources,[5] and pondering long upon a subject before feeling sufficiently sure of himself to undertake its treatment in verse. He
gathers from far and near, and grows weary of the quest, before he
finds his song ;[6] his poem is fitted together;[7] though he attributes
much importance to natural ability in respect to mastery of 'wordcraft,'[8] yet his own wordcraft is deftly woven ;[9] before all things

[1] *El.* 1259; cf. *Jul.* 686 ff.; *El.* 100, 1199.
[2] *El.* 1262–4; cf. *Beow.* 234, 286, 315, 853–6, 864 ff., 916–7, 1035 ff., 1045–9,
1399 ff., 2163 ff., 2174–5; *Run.* 19, 27 ; *Rid.* 15, 20, 23, 78 ; *By.* 188–9, 239–240 ;
Exod. 170–171 ; *An.* 1096–9 ; *Gn. Ex.* 87–88 ; *Husband's Message* 43–45. Note
how often horses and other treasures are associated in the poetry, and the use of
both to reward deeds of prowess.
[3] *Chr.* 668–670.
[4] *El.* 1238–1243ᵃ, 1246–1257ᵃ.
[5] Note his historic sense, *El.* 643 ff., though in dependence upon his source.
[6] *Ap.* 1–2 ; cf. *El.* 1238ᵇ ; *(Ph.* 546–8).
[7] *Ap. runic passage* 3 (*infra*, p. 153).
[8] *El.* 586–595ᵃ ; cf. *El.* 314, 419.
[9] *El.* 1238ᵃ.

wisdom and understanding are necessary for him who would charm
with words ;[1] eventually the theme, the matter, the conduct of one's
song may flash upon him as the result of a divine inspiration, but for
himself, at least, there must be much preliminary searching and long
consideration before he at length produces, with a certain feeling of
pleasure, what he is willing to give to the world.[2]   He evidently has
a great admiration for skill in the other arts,[3] as well as in writing,[4]
and indeed for skill and dexterity of all kinds.[5] And what he
avows is borne out by the character of his own writing.   We see
how widely and thoughtfully he reads — this is peculiarly true of the
Christ — how he adapts a bit from one source to another from a
different source, how he makes each subservient to the scheme of
the whole.   We see, too, with what care he sometimes chooses an
epithet, as, for instance, when he applies to flame an adjective —
heorugifre, ' sword-greedy,' 'greedy for destruction as the sword ' —
which elsewhere occurs only once in the poetry,[6] and is there applied
to a living being, namely, Grendel's mother.   One may think the
epithet bold, even to the verge of frigidity, yet must admit that it
was deliberately chosen and applied, and that, if it does not pass the
limit prescribed by good taste, it is highly effective.

But if Cynewulf is a student of poetry and a lover of learning
rather than an improvisator such as we hear of in the *Beowulf*, who
on the completion of the hero's first exploit immediately celebrates
it in hall ;[7] and if everything points to his maturity as the epoch in
which he developed the reflective habit, and practised his exacting
art, there can be no difficulty in assuming that he had experience of
military adventures in his youth.   In this way he would have accu-
mulated the fund of exact knowledge concerning war, and all its
pomp and circumstance, which he exhibits in his poems, while at the
same time he would be performing the deeds of valor for which he
was to receive guerdon from his lord.   That he was familiar with
armies and battle can hardly be doubted by any one who reads the

---

[1] *Chr.* 664–8ª; cf. *El.* 418 ; *Chr.* 713.

[2] *El.* 1238 ff., 1252ᵇ ff.   It will be noted that his frequent meditation on the
cross must have occurred after his conversion, and not during the period when he
was 'fettered by sins.'

[3] In architecture, *El.* 1018 ff.; *Chr.* 9 ff.; in jewelry, *El.* 1023ᵇ ff., (*Ph.* 302–4) ;
(in sculpture, *An.* 712).

[4] *Chr.* 672.   [6] *Beow.* 1498.

[5] *Chr.* 664–680.   [7] *Beow.* 867 ff.

opening of the *Elene*, and who bears in mind that of all the splendor and movement depicted by the poet there is virtually nothing in the original.[1] Admirable are his graphic descriptions of arms and armor,[2] of the assembling of a host,[8] of an army on the march,[4] with trumpeters sounding,[5] heralds shouting,[6] shields clashing,[7] horses stamping,[8] and over all the ominous cry of the black raven [9] and dewy-feathered eagle,[10] and from the distant forest the long howl of the expectant wolf.[11] Now the banner is advanced,[12] the arrows begin to fly,[18] swords crash through shields.[14] At length Constantine orders the labarum to be raised on high [15] and the war-cry to be shouted ; [16] at this the enemy takes to flight, seeking refuge among the rocky fastnesses,[17] or drowned in attempting to swim the river,[18] while after them the javelins dart like angry serpents,[19] and the host pursues from daylight till dark.[20]

Perhaps to Cynewulf the Welsh represented the heathen against whom Constantine fought, and he may have figured to himself the Roman Emperor as a prototype of Offa, who, like Constantine, possessed fearlessness, decision, and political sagacity, and aimed at some such imperial position in Britain as that held by the son of the British Helena in the East. Perhaps it was in the battles beyond the Severn, waged by Offa after 779, that Cynewulf witnessed the magnificence and horror of war. And perhaps the destruction of towns by fire on some such ravaging expedition may have inspired the terrible pictures of conflagration in the *Christ*.[21]

But Cynewulf has not merely, nor even chiefly, the soldier's enthusiasm for war. He has the poet's love for beauty — the beauty of

---

[1] For example, lines 110–143 are represented by the following : 'Et veniens cum suo exercitu super barbaros, coepit caedere eos proxima luce ; et timuerunt barbari, et dederunt fugam per ripas Danubii, et mortua est non minima multitudo' (cf. Glöde, in *Angl.* 9. 277).

[2] *El.* 23–25, 125, 234–5, 256 ff.   [11] *El.* 28, 112–3.
[8] *El.* 19.   [12] *El.* 107, 113.
[4] *El.* 35 ff., 50 ff.   [14] *El.* 114, 122.
[5] *El.* 54, 109.   [15] *El.* 128–9.
[6] *El.* 54 ; cf. 550.   [17] *El.* 133–5.
[7] *El.* 50.   [18] *El.* 136–7.
[8] *El.* 55.   [19] *El.* 140–1.
[9] *El.* 52 ; cf. 110 ff.   [20] *El.* 139–140.
[10] *El.* 29 ; cf. 111.   [21] See p. xciv, and cf. *An.* 1542 ff.
[18] *El.* 116 ff. ; cf. the malignant archer of *Chr.* 761 ff., and *Jul.* 384 ff., 471.
[16] Or the song of victory to be sung, *sigeléoð galen*, *El.* 124.

the world, the splendor of art, the loveliness of woman, the glory of manhood. His eye is caught by the gleam of gold in ornaments [1] or on apparel,[2] and he mentions a second time the golden gates [8] which serve him as a metaphor. To him the earth is all green.[4] At the crucifixion the trees weep bloody tears,[5] and at the Judgment the mighty Cross is all bedewed with the pure blood of heaven's King,[6] though it shines like a sun in the heavens.[7] It is the white hands of Christ that are pierced by the nails.[8] These notes of color, though so simple, are, it must be confessed, effective out of all proportion to their simplicity.[9] The veil of the temple is a wonderful tissue of colors.[10] The nails of Christ's cross, newly discovered in the earth, shine like stars, or glitter like precious stones.[11] On the sword that keeps the way of the tree of life there is a shifting play of color as it turns this way and that in the strong grasp of the cherubic guard,[12] and the earthly Paradise is resplendent with hues.[18] The sign that Constantine sees in the heavens is set with gold and lucent with gems ;[14] the true cross found by Helena is similarly adorned by her.[15]

I have said that Cynewulf loves the beauty of the world. This is shown by the fact that, though he has a utilitarian sense of the earth as bringing forth food for men, and as producing wealth of all kinds,[16] he yet conceives of it in its array[17] — no doubt as dressed in living green, with grass and trees,[18] and among them flowers and fruits.[19]

[1] *Chr.* 995; cf. 292.
[2] *El.* 992.
[8] *Chr.* 250; 308 ff., esp. 318.
[4] *Chr.* 1128.
[5] *Chr.* 1175.
[6] *Chr.* 1085-6.
[7] *Chr.* 1101-2.
[8] *Chr.* 1110.

[9] If we may attribute the *Phoenix* to Cynewulf (see p. lxiii), we shall discover a greater profusion and variety of color. Thus the trees (36), groves (13, 78), and earth (154) are green, and there are numerous references to herbs, blossoms, leaves, and fruits. Flame (218) and the feet of the phoenix (310) are yellow. And various parts of the bird's plumage are at first gray (121, 153), and then green, crimson, brown, purple, and white (293-8), while the phoenix himself is compared to a peacock (312).

[10] *Chr.* 1139.
[11] *El.* 1113-6.
[12] *El.* 758-760.
[18] *Chr.* 1391.
[15] *El.* 1023-6.

[14] *El.* 90. Precious stones greatly attract Cynewulf ; thus he informs us of one notable specimen in the army of Queen Helena (*El.* 264-5), and, like Shakespeare, he alludes to eyes as the jewels of the head (*Chr.* 1330; so *An.* 31 ; *Gu.* 276).

[16] *Chr.* 604-5, 609-611 ; cf. *Jul.* 42-44, 100 ff.

[17] *Chr.* 805 (probably with allusion to Gen. 2. 1 Vulg.) ; cf. *El.* 1271.

[18] Cf. *Chr.* 1169; *Jul.* 6; (*Ph.* 13 ff.).

[19] *Chr.* 1389 ; (*Ph.* 20 ff., 34 ff., 71 ff.).

On it fall the dew and the rain;[1] it is blessed with serene weather;[2] the stars, fixed in their places,[3] circle round it,[4] and blaze in the heavens[5] with mild beauty;[6] and over it stand the sun and moon, the candles of the sky,[7] shining aloft like jewels.[8]

Cynewulf's sense of color is somewhat obscured, as the reader will already have noted, by his passion for light. Misery is to him synonymous with the deprivation of light, and bliss with its intensity and abundance.[9] He is a sort of Zoroastrian, and worships the sun. Christ himself is the sunburst out of the East,[10] flooding the world with day, and the presence of divinity,[11] of angels,[12] and even of good men,[13] is attested by a glory of light. When Christ comes to the Judgment, his approach is heralded by a sunbeam of unimaginable brightness from the southeast.[14] Even when the poet uses the word 'white,' we must not think of the ordinary acceptation, but of a dazzling whiteness, a brilliancy.[15] On the other hand, his devils and wicked men are painted an unrelieved black,[16] and the flames of hell[17] and of the Judgment Day[18] are of a corresponding hue, though not necessarily of pitchy blackness.[19]

Among natural objects, Cynewulf is much impressed by the sea. This is natural, on the supposition that he lived as priest at Dunwich;[20] perhaps, too, he may have crossed the strait on some visit to the court of Charlemagne, which his relation to Alcuin renders not improbable;[21] or he may have coasted along the shores of England or

---

[1] *Chr.* 609.

[2] *Chr.* 605.

[3] *Chr.* 933.

[4] *Chr.* 671, 883; *Jul.* 498.

[5] *Chr.* 968, 1149–1150.

[6] *Chr.* 1148.

[7] *Chr.* 606–8.

[8] *Chr.* 692, 695; cf. 935–6.

[9] Cf. *Jul.* 333, 419, 503, 524, 554–5, 683; *El.* 310–312, 767; *Chr.* 26 ff., 92, 116–8, 742, 1247, 1346, 1385, 1409, 1422–3, 1541, 1656–7. For the Biblical conception, cf., e.g. 2 Pet. 2. 4, 17; Jude 6, 13, with Ps. 36. 9; 1 Tim. 6. 16; Jas. 1. 17; 1 Jn. 1. 5; Rev. 22. 5.

[10] *Chr.* 104 ff., 696 ff., 1651; cf. 230 ff.

[11] *Chr.* 204, 504 ff.; cf. *El.* 94; *Chr.* 483, 519, 1085 ff., 1101–2.

[12] *Jul.* 564; *El.* 73; *Chr.* 447 ff., 507, 545, 880, 928, 1011 ff., 1018, 1276.

[13] *Chr.* 879, 1238 ff., 1467; cf. 896 ff.

[14] *Chr.* 899 ff.; cf. 1009, 1334 ff.

[15] So *El.* 73; *Chr.* 447, 454, 545, 897, 1018, 1110; cf. the Gr. λευκός, as, e.g. in Mt. 17. 2; Jn. 20. 12; Acts 1. 10; Rev. 3. 5; so Lat. *candidus.*

[16] *Chr.* 257, 269, 896–7, 1522, 1564; cf. 1104, 1560.

[17] *Chr.* 1532; cf. *El.* 931; *Chr.* 871.

[18] *Chr.* 965–6, 994.

[19] Cf. *Chr.* 934.

[20] See p. lxxv.

[21] See pp. lxix, lxxiv.

Wales in some military expedition, if the theory suggested above is true.[1] At all events, his familiarity with the ocean seems to imply personal experience.

In the *Christ* he refers to the extent of the ocean,[2] its depth,[3] its roughness,[4] its power and rage,[5] its coldness,[6] its perilousness,[7] its multitudinous billows,[8] and the rush of its floods.[9] In the *Juliana* there is a brief account of an ocean voyage.[10] But it is in the *Elene* that the true zest of the sailor is displayed. There, when the journey in search of the cross has been decided on, a multitude of men hasten to the shore, where the vessels stand ready, swinging at anchor. Band after band go on board, and load the ships with coats of mail, shields, and spears. The foam spouts from the high prows ; the waves beat against the sides ; loud is the din of ocean. Under the bellying sails the vessels rush forward ; the chargers of the sea dance upon the waves. Soldiers and queen alike are in high spirits over the voyage as they moor the vessels, and prepare to start for Jerusalem.[11] If we may attribute the *Andreas* to Cynewulf,[12] we shall have materials for a still completer and finer account of an ocean voyage,[13] beginning with a picture of sunrise over the sea, and containing, among other things, a notable description of a storm.[14]

Cynewulf is susceptible to the beauty of woman, though he expresses his admiration in general phrases, and preferably in terms of light.[15] The Virgin Mary is the joy of women, the fairest maiden.[16] In the *Juliana* the people gaze with wonder on the maiden's beauty,[17] and she is repeatedly called 'sunshine' or 'sun.'[18] Her bridegroom addresses her with : 'My sweetest sunshine, Juliana ! What radiant beauty hast thou, the flower of youth !'[19] And her father, with still greater tenderness, says to her : 'Thou art my daughter, dearest and sweetest to my heart, the light of my eyes, my only one on earth, Juliana !'[20]

Of manly beauty he has less to say, and then, indeed, it is an angel he is describing : to Constantine 'there appeared a certain

---

[1] See p. lxxxv.
[2] *Chr.* 852, 1144, 1164; cf. *Jul.* 112.
[3] *Chr.* 856.
[4] *Chr.* 858 ; cf. *Jul.* 401.
[5] *Chr.* 1145-6.
[6] *Chr.* 851.
[7] *Chr.* 853.
[8] *Chr.* 854.
[9] *Chr.* 985.
[10] *Jul.* 671-5.
[12] See p. lx.
[13] *An.* 235-536.
[14] *An.* 369 ff.
[15] Cf. p. lxxxvii.
[16] *Chr.* 72.
[17] 162-3.
[18] Thus, e.g. 229, 454.
[19] 166-8.
[20] 93-95.

[11] *El.* 225-255. Of all this there is not a word in the original.

hero in the form of a man, beautiful, radiant, and bright of hue, more glorious than he ever saw under heaven before or since.'[1] On the other hand, for the virtues and accomplishments of manhood he has great admiration. Constantine 'was a true king, a guardian of men in war.' Through God's help 'he became a stay to many men throughout the world, an avenger on the nations.'[2] The courage, gayety, activity, staunchness, and fidelity of soldiers are dwelt upon in the *Elene*.[3] But it is in the *Christ* that Cynewulf intimates his delight in skill and science of various sorts. His gamut of appreciation is a wide one, and includes the bodily activities of the athlete, the soldier, and the sailor ; the art of the armorer and the musician ; the knowledge of the traveler, the astronomer, and the theologian ; the deftness of the author, and the power and persuasiveness of the orator.[4] Energy, coupled with knowledge, directed by skill, and manifest in action — such seems to be, in this notable passage, his ideal for men.[5] But in order to touch the heart to fine issues, and thus nobly to direct the activities of others, wisdom is the supreme endowment, the wisdom that cometh from on high.[6]

Cynewulf had himself, as we have seen, probably known the activities of the soldier and seaman, and hence of the traveler ; he was keenly alive to the thrill of song and the music of the harp ;[7] he was a zealous student of the Bible ; of the poetry, or poetical prose, of Bede, Gregory the Great, Jerome, Augustine, Prudentius, Caesarius of Arles, and Alcuin ; of the creeds, the antiphons, and the hymns of the church. So familiar does he become with Latin that words from that language slip unobserved, as it were, into his lines.[8] He practises himself in various forms of poetic art — in

---

[1] *El.* 72-75.   [2] *El.* 13-17; cf. 99 ff., 202 ff.

[3] 22, 38, 46b ff., 64, 121, 242, 246, 261, 273, etc. Among vices, he points out the danger of drunkenness, *Jul.* 483 ff.

[4] *Chr.* 664-681.

[5] (Cf. *Gu.* 948-950.)

[6] *Chr.* 664-8ª ; cf. *El.* 1241 ff.; (*Gu.* 502-4, 620-2, 1245 ff.).

[7] *El.* 744 ff.; *Chr.* 387 ff., 400 ff., 502 ff., 668 ff., 1649 ; (*An.* 719 ff., 869 ff. In the *Phoenix* there are some lovely lines, 131 ff., from which Tennyson may have derived the suggestion for Percivale's description of the music accompanying the Holy Grail, and which he has scarcely improved save through condensation ; cf. *Ph.* 11-12, 539 ff., 615 ff., 635 ; *Gu.* 1288 ff.). See Padelford's *OE. Musical Terms*, Bonn, 1899.

[8] Thus *rex*, *El.* 1042 ; *culpa*, *Chr.* 177 ; *sancta*, *Chr.* 50, 88 ; (and *Ph.* 667-677).

didactic [1] and dramatic [2] dialogue, and even dramatic monologue, [3] thus in some sense anticipating Browning; in poetical enumeration, brightened only by brief characterizations; [4] in narration; [5] and incidentally in description. [6] He employs all the figures of speech known to the Germanic rhetoric, and many borrowed from the ancients, [7] even producing elaborate similes by expanding his Latin originals. [8] Yet withal he seems to possess a good sense of values in his authors, [9] clear vision of realities, and lyric susceptibility and intensity, rather than the higher order of constructive ability and epic breadth of vision.

The fault of Cynewulf is in harmony with the tendency of the Old English poets in general, a tendency to dwell too much upon details, and neglect the architectonics, the perspective of the whole. The more intensely a poet feels, the greater is this danger, especially if a sufficient outline has not been provided for him by an author on whom he is dependent. Thus it is that the construction of Parts I and II of the *Christ* is better than that of Part III: the

---

[1] *Juliana* (and *Guthlac*).

[2] *Chr.* 164-213.

[3] *Chr.* 510 ff., 558 ff., 1376-1523.

[4] *Fates of the Apostles.*

[5] *Elene*, and Part III of the *Christ; (Andreas).*

[6] Especially in *Elene, Christ; (Andreas; Phoenix).*

[7] Cf. Jansen's collection, covering 143 pages, in his book, *Beiträge zur Synonymik*, etc.; he includes the *Riddles*, it is true. For rime see 591 ff., 757, 1320, 1481-2, 1496, 1570-1, 1646.

[8] So *Chr.* 850 ff., 867 ff.; Jansen adds *El.* 355 ff., *Chr.* 744 ff.

[9] Take, for example, his choice of Caesarius, whom he employs as a source for some of the finest passages in Part III. Of this author his biographer says (Arnold, *Caesarius von Arelate*, p. 122): 'Cäsarius besitzt in hohem Grade die Gabe der Anschaulichkeit und des bildlichen Ausdrucks. Seine Sprache ist populär, weil sie konkret ist; seine Ermahnungen wirken packend, weil sie sich auf bestimmte Vorgänge der wirklichen Lebens beziehen, und sich nicht in abstrakten Allgemeinheiten bewegen. Auch das Innerlichste und Geistigste sucht er greifbar zu gestalten. Seine Bilder sind nicht rasch wechselnd und kurz angedeutet, sondern meist eingehend behandelt und sorgfältig ausgeführt. Sie sind nicht überraschend und blendend, aber treffend und eindringlich, erinnernd an die Art des Ezechiel.' It is no small merit to have made choice of such a model for style and matter, a man who, as Arnold says, 'in virtue of his noble dignity, simplicity, and naturalness came as near to the classicity of the ancients as in his age was possible.'

two together are not much longer than the third, and the originals selected were in each of those two cases sufficient to provide the framework of the division, while in Part III, notwithstanding the preponderance of the Latin Judgment Hymn as a source, much material, not greatly inferior in extent and interest, is drawn from other authors. It is true that Part I, being based upon a series of Antiphons, is essentially lyrical in character, and the only unity demanded is that secured through the character of the Advent season to which the Antiphons belong. In Part II the lyrical and dramatic passages introduced do not seriously interrupt the steady flow of meditative discourse, and it is with commendable art that the prefigurement of Part III is introduced near the end without seriously marring the harmony imposed by adherence to the general tenor of Gregory's homily.

It is in Part III, as already intimated, that the faults of construction are most obvious and flagrant. Thus the circumstances attending the passion of Christ are twice introduced, once as suggested to the mind by the sight of the visionary Rood,[1] and once as touched upon by Christ himself in his address to the wicked.[2]   Hence it is there that there is a twofold reference to the buffeting and spitting,[3] to the crown of thorns,[4] to the wounds in hands and feet,[5] and even a threefold reference to the wounds in the side.[6]   On each occasion the references are appropriate, but the repetition of them is only confusing and weakening.   Nor is this a solitary instance.   Three times do the stars fall[7] at the Judgment Day; twice the trumpets sound;[8] twice the winds storm;[9] twice is there the crash of the universe;[10] twice do the dead arise;[11] twice the deeds of men are made manifest;[12] three times the devouring flame rages;[13] five times the wicked lament;[14] and four times does Christ come to Judgment,[15] on three occasions with attendant hosts.   Within a single sentence we have 'the bright sign' and 'the high rood,'[16] where evidently the

---

[1] 1084 ff.

[2] 1433 ff.

[3] 1121–4; 1433–6.

[4] 1125–6; 1444.

[5] 1109–1110; 1454–6.

[6] 1111–2; 1447–9; 1457–8.

[7] 933; 939; 1043.

[8] 878–889a; 947b–8.

[9] 940; 949–951.

[10] 930; 953–5.

[11] 886–898; 1022–1042 (perhaps only allusive).

[12] 1036b–8; 1045a–1056a.

[13] 930–932; 964–1003; 1043b–4a.

[14] 889b–892a; 961 (cf. 1015–7); 991 ff.; 1229; 1567; cf. 833 ff.

[15] 899–906; 924–9 (incidental mention); 941–7a; 1007–1021.

[16] 1061, 1064.

same thing is meant, and in this very sentence 'the exalted multitude' and 'the band of angels';[1] besides, in alternate lines there
occur 'sēo hēa duguð' and 'sēo hēa rōd,' and the abstract 'se
egsan þrēa' (cf. 'se hearda dæg') side by side with concrete objects
and the sound of the trumpet. In this same sentence, too, much is
resumptive, while the rest is clearly anticipatory. Yet the effect of
the passage is not so bad as the analysis would indicate, since the
confusion in some way reflects the agitation of the waiting multitudes, compelled forward alike by fire, trumpet, angel-host, and the
glittering crimson cross. Occasionally an excess of mere parallelism becomes cloying, though the synonyms may be varied with considerable skill.[2] But more wearisome than this are the frequent
didactic passages,[3] in some cases, however, not distinguishable
from the lyrical reflections which the situations extort from the
poet.

But there are other faults quite as serious. Thus, immediately
after the opening simile of this Part, we are told that a host of the
faithful 'so ascend to Zion's hill,'[4] but neither here nor elsewhere are
we told why they ascend or who they are, whether angels or righteous men. Lines 956–9, relating how sinners pass into the flame
of the Last Day, weaken the effect of 994, where the flame seizes
upon them. In the account of the signs that accompany the crucifixion of Christ, the heaven is represented as discerning who made it
bright with stars,[5] and the sea as discovering who set it in its bed,[6]
reference being made in the former case to the Star in the East, and
in the latter to Christ's walking on the water; both are totally irrelevant, and are due to an unpardonable transposition of matter in
Gregory's homily. In the same passage not only does the earth give
up those whom she contains, but so does hell;[7] the former is based
upon the Biblical account, the latter apparently upon the homily, by
a confusion between the sense of *infernus* as 'the hidden parts of
the earth,' and as 'the abode of departed spirits.' Accordingly, we
have the crucifixion confused with the resurrection, in so far as
there is reference both to the local resurrection and to the Harrowing of Hell. Again, lines 1316–1326 seem to be wholly irrelevant

---

[1] 1062–3.   [4] 875–7.   [6] 1163–8.
[2] Thus 1531–6a.   [5] 1148–1152.   [7] 1157–1163.
[3] Thus 921–4, 1056b–1060, 1079b–1080, 1199–1203, 1301–1333, 1549–1590,
1598b–1602a.

to the context ; [1] and elsewhere there is an excess of emphasis in calling sinners devils,[2] and in designating them as black.[3]

But it would be leaving a wrong impression not to add that both
faults of structure and verbal infelicities are to be found in the other
two Parts, and indeed in Cynewulf's remaining poems.   Some of
these have been mentioned above,[4] but one or two may be touched
upon here.   Whatever interpretation we may put upon *wōpes hring,*[5]
it is a conceit which, though not unparalleled in modern poetry, is
almost as frigid as many in the Scaldic verse ; and one's condemnation is intensified by the fact that Cynewulf is so fond of it as to
repeat it.   A typical instance of bad art is to be found in a superfluous line and a half of Part II.[6]   In this same Part we have an inartistic repetition of a word at the end of two neighboring lines ; [7] an
even worse instance, because here the lines are contiguous, is to be
found in the repetition of *Wāldend,* 555, 556, unless the second is
corrupt.   This last is paralleled, however, in the *Elene.*[8]   The cross
of Christ is several times referred to, in the *Elene* and the *Dream of
the Rood,* as the *sigebēam,* an entirely appropriate designation ; but
the poet is so under the influence of convention as to include the
crosses of the two thieves with that of Christ under the same
kenning.[9]

It is pleasant to turn from lapses such as these, from which no poet
is altogether free, to the undeniably great qualities which Cynewulf
manifests in the poem before us.   In the First Part he is full of reverence, of attachment to what he regards as essential verities, of enthusiasm, of passionate, mystical longing, and even of a tenderness [10]
like that of a Preraphaelite painter.   This section ends with the
thought of the home-coming to the Christian's fatherland.

In the Second Part we come closer to the ordinary life of men,[11]
lighted up, however, by reflections from the glistering raiment of
angels, and the pure brightness of the ascending Son of God.   Then,
preluding on the terrors of the Day of Doom, the poet discloses him-

---

[1] Cf. note.

[2] E.g. 895, 1532.

[3] 896, 1560, 1565, 1607.

[4] See p. xliv.

[5] *Chr.* 537 ; *El.* 1232 ; cf. *An.* 1281 ; *Gu.* 1313.

[8] 545b–6.

[7] 760, 764.

[8] Repetition of *cræftige,* 314, 315.

[9] *El.* 847.

[10] *Chr.* 341 (cf. note); see also *Jul.* 93–96.

[11] For example, 664 ff.

self to us in the attitude of a trembling sinner apprehensive for his own fate. But at the close we perceive the heavenly port to which our course is directed, a haven prepared for our reception by our ascended Lord.

Finally, in the Third Part, though the faults are more numerous, it is partly because the strain is of a higher mood. Here there are such sublimities as have rarely been united within the same compass. Each individual one may be approached, may perhaps be equaled, somewhere in the compass of the *Divina Commedia*, but nowhere within the same space does Dante assemble so many and such varied traits of stern beauty and tremendous power. The concordant singing of the angelic trumpets that wake the dead, swelling from each of the four corners of the earth, and shivering to the very stars; the splendor of light from the southeast, announcing the coming of the Son of God; the mingled majesty and sweetness of his countenance; the throngs of attendant angels; the torrent of flame that issues, with the noise of the falling heavens and the hurtling stars, from before the presence of the King, while the sun is turned to blood; the upward and forward rush of the risen dead, encountering the conflagration that is devouring heaven, earth, and sea, burning the waters of the great deep like wax, and melting with its impetuous onset the mountains [1] and the ocean-guarding cliffs; and the lamentations of the rising multitudes, blended with the din of trumpets, winds, flames, and a ruining universe; this forms the appropriate prelude to the scene of Judgment. That scene discloses Christ on Mount Zion, surrounded by the chivalry of heaven, and high above the illimitable throng that waits, in fear and anguish, the sentence of doom. All eyes are fixed alternately upon the Son of Man and upon his Sign in the heavens. For the Cross towers like the mythic Yggdrasil, dripping with blood, but flooding the whole world with a blaze like sunlight.[2] Yet the sight of the Rood only impels men to look on Him whom they pierced, and to behold in his white hands and holy feet the print of the nails. Then they recall the scene of *his* judgment, when he was mocked and crowned with thorns, and of his crucifixion, when earth, sea, and hell were moved by his sufferings, when the sun was darkened and rocks were rent, while only men were untouched by the agony of their God.

---

[1] Cf. Ovid, *Met.* 2. 216 ff.; with l. 987, *Met.* 2. 265 ff.
[2] Cf. Dante, *Paradiso*, Canto 14, esp. v. 94.

At once penetrating in its compassionate sweetness, and awful in its justice, is Christ's address to the sinner; and of unexampled energy are the two lines in which the sweep of the victor-sword in the right hand of the Judge hurls the whole multitude of the lost to the pit of hell. But again, as at the close of Parts I and II, the poet, after a description of the abode of endless misery, where darkness and serpents, torturing flame and piercing frost, combine to execute the just vengeance of the Almighty, returns to his favorite theme of the reward of the faithful, the Beatific Vision, eternal youth and joy, the hymning of angels in a day without night. Thus, in a space of less than eight hundred lines, Cynewulf brings together elements which remind us successively or alternately of the terrors of the *Inferno*, the sweet humanity of the *Purgatorio*, and the splendors of the closing cantos of the *Paradiso*, presenting them with the utmost vividness and poignancy, in a style of uniform elevation.

So much may fairly be said without challenging for Cynewulf a comparison with Dante which he would be unable to sustain. In grasp, in variety, in narrative skill, in the development of a difficult thought, in architectonic power, Cynewulf is hopelessly inferior; but in compunction, gratitude, hope, love, awe, and tenderness, he belongs to the same order; and in his sense of the sublime and the ability to convey it to his readers, he need not shrink from a comparison with either Dante or Milton, in other words, with the very prophets of the sublime among the poets of Christianity.

We have considered the inner life of Cynewulf as reflected in his poetry, but how shall we picture the author of the *Christ* in his habit as he lived? What were the congenial avocations of his riper years, whose business and burden was the utterance of that nervous, vivid, tender rhythmic speech, fraught with suggestions of a heroic past, which strove to disclose the kingdoms of life and death, to pierce the darkness of heathenism with a lyric cry, and to invest the lives of others with the heaven which lay habitually about his own soul? In what relations did he stand to the men who surrounded him, and to the fatherland whose mighty career lay wrapped in embryo, conditioned by the religion of which he was a passionate devotee, nay in some sense by the very song he sung?

At some time in his life, whether earlier or later, he had come, in a peculiar sense, under the sway of religion.[1]   Whether or not he became a monk we have no means of knowing; but we do know that the monastic life was the natural resort of the elect souls of that age, and that the Antiphons which he loved bear traces of monastic influence.[2]   That he eventually became a priest at Dunwich is by no means improbable.[3]   Here, within sound of the sea, he would listen to the music in which he delighted,[4] and would, on the recurrence of each Advent season, join in the chanting of the Antiphons which he so aptly paraphrased.   Here he would be surrounded by memories of St. Felix, would have leisure for study and composition, and would no doubt enjoy the intimacy of his bishop, his fellow-priests, and the teachers of the famous school.   Stirring events would occur, from time to time, in the world about him,[5] but they would not disturb the tenor of his peaceful life; for as yet the Danes had not begun to ravage the East Anglian territory, and to constitute themselves its absolute masters.   Yet he would not forget the interests of his youth and early manhood; all would live again in his pages — battle and voyage, mead-hall and race-course, jewels and fair women — but subordinated to his poetic purpose, heightened and transfigured by the vision and the faculty divine.   As his lifetime fell within the reigns of two notable English kings, Offa and Egbert; as he was a contemporary of Charlemagne and probably outlived him; and as we cannot suppose that he was wholly blind to the course of events in his own day, he may have had some premonition of the influence which his poetry would exert, and therefore have taken precautions that his name should not perish, by interweaving it into the very substance of his verse.[6]   That he, like Alfred, loved the poetry of his native tongue, is beyond question.   Cædmon, who knew no Latin, could only sing in English, if at all; Aldhelm, who knew Latin, wrote only in that language; Bede has left us but one brief English poem, though the vigor which that displays is evidence that he was under no necessity of writing in Latin; so that Cynewulf is the first Christian poet who, being thoroughly conversant with Latin,

---

[1] Cf. pp. lxvi ff.
[2] Cf. p. xxxix.
[3] Cf. p. lxxiv.
[4] Cf. p. lxxxix, note 7.
[5] Cf. pp. lxxx ff.
[6] Cf. pp. 152–4, esp. 153, top.

deliberately adopted the vernacular as the vehicle for a considerable body of poetry, and in this showed himself at once a good scholar, a good Christian, and a good patriot.[1]

As to the fate of his poetry in the period which followed, we are reduced almost wholly to conjecture. That Egbert may have conveyed it to Wessex after his victory over the Mercians is a plausible hypothesis;[2] and that these poems were among those which were taught to Alfred's children, and which he himself learned by heart in his rare moments of leisure, is at least equally probable. What we know is that they were still prized at the beginning of the eleventh century, since they are contained in the two great collections of Old English poetry, part in the Exeter, and part in the Vercelli Book; and we may infer that they were rather frequently transcribed, since side by side with forms which are clearly Anglian, and others which are manifestly Late West Saxon, there are others, though comparatively few in number, which are no less evidently Early West Saxon,[3] that is, belong to the age of Alfred. If we consider these facts, and the undoubted influence exerted by Cynewulf upon subsequent poets, we shall not hesitate to conclude that he was known and prized throughout the Old English period. When the Norman Conquest was imminent, and the religious revival of the older England was still in progress, his poems were embodied in collections of Old English verse, and, by the piety of ecclesiastics whose education was Continental,[4] have been preserved for the English race and for the world.

[1] For a somewhat exaggerated view of his Germanism, see Price's *Teutonic Antiquities in the generally acknowledged Cynewulfian Poetry;* cf. Kent, *Teutonic Antiquities in Andreas and Elene.*

[2] Cf. p. lxxiii.

[3] Cf. p. xlvii. In Ælfric's *Homilies* there is no *ie;* see Fischer, *The Stressed Vowels of Ælfric's Homilies,* Vol. 1 (*Pub. Mod. Lang. Assoc. of America,* Vol. 4, No. 2).

[4] See my *Cardinal Guala and the Vercelli Book* (Library Bulletin No. 10, University of California, 1888).

TABLE OF SIGNIFICANT DATES.

—•◦•—

755. St. Boniface dies.

757–796. Offa king of the Mercians.

759–829. Deterioration and anarchy of Northumbria.

766. Alcuin head of Egbert's school at York.

771. Charlemagne sole king of the Franks.

781. Alcuin settles at Charlemagne's court.

786–809. Caliphate of Haroun-al-Raschid.

787. First landing of the Danes in England.

789. King Egbert at the court of Charlemagne.

794. Offa seizes East Anglia.

800. Charlemagne crowned emperor by Pope Leo III.

802. Egbert king of Wessex. Alcuin's work on the Trinity.

804. Alcuin dies.

820. Macregol, who wrote the Latin text of the Rushworth Gospels, dies.

825 (ca.). Cynewulf dies.

829. Egbert overlord of all England.

849. King Alfred born.

856. OE. *Judith* written (or perhaps 918?).

871. Alfred king of Wessex.

901. King Alfred dies.

924. St. Dunstan born.

937. Battle of Brunanburh.

950 (ca.). Northumbrian gloss in Durham Book.

955 (ca.). Ælfric born.

957. St. Dunstan bishop of Worcester.

963. St. Æthelwold bishop of Winchester.

984. St. Æthelwold dies.

988. St. Dunstan dies.

990–995. Ælfric's Homilies.

990–1000. West Saxon translation of the Gospels.

991. Battle of Maldon.

998. Ælfric's translations from the Old Testament.

1020–1025. Ælfric dies.

1066. Battle of Hastings.

TABLE OF ABBREVIATIONS.

———•◦•———

ci

Gen. Genesis.

Gn. C. Cotton Gnomes.

Gn. Ex. Exeter Gnomes.

Go. Go.[1] and Go.[2] in agreement.

Go.[1] Gollancz, *Cynewulf's Christ.* 1892.

Go.[2] Gollancz, *The Exeter Book, Part I.* 1895.

Goth. Gothic.

Gr.[1] Grein, *Bibliothek der Angelsächsischen Poesie.* 1857.

Gr.[2] Grein, in *Germania*, Vol. 10. 1865.

Gram., Gr. Sievers' *Old English Grammar*, translated by Albert S. Cook. *Gram.*[8] = Sievers, *Angelsächsische Grammatik.* Dritte Ausgabe. 1898.

Greg. Magn. Gregory the Great.

Gu. Guthlac.

Hammerich (-Michelsen). In his *Aelteste Christliche Epik der Angelsachsen, Deutschen, und Nordländer.* 1874.

Haupt's Zs. Zeitschrift für Deutsches Alterthum.

Hel. Heliand.

Hertel. In his *Der Syntaktische Gebrauch des Verbums in dem Angelsächsischen Gedichte 'Crist.'* 1891.

Hist. Dun. Historia Dunelmensis.

Hom. Homilies.

Hy. Hymn.

Ind. Forsch. Indogermanische Forschungen.

Jansen. In his *Beiträge zur Synonymik und Poetik der allgemein als ächt anerkannten Dichtungen Cynewulfs.* 1883.

Joan. Diac. Joannes Diaconus, in *Migne*, Vol. 75.

Jud. Judith.

Jul. Juliana.

K. Körner, *Angelsächsische Texte.* 1880.

Kirkland. In his *Study of the Anglo-Saxon Poem, The Harrowing of Hell.* 1885.

Lehner. In his *Die Marienverehrung in den Ersten Jahrhunderten.* 1881.

Lind. The Lindisfarne Gospels, or Durham Book, in Skeat, *The Gospels*, etc. 1871–87.

Lit. Centrbl. Literarisches Centralblatt.

Livius. In his *The Blessed Virgin in the Fathers of the First Six Centuries.* 1893.

LWS. Late West Saxon.

M. Müller (L. C.), *Collectanea Anglo-Saxonica.* 1835.

Men. Menologium.

Metr. Metre.

Migne. In his *Patrologia Latina.*

M. L. N. Modern Language Notes.

Mod. Moods of Men.

Mon. Alcuin. Monumenta Alcuiniana.

Mone. In his *Lateinische Hymnen des Mittelalters.* 1853–55.

Morley. In his *English Writers.* 1887–95.

NED. New English Dictionary.

OET. Oldest English Texts, ed. Sweet. 1885.

Part. Partridge.

Patr. Gr. Patrologia Graeca, ed. Migne.

PBB. Paul und Braune's *Beiträge zur Geschichte der Deutschen Sprache und Literatur.*

Ph. Phoenix.

Ps. Psalm.

R. Rieger, *Alt- und Angelsächsisches Lesebuch.*

Rid. Riddle.

Robinson (W. C.). In his *Our Early English Literature.* 1885.

Rim. Poem. Riming Poem.

Rose. In his *Darstellung der Syntax in Cynewulfs Crist.* 1890.

Run. Runic Poem.

Rush.[2] The Rushworth Mark, Luke, and John, in Skeat, *The Gospels,* etc. 1871–87.

S. Schipper, in *Germania,*Vol. 19. 1874.

Sal. Salomon and Saturn.

Salzer. In his *Die Sinnbilder und Beiworte Mariens.* Linz, 1888–92.

Sat. Christ and Satan.

Schubert. In his *De Anglosaxonum Arte Metrica.* 1870.

Seaf. Seafarer.

Siev. Sievers, in Paul und Braune's *Beiträge.*

Spr. Sprachschatz.

Th. Thorpe, *Codex Exoniensis.* 1842.

tr. translates, translated.

W. Wanley, *Catalogus.*

Wand. Wanderer.

Wid. Widsith.

Wond. Creat. Wonders of Creation.

Wü. Wülker, in Grein-Wülker, *Bibliothek der Angelsächsischen Poesie,* Vol. 3. 1897.

Wülfing. In his *Die Syntax in den Werken Alfreds des Grossen,* I. Teil. 1894.

WW. Wright-Wülker, *Anglo-Saxon and Old English Vocabularies.* 1884.

Zacher's Zs., Zs. f. D. Phil. Zeitschrift für Deutsche Philologie.

+   All editors after the one named.

CHRIST.

PART I. — THE ADVENT.

. . . . . Cyninge.

Ðū eart sē weallstān   þe ðā wyrhtan īu
wiðwurpon tō weorce ;   wel þē gerīseð
þæt þū hēafo[d] sīe   healle mǣrre,

5   ond gesomnige   sīde weallas
fæste gefōge,   flint unbrǣcne,
þæt geond eorðb[yri]g eall   ēagna gesihþe
wundrien tō worlde   wuldres Ealdor.

Gesweotula nū þurh searocræft   þīn sylfes **weorc**,

10 sōðfæst, sigorbeorht,   ond sōna forlǣt
weall wið wealle.   Nū is þām weorce þearf
þæt se Cræ[f]tga cume   ond se Cyning sylfa,
ond þonne gebēte —   nū gebrosnad is —
hūs under hrōfe.   Hē þæt hrā gescōp,

15 leomo lǣmena ;   nū sceal Līffrēa
þone wērgan hēap   wrāþum āhreddan,
earme from egsan,   swā hē oft dyde.

Ēalā þ[ū] Reccend   ond þū riht Cyning —
se þe locan healdeð,   līf ontȳneð —

4 *MS.* heafoð. — 5 'and' *always represented by u contraction, except in 927, 1011, 1225, where* ond *occurs ; hence* ond *has been substituted for the contraction in all cases, including prefixes.* — 7ᵃ *MS.* eorðb . . . g ; *Th.* eorðb[uend] (?) ; *Gr.*¹ eorðan ; *note* eorðweall (?) (*for* eorðan eall) ; *Gr.*² eorðb[yri]g. — 7ᵇ *MS.* eagnan *with erasure of final* n. — 8ᵇ *M.* begins sentence. — 9 *M.* geswutula ; þin *in first hemistich.* — 10 *MS.* forlęt (ę *rare, and probably always a correction*) ; *M.* forlet. — 11 *M.* wid. — 12 *MS.* cræstga ; *M.* cræftiga. — 13 *M.* þone. — 14 *M. om.* hra. — 15 *M.* leoma ; *Th. note* læmenu (?) ; *Gr.*¹ læmenu. — 16 *From here to 26 there was much that I found scarcely legible in September, 1894 (A. S. C.).* — 17 *M.* earma. — 18ᵃ *MS.* þa. — 19 *Th.* ontyned.

20   ēadga ūs siges,   ōþrum forwyrned,
      wlitigan wilsīþes,   gif his weorc ne dēag.
      Hūru wē for þearfe   þās word sprecað,
      ...... giað   þone þe mon gescōp
      þæt hē ne hete ...... ceose sprecan
25   cearfulra þing,   þe wē in carcerne
      sittað sorgende   sunnan wilsīð,
      hwonne ūs Līffrēa   lēoht ontȳne,
      weorðe ūssum mōde   tō mundboran,
      ond þæt tȳdre gewitt   tīre bewinde ;
30   gedō ūsic þæs wyrðe,   þe hē tō wuldre forlēt,
      þā wē hēanlīce   hweorfan sceoldan
      tō þis enge lond,   ēðle bescyrede.
          Forþon secgan mæg   sē ðe sōð spriceð
      þæt hē āhredde,   þā forhwyrfed wæs,
35   frumcyn fīra.   Wæs sēo fǣmne geong,
      mægð mānes lēas,   þe hē him tō mēder gecēas ;
      þæt wæs geworden   būtan weres frīgum,
      þæt þurh Bearnes gebyrd   brȳd ēacen wearð.
      Nǣnig efenlīc þām,   ǣr nē siþþan,

20ᵃ *Th.* eadga ... us siges ; *Gr.*[1] eadgað us siges ; *Siev. suggests* sigores (*PBB. x. 485*) ; *Go.*[2] *After* ga, *which comes at the end of the line, a small piece of parchment has been cut out ; at most one letter could have been on it, but probably none at all.*— 20ᵇ *Gr.*[1] forwyrneð.— 21 *Go.*[1] wilsīþes, *the last two letters can scarcely be read, the whole word is barely visible.*— 22 *M.* nu we.— 23ᵃ *MS.* ...... giað ; *Gr.*[1] [modgeomre halsi] giað ; *S., A. think the last letter before* g *looks like* o ; *Go.*[1] [nu gemærsi]giað, *and declares the space in the MS. renders Grein's reading impossible.* — 23ᵇ *Gr.*[1] þone, *but restores* þe *in Appendix, p. 414.*— 24 *M.* hete ... ofe ; *Gr.*[1] heose ; *and in note conjectures a verb* hēosan, 'hasten,' *on the analogy of a Bavarian* hosen, hoseln, hosnen, *and adj.* husig, *but this is rejected by Sievers on metrical grounds (PBB. x. 515*) ; *Gr.*[2] hēte [hēo]fe, *interpreting* þing *as* 'concionem,' 'multitudinem' ; *S.* hete to hofe ceose, *but Go.*[1] *states that there is no trace of* hofe, *and A. that there is not sufficient room ; Go.*[1] *two or three letters are obliterated before* ceose, *the first probably* h, *and suggests* her ; *Edd. agree as to general illegibility ; of* sprecan *A. reads only* s .... an.— 26ᵇ *M.* sunnan wirnde ; *Th. note very doubtful in MS. ; Gr.*[2] sunnan wyrnde (*part. pl.*) ; *Go.* wil-sīð, l-s *almost obliterated, but* ið *quite legible.*— 27 *Siev.* frīga.— 28 *M.* weorde.— 30ᵇ *Th. note* þ (?).— 31 *MS., Th.* þā þe.— 33 *Go., A.* se ðe *hardly legible.*— 35 *Gr.*[1] *note* fromcyn (?).

40 in worlde gewearð　　wīfes ge[ē]a[c]nung ;
　　þæt dēgol wæs　　Dryhtnes gerȳne.
　　Eal giofu gæstlīc　　grundscēat geondsprēot;
　　þǣr wisna fela　　wearð inlīhted,
　　lāre longsume,　　þurh līfes Fruman,
45 þe ǣr under hoðman　　biholen lǣgon,
　　wītgena wōðsong,　　þā se Wāldend cwōm,
　　se þe reorda gehwæs　　ryne gemiclað
　　ðāra þe geneahhe　　noman Scyppendes
　　þurh ho[r]scne hǎd　　hergan willað.

50 Ēalā sibbe gesihð,　　sancta Hierūsalēm,
　　cynestōla cyst,　　Crīstes burglond,
　　engla ēþelstōl,　　ond þā āne in þē
　　sāule sōðfæstra　　simle gerestað,
　　wuldrum hrēmge.　　Nǣfre wommes tācn
55 in þām eardgearde　　ēawed weorþeð,
　　ac þē firina gehwylc　　feor ābūgeð,
　　wærgðo ond gewinnes.　　Bist tō wuldre full
　　hālgan hyhtes,　　swā þū gehāten eart.
　　Sioh nū sylfa þē geond　　þās sīdan gesceaft
60 swylce rodores hrōf　　rūme geondwlītan
　　ymb healfa gehwone,　　hū þec heofones Cyning
　　sīðe gesēceð,　　ond sylf cymeð,
　　nimeð eard in þē,　　swā hit ǣr gefyrn
　　wītgan· wīsfæste　　wordum sægdon,
65 cȳðdon Crīstes gebyrd,　　cwǣdon þē tō frōfre,
　　burga betlīcast.　　Nū is þæt Bearn cymen,
　　āwæcned tō wyrpe　　weorcum Ebrēa,
　　bringeð blisse þē,　　benda onlȳseð

---

40 *MS., Edd.* gearnung ; *Gr.*[1] *note* geeacnung (?). — 42 *Gr.*[1] geondspreat, *but restores* -spreot *in Gr.*[2] — 47 *Gr.*[1] (*App., p. 369*) rȳne, 'mysterium' (*so in Sprach-schatz*). — 49 *MS.* hoscne. — 53 *Th. note* saula (?). — 59 *Gr.*[1] sylfan; *Gr.*[2] sylfa, *nsf.* — 61 *Th., Gr.* healsa.

niþum genēðde,   nearoþearfe conn, —
70 hū se earma sceal   āre gebīdan.

'Ēalā wīfa wynn   geond wuldres þrym,
fǣmne frēolīcast   ofer ealne foldan scēat
þæs þe ǣfre sundbūend   secgan hȳrdon ;
ārece ūs þæt gerȳne   þæt þē of roderum cwōm,
75 hū þū ēacnunge   ǣfre onfēnge
Bearnes þurh gebyrde,   ond þone gebedscipe
æfter monwīsan   mo[t] ne cūðes.
Ne wē sōðlīce   swylc ne gefrugnan
in ǣrdagum   ǣfre gelimpan,
80 þæt ðū in sundurgiefe   swylce befēnge,
nē wē þǣre wyrde   wēnan þurfon
tōweard in tīde.   Hūru trēow in þē
weorðlicu wunade,   nū þū wuldres Þrym
bōsme gebǣre,   ond nō gebrosnad wearð
85 mægðhād se micla.   Swā eal manna bearn
sorgum sāwað,   swā eft rīpað, —
cennað tō cwealme.'—   Cwæð sīo ēadge mǣg
symle sigores full,   Sancta Marīa : —
'Hwæt is þēos wundrung   þe gē wāfiað,
90 ond gēomrende   gehþum mǣnað,
sunu Sōlimæ   somod his dohtor ?
fricgað þurh fyrwet   hū ic fǣmnanhād,
mund mīnne, gehēold,   ond ēac mōdor gewearð
mǣr[an] Meotudes Suna?   Forþan þæt monnum nis
95 cūð gerȳne,   ac Crīst onwrāh
in Dāuīdes   dȳrre mǣgan

69 *Gr.*² nīðum ; *Gr.*¹ genedde; *Th. says that a leaf is obviously wanting between*
nearo *and* þearfe; *S. says there is no sign of this.*—70 *Gr.*¹ nu.—73 *Th. note*
sand- (?).—77 *MS.* mod ; *Th. note, Gr. Sprachschatz* mōdê; *Gr.*¹ mōt; *Gr.*¹ *note*
mōt, *in the sense of* 'meeting,' *appositional with* gebedscipe ; *Go.*¹ *note* mōd
(= 'desire') ; *A.* mot.—78 *Th.* swylcne.—91 *MS.* solimę.—93 *Th., Gr.*¹ inne,
but Th. translates 'my'; *Gr.*¹ *note* mīnne *or* mīne (?); *Gr.*² minne (*so MS.*).—
94 *MS., Edd.* mære.

þæt is Ēuan scyld eal forpynded,
wærgð[o] āworpen, ond gewuldrad is
se hēanra hād. Hyht is onfangen
100 þæt nū blētsung mōt bǣm gemǣne,
werum ond wīfum, ā tō worulde forð
in þām ūplīcan engla drēame,
mid Sōðfæder symle wunian.'

Ēalā Ēarendel, engla beorhtast
105 ofer middangeard monnum sended,
ond sōðfæsta sunnan lēoma,
torht ofer tunglas, — þū tīda gehwane
of sylfum þē symle inlīhtes.
Swā þū, God of Gode gearo ācenned,
110 Sunu sōþan Fæder, swegles in wuldre
būtan anginne ǣfre wǣre,
swā þec nū for þearfum þīn āgen geweorc
bideð þurh byldo, þæt þū þā beorhtan ūs
sunnan onsende, ond þē sylf cyme,
115 þæt ðū inlēohte þā þe longe ǣr
þrosme beþeahte, ond in þēostrum, hēr
sǣton sinneahtes synnum bifealdne,
deorc dēapes sceadu drēogan sceoldan.
Nū wē hyhtfulle hǣlo gelȳfað
120 þurh þæt Word Godes weorodum brungen,
þe on frymðe wæs Fæder ælmihtgum
efenēce mid God, ond nū eft gewearð
flǣsc firena lēas, þæt sēo fǣmne gebær
gēomrum tō gēoce. God wæs mid ūs
125 gesewen būtan synnum ; somod eardedon
mihtig Meotudes Bearn ond se monnes Sunu,

---

97 *Th. note* forwended (?).—98 *MS.* wærgða ; *Gr.*[1] wærgðu.—108 *Gr.*[1] inlihtest.—
113 *Th. tr.* bideð *by* 'awaiteth' ; byldo *in MS. from* hyldo (*Go.*). — 114 *Th. note* þu
sylfa (?). — 118 sceadu *in MS. from* sceaðu. — 121 *MS., Edd.* ælmihtigum.

geþwǣre on þēode.   Wē þǣs þonc magon
secgan Sigedryhtne   symle bi gewyrhtum,
þǣs þe hē hine sylfne ūs   sendan wolde.

130   Ēalā gǣsta God,   hū þū glēawlīce
      mid noman ryhte   nemned wǣre
      Emmānūhēl,   swā hit engel gecwǣð
      ǣrest on Ebrēsc;   þæt is e[f]t gereht
      rūme bi gerȳnum :   ' Nū is rodera Weard,
135   God sylfa mid ūs';   swā þæt gomele gefyrn
      ealra cyninga Cyning   ond þone clǣnan ēac
      Sācerd sōðlīce   sǣgdon tōweard.
      Swā se mǣre iu   Melchīsedech,
      glēaw in gǣste,   godþrym onwrāh
140   ēces Alwāldan.   Sē wæs ǣ bringend,
      lāra lǣdend   þām longe his
      hyhtan hidercyme,   swā him gehāten wæs
      þætte Sunu Meotudes   sylfa wolde
      gefǣlsian   foldan mǣgðe,
145   swylce grundas ēac   Gǣstes mægne
      sīþe gesēcan.   Nū hīe sōfte þæs
      bidon in bendum   hwonne Bearn Godes
      cwōme tō cearigum.   Forþon cwǣdon swā
      sūslum geslǣhte :   'Nū þū sylfa cum,
150   heofones Hēahcyning.   Bring ūs hǣlolīf
      wērgum witeþēowum   wōpe forcymenum,
      bitrum brynetēarum.   Is sēo bōt gelong
      eal æt þē ānum   [æfter] oferþearfum.

133b *MS.*, *Th.* est; *Th. renders* by 'grace.'—134 *Th. note* runa (?).—138 *Gr.*[1]
note mǣra (?).—141b *Th. note* þam þe (?); *Gr.*[1] *note* þam *attraction for* þam þe.
—151 *MS.*, *Edd.* werigum.—152 *Th.* bryne tearum.—153 *Th. assumes a gap
before* oferþearfum; *Gr.*[1] *does not* ; *S.*, *Go. about five letters obliterated* ; *Siev.* for (?);
Th., *S. divide.* ofer þearfum ; *Holthausen* (*Ind. Forsch.* iv. *384*) æfter o.

Hæftas hygegēomre   hider [gesēce;
155 ne lǣt] þē behindan,   þonne þū heonan cyrre,
    mænigo þus micle;   ac þū miltse on ūs
    gecȳð cynelīce,   Crīst nergende,
    wuldres Æþeling ;   ne lǣt āwyrgde ofer ūs
    onwāld āgan.   Lǣf us ēcne gefēan
160 wuldres þīnes,   þæt þec weorðien,
    weoroda Wuldorcyning,   þā þū geworhtes ǣr
    hondum þīnum.   þū in hēannissum
    wunast wideferh   mid Wāldend Fæder.'

    ' Ēalā Iōsēph mīn,   Iācōbes bearn,
165 mǣg Dāuīdes   mǣran cyninges,
    nū þū frēode scealt   fæste gedǣlan,
    ālǣtan lufan mīne!'
                            ' Ic lungre eam
    dēope gedrēfed,   dōme berēafod,
    forðon ic worn for þē   word[a] hæbbe
170 sīdra sorga   ond sārcwida
    hearmes gehȳred,   ond mē hosp sprecað,
    tornworda fela.   Ic tēaras sceal
    gēotan gēomormōd.   God ēaþe mæg
    gehǣlan hygesorge   heortan mīnre,
175 āfrēfran fēasceaftne.   Ēalā fǣmne geong,
    mægð Marīa!'
                            ' Hwæt bemurnest ðū,

154ª Th. hyge geomre. — 154ᵇ Th. hider . . . ; Gr.¹ hider [gesohtest] ; S., Go., A.
ten or eleven letters obliterated or faded ; S. no s or f among the lost letters ; A. the
first letter may have been g, the sixth e, traces of both being visible, then two gone,
then the upper part of l or þ (?) ; Go. as above in text, by conjecture. — 155ª Th.
þe behindan . . es nu læt ; Gr.¹ [ne] þe behindan nu læt ; S. No gap between
behindan and þonne, es nu læt not in MS. — 161 A. geworhte. — 162 Gr. heahnis-
sum. — 163 Th., Gr.¹ wide ferð ; Gr.² wideferð ; MS. wide ferh. — 166 Gr.¹ note
hu þu (?). — 169 Th. note worda (?); Gr., R., K. worda ; Gr.¹ note worde (inst.);
Go.¹ Probably a scribal error for worda, or else worde, 'in word,' construed with
hæbbe gehyred ; MS. worde. — 171 Th. hospsprecað.

cleopast cearigende?   Ne ic culpan in þē,

incan ǣnigne   ǣfre onfunde,

womma geworhtra;   ond þū þā word spricest

180 swā þū sylfa sīe   synna gehwylcre

firena gefylled.'

   'Ic tō fela hæbbe

þæs byrdscypes   bealwa onfongen.

Hū mæg ic lādigan   lāþan sprǣce,

oþþe ondsware   ǣnge findan

185 wrāþum tōwiþere?   Is þæt wīde cūð

þæt ic of þām torhtan   temple Dryhtnes

onfēng frēolīce   fǣmnan clǣne,

womma lēase,   ond nū gehwyrfed is

þurh nāthwylces.   Mē nāwþer dēag,

190 secge nē swīge.   Gif ic sōð sprece,

þonne sceal Dāuīdes   dohtor sweltan,

stānum āstyrfed.   Gēn strengre is

þæt ic morþor hele :   scyle mānswara

lāþ lēoda gehwām   lifgan siþþan,

195 fracoð in folcum.'

   Þā sēo fǣmne onwrāh

ryhtgerȳno,   ond þus reordode : —

'Sōð ic secge   þurh Sunu Meotudes,

gǣsta Gēocend,   þæt ic gēn ne conn

þurh gemǣcscipe   monnes ōwer

200 ǣnges on eorðan;   ac mē ēaden wearð,

geongre in geardum,   þæt mē Gabrihēl,

heofones hēagengel,   hǣlo gebodade,

---

184 *MS., Edd.* ænige.— 185 *R.* to wiþere.— 188 *R. assumes loss of two hemistichs,* 188b *and* 189a, *after* lēase, *and conjectures:* weres ne cuðe, hal wæs þære mægðe had ; *Gr.*[1] gewyrped, *on account of alliteration.*— 189 *The text is here apparently corrupt; Gr.* nathwylces [searo], *to which Siev.* (*PBB. x. 515*) *objects on metrical grounds; R. indicates omission; K.* nathwylcne.— 190 *Th.*, *Gr.*[1] spræce.— 194 *Gr.*, *K.* lifian.— 196 *Gr.*, *R.*, *K.*, *A.* ryht geryno.— 199 *Gr.*[1] [mān] gemǣcscipe ; *Gr.*[2] *retracts, and Siev. likewise* (*PBB. x. 515*) *objects.*— 202 *Gr.*[1] heahengel.

sægde sōðlīce   þæt mē swegles Gǣst
lēoman onlȳhte ;   sceolde ic lifes Þrym
205 geberan, beorhtne Sunu,   Bearn ēacen Godes,
torhtes Tīrfruma[n].   Nū ic his tempel eam
gefremed būtan fācne ;   in mē frōfre Gǣst
geeardode.   Nū þū ealle forlǣt
sāre sorgceare.   Saga ēcne þonc
210 mǣrum Meotodes Sunu   þæt ic his mōdor ge-
          wearð,
fǣmne forð se-þēah,   ond þū fæder cweden
woruldcund bi wēne ;   sceolde wītedōm
in him sylfum bēon   sōðe gefylled.'

Ēalā þū sōða   ond þū sibsuma
215 ealra cyninga Cyning,   Crīst ælmihtig,
hū þū ǣr wǣre   eallum geworden
worulde þrymmum   mid þīnne Wuldorfæder
cild ācenned   þurh his cræft ond meaht !
Nis ǣnig nū   eorl under lyfte,
220 secg searoþoncol,   tō þæs swīðe glēaw
þc þæt āsecgan mægc   sundbūcndum,
āreccan mid ryhte,   hū þē rodera Weard
æt frymðe genōm   him tō Frēobearne.
Þæt wæs, þāra þinga   þe hēr þēoda cynn
225 gefrugnen mid folcum,   æt fruman ǣrest
geworden under wolcnum,   þæt wītig God,
lifes Ordfruma,   lēoht ond þȳstro
gedǣlde dryhtlīce,   ond him wæs dōmes geweald,
ond þā wisan ābēad   weoroda Ealdor : —
230 'Nū sīe geworden, forþ   ā tō wīdan fēore,

---

204 *Gr.*,[1] *K.* scolde. — 206 *MS.*, *Th.* -fruma ; *Th. note* tir fruman, *adopted by R.*,
Gr.,[1] *K.*, *and A.* ; *Go.* tirfruma[n]. — 210 *Th.*, *Gr.*[1] suna. — 211 *Th.*, *Gr.*, *R.*, *A.* se
þeah. — 229 *Gr.*[1] weroda. — 230 *MS.* forþa (*S.*), forþ a (*Go.*, *A.*) ; *Th.* forþā ; *Gr.*[1]
furðum ; *Gr.*[1] *note* forþam *as MS. reading* (*after Thorpe*).

lēoht līxende, gefēa   lifgendra gehwām
þe in cnēorissum   cende weorðen.'

Ond þā sōna gelomp,   þā hit swā sceolde ;
lēoma lēohtade   lēoda mǣgþum,
235 torht mid tunglum,   æfter þon tīda bīgong ;
sylfa sette   þæt þū Sunu wǣre
efeneardigende   mid þīnne ēngan Frēan
ǣrþon ōht þisses   ǣfre gewurde.
Þū eart sēo Snyttro   þe þās sīdan gesceaft,
240 mid þī Wāldende,   worhtes ealle.
Forþon nis ǣnig þæs horsc,   nē þæs hygecrǣftig,
þe þīn fromcyn mǣge   fīra bearnum
sweotule gesēþan.   Cum nū, sigores Weard,
Meotod moncynnes,   ond þīne miltse hēr
245 ārfæst ȳwe ;   ūs is eallum nēod
þæt wē þīn mēdrencynn   mōtan cunnan,
ryhtgerȳno,   nū wē āreccan ne mǣgon
þæt fǣdrencynn   fier ōwihte.
Þū þisne middangeard   milde geblissa
250 þurh ðīnne hērcyme,   hǣlende Crīst,
ond þā gyldnan geatu,   þe in gēardagum
ful longe ǣr   bilocen stōdan,
heofona Hēahfrēa,   hāt ontȳnan ;
ond ūsic þonne gesēce,   þurh þīn sylfes gong
255 ēaðmōd tō eorþan.   Ūs is þinra ārna þearf.
Hafað se āwyrgda   wulf tōstenced,
deor[c] d[ēað]scūa,   Dryhten, þīn ēowde,

---

231 *Th.* leohtlixende; *Gr.*, *A.* leoht, lixende; *Go.*[1] *tr.* '*bright-shining.*' — 237 *Th.* note agan *or* agen (?); *Gr.*[1] angenfrean; *Gr.*[1] *note* angen-frea (dominus dilectus). *comparing* Angenþēow, *etc.*; *Gr.*[2] *as in text.* — 238 *MS.*, *Edd.* ær þon. — 242 *Th.* note frumcyn (?); *Gr.*[1] frumcyn; *Gr.*[2] fromcyn. — 243 *Th.* note (*p. 501*) geseþan, *probably an error for* gesecgan, *but Gr.*[1] *note rejects this.* — 244 *MS.* milstse. — 245 *Siev.* suggests eowa, eawa, *for MS.* ywe. — 247ª *Th.*, *Gr.*, *A.* ryht geryno ; 247b *Th.*, *Gr.* magon. — 253 *Th.*, *Go.* heah frea. — 257. *MS.*, *Edd.* deor dædscua ; *Th. note* deorc deaðscufa, *which Gr.*[1] *note rejects.*

wīde tōwrecene; þæt ðū, Wāldend, ǣr
blōde gebohtes, þæt se bealofulla
260 hȳneð heardlīce, ond him on hæft nimeð
ofer ūss[a] nīoda lust. Forþon wē, Nergend, þē
biddað geornlīce brēostgehygdum
þæt þū hrædlīce helpe gefremme
wērgum wreccan; þæt se wītes bona
265 in helle grund hēan gedrēose;
ond þīn hondgeweorc, hæleþa Scyppend,
mōte ārīsan, ond on ryht cuman
tō þām ūpcundan æþelan rīce,
þonan ūs ǣr þurh synlust se swearta gǣst
270 fortēah ond forty[ht]e, þæt wē, tīres wone,
ā būtan ende sculon ermþu drēogan,
būtan þū ūsic þon ofostlīcor, ēce Dryhten,
æt þām lēodsceaþan, lifgende God,
Helm alwihta, hreddan wille.

275 Ēalā þū mǣra middangeardes,
sēo clǣneste cwēn ofer eorþan
þāra [þ]e gewurde tō wīdan fēore,
hū þec mid ryhte ealle reordberend
hātað ond secgað, hæleð geond foldan,
280 blīþe mōde, þæt þū brȳd sīe
þæs sēlestan swegles Bryttan!
Swylce þā hȳhstan on heofonum ēac
Crīstes þegnas cweþað ond singað
þæt þū sīe hlǣfdige hālgum meahtum
285 wuldorweorudes, ond worl[d]cundra

Cf. Litany [...]
Lu Pearl 441 [...]

---

270 *MS., Edd.* fortylde; *Th. note* fortealde, ' seduced by false stories ' (?) ; *Gr.*[1]
note fortylde = fortilde; *Cos.* fortyhte. — 275 *MS., Th., Go.* mæra; *Th. note* mæra
is, undoubtedly, an error of the scribe for maria. — 276ᵃ *Th. note suspects the loss of
a leaf, but Gr.*[1] *note rejects.* — 277 *MS.* þara ege wurde; *Th. note* l. gewurden; *S.*
reads gege, *but first g erased; A. assumes that the scribe neglected to write* þ *on the
erasure.* — 281 *Go.*[1] *note MS.* selesten. — 285 *MS.* worlcundra.

hāda under heofonum,   ond helwara ;
forþon þū þæt, āna   ealra monna,
geþōhtest þrymlīce,   þrīsthycgende,
þæt þū þīnne mægðhād   Meotude brōhtes,
290 sealdes būtan synnum.   Nān swylc ne cwōm
ænig ōþer   ofer ealle men,
brȳd bēaga hroden,   þe þā beorhtan lāc
tō heofonhāme   hlūtre mōde
siþþan sende.   Forðon heht sigores Fruma
295 his hēahbodan   hider geflēogan
of his mægenþrymme,   ond þē meahta spēd
snūde cȳðan,   þæt þū Sunu Dryhtnes
þurh clǣne gebyrd   cennan sceolde,
monnum tō miltse,   ond þē, Marīa, forð
300 efne unwemme   ā geheald[a]n.

Ēac wē þæt gefrugnon,   þæt gefyrn bi þē
sōðfæst sægde   sum wōðbora
in ealddagum,   Ēsaias,
þæt hē wǣre gelǣded   þǣ[r] hē līfes gesteald
305 in þām ēcan hām   eal scēawode.
Wlāt þā swā wīsfæst   wītga geond þēodland
oþþæt hē gestarode   þǣr gestaþelad wæs
æþelīc ingong.   Eal wæs gebunden
dēoran since   duru ormǣte,
310 wundurclommum bewriþen.   Wēnde swīðe
þæt ænig [ǣ]lda   æfre [ne] meahte
swā fæstlīce   forescyttelsas
on ēcnesse   ō inhebba[n],

---

300 *MS., Th., Go.* gehealden; *Th. note* gehealdan (?). — 304[b] *MS., Edd.* þæt; *Th.
note* þær (?). — 306 *MS.* wisfæft (*A., but not Th., Go.*). — 307 *Gr.*[1] oð þæt. —
310 *Th. note assumes the loss of an adverb after* swīðe. — 311 *MS., Edd.* elda; *MS.
omits* ne, *and so Th., Go.; Th. note* ne *is obviously wanting after* æfre; *Gr.*[1] [ne];
A. ne. — 313 *MS., Th.* o in hebba; *Th. note* owiht hebban (?); *Gr.,*[1] *A.* in hebban;
Go. in-hebba.

oþþe ðæs ceasterhlides   clūstor onlūcan,
315 ǣr him Godes engel,   þurh glædne geþonc,
þā wīsan onwrāh,   ond þæt word ācwæð : —
'Ic þē mæg secgan   þæt sōð gewearð
þæt ðās gyldnan gatu   gīet sume sīþe
God sylf wile,   Gǣstes mægne,
320 gefǣlsian,   Fæder ælmihtig,
ond, þurh þā fæstan locu,   foldan nēosan ;
ond hīo þonne æfter him   ēce stond[a]ð
simle singāles   swā beclȳsed
þæt nǣnig ōþer,   nymþe Nergend God,
325 hȳ ǣfre mā   eft onlūceð.'
Nū þæt is gefylled   þæt se frōda þā
mid ēagum þǣr   on wlātade.
Þū eart þæt wealldor ;   þurh þē Wāldend Frēa
ǣne on þās eorðan   ūt sīðade,
330 ond efne swā þec gemētte   meahtum gehrodene
clǣne ond gecorene   Crīst ælmihtig ;
swā ðē æfter him   engla Þēoden
eft, unmǣle   ælces þinges,
lioþucǣgan bilēac,   līfes Brytta.
335 Īowa ūs nū þā āre   þe se engel þē,
Godes spelboda,   Gābriēl, brōhte.
Hūru þæs biddað   burgsittende
þæt ðū þā frōfre   folcum cȳðe,
þīnre sylfre Sunu.   Siþþan wē mōta[n]
340 ānmōdlīce   ealle hyhtan,
nū wē on þæt bearn foran   brēostum stariað.
Geþinga ūs nū   þrīstum wordum
þæt hē ūs ne lǣte   leng ōwihte
in þisse dēaðdene   gedwolan hȳran,

315 *Th. note* glæwne (gleawne) (?). — 322 *MS., Th., Go.* stondeð. — 339 *MS., Th.*
motam.

345　ac þæt hē ūsic geferge　　in Fæder rīce,
　　þǣr wē sorglēase　　siþþan mōtan
　　wunigan in wuldre　　mid weoroda God.

　　Ēalā þū hālga　　heofona Dryhten,
　　þū mid Fæder þīnne　　gefyrn wǣre
350　efenwesende　　in þām æþelan hām.
　　Næs ǣnig þā gīet　　engel geworden,
　　nē þæs miclan　　mægenþrymmes nān
　　ðe in roderum ūp　　rīce biwitigað,
　　þēodnes þrýðgesteald　　ond his þegnunga,
355　þā þū ǣrest wǣre　　mid þone ēcan Frēan
　　sylf settende　　þās sīdan gesceaft,
　　brāde brytengrundas.　　Bǣm inc is gemǣne
　　Hēahgǣst hlēofæst.　　Wē þē, Hǣlend Crīst,
　　þurh ēaðmēdu　　ealle biddað
360　þæt þū gehȳre　　hæfta stefne
　　þīnra nīedþīowa,　　nergende God, —
　　hū wē sind geswencte　　þurh ūre sylfra gewill.
　　Habbað wræcmæcgas　　wērgan gǣstas,
　　het[e]l[a]n helsceaþa[n],　　hearde genyrwad,
365　gebunden bealorāpum.　　Is sēo bōt gelong
　　eall æt þē ānum,　　ēce Dryhten.
　　Hrēowcearigum help,　　þæt þīn hidercyme
　　āfrēfre fēasceafte,　　þēah wē fæhþo wið þec
　　þurh firena lust　　gefremed hæbben.
370　Āra nū onbehtum,　　ond ūsse yrmþa geþenc, —
　　hū wē tealtrigað　　tȳdran mōde,
　　hwearfiað hēanlīce.　　Cym nū, hæleþa Cyning ;
　　ne lata tō lange.　　Ūs is lissa þearf, —
　　þæt þū ūs āhredde,　　ond ūs hǣlogiefe

345 *Go.* fæderrice. — 353 *Th., Gr.*[1] bewitigað. — 358 *Th.* heah gæst. — 361 *MS.*
med; *Th., Gr.*[1] nied *without remark.* — 364a *MS.* hetlen helsceaþa ; *Th. note* hetlan
(hetolan) helsceaþas (?); *Ettm.* (*Lex.*) hetlan helsceaðan ; 364b *MS.* genyrwað
(*A.*; *not Th., Go.*). — 371 *MS.* hu þe.

375 sōðfæst sylle,   þæt wē siþþan forð
     þā sēllan þing   symle mōten
     geþēon on þēode,   þīnne willan.

     Ēalā sēo wlitige,   weorðmynda full,
     hēah ond hālig,   heofoncund Þrȳnes,
380 brāde geblissad   geond brytenwongas,
     þ[ec] mid ryhte sculon   reordberende,
     earme eorðware,   ealle mægene
     hergan hēalīce,   nū ūs Hǣlend God
     wǣrfæst onwrāh   þæt wē hine witan mōtan.
385 Forþon hȳ, dǣdhwǣte,   dōme geswīðde,
     þæt sōðfæste   seraphinnes cynn,
     uppe mid englum   ā brēmende,
     unāþrēotendum   þrymmum singað
     ful hēalīce,   hlūdan stefne,
390 fægre feor ond nēah.   Habbaþ folgoþa
     cyst mid Cyninge.   Him þæt Crīst forgeaf,
     þæt hȳ mōtan his ætwiste   ēagum brūcan,
     simle singāles,   swegle gehyrste,
     weorðian Wāldend   wide ond sīde;
395 ond mid hyra fiþrum   Frēan ælmihtges
     onsȳne wear[dia]ð,   ēcan Dryhtnes,
     ond ymb þēodenstōl   þringað georne,
     hwylc hyra nēhst mǣge   ūssum Nergende
     flihte lācan   friðgeardum in.
400 Lofiað Lēoflīcne,   ond in lēohte him
     þā word cweþað,   ond wuldriað
     æþelne Ordfruman   ealra gesceafta : —
     ' Hālig eart þū, hālig,   hēahengla Brego,
     sōð sigores Frēa;   simle þū bist hālig,

---

381 *MS., Edd.* þa. — 385 *Gr.*[1] dædhwate. — 393 *Th. note* swegles (?). — 394 *Th. note* weorðiað (?). — 395 *Th., Gr.*[1] ælmihtiges. — 396 *MS., Th.* wearð; *Th. note* weardiað (?), *and so Edd.* — 399 *Gr.*[1] flyhte.

405 dryhtna Dryhten ;   ā þīn dōm wunað
    eorðlīc mid ældum   in ǣlce tīd
    wīde geweorþad.   Þū eart weoroda God,
    forþon þū gefyldest   foldan ond rodoras,
    wīgendra Hlēo,   wuldres þīnes,
410 Helm alwihta.   Sīe þē in hēannessum
    ēce hǣlo,   ond in eorþan lof,
    beorht mid beornum.   Þū geblētsad leofa,
    þe in Dryhtnes noman   dugeþum cwōme
    hēanum tō hrōþre.   Þē in hēahþum sīe
415 ā būtan ende   ēce herenis.'

    Ēalā ! hwæt þæt is wræclīc wrixl   in wera līfe,
    þætte moncynnes   milde Scyppend
    onfēng æt fǣmnan   flǣsc unwemme,
    ond sīo weres frīga   [w]iht ne cūþe,
420 nē þurh sǣd ne cwōm   sigores Āgend
    monnes ofer moldan ;   ac þæt wæs mā[ra] cræft
    þonne hit eorðbūend   ealle cūþan
    þurh gerȳne,   hū hē, rodera þrim,
    heofona Hēahfrēa,   helpe gefremede
425 monna cynne   þurh his mōdor hrif.
    Ond, swā forð gongende,   folca Nergend
    his forgifnesse   gumum tō helpe
    dǣleð dōgra gehwām,   Dryhten weoroda.
    Forþon wē hine dōmhwate,   dǣdum ond wordum,
430 hergen holdlīce.   Þæt is hēalīc rǣd
    monna gehwylcum   þe gemynd hafað,
    þæt hē symle oftost   ond inlocast
    ond geornlīcost   God weorþige.

---

410 *Gr.*[1] heahnessum. — 416 *Th. note assumes a gap of more than a line after*
hwæt, *but against the MS.* — 419 *MS.* niht. — 421 *MS., Edd.* ma ; *Siev.* (*PBB. x.*
515) *suggests* mara. — 423 *Gr.*[1] þrym. — 426 *MS., Edd.* forð gongende. — 432 *Gr.*[1]
note inlicast (?).

He him þære lisse   lean forgildeð,

435 se gehalgoda   Hælend sylfa,

efne in þam eðle   þær he ær ne cwom,

in lifgendra   londes wynne,

þær he gesælig   siþþan eardað,

ealne widan feorh   wunað butan ende. Amen.

PART II. — THE ASCENSION.

440 Nū ðū geornlīce   gǣstgerȳnum,
mon se mǣra,   mōdcræfte sēc
þurh sefan snyttro,   þæt þū sōð wite
hū þæt geēode —   þā se Ælmihtga
ācenned wearð   þurh clǣnne hād,
445 siþþan hē Marīan,   mægða weolman,
mǣrre mēowlan,   mundheals gecēas —
þæt þǣr in hwītum   hræglum gewerede
englas ne oðēowdun,   þā se Æþeling cwōm
Beorn in Betlēm.   Bodan wǣron gearwe,
450 þā þurh hlēoþorcwide   hyrdum cȳðdon,
sǣgdon sōðne gefēan,   þætte Sunu wǣre
in middangeard   Meotudes ācenned,
in Betlēme.   Hwæþre in bōcum ne cwið
þæt hȳ in hwītum þǣr   hræglum oðȳwden
455 in þā æþelan tīd,   swā hīe eft dydon
ðā se Brega mǣra   tō Bethānia,
Þēoden þrymfæst,   his þegna gedryht
gelaðade, lēof weorud.   Hȳ þæs Lārēowes
on þam wildæge   word ne gehyrwdon
460 hyra Sincgiefan.   Sōna wǣron gearwe
hæleð mid Hlāford   tō þǣre hālgan byrg,
þǣr him tācna fela   tīres Brytta
onwrāh, wuldres Helm,   wordgerȳnum,
ǣrþon ūp stige   āncenned Sunu,
465 efenēce Bearn   āgnum Fæder,

---

440 W., Go.[1] gæst gerynum. — 443 MS., Edd. ælmihtiga. — 445 Gr.[1] *note* mægðe (:). — 453 *Siev. suggests* cwiðeð (*PBB. x. 475*). — 456 *Th.*, Gr. brego. — 465 *Siev. suggests* Fædere (*PBB. x. 483*), *and so in 532.*

þæs ymb fēowertig,   þe hē of foldan ǣr

from dēaðe ārās,   dagena rīmes ; —

hæfde þā gefylled,   swā ǣr biforan sungon,

wītgena word,   geond woruld innan,

470 þurh his þrōwinga.   Þegnas heredon,

lufedun lēofwendum,   līfes Āgend,

Fæder frumsceafta.   Hē him fǣgre þæs

lēofum gesīþum   lēan æfter geaf,

ond þæt word ācwæð   Wāldend engla,

475 gefȳsed, Frēa mihtig,   tō Fæder rīce :

'Gefēoð gē on fērðe ;   nǣfre ic from hweorfe,

ac ic lufan symle   lǣste wið ēowic,

ond ēow meaht giefe,   ond mid wunige

āwo tō ealdre,   þæt ēow ǣfre ne bið

480 þurh gife mīne   gōdes onsīen.

Farað nū geond ealne   yrmenne grund,

geond wīdwegas ;   weoredum cȳðað,

bodiað ond brēmað,   beorhtne gelēafan,

ond fulwiað   folc under roderum,

485 hweorfað tō heofonum ;   hergas brēotaþ,

fyllað ond fēogað ;   fēondscype dwǣscað,

sibbe sāwað,   on sefan manna,

þurh meahta spēd.   Ic ēow mid wunige

forð on frōfre,   ond ēow friðe healde

490 strengðu staþolfæstre   on stōwa gehwā[m].'

Ðā wearð semninga   swēg on lyfte

hlūd gehȳred ;   heofonengla þrēat,

weorud wlitescȳne,   wuldres āras,

cwōmun on corðre.   Cyning ūre gewāt

---

471 *Th. note* lofedun (?), *with reference to 504.* — 469 *Gr.*[1] woruld-innan ; *A*, woruldinnan. — 476 *MS., Edd.* ferððe. — 479 *Th., Gr.*[1] awa. — 482 *MS.* wid wegas ; *Th., Gr.*[1] wide wegas ; *Gr.*[1] *note* wid-wegas (?) ; *Gr.*[2] widwegas. — 485 *Gr.*[1] *note* hweorfað hi (?). — 490 *Th. note l.* strengðe, *unless the word be sometimes indeclinable ; Th., Gr.* stowe ; *MS., Edd.* gehware ; *Siev.* (*PBB. x. 485*) gehwæm. — 493 *Th.* wlite scyne.

495 þurh þæs temples hróf,   þær hȳ tō sēgun,—
þā þe lēofes þā gēn   lāst weardedun
on þām þingstede,   þegnas gecorene.
Gesēgon hī on hēahþu   Hlāford stīgan
Godbearn of grundum.   Him wæs gēomor sefa,
500 hāt æt heortan   hyge murnende,
þæs þe hī swā lēofne   leng ne mōstun
gesēon under swegle.   Song āhōfun
āras ufancunde,   Æþeling heredun,
lofedun Līffruman,   lēohte gefēgun
505 þe of þæs Hǣlendes   heafelan līxte.
Gesēgon hȳ ælbeorhte   englas twēgen
fægre ymb þæt Frumbearn   frætwum blican,
cyninga Wuldor.   Cleopedon of hēahþu
wordum wrǣtlīcum   ofer wera mengu
510 beorhtan reorde :   'Hwæt bīdaðgē,
Galilēsce   guman, on hwearfte ?
Nū gē sweotule gesēoð   sōðne Dryhten
on swegl faran,   sigores Āgend ;
wile ūp heonan   eard gestīgan
515 æþelinga Ord   mid þās engla gedryht,
ealra folca Fruma,   Fæder ēþelstōll.

'Wē mid þyslīce   þrēate willað
ofer heofona gehlidu   Hlāford fergan
tō þǣre beorhtan byrg   mid þās blīðan gedry[h]t, —
520 ealra sigebearna   þæt sēleste
ond æþeleste, —   þe gē hēr on stariað,
ond in frōfre gesēoð   frætwum blican ;
wile eft swā-þēah   eorðan mǣgðe
sylfa gesēcan   sīde herge,

496 *MS., Th.* weardedum.—503 *MS., Th.* heredum.—508 *Th.* heahþū; *Gr.*[1]
heahðum.—519 *Con.*[2] byrig *always; MS., Edd.* gedryt, *except Gr.*[1] gedryht.—
521 *Gr.*[1] þæt *for* þe; *Con.*[2] ðæge.

525 ond þonne gedēman   dǣda gehwylce
þāra ðe gefremedon   folc under roderum.'
Ðā wæs wuldres Weard   wolcnum bif[o]ng[e]n,
hēahengla Cyning,   ofer hrōfas upp,
hāligra Helm.   Hyht wæs genīwad,
530 blis in burgum,   þurh þæs Beornes cyme.
Gesæt sigehrēmig   on þā swīþran hand
ēce Ēadfruma   āgnum Fæder.
Gewitan him þā gongan   tō Hierūsalēm
hæleð hygerōfe   in ðā hālgan burg
535 gēomormōde,   þonan hȳ God nȳhst
ūp stīgende   ēagum sēgun,
hyra Wilgifan.   Þǣr wæs wōpes hring;
torne bitolden   wæs sēo trēowlufu,
hāt æt heortan ;   hre[ð]er innan wēoll,
540 beorn brēostsefa.   Bidon ealle þǣr
þegnas þrymfulle   Þēodnes gehāta
in þǣre torhtan byrig   tȳn niht þā gēn,
swā him sylf bibēad   swegles Āgend,
ǣrþon ūp stige   ealles Wāldend
545 on hcofona gchyld.—   Hwīte cwōman
eorla Ēadgiefan   englas tōgēanes.
Ðæt is wel cweden,   swā gewritu secgað,
þæt him ælbeorhte   englas tōgēanes
in þā hālgan tīd   hēapum cwōman,
550 sīgan o[f] swegle.   Þā wæs symbla mǣst
geworden in wuldre.   Wel þæt gedafenað

526 Con.² ða.— 527 MS., Con.² (p. xxx), Th. bifengun; Con.² bifengum; Th.
note bifangen (?); Gr.¹ bifangen; Go.¹ bifongen, but, in his note, calls the MS. reading an error for bifangen; Go.² bifen.— 535 Con.² geomor mode; Siev. neist.—
536 Th. note more correctly up-stigendne; Gr.¹ up stigende.— 537 Con.² wofes.—
539 MS., Con. hreder.— 540 MS. beorn, with erasure between b and o; Con.,² Gr.¹
bearn, Con.² tr. by 'filii'; MS. bidån ; Con. ðære.— 542 Con. tyr riht; Go. pa-gen.
— 543 Con.² himself.— 544 MS., Edd. ær þon.— 545 Th. note gehlyd (?).—
548 MS. ælbeorhte ; Go. albeorhte — 550 MS., Edd. on.

ðæt tō þǣre blisse   beorhte gewerede
in þæs Þēodnes burg   þegnas cwōman,
we orud wlitescȳne ;   gesēgon wilcuman
555 on hēahsetle   heofones Wāldend,
folca Feorhgiefan,   frætwum ealles wāldend
middangeardes   ond mægenþrymmes.

' Hafað nū se Hālga   helle birēafod
ealles þæs gafoles   þe hī gēardagum
560 in þæt orlege   unryhte swealg.
Nū sind forcumene,   ond in cwicsūsle
gehȳnde ond gehæfte,   in helle grund
duguþum bidæled,   dēofla cempan.
Ne meahtan wiþerbr[eoc]an   wīge spōwan,
565 wǣpna wyrpum,   siþþan wuldres Cyning,
heofonrīces Helm,   hilde gefremede
wiþ his ealdfēondum   Ānes meahtum,
þǣr hē of hæfte āhlōd   hūþa mǣste,
of fēonda byrig   folces unrīm,
570 þisne ilcan þrēat   þe gē hēr on stariað.
Wile nū gesēcan   sāwla Nergend
gǣsta giefstōl,   Godes āgen Bearn,
æfter gūðplegan.   Nū gē geare cunnon
hwæt se Hlāford is   se þisne here lǣdeð.—
575 Nū gē fromlīce   frēondum tōgēanes
gongað glædmōde.—   Geatu, ontȳnað ;
wile in tō ēow   ealles Wāldend,
Cyning on ceastre,   corðre ne lȳtle,
fyrnweorca Fruma,   folc gelǣdan
580 in drēama drēam,   ðe hē on dēoflum genōm
þurh his sylfes sygor.   — Sib sceal gemǣne

554 *Th.* wlite scyne. — 556b *Siev. suggests* (*PBB. x. 515*) *that* Waldend *is from
the preceding line, and would read* Frætwan (as.) ealles. — 559 *Gr.*[2] þe heo. —
564 *MS.* nē͟ahtan, me *by another hand*; *MS.*, *Edd.* wiþerbrogan ; *Cos.* wiþerbreocan. — 577 *Con.*[2] (*p. xxx*) hi to; *Gr.*,[1] *A.* in to. — 578 *Con.*[2] corðrene, *tr.* 'coronam.' — 580 *Con.*[2] drǣma drǣm. — 581 *Gr.*[1] sigor.

englum ond ǣldum   ā forð heonan
wesan wīdeferh.   Wǣr is ætsomne
Godes ond monna,   gǣsthālig trēow, —
585 lufu, līfes hyht,   ond ealles lēohtes gefēa.' —

   Hwæt ! wē nū gehȳrdan   hū þæt Hǣlubearn
þurh his hydercyme   hāls eft forgeaf,
gefrēode ond gefreoþade   folc under wolcnum,
mǣre Meotudes Sunu,   þæt nū monna gehwylc
590 cwic þendan hēr wuna[ð],   gecēosan mōt
swā helle hīenþu   swā heofones mǣrþu,
swā þæt lēohte lēoht   swā ðā lāþan niht,
swā þrymmes þrǣce   swā þȳstra wrǣce,
swā mid Dryhten drēam   swā mid dēoflum hrēam,
595 swā wīte mid wrāþum   swā wuldor mid ārum,
swā līf swā dēað,   swā him lēofre bið
tō gefremmanne,   þenden flǣsc ond gǣst
wuniað in worulde.   Wuldor þæs āge
Þrȳnysse þrym,   þonc būtan ende!

600   Ðæt is þæs wyrðe   þætte werþēode
secgen Dryhtne þonc   duguða gehwylcre
þe ūs sið ond ǣr   simle gefremede
þurh monigfealdra   mægna gerȳno.
Hē ūs æt giefeð,   ond ǣhta spēd,
605 welan ofer wīdlond,   ond weder līþe
under swegles hlēo.   Sunne ond mōna,
æþelast tungla,   eallum scīnað,
heofoncondelle,   hæleþum on eorðan.
Drēoseð dēaw ond rēn ;   duguðe weccaþ

---

586 *Th.* hælu bearn. — 587 *Th. note* heals-hæft (?), *for* hals eft. — 590 *MS., Go.,*[1]
Go.[2] wunat.— 593 *MS.* (*A.*) þystra ; *Th., Gr.,*[1] *Go.* þrystra (*as if MS.*); *R.* þystra,
but assumes þrystra *as MS. reading*; *Gr.*[1] *note* þrīstra (?) þystra (?). — 600b *Con.,*[1]
Con.[2] ðæt ðe ; *Ettm.* -ðeoda. — 601 *Con.*[1] drythne þone ; *Con.*[2] secgan dryðne. —
604 *Con.,*[1] *Con.*[2] giefed ; æhta-sped.— 605 *Con.,*[1] *Con.,*[2] *Th., Ettm., Gr.,*[1] *R.* wid
lond ; *Gr.*[2] widlond. — 608 *Con.,*[1] *Con.*[2] heofon candelle, *and frequently separates
compound words.* — 609 *Con.*[2] *translates* ren duguðe *by* 'pluvia bona.'

610 tō feorhnere　　　fīra cynne,

　　īecað eorðwelan.　　Þæs wē ealles sculon

　　secgan þonc ond lof　　Þēodne ūssum,

　　ond hūru þǣre hǣlo　　þe hē ūs tō hyhte forgeaf,

　　ðā hē þā yrmðu　　eft oncyrde,

615 æt [h]is ūpstige,　　þe wē ǣr drugon,

　　ond geþingade　　þēodbūendum

　　wið Fæder swǣsne　　fǣhþa mǣste

　　Cyning ānboren.　　Cwide eft onhwearf

　　sāulum tō sibbe,　　se þe ǣr sungen [wæs]

620 þurh yrne hyge　　ældum tō sorge : —

　　'Ic þec of eorðan geworhte ;　　on þǣre þū scealt yrmþum lifgan,

　　wunian in gewinne　　ond wrǣce drēogan,

　　fēondum tō hrōþor　　fūslēoð galan,

　　ond tō þǣre ilcan scealt　　eft geweorþan

625 wyrmum āweallen ;　　þonan wītes fȳr

　　of þǣre eorðan scealt　　eft gesēcan.'

　　Hwæt ! ūs þis se Æþeling　　ȳðre gefremede,

　　þā hē leomum onfēng　　ond līchoman,

　　monnes magutūdre.　　Siþþan Meotodes Sunu

630 engla ēþel　　ūp gestīgan

　　wolde, weoroda God,　　ūs se willa bicwōm

　　hēanum tō helpe　　on þā hālgan tīd.

　　　Bi þon giedd 'āwræc　　Iōb, swā hē cūðe,

　　herede Helm wera,　　Hǣlend lofede,

635 ond mid siblufan　　Sunu Wāldendes

---

611 *Con.*[2] secath.—612[b] *Ettm.*, *Gr.*[1] dryhtne.—614 *Gr.*[1] yrmða; *Ettm.* oncirde; *Th.*, *Go.* eftoncyrde, *and so usually in verbs with separable prefix ; variations in this respect will not be noted.*—615 *MS.* is.—619 *Ettm.* sawlum ; *Th. note* wæs add (?); *Ettm.*, *Gr.*,[1] *R.*, *Go.*[1] *supply* wæs *or* [wæs]; *Con.*,[1] *Con.*[2] *omits, with MS.*—620 *Ettm.* ealdum.—621 *MS.* ofer, *and so Edd. except R.* of.—623 *Con.*,[1] *Con.*[2] hroðer, fus leoðgalan (*translating the last two words by* promptis hominum inimicis).— 624 *Ettm.* ylcan.—626 *Con.*[1] thæeore.—627 *Con.*,[1] *Con.*[2] *om.* se.— 629 *Ettm.*, *Gr.*[1] meotudes.—631 *Ettm.* weoruda.—634 *Ettm.* lofode.—635 *Th.* suna (?); *Ettm.*, *Gr.*[1] suna.

frēonoman cende,   ond hine fugel nemde,
þone Iūdēas   ongietan ne meahtan
in ðǣre godcundan   Gǣstes strengðu ;
wæs þæs fugles flyht   fēondum on eorþan
640 dyrne ond dēgol,   þām þe deorc gewit
hæfdon on hreþre,   heortan stǣnne ;
noldaɲ hī þā torhtan   tācen oncnāwan
þe him beforan fremede   Frēobearn Godes,
monig, mislic[u],   geond middangeard.

645 Swā se fǣla fugel   flyges cunnode :
hwīlum engla eard   ūp gesōhte,
  ˙mōdig, meahtum strang,   þone m[ǣ]ran hām ;
hwīlum hē tō eorþan   eft gestylde,
þurh Gǣstes giefe   grundscēat sōhte,
650 wende tō worulde.   Bi þon se wītga song :
' Hē wæs upp hafen   engla fæðmum
in his þā miclan   meahta spēde,
hēah ond hālig,   ofer heofona þrym.'

Ne meahtan þā þæs fugles   flyht gecnāwan
655 þe þæs ūpstiges   ondsæc fremedon ;
ond þæt ne gelȳfdon,   þætte Līffruma
in monnes hīw   ofer mægna þrym,
hālig from hrūsan,   āhafen wurde.

Ðā ūs geweorðade   sē þās world gescōp,
660 Godes Gǣstsunu,   ond ūs giefe sealde,
uppe mid englum   ēce staþelas,
ond ēac monigfealde   mōdes snyttru
sēow ond sette   geond sefan monna.
Sumum wordlaþe   wīse sendeð

---

636 *Th.* freo noman.—637 *Ettm.* meahton, *and so* -on *elsewhere.*—638 *Ettm.*
gastes, *and so elsewhere.*—641 *Gr.*[1] *note* stænene (?).—642 *Th. note* r. tacnu or
tacna ; *Ettm.* tacnu.—645 *Go.*[1] fæle.—647 *MS., Edd.* maran, *except Gr.*[1] *note*
mæran (?).—651 *Th., Go.,*[1] *A.* upphafen.—654 *MS.* flȳt.—657 *Gr.*[1] hiwe (?).—
659 *Con.,*[1] *Con.*[2] ðis.—660 *Con.*[1] sealede.—664 *Th. note* wordlace (?); *Ettm.*
wordlade, *comparing* OHG. wortleita.

665 on his mōdes gemynd   þurh his mūþes Gǣst,
     æðele ondgiet ;   sē mæg eal fela
     singan ond secgan ;   þām bið snyttru cræft
     bifolen on fērðe.   Sum mæg fingrum wel
     hlūde fore hæleþum   hearpan stirgan,
670 glēobēam grētan.   Sum mæg godcunde
     reccan ryhte ǣ.   Sum mæg ryne tungla
     secgan, sīde gesceaft.   Sum mæg searolīce
     wordcwide wrītan.   Sumum wīges spēd
     giefeð æt gūþe,   þonne gārgetrum
675 ofer scildhrēadan   scēotend sendað,
     flacor flāngeweorc.   Sum mæg fromlīce
     ofer sealtne sǣ   sundwudu drīfan,
     hrēran holmþræce.   Sum mæg hēanne bēam
     stǣlgne gestīgan.   Sum mæg stȳled sweord,
680 wǣpen, gewyrcan.   Sum cǫn wonga bīgong,
     wegas wīdgielle.   Swā se Wāldend ūs,
     Godbearn, on grundum   his giefe bryttað.
     Nyle hē ǣngum ānum   ealle gesyllan
     gǣstes snyttru,   þȳ-lǣs him gielp sceþþe
685 þurh his ānes cræft   ofer ōþre forð.

     Ðus God meahtig   geofum unhnēawum,
     Cyning alwihta,   cræftum weorðaþ
     eorþan tuddor ;   swylce ēadgum blǣd
     seleð on swegle ;   sibbe rǣreþ
690 ēce tō ealdre   engla ond monna.

665 *Th.* gæst (= ' guest '). — 666 *Con.*[2] ongiet. — 667 *Ettm.* byð, *and so always;*
Th., *Ettm.*, *Gr.*,[1] *K.*, *Go.* snyttru cræft ; *Con.*,[1] *Con.*,[2] *Gr.*,[2] *A.* snyttrucræft. —
668 *Ettm.* befolhen. — 669 *Con.*[2] styrgan, *Ettm.* stŷrjan. — 671 *Ettm.* rihte, *and
so elsewhere.* — 672 *Con.*,[1] *Con.*[2] learolice. — 673 *Con.*,[1] *Con.*[2] word cwide; *MS.*
sum[n], *S. and A. say the* ū *by another hand.* — 674 *Con.*,[1] *Con.*[2] giefed, ðon. — 675
Th. note 1. hreoðan ; *Ettm.* scildhreoðan ; *Con.*,[1] *Con.*[2] sendeð. — 677 *Con.*[1] sund
wudu ; *Ettm.* þrifan. — 678 *Ettm.*, *Gr.*,[1] *K.* heahne. — 680 *Con.*,[1] *Con.*[2] begong. —
681 *Con.*,[1] *Con.*[2] wið gielle (= ' elata voce '). — 682 *Con.*,[1] *Con.*[2] bryttad. — 683 *Con.*
gefyllan (= ' replere '). — 684 *MS.* hī, *not* hi, *as Th.*, *Ettm.*, *Gr.*[1] *read ; Con.* sceðe
— 685 *Con.*,[1] *Con.*[2] ford.

Swā hē his weorc weorþað.   Bi þon se wītga cwæð
þæt āhæfen wǣren   hālge gimmas,
hǣdre heofontungol,   hēalīce upp,
sunne ond mōna.   Hwæt sindan þā
695 gimmas swā scȳne   būton God sylfa?
Hē is se sōðfæsta   sunnan lēoma,
englum ond eorðwarum   æþele scīma.
Ofer middangeard   mōna līxeð,
gǣstlīc tungol ;   swā sēo Godes circe
700 þurh gesomninga   sōðes ond ryhtes
beorhte blīceð, —   swā hit on bōcum cwiþ —
siþþan of grundum   Godbearn āstāg,
Cyning clǣnra gehwæs.   Þā sēo circe hēr
æfyllendra   eahtnysse bād
705 under hǣþenra   hyrda gewealdum.
Þǣr ðā synsceaðan   sōþes ne gīemdon,
gǣstes þearfe ;   ac hī Godes tempel
brǣcan ond bærndon,   blōdgyte worhtan,
fēodan ond fyldon.   Hwæþre forð bicwōm
710 þurh Gǣstes giefe   Godes þegna blǣd,
æfter ūpstige   ēcan Dryhtnes.
Bi þon Salomon song,   sunu Dāuīþes,
giedda gearosnottor   gǣstgerȳnum,
wāldend werþēoda,   ond þæt word ācwæð : —
715 ‘ Cūð þæt geweorðeð   þætte Cyning engla,
Meotud, meahtum swīð,   munt gestylleð,
gehlēapeð hēadūne,   hyllas ond cnollas
bewrīð mid his wuldre,   woruld ālȳseð,

---

692 *Ettm.* ahafen. — 693 *Ettm.* up. — 695 *Ettm.* silfa. — 698 *MS.* līxed. — 699
Gr.[1] se ; *Ettm.* swa seo Godes cyrce, gæstlic tungol. — 701 *Siev. suggests* cwiðeð.
— 703 *Ettm.* cyrce. — 704 *Ettm.* eahtnisse (*note* ēhtnisse (?)). — 705 *Ettm.* hirda. —
709 *MS.* feodan, *between* o *and* d *a letter erased.* — 710 *MS.* blǣð. — 712 *Ettm.*
Davides ; *Gr.*,[1] *A.* Dauides. — 713 *Th.*, *Ettm.* gearo snottor. — 717 *Gr.*,[1] *A.* hea
dune.

ealle eorðbūend, þurh þone æþelan styll.'

720 Wæs se forma hlȳp þā hē on fǣmnan āstāg,
mægeð unmǣle, ond þǣr mennisc hīw
onfēng būtan firenum ; þæt tō frōfre gewearð
eallum eorðwarum. Wæs se ōþer stiell
bearnes gebyrda, þā hē in binne wæs,
725 in cildes hīw clāþum bewunden,
ealra þrymma þrym. Wæs se þridda hlȳp,
Rodorcyninges rǣs, þā hē on rōde āstāg,
Fæder, frōfre Gǣst. Wæs se fēorða stiell
in byrgenne — þā hē þone bēam ofgeaf —
730 foldærne fæst. Wæs se fīfta hlȳp
þā hē hellw[a]rena hēap forbȳgde
in cwicsūsle, cyning inne gebond,
fēonda foresprecan, fȳrnum tēagum,
gromhȳdigne, þǣr hē gēn ligeð
735 in carcerne, clommum gefæstnad,
synnum gesǣled. Wæs se siexta hlȳp,
Hālges hyhtplega, þā hē tō heofonum āstāg
on his ealdcȳððe. Þā wæs engla þrēat
on þā hālgan tīd hleahtre blīþe
740 wynnum geworden. Gesāwan wuldres Þrym,
æþelinga Ord, ēþles nēosan,
beorhtra bolda. Þā wearð burgwarum,
ēadgum, ēce gefēa Æþelinges plega.
Þus hēr on grundum Godes ēce Bearn
745 ofer hēahhleoþu hlȳpum stylde,
mōdig æfter muntum. Swā wē men sculon
heortan gehygdum hlȳpum styllan
of mægne in mægen, mǣrþum tilgan,

719 *Th.* eall. —724 *Ettm.* gebyrdo; *Gr.*[1] gebyrd; *Gr.*[2] gebyrdu. —725 *Th.*,
Ettm., *Gr.*[1] biwunden. —728 *Ettm.*, *Gr.*[1] gast. —731 *MS.*, *Th.* hellwerena. —
737 *MS.*, *Edd.* haliges. — 738 *Th.* eald cȳððe. —740 *Th.*, *Ettm.*, *Gr.*[1] gesawon. —
743 *Th.* eadgu. —748 *Ettm.* tiljan.

þæt wē tō þām hȳhstan   hrōfe gestīgan,
750 hālgum weorcum,   þǣr is hyht ond blis,
geþungen þegnweorud.   Is ūs þearf micel
þæt wē mid heortan   hǣlo sēcen,
þǣr wē mid gǣste   georne gelȳfað
þæt þæt Hǣlobearn   heonan ūp stige
755 mid ūsse līchoman,   lifgende God.
    Forþon wē ā sculon   īdle lustas,
synwunde, forsēon,   ond þæs sēllran gefēon.
Habbað wē ūs tō frōfre   Fæder on roderum
ælmeahtigne.   Hē his āras þonan,
760 hālig of hēahðu,   hider onsendeð,
þā ūs gescildaþ   wið sceþþendra
eglum earhfarum,   þi-lǣs unholdan
wunde gewyrcen,   þonne wrōhtbora
in folc Godes   forð onsendeð
765 of his brægdbogan   biterne strǣl.
    Forþon wē fæste sculon   wið þām fǣrscyte
symle wærlīce   wearde healdan,
þȳ-lǣs se āttres ord   in gebūge,
biter bordgelāc,   under bānlocan,
770 fēonda fǣrsearo.   Þæt bið frēcne wund,
blātast benna.   Utan ūs beorgan þā,
þenden wē on eorðan   eard weardigen!
Utan ūs tō Fæder   freoþa wilnian,
biddan Bearn Godes   ond þone blīðan Gǣst,
775 þæt hē ūs gescilde   wið sceaþan wǣpnum,
lāþra lygesearwum,   se ūs līf forgeaf,

752 *Ettm.* secan. — 753 *Th. note* þæt (?); *Ettm.* þæt; *Ettm. note* þær þæt, *MS.* — 754 *Th., Ettm., Go., A.* upstige. — 757 *Ettm.* synwunda; *MS.* sellᵣan; *Ettm.* selran. — 758 *Th. note* we *seems redundant.* — 760 *Th.* heahðū; *Ettm.* heahðum. — 762 *MS., Th.* englum; *Th. note* eglum (?); *Ettm.* þy. — 765 *Siev.* bitterne (*PBB. x. 496*). — 767 *Ettm.* simle, *and elsewhere.* — 768 *Th., Ettm.* ingebuge. — 770 *Ettm.* byð, *and elsewhere.* — 771 *Ettm.* uton. — 773 *Siev. suggests* Fædere (*PBB. x. 483*) *and so in 532.*

leomu, lic, ond gǣst !   Sī him lof symle,
þurh woruld worulda   wuldor on heof[o]num.

Ne þearf him ondrǣdan   dēofla strǣlas
780 ǣnig on eorðan   ǣlda cynnes,
gromra gārfare,   gif hine God scildeþ,
duguða Dryhten.   Is þām dōme nēah
þæt wē gelīce sceolon   lēanum hlēotan,
swā wē wīdefeorh   weorcum hlōdun
785 geond sīdne grund.   Ūs secgað bēc
hū æt ǣrestan   ēadmōd āstāg
in middangeard   mægna Goldhord,
in fǣmnan fæðm   Frēobearn Godes,
hālig of hēahþu.   Hūru ic wēne mē
790 ond ēac ondrǣde   dōm [ð]ȳ rēþran —
ðonne eft cymeð   engla Þēoden —
þe ic ne hēold teala   þæt mē Hǣlend mīn
on bōcum bibēad.   Ic þæs brōgan sceal
gesēon synwræce,   þæs þe ic sōð talge,
795 þǣr monig[e] bēoð   on gemōt lǣded
fore onsȳne   ēces Dēman.

Þonne ᚻ cwacað,   gehȳreð Cyning mæðlan,
rodera Ryhtend,   sprecan rēþe word
þām þe him ǣr in worulde   wāce hȳrdon,
800 þendan ᚠ ond ᚦ   ȳþast meahtan
frōfre findan.   Þǣr sceal forht monig
on þām wongstede   wērig bīdan

---

777 *Con.*[1] leomulic; sel him; *MS.* seⁱ (i *by another hand*), *according to S. and A.*; *but, according to* Go.[1] sⁱ, *and to* Go.[2] s^e. — 778 *Con.*,[1] *Ettm.* heofonum; *MS.*, *other Edd.* heofnum. — 780 *Ettm.* alda. — 783 h *of* hleotan *by another hand.* — 784 *Th.*, *Ettm.* wide feorh. — 786 Go.[1] ead mod. — 788 *Th.* freo bearn. — 789 *Th.* heahþū; *Ettm.* heahðum; *R.* heahþum. — 790 *MS.* dyreþran. — 794 *Th. note Perhaps* sinwræce, '*eternal vengeance*,' *which* Gr.[1] *rejects*; *Ettm.* talige. — 795 *MS.* lædað. — 797 *For the runes* Gr.[1] *prints the corresponding Roman letters.* — 798 *Ettm.* rodora rihtend. — 802 *Th.*, *Ettm.*, Gr.,[1] Go.[1] wērig; Gr.[2] werig.

hwæt him æfter dǣdum   dēman wille

wrāþra wīta. Biþ se ᛈ scæcen

805 eorþan frætwa. ᚾ wæs longe

ᚱ flōdum bilocen, līfwynna dǣl,

ᚠ on foldan. þonne frætwe sculon

byrnan on bǣle ; blāc rāsetteð

recen rēada lēg, rēþe scrīþeð

810 geond woruld wīde. Wongas hrēosað,

burgstede berstað. Brond bið on tyhte ;

ǣleð ealdgestrēon   unmurnlīce

gǣsta gīfrast, þæt gēo guman hēoldan,

þenden him on eorþan   onmēdla wæs.

815 Forþon ic lēofra gehwone   lǣran wille

þæt hē ne āgǣle   gǣstes þearfe,

nē on gylp gēote, þenden God wille

þæt hē hēr in worulde   wunian mōte,

somed sīþian   sāwel in līce,

820 in þām gæsthofe. Scyle gumena gehwylc

on his gēardagum   georne biþencan

þæt ūs milde bicwōm   meahta Wāldend

---

803 *Th. note Absence of the rune E, and the want of connexion in the sense, prove the loss of a couplet* [i.e. *long line*] *between ll. 22 and 23* [i.e. *after* wīta]; *Ettm. note Literæ deficientis nomen est* Eh, *ejusque notio: equus ; Gr.*[1] *inserts as 804, after* wille : [on þam E. fullan dæge engla dryhten], *which Siev. criticizes (PBB. x. 515*); *Gr.*[1] *note 804 habe ich eingeschaltet, weil sonst nicht nur der Buchstabe E. fehlt, sondern auch der Zusammenhang unterbrochen ist ;* E. full = eh -full, egefull *terribilis (sonst ist* E = Eh *equus*) ; *R. indicates omission after* wille; *R. note In der ausgefallenen Zeile muss die erune vorgekommen sein, etwa mit der Bedeutung* ege ; *Go. indicates no omission in text ; Wü. leaves a space for the line ; Gr. and Wü. of course number all succeeding lines one higher than the other Edd.*—804 *Ettm.* scacen ; *Gr.*[1] sceacen, *but notes MS. reading ; Gr.*[2] scæcen.—806 *Gr.*[1] bilocan ; *Gr.*[2] bilocen.—807 *Ettm.* frætwa. — 808 *Ettm.* birnan, *and elsewhere ; MS., Th.* blacra setteð (*Th., tr., according to Kenble's emendation, 'dusk shall crackle'*); *Kenble, quoted by Th. (note, and p. 502), and by Gr.*[1] *note, emends to* blac (blæc, blāc) ræscetteð ; *Ettm.* blâc ræscetteð ; *other Edd.* blâc rasetteð.—809 *Th. Ettm.* recenreada ; *R.* recene reada ; *Th., Ettm., Gr.*,[1] *R.* lig.—812 *Th.* ontyhte (*tr. 'kindled'*). — 813 *Th.* gæsta (*tr. 'of guests'*); *Ettm.* gâsta ; *R.* geoguman.—814 *Ettm.* unmedla —817 *Ettm.* gilp. —819 *Ettm.* sawl.—820 *Th., Gr.*[1] gasthofe ; *R.* gâsthofe.—821 *Gr.*[1] in.

æt ǣrestan   þurh þæs engles word;
bið nū eorneste   þonne eft cymeð,
825 rēðe ond ryhtwīs.   Rodor bið onhrēred,
ond þās miclan gemetu   middangeardes
beofiað þonne ;   beorht Cyning lēanað
þæs þe hȳ on eorþan   eargum dǣdum
lifdon leahtrum fā.   Þæs hī longe sculon,
830 fērðwērge, onfōn   in fȳrbaðe,
wǣlmum biwrecene,   wrāþlīc ondlēan.

Þonne mægna Cyning   on gemōt cymeð
þrymma mǣst[e],   þēodegsa bið
hlūd gehȳred   bi heofonwōman,
835 cwānendra cirm ;   ce[a]r[i]ge rēotað
fore onsȳne   ēces Dēman,
þā þe hyra weorcum   wāce trūwiað.

Ðǣr biþ oðȳwed   egsa māra
þonne from frumgesceape   gefrægen wurde
840 ǣfre on eorðan.   Þǣr bið ǣghwylcum
synwyrcendra   on þā snūdan tīd
lēofra micle   þonne eall þēos lǣne gesceaft
þæ[t] hē hine sylfne   on þām sigeþrēate
behȳdan mæge,   þonne herga Fruma,
845 æþelinga Ord,   eallum dēmeð,
lēofum ge lāðum,   lēan æfter ryhte,
þēoda gehwylcre.   Is ūs þearf micel
þæt wē gǣstes wlite   ǣr þām gryrebrōgan

---

825 *Ettm.* rihtwis.—826 *Ettm.* gemêtu.—827 *MS.*, *Th.* (*tr.* 'wail'), *Ettm.*, *Wü.* beheofið; *Gr.*,[1] *R.* beofið ; *R. indicates a break after* beofið; *R. note Offenbar ist das beziehungswort des* hȳ *in v. 13* [*828*] *ausgefallen.*—828 *Ettm.* hī, *and elsewhere.*—830 *MS.* fyr baðe, *the* y *corrected from* i (*so A.*); *not* fyr bade, *as Th., Ettm., Gr.*,[1] *Go. read* (*so A.*).—830 *MS., Edd.* ferðwerige.—831 *Ettm.* welmum; *Th. note* biwrigene *or* biwrogene (?).—833 *MS.* mæsta (*so Go.*,[1] *Go.*[2]); *Go.*[2] mæsta.—835 *MS.* cwanīendra; *Th., Ettm. Frucht* cwanendra; *MS.* cerge ; *Ettm., Gr.*[1] cearge.—837 *Ettm.* hira, *and elsewhere*; *Siev.* (*PBB. x. 486*) *for metrical reasons prefers* treowað *to* truwiað.—839 *Ettm.* gefregen.—842 *MS., Th., Wü.* leofra; *Ettm., Gr.*[1] eal.—843 *Ettm.* þæt; *MS., other Edd.* þær.

on þās gǣsnan tīd,   georne biþencen.

850   Nū is þōn gelīcost,   swā wē on laguflōde

      ofer cāld wæter   cēolum līðan,

      geond sīdne sǣ   sundhengestum,

      flōdwudu[m], fergen.   Is þæt frēcne strēam,

      ȳða ofermǣta,   þe wē hēr on lācað

855   geond þās wācan woruld,   windge holmas

      ofer dēop gelād.   Wæs se drohtað strong

      ǣrþon wē tō londe   geliden hæfdon

      ofer hrēone hrycg ;   þā ūs help bicwōm,

      þæt ūs tō hǣlo   hȳþe gelǣdde

860   Godes Gǣstsunu,   ond ūs giefe sealde,

      þæt wē oncnāwan magun   ofer cēoles bord

      hwǣr wē sǣlan sceolon   sundhengestas,

      ealde ȳðmēaras,   ancrum fæste.

      Utan ūs tō þǣre hȳðe   hyht staþelian,

865   ðā ūs gerȳmde   rodera Wāldend,

      hālge on hēahþu,   þā hē [tō] heofonum āstāg.

---

853 *Ettm.* flodwudum.— 854 *R.* ofermætu; *Th.* onlacað.— 862 *Ettm.* hwar.—
866 *Th.* heahþū; *Ettm., Gr.,*[1] *R.* heahðum; *Ettm. note* to heofonum (?), *MS.,*
Edd. om. to.

PART III.— DOOMSDAY.

Ðonne mid fēre   foldbūende
se micla dæg   meahtan Dryhtnes
æt midre niht   mægne bihlæm[m]eð,
870 scīre gesceafte,   swā oft sceaða fǣcne,
þēof þrīstlīce,   þe on þȳstre fareð,
on sweartre niht   sorglēase hæleð
semninga forfēhð   slǣpe gebundne,
eorlas ungearwe   yfles genǣgeð.
875 Swā on Sȳne beorg   somod ūp cymeð
mægenfolc micel,   Meotude getrȳwe,
beorht ond blīþe ;   him weorþeð blǣd gifen.
Þonne from fēowerum   foldan scēatum,
þām ȳtemestum   eorþan rīces,
880 englas ælbeorhte   on efen blāwað
bȳman on brehtme ;   beofað middangeard,
hrūse under hæleþum.   Hlȳdað tōsomne,
trume ond torhte,   wið tungla gong,
singað ond swinsiaþ   sūþan ond norþan,
885 ēastan ond westan,   ofer ealle gesceaft ;
weccað of dēaðe   dryhtgumena bearn,
eall monna cynn,   tō meotudsceafte
egeslīc of þǣre ealdan moldan ;   hātað hȳ upp āstandan
snēome of slǣpe þȳ fæstan.   Þǣr mon mæg sorgende folc
890 gehȳran, hygegēomor,   hearde gefȳsed,
cearum cwīþende   cwicra gewyrhtu

---

868 *Ettm.* meahtum.—869 *Th. note* bihlemmeð (?); *Ettm.* bihlemmeð.—
871 *Th., Ettm., Gr.*¹ fǣreð.—875 *Ettm. om.* up.—878 *Ettm.* fram.—885 *MS.*
healle.—888 *Gr.*¹ *note* egeslice (?); *Th., Ettm., Go., A.* uppastandan.—890 *Th.*
hyge geomor.

forhte āfǣrde. Þæt bið foretācna mǣst
þāra þe ǣr oþþe sīð ǣfre gewurde
monnum oþȳwed. Þǣr gemengde bēoð
895 onhǣlo gelāc engla ond dēofla,
beorhtra ond blacra ; weorþeð bēga cyme,
hwītra ond sweartra, swā him is hām sceapen
ungelīce englum ond dēoflum.

Þonne semninga on Sȳne beorg
900 sūþanēastan sunnan lēoma
cymeð of Scyppende scȳnan lēohtor
þonne hit men mǣgen mōdum āhycgan,
beorhte blīcan, þonne Bearn Godes
þurh heofona gehleodu hider oðȳweð.

905 Cymeð wundorlīc Crīstes onsȳn,
æþelcyninges wlite, ēastan fram roderum,
on sefan swēte sīnum folce,
biter bealofullum, geblēod wundrum,
ēadgum ond earmum ungelīce.

910 Hē bið þām gōdum glædmōd on gesihþe,
wlitig, wynsumlīc, weorude þām hālgan —
on gefēan fæger, frēond ond līoftǣl ;
lufsum ond līþe lēofum monnum
tō scēawianne þone scȳnan wlite,

915 wēðne mid willum, Wāldendes cyme,
Mægencyninges, þām þe him on mōde ǣr
wordum ond weorcum wel gecwēmdun.
Hē bið þām yflum egeslīc ond grimlīc
tō gesēonne, syngum monnum,
920 þām [þe] þǣr mid firenum cumað forð forworhte.

892 *Siev. suggests* (*PBB. x. 515*) foretacn, *for metrical reasons.* —894 *Th., Gr.,*[1]
Go. þar. —895 *Ettm.* unhælo. —896 *Ettm.* blâcra. —897 *Ettm.* hama. —900 *Th.*
suþan eastan. —901 *Ettm.* scippende scinan. —903 *Ettm. note* beorhte (?). —906
Gr.[1] from. —913 *Ettm. note* bȳð lufsum (?); *Ettm.* mannum. —914 *Ettm.* sceawanne.
—919 *MS., Edd.* synnegum ; *but cf. Siev.* (*PBB. x. 459*). —920 *Ettm.* þam þe.

Þæt mæg wītes tō wearninga   þām þe hafað wīsne geþōht,
þæt sē him eallunga   ōwiht ne ondrǣdeð;
sē for ðǣre onsȳne   egsan ne weorþeð
forht on fērðe,   þonne hē Frēan gesihð
925 ealra gesceafta   ondweardne faran
mid mægenwundrum   mon[i]gum tō þinge,
ond him on healfa gehwo[n]e   heofonengla þrēat
ymbūtan farað,   ælbeorhtra scolu,
hergas hāligra,   hēapum geneahhe.
930 Dyneð dēop gesceaft,   ond fore Dryhtne fǣreð
wǣlmfȳra mǣst   ofer wīdne grund,
hlemmeð hāta lēg;   heofonas berstað;
trume ond torhte   tungol ofhrēosað.
Þonne weorþeð sunne   sweart gewended
935 on blōdes hīw,   sēo ðe beorhte scān
ofer ǣrworuld   ælda bearnum ;
mōna þæt sylfe,   þe ǣr moncynne
nihtes lȳhte,   niþer gehrēoseð ;
ond steorran swā some   strēdað of heofone,
940 þurh ðā strongan lyft   stormum ābēatne.
Wile Ælmihtig   mid his engla gedryht,
mægencyninga Meotod,   on gemōt cuman,
þrymfæst Þēoden.   Bið þǣr his þegna ēac
hrēþēadig hēap.   Hālge sāwle
945 mid hyra Frēan farað,   þonne folca Weard
þurh egsan þrēa   eorðan mǣgðe
sylfa gesēceð.   Weorþeð geond sīdne grund
hlūd gehȳred   heofonbȳman stefn ;

---

921 *Gr.,*[1] *Go., Wü.* wites, *with short vowel, but cf. Siev. (PBB. x. 456) on this
and 264; Th. note* wearninge (?); *Ettm.* wearninge; *Ettm.* habbað.—924 *Th.*
þon. — 926 *MS., Edd.* mongum.—927 *MS., Ettm.* gehwore.—931 *Ettm.* welmfyra.
—936 *Ettm.* ealda.—937 *Th. note* se sylfa (?); *Ettm. note* Si þæt silfe '*item,
pariter' exprimere non posset (cf.* þæt ān='*solum* '), mona, þæt silfe leoht, *legerem.*
— 938 *Ettm.* gehweorfeð.—942 *Ettm.* meotud.—944 *Th. note, Ettm.* sawla.

ond on seofon healfa   swōgað windas,
950 blāwað brecende   bearhtma mǣste,
w_eccað ond woniað   woruld mid storme,
fyllað mid f[ȳ]re   foldan gesceafte.
Ðonne heard gebrec,   hlūd, unmǣte,
swār ond swiðlīc,   swēgdynna mǣst,
955 ǣldum egeslīc,   ēawed weorþeð.

Þǣr mægen wērge   monna cynnes
wornum hweorfað   on wīdne lēg,
þā þǣr cwice mēteð   cwelmende fȳr,
sume ūp, sume niþer,   ǣldes fulle.
960 Þonne bið unt[w]ēo   þæt þǣr Ādāmes
cyn, cearena full,   cwīþeð gesārga[d],
nāles fore lȳtlum,   lēode gēomre,
ac fore þām mǣstan   mægenearfeþum,
ðonne eall þrēo   on efen nimeð
965 won fȳres wǣlm   wīde tōsomne
se swearta līg, —   sǣs mid hyra fiscum,
eorþan mid hire beorgum,   ond ūpheofon
torhtne mid his tunglum.   Tēonlēg somod
þrȳþum bærneð   þrēo eal on ān
970 grimme tōgædre.   Gornnað gesārgad
eal middangeard   on þā mǣran tīd.

Swā se gīfra gǣst   grundas geondsēceð,
hiþende lēg   hēahgetimbro ;
fylleð on foldwong   fȳres egsan,

---

952 *MS.* feore, *and so Edd.; Ettm. note* fyre (?); *Th., Go. tr.* 'with their breath,' *Gr.* (*Dichtungen*) 'mit Feuer,' *Gr.*[2] feore 'vitâ' (*vgl. v. 975* [*i.e.* 974]); *but cf. 867; Ettm.* gesceafta.—955 *Ettm.* ealdum.—956 *Th., Ettm.* mægenwerge (*Th. tr.* 'most accursed').—958 *Ettm.* metað cwealmende.—959 *Th. note* fylle (?), *which Ettm. note rejects.*—960 *MS., Th.* untreo (*Th. tr.* 'faithless'); *Ettm.* + untweo.—961 *MS.* gesargað.—963 *Ettm.* mæstum.—965 *Gr.*[1] *note* wonfyres (?); *Ettm.* welm ; *Ettm.* to somne.—970 *Ettm.* to gædre grornað ; *MS.* gesargad, *corr. from* gesargað.—973 *Ettm.* hyðende.

975 wīdmǣre blǣst,   woruld mid ealle,
    hāt, heorogīfre.   Hrēosað geneahhe
    tōbrocene burgweallas.   Beorgas gemeltað
    ond hēahcleofu,   þā wið holme ǣr
    fæste wið flōdum   foldan sce[l]dun,
980 stīð ond stæðfæst,   staþelas wið wǣge,
    wætre windendum.   Þonne wihta gehwylce
    dēora ond fugla   dēaðlēg nimeð ;
    færeð æfter foldan   fȳrswearta lēg,
    weallende wiga.   Swā ǣr wæter flēowan,
985 flōdas āfȳsde,   þonne on fȳrbaðe
    swelað sǣfiscas   sundes getwǣfde ;
    wǣgdēora gehwylc   wērig swelteð ;
    byrneþ wæter swā weax.   Þǣr bið wundra mā
    þonne hit ǣnig on mōde   mǣge āþencan, —
990 hū þæt gestun, ond se storm,   ond sēo stronge lyft,
    brecað brāde gesceaft.   Beornas grētað,
    wēpað wānende   wērgum stefnum,
    hēane, hygegēomre,   hrēowum gedreahte.
    Sēoþeð swearta lēg   synne on fordōnum,
995 ond goldfrætwe   glēda forswelgað,
    eall ǣrgestrēon   eþelcyninga.
    Ðǣr bið cirm, ond cearu,   ond cwicra gewin,
    gehrēow, ond hlūd wōp,   bi heofonwōman,
    earmlīc ælda gedreag.   Þonan ǣnig ne mæg
1000 firendǣdum fāh   frið gewinnan,
    lēgbryne losian   londes ōwer ;

975 *Gr.*² blæst, *with short* æ ; *Th., Go.* mid-ealle.—977 *Ettm.* burhweallas.—
978 *Gr.*¹ heah. cleofu ; *MS.* þu.—979 *MS.* scehdun ; *Th. note* sceldun (scyldon)
(?) ; *Ettm.* sceldun ; *Gr.*¹ *note* etwa scêndun (?) (vergl. Ahd. scônian 'schonen');
Gr. (*Sprachschatz*) *adopts Th.'s suggestion* ; *Go.*¹ *note Probably* = scédun, *past tense of*
scéadan, '*to separate*'; *Go.*² scetdun.— 981 *Th. note* winnendum.—984 *Th.* wæter-
fleowan (*tr.* '*the rivers*'); *Ettm.* fleowun.—988 *Ettm.* birneð.—991 *Ettm.* grætað.—
993 *Th., Go.*¹ hyge geomre.— 994 *Ettm. note* synnum fordone (?).—995 *Ettm.* -frætwa.
—998 *Gr.*¹ ano.—999 *Ettm.* ealda ; *Ettm. note* gedræg (?).— 1001 *Ettm.* ohwer.

ac þæt fȳr nimeð   þurh foldan gehwæt,
græfeð grimlíce,   georne āsēceð
innan ond ūtan   eorðan scēatas,
1005 oþþæt eall hafað · ældes lēoma
woruldwidles wom   wǣlme forbærned.

Ðonne mihtig God   on þone mǣran beorg
mid þȳ mǣstan   mægenþrymme cymeð,
heofonengla Cyning   hālig scīneð
1010 wuldorlíc ofer weredum,   wāldende God;
ond hine ymbūtan   æþelduguð betast,
hālge herefēðan,   hlūtre blīcað,
ēadig engla gedryht ;   ingeþoncum
forhte beofiað   fore Fæder egsan.

1015 Forþon nis ǣnig wundor   hū him woruldmonna
sēo unclǣne gecynd   cearum sorgende
hearde ondrēde,   ðonne sīo hālge gecynd,
hwīt ond heofonbeorht, hēagengla mǣgen,
for ðǣre onsȳne bēoð   egsan āfyrhte,
1020 bīdað beofiende   beorhte gesceafte
Dryhtnes dōmes.   Daga egeslicast
weorþeð in worulde,   þonne Wuldorcyning
þurh þrym þrēað   þēoda gehwylce,
hāteð ārīsan   reordberende
1025 of foldgrafum,   folc ānra gehwylc
cuman tō gemōte,   moncynnes gehwone.

Þonne eall hraðe   Ādāmes cynn
onfēhð flǣsce,   weorþeð foldræste
eardes æt ende.   Sceal þonne ānra gehwylc
1030 fore Crīstes cyme cwic ārīsan,
leoðum onfōn   ond lichoman,

1005 *Ettm., Gr.*¹ oð þæt.—1006 *Ettm.* welme.—1017 *Ettm., Gr. (Sprachschatz)*
ondræde.—1018 *Gr.*¹ heahengla.—1020 *Ettm.* gesceafta.—1023 *Siev. (PBB. x.*
477) suggests that the metre requires a disyllabic form for þreað.—1031 *Siev.*
(PBB. x. 476) would have onfon *uncontracted.*

edgeong wesan;   hafað eall on him
þæs þe hē on foldan   in fyrndagum
gōdes oþþe gāles   on his gǣste gehlōd,
1035 gēara gongum.   Hafað ætgædre bū,
līc ond sāwle.   Sceal on lēoht cuman
sīnra weorca wlite,   ond worda gemynd,
ond heortan gehȳgd,   fore heofona Cyning.
Ðonne biþ geȳced   ond geednīwad
1040 moncyn þurh Meotud;   micel ārīseð
dryhtfolc tō dōme,   siþþan dēaþes bend
tōlēseð Līffruma.   Lyft bið onbærned;
hrēosað heofonsteorran;   hȳþað wīde
gīfre glēde.   Gǣstas hweorfað
1045 on ēcne eard.   Opene weorþað
ofer middangeard   monna dǣde:
ne magun hord wera[s],   heortan geþōhtas,
fore Wāldende   wihte bemīþan;
ne sindon him dǣda dyrne,   ac þǣr bið Dryhtne cūð,
1050 on þam miclan dæge,   hū monna gehwylc
ǣr earnode   ēces līfes,
ond eall ondweard   þæt hī ǣr oþþe sīð
worhtun in worulde.   Ne bið þǣr wiht forholen
monna gehygda,   ac se mǣra dæg
1055 hreþerlocena hord,   heortan geþōhtas,
ealle ætȳweð.   Ǣr sceal geþencan
gǣstes þearfe,   se þe Gode mynteð
bringan beorhtne wlite,   þonne bryne costað,
hāt, heorugīfre,   hū gehealdne sind
1060 sāwle wið synnum   fore Sigedēman.

1035 *Ettm.* æt gædre, *and begins 1036 with* bu.—1042 *MS.* liffruman.—
1044 *Ettm.* gleda.—1047 *Th.*, *Ettm.*, *Gr.*[1] magon; *MS.*, *Go.* wera; *Th. note*
weras (?); *Ettm.*, *Gr.*,[1] *Wü.* weras; *Th. note* hord, *i.e.* breost-hord = heortan
geþohtas; *Ettm. note* geþohta, *gen. plur.* ab hord *dependens, mihi placeret; Go.*[1]
The change [to weras] *seems unnecessary, if* bemiþan *is construed intransitively.—*
1059 *Th.* heoru gifre.—1060 *Ettm.* sawla.

Ðonne sīo bȳman stefen,   ond se beorhta segn,
ond þæt hāte fȳr,   ond sēo hēa duguð,
ond se engla þrym,   ond se egsan þrēa,
ond se hearda dæg,   ond sēo hēa rōd,
1065 ryht ārǣred,   rices tō bēacne,
folcdryht wera   biforan bonnað,
sāwla gehwylce,   þāra þe sīð oþþe ǣr
on līchoman   leoþum onfēngen.
Ðonne weoroda mǣst   fore Wāldende,
1070 ēce ond edgeong,   ondweard gǣð,
nēode ond nȳde   bi noman gehātne,
berað brēosta hord   fore Bearn Godes,
fēores frætwe.   Wile Fæder eahtan
hū gesunde suna   sāwle bringen
1075 of þām ēðle   þe hī on lifdon.
Ðonne bēoð bealde   þā þe beorhtne wlite
Meotude bringað;   bið hyra meaht ond gefēa
swīðe gesǣliglīc   sāwlum tō gielde,
wuldorlēan weorca.   Wel is þām þe mōtun
1080 on þā grimman tīd   Gode līcian.

Þǣr him sylfe gesēoð   sorga mǣste
synfā men   sārigfērðe.
Ne bið him tō āre   þæt þǣr fore ellþēodum
ūsses Dryhtnes rōd   ondweard stondeð,
1085 bēacna beorhtast,   blōde bistēmed
Heofoncyninges,   hlūtran drēore,
bisēon mid swāte,   þæt ofer sīde gesceaft
scīre scīneð.   Sceadu bēoð bidyrned

1063 Th. þry.—1064 Siev. (PBB. x. 478) would have hea uncontracted.—
1070 Siev. (PBB. x. 477) would have gæð uncontracted.—1073 Ettm. frætwa;
Ettm. eahtjan.—1074 Th. note sawle altered from sawla.—1075 Th. onlifdon.—
1079 MS. motum.—1081 W. sylf.—1082 Siev. (PBB. x. 478) would have synfa
uncontracted.—1085 Th., Gr.,[1] Go. bestemed.—1087 Th. note biseoð (?).—1088
MS. bydyrned, the i by another hand.

þǣr se lēohta bēam   lēodum byrhteð.

1090 Þæt, þēah, tō tēonum   [getēod] weorþeð
þēodum tō þrēa,   þām þe þonc Gode
womwyrcende   wi[h]t[e] ne cūþun,
þæs hē on þone hālgan bēam   āhongen wæs
fore moncynnes   mānforwyrhtu,

1095 Þǣr hē lēoflīce   līfes cēapode,
Þēoden moncynne,   on þām dæge,
mid þȳ weorðe —   þe nō wom dyde
his līchoma   leahtra firena —
mid þȳ ūsic ālȳsde.   Þæs hē eftlēan wile

1100 þurh eorneste   ealles ge[m]o[n]ian,
ðonne sīo rēade   rōd ofer ealle
swegle scīneð,   on þǣre sunnan gyld.

On þā forhtlīce   firenum fordōne
swearte synwyrcend   sorgum wlītað ;

1105 gesēoð him tō bealwe   þæt him betst bicwōm,
þǣr hȳ hit tō gōde   ongietan woldan.

Ond ēac þā ealdan wunde   ond þā openan dolg
on hyra Dryhtne gesēoð   drēorigfērðe,
swā him mid næglum þurhdrifan   nīðhycgende

1110 þā hwītan honda   ond þā hālgan fēt,
ond of his sīdan swā some   swāt forlētan,
þǣr blōd ond wæter   būtū ætsomne
ūt bicwōman   fore ēagna gesyhð,
rinnan fore rincum   þā hē on rōde wæs.

1115 Eall þis magon him sylfe   gesēon þonne,
open, orgete,   þæt hē for ælda lufan,
firenfremmendra,   fela þrōwade.

1090 Gr.,[1] Go.,[2] Wü. [geteod] ; Go.[1] note The line is evidently defective.—
1092 Th. note wom-wyrcendum (?) ; MS., Edd. wita ; Th. note wihte (?).—1093 Th.,
Gr.[1] þæs þe he.—1094 Th., Gr.[1] manforwyrhtum.—1095 Siev. (PBB. x. 484)
suggests cypte for ceapode, comparing gecypte, 1471.—1098 Th. note leahtor-f. (?).
—1100 Perhaps we should read eornesse (cf. Bl. Hom. 123 8) ; MS., Th., Go.
genomian.—1106 Th. note þæt (?).—1115 Th. ends line with geseon.

Magun lēoda bearn   lēohte oncnāwan
hū hine lȳgnedon   lēase on geþoncum,
1120 hysptun hearmcwidum,   ond on his hlēor somod
hyra spātl spēowdon;   spræcon him edwīt;
ond on þone ēadgan   ondwlitan swā some
helfūse men   hondum slōgun,
folmum āreahtum,   ond fȳstum ēac,
1125 ond ymb his hēafod   heardne gebīgdon
bēag þyrnenne   blinde on geþoncum,
dys[i]ge ond gedwealde.
                    Gesēgun þā dumban gesceaft, —
eorðan ealgrēne   ond ūprodor, —
forhte gefēlan   Frēan þrōwinga;
1130 ond mid cearum cwīðdun,   þēah hī cwice næron,
þā hyra Scyppend   sceaþan onfēngon
syngum hondum.   Sunne wearð ādwæsced,
þrēam āþrysmed,   þā sīo þēod geseah
in Hierūsalēm   godwebba cyst,
1135 þæt ær ðām hālgan   hūse sceolde
tō weorþunga   weorud scēawian : —
utan eall forbærst,   þæt hit on eorþan læg
on twām styccum :   þæs temples segl,
wundorblēom geworht   tō wlite þæs hūses,
1140 sylf slāt on tū,   swylce hit seaxes ecg
scearp þurhwōde.   Scīre burstan
mūras ond stānas   mon[i]ge æfter foldan;
ond sēo eorðe ēac,   egsan myrde,
beofode on bearhtme;   ond se brāda sæ
1145 cȳðde cræftes meaht,   ond of clomme bræc
ūp yrringa   on eorþan fæðm;
ge on stede scȳnum   steorran forlēton

hyra swǣsne wlite.   On þā sylfan tīd
heofon hluttre ongeat   hwā hine hēalīce
1150 torhtne getremede   tungolgimmum;
forþon hē his bodan sende   þā wæs geboren ǣrest
gesceafta scīr Cyning.   Hwæt! ēac scyldge men
gesēgon tō sōðe,   þȳ sylfan dæge
þe [hē] on þrōwade,   þēodwundor micel, —
1155 þætte eorðe āgeaf   þā hyre on lǣgun:
eftlifgende   ūp āstōdan
þā þe hēo ǣr fæste   bifēn hæfde,
dēade, bibyrgde,   þe Dryhtnes bibod
hēoldon on hreþre.   Hell ēac ongeat,
1160 scyldwreccende,   þæt se Scyppend cwōm,
wāldende God,   þā hēo þæt weorud āgeaf,
hlōþe of þām hātan hreþre;   hyge wearð mon[i]gum blissad,
sāwlum sorge tōglidene.   Hwæt! ēac sǣ cȳðde
hwā hine gesette   on sīdne grund,
1165 tīrmeahtig Cyning,   forþon hē hine tredne him
ongēan gyrede,   þonne God wolde
ofer sīne ȳðe gān: ēahstrēam ne dorste
his Frēan fēt   flōde bisencan.
Ge ēac bēamas onbudon   hwā hȳ mid blēdum scēop,
1170 mon[i]ge, nāles fēa,   ðā mihtig God
on hira ānne gestāg,   þǣr hē earfeþu
geþolade fore þearfe   þēodbūendra,
lāðlicne dēað   lēodum tō helpe.
Ðā wearð bēam monig   blōdgum tēarum
1175 birunnen under rindum,   rēade ond þicce;
sæp wearð tō swāte.   Þæt āsecgan ne magun

1152 Th., Go.¹ Go.² scir-cyning. — 1154 Gr.¹ þe [he]; MS., other Edd. þe. —
1156 MS., Edd. eft lifgende; Th. upastodan. — 1157 Th. bifengen. — 1158 MS.
bibyrgde; Th., Gr.¹ bibyrgede. — 1162 MS., Edd. mongum. — 1165 Th. carries
him over to 1166. — 1166 Th. note r. gyrwede (gearwode). — 1168 MS. fream. —
1170 MS., Edd. monge; Siev. (PBB. x. 480) proposes feawe. — 1174 MS., Edd.
blodigum. — 1175 Th., Gr.¹ roderum. — 1176 Go.² æp; MS. magum.

foldbūende, þurh frōd gewit,
hū fela þā onfundun þā gefēlan ne magun
Dryhtnes þrōwinga, dēade gesceafte.
1180 Þā þe æþelast sind eorðan gecynda,
ond heofones ēac hēahgetimbro, —
eall fore þām ānum unrōt gewearð,
forht āfongen. Þēah hī fērðgewit
of hyra æþelum ǣnig ne cūþen,
1185 wēndon swā-þēah wundrum, þā hyra Wāldend fōr
of līchoman. Lēode ne cūþan,
mōdblinde men, Meotud oncnāwan,
flintum heardran, þæt hī Frēa nerede
fram hellcwale hālgum meahtum,
1190 alwālda God. Þæt æt ǣrestan
foreþoncle men from fruman worulde,
þurh wīs gewit wītgan Dryhtnes,
hālge, higeglēawe, hæleþum sægdon
oft, nāles ǣne, ymb þæt æþele Bearn, —
1195 ðæt se Earcnanstān eallum sceolde
tō hlēo ond tō hrōþer hæleþa cynne
weorðan in worulde, wuldres Āgend,
ēades Ordfruma, þurh þā æþelan cwēnn.

Hwæs wēneð sē þe mid gewitte nyle
1200 gemunan þā mildan Meotudes lāre,
and eal ðā earfeðu þe hē fore ǣldum ādrēag,
forþon þe hē wolde þæt wē wuldres eard
in ēcnesse āgan mōsten?
Swā þām bið grorne, on þām grimman dæge
1205 dōmes þæs miclan, þām þe Dryhtnes sceal
dēaðfirenum fordēn dolg scēawian,
wunde ond wīte. On wērgum sefan

1185 *Gr.*[1] wendon, *with short* e (*but not Dichtungen nor Sprachschatz*); *Th.*
ends the line with waldend. — 1195 *Th., Go.* earcnan stan. — 1206 *Th., Gr.*[1] deað
firenum; *Gr.*[2] deaðfirenum. — 1207 *MS., Edd.* werigum.

gesēoð sorga mǣste : h[ȳ] se sylfa Cyning
mid sīne līchoman lȳsde of firenum,
1210 þurh milde mōd, þæt hȳ mōstun mānweorca
tōme lifgan, ond tīres blǣd
ēcne āgan ; hȳ þæs ēðles þonc
hyra Wāldende wi[*h*]t[*e*] ne cūþon ;
forþon þǣr tō tēonum þā tācen geseōð
1215 orgeatu on gōd[*um*] ungesǣlge.

Þonne Crīst siteð on his cynestōle,
on hēahsetle, heofonmægna God,
Fæder ælmihtig, folca gehwylcum,
Scyppend scīnende, scrīfeð bi gewyrntum
1220 call æfter ryhte, rodera Wāldend.
Þonne bēoð gesomnad on þā swīþran hond
þā clǣnan folc, Crīste sylfum
gecorene bi cystum, þā ǣr sīnne cwide georne
lustum lǣstun on hyra līfdagum ;
1225 ond þǣr womsceaþan on þone wyrsan dǣl
fore Scyppende scyrede weorþað :
hāteð him gewītan on þā winstran hond
sigora Sōðcyning synfulra weorud.
Þǣr hȳ ārāsade rēotað ond beofiað
1230 fore Frēan forhte ; swā fūle swā gǣt,
unsȳfre folc, ārna ne wēnað.
Ðonne bið gǣsta dōm fore Gode scēaden
wera cnēorissum, swā hī geworhtun ǣr.
Þǣr bið on ēadgum ēðgesȳne
1235 þrēo tācen somod, þæs þe hī hyra Þēodnes wel
wordum ond weorcum willan hēoldon : —
Ān is ǣrest orgeate þ̵ǣr, —
þæt hȳ fore lēodum lēohte blīcaþ,

1208 *Gr.*[1] hy ; *MS., other Edd.* hu. — 1210 *Th. divides this into three short lines.* — 1213 *MS., Edd.* wita ; *Th. note* wihte (?). — 1215 *MS., Edd.* gode. — 1223 *Th. ends the line with* cwide. — 1228 *Go.*[2] soð cyning. — 1231 *MS.* wenéað. — 1234 *Th., Go.* eð gesyne.

blǣde ond byrhte,　　　ofer burga gesetu;
1240 him on scīnað　　ǣrgewyrhtu
on sylfra gehwām　　sunnan beorhtran.

Ōþer is tōēacan　　ondgete swā some, —
þæt hȳ him in wuldre witon　　Wāldendes giefe,
ond on sēoð,　　ēagum tō wynne,
1245 þæt hī on heofonrīce　　hlūtre drēamas,
ēadge mid englum,　　āgan mōtun.

Ðonne bið þridde, —　hū, on þȳstra bealo,
þæt gesǣlge weorud　　gesihð þæt fordōne
sār þrōwian,　　synna tō wīte —
1250 weallendne līg　　ond wyrma slite
bitrum ceaflum —　　byrnendra scole;
of þām him āweaxeð　　wynsum gefēa.

Þonne hī þæt yfel gesēoð　　ōðre drēogan,
þæt hȳ þurh miltse　　Meotudeś genǣson,
1255 ðonne hī þȳ geornor　　Gode þonciað
blǣdes ond blissa,　　þe hȳ bū gesēoð, —
þæt hē hȳ generede　　from nīðcwale,
ond ēac forgeaf　　ēce drēamas:
bið him hel bilocen,　　heofonrīce āgiefen.
1260 Swā sceal gewrixled　　þām þe ǣr wel hēoldon
þurh mōdlufan　　Meotudes willan.

Ðonne bið þām ōþrum　　ungelīce
willa geworden:　　magon wēana tō fela
gesēon on him selfum, —　　synne genōge,
1265 atolearfoða　　ǣr gedēnra.

Þǣr him sorgendum　　sār oðclīfeð
þroht þēodbealu　　on þrēo healfa: —

1240 *Th.*, *Go.* onscinað. — 1242 *Th. note* orgete (?); *Gr.*,[1] *Wü.* to eacan. —
1244 *Th.*, *Go.* onseoð; *Siev.* (*PBB. x. 476*) *would have* seoð *uncontracted.* —
1245 *MS.*, *Th.*, *Go.* hlutru. — 1246 *MS.* motum. — 1248 *MS.*, *Edd.* gesælige. —
1250 *Go.*,[1] *Go.*[2] wlite (*Go.*[1] *asserting this to be the MS. reading*). — 1265 *Gr.*,[1] *Go.*,[1]
Wü. atol earfoða.

Ān is þāra   þæt hȳ him yrmþa tō fela,
grim hellefȳr,   gearo tō wīte
1270 ondweard sēoð,   on þām hī āwo sculon
wræc winnende   wærgðu drēogan.

Þonne is him ōþer   earfeþu swā some
scyldgum tō sconde, —   þæt hī þær scoma mǣste
drēogað fordōne :   on him Dryhten gesihð
1275 nāles fēara sum   firenbealu lāðlīc ;
ond þæt ællbeorhte   ēac scēawiað
heofonengla here,   ond hæleþa bearn,
ealle eorðbūend,   ond atol dēofol,
mircne mægencræft,   mānwomma gehwone.

1280 Magon þurh þā līchoman   leahtra firene
gesēon on þām sāwlum :   bēoð þā syngan flǣsc
scandum þurhwaden[e],   swā þæt scīre glæs,
þæt mon ȳþæst mæg   eall þurhwlītan.

Ðonne bið þæt þridde   þearfendum sorg,
1285 cwīþende cearo,   þæt hȳ on þā clǣnan sēoð
hū hī fore gōddǣdum   glade blissiað,
þā hȳ, unsælge,   ær forhogdun
tō dōnne,   þonne him dagas lǣstun ;
ond be hyra weorcum   wēpende sār
1290 þæt hī ær frēolīce   fremedon unryht.

Gesēoð hī þā betran   blǣde scīnan :
ne bið him hyra yrmðu   ān tō wīte,
ac þāra ōþerra   ēad tō sorgum,
þæs þe hȳ swā fægre gefē[a]n   on fyrndagum,
1295 ond swā ǣnlīce,   ānforlētun

1269 *Gr.*[1] wite (*but not Sprachschatz nor Dichtungen*). — 1270 *Siev.* (*PBB. x. 476*) *would have* seoð *uncontracted; Go.*[2] þa (*Go.*[1] *asserting this to be the MS. reading*). — 1271 *Th.*, *Gr.*,[1] *Go.*,[1] *Go.*[2] wræc-winnende ; *Gr.*[2] (*and Sprachschatz*) wræc winnende. — 1280 *Th. note* leahtorfirene (?). — 1282 *MS., Edd.* þurhwaden ; *Frucht* þurhwadene (?). — 1283 *Gr.*[1] yðast. — 1288 *Siev.* (*PBB. x. 477*) *would have* donne *uncontracted*. — 1290 *Gr.*[1] þât. — 1294 *MS., Th., Gr.*[1] gefeon.

þurh lēaslīce   līces wynne,
earges flǣschoman   īdelne lust.
Þǣr hī āscamode,   scondum gedreahte,
swiciað on swīman;   synbyrþenne,
1300 firenweorc berað;   on þæt þā folc sēoð.

Wǣre him þonne betre   þæt hȳ bealodǣde,
ǣlces unryhtes,   ǣr gescomeden
fore ānum men,   eargra weorca,
Godes bodan sǣgdon   þæt hī tō gyrne wiston
1305 firendǣda on him.   Ne mæg þurh þæt flǣsc se scrift
gesēon on þǣre sāwle,   hwæþer him mon sōð þe lyge
sagað on hine sylfne,   þonne hē þā synne bigǣð.
Mæg mon, swā-þēah, gelācnigan   leahtra gehwylcne,
yfel unclǣne,   gif hē hit ānum gesegð;
1310 ond nǣnig bihelan mæg   on þāṃ heardan dæge
wom unbēted;   ðǣr hit þā weorud gesēoð.

Ēalā! þǣr wē nū magon   wrāþe firene
gesēon on ūssum sāwlum,   synna wunde,
mid līchoman,   leahtra gehygdu,
1315 ēagum,   unclǣne ingeþoncas!

— Ne þæt ǣnig mæg   ōþrum gesecgan
mid hū micle elne   ǣghwylc wille
þurh ealle list   līfes tiligan,
fēores forhtlīce   forð āðolian,
1320 synrūst þwēan   ond hine sylfne þrēan,

1296 *Th.* þurhleaslice (*tr.* ‘*all-deceiving*’). — 1298 *Gr.*[1] *note* þæs (?). — 1299 *Th.* *note* 1. byrþene. — 1300 *Siev.* (*PBB. x. 476*) *would have* seoð *uncontracted.* — 1301 *Go.*,[1] *Go.*[2] þon (*Go.*[1] *asserting this to be the MS. reading*). — 1302 *Gr.*[1] gescomedon. — 1305 *Th. ends the line with* flæsc. — 1306 *Th. ends the line with* soð. — 1307 *Th. ends the line with* sagað. — 1309 *Siev.* (*PBB. x. 475*) *assumes that the Anglian original had* gesagað. — 1311 *MS.* unbeted *from* unbeteð; *Th. note* 1. weorudas. — 1312 *Th. note* þæt (?); *Gr.*[1] *note* þær weras magon (?). — 1314 *Th. note* leahtor-gehygdu (?). — 1317 *Gr.*[1] *note* scyle (?). — 1319 *Gr.*[1] *note* aðolian *übersetzt Th. durch* endure, *als wäre es* â-þolian: *es ist das Ahd.* adaljan *Mhd.* edelen *nobilitare.* — 1320ª *Siev.* (*PBB. x. 515*) *would have* þwean *uncontracted; Gr.*[1] þrean.

ond þæt wom ǣrran   wunde hǣlan,
þone lȳtlan fyrst   þe hēr lifes sȳ ;
þæt hē mǣge fore ēagum   eorðbūendra,
unscomiende,   ēðles mid monnum
1325 brūcan bysmerlēas,   þendan bū somod
līc ond sāw[el]   lifgan mōte. —

    Nū wē sceolon georne   glēawlīce þurhsēon
ūsse hreþercofan   heortan ēagum
innan uncyste.   Wē mid þām ōðrum ne magun
1330 hēafodgimmum   hygeþonces fērð,
ēagum, þurhwlītan   ǣnge þinga,
hwæþer him yfel þe gōd   under wunige,
þæt hē on þā grimman tīd   Gode līcie.

    Þonne hē ofer weoruda gehwylc   wuldre scīneð
1335 of his hēahsetle,   hlūtran lēge,

þǣr hē, fore englum   ond fore elþēodum,
tō þām ēadgestum   ǣrest mǣðleð,
ond him swǣslice   sibbe gehāteð,
heofona Hēahcyning,   hālgan reorde
1340 frēfreð hē fægre,   ond him friþ bēodeð ;
hāteð hȳ gesunde   ond gesēnade
on ēþel faran   engla drēames,
ond þæs tō wīdan fēore   willum nēotan : —
    ' Onfōð nū mid frēondum   mīnes Fæder rīce,
1345 þæt ēow wæs ǣr woruldum   wynlīce gearo,
blǣd mid blissum,   beorht ēðles wlite,
hwonne gē þā līfwelan   mid þām lēof[s]tum,
swāse swegldrēamas,   gesēon mōsten.
Gē þæs earnedon   þā gē earme men,

<hr/>

1326 *Th. note* (p. 503) *Read either* sawl *and* moton, *or for* 7 *read* mid. —
1329 *MS.* mnan (*so Go.,*[1] *Go.*[2]), *but A. says Hs. doch wohl* innan. — 1331 *Th.*
ængeþinga. — 1337 *MS.* mædleð. — 1340 *Gr.*[1] hi. — 1346 *Th. note* beorhtne (?). —
1347 *Gr.*[1] þonne ; *MS., Th.* leoftum ; *Th. note* r. leofestum ; *Gr.*[1] leofestum.

1350 woruldþearfende,　　willum onfēngu[n]
　　　on mildum sefan.　　Ðonne hȳ him þurh mīnne noman
　　　ēaðmōde tō ēow　　ārna bǣdun,
　　　þonne gē hyra hulpon,　　ond him hlēoð gēfon,
　　　hingrendum hlāf,　　ond hrægl nacedum ;
1355 ond þā þe on sāre　　sēoce lāgun,
　　　æf[n]don unsōfte,　　ādle gebundne,
　　　tō þām gē holdlīce　　hyge staþeladon
　　　mid mōdes myne.　　Eall gē þæt mē dydon,
　　　ðonne gē hȳ mid sibbum sōhtun,　　ond hyra sefan trymedon
1360 forð on frōfre.　　Þæs gē fǣgre sceolon
　　　lēan mid lēofum　　lange brūcan.'

　　　Onginneð þonne tō þām yflum　　ungelīce
　　　wordum mǣðlan,　　þe him b[ēo]ð on þā wynstran hond,
　　　þurh egsan þrēa,　　alwālda God.
1365 Ne þurfon hī þonne tō Meotude　　miltse gewēnan,
　　　līfes nē lissa,　　ac þǣr lēan cumað
　　　werum bi gewyrhtum　　worda ond dǣda,
　　　reordberendum ;　　sceolon þone ryhtan dōm
　　　ænne geæfnan,　　egsan fulne.
1370 Bið þǣr sēo miccle　　milts āfyrred
　　　þēodbūendum,　　on þām dæge,
　　　þæs Ælmihtgan,　　þonne hē yrringa
　　　on þæt frǣte folc　　firene stǣleð
　　　lāþum wordum,　　hāteð hyra līfes riht
1375 ondweard ȳ[w]an　　þæt hē him ǣr forgeaf,
　　　syngum tō sǣlum.　　Onginneð sylf cweðan,

1350 MS. onfengum. — 1354 Go.¹ nace dum. — 1356 MS., Th., Gr.¹ æfdon; Gr. (Sprachschatz) from æfian (æfan?) laborare, but suggests, as an alternative, that it = æfndon. — 1359 Gr.¹ tyrmedon (misprint). — 1363 Gr.¹ wordun (misprint). — 1369 MS. anne (S.), but denied by A. — 1370 MS. miĕcle, e by another hand (S.), miccle (Go.¹), miͨcle (Go.²) ; A. das I. c in miccle darübergeschrieben wohl von andrer Hand. — 1372 MS., Edd. ælmihtigan ; cf. Siev. (PBB. x. 460). — 1373 Gr.¹ frǣte (with short vowel). — 1375 MS., Th. yðan (tr. 'to flow ').

swā hē tō ānum sprece,   ond hwæþre ealle mǣneð,
firensynnig folc,   Frēa ælmihtig : —
    ' Hwæt ic þec, mon,   hondum mīnum
1380 ǣrest geworhte,   ond þē ondgiet sealde ;
    of lāme ic þē leoþ[o] gesette,   geaf ic ðē lifgendne gǣst ;
    ārode þē ofer ealle gesceafte,   gedyde ic þæt þū onsȳn hæfdest,
    mægwlite, mē gelīcne ;   geaf ic þē ēac meahta spēd,
    welan ofer wīdlonda gehwylc ;   nysses þū wēan ǣnigne dæl,
1385 ðȳstra, þæt þū þolian sceolde.   Þū þæs þonc ne wisses.
    Þā ic ðē swā scīenne   gesceapen hæfde,
    wynlīcne geworht,   ond þē welan forgyfen
    þæt ðū mōstes wealdan   worulde gesceaftum,
    ðā ic þē on þā fægran   foldan gesette
1390 tō nēotenne   neorxnawonges,
    beorhtne blǣdwelan,   blēom scīnende ;
    ðā þū līfes word   lǣstan noldes,
    ac mīn bibod brǣce   be þīnes bonan worde ;
    fǣcnum fēonde   furþor hȳrdes,
1395 sceþþendum sceaþan,   þonne þīnum Scyppende.
    Nū ic ðā ealdan race   ānforlǣte,
    hū þū æt ǣrestan   yfle gehogdes,
    firenweorcum forlure   þæt ic ðē tō fremum sealde.
    Þā ic þē gōda swā fela   forgiefen hæfde,
1400 ond þē on þām eallum   ēades tō lȳt[el]
    mōde þūhte,   gif þū meaht[a] spēd
    efenmicle Gode   āgan ne mōste,
    ðā þū of þān gefēan   fremde wurde,
    fēondum tō willan   feor āworpen ;

1379 *MS., Edd.* minum hondum. — 1380 *MS.* sâlde, *the* e *by another hand.* —
1381 *MS., Th., Go.,*[1] *Go.*[2] leoþe. — 1386 *Th.* þe. — 1387 *Th. ends line with* þe. —
1390 *MS., Th., Go.,*[1] *Go.*[2] neorxna wonges. — 1398b *Th.* þe; *Th.* firenum (*tr.*
'comfort'); *Th. note* frefrunge *or* frofre *for* firenuṁ (?) ; *MS.* sâlde, *the* e, *accord-*
ing to A., by another hand. — 1399 *Gr.*[1] goda, *with short* o (*misprint*). — 1400 *MS.,*
Edd. lyt. — 1401 *Th. note* 1. meahta; *MS., other Edd.* meahte. — 1403 *Siev.*
(*PBB. x. 478*) *would have* gefean *uncontracted.*

1405 neorxnawonges wlite   nȳde sceoldes
    āgiefan, gēomormōd,   gǣsta ēþel,
    earg ond unrōt,   eallum bidǣled
    dugeþum ond drēamum;   ond þā bidrifen wurde
    on þās þēostran woruld,   þǣr þū þolades siþþan
1410 mǣgenearfeþu   micle stunde,
    sār ond swār gewin   ond sweartne dēað,
    ond æfter [h]ingonge   hrēosan sceoldes
    hēan in helle,   helpendra lēas.

    'Ðā mec ongon hrēowan   þæt mīn hondgeweorc
1415 on fēonda geweald   fēran sceolde,
    moncynnes tuddor   māncwealm sēon,
    sceolde uncūðne   eard cunnian,
    sāre sīþas.   Þā ic sylf gestāg,
    māga in mōdor,   þēah wæs hyre mægdenhād
1420 ǣghwæs onwālg.   Wearð ic āna geboren
    folcum tō frōfre.   Mec mon folmum biwond,
    biþeahte mid þearfan wǣdum,   ond mec þā on þēostre ālegde
    biwundenne mid wonnum clāþum, —   hwæt! ic þæt for wor-
        ulde geþolade!
    Lȳtel þūhte ic lēoda bearnum;   læg ic on heardum stāne,
1425 cildgeong on crybbe,   mid þȳ ic þē wolde cwealm āfyrran,
    hāt hellebealu;   þæt þū mōste hālig scīnan
    ēadig on þām ēcan līfe,   forðon ic þæt earfeþe wonn.

    'Næs mē for mōde,   ac ic on magugeoguðe
    yrmþu geæfnde,   ārlēas licsār,
1430 þæt ic þurh þā   wǣre [þ]ē gelīc,
    ond þū meahte   mīnum weorþan
    mǣgwlite gelīc,   māne bidǣled;

1405 *As in 1390.* — 1408 *Gr.*[1] bedrifen. — 1409 *MS.*, *Go.* weoruld; *Th.*, *Wü.*
weorulde; *Gr.*[1] worulde. — 1412 *MS.* ingonge. — 1416 *Siev.* (*PBB. x. 476*) *would
have* seon *uncontracted.* — 1422 *Gr.*[1] biþeahte mec mid. — 1424 *Th.*, *Gr.*[1] *om. second*
ic. — 1425 *Th.*, *Go.*,[1] *Go.*[2] cild geong. — 1426 *Th.*, *Go.*,[1] *Go.*[2] helle bealu. — 1429
Gr.[1] geæfnede — 1430 *MS.* wege lic; *Edd.* þe gelic.

ond fore monna lufan   mīn þrōwade

hēafod hearmslege.   Hlēor geþolade ;

1435 oft ondlata   ārlēasra spātl

of mūðe onfēng   mānfremmendra.

Swylce hī mē geblendon   bittre tōsomne

unswētne drync   ecedes ond geallan.

Ðonne ic fore folce onfēng   fēonda genīðlan ;

1440 fylgdon mē mid firenum—   fǣhþe ne rōhtun —

ond mid sweopum slōgun.   Ic þæt sār for ðē

þurh ēaðmēdu   eall geþolade,

hosp ond heardcwide.   Þā hī hwæsne bēag

ymb mīn hēafod   heardne gebȳgdon,

1445 þrēam biþrycton ;   sē wæs of þornum geworht.

Ðā ic wæs āhongen   on hēanne bēam,

rōde gefæstnad.   Ðā hī ricene mid spere

of mīnre sīdan   swāt ūt g[u]tun,

drēor tō foldan,   þæt þū of dēofles þurh þæt

1450 nȳdgewalde   genered wurde.

Ðā ic, womma lēas,   wīte þolade,

yfel earfeþu,   oþþæt ic ānne forlēt

of mīnum līchoman   lifgendne gǣst.

'Gesēoð nū þā feorhdolg   þe gefremedun ǣr

1455 on mīnum folmum,   ond on fōtum swā some,

þurh þā ic hongade,   hearde gefæstnad ;

meaht hēr ēac gesēon,   orgete nū gēn,

on mīnre sīdan   swātge wunde.

1435 *Th.* and lata (*tr.* 'and late'), *and so Gr.*[1]; *Th. note* late (?); *Gr.*[1] *note* andlata (?) *man erwartet die Bedeutung* '*Backenstreiche*' *oder* '*Beschimpfung*'; *Gr.* (*Sprachschatz*) andlata (?); *Go.*,[1] *Go.*,[2] *Wü. follow Grein's suggestion and unite the words.* — 1439 *Gr.*[2] þone. — 1443 *Th.*, *Go.*,[1] *Go.*[2] heard cwide. — 1446 *MS.* heanne, ne *by another hand ; Gr.*[1] heahne, *but notes MS. reading.* — 1448 *Th.*, *Go.*,[1] *Go.*[2] *end 1447 with* ricene; *MS.*, *Th.*, *Go.*,[1] *Go.*[2] gotun; *Gr.*[1] guton; *Wü.* gutun. — 1451 *MS.* wite *corrected from* wita. — 1452 *Th.* anneforlet (*tr.* 'sent forth').— 1454 *Th.*, *Gr.*[1] gefremedon; *Gr.*[2] ge fremedon; *MS.* gefremedun, *not as S. reads*, gefremedum (*so A.*). — 1457 *Th. r.* meahte. — 1458 *Th.* swat-gewunde (*tr.* 'the gory wound').

' Hū þǣr wæs unefen racu		unc gemǣne |
1460 Ic onfēng þīn sār, þæt þū		mōste gesǣlig mīnes
	ēþelrīces		ēadig nēotan;
	ond þē mīne dēaðe		dēore gebohte
	þæt longe līf,		þæt þū on lēohte siþþan,
	wlitig, womma lēas,		wunian mōste.
1465 Læg mīn flǣschoma		in foldan bigrafen,
	niþre gehȳded —		se ðe nǣngum scōd —
	in byrgenne,		þæt þū meahte beorhte uppe
	on roderum wesan,		rīce mid englum.
	' Forhwon forlēte þū		līf þæt scȳne,
1470 þæt ic þē for lufan		mid mīne līchoman,
	hēanum tō helpe,		hold gecȳpte?
	Wurde þū þæs gewitlēas		þæt þū Wāldende
	þīnre ālȳsnesse		þonc ne wisses.
	Ne āscige ic nū		ōwiht bi þām bitran
1475 dēaðe mīnum		þe ic ādrēag fore þē;
	ac forgield mē þīn līf,		þæs þe ic īu þē mīn
	þurh woruldwīte		weorð gesealde;
	ðæs līfes ic manige		þe þū mid leahtrum hafast
	ofslegen synlīce,		sylfum tō sconde.
1480 Forhwan þū þæt selegescot,		þæt ic mē swǣs on þē
	gehālgode,		hūs tō wynne,
	þurh firenlustas,		fūle synne,
	unsȳfre bismite,		sylfes willum?
	Ge þū þone līchoman		þe ic ālȳsde mē
1485 fēondum of fæðme,		ond þā him firene forbēad,
	scyldwyrcende		scondum gewemdest.
	Forhwon āhēnge þū mec hefgor		on þīnra honda rōde
	þonne īu hongade?		Hwæt! mē þēos heardra þynceð.
	Nū is swǣrra mid mec		þīnra synna rōd,

1460 *Gr.*[1] *alone ends line with* mines, *but cf. Holthausen, Angl. Beibl. xii. 355.* —
1464 *MS., Edd.* mostes. — 1467 *Th. ends line with* beorhte. — 1487 *Gr.*[1] me. —
1488 *Th. note r.* heardre; *Gr.*[1] heardre. — 1489 *Th. note r.* swærre; *Gr.*[1] swærre.

1490 þe ic unwillum   on bēom gefæstnad,

þonne sēo ōþer wæs   þe ic ǣr gestāg

willum mīnum,   þā mec þīn wēa swīþast

æt heortan gehrēaw,   þā ic þec from helle ātēah —

þǣr þū hit wolde sylfa   siþþan gehealdan!

1495 'Ic wæs on worulde wǣdla,   þæt ðū wurde welig in heofonum;

earm ic wæs on ēðle þīnum,   þæt þū wurde ēadig on mīnum.

Þā ðū þæs ealles   ǣnigne þonc

þīnum Nergende   nysses on mōde.

'Bibēad ic ēow,   þæt gē brōþor mīne

1500 in woruldrīce   wel ārētten

of þām ǣhtum þe ic ēow   on eorðan geaf,

earmra hulpen.   Earge gē þæt lǣstun:

þearfum forwyrndon   þæt hī under ēowrum þæce mōsten

in gebūgan,   ond him ǣghwæs oftugon,

1505 þurh heardne hyge,   hrægles nacedum,

mōses metelēasum.   Þēah hȳ him þurh mīnne noman,

wērge, wonhāle,   wǣtan bǣdan,

drynces, gedreahte,   duguþa lēase,

þurste geþegede,   gē him þrīste oftugon.

1510 Sārge gē ne sōhton,   nē him swǣslīc word,

frōfre, gesprǣcon,   þæt hȳ þȳ frēoran hyge

mōde gefēngen.   Eall gē þæt mē dydan,

tō hȳnþum Heofoncyninge.   Þæs gē sceolon hearde ādrēogan

wīte tō wīdan ealdre,   wræc mid dēoflum geþolian.'

1515 Ðonne þǣr ofer ealle   egeslicne cwide

sylf sigora Weard,   sāres fulne,

ofer þæt fǣge folc   forð forlǣteð, —

1490 gefæstnad *in MS. from* gefæstnað. — 1495 *Go.* weadla; *Th.*, *Gr.*[1] on. —
1496 *MS.*, *Th.* worde. — 1497 *Th.* Ða. — 1499 *Th.* geþroþor. — 1503 *Th. ends
line with* eowrum. — 1504 *Th.*, *Go.*[1], *Go.*[2] in-gebugan. — 1509 *Th. note* geþregede
(?). — 1511 *Th.* ge spræcon. — 1512 *Th.*, *Gr.*[1] dydon. — 1513 *Th. ends line with*
hynþum.

cwið tō þāra synfulra   sāwla fēþan : —

'Farað nū, āwyrgde,   willum biscyrede

1520 engla drēames,   on ēce fīr,

þæt wæs Sātāne   ond his gesīþum mid,

dēofle gegearwad   ond þǣre deorcan scole,

hāt ond heorogrim ;   on þæt gē hrēosan sceolan.'

Ne magon hī þonne gehȳnan   Heofoncyninges bibod,

1525 rǣdum birofene ;   sceolon raþe feallan

on grimne grund,   þā ǣr wiþ Gode wunnon.

Bið þonne rīces Weard   rēþe ond meahtig,

yrre ond egesful.   Ondweard ne mæg

on þissum foldwege   fēond gebīdan.

1530   Swāpeð sigemēce   mid þǣre swī[ð]ran hond

þæt on þæt dēope dæl   dēofol gefeallað,

in sweartne lēg   synfulra here,

under foldan sceat   fǣge gǣstas,

on wrāþra wīc   womfulra scolu,

1535 wērge tō forwyrde   on wītehūs,

dēaðsele dēofles.   Nāles Dryhtnes gemynd

siþþan gesēcað ;   synne ne āspringað,

þǣr hī leahtrum fā,   lēge gebundne,

swylt þrōwiað.   Bið him synwracu

1540 ondweard, undyrne ;   þæt is ēce cwealm.

Ne mæg þæt hāte dæl   of heoloðcynne

in sinnehte   synne forbærnan,

tō wīdan fēore   wom of þǣre sāwle ;

ac þǣr se dēopa sēað   drēorge fēdeð,

1545 grundlēas gīemeð   gǣsta on þēostre,

ǣleð hȳ mid þȳ ealdan līge   ond mid þȳ egsan forste,

1526 grimne *in MS. from* grimme. — 1530 *MS.* swiran. — 1533 *MS.* scåt. —
1535 *Th.* wite hus. — 1536 *MS.* deofǫles ; *Th., Gr.*[1] deofoles. — 1539 *Th. note*
or eternal vengeance [i.e. sin-wracu, *as interpreted by Grein in his note*]. — 1541 *Th.*
r. hæleð. — 1542 *Th., Gr.*[1] sin nihte.

wrāþum wyrmum   ond mid wīta fela,
frēcnum feorhgōmum,   folcum sce[ðð]eð.

Þæt wē magon eahtan,   ond on ān cweþan,
1550 sōðe secgan,   þæt sē sāwle weard,
lifes wisdōm,   forloren hæbbe,
se þe nū ne gīemeð   hwæþer his gǣst sie
earm þe ēadig,   þǣr hē ēce sceal
æfter hingonge   hāmfæst wesan.
1555 Ne bisorgað hē   synne tō fremman,
wonhȳdig mon,   nē hē wihte hafað
hrēowe on mōde,   þæt him Hālig Gǣst
losige þurh leahtras   on þās lǣnan tīd.

Ðonne mānsceaða   fore Meotude forht,
1560 deorc on þām dōme standeð,   ond dēaðe fāh,
wommum āwyrged ;   bið se wǣrloga
fȳres āfylled,   fēores unwyrðe,
egsan geþrēad   ondweard Gode ;
won ond wlitelēas,   hafað wērges blēo,
1565 fācentācen fēores.   Ðonne firena bearn
tēar[as] gēotað   þonne þæs tīd ne biþ,
synne cwīþað ;   ac hȳ tō sīð dōð
gǣstum helpe,   ðonne þæs gīman nele
weoruda Wāldend,   hū þā womsceaþan
1570 hyra ealdgestrēon   on þā openan tīd
sāre grēten.   Ne biþ þæt sorga tid
lēodum ālȳfed,   þæt þǣr lǣcedōm
findan mōte   se þe nū his fēore nyle
hǣlo strȳnan   þenden hēr leofað.
1575 Ne bið þǣr ængum gōdum   gnorn ætȳwed,

1548 MS. scendeð; Gr.[1] note sceððeð (?), and so Spr. — 1549 Gr.,[1] Go.,[1] Go.[2]
cweðan. — 1563 Siev. (PBB. xii. 477) would have geþread uncontracted. — 1564 Gr.[1]
wêrges ; Gr.[2] werges. — 1565 Th. facen tacen; Th. note r. fira (tr. 'children of
men '); Go.,[1] Go.[2] tr. 'sons of men.' — 1566 MS., Edd. tearum ; Th. note tearas (?).
— 1567 Siev. (PBB. x. 477) would have doð uncontracted.

nē nǣngum yflum wel ;   ac þǣr ǣghwæþer
ānfealde gewyrht   ondweard wigeð.

   Forðon sceal ōnettan   se þe āgan wile
lif æt Meotude,   þenden him [lic] ond gǣst
1580 somodfæst[e] s[ie]n.   Hē his sāwle wlite
georne bigonge   on Godes willan,
ond [w]ær weorðe   worda ond dǣda,
þēawa ond geþonca,   þenden him þēos woruld,
sceadum scrīþende,   scīnan mōte,
1585 þæt hē ne forlēose   on þās lǣnan tīd
his drēames blǣd,   ond his dagena rīm,
ond his weorces wlite,   ond [his] wuldres lēan,
þætte heofones Cyning   on þā hālgan tīd   •
sōðfæst syleð   tō sigorlēanum,
1590 þām þe him on gǣstum   georne hȳrað.

   Þonne heofon ond hel   hæleþa bearnum
fira fēorum   fylde weorþ[a]ð.

   Grundas swelgað   Godes ondsacan;
lācende lēg   lāðwende men
1595 þrēað, þēodsceaþan,   ond nō þonan lǣt[e]ð
on gefēan faran   tō feorhnere ;
ac se bryne bindeð   bīdfæstne here,
fēoð firena bearn.   Frēcne mē þinceð
þæt þās gǣstberend   gīman nellað,
1600 men on mōde,   þonne mān [fremmað],
hwæt him se Wāldend   tō wrace gesette,
lāþum lēodum.   Þonne lif ond dēað

1576 *Gr.*,[1] *Wü.* ængum. — 1577 *Th. note* [*for* wigeð] ætyweð (?). — 1578
MS. on nettan (*A.*). — 1579[b] *Gr.*[I] lic ; *MS., other Edd.* leoht. — 1580 *Th.* somod
fæst; *Th. note r.* fæste; *MS., Edd.* seon. — 1582 *MS., Th., Gr.*,[1] *Go.*[1] þær;
Gr.,[2] *Go.*,[2] *Wü.* wær. — 1584 *Th. note* scriþendum. 'For man walketh in a vain
shadow.' — 1592 *MS., Edd.* weorþeð. — 1595 *MS., Th., Go.*,[1] *Go.*[2] lætað; *Gr.*,[1]
Wü. læteð. — 1597 *MS., Th.* bið fæstne; *Th. note* bit (?); *Gr.*[1] bīd-fæstne. —
1600 *Gr.*[1] þonne man [fremmað] ; *other Edd. end the line with* hwæt, *and leave
MS. reading.* — 1601 *Th. ends line with* to. — 1602 *Schubert* (*p. 59*) lig.

sāwlum swelgað,　　bið sūsla hūs
open ond oðēawed　　āðlogum ongēan ;
1605 ðæt sceolon fyllan　　firengeorne men
sweartum sāwlum.　　Þonne, synna [tō] wrac[e],
scyldigra scolu　　āscyred weorþeð,
hēane from hālgum,　　on hearmcwale.
Ðǣr sceolan þēofas　　ond þēodsceaþan,
1610 lēase ond forlegene,　　līfes ne wēnan,
ond mānsworan　　mo[r]þorlēan sēon,
heard ond heorogrim.　　Þonne hel nimeð
wǣrlēasra weorud,　　ond hī Wāldend giefeð
fēondum in forwyrd ;　　fā þrōwiað
1615 ealdorbealu egeslīc.　　Earm bið sē þe wile
firenum gewyrcan　　þæt hē, fāh, scyle
· from his Scyppende　　āscyred weorðan
æt dōmdæge　　tō dēaðe niþer,
under helle cinn　　in þæt hāte fȳr,
1620 under līges locan ;　　þǣr hȳ leomu rǣcað
tō bindenne　　ond tō bærnenne
ond tō swingenne,　　synna tō wīte.
Ðonne Hālig Gǣst　　helle bilūceð,
morþerhūsa mǣst,　　þurh meaht Godes,
1625 fȳres fulle　　ond fēonda her[g]e[s],
Cyninges worde.　　Sē biþ cwealma mǣst,
dēofla ond monna.　　Þæt is drēamlēas hūs.
Ðǣr ǣnig ne mæg　　ō[w]er losian
cāldan clommum.　　Hȳ brǣcon Cyninges word,
1630 beorht bōca bibod ;　　forþon hȳ ābīdan sceolon
in sinnehte,　　sār endelēas

1606 MS. wracu ; Th. note wrace (?). — 1611 MS. moþorlean. — 1612 Th. heoro
grim.— 1614 Frucht (p. 74) suggests forwyrde as a possible reading.— 1618 MS. dom
dæge (S.).— 1621 MS. bindeňne, the m, or three strokes resembling it, perhaps by
another hand. — 1624 Gr.¹ morðorhusa.— 1625 MS., Edd. here.— 1628 MS. oþer ;
Th. note oþerne leosan (tr. 'other loosen'); Gr.¹ + ower.— 1631 Th., Gr.¹ sinnihte ;
Th. ende leas.

firendǣdum fā forð þrōwian,

ðā þe hēr [for]hogdun heofonrīces þrym.

Þonne þā gecorenan fore Crīst berað

1635 beorhte frætwe; hyra blǣd leofað

  æt dōmdæge; āgan drēam mid Gode

  līþes līfes, þæs þe ālȳfed biþ

  hāligra gehwām on heofonrīce.

  Ðæt is se ēþel þe nō geendad weorþeð,

1640 ac þǣr symle forð synna lēase

  drēam weardiað, Dryhten lofiað,

  lēofne līfes Weard, lēohte biwundne,

  sibbum bisweðede, sorgum biwerede,

  drēamum gedȳrde, Dryhtne gelȳfde;

1645 āwo tō ealdre engla gemānan

  brūcað mid blisse, beorhte mid lisse,

  frēogað folces Weard. Fæder ealra geweald

  hafað ond healdeð hāligra weorud[a].

  Ðǣr is engla song, ēadigra blis;

1650 þǣ[r] is sēo dȳre Dryhtnes onsīen

  eallum þām gesǣlgum sunnan lēohtra;

  ðǣr is lēofra lufu; līf būtan dēaðe;

  glæd gumena weorud; gioguð būtan ylde;

  heofonduguða þrym; hǣlu būtan sāre;

1655 ryhtfremmendum ræst būtan gewinne;

  dōm ēadigra; dæg būtan þēostrum,

  beorht, blǣdes full; blis būtan sorgum;

  frið frēondum bitwēon forð būtan æfestum

  gesǣlgum on swegle; sib būtan nīþe

1633 *MS.* hogdun; *Gr.*[1] *note* forhogdun (?); *Go.*,[1] *Go.*,[2] *Wü.* forhogdun; *Go.*[1] *note evidently an error for* forhogdun, *or* ne hogdun. — 1635 *Gr.*[1] leófað; *Gr.*[2] leofað. — 1636ª *Go.*[2] *ends hemistich with* agan. — 1645 *Go.*[1] awa. — 1646 *Th.*, *Gr.*[1] beorht. — 1647 *Th.*, *Go.*,[1] *Go.*[2] *end line with* ealra. — 1648 *MS.*, *Edd.* weorud. — 1650 *MS.* þæs. — 1651 *Gr.*[1] þæm; *Gr.*[1] leohtre. — 1652 *MS.*, *Edd.* endedeaðe; Schubert (*p.* 49) *and* Siev. *suggest* (*PBB. xii. 477*) *that* ende *should be omitted.* — 1655 *Gr.*[2] *has no comma after* gewinne. — 1656 *Th.*, *Gr.*,[2] *Go.*,[1] *Go.*[2] dom-eadigra; *Gr.*[1] dom eadigra.

1660 hālgum on gemonge.   Nis þǣr hungor nē þurst,
    slǣp nē swār leger,   nē sunnan bryne,
    nē cyle nē cearo ;   ac þǣr Cyninges gief[e]
    āwo brūcað   ēadigra gedryht,
    weoruda wlitescȳnast,   wuldres mid Dryhten.

1663 *MS.* gief, *after which is an erasure.* — 1664 *Th.* wlite scynast.

CHRIST 1665–1693.

[Thus according to some reckonings. Gollancz regards this passage as the beginning of *Guthlac*, and so prints it. Cosijn considered it an independent poem.]

1665   Sē bið gefēana fǣgrast   þonne hȳ æt frymðe gemētað —
    engel ond sēo ēadge sāwl ;   ofgiefeþ hīo þās eorþan wynne,
    forlǣteð þās lǣnan drēamas,   ond hīo wiþ þām līce gedǣleð.
    Ðonne cwið se engel —   hafað yldran hād —
    grēteð gǣst ōþerne,   ābēodeð him Godes ǣrende : —
1670   ' Nū þū mōst fēran   þider þū fundadest
    longe ond gelōme ;   ic þec lǣdan sceal.
    Wegas þē sindon wēþe,   ond wuldres lēoht
    torht ontȳned.   Eart nū tīdfara
    tō þām hālgan hām   þǣr nǣfre hrēow cymeð;
1675   edergong fore yrmþum ;   ac þǣr biþ engla drēam,
    sib, ond gesǣlignes,   ond sāwla ræst ;
    ond þǣr ā tō fēore   gefēon mōtun,
    drȳman mid Dryhten,   þā þe his dōmas hēr
    æfnað on eorþan.   Hē him ēce lēan
1680   healdeð on heofonum,   þǣr se hȳhsta
    ealra cyninga Cyning   ceastrum wealdeð.
    Ðæt sind þā getimbru   þe nō tȳdriað,
    nē þām fore yrmþum   þe þǣr in wuniað
    līf āspringeð,   ac him bið lenge hū sēl ;
1685   geoguþe brūcað   ond Godes miltsa.
    Þider sōðfæstra   sāwla mōtun
    cuman æfter cwealme,   þā þe ǣr Crīstes ǣ
    lǣrað ond lǣstað,   ond his lof rǣrað,
    oferwinnað þā āwyrgdan gǣstas,   bigytað him wuldres ræste.'

1690 Hwider sceal þæs monnes mōd āstīgan
   ǣr oþþe æfter, þonne hē his ænne hēr
   gǣst bigonge þæt sē Gode mōte
   womma clǣne in geweald cuman?

NOTES.

NOTES.

PART I.

The superscriptions suggested by editors and commentators for this Part are as follows :—

Wanley : 1. Poema sive Hymnus de Nativitate D. N. I. C. et de B. V. Maria.
Thorpe : To Jesus Christ.
Dietrich : Die Ankunft Christi auf Erden.
Grein : I.
Gollancz[1] : Primus Passus de Nativitate, I.
Gollancz[2] : A. The Nativity, I.
Wülker : 1. Teil : Die Ankunft Christi auf Erden.

The divisions of the poem recognized by the several editors are these (the line-number is that of the line with which the new section begins) : —
Wanley : 2. Poema sive Hymnus in laudem B. V. Mariae, Earendelis Angeli (sive Luciferi), Melchisedechi, et D. N. Jesu Christi : 71.
3. Poema sive Hymnus maxime de B. V. Maria : 164.
4. Poema sive Hymnus ad B. V. Mariam : 275.
5. Hymnus de Deo, qui Filium suum misit in mundi redemptionem : 378.
1. Liber II, cujus Hymnus prior est de Nativitate D. N. Jesu Christi : 440.
2. Poema de die Judicii : 517.
3. Poema de mundi Creatione : 600.
4. Poema de Christi Incarnatione, etc. : 686.
5. Poema de die judicii, ex quo desumpsit Dns Hickesius illud specimen, Litteris Runicis insignitum, quod designatur littera C, ad pag. 4. Gramm. Islandicae : 779.
Liber III in quo habentur
1. Descriptio Poetica diei Judicii : 867.
2. Adhuc de die Judicii : 972.
3. Adhuc de die Judicii : 1081.
4. Adhuc de die Judicii : 1199.
[5.] Adhuc de die Judicii : 1327.
6. Adhuc de die Judicii, et damnatione Impiorum : 1428.
7. De supplicio Peccatorum, et gaudio beatorum in coelis : 1530.
Wanley begins the next section (1665–*Guth.* 790 [818]) thus : — ' Liber IV, octo constans Capitibus, agit de Gaudiis quae paravit Deus pro iis qui amaverunt eum et mandata ejus impleverunt ; cum narratione Poetica eorum quae in spiritu viderit in caelos raptus Guthlacus. (Vid. visiones Guthlaci Anachoretae.)'

Conybeare agrees with Wanley, except that he entitles the second poem of
Bk. II. 'A Description of the Entrance of the Saints into the Glory of Heaven';
the third, 'An Hymn of Thanksgiving for the General Mercies of God'; while
the fourth is described as 'the sequel of the former poem' (p. 202).

Thorpe: [2.] To the Virgin Mary: 71.
   [3.] On the Nativity: 164.
   [4.] On the Nativity: 275.
   [5.] To the Trinity: 378.
   [6] On the Nativity: 416.
   [7.] On the Nativity and Ascension : 440.
   [8.] On the Ascension, and the Harrowing of Hell[1]: 517.
   [9.] Hymn of Praise and Thanksgiving: 600.
   [10.] Hymn in Continuation of the Foregoing: 686.
   [11.] Poems on the Day of Judgment: I. 779; II. 867; III. 972.
   [12.] On the Crucifixion : 1081.
   [13.] On the Day of Judgment: I. 1199; II. 1327.
   [14.] On the Crucifixion, etc. : 1428.
   [15.] Of Souls after Death, etc.: I. 1530; [II. 1665.]

Ettmüller classifies as follows (p. xvi) : 'Alterum est carmen in laudem benig-
nitatis dei, magis ornatum quidem quam Cædmonis, sed idem consuetam cleri-
corum rationem non deserens [600-778].

Tertium locum hymni merentur, quorum etiamsi unus alterve latini poematis
versio judicaretur, non nulli tamen magni sunt pretii maximeque decori, idque
poetae Saxonici cum. Sunt autem
   a) Hymnus in Christum [1].
   b) Hymni duo in Christum natum [164?; 275?].
   c) Hymnus in Christi ascensionem [440].
   d) Hymnus in Christi resurrectionem et descensionem in infernum [517].
   e) Hymnus in Trinitatem [378].
   f) Hymnus in Mariam virginem salvatoris matrem [71].
   g) Hymnus in laudem dei fautoris hominum [416?].
Quartum locum concedimus carmini de judicio supremo, Cynevulfo auctore
supra jam laudato. Tres habet cantus [779, 867, 972] carmen amplissimum.

Praeter hoc Cynevulfi carmen quo alia de judicio supremo poemata habemus,
quorum primum duos [1199, 1327] habet cantus. Auctores ignorantur. . . .

Denique carmen in Christum crucifixum [1081] et carmen in Christi resurrectionem et descensum in infernum [1428–1530] recenseri debent, utrumque medio-
cris pretii; qui pepigerit ea, nescimus.'

The 'alterum carmen' he prints on pp. 223–7, under the title of 'Lofsang.'
That to which he assigns the 'quartum locum' he prints on pp. 239–246, under
the title, 'Be þam domes dæge.' It will be observed that he makes no account
of 1530 ff.

---

[1] Thorpe added in a note: 'This poem evidently forms a continuation of the one preceding.'

Dietrich: II. 71; III. 164; IV. 275; V. 378; VI. 416; VII. 440; VIII. 517; IX. 600; X. 686; XI.[1] 779; XI.[2] 867; XI.[3] 972; XII.[4] 1081; XIII.[5] 1199; XIII.[6] 1327; XIV.[7] 1428; XV.[8] 1530; [XV.[9] 1665.]

It will be seen that Wanley, Thorpe, and Dietrich divide at the same places, except that Wanley does not recognize the division at 416.

Dietrich has:
[2.] Seine Himmelfahrt [v. 440].
[3.] Seine Wiederkunft zum Gericht [v. 779].

Grein: II. 50; III. 71; IV. 104; V. 130; VI. 164; VII. 214; VIII. 275; IX. 348; X. 378; XI. 416; XII. 440; XIII. 558; XIV. 586; XV. 691; XVI. 779; XVII. 867; XVIII. 1007; XIX. 1216; XX. 1336; XXI. 1362; XXII. 1549.

Rieger is curiously eclectic in his procedure. While his text is based upon Thorpe's, his 'Parts' are those of Dietrich, and his 'Songs' follow the divisions of Grein, except that in one case he reverts to Thorpe. Accordingly, his 'Sechster gesang des ersten teiles' (p. 116) is vv. 164–213; his 'Dritter gesang des zweiten teiles' (p. 118) is vv. 586–685 (not 690, with Grein); and his 'Erster gesang des dritten teiles' (p. 121) is vv. 779–866.

Körner (pp. 136–138) gives Grein's No. VI as 'Gespräch zwischen Maria und Joseph'; and the latter part of Grein's No. XV (vv. 659–690), as 'Lobgesang auf die Weisheit des Schöpfers' (pp. 138–140).

Sievers (*PBB*. 12. 455–6) begins Part III with v. 779, and believes that the three parts were not conceived as divisions of one whole.

Cremer (*Untersuchung*, pp. 47–48) divides into *Christ* A (1–778) and *Christ* B (779–end).

Gollancz[1]: II. 71; III. 164; IV. 275; V. 378.
Secundus Passus de Ascensione: I. 440; II. 517; III. 600; IV. 686; V. 779.
Tertius Passus de Die Judicii: I. 867; II. 972; III. 1081; IV. 1199; V. 1327; VI. 1428; VII. 1530.

Gollancz[2]: Like Gollancz[1], except:
B. The Ascension.
C. The Day of Judgment.

Trautmann (*Anglia* 18. 382–8) recognizes the divisions 1–439, 440–866, 867–end, but assumes that they constitute three separate poems.

Blackburn (*Anglia* 19. 89–98) recognizes the divisions 1–439, 440–866, 867–1664, and subdivides as follows:
Part I. 1. a: 1–32; b: 33–49; c: 50–70; 2. a: 71–103; b: 104–163; 3. a: 164–213; b: 214–274; 4. a: 275–347; b: 348–377; 5. a: 378–402; b: 403–439.
Part II. 1: 440–546; 2: 547–743; 3: 744–778; 4: 779–866.
Part III.

Wülker: Like Grein, except:
2. Teil: Christi Himmelfahrt [v. 440].
3. Teil: Christi Wiederkunft zum jüngsten Gericht [v. 779].

The following general table will show at a glance the divisions recognized by those who have dealt with the poem as a whole.

Wanley Gollancz	Thorpe Dietrich	Grein Wülker	Cook
			18
		50	50
71	71	71	71
		104	104
		130	130
164	164	164	164
		214	214
275	275	275	275
		348	348
378	378	378	378
	416	416	416
440	440	440	440
517	517		[See pp. 115–116]
		558	
		586	
600	600		
686	686		
		691	
779	779	779	
867	867	867	867
972	972		
		1007	
1081	1081		
1199	1199		[See pp. 170–171]
		1216	
1327	1327		
		1336	
		1362	
1428	1428		
1530	1530		
		1549	

The manuscript evidence for divisions is as follows (after Gollancz[2], and Assmann, in Wülker):

Three-line space: [1665].
Two-line space: 440, 867.
One-line space: 71, 164, 378, 517, 600, 972, 1530.
Half-line space: 779, 1327, 1428.
About a third of a line space: 275, 1199.
Part of line blank (only one word in line): 686, 1081.
Other indications are the *Amen* at 440, the : 7 at 71, 164, 275, 378, 440, 517, 600, 686, 779, 972, 1081, 1199, 1428, 1530, 1664; the : at 1327; the : 7 : 7 : 7 at 867 (after Gollancz[2]); and the whole line of capitals at the beginning of 867, and of [1665].

Accordingly, the divisions in any way indicated in the manuscript are those of Wanley – Gollancz, which are evidently insufficient, since they do not take account of all the Antiphons. *My* omission of subdivisions (I indicate those of other editors) in Parts II and III has reference merely to what I can discern of the structure of these parts; in other words, the manuscript divisions are not, in my opinion, structurally inevitable, as they are in I.

Part I consists, to a large extent, of variations on a series of antiphons. These comprise

(a) The Greater Antiphons of Advent, sometimes called the O's;

(b) Four Antiphons included by certain mediæval churches among the Greater Antiphons, or associated with them;

(c) Two of the Antiphons for Lauds on Trinity Sunday (here counted as one) according to the Sarum Use.

For convenience of reference, these twelve antiphons are subjoined, in the order just given. The Greater Antiphons follow the order in which they are sung at vespers from Dec. 17 to Dec. 23 inclusive, and all, except the last, follow the order in which they are found in the St. Gallen MS. edited by Tommasi (Thomasius) in his *Opera Omnia* 4. 182–3 (cf. Guéranger, *The Liturgical Year*, Advent, pp. 515, 529, 531). The last consists of the two for Trinity Sunday. After the eighth, ' O Virgin of Virgins,' there occurs in the St. Gallen MS. another, ' O Gabriel,' which is here omitted.

To each is prefixed a number, indicating the order in which it is used in Part I ; the numbers added in parentheses are those of the lines based on the respective antiphons. The translations of the first seven are by Cardinal Newman (*Tracts for the Times*, No. 75 (Vol. 3), pp. 183, 206–7) ; those of the next two from the English translation of Guéranger ; of the next by myself, the penultimate from Guéranger, and the last by myself.

(9) O eternal Wisdom, which proceedest from the mouth of the Most High, reaching from one end of creation unto the other, mightily and harmoniously disposing all things : come Thou to teach us the way of understanding. (239–240 ?)

(1 ?) O Lord, and Ruler of the House of Israel, who appearedst unto Moses in the flame of a burning bush, and gavest to him the Law in Sinai : come to redeem us with a stretched out arm. (Possibly preceding the present beginning.)

(11 ?) O Root of Jesse, who art placed for a sign of the people, before whom kings shall shut their mouths, whom the Gentiles shall supplicate : come Thou to deliver us, do not tarry. (348–377 ?)

(3) O Key of David and Sceptre of the house of Israel, who openest and none shutteth, who shuttest and none openeth : come Thou, and bring forth the captive from the house of bondage, who sitteth in darkness and in the shadow of death. (18–49.)

(6) O Rising Brightness of the Everlasting Light and Sun of Righteousness : come Thou and enlighten those who sit in darkness and in the shadow of death. (104–129.)

(2) O King and the Desire of all nations, and chief Corner-stone, who makest two to be one : come Thou and save man whom Thou formedst from the clay. (1–17.)

(7) O Emmanuel, our King and Lawgiver, the gatherer of the people and their
Saviour: come Thou to save us, O Lord our God. (130-163.)

(5) 'O Virgin of Virgins, how shall this be? for never was there one like thee,
nor will there ever be.' — 'Ye daughters of Jerusalem, why look ye wondering at
me? What ye behold is a divine mystery.' (71-103.)

(8) O King of peace, that wast born before all ages: come by the golden gate,
visit them whom thou hast redeemed, and lead them back to the place whence
they fell by sin. (214-274; cf. (9).)

(10) O mistress of the world, sprung of royal seed: from thy womb did Christ
go forth as a bridegroom from his chamber; here he who ruleth the stars lieth
in a manger. (275 ff.)

(4) O Jerusalem, city of the great God: lift up thine eyes round about, and
see thy Lord, for he is coming to loose thee from thy chains. (50-70.)

(12) O holy, blessed, and glorious Trinity, Father, Son, and Holy Spirit:
Thee do all thy creatures rightly praise, adore, and glorify, O blessed Trinity.

(378 ff.)

The correspondence of the seven Antiphons with the sevenfold gifts of the
Holy Spirit (Isa. 11. 2, 3), and of the twelve Antiphons with the twelve prophets
who foretold Christ's coming, is mystically pointed out by Honorius of Autun,
Gemma Animae, lib. 3. cap. 5 (Migne 172. 644): 'Septem O admirando potius
quam vocando cantantur, in quibus septem dona Spiritus sancti notantur, per
quae haec administratur incarnatio, et per quae Christus ab Ecclesia invita-
tur. Ipse quippe est *sapientia*, in qua Pater fecit omnia, qui venit in spiritum
sapientiae, docere nos viam prudentiae. Ipse *Adonai*, quod nomen Moysi indicavit, cui legem in Sina dedit, qui venit per spiritum intelligentiae nos redimere.
Ipse *radix Jesse*, qui in signum populorum stetit, dum per signum crucis ubique
adorari voluit ; qui in spiritu consilii nos liberare venit. Ipse *clavis David*, qui
caelum justis aperuit, infernum clausit, et per spiritum fortitudinis vinctos de
domo carceris educere venit. Ipse *Oriens* et *Sol justitiae*, qui venit nos illuminare
spiritu scientiae. Ipse *Rex gentium* et *lapis angularis*, qui venit salvare hominem
per spiritum pietatis. Ipse est *Emmanuel* veniens ad nos per Israel, qui venit
ad salvandum nos per spiritum timoris, dans cunctis charismata amoris.

'Si duodecim O cantantur, tunc duodecim prophetae exprimuntur, qui Christi
adventum praedicasse leguntur.' On this last point, cf. Durandus, *Rationale
Divinorum Officiorum*, lib. 4. cap. 11.

See also *infra*, on 71-103, p. 84.

Perhaps the last portion, preceding the first lines of the present poem, may
have been based upon the Antiphon of the Magnificat for December 18 :

O ADONAI, ET DUX DOMUS ISRAEL, QUI MOYSI IN IGNE FLAMMAE RUBI APPA-
RUISTI, ET EI IN SINA LEGEM DEDISTI : VENI AD REDIMENDUM NOS IN
BRACHIO EXTENTO.

It is conceivable, too, that the early part of the poem may have contained a variation upon the Gabriel antiphon mentioned above :

O GABRIEL, NUNTIUS CAELORUM, QUI JANUIS CLAUSIS AD ME INTRASTI, ET VER-
BUM NUNTIASTI : ' CONCIPIES, ET PARIES ; EMMANUEL VOCABITUR.'

There being such slight traces discernible in the poem of the Antiphon No. 3 in our list, it might even be thought that this had been treated in the missing portion, though such an assumption would be fully as doubtful as the preceding conjecture.

1–17. Based upon the Antiphon of the Magnificat for December 22 :

O REX GENTIUM, ET DESIDERATUS EARUM, LAPISQUE ANGULARIS, QUI FACIS
UTRAQUE UNUM : VENI, ET SALVA HOMINEM, QUEM DE LIMO FORMASTI.

The first source of the Antiphon is Jer. 10. 7 : 'Quis non timebit te, *O Rex gentium ?*' Then Hag. z. 7 (Vulg. 8): 'Et veniet *desideratus cunctis gentibus*'; Eph. z. 20: '. . ipso *summo angulari lapide* Christo Jesu'; Eph. 2. 14: '. . . qui *fecit utraque unum*'; Gen. 2. 7 : '*Formavit* igitur Dominus Deus *hominem de limo* terrae'; Tob. 8. 8 : 'Tu fecisti Adam *de limo* terrae.'

1. Cyninge. With two exceptions, 165 and 732, *cyning* always denotes God or Christ. Here the reference must be to the 'Rex' of the Antiphon. What is lost in this paragraph must cover the 'O Rex gentium, et desideratus earum' of the Antiphon, and can scarcely have exceeded a dozen lines, at most. Cf. the length of the other divisions which severally correspond to the Antiphons.

Go.¹ says of *Cyninge :* 'I have purposely omitted it, so as to give the appearance of completeness to the poem.' [!]

2. weallstān. On the use of stone in church architecture among the English, cf. Bede on Benedict Biscop, *Hist. Abb.* 5 (the date being *ca.* 676): 'Nec plusquam unius anni spatio post fundatum monasterium interjecto, Benedictus oceano transmisso Gallias petens, caementarios qui *lapideam* sibi *ecclesiam* juxta Romanorum quem semper amabat morem facerent, postulavit, accepit, attulit.' In 710 Naiton, king of the Picts, sends to Ceolfriŏ for architects capable of building a stone church (*Hist. Eccl.* 5. 21). Cf. Mayor and Lumby's Bede, p. 222 ; Traill, *Social England,* 1. 197–8 ; and especially the articles by C. C. Hodges in *The Illustrated Archæologist* for March, 1894, and *The Reliquary* for January, April, and July, 1893, and January, April, and October, 1894.

For the high estimate placed upon stone buildings in Germany, see *Heliand* 5577–8 :

> that hōha hūs hebankuninges,
> stēnwerko mēst.

For German contemporary building in stone, cf. Lauffer, *Das Landschaftsbild Deutschlands im Zeitalter der Karolinger* (Göttingen, 1896), pp. 3–4. Cf. *El.* 1020.

3. wiŏwurpon. The reference is to Ps. 118. 22 : 'Lapidem, quem reprobaverunt aedificantes, hic factus est in caput anguli.' Cf. also Mt. 21. 42 ; Mk. 12. 10 ; Lk. 20. 17 ; Acts 4. 11 ; 1 Pet. 2. 7. Ælfric has (*Hom. z.* 580) : 'Crīst is se lybbenda stān þone āwurpon ŏā ungeleaffullan Iūdēi.' Cf. *Jul.* 654.

4. **hēafod.** A Hebraism. See *caput*, above. The N. T. Greek is κεφαλὴ γωνίας; similarly λίθος ἀκρογωνιαῖος, Lat. *lapis (summus) angularis*, Eph. 2. 20; I Pet. 2. 6; from Isa. 28. 16.

healle. The word must here virtually signify 'temple.'

5. **sīde.** Is reference made to the dimensions of the symbolical temple, such as are indicated in Ezek. 40 ff. (cf. Rev. 11. 1; 21. 10, 15, 16)? The living temple may be expected to cover the whole earth.

6. **fæste gefōge.** Cf. the 'fitly framed together' of Eph. 2. 21, Lat. *constructa*, Gr. συναρμολογουμένη. The same Greek word is found Eph. 4. 16, referring to the body, where the Latin is *compactum*.

flint unbræcne. The hardness of flint is referred to in 1188; cf. Ezek. 3. 9. The adamantine indestructibility of this divine temple seems to be the notion which the poet is seeking to convey.

7. **eorōb[yri]g.** None of the readings is satisfactory. *Wundrien* needs a subject, and a different sort of subject might be looked for than *eall*, in the sense of 'all things'; one would rather expect *ealle* (see the references in Glossary). If *eall* is adverbial, we lack a subject for the verb, unless, with Grein, we take *gesihþe* as nom. plur.; but the plur. is not elsewhere found in the poetry, and one would hardly expect the 'sights of the eyes' to wonder. Thorpe's emendation would seem probable, in the light of 422, 1278, were it not for the MS. *g*, and the fact that *geond* needs an object. *Eorðburg* is not found in the poetry; in its two prose instances, it seems to render Lat. *agger*. Go.[2] translates *earth's cities*.

ēagna gesihþe. Cf. 1113.

8. **tō worlde.** Perhaps we should read *tō worulde*, the forms with *u* far outnumbering the syncopated ones. The phrase clearly means 'for ever'; cf. 101, 'ā tō worulde forð.' So the Vulgate *in saeculum*, Exod. 21. 6, etc.

wuldres Ealdor. Cf. 158, 463, 493, 527, 565, 740, 1197. For the sense, see Ps. 24. 7; I Cor. 2. 8; Jas. 2. 1. Thayer (*N. T. Lexicon*) interprets δόξα in the last two instances as 'the absolutely perfect inward or personal excellence of Christ.' Otherwise one would be inclined to think of Mk. 10. 37 ('majestic state'); Lk. 24. 26 ('exalted condition'), etc. The exact meaning is very difficult to fix.

The edd. construe *Ealdor* as vocative. It is quite as likely that it is accusative after *wundrien*; cf. *Ph.* 331; *Gu.* 1205. *Wundrian* is usually construed with the gen., but even in prose with the acc.; cf. Wülfing, *Syntax* I. 262. Gr. finds no other instance of its absolute use. Then, too, a vocative is not so likely to be found at the end of a paragraph as at the beginning, after *ēald*. For these reasons I prefer to regard *Ealdor* as acc.

Brooke translates *wuldres Ealdor* as 'Master of Magnificence,' and connects it with the following.

10. **sōðfæst, sigorbeorht.** Brooke translates 'true-fast and triumphant-clear' — whatever that may mean.

forlǣt. Gr. assumes ellipsis of a dependent infinitive, and so in 30, 1111; he translates (*Dichtungen*) by *lass . . . steigen*; Th., Go.[2] by *leave*; Go.[1] by *leave . . . erect*. Thorpe's rendering is probably the best, understanding *leave* as *leave remaining, leave standing*, like ἀφεῖναι, *relinquere*, in Matt. 24. 2; Mk. 13. 2; Lk. 19. 44; 21. 6. In all these instances, Lind. and Rush.[2] have *forlēta*, while the WS.

Gospels and Rush.[1] have *lǣfan*, Wycliffe *leeve*. Ælfric has *forlǣtan*, Lk. 19. 44 (see my *Biblical Quotations*, p. 204). Goth. goes with Lind.: *lètand*, Lk. 19. 44.

11. **weall wiŏ wealle.** According to Gregory, the two walls signify (1) the Jews and the Gentiles, (2) the church on earth and the angels in heaven. Thus in his *Moralia*, commenting on Job 38. 6 (Migne 76. 458): ' Jam per divinam gratiam omnibus liquet, quem Scriptura sacra angularem lapidem vocet, illum profecto qui, dum in se *hinc Judaicum illinc gentilem* populum suscipit, in una Ecclesiae fabrica quasi *duos parietes* jungit, illum de quo scriptum est: *Fecit utraque unum* (Ephes. 2. 14). Qui angularem se lapidem non solum in inferioribus, sed et in supernis exhibuit, quia et in terra plebi Israeliticae nationes gentium et *utram que simul angelis in caelo sociavit*. Eo quippe nato clamaverunt angeli: *In terra pax hominibus bonae voluntatis* (Luc. 2. 14). In ortu enim Regis nequaquam pro magno offerrent hominibus pacis gaudia, si discordiam non haberent.' This is interesting: If reconciliation between angels and men had not been needed, the former would never have sung peace on earth, for that song implied that there had been, if not antagonism, at least variance. Cf. also Migne 79. 617 ; Ælfric, *Hom*. 1. 38.

Jerome likewise recognizes the twofold interpretation. He says (Migne 26. 476) that, according to the second of these, Christ 'caelestia jungat atque terrena.' Amalarius (Migne 105. 1269) gives only the first interpretation.

Ælfric on Ps. 118. 22 (*Hom*. 1. 106) follows Gregory's first interpretation: ' Sóŏlice se sealmsceop āwrāt se Crīste þæt hē is se hyrnstān þe gefēgŏ þā twēgen weallas tōgædere, forŏanŏe hē geþéodde his gecorenan of Iūdēiscum folce and þā gelēaffullan of hǣŏenum, swilce twēgen wāgas tō ānre gelaŏunge. . . þā Iudēiscan ŏe on Crīst gelȳfdon wǣron him gehendor stōwlice, and eac ŏurh cȳŏŏe þǣre ealdan ǣ : wē wǣron swīŏe fyrlyne, ǣgŏer ge stōwlice ge ŏurh uncȳŏŏe; ac hē ūs gegaderode mid ānum gelēafan tō ŏǣm hēalicum hyrnstāne, þæt is, tō ānnysse his gelaŏunge.' In *Hom*. 2. 578–580, Ælfric adopts Gregory's second interpretation : ' Hē (Salomon) hæfde gētācnunge ūres Hǣlendes Crīstes, seŏe forŏī āstāh of heofenum tō ŏisum middanearde, þæt hē wolde mancynn gesibbian and geŏwǣrlǣcan tō þām heofenlicum werode, swā swā Paulus, ŏēoda lārēow, cwæŏ: "Ipse est pax nostra, qui fecit utraque unum — Sē is ūre sib, seŏe dyde ǣgŏer tō ānum "; þæt is, engla werod and mancynn tō ānum werode.'

weorce. Rather as in 3 than as in 9; almost = *cause*.

12. **Cræftga.** The figure does not dominate the thought ; Christ throughout is represented as a person, notwithstanding the use of metaphors. Cf. 14 b.

13. **gebrosnad.** Cf. the OE. poem, *The Ruin*. Dietrich refers to Amos 9. 11 ; Acts 15. 16.

14. **hūs.** Ælfric recognizes *hūs*, as a metaphor, in two senses : (a) The one church universal ; (b) the individual Christian. Both are touched upon in the following passage (*Hom*. 2. 580): ' Se gesibsuma Salomon ārǣrde þæt mǣre hūs of eorŏlicum antimbre Gode tō wurŏmynte, and se gesibsuma Crīst getimbrode ŏā gāstlican cyrcan, nā mid dēadum stānum, ac mid lybbendum sāwlum. . . . Ealle Godes cyrcan sind getealde tō ānre cyrcan, and sēo is gehāten "gelaŏung," ŏā getācnode þæt ān tempel ŏe Salomon ārǣrde on ŏǣre ealdan ǣ. Nū sind wē crīstene menn Godes hūs gehātene, swā swā se apostol Paulus cwæŏ, "Templum Dei sanctum est, quod estis uos "; þæt is, "Godes tempel is hālig, þæt gē sind."

... Fram ðǣre tíde ūres fulluhtes wunað se Hālga Gāst on ūs, and ealle englas
and ealle rihtwīse men sindon his tempel; forðī sceolon crīstene men þā fūlan
leahtras forsēon þe se swicola dēofol tǣcð, þæt hī mōton bēon wurðe þæs Hālgan Gāstes onwununge. ... Fela sind nū Godes hūs, ac swā-ðēah ān, for ðǣre
ānnysse þæs sōðan gelēafan ðe hī ealle andettað. Fela ðēoda sind þe mid mislicum gereordum God heriað, ac swā-ðēah hī habbað ealle ænne gelēafan, and
ænne sōðne God wurðiað, þēah-ðe heora gereord and gebedhūs manega sind.' Cf.
also 1. 368.

hrā. Not to be identified with *hūs;* we have now passed to the second half
of the Antiphon.

15. lǣmena. On the retention of the middle vowel see Sievers, *PBB.* 10.
461.

Līffrēa. An appropriate title in this place; cf. Acts 3. 15. For metrical
reasons, Sievers (*PBB.* 10. 479) would read *Līffrīga.*

16. hēap. Seems to mean *mankind* (cf. the Antiphon); but the transition
from the sing. *hrā* is abrupt. Dietrich refers to Lk. 1. 71.

17. swā hē oft dyde. So *Gen.* 2586; *Beow.* 444; cf. 455; *Beow.* 1238.

18–49. Based upon the Antiphon of the Magnificat for December 20:

O CLAVIS DAVID, ET SCEPTRUM DOMUS ISRAEL; QUI APERIS, ET NEMO CLAUDIT,
  CLAUDIS, ET NEMO APERIT: VENI, ET EDUC VINCTUM DE DOMO CARCERIS,
  SEDENTEM IN TENEBRIS ET UMBRA MORTIS.

From Isa. 22. 22 : 'Et dabo *clavem* domus *David* super humerum ejus; et
aperiet, et nemo erit qui claudat; et claudet, et non erit qui aperiat'; Rev. 3. 7:
'... qui habet clavem David; *qui aperit, et nemo claudit; claudit, et nemo
aperit*'; Gen. 49. 10: 'Non auferetur *sceptrum* de Juda'; Isa. 42. 7: 'Ut ...
educeres de conclusione *vinctum, de domo carceris sedentes in tenebris.*'

This Antiphon was a favorite with Alcuin, who frequently recited it in the
closing days of his life. Cf. *Alcuini Vita*, cap. xiv, in Migne 100. 104–5: 'Jam
ergo Albinus corpore dissolvi cupiens et cum Christo esse desiderans, exorabat
eum ut die quo in linguis igneis Spiritus sanctus super apostolos venisse visus
est et eorum corda replevit, si fieri posset, migraret e mundo. Vespertinum siquidem pro se officium in loco quo elegerat post obitum quiescere, juxta videlicet
ecclesiam sancti Martini, hymnum sanctae Mariae evangelicum cum hac antiphona
decantabat. ... Tertia tandem antequam migraret die, solitam exsultationis voce
decantavit antiphonam, *O clavis David.*' Cf. Bede, *Works* 8. 162–3.

18. Ēalā. Translating *O.* In the *Surtees Hymns* frequently found to denote
the vocative, even where *O* is lacking in the original, in the combination *O ēalā
þū;* thus 3. 16; 6..1; 7. 7, etc. The liturgiologist Amalarius, early in the ninth
century, thus comments on the *O* (Migne 105. 1265) : 'Per illud O voluit cantor
intimare verba sequentia pertinere ad aliquam mirabilem visionem, quae plus pertinet ad mentis ruminationem quam ad concionatoris narrationem. Et quoniam
per conceptionem et partum sanctae Mariae facta est haec admiratio, amplius congruunt memoratae antiphonae hymno sanctae Mariae quam Zachariae.' Yet these
antiphons were sometimes used for the Benedictus, instead of the Magnificat; cf.

Tommasi, *Opera* 4. 27. That the O was a cry of admiration rather than a summons, seems to be borne out by the Gabriel Antiphon above, which contains no verb in the imperative. — With the line cf. *Rid.* 41³.

19. **locan.** Grein (*Dichtungen*) has ' die Schlüssel,' Kemble's emendation in *Solomon and Saturn* 184–5 would apparently equate *cǣgan* with *locan*, and the Antiphon shows that the word must stand for *clavis ;* besides, how could locks or bars be *held?* It is doubtful whether *locan* is sing. or plur., probably the former. *Riddle* 87 is interpreted as ' key '; see Dietrich in *Haupt's Zs.* 11. 486.

21. **wilsīþes.** Th. leaves untranslated; Gr. 'wolergehen'; Go. 'career.' The general sense is determined by the apposition with *siges (sigores)*.

23-26. Gr. translates:

> beschwören mutbekümmert den, der den Menschen schuf,
> dass er nicht eile mit Hass das Urteil zu sprechen
> der Kummervollen, die wir im Kerker hier
> sitzen voller Sorgen während der Sonne Lustfahrt.

Go.[1] has:

> Him who created man we supplicate,
> that He elect not to declare in hate
> the doom of us who sad in prison here
> sit yearning for the sun's propitious course.

Similarly Go.[2]

23. Go.'s emendation, *gemǣrsigiað*, will not admit of his translation, ' supplicate,' ' beseech.'

24. I can make nothing of this line. **Hete** as *hēte*, opt. pret. 3 sing. of *hātan*, can hardly follow a verb in the present, to which -giað points ; besides, the form would be *hehte* (cf. 294). For *hete* as inst. sing. of the noun there is no parallel in the poetry ; in *Gen.* 757 the word is preceded by *mid ;* besides, *hete*, with a short syllable, would not scan.

As for *cēose*, if we retain it, it is an opt. pres., and therefore inconsistent with *hēte*, if we suppose this to be an opt. pret.; it cannot have a simple infinitive dependent on it; and there is no alliteration. The metre, too, would be very exceptional (cf. *PBB.* 10. 231).

With regard to **hēofe**, whether as verb or noun, it is difficult to see how it is to be construed with the rest of the line, even if the MS. favored the conjecture.

25. **þing.** Gr. (*Spr.*) renders by 'Versammlung,' 'Gerichtsversammlung'; under *hēof* by ' coetum,' ' multitudinem '; in *D.* by ' Urteil '; Go. by ' doom.' The sense of ' doom' derives some support from 926, though it verges on the inadmissible.

þe wē. Perhaps to be understood as *wē þe*, in which case *wē* would be anacoluthic after *cearfulra.*

carcerne. Cf. Wulfstan, *Hom.* 3. 14 ff.: ' Ðæt is þonne þǣm gelīcost, þe wē nū on carcerne sȳn betȳnede on þisse worulde ; and eft, þonne se gāst wyrð ūt of ðām līchoman ālǣd, þe hē nū mid befangen is, þonne bið ūs gesawen þæt ūs ǣr gesǣd wæs, þēah-þe wē hit nū geortrȳwan, forðȳ wē hit gesēon ne magon.'

26. **sorgende.** Go. translates' yearning for,' and is followed by Brooke. This is perhaps correct, though I know of no instance where *sorgian* governs the

acc., and 'yearn for' is an unusual extension of the ordinary senses of the word. Sievers (*PBB* 10. 482) notes that the form is for *-iende*. Cosijn assumes the loss of a line, which, adducing 147, he would make something like : *bīdaþ in bendum* + hemistich.

wilsīð. Th. Gr.[1] take this as an acc. of extent of time. Gr. (*Spr.*) translates, 'während des Laufes der Sonne, den ganzen Tag lang'; (*D.*) 'Während der Sonne Lustfahrt.' Examples of this acc. occur 439, 542, 1322, 1410. There must be an allusion to the period of Advent, conceived as one of expectation, with transference to any period of solicitous waiting for spiritual aid.

27. hwonne. So 147, 1347. This use, found elsewhere in the poetry, occurs also in prose. A typical instance is Lk. 12. 36: 'ābīdað hwænne hē sȳ fram gyftum gecyrred,' where the Latin has : 'expectantibus ... quando revertatur a nuptiis '; in this case the Greek has πότε, for ὁπότε (cf. Buttmann, *Grammar of N. T. Greek*, p. 251). Other instances are *Bede* (ed. Miller) 178. 22 ; 186. 23 ; 440. 16 ; *Cura Past.* 120. 12 ; *Bl. Hom.* 97. 25 ; 109. 32 ; *Oros.* 88. 14 ; Wulfstan 236. 11 ; *Boeth.* (ed. Fox) 26. 13 ; 212. 2 ; *Homilies* (ed. Assmann) 157. 130 ; 202. 228.

28. tō. This use of *tō* is common in the *Christ ;* Rose gives a list, pp. 28–9. There are 6 in Part I, 8 in Part II, and 17 in Part III.

29. Th. 'and the weak understanding surround with honor '; Gr. 'und den zaghaften Sinn mit Zierglanz uns bewinde '; Go.[1] 'and wreathe the feeble mind with radiant grace' (Go.[2] 'splendor').

tȳdre gewitt. Cf. *tȳdran mōde*, 371.

30–32. Professor Bright would translate : ' Make us worthy of this (what has preceded), us, whom he hath [denied] shut out from glory, when we were doomed in wretchedness, deprived of our home (heaven), to sojourn in this narrow world (earth)'.

Thorpe had rendered : 'Make us thus worthy, whom he to glory hath admitted, those who humbly must return to this narrow land, deprived of country.'

Gr. translated :

> und uns des würdig mache, die er erwählte zur Glorie,
> da wir wehvoll erniedrigt uns wenden sollten
> des Erbsitzes bar zu diesem engen Lande.

Go.[1] thus :

> May he glorify us thus, His favored ones,
> when we must needs depart in abject plight
> unto this narrow land, bereft of home.

Go.[2] renders v. 30:

> May he make us thus worthy, whom he hath admitted unto glory.

Brooke translates vv. 31–2 : 'who must turn us to the narrow shore, cut off from our Fatherland.' Dietrich's condensed paraphrase should also be mentioned : ' Er selbst möge die in Finsternis sitzenden (Luc. 1. 79) und der Heimat beraubten, der Zulassung seiner Herrlichkeit werth machen.' Of these renderings, Grein's seems most defensible, though 'admit,' rather than 'choose,' is the sense of the verb.

The whole passage (25 ff.) must, I believe, be regarded as containing a motive from the Harrowing of Hell, a motive which may be represented by the following passage from the OE. *Evangelium Nicodemi*, chap. 24 (p. 129 of Bright's *Reader*), which is a rendering of a portion of chap. 2 of the *Descensus Christi ad Inferos*, as found in Tischendorf's *Evangelia Apocrypha*, pp. 391–2 (cf. Cowper's *Apocryphal Gospels*, p. 349): 'Efne, þā wē wǣron myd eallum ūrum fæderum on þǣre hellican dēopnysse, þǣr becōm sēo beorhtnys on þǣre þēostra dymnysse, þæt wē ealle geondlȳhte and geblyssigende wǣron. Þǣr wæs fǣringa geworden on ansȳne swylce þǣr gylden sunna onǣled wǣre, and ofer ūs ealle geondlȳhte. And Sātanas þā, and eall þæt rēþe werod, wǣron āfyrhte, and þus cwǣdon: "Hwæt ys þys lēoht þæt hēr ofer ūs swā fǣrlice scȳneð?" Þā wæs sōna eall þæt mennisce cynn geblyssigende — ūre fæder Ādām myd eallum hēahfæderum, and myd eallum wȳtegum — for þǣre myclan beorhtnysse; and hig þus cwǣdon: "Þys lēoht ys ealdor þæs ēcan lēohtes, call swā ūs Dryhten behēt þæt hē ūs þæt ēce lēoht onsendan wolde." Þā clypode Ȳsaias se wȳtega and cwæþ: "Þys ys þæt fæderlice lēoht, and hyt ys Godes Sunu, eall swā ic foresǣde þā ic on eorðan wæs, þā ic cwæð and forewītegode þæt ðæt Zabulōn, and þæt land Neptalīm, wyþ þā ēa Iordānen, and þæt folc þæt on þām þȳstrum sæt sceoldon mǣre lēoht gesēon, and þā ðe on dymmum rȳce wunedon ic wītegode þæt hig lēoht sceoldon onfōn; and nū hyt ys tōcumen, and ūs onlȳht þā ðe gefyrn on dēaðes dymnysse sǣton. Ac uton ealle geblyssian þæs lēohtes."'

I find this suggestion borne out by an Advent hymn quoted in Mone I. 51, of which the first four and the last stanzas are :

> Veni, veni, rex gloriae,
> educque nos de carcere
> mordentis conscientiae,
> dimisso cuncto crimine.

> Quamvis vero instruxeris,
> emeris, liberaveris,
> quid prodest ni eduxeris
> nos de squalore carceris?

> Est carcer multum horridus,
> tenebrosus ac foetidus,
> impurus omnis animus
> criminis sibi conscius.

> Hic multam fert miseriam,
> panis vitae carentiam,
> aquae vivae penuriam,
> verae lucis inopiam.

> Ei, educ hunc de tenebris
> hujus foetentis carceris,
> ut te in regno luminis
> semper laudet cum angelis.

According to Mone, *carcer* is here used in a twofold sense, partly as in 1 Pet. 3. 19: 'By which also he went and preached unto the spirits in *prison*'; and partly as in Ps. 142. 7: 'Bring my soul out of *prison*, that I may praise thy name.' The hymn assumes a parallel, according to Mone, 'between the patriarchs and prophets, who yearned in their limbo for the birth of Christ, and such as implore the coming of the kingdom of Christ after the end of this sinful world, this prison of the body.' He quotes Gregory, *Moral.* 11. 9. 12: 'Omnis homo, per id quod male agit, quid sibi aliud quam conscientiae suae *carcerem* facit, ut hanc animi reatus premat, etiamsi nemo exterius accuset?' and Augustine, *Ep.* 165. 16: 'animae, quae ignorantiae tenebris velut *carcere* clauduntur.' Cf. the Advent hymn in Mone 1. 47 (st. 2):

> Adesto nunc propitius
> et parce supplicantibus,
> tu dele nostra crimina,
> tu tenebras illumina.

The imagery would therefore be based upon the condition of the patriarchs in the underworld just before the advent of Christ, but would picture the longing of the soul for any of the comings of the Savior, especially for his spiritual entrance into the believer.

For the recurrence of the motives drawn from the Harrowing of Hell, see 145 ff., 558 ff., 730 ff., 1159 ff.

30. þe hē tō wuldre forlēt. Go. 'whom he hath admitted to glory.' With *tō wuldre forlēt* Professor Bright compares *wiðwurpon tō weorce*, 3, and thence infers for *forlǣtan* the sense 'reject,' 'exclude,' 'deny.' See above.

This view is confirmed by Ælfric, *Hom.* 1. 154: 'þēs ān blinda man getācnode eall mancynn, þe wearð āblend þurh Ādāmes gylt, and āsceofen of myrhðe neorxenawanges, and gebrōht tō ðisum līfe, þe is wiðmeten cwearterne. Nū sind wē ūte belocene fram ðām heofenlican lēohte, and wē ne magon on ðissum līfe þæs ēcan lēohtes brūcan; nē wē his nā māre ne cunnon būton swā micel swā wē ðurh Crīstes lāre on bōcum rǣdað. þēos woruld, þēah-ðe hēo myrige hwīltīdum geðūht sȳ, nis hēo hwæðere ðē gelīccre ðǣre ēcan worulde, þe is sum cweartern lēohtum dæge. Eal mancyn wæs, swā wē ǣr cwǣdon, āblend mid gelēaflǣste and gedwylde; ac þurh Crīstes tōcyme wē wurdon ābrodene of ūrum gedwyldum, and onlīhte þurh gelēafan. Nū hæbbe wē þæt lēoht on ūrum mōde, þæt is Crīstes gelēafa; and wē habbað þone hiht þæs ēcan līfes myrhðe, þēah-ðe wē gȳt līchamlice on ūrum cwearterne wunian.'

31. hweorfan sceoldan. Cf. *Sat.* 419: 'þā wit in þis hāte scræf *hweorfan sceoldon*.'

32. þis enge lond. Gr. renders (*Spr.*): 'hunc mundum anxietatis plenum.' But cf. also what has been said above concerning the *limbus Patrum*, and *Sat.* 106: 'helle, engestan ēðelrīces.'

bescyrede. Note the number of words expressive of deprivation; cf. *Gen.* 63.

33. sē ðe sōð spriceð. Cf. 190.

35. frumcyn. Perhaps both (*a*) *original race*, and (*b*) *race*, i.e. (*a*) the patriarchs and prophets, (*b*) mankind. *Frumcyn* has not been taken in the former sense, but the context seems to favor this as one interpretation.

38. gebyrd. Here, and in 298 (cf. 76), one can only understand 'birth' by taking *þurh* in the sense of 'with reference to,' 'in anticipation of,' 'in order to.'

An argument in favor of the latter alternative is that the former renders the line somewhat tautological.

39. Nǣnig. Modifies *geēacnung*.

40. worlde. See note on 8. — **geēacnung.** Cosijn adduces 75, and *Bl. Hom.* 143. 24, as arguments for reading *geēacnung*, with Grein.

41. dēgol. Anglian vowel (*Gr.* 159. 3); cf. 640. The adjective belongs in the predicate, modifying *gerȳne*.

42. gīofu. For the variations in spelling, see the Glossary, *s. v.* **gīefu.**

geondsprēot. For **-sprēat.** Anglian confusion of *ēa* and *ēo* (*Gram.* 150. 3). Cosijn compares Netherl. *spruiten*, and postulates the inf. *geondsprūtan*.

43 ff. The fulfilment of prophecy is meant.

45. hōðman. The word occurs only once elsewhere, *Beow.* 2458 : ' swefað hæleð in *hoðman*,' where it = ' the grave.' Grein refers to Dietrich's etymology in *Haupt's Zs.* 5. 219.

47. Cf. 2 Thess. 3. 1.

48. ðāra. Dependent on **gehwæs ;** the logical order is : ' ryne reorda gehwæs ðāra þe willað.'

49. þurh horscne hād. Cf. 444, *þurh clǣnne hād.*

50–70. Based upon an occasional Antiphon of the Magnificat :

O HIERUSALEM, CIVITAS DEI SUMMI : LEVA IN CIRCUITU OCULOS TUOS, ET VIDE DOMINUM TUUM, QUIA JAM VENIET SOLVERE TE A VINCULIS.

Among the sources of the Antiphon may be reckoned Ps. 48. 2 : 'mons Sion, . . . *civitas Regis magni* '; Isa. 49. 18 : ' *Leva in circuitu oculos tuos*, et vide ' (so Isa. 60. 4); Isa. 52. 2 : ' *Solve vincula* colli tui, captiva filia Sion.'

The conception seems to fluctuate between the following :

(*a*) The earthly Jerusalem ;

(*b*) The church on earth ;

(*c*) The heavenly Jerusalem, the abode of the blessed, partly conceived as the bride, the Lamb's wife (Rev. 21. 9 ff.); cf. Gregory, in Migne 76. 938 ;

(*d*) The Virgin Mary (see my article in the *Festgabe für Eduard Sievers*, Halle, 1896).

It is impossible to distinguish these several meanings with authority and accuracy, but 50–54a may primarily refer to (*c*) ; 54b–58 to (*c*) or (*d*); 59–66a to (*a*) or (*d*) ; 66b–70 to (*b*).

On the specific reference to Jerusalem in the Second Sunday of Advent cf. Honorius of Autun, *Gemma Animæ*, lib. 3, cap. 2 (Migne 172. 643) : ' Secunda Dominica praedicatio prophetarum de Christi adventu ad Hierusalem denotatur, ubi cantatur, *Hierusalem cito veniet*, et *Civitas Hierusalem*, et *Hierusalem, surge*.'

The Biblical passages on which the mediæval Church founded the symbolical interpretation of Jerusalem as the Virgin Mary are such as Ps. 46. 5; 87. 3 ; 132. 13, 14; Cant. 6. 3; Isa. 12. 6 ; 60. 3. Cf. Livius, pp. 79 ff.; Salzer, p. 118, n. 3, and p. 377.

50. sibbe gesihð. Translating the Lat. *pacis visio*, by which the word ' Jerusalem ' was generally interpreted in the Middle Ages. This interpretation is found as early as Origen (*Hom.* 9. 2), and is illustrated in the opening line of a well-known Latin hymn (Mone I. 319; Daniel I. 239): 'Urbs beata Ierusalem, dicta pacis visio.' Cf. also Athan. *In Psalm* 64. 2; Greg. Magn., *Hom. in Ezech.* I. 12. 23; Mone 2. 184 (Hymn 470. 1–3). Mone says (I. 320–1): '*Pacis visio* ist die Uebersetzung des Namens Jerusalem, . . . und bedeutet die *sichtbare* christliche Kirche, deren irdisches Vorbild das geschichtliche Jerusalem und deren Vollendung das zukünftige himmlische Jerusalem ist. . . . Die Benennung *pax* für die Kirche ist biblisch, denn in ihr ist Gottes Frieden.' Ælfric has (*Hom.* 2. 66): 'Hierūsalēm is gecweden *visio pacis*, þæt is, *sibbe gesihð*'; and again (I. 210): 'Sion is ān dūn, and hēo is gecweden, *Scēawungstow ;* and Hierū-salēm, *Sibbe gesihð.* Siones dohtor is sēo gelaðung gelēaffulra manna, þe belimpð tō ðære heofenlican Hierūsalēm, on þære is symle sibbe gesihð, būtan ælcere sace, tō ðære ūs gebrincð se Hælend, gif wē him gelæstað.' See Sweet's *Cura Past.* 161. 16, and cf. *Gu.* 783–790 (811–18):

> Him þæt ne hrēoweð æfter hingonge,
> ðonne hy hweorfað in þā hālgan burg,
> gongað gegnunga tō Hierusalem,
> þær hī tō worulde wynnum mōtun
> Godes onsȳne georne bihealdan,
> *sibbe and gesihðe,* þær hēo sōð wunað,
> wlitig, wuldorfæst, ealne wīdan ferh,
> on lifgendra londes wynne.

One of the clearest explanations is by Greg., *Hom. in Ezech.* I. 8 (Migne 76. 857). In the glosses on Aldhelm's *De Laudibus Virginitatis*, published by Bouterwek in *Haupt's Zs.*, there occur, as a gloss on '[per portas] coelestis Hierosolymae' (p. 24, l. 9. ed. Giles) the words (9. 447): 'þære heofonlicra sibgesyhðe.' Grein refers to this. Cf. note on 53.

sancta. Cf. 88.

52–53. Anacoluthon. Th. 'native seat of angels ! and alone in thee the souls of the just ever rest '; Gr. 'der Engel Erbsitz und derer, die allein in dir immer selig ruhen '; Go. 'the native seat of angels and of the just, the souls of whom alone rest in thee ever '; Br. ' Native seat of angels, of the soothfast souls that for ever sit, they alone, at rest in thee.'

53. sāule sōðfæstra simle gerestað. Cf. *Bl. Hom.*, pp. 79, 81: 'Hē hīe gelædeþ on sibbe gesyhþe; forþon þære burge nama þe is nemned Gerūsalēm is gereht *sibbe gesyhþ*, forþon þe hālige sāula þær restaþ.'

54. wuldrum hrēmge. Brooke renders : 'In their splendors, singing joy' [!].

54b–58. Perhaps based on Eph. 5. 27: 'That he might present it to himself a glorious church, not having spot, or wrinkle, or any such thing; but that it should be holy and without blemish '; cf. Cant. 4. 7.

56. firina. Note the rare *-ina* for *-ena.*

57. tō wuldre. The translators render by 'gloriously'; the construction is peculiar, but this may be the sense.

58b. swā þū gehāten eart. Possibly referring to Ps. 87. 3.

59–61a. 'Leva in circuitu oculus tuos.' Th. 'See now thyself over this wide creation, as also heaven's height, widely look o'er, around each side '; Gr. 'Nimm du nun wahr, wie diese weite Schöpfung und das Dach des Himmels in

dir umher allenthalben schauen '; Go.[2] ' See now thyself how the wide creation
and heaven's roof surveyeth thee all about on every side '; Br. ' The wide creation and the roof of heaven look on it from every side.' Michelsen, in Hammerich : ' Hebe dein Auge : die weite Welt, das Gewölbe des Himmels, siehe, sie
achten rings auf dich.' Cf. Baruch 4. 36; 5. 5.

None of the translations agrees with the Antiphon. The interpretation, if it
is to conform in any sense to the Antiphon, must take *geond* with *þē*, as Grein
recommends (rendering κατά σε), and Frucht (p. 65) scans, and translate these
two words by ' about thee.' The real difficulty is in the verb *geondwlītan*, for
which one would like to substitute *geondwlīt*, parallel with *sioh*. Then, instead
of construing *gesceaft* as the subject of *geondwlītan*, it would be the object of
sioh, as *hrōf* would be the object of *geondwlīt* (cf. *Sat.* 9; *Beow.* 2771; *Ph.* 211 ;
Jul. 399). We should then have complete parallelism, for 61ᵃ would be the
equivalent of *þē geond*. According to the Antiphon, it is not the creation that
gazes ; nor is it easy to make sense out of the passage with *gesceaft* as subject
accusative. It would be possible, however, to regard it as the object of *geond*, in
which case *sylfa þē* would = ' thyself.' With reference to this construction, cf.
Gen. 1564, *him selfa ; An.* 1350, *þē sylfa ;* Wülfing, I. 355; Kellner, *Hist. Out-
lines of Engl. Syntax,* pp. 184-5 ; Mätzner I. 318. Wülfing quotes, *e.g.* from
Boeth. 266. 16 : ' þū miht ðē self ongitan þæt,' etc. ; *Oros.* 164. 3 : ' Romane him
self þyllic writon.' Dr. F. H. Chase makes *geond* adv. = ' round about.'

Professor Bright would construe *sioh* ... *geondwlītan* as formed upon the analogy
of expressions like *gā gesittan, cum nēosian,* etc. (cf. Wülfing 2. 193-4), where a
verb of *motion* is more specifically defined by a following verb in the inf. He
would then translate : ' Lift up thine eyes (*sioh*) to look widely (*rūme geondwlītan*)
over the broad creation,' etc. This conjecture seems to me quite too venture-
some, as the construction is otherwise found only with *gān* (*gangan*) and *cuman.*

59. sylfa. This form is elsewhere used as nsf. : *Gen.* 2648 (nsn.?) ; *Rid.* 82 ;
even as nsn. : *Sat.* 355.

sīdan gesceaft. Cf. 239, 356, 672, 1087 ; *Gen.* 675 ; *Men.* 227.

60. rodores hrōf. Cf. 518, 904.

63. nimeð eard in þē. Cf. Ps. 68. 16 ; 132. 13, 14.

65. tō frōfre. Cf. 722, 758, 1421, and Ælfric, *Hom.* 2. 14 : ' Ezechiel wītegode
be ðære byrig Hierūsalēm and be Crīste, ðus cweðende, " þīn Cyning cymð tō
ðē ēadmōd, and geedstaðelað þē." '

66. cymen. See *Gram.* 378.

67. The following passages from Ælfric's *Homilies* will illustrate Cynewulf's
probable meaning :

Hom. I. 522 : ' Hit is þus āwriten on þære ealdan ǣ : " Lufa ðīnne frēond, and
hata ðīnne fēond." þus wæs ālȳfed þām ealdum mannum þæt hī mōston Godes
wiðerwinnan and heora āgene fȳnd mid stranglicere mihte ofsittan, and mid
wǣpne ācwellan. Ac se ylca God þe þās lēafe sealde þurh Moyses gesetnysse ǣr
his tōcyme, se ylca eft, ða-ða hē þurh menniscnysse tō middangearde cōm, āwende
ðone cwyde, þus cweðende : " Ic bebeode ēow, Lufiað ēowre fȳnd," ' etc.

Hom. I. 186: ' Wē ne magon nū ealle þā fīf bēc āreccan, ac wē secgað ēow
þæt God sylf hī dihte, and Moyses hī āwrāt, tō stēore and tō lāre ðām ealdan
folce Israhel, and ēac ūs on gāstlicum andgite. þā bēc wǣron āwritene be

Crīste, ac þæt gāstlice andgit wæs þām folce dīgle, ōð þæt Crīst sylf cōm tō mannum, and geopenede þæra bōca dīgelnysse æfter gāstlicum andgite.'

Hom. 2. 56: 'Et ðām giftum āscortode wīn, forðan ðe sēo ealde gecȳðnys
āteorode on Crīstes andwerdnysse fram flæsclicum weorcum, and wearð āwend
tō gāstlicum ðēawum. Swā micclum swā wīn is dēorwurðre þonne wæter, swā
micclum is Crīstes lār, þe hē þurh his andwerdnysse his apostolum tæhte, dēorwurðre ðonne wǣre sēo ealde gesetnys ðe hē þurh Moysen gedihte; forðan ðe
Moyses ǣ wæs flæsclic, and Crīstes gesetnys is gāstlic. Sēo ealde ǣ wæs swilce
scadu and getācnung; Crīstes bodung is sōðfæstnys, and gefylð gāstlice swā
hwæt swā sēo ealde gecȳðnys mid mislicum gesetnyssum getācnode.'

    68. benda onlȳseð. 'Veniet solvere te a vinculis.'

    69. niþum genēðde, nearoþearfe conn. Th. tr. the first two words as
'hostilely subdued,' leaving the others untranslated; Gr. '(Fesselbande) geknüpft
für die Menschen ; er kennt die Nöte '; Go. 'He hath adventured him for men;
He knoweth their (Go.[2] dire) need.' In the *Spr.*, s. v. *nīð*, Gr. hesitates between
nið and *nīð*, *genēðde* and *genēdde*, though he had already admitted the last form
under *genēdan*, 'force,' 'compel.' Hertel (p. 47) reads *nīðum genēdde*, and
renders *genēdan* by 'binden,' 'bezwingen.' Professor Bright would read *niþum
genēdde*, and render, *imposed by sin* (*iniquities*). Cosijn calls *genēðde* nonsense,
and would read *genēdde*.

    Genēdan cannot = 'geknüpft,' were we to make the change of a letter; but
neither can *niþum genēðde* mean 'adventured (him) for men,' if analogy is to be
considered, since *genēðan* with the inst. means 'risk (life),' *An.* 1353, *Beow.* 1469,
2133, and an intransitive *genēðan* with dat. of interest is unknown. In sheer
desperation, one is tempted to read *niþum genēhwað* (*genēawað*), basing the
emendation upon the use of this Northumbrian verb in Lind. Mt. 19. 5; Lk. 15.
15; 16. 13; and especially Mt. 10. 7. The verb means 'cleave,' 'hold to,' 'join
oneself,' 'draw nigh,' Lat. *adhaerere, appropinquare*. This would suit the metre
as well ; it does not interrupt the sequence of present tenses by a verb in the
preterit ; the verb continues the general sense of *cymen* and *bringeð*, and provides
a motive for *nearoþearfe conn* — he draws nigh to men, because he knows their
need, how they have been looking for sympathy and succor.

    nearoþearfe conn. Cf. *Beow.* 422, *nearoþearfe drēah;* *El.* 1261 (in the
Rune passage), *nearusorge drēah.*

    70. se earma. In a generalized sense. Cf. Matt. 15. 14: 'If the blind lead
the blind, both shall fall into the ditch '; in OE. (*Cura Past.* 28. 8), 'Gif se blinda
ðone blindan lædeð, hī feallað bēgen on ænne pytt.' See Wülfing 1. 291–2.

    sceal. Must needs.

    71–103. Based upon the Antiphon of the Magnificat for December 24 :

'O VIRGO VIRGINUM, QUOMODO FIET ISTUD? QUIA NEC PRIMAM SIMILEM VISA
    ES, NEC HABERE SEQUENTEM.' — 'FILIAE HIERUSALEM, QUID ME ADMIRA-
    MINI? DIVINUM EST MYSTERIUM HOC QUOD CERNITIS.'

    This Antiphon is not so directly based upon Scripture as the preceding, but at
least two phrases are Biblical. Lk. 1. 34: '. . . *Quomodo fiet istud ?* . . .' Cant. 1.
5, etc. : '. . . *Filiae Jerusalem.* . . .' The Antiphon is found in the *Liber Responsalis,*

or *Antiphonarius*, attributed to Gregory the Great (Migne 78. 733), and is the only one there found besides the seven Greater Antiphons, if we except the one immediately following it, which runs : ' Orietur sicut sol Salvator mundi, et descendet in utero Virginis sicut imber super gramen. Alleluia.' Tommasi (*Opera* 4. 28) is not willing to allow the last to be an Antiphon, but rather a ' Declinatory.' On the propriety of ascribing to Gregory this *Antiphonary*, see Bäumer, *Geschichte des Breviers*, pp. 203 ff. Amalarius knows our Antiphon (Migne 105. 1269), and thus comments on it : ' Haec antiphona monstrat illum hominem qui ex Maria carnem assumpsit solum et perfectum esse inter caeteros homines, quia in ipso solo habitat septiformis Spiritus, qui superius memoratus est. De qua re scribit sanctus Augustinus in libro primo de sermone Domini in monte. Septum sunt ergo quae perficiunt, nam octava clarificat et quod perfectum est demonstrat.' With Amalarius, this Antiphon is the eighth and last. It is likewise contained in the Vatican *Antiphonary* (Tommasi 4. 28). Martène (*De Antiquis Ecclesiae Ritibus*, lib. iv, cap. 10) says of it: ' Octavam ... addit ordinarium Cabilonense.'

As bearing upon the connection between Parts I and II, with special reference to vv. 660 ff., I quote the following from Amalarius on the correspondence between the seven Greater Antiphons and the sevenfold gift of the Holy Spirit (cf. Honorius of Autun, *supra*, p. 72): ' Et disponis illis omnia dona Spiritus sancti in uno eodemque spiritu suaviter. Quoniam praesentes antiphonae dulcedine sua decorant septem ferias vel octo in quibus recolitur septiformis Spiritus, qui in Christo homine semper habitavit ex quo coepit homo esse, et *Verbum caro factus est* ut habitaret in nobis, fas est ut demonstrem, in quantum possum, quam consonantem habeant singulae cum singulis gradibus Spiritus sancti. Licet alter ordo scriptus inveniatur praesentium antiphonarum in Romano Antiphonario et in Metensi.' Amalarius then proceeds to show the correspondence in detail. His order is: (1) *O sapientia*, (2) *O clavis*, (3) *O Emmanuel*, (4) *O radix*, (5) *O oriens*, (6) *O Adonai*, (7) *O rex*, (8) *O Virgo;* that is, if the order given above (p. 71), which is that of the Roman Breviary and of the Sarum Use, be represented by the letters A, B, C, D, E, F, G, that in Amalarius will be A, D, G, C, E, B, F ; the 8th, which would correspond to H, occupies the same place in the St. Gallen MS., Amalarius, and the Sarum Use. It is perhaps worth noting here that Ælfric was acquainted with Amalarius (see his *Hom. z.* 84, and Förster, in *Anglia* 16. 48).

According to Gregory (*Hom. in Ezech.* 2. 7), the ascending order of these gifts is here reversed (Migne 76. 1016) : ' Quos gradus, de caelestibus loquens, descendendo magis quam ascendendo numeravit. ... Et cum scriptum est, *Initium sapientiae timor Domini* (Prov. 9. 10), constat procul dubio quia a timore ad sapientiam ascenditur. ... Propheta ergo, quia de caelestibus ad ima loquebatur, coepit magis a sapientia, et descendit ad timorem.'

Wülker, speaking of dramatic dialogue in OE. poetry, says (*Grundriss*, p. 385) : ' Aus dem *Crist* führt man gewöhnlich VI an, das Gespräch zwischen Maria und Joseph, doch ist dies nicht die einzige Stelle dieser Art.

' *Crist* III, v. 71–87ª, ist den Bewohnern von Jerusalem in den Mund zu legen Dies beweist v. 87ᵇ, 88, und ferner v. 91.'

Thorpe and Grein had already shown, by their use of quotation marks, that they fully appreciated this fact.

71. wīfa wynn. So Mary is called in *Hymn* 3[26], *ealra fǣmnena wyn* : cf. a similar use of *æðelinga wyn*, *An.* 1225; *Guth.* 1081; *Jul.* 730; *Harr. of Hell* 121; other phrases of the sort are common in the poetry. The expression comes from the Latin (and no doubt originally from the Greek) hymns. Thus *gaudium sanctorum angelorum*, Mone 2. 514. 11 (cf. *ib.* 21); *angelorum gaudium*, Dreves IX. 57. 1. b; V. p. 342; *mundi gaudium*, Mone 2. 328. 1; 369. 1; *coeli gaudium*, Mone 2. 398. 2; 400. 5; Dreves VI. 25. 33; *laetitia beatorum*, Mone 2. 527. 11; *laetitia angelorum*, Dreves VIII. 91. z. a ; *sanctorum laetitia*, Mone 2. 511. 7; Dreves II. Anh. b. 6. 1 ; *sanctorum angelorum exsultatis*, Dreves I. 1. 3; etc. So in MHG.: *aller engel wunne*, *Ausw. Geistl. Dicht.* VII. 13; see the examples in Salzer, pp. 419 ff.

wuldres þrym. Not as in 83, 740; here probably = *heavenly glory, heaven.* In other words, the line is an address to Mary in heaven, 'in aula caelica,' 'super caelos sublimata,' 'ob immensem fulgorem atque splendorem inaccessa' (Salzer, pp. 421, 422). Brooke's 'In the *glorious glory*, hail !' is not very felicitous either as poetry or as translation. Cf. *Gu.* 1338.

73. þæs þe. As far as. — **sundbūend.** Cf. *Met.* 8[18], 24[21], 26[48]. Brooke translates by 'ocean-rovers.' Cosijn compares 616, 1172, 1371, and thinks the form was coined to vary the uniformity of *eorð-*, *fold-*, *grund-*, *landbūend*, and to provide an alliterative word. He rejects Grein's rendering, *maris accolae*, and says it has nothing to do with Netherl. *de zee bouwen.*

74. gerȳne. Cf. 41, 95.

76. gebyrde. Cf. 38.

77. mot. I reproduce part of a note in the *Journal of Germanic Philology* 1. 247–8 : ' *Gebedscipe* is of course the object of *cūðes*, and *monwīsan* of the preposition *æfter*. Hence, if the manuscript reading is retained, *mōd* is apparently in apposition with *gebedscipe*. But this makes no sense. Thorpe proposed to read *mōde*, 'in mind'; but this is far from convincing. Grein suggested *mōt*, in the sense of 'Begegnung,' 'Zusammensein,' appositional with *gebedscipe ;* but there is no such OE. word, and the two meanings would not be synonymous, if there were. Gollancz interprets *mōd*, in a note, as 'desire,' but leaves it untranslated in his version. Wülker (*Bibliothek* 3. 4) reads *mot*, but without an explanation.

I would suggest *mot*, in the sense of 'mote,' 'atom,' and make *mot ne cūðes* parallel to the *wiht ne cūþe* of 419[b]; the *wiht ne lōgon* of *Beow.* 862[b]; *him wiht ne spēow Beow.* 2854[b]; *nō hē wiht fram mē, Beow.* 541[b]; cf. *Beow.* 1083, 2857. Or it might be taken in the dat. inst. as *mote ;* cf. *Christ* 1048, and *Beow.* 186, 1514.

Mot was known in both North. and WS. as a translation of the Biblical *festuca*, and was employed in ME. in the sense which I would attribute to it here, as strengthening a negation. The ME. examples, collected by Hein (*Anglia* 15· 101), are from (1) *Gawayne and the Green Knight*, v. 2209 ; (2) *Patience*, vv. 455– 6 ; (3) Chaucer, *Tr. and Cr.* 3· 1603; to which he adds (4) Occleve, *De Regimine Principum*, str. 135. These are :

(1) Hit helppes me not a mote.

(2)   þaȝ no schafte myȝt

        þe mount[n]aunce of a lyttel mote,

        vpon þat man schyne.

(3) It mighte nought a mote in that suffyse.

(4) Not wold I rekke as muche as a mote.'

78–82ᵃ. ' Nec primam similem visa es, nec habere sequentem.'

80. swylce. Referring to *ēacnunge.* — **befēnge.** Apparently identical with *onfēnge*, 75.

81. wēnan. Cf. 1610.

82. tōweard. Cf. 137.

83. wuldres Þrym. So 740; cf. 204, 423. This sense of *þrym*, almost = *Lord*, is found only in *Elene, Juliana, Guthlac*, and *Phoenix*, besides *Hymn* 7⁴⁵. As bearing on the unity of authorship, note the identical phrase here and in 740.

84. bōsme. A euphemism. So *Harr. of Hell* 110; *Hy.* 10¹⁹. Cf. *Bl. Hom.*, pp. 5, 105, 165.

86. Cf. Gal. 6. 7 (8) : ' Quae enim seminaverit homo, hoc et metet.'

87. cennaȜ tō cwealme. Cf. Rom. 7. 5. — **mǣg.** Frucht (p. 30) would delete.

89. ' Quid me admiramini ? '

wǣfiaȜ. Elsewhere occurs as tr. of Lat. *obstupescere*, as *wǣfung* of *stupor*. Not ' stare,' as Brooke renders.

90. gehþum mǣnaȜ. *Mǣnan* is combined with the inst. sing. of *gehȜu* in *Jul.* 391, *An.* 1550, 1667, *Beow.* 2267.

The line seems inappropriate to the context.

91. sunu. Evidently an addition. — **Sōlimæ.** Greek occasionally has Σόλυμα (Pausanias, Josephus, etc.) and Latin *Solyma* (Martial, etc.) as a variant of Jerusalem. Cf. Pope's ' Ye nymphs of Solyma, begin the song.'

93. mund. Dietrich (*Haupt's Zs.* 7. 184–5) not only recognizes an ON. *mundr*, ' sum paid for a bride,' and a *mund*, ' hand,' but also an old neut. *mund*, especially in the derivatives *mundang*, found only in compounds and in the adjective and adverbs derived from it. This *mundang* means ' moderation '; thus *mundangsmaȜr*, ' just, moderate man '; *mundangleikr*, ' moderation '; *mundanga*, ' in due measure.' To this neut. *mund* Dietrich attributes the sense ' moderation,' ' temperance,' ' modesty ' (Germ. ' masshaltigkeit,' ' mässigung,' ' bescheidenheit '), and finds it reflected in the Lapp word *muddo*, ' temperantia,' ' modus,' which he considers as an early borrowing from the Norse. Thus allied, our word would here have a meaning like ' continence,' and hence ' chastity,' a sense which admirably harmonizes with *fǣmnanhād* and with the general context. Gollancz's etymology in his note must accordingly be rejected.

94ᵃ. The adjective must agree with *Suna*, which is genitive ; that *mǣre* should be fem. seems to be precluded by 210 and 589, as well as by its own position.

95. gerȳne. ' Divinum est *mysterium* hoc quod cernitis.' The sense is ' a hidden or secret thing, not obvious to the understanding '; cf. 1 Cor. 13. 2.

96. Dāuīdes. Cf. *Dāuīdes dohtor*, 191. Edersheim has (*Jesus the Messiah* I. 149): ' There can be no question that both Joseph and Mary were of the royal lineage of David. Most probably the two were nearly related.' In a footnote he adds: 'The Davidic descent of the Virgin-Mother — which is questioned by some even among orthodox interpreters — seems implied in the Gospel (St. Luke I. 27, 32, 69; 2. 4), and an almost *necessary* inference from such passages as Rom. I. 3; 2 Tim. 2. 8; Hebr. 7. 14.' So he says: 'This' — the theory that Joseph and Mary were nearly related — 'is the general view of antiquity.' Concerning the assumption that the genealogies given by Matthew and Luke are those of both Joseph and Mary, he says : ' The best defense of this view is that by Wieseler, *Beitr. zur Würdig. d. Evang.*, pp. 133, etc. It is also virtually adopted by Weiss (*Leben Jesu*, vol. i. 1882).'

Joseph's descent from David is noted in 165.

97. **þæt.** Perhaps the preceding line should logically be introduced between þæt and **is. — forpynded.** Cosijn refers to *PBB.* 11. 351, and *Bl. Hom.* 7. 14.

Euan. Mary is thought of as the second Eve, and undoing the evil wrought by the first Eve, as early as Justin (A.D. 120–165). See the numerous quotations in Livius, pp. 35–59, 67–74, and *passim*. Also *Bl. Hom.*, p. 3; Ælfric, *Hom.* 1. 194; 2. 22.

98. **wærgðo.** The nom. is required, and *o* or *u* is the ending in this poem; cf. 57, 1271.

gewuldrad. Cf. Proclus (A.D. 434–46), as quoted in Livius, pp. 73–4: 'Through Mary all women are blessed. For no longer is the female sex cursed and under execration; since it has achieved whereby it can surpass in glory even the angels. Now Eve is cured, the Egyptian woman (Agar) reduced to silence, Dalila entombed, Jezebel whelmed in everlasting oblivion, Herodias, too, is lost to memory; and now the roll of women is held in admiration.'

99. **se hēanra hād.** Grein interprets (*Spr.*) *sexus humilior.* Cf. 1 Pet. 3. 7: '. . . quasi *infirmiori vasculo* impartientes honorem.'

100. **blētsung.** Since we find *blētsung* twice associated with *bliss*, as though they were synonymous (*Gen.* 1761, 2331), we may, in the light of 102–3, perhaps here think of Ps. 16. 11: 'Adimplebis me laetitia cum vultu tuo; delectationes in dextera tua usque in fidem.' *Blētsung* would then mean ' joy,' ' happiness,' in this instance.

101. **werum ond wīfum.** Cf. Augustine, *Sermo* 51. 2, 3, quoted in Livius, pp. 237–8 : 'What he showed us is this, that human creatures were not to despair of themselves in any sex, seeing that both males and females belong to a human sex. If then, being a man, as He must needs have been, He were not to be born of a woman, women might despair of themselves, recollecting that the first sin was theirs, because the first man was deceived by a woman, and would fancy that they had no hope in Christ, themselves whatever. He came then a man, to choose first the male sex ; and being born of a woman, to console the female sex.'

Brooke paraphrases inadequately: 'Hope is won that men may dwell with the Father of truth for ever.'

102. **engla drēame.** See, in Part III, 1342, 1520.

103. **Sōðfæder.** Hardly 'true king' (Gr., *D.* 'mit dem wahren Vater '); cf. *Sōðcyning*, 1228 ; on the other hand, cf. 110.

104–129. Based upon the Antiphon of the Magnificat for December 21 :

O ORIENS, SPLENDOR LUCIS AETERNAE, ET SOL JUSTITIAE: VENI, ET ILLUMINA SEDENTES IN TENEBRIS ET UMBRA MORTIS.

Not 'oriens splendor,' but, as punctuated above, 'oriens, splendor'; the former use is unexampled in the Vulgate, whereas the latter manifestly reposes upon
Lk. 1. 78 : 'in quibus visitavit nos *oriens* ex alto.' With this are to be con-
joined, as sources of the Antiphon, Heb. 1. 3 : 'Qui cum sit *splendor gloriae*, et
figura substantiae ejus'; Wisd. 7. 26 : 'Candor est enim *lucis aeternae*, et speculum
sine macula Dei majestatis, et imago bonitatis illius'; Mal. 4. 2 : 'Et *orietur* vobis
timentibus nomen meum *sol justitiae*'; Lk. 1. 79 : '*illuminare his qui in tenebris
et in umbra mortis sedent.*' The latter reposes in turn upon Ps. 107. 10 : '*sedentes
in tenebris et umbra mortis*, vinctos in mendicitate et ferro'; Isa. 42. 6, 7 : '
in lucem gentium, ut aperires oculos caecorum, et educeres de conclusione vinctum, de domo carceris *sedentes in tenebris*'; Isa. 9. 2 : 'Populus, qui ambulabat in
tenebris vidit lucem magnam; habitantibus in regione *umbrae mortis*, lux orta
est eis.'

104. **ēarendel.** The first impulse is to translate the word by 'dawn,' partly
because, in the form *eorendel*, it glosses *Aurora* in the two hymns 'Splendor
paternae gloriae' and 'Aurora jam spargit polum' (*Latin Hymns of the Anglo-
Saxon Church*, called, for brevity, *Surtees Hymns*, from their publication by the
Surtees Society), 16. 18 ; 30. 1. This view might be supported by the general tenor
of the former of these hymns, of which the first and the last stanza are:

> Splendor paternae gloriae,
> De luce lucem proferens,
> Lux lucis et fons luminis,
> Dies dierum inluminans.
>
> .   .   .   .
>
> Aurora cursus provehit,
> Aurora totā prodeat
> In Patre totus Filius,
> Et totus in Verbo Pater.

Finally, one might argue in favor of 'dawn' from the 'dayspring' of Lk. 1. 78,
a word which, first used in this place by Tyndale, has been retained even in the
R. V. The sense of 'dayspring' is sufficiently ascertained by the quotation in
NED. from Eden (1555), *Decades* 264 : 'The day sprynge or dawnynge of the daye
gyueth a certeyne lyght before the rysinge of the soonne.'

Again, one might advocate the rendering 'morning star,' or 'day star,' referring
to 2 Pet. 1. 19, and making use of Gregory the Great's interpretation in his *Moralia*,
in the comment on Job 38. 32 (Migne, *Patr. Lat.* 76. 520) : 'Pater quippe in tempore suo *luciferum* produxit, quia, sicut scriptum est : *Cum venit plenitudo tem-
poris, misit Deus Filium suum, natum ex muliere, factum sub lege, ut eos qui sub
lege erant, redimeret* (Gal. 4. 4). Qui natus ex Virgine, velut *lucifer* inter tenebras
nostrae noctis apparuit, quia fugata obscuritate peccati, aeternum nobis mane nun-
tiavit, *Luciferum* vero se innotuit, quia diluculo ex morte surrexit, et fulgore sui
luminis mortalitatis nostrae terram caliginem pressit. Cui bene per Joannem
dicitur : *Stella splendida et matutina* (*Apoc.* 22. 16). Vivus quippe apparens post
mortem, *matutina* nobis *stella* factus est, quia dum in semetipso exemplum nobis
resurrectionis praebuit, quae lux sequatur indicavit.' With this, too, may be compared Gregory's words at the opening of the *Moralia* (Migne 75. 524) : '. . .

quousque verus *lucifer* surgeret, qui aeternum nobis mane nuntians, stellis caeteris clarius ex divinitate radiaret.' Of this mind is Brooke, p. 394: 'Cynewulf used it to signify Christ, and as he is here speaking of Jesus as descended from David, I have no doubt he was thinking of the text in Rev. xxii, where Jesus says " I am the root and the offspring of David, and the bright and morning star." ' Something like this may have been in Wanley's mind, when he wrote ' Earendelis Angeli (sive Luciferi),' *supra*, p. 67, though it is difficult to see just what his conception was.

As against these interpretations, it must be noted that in the *Blickling Homilies*, p. 163, we have: 'se nīwa ēorendel Sanctus Iōhānnes ; and nū nū se lēoma þǣre sō, an sunnan, God selfa, cuman wille,' according to which John the Baptist was the dawn or the day star preceding Jesus Christ, conceived of as the sun. This is the evident meaning, though the passage seems corrupt. Again, if we regard *earendel* in our text as the translation of ' oriens ' in the Antiphon, then it is important to ascertain the sense in which ' oriens ' is to be taken, or rather the noun, ἀνατολή, of which it is a translation. On this cf. the latest authoritative commentator, Plummer (*St. Luke*, p. 43) : ἀνατολὴ ἐξ ὕψους. " Rising from on high." The word is used of the rising of the *sun* (Rev. 7. 2; 16. 12 ; Hom. *Od.* xii. 4) and of *stars* (Æsch. *P. V.* 457 ; Eur. *Phœn.* 504). Here the rising of the heavenly body is put for the heavenly body itself. Comp. the use of ἀνατέλλω in Is. 60. 1 and Mal. 4. 2.' If the rising of the heavenly body is put for the heavenly body itself, then the heavenly body is here apparently to be interpreted as ' the sun.' But what evidence is there that Cynewulf so understood it ? First, that the Antiphon seems to equate the three expressions, ' oriens,' ' splendor lucis aeternae,' and ' sol justitiae,' and that the dawn or the day star would hardly be invoked to ' come and enlighten those who sit in darkness and in the shadow of death.' Secondly, that Cynewulf calls the *earendel* the ' sōðfæsta sunnan lēoma.' And thirdly, that, after addressing the *earendel*, he goes on to say, ' Thou, of thy very self, dost constantly enlighten every season.' This would be said of the sun, used figuratively, but hardly of the dawn or the day star. Considering, then, that if *earendel* meant ' dawn ' or ' day star ' it would be at least as admissible to understand John the Baptist ; that the ' oriens ' of Lk. 1. 78 connotes the sun ; and that both the Antiphon and Cynewulf immediately go on to name the sun, and attribute to it supreme illuminative power, it would seem that neither ' dayspring ' nor ' day star,' though both most poetical expressions, denotes the full radiance that is suggested.

Since Bede would have been good authority for Cynewulf, we may compare his note on Lk. 1. 78 (*Comm. in Lucam*): ' Et propheta de Domino loquens, *Ecce vir*, inquit, *Oriens nomen ejus* [Zech. 6. 12]. Qui ideo recte Oriens vocatur qui nobis ortum verae lucis aperiens, filios noctis et tenebrarum lucis effecit filios.'

Amalarius (Migne 105. 1268) thus comments on the Antiphon : ' Quinta nempe miratur inauditum orientem, qui non more vicissitudinem temporum mutatur de die in diem, sed est aeternus ; cujus sol non solum corporis oculos illuminat, sed etiam mentis. Justitia enim ad aspectum mentis pertinet.'

Gollancz's note on this word is as follows :

' *earendel*, it is difficult to translate the word adequately ; some bright star is evidently meant, probably the same as *Örwandels-tá*, "Orwendel's toe," mentioned in the Edda. Thor carried Orwendel from Jotunheim in a basket on his back; Orwendel's toe stuck out of the basket, and got frozen; Thor broke it off, and flung it at the sky, and made a star of it, which is called *Örvandels-tá* (*v.* Grimm's *Deutsche Myth.*). That the story of Orwendel was Christianized in mediæval times is attested by the German story of *Orendel* in the *Heldenbuch*, where the hero wins "the seamless coat" of his master. "Earendel" does not occur elsewhere in A. S. poetry as a poetical designation of Christ; the word is interpreted in the Epinal glossary by "jubar."

'The spelling in the Erfurt Gloss "oerendil" is noteworthy. It seems probable that "Earendel" = "Orion," the constellation brightest at winter-time, and "Örvandels-tá" = "Rigel," the chief star of the constellation.

'Cp. the opening lines of *Paradise Lost*, Book iii. : —

> Hail, holy light, offspring of Heaven first-born !
> Or of the Eternal co-eternal beam, etc.

'Cf. John I. 4, 9.'

engla beorhtast. So in *Satan* 586, Christ is called 'hálig encgel.' For the Biblical identification of God or Christ with an angel, compare Gen. 22. 11 with v. 12; Ex. 3. 2 with v. 6; Acts 23. 11 with 27. 23. Christ here surpasses the (other) angels in brightness as the sun surpasses the stars. One might think of 'engla beorhtast' as having been suggested by such a phrase as 'decus angelorum,' in the opening line of a hymn attributed to Rabanus Maurus (*Surtees Hymns*, p. 116): 'Christe sanctorum decus angelorum'; the phrase is there glossed as 'wlite ængla.'

106. **sóðfæsta sunnan leoma.** Cf. *sol justitiae.* See 696, and *Ph.* 587. Ælfric has (*Hom.* I. 36): 'Críst is se sóða dæg, se ðe tódræfde mid his tócyme ealle nytennysse þære ealdan nihte, and ealne middangeard mid his gife onlíhte.'

107. **torht ofer tunglas.** Cf. 235, 968. *Tungol* as masc. is extremely irregular; cf. 933. Perhaps we should assume that this form is LWS., and restore *tungol*.

gehwane. LWS. for *-hwone* (*Gram.*[3] 341, N. 2); Sievers no longer explains it by analogy with the dat. *-hwám*.

108. **sylfum þé.** The position of the pronoun is unusual (but cf. *Gen.* 2713). Is this for emphasis — 'thy very self' — or for metrical reasons?

inlíhtes. The ending earlier than *-est* (*Gram.* 356; cf. 202. 6).

109. **God of Gode.** This can only come from the Nicene Creed, which reads: 'Et in unum dominum Jesum Christum, Filium Dei unigenitum, et ex Patre natum ante omnia saecula, *Deum de Deo*, Lumen de Lumine, Deum verum de Deo vero, genitum non factum, consubtantialem Patri, per quem omnia facta sunt. Qui propter nos homines et propter nostram salutem descendit de caelis, et incarnatus est de Spiritu Sancto ex Maria virgine, et homo factus est.' See Blunt, *Annotated Book of Common Prayer*, p. 375, and Ælfric, *Hom.* 1. 198, 258, 494; 2. 596.

gearo. The context seems rather to require *géara*; cf. *Ps.* 74 (73). 12 : 'géara þú worhtest, ær woruld wære, wíse hælu.'

110. **sóþan Fæder.** Apparently from *Deo vero* of the Creed; see above.

swegles . . . wuldre. So *Jud.* 345.

111. See the Creed. The Athanasian Creed has 'increatus Filius.'

112. **for þearfum.** Cf. 22.

þīn āgen geweorc. Cf. 266, 1414. So, in the *Genesis*, Eve is God's work (822), and both Adam and Eve his handiwork (241, 494, 628, 703).

113. **þurh.** Cf. 92, 359, 1442. — **byldo.** Not 'Mühseligkeit,' as Grein conjectures s. v.; nor 'Dran[g]salen' (*Dichtungen*); nor even Thorpe's 'constancy.' It no doubt corresponds to the παρρησία, *fiducia*, i.e. 'free and fearless confidence,' 'cheerful courage,' of ? Cor. 7. 4; Eph. 3. 12; Phil. 1. 20, etc.; cf. especially Heb. 4. 16.

114. **sunnan.** For the association of Christmas with the winter solstice (the *Menologium* has 'on midne winter'; see Ælfric, *Hom.* 1. 200, 346), cf. *Dict. Christ. Antiqq.* 1. 357–8.

þē sylf. For the dat. (acc.?) with the nom. *sylf*, cf. 59.

115. **inlēohte.** But *inlīht-*, 43, 108. Within Part I is a *lēohtian*, 234. Cf. *-lȳht-*, 204 (I); *lȳht-*, 938 (III).

116. **þēostrum.** Cf. (III) 1247, 1385.

117. **sinneahtes.** Cf. *sinnehte* (sb.), 1542, 1631; Rössger calls this (p. 34) a local genitive. — **synnum bifealdne.** So *synnum gesǣled*, 736. Cf. Ælfric, *Hom.* 1. 208: ' Eal mancyn wæs mid synnum bebunden, swā-swā se wītega cwæð: "Ānra gehwilc manna is gewriðen mid rāpum his synna" [Prov. 5. 22]'; cf. pp. 212, 234, 332.

118. **deorc dēaþes sceadu.** This, like *þrosmc* and *þēostrum,* must no doubt be interpreted figuratively, as referring to the spiritual condition of those who cry; 117[b] would seem to indicate this.

120-1. Gregory quotes Jn. 1. 1, 2 (*Hom. in Evang.* 25. 6: Migne 76. 1193): ' Joannes quoque Redemptorem nostrum manu fidei tetigit, qui ait: *In principio erat Verbum, et Verbum erat apud Deum, et Deus erat Verbum. Hoc erat in principio apud Deum.* . . . Tangit ergo Dominum, qui eum Patri aeternitate substantiae aequalem credit.'

120. **brungen.** Modifies hǣlo, not, as with Th., word.

121-2. **Fæder ælmihtgum efenēce.** Cf. Gregory, *Ib.*: 'Ille ergo Jesum veraciter tangit, qui Patri Filium coaeternum credit.' Cf. (in Part II) 465: ' efenēce Bearn āgnum Fæder'; see also 216 ff.

So Ælfric, *Hom.* 1. 278: . 'Hwæt is se Fæder? Ælmihtig Scyppend, nā geworht nē ācenned, ac hē sylf gestrȳnde Bearn *him sylfum efenēce.* Hwæt is se Sunu? Hē is ðæs Fæder Wīsdōm, and his Word, and his Miht, þurh ðone se Fæder gescēop ealle ðing and gefadode. Nis se Sunu nā geworht nē gesceapen, ac hē is ācenned. Ācenned hē is, and þēah-hwæþere *hē is efeneald and efenēce his Fæder.*' Cf. 1. 198.

Cf. A. V. G. Allen, *Christian Institutions,* pp. 307–8: 'The teaching of Arius, as preserved by Athanasius in quotations from the writings of Arius, known as the *Thalia,* is as follows: "God was not always a Father; once God was alone and not yet a Father, but afterwards He became a Father. The Son was not always; He was made out of nothing; once He was not; He was not before His origination; He had an origin of creation. For God was alone, and the Word as yet was not, nor the Wisdom. Then wishing to form us, thereupon He made a certain one, and named Him Word and Wisdom and Son, that He might form us by means of Him. The Word is not the very God; though He is called

God, yet He is not very God; by participation of grace, He, as others, is God only in name. The Word is alien and unlike in all things to the Father's essence and propriety. Even to the Son the Father is invisible; the Word cannot perfectly either see or know His own Father. He knows not His own essence; the essences of the Father and the Son and the Holy Ghost are separate in nature and estranged and disconnected and alien and without participation of each other; utterly unlike from each other in essence and glory unto infinity" (*Orat.* I., c. 2).' Cf. Ælfric, *Hom.* 1. 290.

Allen remarks, pp. 307–9: 'The doctrine of the Trinity, or of the coequality of the Son with the Father, was incompatible with the spirit of empire resting on force for its sanction; it promoted individual liberty and national freedom, but it meant the ultimate destruction of an imperial despotism. The Arian conception of Deity was identical with the thought of God upon which imperialism rests for its sanction. The God whom Arius proclaimed was not the constitutional sovereign of the universe, whose will was in harmony with truth, and goodness, and justice, as men could read those qualities in human experience, but was rather the arbitrary absolute will, unconditioned and without relationship, incomprehensible to man; a will which no insight could penetrate, which called for absolute unhesitating submission. . . .

'The writings of Athanasius and of the Greek Fathers who carried on his work bear witness in a striking way to the significance of the doctrine of the coequality of the Son with the Father, which had been set forth at Nicæa, as if therein were involved the principle of human freedom, in every form, whether national or individual, the eternal ground and sanction of the dignity of man. . . . Only at a moment of exalted enthusiasm, before the inevitable decline which overtakes all human movements, could words like those of Athanasius have been coined. . . . . "He has become man that He might deify us in Himself." . . . "He first sanctified Himself that He might sanctify us all. The Spirit as a precious ointment is poured forth from Him over all humanity."' On p. 314 he adds: 'The Arian formula stood to the barbarian peoples of the West for the rude conviction that Deity is primarily in its essence omnipotent power and absolute will; as the same formula had also stood in the Roman world for an act of submission to the imperial will of the Roman Emperor. The purpose of the barbarians to substitute another empire, based on the power of conquest, was defeated; and in the obscure history of the time it is evident that the watchword of freedom was the Nicene faith. . . . The dark scenes in which the Ostrogothic kingdom expired in Italy indicated that there was a fatal weakness at the sources of its power which no skill or wisdom or good intentions could overcome.'

121. **on frymðe.** 'In principio.'

122. **mid God.** 'Apud Deum.'

122–3. **ond nū eft gewearð flǣsc.** Jn 1. 14: 'Et verbum caro factum est.'

124. **gēomrum tō gēoce.** Cf. 414, 427, 632, 722, 1196, 1421. — **God wæs mid ūs.** Cf. 135ª, Mt. 1. 23, and my *Biblical Quotations*, p. 137.

125. **būtan synnum.** Cf. Heb. 4. 15: 'absque peccato.'

126. So Greg., *Moral.* 33. 16 (Migne 76. 693): 'Ita vero, ut unus idemque Dei atque hominis filius ipse sit qui inhabitat.'

127. on þēode. May this not possibly mean 'in association,' 'conjunction'? Cf. the senses of *ðēodan, ðīedan,* and of *geðēod* (Hall's second meaning) and its derivatives. See also 377.

128. secgan. So 209, (II) 601, 612; but *ðonc cunnan, witan (nytan),* 1091, 1212, 1385, 1473, 1497 (III).

Sigedryhtne. Cf. 520, 1060 ; 1530. — **bī gewyrhtum.** Cf. 1219, 1367.

130–163. Based upon the Antiphon of the Magnificat for December 23 :

O EMMANUEL, REX ET LEGIFER NOSTER, EXPECTATIO GENTIUM, ET SALVATOR
    EARUM : VENI AD SALVANDUM NOS, DOMINE DEUS NOSTER.

From Isa. 7. 14 ; 8. 8 ; Mt. 1. 23 : '*Emmanuel*'; Isa. 33. 22 : ' Dominus *legifer noster,* Dominus *rex noster* '; ipse salvabit nos ; Gen. 49. 10 : ' ipse erit *expectatio gentium ;* Isa. 37. 20 (?) : ' *Domine Deus noster.*'

Among the Antiphons for Lauds on Thursday of the third week in Advent is Isa. 33. 22, slightly changed (so in the Sarum Use): ' Dominus legifer noster, Dominus rex noster; ipse *veniet* et salvabit nos.'

130. gǣsta God. Cf. 198.

134. rūme. Cf. *Jul.* 314 for this sense. Th. renders the hemistich, ' by mysteries of runes,' adopting his own conjecture, *rūna.* Th. ends the sentence with *gerȳnum.*

rodera Weard. Cf. 222.

135. God sylfa mid ūs. Cf. Ælfric, *Hom. z.* 14.

gomele. The prophets.

136. ealra cyninga Cyning. 1 Tim. 6. 15; Rev. 17. 14; 19. 16. The *ealra* is inserted in Ælfric's version of 1 Tim. 6. 15 (see my *Bibl. Quot.* p. 251) ; cf. his *Hom.* 1. 198; 2. 14. So 215; *Jul.* 289; *Gu.* 16–17 (*Chr.* 1681–2) ; *An.* 980; *Hy.* 3²²; *Sat.* 205. On the idiom, see note on 580.

137. Sācerd. Ps. 110. 4 (Heb. 5. 6) : ' Tu es sacerdos in aeternum, secundum ordinem Melchisedech.' The Roman Breviary adapts this for one of the Responds after the Second Lesson on Thursday of the Third Week in Advent. Cf. Heb. 7. 1, 3 : ' Hic enim Melchisedech, rex Salem, sacerdos Dei summi, . . . assimilatus autem Filio Dei, manet sacerdos in perpetuum.'

138. Melchīsedech. Cf. Gen. 14. 18 (also OE.), and the OE. poetical *Gen.* 2100–2123. The two OE. versions agree in the application to him of the epithet *se mǣra.*

139. godþrym onwrāh. ' The relation between Melchizedek and Christ as type and antitype is made in the Ep. to the Hebrews to consist in the following particulars. Each was a priest, (1) not of the Levitical tribe ; (2) superior to Abraham; (3) whose beginning and end are unknown ; (4) who is not only a priest, but also a king of righteousness and peace ' (Smith's *Dict. of the Bible*).

140. ēces Alwāldan. Cf. *ēce Alwālda, Exod.* 11.

Sē. Christ. — **ǣ bringend.** ' Legifer.' The Spelman Psalter has *ǣlēdend* as a gloss on *legislator* (Ps. 9. 21). One would incline to write this as a compound, were it not for *lāra lǣdend.*

141. lāra lǣdend. For the gen. dependent on a participial noun, cf. *Apollonius of Tyre,* ed. Thorpe, p. 18 : *lāre lufigend.* Here *lār* must signify ' precept,' as equated with *ǣ.* Cf. *An.* 778.

142. hyhtan hidercyme. See note on 154, end. — **gehāten.** Cf. 315 ff.

144. gefǣlsian. Perhaps as in 320. — **foldan mǣgðe.** Cf. *eorðan mǣgðe*, (II) 523, (III) 946.

145. grundas. Cf. 265, 562, 1526, 1593. Here we pass to the motive drawn from the Harrowing of Hell; cf. 25 ff., (II) 558 ff., 730 ff., (III) 1159 ff. *Grund* sometimes denotes the bed of the sea, or its deepest part, as in 1164. Cf. Greg. *Moral.* 29. 12 (Migne 76. 489, 490), commenting on Job 38. 16: ' Profundum maris Dominus petiit, cum inferni novissima, electorum suorum animas erepturos, intravit. Unde et per prophetam dicitur : *Posuisti profundum maris viam, ut transirent liberati* (Isai. 51. 10). Hoc namque *profundum maris* ante Redemptoris adventum non via, sed *carcer fuit*, quia in se etiam bonorum animas, quamvis non in locis poenalibus, clausit. Quod tamen profundum viam Dominus posuit, quia illuc veniens, electos suos a claustris inferni ad caelestia transire concessit. . . . Deambulasse in inferno Dominus dicitur, ut electis animabus in locis singulis per divinitatis potentiam praesens fuisse monstraretur.'

Gǣstes mǣgne. Cf. 319; *Sat.* 550; Lk. 4. 14 (Corpus).

147. bidon in bendum. Cf. *Sat.* 49; *Harr. Hell* 61, 88. According to Gregory, only the righteous were rescued from hell by the descent of Christ; so *Hom. in Evang. ι.* 22 (Migne 76. 1177): ' Per hanc electi, qui quamvis in tranquillitatis sinu, tamen apud inferni claustra tenebantur, ad paradisi amoena reducti sunt. . . De electis suis apud inferos nullum reliquit. . . . Neque etenim infideles quosque, et pro suis criminibus aeternis suppliciis deditos, ad veniam Dominus resurgendo reparavit; sed illos ex inferni claustris rapuit, quos suos in fide et actibus recognovit. . . . Quia vero ex inferno partem abstulit, et partem reliquit, non occidit funditus, sed momordit infernum.' Thus likewise in *Epist. 7. indict.* 15. *ep.* 15 (Migne 77. 870): ' Descendens ad inferos Dominus illos solummodo ab inferni claustris eripuit quos viventes in carne per suam gratiam in fide et bona operatione servavit.' Cf. *Moral.* 12. 11 (Migne 75. 993–4), and Honorius of Autun, *Gemma Animae*, lib. iii, cap. 1 (Migne 172. 641–2): ' In hoc tempore, *Gloria in excelsis* et *Te Deum laudamus* non cantantur, quia justi ante Christi adventum in tristitia inferni tenebantur.'

150. hǣlolīf. See the other unique compounds with *hǣlo-*, 374, (II) 586, 754.

152-3. Is . . . ānum. Cf. 365; less close are *Hy.* 4[109]; *Beow.* 1376.

153. æfter. Cosijn prefers Sievers' *for*, parenthesizing 152[b]–153[a].

154. Hæftas hygegēomre. These two words are associated *Beow.* 2408. For the thought, cf. 360.

gesēce. In favor of Grein's conjecture, *gesōhtest*, is the following passage from the *Blickling Homilies* (p. 87): ' þā sōna instæpes sēo unārīmedlīce menigo hāligra sāula, þe ǣr gehæftnēde wǣron, tō þǣm Hǣlende onluton, and mid wēpendre hālsunga hine bǣdon, and þus cwǣdon : " þū *cōme* tō ūs, middangeardes Ālȳsend, þū cōme tō ūs, heofonwara Hyht and eorþwara, and ēac ūre Hyht, forþon ūs gēara ǣr wītgan þē tōweardne sǣgdon, and wē tō þīnum hidercyme hopodan and hyhtan. þū sealdest on eorþan mannum synna forgifnessa; ālēs ūs nū of dēofles onwǣlde and of helle hæftnēde. Nū þū for ūs āstige on helle grund, ne forlǣt þū ūs nū on wītum wunian, þonne þū tō þīnum ūplican rīce cyrre." '

The preterit, *cōme*, bears out Grein's surmise; but against it is the *cum* of 149. The latter, however, is probably from the Antiphon, and there is very likely con-

tamination with another original. The general correspondences with the prose
passage are striking, and extend even to verbal similarities ; cf. for example,
menigo, hæft (-), *onwāld, grund, þonne . . . þū cyrre.* So *ne forlæt þū ūs* is no
bad confirmation of [*ne lǣt*] *þē behindan.* With *hyhtan hidercyme,* 142, cf. *wē tō
þīnum hidercyme hopodan and hyhtan ;* and see 367.

157. gecȳð. With miltse. *An.* 289; *Exod.* 292.

159. Lǣf. In the poetry, only *Gen.* 1179, 1195, 1214; *Beow.* 1178, 2470.—
gefēan. Cf. *Bl. Hom.* 85: 'Heora līf hē hæfþ tō *gefēan* gecyrred.'

160. þæt. In order that.

164-214. The dramatic character of this section was first noted by J. J. Conybeare, successively Professor of Anglo-Saxon and of Poetry in the University of
Oxford. His brother, W. D. Conybeare, who edited the *Illustrations,* remarks
concerning this part (p. 201):

'The following account of it is extracted from the Lectures delivered by the
late author of this work as Anglo-Saxon Professor in the University of Oxford:
"It is in fact a *dialogue* between the Virgin Mary and Joseph, imitated probably
from some of those apocryphal writings current in the Middle Ages under the
titles of the Life, or the Gospel, of the Virgin. The dialogue commences with an
address of the Virgin to Joseph, expressing her fears lest she should be subjected
by the rigor of the Jewish law to the punishment of an adulteress; and the
answer of Joseph is occupied, partly by the assurance of his steady belief in her
purity, and other expressions calculated to remove her distress; and partly by
prayer and thanksgiving to the power which had so signally favored himself and
his lineage. It will be readily agreed that this subject, from its sacred and myste-
rious nature, is ill adapted to the purposes of poetry. The general absence of
taste and refinement which characterized the age in which the poem was originally
written, may fairly be pleaded in defense of its author; but in the present day no
such excuse could well be discovered for a translator. Indeed, I should have felt
disposed to have passed over the poem without notice, had not the dramatic form
in which it is written rendered it an object of some curiosity. Dialogues of this
kind were probably in our own country, as in Greece, the earliest and rudest
species of the drama; and that here preserved is unquestionably by many years
the most ancient specimen of this kind of poetry existing in our native language."'
To which W. D. Conybeare adds: 'The reader, however, is desired to remember
the remarks of the editor on the dramatic form of parts of the Junian Cædmon.'

Wülker, in a chapter, entitled 'Dramatische Bestrebungen der Angelsachsen'
(*Grundriss,* p. 385), remarks that one might easily assume that these hymns, con-
stituting Part I, were sung in church on certain festival occasions, that vv. 71–103
were presented by a choir of inhabitants of Jerusalem holding converse with
Mary, and that our present section introduced Mary and Joseph before the eyes
of the congregation. On that supposition, he continues, we should here have the
beginning of the mystery play. But as there is no further approach to the mystery
play before the Norman Conquest, he concludes that this assumption would be
unfounded, and supports his view by reference to the meagre vocabulary of
theatrical terms found in the ·OE. glosses.

Ebert (3. 46–7) says concerning this Part: 'Sie [die Darstellung] erinnert an
die mit dem Gottesdienst verbundenen ältesten Mysterien: die zwei Dialoge

der Maria mit den Juden, und derselben mit Josef, worin das Geheimniss der Empfängniss der Gegenstand ist, das wichtigste Moment bei der Geburt Christi, bilden den dramatischen Kern; der Dichter erscheint als der erklärende und betrachtende Prediger, und vertritt zugleich den Chor der Gemeinde in den lobpreisenden, hymnenartigen Stellen : eine höchst merkwürdige Mischung der Didaktik, Lyrik, und Dramatik. Dieser Theil ist gewiss auf Grund einer lateinischen Homilie geschrieben, wie dies vom zweiten selbst nachgewiesen ist.' He adds in a note : ' Dafür spricht wohl auch die theologische Gelehrsamkeit, die sich in manchen einzelnen Zügen kundgibt, und eine solche ist, wie wir sie Cynewulf nicht zutrauen können.'

Gollancz's remarks on the passage are included in those on the sources of Part I (*Cynewulf's Christ*, p. xxi): 'Long and patient search has failed to discover the source of Passus I.; this failure is especially to be deplored as one would much wish to know from what original the poet evolved the earliest dramatic scene in English literature. What a contrast an Anglo-Saxon religious drama would have presented to the homely miracles and mysteries of later centuries ! The original of the greater part of Passus I. must, I think, have been a Latin hymn-cycle, the ' Joseph and Mary' section being derived from an undiscovered hymn arranged for recital by half-choirs.'

In his text, Brooke thinks we may here have the very beginning of the English drama, and proceeds to elaborate his view (pp. 392-4), but, in a note, thus retracts it all : ' Since I first wrote this passage I have seen Wülker's note in his *Grundriss* on the "Dramatische Bestrebungen " of the Anglo-Saxon poems, and though I do not feel inclined to give up the idea that these hymns were sung in parts in the church — which he himself conceives possible — I think that all notion of their being represented on a stage, or dramatized in any true sense of the term, must be given up.'

This section is found in Hammerich, Rieger, and Körner, in the first and last with accompanying translation.

Thorpe divides at 167ᵃ (Joseph), 176ᵇ (Mary), 181ᵇ (Joseph), and this has been generally accepted by the writers on the subject. Cosijn ('Anglosaxonica IV') takes issue squarely with the tradition. His words are : 'Die Einteilung des Dialogs ist nicht in Ordnung. Erst mit *ēalā fǣmne geong*, v. 175, fängt Josephs Rede (bis v. 195) an, und darum ist v. 169 *for þē* in *for þȳ*, und v. 175 *fēasceaftne* in *fēasceafte* zu bessern. Auch lese man, v. 169, mit Thorpe, *worda*. Ein Schluss *ēalā fǣmne geong, mægð Māria* ist unmöglich, und gerade dies *ēalā* weist uns hier den Weg.'

At first sight this is plausible. Against it may be urged the following considerations :

(1) It would then be natural to interpret *nū*, 166, as 'since,' and to punctuate with a comma after *mīne ;* we should, accordingly, have two reasons assigned for the grief — one introduced by *nū*, and one by *forðon*, 169.

(2) If we read, with Cosijn, *for þȳ* for *for þē*, we shall have two causal words in the same line, *forðon* and *for ðȳ* (*forðȳ*); besides, *for ðȳ* is not found in the *Christ*.

(3) Hitherto, vv. 169 ff. have been parallel to 183 ff., and both appropriate in the mouth of Joseph. If the latter be still assigned to him, is the former appro-

priate in the mouth of Mary? And would Mary be so likely to hear derisive gossip as Joseph?

(4) The change of *fēasceaftne* to *fēasceafte* is rather bold, unless for convincing reasons.

(5) 177^b–180^a express a charming *naïveté* on the part of Mary as they stand ; she does not understand what Joseph is talking about, and imagines he is charging himself with wrongdoing. Such a misunderstanding would be less likely on the part of the more experienced Joseph.

(6) Urged to explain himself, Joseph, in uttering the word *byrdscypes*, 182, resolves the suspense, and at the same time gives the key to the rest of his speech. The sentence containing *byrdscypes* would seem unmotived, were it to follow the preceding one in the mouth of Joseph, and therefore pointless.

(7) While it must be conceded that *Ēalā* is extremely rare, if not unexampled, at the close of a speech, this fact can hardly outweigh the objections on the other side. The traditional interpretation of this sentence is decidedly effective.

One consideration in favor of Cosijn's proposed change remains to be adduced. The other dialogues of Part I consist of only one remark and one reply; by retaining the usual division, we should here have Joseph speaking twice, and Mary thrice. But we are not bound to believe that the predominant structure is imperative in all cases.

164. Iācōbes bearn. Brooke tr. 'child of Jacob (old)'; but the reference is not to the patriarch ; cf. Mt. 1. 16.

165. mǣg Dāuīdes. Cf. note on 96, and Mt. 1. 20.

166. frēode. Cf. *frēogan*, 'love,' from which *frēond; Gen.* 1026 has *lufan and frēode.*

fǣste. Cf. *fǣste fyrhð'lufan, An.* 83. — **gedǣlan.** An unusual sense.

167. lungre. The ordinary rendering, 'straightway,' 'at once' (Br. 'this instant ') *may* be right. Against it are: (1) Not all the poetical passages *require* this meaning; (2) OS. *lungar* does not mean 'swift,' but 'strong.' (*Hel.* 987, 5300, 5829); (3) Grimm says (*Andreas u. Elene*, p. 110; on *An.* 518): 'Hier nicht *subito*, sondern *acriter, fortiter*, wie auch das ahd. *lunkar* 'strenuus' ausdrückt; vgl. A. 1472'; (4) the word seems here to be equated with *dēope.*

169. for. Possibly miswritten for *from*, in the sense of 'concerning'; cf. *Beow.* 581, 875. — **worda.** So Cosijn also would read.

170. sorga. Körner : 'Dinge, die gewaltige Sorge bereiten.' See *Beow.* 149.

171. hearmes. Cf. 1120. In this sense *Gen.* 579, 661; *Beow.* 1892; *An.* 671. — **sprecað.** Sudden change of subject.

175. āfrēfran fēasceaftne. Cf. *An.* 367.

176. Hwæt. Like Lat. *quid;* almost = 'why.'

177. culpan. This may yet serve to identify the Latin original.

179. womma geworhtra. Th. 'for perpetrated sins'; Gr. 'kein Werk der Schande'; K. 'wegen begangenen Freveltaten'; Go. 'for evil done.' But on what word is the gen. dependent? hardly on *incan?* Perhaps on an understood *ǣnigne*, repeated from the preceding line.

ond. Almost = 'yet.'

180. swā. So 850, 1377.

181. gefylled. Br. 'thronged' [!]. — **tō fela.** So (III) 1263, 1268.

183. lādigan. Cosijn would read, *þē lādigan.* Th. 'avoid'; Gr. 'mich erledi-gen der leidvollen Reden'; K. 'mich entschuldigen (gegenüber)'; Go. 'escape.' In prose, *lādigan* takes gen. and acc. (Wülfing 1. 43), so that if we accept Cosijn's emendation, *lāþan sprǣce* would be gen.; Grein (*Spr.*) makes it acc., and cites *Ps. Th.* 8³.

186 ff. See the apocryphal *Gospel of James,* chaps. 7–13. Cf. Cowper, *Apoc. Gospels,* p. 15: 'I received her a virgin from the temple of the Lord, and have not kept her. Who hath circumvented me? Who hath done this evil in my house, and defiled the virgin?' (chap. 13). See also the *Gospel of Pseudo-Matthew,* chap. 5 ff.; the *Gospel of the Nativity of Mary,* chap. 6 ff.; the *History of Joseph the Carpenter,* chap. 3 ff.— elǣne, womma lēas. Cf. *Doomsday* 93–4.

188. Note the irregular alliteration — *w: hw.* Cf. Sievers, *Altgermanische Metrik,* p. 37, note.

189. Cosijn would supply *scyld* or some similar word after *nāthwylces;* see the variants. K. says that *nāthwylc* is formed upon the Lat. *nescio quis.*

190 ff. Cf. Cowper, *Apoc. Gospels,* p. 15 (chap. 14): 'And Joseph said, "If I hide her fault, I find myself fighting with the law of the Lord; and if I expose her to the children of Israel, I fear lest . . . I shall be betraying innocent blood to the sentence of death." '

190. swīge. Rather noun than verb in the opt.; the latter advocated by Koch, *Gram. z.* 42; Körner, p. 263.

191. Dāuīdes dohtor. So *Hel.* 255. Cf. Ælfric 2. 12: 'Of Abrahames cynne cōm se mǣra cyning Dāuīd, and of ðām cynecynne cōm sēo hālige Marīa, and of Marīan Crīst wearð ācenned.'

192. stānum. Apparently based upon Deut. 22. 13–21; but the Gospel nar-rative (Mt. 1. 19) refers rather to Deut. 24. 1. Cf. Ælfric, *Hom.* 1. 196: 'þæt Iūdēisce folc hēold Godes ǣ on þām tīman; sēo ǣ tǣhte þæt man sceolde ǣlcne wimman þe cild hæfde būtan rihtre ǣwe stǣnan. Nū ðonne, gif Marīa unbewed-dod wǣre, and cild hæfde, þonne wolde þæt Iūdēisce folc, æfter Godes ǣ, mid stānum hī oftorfian.'

āstyrfed. Causative of *āsteorfan;* cf. *āstęrfed,* Rush. Mt. 15. 13. The *Heliand* mentions the punishment of death, but not the mode.

193. morþor. In this sense *Gu.* 833; *El.* 428; *An.* 19, etc.

194. lifgan. Note the preponderating use of *-gan, -gende,* where a choice is possible: *lifgan,* not *libban; nergan,* not *nerian,* etc.

197. þurh Sunu Meotudes. An oath.

199. monnes. The only instance of *cunnan* with a gen.; perhaps on the analogy of verbs of enjoying, like *brūcan, nēotan.*

200. ēaden. So *Hy.* 4⁴⁶; *Met.* 31ª. Cf. *Hel.* 276–7 : 'thanan skal thi kind ōdan werðan.'

201. geongre in geardum. Similarly *Ph.* 355, 647; *Beow.* 13.

202. Cf. *Men.* 50; from Lk. 1. 28. With hēag- cf. 1018, and *Gram.* 223, N. 1.

204. lēoman onlȳhte. So *Met.* 21³⁶. The reference is to Lk. 1. 35. Plum-mer, *St. Luke,* p. 24: 'It is the idea of the Shechinah which is suggested here (Exod. 40. 38)'; cf. Mt. 17. 5. So the *Heliand* has (278–9): "skal thi *skadowan mid skīmon*' (radiance), and *Bl. Hom.* 7. 35: 'þæs Hēhstan mægen þē ymbscīneþ.'

206. nū ic his tempel eam. 'This reposes upon texts like 2 Chron. 3. 5–7.

Among those who employed this figure may be mentioned Origen (Livius, 123),
Ambrose (52, 105, 130, 132, 260), (Pseudo-) Chrysostom (120), Ephraem (90, 99,
116), Gregory Nazianzen (81), (Pseudo-) Epiphanius (128), Maximus (224), Fortunatus (82), Cyril of Alexandria (220), and Hesychius (99[1]). See also Salzer,
p. 119, n. 2, Lehner, p. 219' (*Festgabe für Eduard Sievers*). Cf. also *Bl. Hom.*
5. 19; 149. 3; 153. 7; 155. 32; 163. 11; Ælfric, *Hom.* I. 546.

207. **frōfre Gǣst.** So 728. The Comforter or Paraclete, Gr. παράκλητος, of
Jn. 14. 16, 26 ; 15. 26 ; 16. 7 ; rendered in the WS. Gospels by *Frēfriend*, except
14. 26 : *se hālga frōfre Gāst* ; Ælfric renders by *Frōforgāst*, Jn. 15. 26 (*Bibl. Quot.*
p. 221) ; Lind. Rush. have *rūmmōd*. Ælfric says (*Hom.* 1. 322) : ' Hē is gehāten
on Grēciscum gereorde " Paraclitus," þæt is, " Frōforgāst," forðī ðe hē frēfra𝛿
þā drēorian, þe heora synna behrēowsia𝛿, and syl𝛿 him forgyfenysse hiht, and
heora unrōtan mōd gelī𝛿ega𝛿.'

209. **sorgceare.** Cf. *Gu.* 939.—þonc. Cf. 1497-8.

211. **fǣmne.** Cf. 1419[b]-1420[a], and *Bl. Hom.* 7. 36 ff. Ælfric has (*Hom.*
1. 42) : 'Hē . . . forlēt hī mǣden nā gewemmed. . . . Hēo . . . þurhwuna𝛿 on
mæg𝛿hāde.'—sē-þēah. Through weakening of stress from *swā-𝛿ēah* ; it occurs
eleven times more in the poetry.

211-12. **ond . . . wēne.** 'And thou reputed his earthly father' — 'his father,
according to supposition'; not 'I ween' (Go.[1]), nor 'according to the hope' (Go.[2]).
Ælfric has, *Hom.* 1. 42 : 'þā *wæs* ge𝛿ūht ðām Iūdēiscum swilce Iōsēph þæs cildes
fæder wǣre, ac hē næs ' ; 1. 196 : 'Gehwā *wēnde* þæt hē ðæs cildes fæder wǣre, ac
hē næs.'

212. **wītedōm.** Cf. Ælfric, *Hom.* 1. 194 : ' þā wītegunga be Crīstes ācennednysse and be ðǣre ēadigan Marīan mæg𝛿hāde sindon swī𝛿e menigfealdlice on
ðǣre ealdan ǣ gesette, and se ðe hī āsmēagan wile, þǣr hē hī āfint mid micelre
genihtsumnysse.' Cf. *Hom.* 2. 12 ff., 20.

214-274. Based in part upon an occasional Antiphon of the Magnificat for
Advent :

O REX PACIFICE, TU ANTE SAECULA NATE : PER AUREAM EGREDERE PORTAM,
REDEMPTOS TUOS VISITA, ET EOS ILLUC REVOCA UNDE RUERUNT PER
CULPAM.

This Antiphon seems but slightly dependent upon Biblical phraseology. The
Nicene Creed has : 'Ex Patre natum ante omnia saecula' (cf. 1 Cor. z. 7).

The section falls into two parts : 214-243[a], 243[b]-274. The first is occupied
with the mystery of the eternal generation of the Son.

214. **sibsuma.** 'Pacifice.' Cf. Ælfric, in note on 14, and 1 Chron. 22. 9:
'Pacificus vocabitur.' So *Bl. Hom.* 11. 21 : 'Se gesibsuma Cyning, ūre Drihten
Hǣlend Crīst.'

216-7[b]. Th. 'how thou wast of old become for all the world's multitudes';
Gr. (*D.*) 'wie warst du eher denn Alle von Anfang an vor aller Welten Schaaren
geworden'; Go. 'how wast thou . (Go.[1] aye) existent before all the worlds
estates !'

217. **mid þīnne Wuldorfæder.** Cf. Ælfric, *Hom.* 1. 32 : 'se ðe mid him wæs
ǣfre būton anginne'; 1. 150 : 'Hē wæs ǣfre God of þām Fæder ācenned, and

wunigende mid þām Fæder and mid þām Hālgan Gāste.'—**Wuldorfæder.** Only
Men. 147.

219. Nis ǣnig. So 241.

222. mid ryhte. So 278, 381.

225. æt fruman. In the next ten lines Cynewulf briefly rehearses the account
of Creation, in order, with allusion to Jn. 1. 1–4, to emphasize that Christ was
then already in existence.

226. under wolcnum. So 588 (II).

227. līfes Ordfruma. Acts 3. 15: *auctorem . . . vitae.*

228. gedǣlde. Gen. 1. 4.

230–35. Gen. 1. 3. Cf. *Gen.* 121–5:

> Metod engla heht,
> līfes Brytta, lēoht forð cuman
> ofer rūmne grund. Raþe wæs gefylled
> Hēahcininges hæs : him wæs hālig lēoht
> ofer wēstenne, swā se Wyrhta bebēad.

231. gefēa. Professor Bright would, for the sake of metre, omit this word,
comparing 234ª; but cf. 743, and especially 585 (II).

235. torht mid tunglum. Cf. 968.

237. efeneardigende. Cf. 122.

239–240. Possibly with some reference to the Antiphon of the Magnificat for
December 17 :

O SAPIENTIA, QUAE EX ORE ALTISSIMI PRODIISTI, ATTINGENS A FINE USQUE AD
  FINEM, FORTITER SUAVITERQUE DISPONENS OMNIA: VENI AD DOCENDUM
  NOS VIAM PRUDENTIAE.

Based upon Ecclus. 24. 5: ' Ego *ex ore Altissimi prodivi* ' ; Wisd. 8. 1 : ' *Attingit*
ergo *a fine usque ad finem fortiter, et disponit omnia suaviter* ' ; Isa. 40. 14: ' . . .
viam prudentiae.'

The connection, if it exists, is here very slight, and is suggested only by the
existence of these Antiphons in one series. It is just possible that the section
based upon this Antiphon is in the part destroyed. See pp. 72, 73.

For the feast given between Martinmas and Christmas, during the later Middle
Ages, by the Master of the Common House, or Calefactory, at Durham Monastery, and called *O Sapientia,* see *Rites of Durham (Surtees Soc. Pub.* 15 (1842),
pp. 75, 85).

239. Snyttro. Cf. Greg. *Moral.* lib. xi. cap. 8 (Migne 75. 958): ' *Christum Dei
virtutem et Dei sapientiam* (1 Cor. 1. 24) ; qui apud ipsum semper est, quia *In
principio erat Verbum, et Verbum erat apud Deum, et Deus erat Verbum* (Jn. 1. 1)?
Cf. Ælfric, *Hom* 1. 40 : ' Word bið wīsdōmes geswutelung ; and þæt Word, þæt
is se Wīsdōm, is ācenned of ðām Ælmihtigum Fæder, būtan anginne ; forðan ðe
hē wæs ǣfre God of Gode, Wīsdōm of ðām wīsan Fæder'; *Hom.* 1. 258 : ' His
Wīsdōm, þe hē mid ealle gesceafta geworhte, sē is his Sunu, se is ǣfre of ðām
Fæder, and mid þām Fæder.' Cf. 1. 248, 500; 2. 42. See also Prov. 3. 19;
8. 22, 23; Ps. 104. 24; 136. 5; and cf. Lk. 11. 49 with Mt. 23. 34.

241. Cosijn compares *Rid.* 2¹.

242. fira bearnum. A Biblical phrase ; cf. my *The Bible and English Prose Style,* p. ix.

243–274. Translated by Morley, *English Writers,* 2. 227–8.

243. From here to the end of the section is a variation upon the second half of the Antiphon, the petition.

245. ȳwe. LWS. form; see variants. — **nēod.** Not to be confounded with *nȳd.*

246. mōtan. Uncertain whether ind. or opt.

247. ryhtgerȳno. Cf. 196.

250. bērcyme. Cf. *hidercyme.* — **hǣlende.** Pres. part.; so *Ph.* 590; *Ps.* 108²⁵; *Ps. C.* 50.

251. gyldnan geatu. Plur. for the sing.: *auream portam.* The reference is undoubtedly to the physical birth of Christ. This is shown by the Responds of the last week in Advent, and the Vigil of Christmas, as given in Gregory's *Liber Responsalis* (Migne 78. 731, 734). The first has: 'Ingressus est per splendidam regionem, aurem Virginis, visitare palatium uteri; et regressus est per auream Virginis portam.' The other has: 'Introivit per aurem Virginis in regionem nostram, indutus stolam purpuream; et exivit per auream portam lux et decus universae fabricae mundi.' Cf. 318. Dietrich thinks the reference here (but not in 318) is to 'das Thor des Himmelreichs oder des Paradieses' (*Haupt's Zs.* 9. 199). Cf. *Sat.* 649.

252. Cf. 308 ff.

253. heofona Hēahfrēa. Cf. 424.

254. gesēce. 'Visita.'. Grein interprets as opt.; but cf. *Gram.* 410, N. 4. The parallelism with *hāt* seems to be decisive in favor of the imp.

þurh þīn sylfes gong. Brooke translates : ' through thy very self a-coming '[!].

256. wulf. With allusion to Jn. 10. 12. Cf. Greg. *Hom. in Evang.* lib. 1, hom. 14 (Migne 76. 1128): 'Sed est alius lupus qui sine cessatione quotidie non corpora, sed mentes dilaniat, *malignus videlicet spiritus,* qui cautas fidelium insidians circuit, et mortes animarum quaerit.'

See Ælfric, *Hom.* 1. 36: 'þām lārēowe gedafenað þæt hē symle wacol sȳ ofer Godes ēowode, þæt se ungesewenlica wulf Godes scēp ne tōstence.' Similarly 1. 238–240 : 'Ælc bisceop and ælc lārēow is tō hyrde gesett Godes folce, þæt hī sceolon þæt folc wið ðone wulf gescyldan. Se wulf is dēofol, þe syrwð ymbe Godes gelaðunge, and cēpð hū hē mage crīstenra manna sāwla mid leahtrum fordōn.' See Bugge, *Home of the Eddic Poems,* pp. lvii, lxxiii ff.

257. deorc dēaðscūa. This is the obvious reading ; cf. *Beow.* 160. It is the personified Shadow of Death, a sublime conception. Cf. *dēaðes scūa, Ps.* 87⁶, 106⁹·¹², *Sat.* 455. Imagine Milton's description of Death, *P. L.* 2. 666–673, applied to Satan. Brooke translates : 'beast that works in darkness.'

259. blōde gebohtes. Cf. Rev. 5. 9.

261. ūssa. We should probably read thus, to agree with *nīoda.* — **nīoda.** Th. tr. *needs ;* Gr. (*Spr.*) *Herzen* (as if *mōda*). The reading of the text is sufficiently confirmed by *Soul's Address* 48 (Exon. *þīnra nēoda lust ;* Verc. *meda,* evidently for *nīeda*). The whole phrase = *against our will.*

264. wreccan. *-an* for *-um* (*Gram.* 237, N. 6). — **wītes.** Possibly we should read *wittes,* as Grein (*Spr.*) and Cosijn suggest, the latter equating it with the *gāstbona* of *Beow.* 177; but cf. *sūslbonan*, *Sat.* 640, which furnishes a fairly good parallel to this, and see *PBB.* 10. 456.

265. Perhaps alluding to Lk. 10. 18, of which Plummer says: 'It refers to the success of the disciples regarded as a symbol and earnest of the complete overthrow of Satan. Jesus had been contemplating evil as a power overthrown.'

266. hondgeweorc. So 1414(III). — **hæleþa Scyþþend.** So *An.* 396; *Hy.* 8[34].

267. on ryht. Cf. *Ph.* 664; *Rid.* 41[3]; *Beow.* 1555.

269-274. Morley's translation is as follows:

> Through love of sin he drew us, that bereft of Heaven's light
> We suffer endless miseries, betrayed for evermore,
> Unless Thou come to save us from the slayer, Lord of Might!
> Shelter of Man! O Living God! come soon, our need is sore!

269. þonan. 'Unde.' — **þurh synlust.** 'Per culpam.'

270. fortyhte. This emendation of Cosijn's seems to deserve the preference over the MS. reading. It would be strange if, side by side with a well-known *fortyhtan*, there should be a *fortyllan* with precisely the same meaning, from a *tyllan* of which nothing could be made. — **tīres wonc.** Cf. *tīrlēas*, *Beow.* 843.

271. ā būtan ende. So 415. — **ermþu.** Elsewhere in the poem, *yrmþu*.

272. ofostlīcor. Where we should use the positive.

273. lifgende God. So 755 (II).

274. Helm alwihta. Cf. 410.

275 ff. Based upon an occasional Antiphon of the Magnificat for Advent:

O MUNDI DOMINA, REGIO EX SEMINE ORTA: EX TUO JAM CHRISTUS PROCESSIT ALVO, TANQUAM SPONSUS DE THALAMO; HIC JACET IN PRAESEPIO QUI ET SIDERA REGIT.

Only one phrase is Biblical, from Ps. 19. 5 (18. 6): 'In sole posuit tabernaculum suum, et ipse *tanquam sponsus* procedens *de thalamo* suo.' For the application to Christ, cf. Pseudo-Jerome in Livius, p. 78, and Augustine, Sedulius, and others, quoted in Salzer, p. 115, N. 4. The hymn of Ambrose, 'Veni, Redemptor gentium,' has:

> Procedit e thalamo suo,
> Pudoris aula regia.

See Neale and Littledale, 1. 265.

275. mǣra. Gollancz comments: 'Th. suggested that the word was due to an error of the scribe, and should properly be *maria*; there is no evidence for this view, but it is probable that the poet used *mǣra* because of its likeness to *maria*, — the sort of popular etymology that the old homilists delighted in.' There is no evidence for *this* view; but cf. 446. *Mǣre* is used alone as a voc. in *Ps.* 118[122].

276. clǣneste. Cf. 187, 331.

cwēn. 'Domina'; cf. 1198. Mary is thus celebrated by Athanasius (Livius, 79, 80, 213), Ephraem (96, 296, 298), Methodius (153), Chrysippus (81), Fortunatus (368), Hesychius (81), and Sophronius (335). See also Salzer, pp. 420-3, and cf. Ælfric, *Hom.* 2. 22: 'Uton bēon ēac gemyndige hū micelre geðincðe sȳ þæt hālige mǣden Marīa, Crīstes mōder; hēo is geblētsod ofer eallum wīfhādes mannum ; *hēo is sēo heofenlice cwēn*, and ealra crīstenra manna frōfer and fultum.' So *Bl. Hom.* 105. 17 : 'ealra fǣmnena cwēn.'

277. tō wīdan fēore. So 1343, 1543 (III).

278. Cf. 381.

280. brȳd. Cf. such Biblical passages as Cant. 4. 8–12; 5. 1. The figure is used by Ephraem (Livius, 99, 383, 386, 419), Ambrose (270), Jerome (97), (Pseudo-) Augustine (276), Prudentius (450), Proclus (98), Cyril of Alexandria (277), Chrysologus (137), and Isidore of Seville (277). Salzer (pp. 99–100) quotes from the hymns such expressions as *sponsa Christi, sponsa summi Regis, cara sponsa Dei, sponsa Creatoris, sponsa Patris aeterni.*

282–3. þā hȳhstan . . . þegnas. Grein (*Spr.*) interprets as 'archangels'; cf. *An.* 726; *Gen.* 15; *Hy.* 7⁵³.

284. hālgum meahtum. So 1189 (III).

285–6. These lines suggest a reminiscence of the triple Hecate, as in Servius on *Aen.* 4. 511 : 'Cum super terras est, creditur esse Luna ; cum in terris, Diana; cum sub terris, Proserpina.' Cf. Chaucer, where, in the Prologue of the *Second Nun's Tale*, he is speaking of Mary's Son

> That of the tryne compas lord and gyde is
> Whom erthe and see and heven, out of relees,
> Ay herien.

This resembles the lines of the Hymn (for Ascension Day), 'Aeterne Rex altissime':

> Ut trium rerum machina,
> Caelestium, terrestrium,
> Et inferorum condita,
> Flectat genu jam subdita.

And see Phil. 2. 10.

288. þrīsthycgende. Only *Gn. Ex.* 50.

289. brōhtes. Cf. *Gram.* 356. We should expect the opt.; cf. Prollius, § 45. 6; § 44. 13. For the thought one might adduce Augustine's statement, as quoted by Livius, p. 199: 'She consecrated her virginity to God.'

292. bēaga hroden. Cf. *bēaghroden, Beow.* 623; *Jud.* 138; *Rid.* 15⁹; and see 330. Elsewhere *hrēodan* takes the inst.: *Beow.* 304, 1151; *Ph.* 79; *Rid.* 81¹⁷; *Jud.* 37; *An.* 1451; *Whole* 74. Perhaps we should read *bēagum.* —lāc. Offering, oblation.

293. heofonhāme. Cf. *Ps.* 102¹⁸, 122¹, 137⁶, 148⁴.—hlūtre mōde. So *Met.* 29²; cf. *Gu.* 77.

295 ff. Cf. 200 ff.

296. meahta spēd. Cf. (II) 488, 652, (III) 1383.

300. Cf. 84, 211.

unwemme. Cf. Chaucer, Prologue to *Second Nun's Tale:*

> Thou, virgin wemmelees,
> Bar of thy body, and dweltest mayden pure,
> The creatour of every creature.

303. Ēsaias. Rather, Ezekiel. In the service for Wednesday of the first week of Advent, according to the Roman Breviary, we read, as the Response to the Second Lesson, the following: 'Ante multum tempus prophetavit Ezechiel: Vidi portam clausam; ecce, Deus ante saecula ex ea procedebat pro salute mundi; et erat iterum clausa, demonstrans Virginem, quia post partum permansit virgo. Porta quam vidisti, Dominus solus transibit per illam.' Cf. Newman, *Tracts for the Times* 3. 186–7. The passage of Ezekiel is 44. 1–2. The confusion between Isaiah and Ezekiel may have arisen, because the Lesson immediately preceding is from Isaiah, chap. 3.

306 ff. Note Cynewulf's highly poetical expansion. Thus the *geond þeodland* suggests the descrying of the gate from afar, as in *The Holy Grail*:

> And eastward fronts the statue, and the crown
> And both the wings are made of gold, and flame
> At sunrise till the people *in far fields*,
> Wasted so often by the heathen hordes,
> Behold it, crying, 'We have still a King.'

308. æþelīc ingong. Brooke translates: 'Glorious an Ingang!'

310. bewriþen. Cf. Tennyson, *Lancelot and Elaine* 808: 'His battle-*writhen* arms and mighty hands.'

312. forescyttelsas. Both *scyt(t)el* and *scyt(t)els* are found in the prose; cf. Bosworth-Toller.

314. clūstor. Cf. Chaucer, as above:

> Within the *cloistre* blisful of thy sydes
> Took mannes shap the eternal love and pees.

315. Godes engel. Cf. Ezek. 40. 3.

316. onwrāh. Also (II) 463.

ond þæt word ācwæð. Also (II) 474, 714.

318. gyldnan gatu. Cf. 251.

320. gefǣlsian. I quote from my note in the *Journal of Germanic Philology*, i. 334–6: 'Thorpe translates it by "make pure"; Grein (*Dichtungen*), by "verherlichen"; Gollancz, by "glorify" (*Cynewulf's Christ*) and "make resplendent" (*Exeter Book*). In the *Sprachschatz*, Grein assigns to *gefǣlsian* the meanings "lustrare, expiare, mundare, purificare, clarificare."

'Professor Bright proposes to read *gefæstnian* for *gefǣlsian*. He says: " *Gefæstnian*, taken with *fæstan* of the next line, reflects in a striking way the special emphasis of the original passage: 'This gate shall be *shut* ... therefore it shall be shut'; cf. also ll. 251–2, which shows that the *closed* gates were particularly in mind."

'I propose to retain *gefǣlsian*, and to translate it by "pass through."

'That Grein is correct in assigning to *gefǣlsian* (and also to *fǣlsian*) the meaning "lustrare" is shown by a comparison with the Wright-Wülcker *Vocabularies*, where (438 ₂₈) we have: "lustrans, fælsende." This, however, does not determine the meaning of *fǣlsende*, since *lustrare* has various definitions. Of these, the commonest in the Vulgate is "pass through," "go through." Thus, too, in the *Vocabularies* (434 ₃): "lustrata, geondhworfen," and (438 ₃₉): "lustraturus, geondferende." Since it has been shown that the well-known Latin meaning of "lustrare" as "traverse," "pass through," must have been familiar to OE. scholars through the Vulgate, and is unmistakably recognized in OE. itself; and since, as we have seen, *fǽlsian* is used in OE. as an equivalent of *lustrare*, we need not hesitate to assign to the OE. verb in our line the meaning of "traverse," "pass through," if the context appears to demand it.

'That the context does demand it is, I think, evident : v. 321 is the gloss on *gefǽlsian;* "ðās gyldnan gatu ... God ... wile ... gefǽlsian" is thus corroborated, explained, and expanded by "þurh þā fæstan locu foldan nēosan."

'So far as *action* is concerned, there is no question anywhere of the shutting of the gate ; the gate is conceived as already shut, and attention is directed to the passage through (cf. the "færð inn" and "ūt færð" of Ælfric). That this is true may be seen from the comment of Ambrose (*Ep.* I. 7): 'Quæ est illa porta sanctuarii, porta illa exterior ad orientem, quæ *manet clausa*, et nemo, inquit, *pertransibit* per eam, nisi solus Deus Israel? Nonne hæc porta Maria est, per quam in hunc mundum Redemptor *intravit?*' Professor Bright's proposed change to *gefæstnian*, so far from giving a better sense, would merely weaken the *fæstan* of the next line : the gate which has just been fastened has not, to the imagination, the same character of impermeability as that which has long been locked (cf. the "ful longe ǣr" of v. 252, if that passage is to be connected with this). And why should the "Father Almighty" fasten the gates in order that immediately, in the next line, he may pass through them? This is neither Scripture nor poetry.' Cf. 145.

328. Dū eart þæt wealldor. Cf. the last note. The same view is represented by Ælfric, *Hom.* I. 194: '"þis geat ne bið nānum menn geopenod, ac se Hlāford āna færð inn þurh þæt geat, and eft ūt færð, and hit bið belocen on ēcnysse." þæt beclȳsede geat on Godes hūse getācnode þone hālgan mægiðhād þǣre ēadigan Marīan. Se Hlāford, ealra hlāforda Hlāford, þæt is Crīst, becōm on hire innoð, and ðurh hī on menniscnysse wearð ācenned, and þæt geat bið belocen on ēcnysse; þæt is, þæt Marīa wæs mǣden ǣr ðǣre cenninge, and mǣden on ðǣre cenninge, and mǣden æfter ðǣre cenninge.'

But the interpretation is much earlier, being found in Gregory Thaumaturgus (Livius, 123), Ephraem (116, 297, 412, 423), Gregory of Nyssa (115), Ambrose (114, 115), Jerome (97, 104, 114 ; cf. Lehner, p. 137), Theodoret (115), Sedulius (444), Proclus (115), Chrysippus (223), Ennodius (454), Julianus Pomerius (116), Arator (454), Fortunatus (459), Hesychius (227), Rufinus (Lehner, p. 141). See also Salzer, p. 117, ll. 7, and the whole of the eighth chapter of Ambrose's *De Institutione Virginis* (Migne 16. 319).

wealldor. Cf. *weallgeat, Jud.* 141 ; *An.* 1205.

331. gecorene. In the Fathers, Mary is often called *electa*. Cf. *Jul.* 613.

334. lioþucǣgan bilēac. Cf. Ambrose, *De Inst. Virginis*, cap. 9 (Migne 16. 321): 'Porta clausa es, virgo; nemo aperiat januam tuam, quam semel clausit Sanctus et Verus, qui habet clavim David, qui aperit et nemo claudit, claudit et nemo aperit.' This carries us back to 19.

līfes Brytta. Cf. *Līffrēa*, 15. So *An.* 823; *Gen.* 122.

336. Cf. 201, 295. — **Godes spelboda.** So *Dan.* 533, 743; *Ph.* 571.

341. 'Now that we look upon the child (lying) on thy breast' (taking *on* and *foran* as separate prepositions). Note the tenderness of the poet, and cf. the close of Milton's *Hymn on the Morning of Christ's Nativity*. Professor Bright, following Thorpe, regards *brēostum stariað*, however, as 'view or look upon with our inmost thoughts,' and interprets the whole sentence : 'Then shall we be able, . . . now that we with our inmost thoughts look on the child before us (*foran*).'

brēostum. Cf. Sweet's note on *Cura Past.* 101. 16 (p. 480), with reference to the dual or plural, and see *Gram.* 274, N. 2.

342. Geþinga. Observe the intercessory character attributed to the Virgin ; cf. Lingard, *Anglo-Saxon Church* 2. 75–8, and Ælfric, *Hom.* 1. 204 : 'Uton biddan nū þæt ēadige and þæt gesǣlige mǣden Marīan þæt hēo ūs geðingige tō hyre āgenum Suna and tō hire Scyppende, Hǣlende Crīst.'

344. gedwolan. This dread of heresy and false doctrine is very significant. Cf. Allen, *Christian Institutions*, pp. 354–5 : 'The largest and most inclusive answer to the problem [of the Atonement], which the church of the Catholic creeds was practically unanimous in rendering, set forth the ignorance of man as the source of the evils in which he was engulfed and out of which he vainly sought to escape, his ignorance of the true nature of God and of His relation to the world; ignorance of the true constitution of man and of his high destiny. Christ came as the enlightener, the light which came forth from the eternal light, to recreate or to rejuvenate humanity, to disclose to men their true relationship to God. In ways which could not be defined, He broke the power of sin and overcame its deadly fascination. It was assumed that the soul was made for God, and that when light was revealed, man by the inner law of his being would respond to light. To know the truth was to be set free; the knowledge which acted through the mind upon the conscience and the heart, involved obedience : *This is life eternal ; to know God and Jesus Christ whom He has sent.* In this way the world was reconciled unto God and God unto the world.' Cf. 106, and note.

347. wunigan. Except in this word, the *i, ig* of such verbs is usually represented in this poem by *g*.

348–377. Perhaps based upon the Antiphon of the Magnificat for December 19:

O RADIX JESSE, QUI STAS IN SIGNUM POPULORUM, SUPER QUEM CONTINEBUNT REGES OS SUUM, QUEM GENTES DEPRECABUNTUR : VENI AD LIBERANDUM NOS, JAM NOLI TARDARE.

The Biblical sources are : Isa. 11. 10 : 'In die illa *radix Jesse, qui stat in signum popularum, ipsum gentes deprecabuntur . . .*'; Isa. 52. 15 : '*. . . super ipsum continebunt reges os suum . . .*'; Heb. 10. 37 : '*. . .* qui venturus veniet, et *non tardabit.*' A great part of this section has no obvious relation to the Antiphon ; but certain lines seem to point to it. There may be 'contamination' with the next, as well as with some of the preceding.

349–357. Cf. 109–111, 121–2, 216–240.

350. efenwesende. Cf. *efeneardigende*, 237 ; cf. Ælfric, *Hom.* 1. 282 : 'Godes Sunn is ǣfre of ðām Fæder ācenned, and ǣfre mid him wunigende.'—**hām.** Cf. 305, 647.

355. mid þone ēcan Frēan. Cf. *mid þinne ēngan Frēan*, 237.

356. þās sīdan gesceaft. Cf. 239b.

357–8. Bǣm . . . hlēofæst. Here, in the introduction of the Holy Spirit, is the first suggestion of the Trinity, which is to be the theme of the next section.

gemǣne. Cf. the Nicene Creed : ' qui ex Patre Filioque procedit.' See Blunt, p. 375 : ' The words "et Filio" or " Filioque" of the Procession of the Holy Ghost have, as is well known, never been admitted into the Creed by the Eastern Church. They were first introduced, probably, as an additional protest against the Arian denial of the full Godhead of the Son, by the Spanish Church, at the great Council of Toledo in 589; or, according to Bingham, at the still earlier Council of Bracara in 411. Some, however, think that they cannot be traced with certainty higher than the Toledan Council of 633. The addition first became of importance towards the end of the eighth century, when the doctrine of the procession of the Holy Ghost from the Son was wielded as a theological weapon against the adoptionist heresy of the Spanish Bishops, Felix and Elipandus. It was then generally adopted through Gaul and Germany, chiefly through the influence of Charlemagne.'

It should not be forgotten that Alcuin, whom I have elsewhere (*Anglia* 15. 9-19) shown to be the author of a conception of purgatorial fire adopted by Cynewulf in his *Elene*, wrote controversial tracts directed against the heresy of Felix and Elipandus, a treatise on the Procession of the Holy Spirit, and another on the Trinity. Chap. 5, Bk. I of the last-named is entitled, *Quod Spiritus sanctus communis est Patris et Filii Spiritus.* Now the word *communis* is precisely the one which would be translated by *gemǣne*, and this is the very treatise with the teaching of which, as I showed in the article cited above, Cynewulf must have been familiar. These coincidences, therefore, are not without significance.

358–372. Cf. 149–154.

359. þurh ēaðmēdu. So 1442 (III) ; *Gu.* 74.

360. hæfta. Cf. 154.

361. nīedþīowa. Cf. *wīteþēowum*, 151.

364. hetelan. Cosijn refers to Bosworth-Toller, and adds Beda-Wheloc, p. 309, and *Saints* 3. 406.

365. gebunden bealorāpum. Cf. 117, and note. — **gelong.** Cf. 152.

367–377. Cf. 249–274. See especially *help*, 366 : *helpe*, 263 ; *hidercyme*, 366 : *hērcyme*, 250 ; *firena lust*, 369 : *synlust*, 269 ; *yrmþa*, 370 : *ermþa*, 271 ; *ne lata tō lange*, 373 : *hrǣdlīce*, 263 ; *ūs is lissa þearf*, 373 ; *ūs is þīnra ārna þearf*, 255 ; *āhredde*, 374 ; *hreddan*, 274.

368. āfrēfre fēasceafte. Cf. 175.

371-2. tȳdran ... hēanlīce. Cf. 29–31. — **tȳdran mōde.** Cf. *Gu.* 729.

372. Cym. But *cum*, 149, 243.

373. ne lata tō lange. ' Jam noli tardare.'

374. ' Ad liberandum nos.' — **hǣlogiefe.** Cf. *hǣlolīf*, 150.

377. on þēode. Cf. 127. — **þīnne willan.** Cf. 1236, 1261 (III).

378–415. Based upon two of the Antiphons for Lauds on Trinity Sunday, according to the Sarum Use :

O BEATA ET BENEDICTA ET GLORIOSA TRINITAS, PATER ET FILIUS ET SPIRITUS SANCTUS.

TE JURE LAUDANT, TE ADORANT, TE GLORIFICANT OMNES CREATURAE TUAE, O BEATA TRINITAS.

The former of these has been adopted as the invocation of the Trinity near the beginning of the Litany; see Blunt, p. 225.

379. hālig. These adjectives do not strictly render the three of the first Antiphon, though this may stand for *benedicta*, and *wlitige* for *gloriosa*.

þrȳnes. Cf. Ælfric, *Hom.* 1. 10: ' Ðēos þrynnys is ān God: þæt is, se Fæder; and his Wīsdōm, of him sylfum æfre ācenned; and heora bēgra Willa, þæt is se Hālga Gāst; hē nis nā ācenned, ac hē gǣð of þām Fæder and of þām Suna gelīce. Ðās þrȳ hādas sindon ān Ælmihtig God.' Cf. 1. 228, 248, 276–8, 498–500; 2. 42, 56, 362. For other occurrences of the word in the poetry, see 599; *El.* 177; *Jul.* 726; *An.* 1687; *Gu.* 618; *Jud.* 86; *Hy.* 8⁴⁰.

On the comparatively late date of the Feast of Trinity, cf. Burbidge, *Liturgies and Offices of the Church*, pp. 262–3: ' The importance given to the Festival of the Trinity through the numbering of the Sundays for the rest of the year as Sundays after Trinity, is another English custom shared from ancient times with the Gallican Church, but not adopted by the Roman. The observance of Trinity Sunday began in France about the eighth century, being mentioned in a letter to the Emperor Charlemagne. Its observance is also provided for in an ancient MS. of the monastery of S. Denys, and in another belonging to Tours, *circa* A.D. 900. It seems also to be referred to in the Pontifical of Egbert, Archbishop of York, A.D. 732–766. The Festival was not generally admitted into the Roman Service Books until the fifteenth century.'

On the general significance of the doctrine, cf. Allen, *Christian Institutions*, p. 301: ' If the course of Christian history discloses the enduring tendency to distinguish between the revelation of the Father in creation, and in the order of the visible world, the revelation of the Son in the redemption of humanity as a process revealed in history, or the revelation of the Holy Spirit in the inward life of the individual soul, as though either of these might constitute a religion without the others, so also does the history of the church reveal the threefold consciousness and will and purpose in unity, as if no one of the three were to be excluded, or subordinated to the others. These three agree in one. Beneath the diversity there is an underlying unity which, if it be not denied, still asserts its claim, and at least keeps the problem for ever real. When unity is sought for by the customary methods of suppression, the higher unity is reasserted by division and schism. In the ancient church also, when the effort was made to overcome the nature-religions, as by the first Christian apologists, who failed, however, at the same time to do justice to the divine life as revealed in nature, the principle inherent in those old religions came back, and, entering the church in unsuspected ways, revolutionized its cultus. When in the ancient church there was a tendency toward the suppression of the inner personal life by external authority, when prophetism was discouraged and finally banished, there arose in monasticism a protest in behalf of the inner life of the Spirit and its coequal importance when compared with the interests of historic religion, — such a protest as the world has not witnessed before or since. Thus the conflicts of the church and its inner revolutions attest the coequality of the three distinctions in the one divine essence. Natural religion or the Fatherhood of God, historical Christianity or the worship of the Son, the inward experience wrought by the Holy Spirit, these three also agree in one. But no one of them is complete without the others.'

381. mid ryhte. 'Jure.'

382. ealle mægene. So *Beow.* 2667 ; cf. *Ps.* 105²³.

386. seraphinnes cynn. Cf. the description in *Elene* 739–749 :

> Þāra on hāde sint
> in sindrēame syx genemned,
> þā ymbsealde synt mid syxum ēac
> fiðrum, gefrætwad, fægere scīnaþ.
> Þara sint .IIII., þe on flihte ā
> þā þegnunge þrymme beweotigaþ
> fore onsȳne ēces Dēman,
> singallīce singaþ in wuldre
> hǣdrum stefnum Heofoncininges lof,
> wōða wlitegaste, ond þās word cweðaþ
> clǣnum stefnum : — þām is Ceruphīn nama.

Ceruphīn is here 'cherubim,' not 'seraphim'; the mistake is derived from the Latin original.

Ælfric says concerning the seraphim (*Hom.* I. 344) : 'Seraphim sind gecwedene byrnende, oððe onǣlende ; hī sind swā miccle swīðor byrnende on Godes lufe, swā micclum swā hī sind tō him geðēodde ; forðan ðe nāne ōðre englas ne sind betwēonan him and ðām Ælmihtigan Gode. Hī sind byrnende, nā on fȳres wīsan, ac mid micelre lufe þæs wealdendan Cyninges.' This seems to repose on Gregory, *Hom in Evang.* 34. 10 (Migne 76. 1252) : 'Seraphim etiam vocantur illa spirituum sanctorum agmina quae ex singulari propinquitate Conditoris sui incomparabili ardent amore. Seraphim namque ardentes vel incendentes vocantur. Quae, quia ita Deo conjuncta sint ut inter haec et Deum nulli alii spiritus intersint, tanto magis ardent quanto hunc vicinius vident. Quorum profecto flamma amor est, quia, quo subtilius claritatem divinitatis ejus aspiciunt, eo validius in ejus amore flammescunt.'

387. brēmende. Cf. 483 ; *Dan.* 406 ; *Men.* 94.

388. unāþrēoteudum. Cf. the verb *āþrēotan*. — **þrymmum.** Not 'numbers' (Thorpe, Gollancz ²), nor 'notes' (Gollancz ¹).

391. cyst. Cf. the quotation from Ælfric under 386 ; they are closest to God.

392. Cf., under 386, *El.* 745 : 'fore onsȳne ēces Dēman,' and *An.* 719–724 :

> Cheruphīm and Seraphīm,
> þā on swegeldrēamum syndon nemned ;
> fore onsȳne ēcan Dryhtnes
> standað stīðferhðe, stefnum herigað,
> hālgum hlēoðrum, Heofoncyninges þrym,
> Meotudes mundbyrd.

ætwiste. Not 'essence' (Thorpe), nor 'being' (Gollancz).

393–9. Here Brooke's translation is better than usual, though it is marred by the last hemistich :

> Ever and forever   all adorned with the sky,
> Far and wide they worship   God the wielder of the world,
> And with winged plumes   watch around the Presence
> Of the Lord Almighty,   of the Lord Eternal!

All around the throne of God,   thronging they are eager,
Which of them the closest   may to Christ the Saviour
Flashing play in flight,   in the garths of peacefulness!

393. swegle gehyrste. Th., 'these ornaments of heaven'; Go.[1], 'wreathed with celestial light'; Go.[2], 'wrapt in bright harmony'; and see Brooke. Grein (*Spr.*) assumes an adv. *swegle* here, 1102, *Gn. Ex.* 78; *Met.* 28[61]; this is borne out by the adj. *swegle* (OS. *suigli*), *Beow.* 2749, *Ap.* 32. On the other hand, see the compounds *sweglbefǽlden, Sat.* 588 (cf. *Haupt's Zs.* 10. 365); *sweglbeorht, Gu.* 1187; *swegltorht, Gen.* 28, 95, *Gn. Ex.* 41; *An.* 1250; *Met.* 29[24]; *sweglwered, Beow.* 606. Grein does not recognize a simple inst. *swegle*, except in *swegle benumene, Gu.* 597.

395. fiþrum. Cf. Exod. 25. 20; 37. 9; 1 Sam. 4. 4; Ps. 80. 1; 99. 1. The cherubim and seraphim were confused, as we have seen; then the images of the cherubim were confounded with the living angels. But see also Isa. 6. 1, 2.

399. lācan. Cf. *Ph.* 316; *Fates of Men* 23; *Met.* 24[9].

403-415. This is a paraphrase of the hymn variously called the Sanctus, Tersanctus, Triumphal Hymn, Angelic Hymn, or Seraphic Hymn. It is composed of a modification of the hymn of the Seraphim in Isa. 6. 3, and of Mt. 21. 9 (based upon Ps. 118. 26). These are:

'Sanctus, sanctus, sanctus, Dominus Deus exercituum, plena est omnis terra gloria ejus.'

'Hosanna filio David; benedictus qui venit in nomine Domini; hosanna in altissimis.'

The Hymn is regularly found in all Liturgies in the same place, viz. at the conclusion of the Preface, and just before the Consecration (Hammond, *Liturgies Eastern and Western,* p. 381). In the Gregorian Sacramentary it is thus introduced (Migne 78. 25):

'Per quem Majestatem tuam laudant angeli, adorant dominationes, tremunt potestates : caeli, caelorumque virtutes, ac beati seraphim socia exsultatione concelebrant. Cum quibus et nostras voces, ut admitti jubeas, deprecamur, supplici confessione dicentes:

SANCTUS, SANCTUS, SANCTUS, Dominus Deus Sabaoth. Pleni sunt caeli et terra gloria tua. Osanna in excelsis. Benedictus qui venit in nomine Domini. Osanna in excelsis.'

In the Sarum Use it is prefaced as follows (Blunt, p. 387): 'Et ideo cum angelis et archangelis, cum thronis et dominationibus, cumque omni militia caelestis exercitus, hymnum gloriae Tuae canimus, sine fine dicentes' [the Hymn as above].

In the English Prayer Book we read:

'Therefore with angels and archangels, and with all the company of heaven, we laud and magnify thy glorious name, evermore praising thee, and saying: Holy, holy, holy, Lord God of hosts, heaven and earth are full of thy glory ; glory be to thee, O Lord most high.'

Blunt comments (p. 386): 'St. Cyril [315-386] speaks of its long Preface . . . [*Catech. Lect.* xxiii], and then goes on to say: "We make mention also of the Seraphim, whom Isaiah, by the Holy Ghost, beheld encircling the throne of God [cf. *Christ,* v. 395], and with two of their wings veiling their countenances, and with two their feet, and with two flying, who cried: ' Holy, Holy, Holy, Lord God

of Sabaoth.' For this cause, therefore, we rehearse this confession of God, delivered down to us from the Seraphim, that we may join in hymns with the host of
the world above."'

The portion from Isaiah is adapted in the *Te Deum*: 'Tibi Cherubim et Seraphim incessabili voce [cf. *unáþrēotendum þrymmum*, 388, and the 'sine fine
dicentes' of the Sarum Use; Prayer Book, 'continually do cry'] proclamant:
Sanctus, Sanctus, Sanctus, Dominus Deus Sabaoth; pleni sunt caeli et terra
majestatis gloriae Tuae' (Blunt, p. 189). Referring to the words of Isa. 6. 3,
'clamabant alter ad alterum,' the *Mirror of our Lady* says: 'And therefore,
according to the angels, ye sing quire to quire, one Sanctus on the one side, and
another on the other side, and so forth of other verses.'

In *Elene* 750-3 is a much shorter form of the Hymn:

> Hālig is se hālga hēahengla God,
> weoroda Wealdend! Is þæs wuldres ful
> heofun ond eorðe, ond eall hēahmægen
> tīre getācnod!

Ælfric, *On the New Testament* (Grein, *Bibl. der Ags. Prosa*, p. 19), thus introduces the verse of Isaiah: 'þā synd þā twā gecȳðnyssa be Crīstes menniscnysse
and be þǣre hālgan þrīnnysse on sōðre ānnysse, swa Īsaias geseah on his gāstlican
gesihðe hū God sylf gesæt, and him sungon ābūtan duo seraphin, þæt sind twā
engla werod : *Sanctus, sanctus, sanctus, Dominus Deus Sabaoth*, þæt ys on Englisc:
"Hālig, hālig, hālig, Drihten weroda God; mid his wuldre ys āfylled eall eorðan
brādnisse."'

403-412ᵃ. Brooke translates this (p. 395).

403. Cf. *Hy.* 7¹³:

> Hālig eart þū, hālig, heofonengla Cyning.

hālig. Gregory assumed that the threefold repetition of *Sanctus* indicated the
Trinity. So *Hom. in Ezech.* 2. 4 (Migne 76. 977): 'Spiritales quippe illi patres
omnipotentem Deum Trinitatem ita esse crediderunt, sicut eamdem Trinitatem
novi patres aperte locuti sunt. Isaias namque audivit angelica agmina in coelo
clamantia: *Sanctus, Sanctus, Sanctus, Dominus Deus sabaoth*. Ut enim personarum trinitas monstraretur, tertio Sanctus dicitur; sed ut una esse substantia
Trinitatis appareat, non Domini Sabaoth, sed Dominus Sabaoth esse perhibetur.'

404-5. Cf. *An.* 541-2: 'ā þīn dōm lyfað; ... is þīn nama hālig.'

405. dōm. Brooke translates, 'dominion.'

407. weoroda God. So 631 (II), 'Deus Sabaoth.'

408. gefyldest. Cf. 'pleni.'

409. wuldres þīnes. Apparently from the Mass, rather than the *Te Deum*
(see above). Cf. *Ph.* 626-9.

411. ēce hǣlo. 'Hosanna.' *Hǣlo* is the translation of 'hosanna' in Ælfric,
Hom. 1. 214 (cf. my *Biblical Quotations*, p. 164); see also *Bl. Hom.*, p. 81. Brooke
translates by 'everlasting welfare'[!].

ond ... beornum. Here it would appear as if the poet had added part of the
Gloria in excelsis (Lk. 2. 14): 'et in terra pax (though this is not *lof*) hominibus.'

414. tō hrōþre. Cf. 567.

416-439. The last section appears to constitute a sort of climax. It is not a celebration of Trinity Sunday, but the idea, derived from that source, is introduced to round off the treatment of the Advent theme. This general conception has been expressed by Blunt (p. 303) : ' The significance of the festival, as the end of the cycle of days by which our Blessed Lord and His work are commemorated, is very great. . . . On Whitsunday, therefore, we see the crowning point of the work of redemption ; and the feast of Trinity, on the Octave of Pentecost, commemorates the consummation of God's saving work, and the perfect revelation in the Church of the Three Persons in One God, as the sole objects of adoration. . . . In the festival of Trinity all these solemn subjects of belief are gathered into one act of worship, as the Church Militant looks upward through the door that is opened in Heaven, and bows down in adoration with the Church Triumphant, saying, " Holy, Holy, Holy, Lord God Almighty, Which was, and is, and is to come." '

In another sense, the present section is not so much climactic as resumptive. The thought runs thus : Great is the mystery of the Incarnation (416–424ª) ; it was to succor mankind that Christ came, and now he ever liveth to forgive and help (424ᵇ–428) ; therefore let us every one adore him (429–433), and so have a right to the endless joys of heaven (434–9). We shall hardly look for a specific source of these reflections. They are dictated by what has preceded.

Brooke's insight at this point is strangely crossed and rendered ineffective by vagrant fancies. He says : ' And now this first part of the poem is closed by a prayer [!] that, with some feeling for art, refers back to the wonder of the Incarnation with which it began, but which itself is nothing but the same pious thoughts we have so often had before. This repetition is so frequent in the *Christ* that I am more and more inclined to think that these tails at the end of the narrative or dialogue passages were sung by full choirs in church [!], by the listeners in the monastery halls, or perhaps by the whole band of some mission expedition in town or village, when the chief singers had first sung the narrative and dialogue.'

416. **wræclīc.** This should probably be *wrǣtlīc*. I suspect that all the instances of *wræclīc* in this sense are miswritings, due to the resemblance, in the manuscripts, of *c* and *t*.

wrixl. Probably points forward to 424 ff.

418. Cf. 123.

419. **frīga.** Possibly acc., in which case *wiht* would be adverbial. For the thought, cf. 37 ; *Jul.* 103 ; *El.* 341.

420. **sigores Āgend.** So 513 (II) ; *Sat.* 678.

421. **māra.** Cf. 219 ff.

424. **heofona Hēahfrēa.** Cf. 253. — **helpe gefremede.** Cf. 263.

425. **monna cynne.** Cf. 35ª, 124ª.

427. **helpe.** Cf. 424.

429. **dǣdum ond wordum.** So *Gen.* 2249, *Sat.* 552 (?), but esp. *Chr.* 1367, 1582.

432. **inlocast.** The *-loc-* due to lack of stress ; this would seem to point to a short *i* before the change, and so to *-lic-* in the next line ; cf. Trautmann, *Kynewulf*, p. 78.

434. Cf. 268, 345-7. — **lisse.** Points back to *hergen* and *weorþige.* — **leān.** Cf. 846.

436. hē. Such a man.

437-9. Cf. *Gu.* 788-790 :

> þǣr hēo sōð wunað
> wlitig, wuldorfæst, ealne wīdan ferh,
> on lifgendra londes wynne.

437. lifgendra londes. Cf. Ps. 27. 13; 142. 5; *Ps.* 141⁵; *Ps. C.* 157. — **londes wynne.** So *Gu.* 110; Isa. 24. 11. For the line see *Gu.* 790.

Dietrich thus closes his consideration of this Part (p. 200) : ‘Dass sich Nr. V und VI als zweigliedriger Abschluss zu dem bisherigen Ganzen verhalte ist unverkennbar ; ebenso dass, indem zuletzt der Blick auf die während des Erdenlebens von Christus noch nicht betretene Heimat hingerichtet wird, das folgende Gedicht von seiner Rückkehr in die himmlische Heimat, von der aus er den Menschen Gaben giebt, vorbereitet wird.’

PART II.

As Dietrich pointed out in 1853 (*Haupt's Zs.* 9. 204), the chief source of this Part is the close of Gregory the Great's homily on the Ascension, being No. 29 of his Homilies on the Gospels (Migne 76. 1218–9). What Dietrich did not observe, but what is of singular interest and importance, these extracts are taken from the Breviary, under the season of Ascension. The relevant portions will be given in their appropriate places, as well as the supplementary sources.

If we follow Gregory somewhat closely, we shall recognize an eightfold division, as follows :

A. The significance of the white robes of the angels who appeared at the Ascension (440–599).

B. (*a*) Our human nature, our very flesh, rose to heaven in the person of Christ ; (*b*) and this fact Job expressed under the symbol of a bird's flight (600–658).

C. Not only did Christ thus ennoble our humanity, but he, by his Spirit, gave gifts unto men (659–690).

D. Christ's Ascension strengthened and emboldened his Church (691–711).

E. The Church, by the mouth of Solomon, figures the Ascension as the last of five leaps or bounds made by the Savior : (1) to the Virgin ; (2) into the manger ; (3) to the cross ; (4) into the tomb ; (5) to heaven. To these Cynewulf makes an original addition, the Descent into Hell ; this is inserted before (5), making six in all (712–743).

F. We ought to follow Christ whither he has ascended (744–778, or 782ª).

G. We ought the rather to heed Christ's words, since he who was gentle at his Ascension will be terrible when he comes to the Judgment (782ᵇ–849).

H. But let hope, as an anchor of the soul, fixed within the heavenly country, whither Jesus as our forerunner is entered, hold us steadfast amidst the fluctuations of this mortal life (850–866).

With the interpolations which Cynewulf has introduced, the foregoing scheme requires subdivision and amplification. With these, it will stand somewhat as follows :

ANALYSIS.

1. = A (440–455).

2. The Ascension described, following the Scripture, with some legendary and poetical additions (456–532).

3. The return of the disciples to Jerusalem, according to Scripture (533–545ª).

4. = A, resumed (545ᵇ–557).

5. The Harrowing of Hell (558–585).

6. Lyrical reflections on the preceding (586–599).

7. God's gifts of nature and providence, perhaps as prefiguring the gifts of his Spirit (600–612).

8. The redemption and glorification of our fallen humanity = Bᵃ (613–632).

9. The figure of a bird, by which Job expressed this thought = Bᵇ (633–658).

10. Christ gave the gifts of his Spirit unto men = C (659–690).

11. = D (691–711).

12. = E (712–743).

13. = F (744–755).

14. Angel guards, watching, and prayer must shield us against the fiery darts of our adversaries (756–782ᵃ).

15. = G, with personal application (782ᵇ–796).

16. Rune passage (797–807ᵃ).

17. The terrors of the Judgment = G (807ᵇ–849).

18. = H (850–866).

So much light is thrown upon this Part by an Ascension hymn ascribed to Bede that it seems desirable to print it in its entirety. The text is from Migne 94. 624–6; Giles, *Misc. Works of Venerable Bede* 1. 83–86. As the whole is too long for use in the Church Service, extracts, sometimes considerably modified, from the complete text, have been made for this purpose (see Julian's *Dict. of Hymnology*, p. 554). Such a hymn, with interlinear gloss to certain stanzas, is found in the *Surtees Hymns*, p. 87, with the title, *Ymnus in Ascensione Domini ad Vesperam*. This contains vv. 1–8, 53–68, 117–124, together with four adapted lines introduced before 117, and six and a half different lines at the end. That in Daniel (1. 208) consists of vv. 1–4, 53–6, 61–4, 121–4, the adapted and added lines being the same as in the *Surtees Hymns*. In the latter, the stanzas which are not glossed correspond to those which are omitted by Daniel. The variants from the complete poem are also the same in both.

As illustrating the phraseology of the *Christ*, we may note: the frequent occurrence of *gloria*, 1, 5, 56, 76, 79, 84, 91, 95, 100, 101, 104, 113; *triumphus*, 5, 50, 64; *lustrans*, 11; *Auctor aetheris*, 44 (cf. *swegles Bryttan*, 281; *swegles Agend*, 543); *Auctor virtutum*, 98 (cf. *meahta Wāldend*, 822); *consempiternus Filius*, 112 (cf. *efenēce Bearn*, 465). Then this is a lyric, with long descriptive and dramatic passages, among the latter being the adaptation of Psalm 24 (75 ff.; cf. *Chr.* 575ᵇ ff.); it introduces the Harrowing of Hell (7, 9, 28, 106), followed immediately by the account of Christ's Ascension with the attendant hosts (29–36, 49–52, 69–72); the address of the two angels (62 ff.); the connection with the Last Judgment (67–8, 113–6); and the aspiration in 121–4, compared with *Chr.* 751ᵇ–755; to which may be added the allusion to the Nativity, 55.

The complete poem is as follows :

Hymnum canamus gloriae,[1]		Nam diri leti limina,
hymni novi nunc personent;		caecas et umbras inferi 10
Christus novo cum tramite		lustrans sua potentia,
ad Patris ascendit thronum.		leti ligarat principem;
Transit triumpho gloriae 5		et quos suos in actibus
poli potenter culmina		fideque lectos noverat,
qui morte mortem absumpserat,		omnes Averni faucibus 15
derisus a mortalibus.		salvavit a ferocibus;

[1] *Surtees*, Domino.

laetamque vitae januam
pandit Redemptor omnibus
quos lex amara corporis
vita pios privaverat. 20
O mira rerum claritas!
miranda Salvatoris est
virtus gemella gratiæ
quae regna leti destruit;
nam plurimos ab inferi 25
portis reduxit spiritu,
multos et ipso corpore
de fauce mortis eruit,
surgentis ut de mortuis
Christi sonarent gaudia 30
binos[1] choros paschalia
vita nova laetantium,
binae cohortes aethera
Christum secutae ascenderent,
sedesque caelo perpetes 35
inter tenerent angelos.
Hunc ergo cuncti consonis
diem feramus laudibus
victor petit quo fulgidi
Jesus Olympi januas; 40
quo nobis ipse apud Patrem
toros beatos[2] praevius
ac mansiones plurimas
paravit Auctor aetheris;
quo tota praecedentium 45
a saeculo fidelium
caterva caeli regiam
pandente Christo subiit.
Erant in admirabili
Regis triumpho altithroni 50
coetus simul caelestium
polum petentes agminum —
apostoli tum[3] mystico
in monte stantes chrismatis
cum matre claram[4] virgine 55
Jesu videbant gloriam —
ac, prosecuti lumine
laeto petentem sidera,
laetis per auras cordibus
duxere Regem saeculi. 60
Quos alloquentes angeli:
'Quid astra stantes cernitis?
Salvator hic est,' inquiunt,
'Jesus triumpho nobilis,[5]

a vobis ad caelestia 65
qui regna nunc assumptus est,
venturus inde saeculi
in fine Judex omnium.'
Haec dixerant, et non mora
juncti choris felicibus, 70
cum Rege regum lucidi
portis Olympi approximant.
Emissa tunc vox angeli:
'Portas,' ait, 'nunc pandite,
et introibit perpetis 75
Dux pacis et Rex gloriae.'
Respondit haec ab intimis
vox urbis almae moenibus:
'Quis iste Rex est gloriae
intret poli qui januas? 80
nos semper in caelestibus
Christum solemus cernere,
et ejus una cum Patre
pari beamur gloria.'
At praeco magni Judicis: 85
'Dominus potens et fortis est,
qui stravit atrum in praelio
mundi triumphans principem;
quapropter elevamini
portae perennes aetheris, 90
introeat Rex gloriae,
virtutis atque gratiae.'
Mirata adhuc caelestium
requirit aula civium:
'Quis,' inquit, 'est Rex gloriae, 95
Rex iste tam laudabilis?'
Herilis at mox buccina
respondit: 'Auctor omnium
altissimus virtutum, et is
Rex ipse fulget gloria.' 100
Dictis quibus, Rex gloriae,
cum glorioso milite,
ingressus est in aethere
sublime regnum gloriae.
Qua mansiones singulis 105
quos de profundis inferi
abduxerat, pro congruis
donavit almus actibus.
Ac[6] ipse cuncta transiens
caeli micantis culmina, 110
ad dexteram sedit Patris
consempiternus Filius,

[1] bini chori?
[2] *Migne, Giles*, beatus.
[3] *Surtees*, tunc.
[4] *Surtees*, clara.

[5] *Surtees*, nobili.
[6] *Surtees* apparently adapts the next five lines, changing and condensing them to four.

venturus inde in gloria		da nobis illuc sedula	
vivos simul cum mortuis		devotione tendere	
dijudicare pro actibus,	115	qua [3] te sedere cum Patre	
justo potens examine.		in arce regni credimus ;	
Quo nos precamur tempore,		nostris ibi tum cordibus	125
Jesu, Redemptor unice,		tuo repleti [4] Spiritu	
inter tuos in aethere [1]		ostende Patrem, et sufficit	
servos benignus [2] aggrega ;	120	haec nobis una visio.	

We may remember that Bede died on Ascension eve, probably May 9, 742 (see the learned note in Mayor and Lumby's Bede, pp. 401–2), and that he used on his deathbed to sing Antiphons, the one for the Second Vespers of Ascension Day being apparently his favorite. As there is no accurate translation of Cuthbert's letter on Bede's death (both that in Lingard's *Anglo-Saxon Church* 2. 177–182, and that in Stevenson's Bede, 1. lxxix–lxxxiii, reposing on an inferior text and being inaccurately translated, and that in Montalembert's *Monks of the West* 5. 90–93 being incomplete), I transcribe the most important passages from the St. Gallen MS. of the ninth century, the oldest known, as printed by Mayor and Lumby, pp. 176 ff.: 'Postea letus et gaudens graciasque agens omnipotenti Deo omni die et nocte, immo horis omnibus usque ad diem Ascensionis Dominicae, id est vii id. Maī vitam ducebat. . . . Cantabat etiam antiphonas ob nostram consolationem et suam, quarum una est: "O Rex gloriae, Domine virtutum, qui triumphator hodie super omnes caelos ascendisti, ne derelinquas nos orphanos," usque "veritatis. Alleluia." Cum venisset autem ad illud verbum, "Ne derelinquas nos orphanos," prorupit in lacrimas et multum flebat. Et post horam cepit repetere quae incoaverat. Et sic tota die faciebat. . . . In tali leticia quinquagesimales dies usque ad diem praefatum deduximus. . . . In letitia diem ultimum usque ad vesperum duxit.' The words omitted from the Antiphon are : 'sed mitte promissum Patris in nos Spiritum [veritatis].'

440–455. See *Analysis*, 1 (p. 115).

As the source of this section (and 545[b]–557), cf. Gregory, *Hom. in Evang.* 29. 9: 'Hoc autem nobis primum quaerendum est, quidnam sit quod nato Domino apparuerunt angeli, et tamen non leguntur in albis vestibus apparuisse; ascendente autem Domino, missi angeli in albis leguntur vestibus apparuisse. Sic etenim scriptum est : *Videntibus illis elevatus est, et nubes suscepit eum ab oculis eorum. Cumque intuerentur in caelum euntem illum, ecce duo viri steterunt juxta illos in vestibus albis* (Act. 1. 9). In albis autem vestibus gaudium et solemnitas mentis ostenditur. Quid est ergo quod, nato Domino, non in albis vestibus, ascendente autem Domino, in albis vestibus angeli apparent, nisi quod tunc magna solemnitas angelis facta est, cum caelum Deus homo penetravit? Quia, nascente Domino, videbatur divinitas humiliata ; ascendente vero Domino, est humanitas exaltata. Albae etenim vestes exaltationi magis congruunt quam humiliationi. In Assumptione (*Breviary*, Ascensione) ergo ejus angeli in albis vestibus videri debuerunt, quia qui in Nativitate sua apparuit Deus humilis, in Ascensione sua ostensus est homo sublimis.' Tr. by Ælfric, 1. 298.

---

[1] *Surtees*, aethera.
[2] So *Surtees* ; Migne, Giles, benignos.

[3] *Surtees*, quo.
[4] repletis ?

This is from the Lesson for the Third Nocturn of Wednesday in the Octave of Ascension (Feria Quarta infra Octavum Ascensionis). The homily is continued at the Third Nocturn of the Octave, ending with the word *praerogavit* (see note on 783ᵇ–796).

440. gǣstgerȳnum. So 713; *An.* 860; *El.* 189, 1148; *Gu.* 1086. In another sense *Gu.* 219.

441. mon se mǣra. If we could but know whom Cynewulf is here addressing, what light might be thrown upon the circumstances of his life! It may perhaps have been an ecclesiastic, though such a person might be presumed to have reflected upon these matters as deeply as Cynewulf. It may have been a king, or perhaps a nobleman ; cf. Ælfric's relations with laymen eminent for their virtue (chaps. 3 and 4 of Dr. Caroline L. White's *Ælfric, a New Study of his Life and Writings*, Boston, 1898).

For *mǣre* as employed in the voc. by itself, see 275, and *Ps.* 118¹⁸²; with *se* preceding, *Beow.* 1474.

444. Cf. 298 (I). — **þurh clǣnne hād.** Th. 'through state of purity'; Gr. (*D.*) 'durch reine Geburt'; (*Spr.*) 'a virgine'; Go. 'in purity.'

445. Marīan. Gen., not acc.

446. mundheals. Sanctuary, shelter; cf. *mundbora*, 28, and *hāls*, 587. Gollancz mentions this interpretation, though he adds : 'but cp. *mund*, l. 92, and the special use of *heals* in such compounds as *healsmægeð*, *Gen.* 2155; *healsgebedda*, *Beow.* 63; *mundheals* may have had a similar meaning, "beloved maiden."' — gecēas. Cf. 36.

447. gewerede. Cf. 552; *El.* 263; *Gen.* 462.

449. Beorn. Possibly we should read *Bearn;* cf. *El.* 391.

450. hlēoþorewide. Cf. *Dan.* 155; *An.* 820. — **hyrdum.** Cf. Lk. 2. 8 ff.

453. cwið. For this impersonal use, cf. 701.

456–532. See *Analysis*, 2 (p. 115).

456. Bethānia. Cf. Lk. 24. 50.

459. wildæge. So *wilboda*, *Gu.* 1220; *wilgæst*, *Mōd.* 7 ; *wilgedryht*, *An.* 916; *Ph.* 342; *wilgesið*, *Beow.* 23, *Gen.* 2003; *wilhrēðig*, *El.* 1117; etc.

460. gearwe. For the construction with *tō*, see *El.* 23; *An.* 1371; here there seems to be an ellipsis of a verb of motion.

462. tācna. In this sense *Dan.* 447; *El.* 319, 854; etc. The reference is to Lk. 24. 27, 44–48.

464. ūp stige. Not as in 651, 711; cf. the parallel expression, 544.

465. efenēce. So 122 (I); cf. *Bl. Hom.* 29³, 111⁸. — **āgnum Fæder.** So 532. With the whole line cf. *Hy.* 8²¹ : 'efenēadig Bearn āgenum Fæder.' On the thought, cf. Allen, *Christian Institutions*, p. 296 : 'It can be shown that the faith in Christ as the incarnate and coequal Son of God has never lost its hold upon the Christian consciousness, that it has been the antecedent of the changes which have modified, if not created, our modern civilization.'

Fæder. Here, and in 211, 532, 773, Trautmann (*Kynewulf*, p. 77) would read *Fædder.*

466. fēowertig. Cf. Acts 1. 3.

468–469. The word-order is indicated in Gollancz' translation : 'Then had He fulfilled the prophets' words, as they had sung before throughout the world.'

Not as in Grein (*D.*): 'Er hatte da erfüllet, wie zuvor gesungen der Wahrsager Worte durch die Weltbehausung,' where he makes *Worte* nom., instead of acc.

468. gefylled. Cf. 213, 326.

469. geond . . . innan. This must be interpreted in the light of *on innan*, sometimes found in this form, and sometimes separated by the governed word. The simple *innan* is either adv., or prep. with dat. or acc., the acc. occurring only once (with variant *inne*). The combination *on* (*in*) *innan* is rather numerous. For analogues to our phrase, cf. *Dan.* 238: 'engel in þone ofn innan becwōm'; *Gen.* 839: 'uton gān on þysne weald innan'; *Ph.* 200: 'bireð in þæt trēow innan torhte frætwe'; where the combination is sufficiently rendered by *into*. *Geond . . innan* is found *Gu.* 855: 'mǣre wurdon his wundra geweorc . geond Bryten innan'; *Panther* 4: 'wīde sind geond world innan fugla and dēora . . . wornas'; in both of these, *throughout* expresses the whole sense, and so, I believe, in our passage.

470. þrōwinga. Cf. 1129, 1179 (III).

471. See *Hy.* 8³: 'lufian lēofwendum līfes Āgend.' Hence Cosijn's emendation, *lēofwendne* (comparing 400) is unnecessary. Cosijn adds : 'Die Verwechselung von *lofian* und *lufian* kommt auch sonst vor, z. B. Beda-Miller 212. 7 var.; v. 504 steht richtig *heredun, lofedun* '; but cf. *Az.* 100; *Ps.* 77³⁵.

476-490. Cf. Mt. 28. 19, 20; Mk. 16. 15 ff.; Mt. 10. 7 ff.; Lk. 9. 2 ff.

476. Gefeoð. Based upon Jn. 16. 22, according to Dietrich. — **ferðe.** Cf. *Gram.* 222. 1. *Ferhð* is common in the poetry : *Beow.* 1166; *El.* 1037; etc.

478. mid wunige. So 488.

479. āwo tō ealdre. So 1645 (III); *Gu.* 758. *Āwa tō ealdre* occurs five times more.

480. onsīen. The word *onsīen, -sȳn*, meaning 'countenance,' is common in OE. Thorpe, when he had reached this point (*Cod. Exon.* 30. 16), did not suspect any other sense, and so rendered by 'God's countenance,' adding in a note: 'Here two or more lines are obviously wanting.' In *Gu.* 800 (*Cod. Exon.* 151. 24) he rendered by 'madness '; *Ph.* 55 (201. 13), 'desire'; but *Ph.* 398 (225. 32) he discerned the true sense, and rendered 'lack.' Dietrich called attention to these facts (*Haupt's Zs.* 9. 211), and added that neither alliteration nor context requires the assumption of a gap.

481 ff. A parallel to this is *An.* 332-9 :

'Fara nū geond ealle eorðan scēatas
emne swā wīde swā wæter bebūgeð
oðð e stedewangas strǣte gelicgað.
Bodiað æfter burgum beorhtne gelēafan
ofer foldan fæðm; ic ēow freoðo healde.
Ne þurfan gē on þā fōre frætwe lǣdan,
gold ne seolfor ; ic ēow gōda gehwæs
on ēowerne āgenne dōm ēst āhwette.'

Cf. the OS. *Heliand* 1837-1914.

481. ealne yrmenne grund. So *Jul.* 10; cf. *eormengrund, Beow.* 859. Cf. the OS. *irmin-*, in *Hel.* 340, etc., and the ON. mythical names Jörmungandr, Jörmunrekr, Jörmunþrjōtr, but especially *Jörmundgrund*, in *Grimnismal* 20. See also Grimm, *Teut. Myth.*, pp. 115–9; Müllenhoff, in *Haupt's Zs.* 23. 1 ff. ; and cf. the references in Golther, *Handbuch der Germ. Mythologie*, p. 207, note.

482. geond wīdwegas. So *Beow.* 840, 1704; *Ps.* 144²⁰.

483. Cf. *An.* 335. — **beorhtne gelēafan.** So *Gu.* 770.

484. folc under roderum. So 526.

485. hergas. Grein defines *hearg* as *fanum, delubrum, idolum.* Grimm (*Teut. Myth.*, p. 68) says that the OHG. *haruc* stands for *fanum, delubrum, lucus,* and *nemus.* ' It includes,' he continues, ' on the one hand the notion of *templum, fanum,* and on the other that of *wood, grove, lucus.*' Cf. Bede, *Eccl. Hist.*, Bk. 2, chaps. 13, 15. In the *Cura Past., hearg* is once used for *idolum,* and once for *simulacrum* (*Bibl. Quot.*, pp. 28, 52). On ON. *hörgr,* cf. the Cleasby-Vigfusson *Dictionary,* though perhaps their conclusions are not to be affirmed of OE. *hearg:* ' Distinction is to be made between hof (*temple*) and horg; the hof was a house of timber, whereas the horg was *an altar of stone* erected on high places, or *a sacrificial cairn,* built in open air, and without images, for the horg itself was to be stained with the blood of the sacrifice; hence such phrases as, to " break " the horgs, but " burn " the temples. The horg worship reminds one of the worship in high places of the Bible. . . . In provincial Norse a dome-shaped mountain is called *horg.* The worship on horgs seems to be older than that in temples, but was in after times retained along with temple worship. . . Many of the old cairns and *hows* are no doubt horgs or high places of worship of the heathen age.' Under *hof, hörgr* is defined as, ' *an altar, holy circle,* or *any roofless place of worship.*' Golther has (*Handbuch der Germ. Myth.*, p. 591): ' Im Nordischen bedeutet *hǫrgr* ursprünglich Steinhaufen, vielleicht geschichteter Steinaltar oder Steinkreis als Hag um den Opferplatz, wie solche noch in England und Skandinavien zu sehen sind. Zugleich aber nimmt *hǫrg* die allgemeine Bedeutung "Heiligtum," die besondere " kleinere Tempel " an.'

brēotaþ. ON. *brjōta* is used in the same sense.

486. fyllað ond fēogað. Brooke's rendering is vigorous : ' overthrow them, abhor them.'

487. sāwað. For the verb with an abstract noun as object, see Ps. 97. 11 ; Prov. 6. 14, 19 ; 11. 18 ; 16. 28 ; 22. 8 ; Mk. 4. 14. Prov. 6. 14 is translated in the *Cura Past.* (see my *Bibl. Quot.*, p. 19); for other examples of *sāwan* in a figurative sense, see Bosworth-Toller, II, and *Chr.* 86, 663.

488. meahta spēd. So (I) 296, (III) 1383, 1401; cf. 652, and *mihta spēd, Gen.* 1696; *Dan.* 335; *El.* 366. — **ic ēow mid wunige.** Cf. *An.* 99.

489. forð on frōfre. So 1360 (III).

friðe healde. So *An.* 336, 917, 1434, *Gu.* 281 ; cf. *Gen.* 2528.

490. Cf. *An.* 121.

492. hlūd gehȳred. So *Gu.* 1289. — **heofonengla þrēat.** So 927 (III).

493. weorud wlitescȳne. So 554. — **wuldres āras.** So *El.* 738.

494. cwōmun. This is not in the New Testament, and must be sought in the Fathers and the hymns. Cf., for example, the passages mentioned above (p. 116), and Mone's Hymn No. 176:

> Officiis te angeli
> atque nubes stipant
> ad Patrem reversurum.

Alban Butler (*The Movable Feasts, Fasts*, etc., p. 319) thinks the cloud itself
denotes the presence of angels, comparing Lev. 16. 2 with Exod. 25. 22. According to Neale and Littledale, *Commentary on the Psalms* i. 336, this attendance
of angels is recognized by Basil, Theodoret, Cyril of Alexandria, Tertullian,
and Cyprian. I have found it in none but Theodoret (on Ezek. 11. 22, 23 : *Patr.
Gr.* 81. 902). In the Latin translation it runs : ' His ita dictis, inquit, recesserunt
de civitate cherubim gloriam Dei insidentem vehentia, steterunt super montem e
regione Hierosolymae. Est autem hic mons qui vocatur Olivarum, unde etiam
secundum carnem facta est in caelum Ascensio Salvatoris nostri. . . . In montem
illum cum discipulis profectus, ab intelligentibus et quae cerni nequeunt potesta-
tibus latus in caelos assumptus est.' We have it, however, in Gregory of Nyssa,
Orat. de Ascens. Dom. (Lesson 4 of the Second Nocturn for Wednesday of the
Octave of Ascension, according to the Roman Breviary) : ' Cum in caelum rede-
untem Dominum ipsae [caelestes potestates] comitantes angelis . . . imperant ad
hunc modum ; *Tollite portas*,' etc. . . . (Lesson 6) : ' Itaque rursus comites ejus . . .
interrogantur : *Quis est iste Rex gloriae ?* ' As Bede recognized it in the Hymn
quoted above, it is interesting to compare a passage from his *Hom. in Ascensione*
(Migne 94. 180) : 'Elevatus est, etsi non angelico fultus auxilio, angelico tamen
comitatus obsequio, vereque assumptus est in caelum.' Cf. Ps. 18. 10 ; 47.5
(used as Antiphon, and as Versicle and Response on Ascension Day). See also
Adam of St. Victor's Sequence on the Ascension :

> Postquam hostem et inferna
> Spoliavit, ad superna
>   Christus redit gaudia,
> Angelorum ascendenti,
> Sicut olim descendenti,
>   Parantur obsequia.

And add, from Bede's Hymn, *De Universis Dei Operibus* (Migne 94. 622), the
lines :

> Vitaeque prima Sabbati
> Surgendo pandit januam,
> *Suisque congaudentibus*
> Ascendit ad thronum Patris.

But perhaps the finest passage on this theme is that from Giles Fletcher, quoted
in the note on 576 ; see also Wesley's hymn, ' Our Lord is risen from the dead.'
  Cf. the account of the Ascension in *Sat.* 563–9.

  495. þurh þæs temples hrōf. The difficulty which this occasions was solved
by Professor Bright in *Modern Language Notes* for January, 1898. He says
(p. 14) : ' The poet, as it would appear, was familiar with the first traveller's
account of the Holy Land brought to England, in which the place of the Ascension is thus described : "The Mount of Olives is five miles distant from Jerusalem, and is equal in height to Mount Sion, but exceeds it in breadth and length ;
it bears few trees besides vines and olive-trees, and is fruitful in wheat and bar-
ley, for the nature of that soil is not calculated for bearing things of large or
heavy growth, but grass and flowers. On the very top of it, where our Lord
ascended into heaven, is a large round church, having about it three vaulted

porches.　For the inner house could not be vaulted and covered, because of the passage of our Lord's body; but it has an altar on the east side, covered with a narrow roof.　In the midst of it are to be seen the last prints of our Lord's feet, and the sky appearing open above where he ascended; and though the earth is daily carried away by believers, yet still it remains as before, and retains the same impression of the feet."　This is extracted (in Giles's translation) from an abridged treatise entitled *De Locis Sanctis* attributed to Bede (Giles, vol. iv, p. 416).　The passage is also reproduced in Bede's *Eccl. Hist.*, lib. v. cap. 17, where it is preceded by an account of the composition of the original work by Adamnan, at the dictation of Arculf (cap. 15).　These chapters (15–17) are omitted by the West Saxon translator of the *History*, whether for the reason assigned by Wheloc, or for that assigned by Schmidt (*Untersuchungen über K. Ælfred's Bedaübersetzung*), or for neither.'

The account is given in Old English, though not in the translation of the *Eccl. Hist.* I subjoin the passage from Cockayne's *Shrine*, pp. 80–82 :

'On ðone fīftan dæg þæs mōnðes [i.e. May] bið se dæg þe ūre Dryhten tō heofonum āstāg. Ðȳ dæge hine gesēgon nȳhst his þegnas on Oliuetes dūne,[1] ðǣr hē blētsade hī, ond ðā gewāt mid þȳ līchoman on heofonum. Ðȳ dæge ēode sēo eorðe on heofon, ðæt is, se mon ofer engla ðrym. Ond on Oliuetes dūne syndon nū gȳt ðā swæþe Drihtnes fōtlāsta. Ymb þā Drihtnes fōtlāstas timbredon crīstne men seonewalte cirican wunderlice. Ne mihte sēo his swaðu nǣfre mid nǣnigre ōðre wīsan bēon þǣm ōðrum flōrum geonlīcod ond gelīce gehīwad. Gif þǣr mon hwæt mænnisces on āsette, ðonne sēo eorðe him on ufan scealde; ðēah hit wǣre marmanstānas, ðā wǣron āswengde on ðāra onsȳn þe þǣr onsǣton.[2]

'Ðæt dūst ðæt God ðǣr ontrǣd, ond þā his swaða ðe þǣr onþricced sendon, ðā syndon monnum tō ēcre lāre. Ond dæghwamlice gelēaffulle men nimað ðæt sand, ond þǣr hwæðre ne bið nǣnig wonung on þǣm sande ðǣre Drihtnes[3] fōtswaða. Sanctus Arculfus sǣde þæt þǣr ne mihte nǣnig hrōf on bēon on ðǣre cirican on ðǣre stōwe ðe ūre Drihten on stōd þā hē tō heofonum āstāg, ac þæt se weg ðǣr wǣre ā tō heofonum open, þāra monna ēagum þe him þǣr gebǣdan on ðǣre ylcan stōwe. Ond hē sǣde þæt þā Drihtnes fōtlāstas wǣron beworht mid ǣrne hwēole, ond þæs hēanes wǣre oð monnes swȳran; ond þǣr wǣre ðȳrel on middum þǣm hwēole, ðurh þæt mihton men ufan beorhtlice scēawian Drihtnes fōta swaðe; ond þæt hī mihton mid heora handum rǣcean ond niman þæs hālgan dūstes dǣl. Ond Sanctus Arculfus sǣde þæt þǣr hangade ūþmǣte lēohtfæt ond ðwǣre byrnende dæges and nihtes ofer þāra Drihtnes fōta swaða. Ond hē sǣde þæt ǣghwelce gēare, ðȳ dæge æt Crīstes uppāstignesse, on middes dæges tīde, æfter-þon-þe mæssesangas wǣron geendode on þǣre ylcan cirican, þæt þǣr tō

---

[1] Cockayne, 'done' (misprint).

[2] Quoted expressly from Arculf, in whose account, as given by Adamnan, they occur : but partly a citation from an earlier author. Illud mirum, quod locus ille, in quo postremum institerat divina vestigia, cum in caelum Dominus nube sublatus est, continuari pavimento cum reliqua stratorum parte non potuit: siquidem quaecunque applicabantur, insolens humana suscipere terra respueret, excussis in ora apponentium saepe marmoribus. Sulpicius Severus, *Sacr. Hist.* II. 61 and more. (Cockayne's note.)

[3] MS. drihtne.

cōme þæs strongestan windes ȳste, ond þæt sē swā stronglice hrure on þā circan þæt þǣr ne mihte nǣnig mon ǣnge gemete on ðǣre circean oððe on hire nēah-stōwe gestandan oþþe gesittan, ac þæt ealle þā men ðe þǣr þonne wǣron lāgon āþænede on þǣre eorðan mid ofdūnehealdum ondwleotan oþ-þæt sēo ondrysnlice[1] ȳst forð gelēoreð. Se ondrysnlica wind þæt dēð, þæt sē dǣl ðǣre ciricean ne mæg habban ðone hrōf ðǣr þæs Hǣlendes fōtlāstas syndon under. Sanctus Arculfus sǣde þæt hē self ðǣr wǣre ondweard æt þǣre ylcan cyricean, ðȳ dæge æt Crīstes uppāstignesse ðā se stranga ond se forhtlica wind þǣr onrǣsde.'

Other accounts are by Eusebius, *Vit. Const.* 3. 42 (*Patr. Gr.* 20. 1102) ; Pauli-nus of Nola, *Epist.* 31. 4 (Migne 61. 328) ; John of Würzburg (A.D. 1165), quoted in T. Tobler, *Descriptiones Terrae Sanctae*, Leipzig, 1874, p. 156; Maundrell, in Wright, *Early Travels in Palestine*, pp. 470–1; and especially Willibald (A.D. 723-6), quoted in Tobler, p. 33. The passage from Willibald is perhaps quite as likely to have been in Cynewulf's mind as that from Bede. Cf. *Bl. Hom.*, pp. 125-9.

496. lāst weardedun. We have seen how, for ages, his 'footsteps' were ' watched,' by the passages quoted above.

497. þingstede. So *An.* 1100.

498. Cf. Lk. 24. 51 ; Acts 1. 9.

499. Godbearn of grundum. Cf. 702; also 682; *An.* 640.

Him wæs gēomor sefa. So *Beow.* 49, 2419; *El.* 627; cf. *Beow.* 2632; *Hy.* 4[94].

500. hāt æt heortan. So 539; *An.* 1711; *Gu.* 1182, 1310; *El.* 628.

505. One is reminded of Homer, *Il.* 5. 4-7 : ' She [Pallas Athene] kindled flame unwearied from his helmet and shield, like to the star of summer that above all others glittereth bright after he hath bathed in the ocean stream. In such wise kindled she flame *from his head* and shoulders.'

Possibly there may be a reference here to the passage from the *Evangelium Nicodemi*, of which the OE. translation is given in the note on 30–32.

506-526. Acts 1. 10, 11. For the prose account by Ælfric, see *Bibl. Quot.*, p. 227.

507. ymb þæt Frumbearn. This, like *of hēahþu*, 508, and the whole of 499[b]-505, 516-522, is poetical embellishment, though perhaps not original with Cynewulf.

508. Wuldor. Matthew Arnold calls Sophocles (*To a Friend*) ' The mellow *glory* of the Attic stage.'

510. beorhtan reorde. Cf. *An.* 96, but especially *Ph.* 128.

511. on hwearfte. Th. 'about'; Gr. 'da'; Go. 'about.' Cosijn would read *hwearfe*, = *þrēate*. It is true that *hwearfte* is not altogether satisfactory. Grein (*Spr.*) renders *hwearft* by ' ambitus,' ' circuitus,' adduces *Az.* 38, 41, *Rid.* 41[33], and interprets our passage by ' quid circumstantes exspectatis ?' Sweet renders *hwearft* by ' circuit,' ' expanse,' ' lapse of time.' *Hwearf*, ' caterva,' ' con-gregatio' (Grein), ' crowd ' (Sweet), *Gu.* 234, *Jud.* 249, is perhaps justified by such expressions as Ælfric, *Hom.* 1. 28 : ' Drihten . . . āstāh tō heofenum ætforan heora *ealra* gesihðe'; *Bl. Hom.* 91. 3: ' On *manigra manna* gesyhþe hē āstāg on heofenas.'

515. æþelinga Ord. So 741, 845. —**mid þās engla gedryht.** Cf. 519.

---

[1] Cockayne, ' ondrynslice ' (misprint).

517-8. Gollancz says : ' I take these lines to be the reply of Galileans ; another interesting instance of the dramatic bent of Cynewulf's genius. Grein takes ll. 509-525 as one long speech. The MS. is in favor of my view of the passage, as a new section begins with l. 516.' The Galileans, then, if grammar is to be heeded, must have been provided with wings ! Brooke, misled, as on some other occasions, by his guide, renders :

> O how fain would we   in this fashion, with this band,
> With this cheerful company,   o'er the cover of the Heaven,
> To the brightening Burg,   bring the Lord along.

As against this, cf. the use of *willan*, 514, 523, 571, 577, 941, 1073, 1099, etc. A wish is expressed by the opt. pret., as in *El.* 1080 : ' wolde ic þæt þū funde,' or as in *Chr.* 410, 414, 598, 777. Even Conybeare had a clearer perception of the truth, as appears from his thus introducing his translation (p. 215) : ' It commences thus abruptly with what I should apprehend to be a song of the attendant angels :

> Thus in glad triumph o'er the aetherial vault
> To Zion's holy towers, with this fair pomp
> Of Heaven's all-glorious sons we bear our Lord.'

However, he immediately adds : ' The poet now appears to return to his narrative.' Dietrich is right in saying : ' Offenbar nicht Worte des Dichters an die Leser (Thorpe), sondern weitere Rede der beiden Engel an die Jünger '; but he apparently makes the mistake of following Thorpe, who begins a new sentence with 520, and regards *sēleste* as nom. Grein considers *sēleste* as acc.; in favor of this view it is scarcely necessary to do more than adduce the parallelism of *frætwum blīcan*, 507, 522, as applied to the angels, not to Christ (note *gesēgon*, 506; *gesēoð*, 522).

518. heofona gehlidu. Cf. 904; *Gen.* 584.

519. gedryht. It is not perfectly clear whether this band consists wholly of angels, or includes the Old Testament saints delivered from hell; the latter is more probable. Neale and Littledale (2. 389) thus interpret Ps. 68. 25, referring to Jerome : ' If we take the words of the triumphal Ascension of Christ, then the Princes will be the Angels who formed His court, the minstrels the train of ransomed Fathers.'

520ᵃ. Conybeare ends the sentence here, so that *sigebearna* designates the angels. — **520ᵇ.** Con. renders *þæt* by *illum*, and translates 520ᵇ-525. Note how Cynewulf occasionally introduces parenthetical passages which break the sense; *þæt* of course = **Hlāford.** Cf. 1097-8, 1316-26.

521ᵇ. So 570; cf. *Beow.* 2796.

522. frætwum blīcan. So 507. Con. ends the sentence here.

523-4. eorðan mægðe sylfa gesēcan. Hear the admirable echo, 946-7 (III). Con. renders *gesēcan* by *convocare*, and *side herge* by *immensam (latam) coronam* [!].

524. sīde herge. Cf. 2 Thess. 1. 7 ; *Beow.* 2347 has *sīdan herge.*

525. Cf. 803.

527-532. Conybeare says : ' The next paragraph affording a good example of the peculiar construction of the Anglo-Saxon poetical sentence, I have rendered it line for line into a Latin dimeter iambic :

Sedebat illic Filius
Tremente caeli fornice,
Rex angelorum altissimus
Supra aetheris fastigium,
Tutela devotae gregis,
Tunc aucta spes fidelium,
In urbe sancta gaudium
Praesente tandem Filio.'

527. wolcnum. Acts 1. 9.

529ᵇ-530ᵃ. Cf. *Gu.* 927, but especially *Dream of the Rood* 148-156:

Hiht wæs genīwad
mid blēdum ond mid blisse, þām þe þær bryne þolodan.
Se Sunu wæs sigorfæst on þām sīðfate,
mihtig ond spēdig, þā he mid manigeo cōm,
gāsta weorode on Godes rīce,
Anwealda ælmihtig, englum tō blisse
ond eallum ðām hālgum, þām þe on heofonum ǣr
wunedon on wuldre, þā heora Wealdend cwōm,
ælmihtig God, þǣr his ēðel wæs.

531. Mk. 16. 19. Cf. *Hy.* 8⁸⁰.

533-540ᵃ. See *Analysis*, 3 (p. 115). Conybeare renders all but the last line (pp. 216-7).

534. hæleð hygerōfe. So *Gen.* 1550, 1709; *Jud.* 303; *An.* 1056. Con. renders: 'heals every sorrow.'

537ᵇ-540ᵇ. Conybeare translates:

The crowd of mourners there forgot their pain,
And love glow'd quickening at their inmost soul
Responsive to their master's.

537. wōpes hring. This difficult phrase must be interpreted in the light of its four occurrences. The other three are:
An. 1280:

þā cwōm *wōpes hring*
þurh þæs beornes brēost blāt ūt faran,
wēoll waðuman strēam.

El. 1132:

þā wæs *wōpes hring,*
hāt hēafodwylm, ofer hlēor goten,
nälles for torne; teāras fēollon.

Gu. 1313:

Him þæs *wōpes hring,*
torne gemonade; teagor yðum wēoll,
hāte hlēordropan, and on hreðre wæg
micle mōdceare.

Grimm, on the passage of *Andreas*, says that it does not mean *coetus flentium*, but rather *fletus intensissimus, quasi circulatim erumpens;* and this is approved by Bosworth-Toller, 'though the connection with *hring* is not very evident.' Conybeare translates by 'lamentationis circulus.' Grein renders *hring* by

' sonus,' and Zupitza (Glossary to *Elene*) by ' getön, schall, laut.' Kent (Glossary
to *Elene*) renders by ' ring, sound,' and *wōpes hring* by ' sound of weeping,' which
is the expression adopted by Garnett in his translation.

What are the equivalents of *wōpes hring* and of what verbs is it the direct
or indirect subject? It appears to be synonymous with *strēam* (*An.*); with
hāt hēafodwylm and *tēaras* (*El.*); and with *teagor* and *hāte hlēordropan* (*Gu.*).
It comes issuing through the breast as a welling stream (*An.*); is shed over
the face, and falls as tears (*El.*); and gushes, as tears and hot face-drops, in
waves (*Gu.*). In so rendering, use is of course made of the synonymous kennings. Thus the notion of sound or noise seems to be excluded, or at all events
is not prominent. If, then, *wōpes hring* signifies tears, represented as issuing
from the troubled bosom, and gushing from the eyes, why might not the succession of drops be thought of as pearls upon a string, or as beads in a necklace or
rosary? As for *wōp*, though in the poetry it generally means ' wailing,' 'loud
lament,' yet *wōpdropa* and *wōpig* indicate tears, to which may be added the
wōplic(e) of prose.

It is no argument to say that such a rendering is far-fetched ; any rendering of
the phrase must be somewhat far-fetched, and not of this phrase only in the
poetry. The kennings of Norse poetry, as is well known, go much further in this
direction, like the phraseology of such writers as Nonnus and Lycophron in the
Greek decadence. Indeed, one need not look further than Shelley and Tennyson
for instances. Of Tennyson take this (*Princess* III. 112):

> Up went the *hushed amaze* of hand and eye;

or this (*ib.* VII. 201–2) :

> *Azure pillars of the hearth*
> Arise to thee ;

or this (*Audley Court* 15) :

> The *pillared dusk* of sounding sycamores ;

or where he speaks of a moon (*Audley Court* 80–81) that

> *Dimly rained* about the leaf
> *Twilights of airy silver.*

Here is a conceit which the ancients would probably have called 'frigid' (*In
Mem.* IV) :

> Break, thou deep vase of chilling tears
> That grief hath shaken into frost.

As a suggestive parallel to the rendering proposed above, cf. Shelley, *Adonais*
XI. 4–5 :

> An anadem
> Which frozen tears, instead of pearls, begem.

Remoter, but somewhat to the purpose, is Browning's (*By the Fireside* 149–150)

> Break the *rosary in a pearly rain*,
> And gather what we let fall.

Perhaps the idea of *wōpes hring* might be suggested to the modern reader by
' circling fountain of tears.'

539. hreðer innan wēoll. So *Beow.* 2113; *Gu.* 952; cf. *Beow.* 2593. Con. renders *hreðer* by ' velocius.'

540. beorn. Wyatt is evidently wrong in saying, on *Beow.* 1880 : '*Beorn* is an unexampled form of the pret. of *beornan* (*Grammar* § 386, N. 2).' Con. renders by 'filii'!

541. Þēodnes gehāta. Con. renders by 'Domini electorum,' 'of those whom God hath called.'

542ᵃ. byrig. Here, and in 569, Trautmann (*Kynewulf,* p. 82) would read *byrg;* cf. 461, 519.

542ᵇ. Con. writes: *Tyr riht ðagen,* and renders: 'Dei justi ministri,' 'the servants of his justice.' He evidently understands *ðagen* as *ðegen,* i.e. *ðegnas,* and *Tyr* as Tīw (in ON. Tȳr), the god Mars, whose name is preserved in Tuesday (cf. Grimm, *Teut. Myth.,* pp. 193–208 ; Golther, *Germ. Myth.,* pp. 200 ff.). For the time, cf. Acts 1. 3 and 2. 1.

545. on heofona gehyld. Th. ' in heaven's vault ' [evidently his suggested *gehlyd = gehlid*] ; Gr. ' zu der Himmel Höhen ' ; Go. ' to heaven's keeping.' Gr. (*Spr.*) separates *gehyld,* ' keeping,' ' protection,' from *gehyld,* (?) ' recessus,' ' res abditae,' ' arcanum,' for which he doubtfully adduces *Beow.* 3056, and the gloss on Ps. 16¹³, ' on gehyldum *in abditis* (cf. Bosworth-Toller s. v. *gehild.* B.-T. does not distinguish two words, and doubtfully renders by 'protection ' in our passage). Sweet has five meanings under (*ge*) *hield :* (1) watching ; (2) observance (of festival) ; (3) protection ; (4) guardian ; (5) secret place. *Gehlid(u)* is, of course, out of the question here ; 518 and 904 are not parallel to this: the *ofer* and *þurh* are intelligible with *gehlid(u),* but not *on.* One might think of Ps. 91. 1 : ' Qui habitat in adjutorio Altissimi, *in protectione Dei caeli* commorabitur.'

545ᵇ–557. See *Analysis* 4 (p. 115).

545ᵇ. Hwīte. One hardly knows whether to think of 447, 454, or of 506.

546. Ēadgiefan. Cf. *An.* 74, 451.

548–9. Cf. 928–9 (III).

548. ælbeorhte englas. So 506.

549ᵃ. See 632ᵇ, 739ᵃ.

551. Wel þæt gedafenað. Cf. *Blickling Homilies,* pp. 121, 123: ' þæt wæron Drihtnes englas ; þā hwītan hrægl þāra engla getācniaþ þone gefēan engla and manna, þe þā geworden wæs ; forþon þær þæt æfre wære þæt englas on heofenum māran gefēan and māran blisse hæfdon þonne hīe ealne weg ær hæfdon, þonne wære þæt on þās hālgan tīd geworden þā hīe þone heora Scyppend gesēgon, and þone sōþan Cyning ælmihtigne God ealra gesceafta mid þære menniscan gecynd tō þæm fæderlican setle āhafenne, þonon hē næfre ne gewāt þurh his þā ēcean godcundnesse. And him þā wæs ēac heora gefēa and heora blis geēced þā hīe wiston þæt heora ēþel þær on heofenum sceolde eft gebūen and geseted weorþan mid hālgum sāwlum, and þā hālgan setl eft gefylde mid þære menniscan gecynde, þe deofol ær for his oforhygdum of āworpen wæs. Hwæt, wē witon þæt æghwylcum men biþ lēofre swā hē hæbbe holdra frēonda mā.'

556. folca Feorhgiefan. Cf. *Gu.* 1213.

frætwum ealles ' wāldend. Against Sievers' suggestion we may adduce *ealles Wāldend,* 544, 577, while *frætwum* is demanded by the alliteration besides, *Frætwan ?*

557. So *Ph.* 665; *Jul.* 154.

558–585. See *Analysis*, 5 (p. 115). Wanley, Thorpe, Dietrich, and Gollancz recognize no break here (see p. 70). Dietrich even connects this intimately with the preceding : ' Darum mussten weissgekleidete Engel ihn abholen, da dass grösste der Feste gekommen war, denn es hätte der Heilige, der Siegesfrohlock-ende, die Hölle alles Tributs beraubt.' Grein (*Dichtungen*, p. 164, note) has : ' Hier redet wol der Dichter im Geiste die bei der Himmelfahrt im Himmel gebliebenen Engel an; denn wegen v. 574–581 kann man es nicht füglich als Anrede an die Leser auffassen.' Wülker (*Grundriss*, p. 186) remarks : 'So einfach als es nach Dietrich scheinen könnte ist das Sachverhältniss nicht. XIII ist jedenfalls auch eine Rede (der Engel vielleicht, oder der erlösten Altväter und Weissagen, welche mit Christus in den Himmel einziehen). V. 570, 573 ff. Dass v. 570 an die " Hörer " vom Sänger gerichtet sei [see note on 570] kann ich nicht glauben. Und wie erklärten sich alsdann v. 575 und 576?' Cf. *Grundriss*, p. 385.

Speaking of the *Harrowing of Hell*, Grein said (*Kurzgefasste Ags. Gram.*, p. 12) : ' Vielleicht bildete dies Lied ursprünglich einen integrierenden Teil des *Crist* (vor v. 558).' On this Wülker remarks (*Grundriss*, p. 186) : ' Dies scheint mir unglaublich. Jetzt finden wir eine eigentliche Beschreibung der Höllenfahrt Christi in dem *Crist* nicht, denn v. 558–586 kann man nicht als ein solches Gedicht bezeichnen. Die Situation ist hier nicht ganz klar, wahrscheinlich aber, wenn überhaupt XIII nicht wo anders im *Crist* zu stehen hat, müssen wir diesen Abschnitt als Rede auffassen. Darin soll kurz die Höllenfahrt Christi und sein Sieg über die Hölle erwähnt werden, um die Freude im Himmel zu begründen ; ganz unpassend aber wäre an dieser Stelle eine so ausgeführte Schilderung, wie sie die *Höllenfahrt Christi* giebt. Auch passte die Einleitung, *Höllenfahrt* 1–20, gar nicht in den *Crist* an dieser Stelle herein.' Dietrich had already said (*Haupt's Zs.* 9. 214) : ' . . da der gute Verband dieser drei Lieder keine Stelle zeigt wo es gleich anfangs hätte eingereiht sein können.'

Grein is of course wrong about the possibility of regarding the *Harrowing of Hell* as a part of the *Christ.* Surely a given literature may contain more than one poem on the same subject. Nor can this speech be one by the patriarchs and prophets, as Wülker would admit; it is most natural in the mouth of the angels who have already spoken.

Ebert's view is as follows (3. 47) : ' Die Engel aber ziehen im Himmel Christus entgegen, indem sie ihn durch ein Loblied als Besieger der Hölle bewillkommnen, und zur Feier dieses *höchsten* Festes erscheinen sie in weissen Gewändern. . . . Christus aber, der siegreiche Held, führt die dem Teufel entrissenen Seelen in seinem Gefolge.' He adds in a footnote: ' Die Verse 558–585 sind der v. 554 angezeigte *wilcuman*, wie v. 570 und 573 klar zeigen. Der Sänger selbst spricht sie nicht, wie Dietrich annimmt.'

Morley has (2. 228) : ' The next part celebrates the higher festival at which the angels, all arrayed in white, go forth to meet the Saviour of Man as He ascends to Heaven, bringing with Him the great company of the redeemed whom He has saved from death and hell.'

Brooke remarks (p. 396), but without producing conviction : ' The order of the poem now becomes confused. An episode is introduced which concerns the

Harrowing of Hell, an event which the legend always places after the Resurrection, and not after the Ascension. I conjecture that Cynewulf had these lines
by him (ll. 558-585), and that they belonged to another poem, of which the
Descent into Hell, in the Exeter Book, may be a fragment. When he was refitting
the Christ into a whole, he inserted these lines which are full of imagination, and
took no particular pains to fit them properly into their place ; or he thought,
perhaps, that they might represent a hymn sung in heaven after the Ascension.
The hymn would then describe the event, also an ascension, which had taken
place forty days before, when Christ brought up to Paradise the souls from
Hades. Even if that be the case, the passage is most unhappily built together.
The episode is really a choric hymn supposed to be sung by the host of angels
who come forth from the gates of heaven on the day of the Resurrection to
meet and welcome the Old Testament saints as, rising from Hades, they mount
the sky with Christ. The scene is laid in mid-space. The angels from heaven
have met the ascending bands, and when Cynewulf sees this mighty meeting in
his vision, the warrior wakens in him, and the speech the angelic leader makes to
his followers is such as a heathen chief might have made to his Lord returning
from war with the spoils of victory.' But cf. Bede's hymn, above.

With reference to earlier accounts of the Harrowing of Hell, I refer to Kirkland, pp. 16-20, from whom I here draw certain statements and quotations.
Ittigius (*De Evangelio Mortuis annunciato*, Lipsiae, 1699, p. 14) says : 'Haec
enim sententia in scriptis Patrum tam frequens est ut Isidorus Hispalensis
[d. 636] inter haereticos numeraverit qui in Christi ad inferos descensu animarum liberationem factam negant.' Most of the opinions expressed are based
upon such passages as Eph. 4. 8-9 ; 1 Pet. 3. 19; 4. 6, and not till several centuries have elapsed do we find a circumstantial narrative such as is contained in
the *Evangelium Nicodemi*. In Eusebius (whether of Emesa or of Alexandria
has not been decided) a well-developed story meets us almost as soon as in the
Evangelium Nicodemi, and some of the details are even more fully described. In
the works of Epiphanius, who flourished toward the close of the fourth century,
we find the Descensus treated : ' Oratio in Christi sepulturam et Domini in
inferum descensum.' The version here given agrees in many points with the
Evangelium Nicodemi, though there is also much divergence. The Descent is
alluded to in Prudentius, *Cathemerinon* 9. 70 ; Proba Faltonia, *Centones Virgiliani*
(Migne 19. 815-6) ; Sedulius, *Paschale Carmen* 5. 427 ff. (Migne 19. 751), and
Hymn to Christ 86 ff. (19. 769); Aldhelm, *De Laudibus Virg.* (Migne 89. 246) ;
Joannes Scotus Erigena, *Christi Descensus ad Inferos et Resurrectio.* For Bede,
see above.

Besides the quotations from Gregory in the notes on 145, 147, cf. his *Moral.*
4. 29 (Migne 75. 666); 12. 10 (75. 994); 13. 43, 44 (75. 1038); *Hom. in Evang.*
1. 19 (76. 1156); *Ps. Poen.* 6. 6 (79. 637).

Hammerich says (p. 84) : ' Dieses ist aber ein Lieblingsthema geworden für
alle germanischen Sänger, und das eben darum, weil in diesem Kampfe mit den
höllischen Mächten der mannhafte, starkmuthige Siegeskönig ihnen in seiner
ganzen Stärke und Herrlichkeit erschien. Daher begegnen wir Bearbeitungen
desselben Gegenstandes überall in England, in Deutschland, und im Norden.'
He might have added, in Celtic, French, Provençal, Italian, and Spanish ; see

Wülker, *Das Evangelium Nicodemi in der Abendländischen Literatur*, Pader-
born, 1872.

Allusions to the Harrowing of Hell are found *Gu.* 1076; *El.* 181; *Rid.* 56[b].
The subject is treated at considerable length in the *Bl. Hom.*, pp. 85–9; cf.
Ælfric, *Hom.* 1. 28, 216, 480; 2. 6.

My own view on the interpretation of 558–585 is about as follows. This passage would seem to belong immediately after 526, and should be transferred to
that place, were it not that strict chronological order is hardly to be expected in
lyrico-dramatic writing; of this, Bede's hymn is a more than sufficient illustration.
That the two speeches are allied in substance, spirit, and general form is evident
on comparison. The two angels deliver the earlier speech ; and no one can be
conceived more proper than they to deliver this one. Both refer to a *brēat* as
present (517, 570), employ the words, *þe gē hēr on stariað* (521, 570), mention
the throne to which the journey tends (516, 572), and specifically designate a
present time (*nū*, 512 ; 558, 561, 571, 573, 575).

The first part of the discourse (558–574) is apparently addressed to the apostles
on the Mount of Olives, and does not form part of a choric hymn sung in mid-
space by a host of angels who come forth from heaven to meet Christ (Brooke).
On the latter supposition there is no point in the repeated *gē*, 570 and 573 : it
cannot be addressed to the rescued saints, nor to angels conceived as forming the
retinue of Christ. Besides, whether we regard *ontȳnað* as ind. or imp., it cannot
be spoken by angels who have just come forth from the heavenly city, nor after
the gates have already opened to provide for the reception of the risen Lord.
On the other hand, this portion, as addressed to the apostles (cf. Bede's hymn,
63–5) is full of meaning, since it informs them of facts which they are not supposed to know, and accounts for the multitude of the redeemed who are in the
act of ascending the skies. This part appropriately terminates with 573[b]–574:
' Now we have told you who this Lord is, what he has achieved, and why he is
thus attended.'

The two angels, or their spokesman, then turn to the attendant host, saying,
' Go joyfully to meet those who from henceforth are your friends ' (cf. 581[b]–
585). With this they call from afar to the gates of heaven, ' Open, O ye gates,
for the King of glory will come in (Ps. 24. 7); the Lord mighty and victorious
in battle with his hellish foes ' (576[b]–581[a]). This is in the highest degree dramatic
and impressive.

558–573[a]. Translated by Brooke, p. 397.

558. helle birēafod. *Berēafian* seems to have been the OE. term for ' har-
row,' as employed in the 'harrowing' of hell. Cf. *El.* 910, and especially *Bl.
Hom.*, p. 67 : ' Mycelne bite Drihten dyde on helle þā hē þyder āstāg, and *helle
berēafode*, and þā hālgan sāuwla þonon ālǣdde, and hīe generede of dēofles
anwālde, þā hē tō þēowdōme þyder on fruman middangeardes gesamnode wǣron.
Hē hīe eft ālǣdde of helle grunde on þā hēan þrymmas heofona rīces.' See also
Bl. Hom. 87. 23. The noun, *hergung*, is however employed in this sense in OE. :
Ælfric, *Hom.* 1. 228; *Bl. Hom.* 83. 29 ; and the verb occurs early in ME.

559. gafoles. Cf. *Bl. Hom.* 85. 12: 'Ūs dēaþ mycel gafol geald '; 105. 23:
' þurh þā gesamnunga [i.e. of humanity and divinity] wē wǣron gefreoþode feōnda
gafoles.'

gēardagum. So (I) 251, II (821).

560. orlege. Th. '*den of* death'; Gr. (*Spr.*) 'tormentum, cruciatus, tribu-
latio,' (*D.*) 'Abgrund'; Go.¹ 'home (Go.² 'place') of strife'; Br. '(lawless) war.'
Go.¹ comments: '*Orlege*, lit. "war, strife, hostility," also "a place where hostility
is shown," as in this passage; cp.' *Cwǣdon ðæt hē on ðām beorge byrnan sceolde
. . . gif hē monna drēam of ðām orlege eft ne wolde sylfa gesēcan, Guth.* 167; also
Guth. 426; *orlege* in both passages = the place which Guthlac had selected for
his dwelling, wresting it from the evil spirits.' For metrical reasons, Trautmann
(*Kynewulf*, p. 75) would read *orlēge*, comparing OHG. *urliugi.*

swealg. Cf. Bede's hymn, 15, 28. For this sense of *swelgan*, cf. 1593, 1603.

563. duguþum bidǣled. Similarly 1408 (III); *Gen.* 930; *Sat.* 122.

564. Cosijn emends to *wiþerbreocan*, since 'widerschrecken' makes no sense.
He appeals to *Gu.* 265 for the form he adopts, and refers to *Bl. Hom.* 175. 7.
He adds: '*brecan* (denn *wiðerbreca* ist synonym mit *andsaca*) bedeutet hier
"streiten," got. *brikan, brakja,* ἀθλεῖν, πάλη.'

565. wuldres Cyning. Cf. *Bl. Hom.*, p. 67: 'Hit wæs Iūdisc þēaw, þonne
heora ciningas hæfdon sige geworht on heora fēondum, and hīe wǣron eft hām
hweorfende, þonne ēodan hīe him tōgēanes mid blōwendum palmtwigum, heora
siges tō wyorþmyndum. Wel þæt gedafenode þæt Drihten swā dyde on þā gelīc-
nesse, forþon þe hē wæs *wuldres Cyning.* þysne dæg hīe nemdon siges dæg; se
nama tācnaþ þone sige þe Drihten gesigefæsted wiþstōd dēofle, þā hē mid his dēaþe
þone ēcan dēaþ oferswiþde, swā hē sylf þurh þone wītgan sægde; hē cwæþ:
"Ealā dēaþ, ic bēo þīn dēaþ, and ic bēo þīn bite on helle."'

568-9. Dietrich compares Ps. 68. 19 (18); Eph. 4. 8.

568. hūþa mǣste. Cf. *Bl. Hom.* 87. 33: 'þā herehyhþ [herehyþ?] þe on helle
genumen hæfde.'

570. '"Diese Beute ist," so redet nun der Sänger seine Hörer an, "eben diese
Schaar, die ihr hier vor euch seht"—alle erlösten Christen werden ja als der
Hölle beraubt angesehen' (Dietrich). Against this view, see above, on 558-585.

571. sāwla Nergend. So *Ph.* 498; *An.* 549, 923; *El.* 461; *Ps. C.* 16, 59, 83.

572ᵇ. Br. 'He of God the proper Bairn.'

573. æfter gūðplegan. So *Ap.* 22.

574. hwæt. So *Beow.* 233.

575. frēondum. Cf. (III) 1344, 1658.

576. Th. 'go glad of mood, *your* gates unclose.' Gr. 'empfangt sie freundlich,
die Pforten öffnet.' Go. 'go . . . joyful in spirit. Open, O ye gates!' Br. 'March
. . . with a gladdened heart! O, ye gates unclose.'

Geatu, ontȳnað. Ps. 24. 7. The 24th Psalm was read at the First Nocturn
of the Feast of the Circumcision, and the Second Nocturn of Easter Eve, as well
as on other occasions; the Antiphon for the same occasions was: 'Be ye lift up,
ye everlasting doors, and the King of Glory shall come in.' According to Neale
and Littledale, 1. 335, the two chief mystical interpretations of this verse, out of
six enumerated, are the reference of it to the gates of hell, and to the gates of
heaven. Neale says: 'The second, which is received by very great authorities,
would refer it to our Lord's descent into Hell, His bursting the gates of brass,
and smiting the bars of iron in sunder. To this the Latin Church would seem to
appropriate it, by appointing this Psalm as one of those for the Second Nocturn

for Easter Eve, with the antiphon from this verse. . . . The third signification would see in this verse the exclamation of the angels attending our ascended Lord.' He adds: 'The fifth meaning sees in the verse a prophecy of the Incarnation ; and on this account it is that, in the Mass of the Vigil of the Nativity, it forms the offertory. This sense is adopted by S. Jerome ; though here also he would find a spiritual reference to the virtual opening of the gates of heaven by the fact of our Lord's taking flesh upon Himself.' Our authorities still further subjoin : 'The words of Vieyra are well worth notice : " When Christ ascended in triumph to heaven, the angels who accompanied Him said to them that kept the guard, *Lift up, O ye princes, your gates, and the King of Glory shall come in.* They think the term strange ; and before opening the portal, they inquire, *Quis est iste Rex Gloriae?*" '

The primary and all but exclusive reference here is of course to the gates of heaven ; but if we admit that there may be any remoter connotation, we shall at once think of 251, 318, the prophecy of the Advent, and shall not be unwilling to be reminded, in this triumphal entry, of the passage on the Harrowing of Hell which has just preceded.

Interesting, by way of comparison, is a stanza from Giles Fletcher, *Christ's Victory and Triumph*, Part IV :

> ' Toss up your heads, ye everlasting gates,
>   And let the Prince of glory enter in !
>   At whose brave volley of sidereal states
>   The sun to blush, and stars grow pale, were seen,
>   When leaping first from earth He did begin
>   To climb His angels' wings ; then open hang
>   Your crystal doors !' so all the chorus sang
>   Of heavenly birds, as to the stars they nimbly sprang.

See Bede's hymn, 74 ff.

577. ealles Wāldend. So 544, 556.

578. corŏre. So 494.

580. in drēama drēam. So *Ph.* 658. For the idiom, cf. Winer, *New Testament Grammar*, ed. Thayer, p. 246 : "Of the well-known Hebrew mode of expressing the superlative . . . [cf. Deut. 10. 12 ; Josh. 22. 22 ; Ps. 136. 3 ; Dan. z. 47], only the following examples occur in the N. T. . Heb. 9. 3 . . ., Rev. 19. 16 . . ., 1 Tim. 6. 15. But none of these expressions is a pure Hebraism ; in the Greek poets also we find such a doubling of adjectives (used substantively) : Soph. *Electr.* 849 δειλαία δειλαίων, *Oed. R.* 466 ἄρρητ' ἀρρήτων, Soph. *Phil.* 65, κακὰ κακῶν. Soph. *Oed. C.* 1238, see Bhdy. 154 ; Wex, *Antig.* I. 316. The phrase βασιλεὺς βασιλέων too, is very simple, and more emphatic than ὁ μέγιστος βασιλεύς ; cf. Æschyl. *Suppl.* 524 ἄναξ ἀνάκτων, and, even as a technical designation, Theophan. contin. 127. 387 ὁ ἄρχων τῶν ἀρχόντων." To these might be added Plutarch, *Pomp.* 38. 1.

581. sygor. Perhaps we should read *sigor*, with Grein.

582. englum ond ǣlduim. Cf. note on 11, and 697 ; *Beow.* 1855.

586–599. See *Analysis*, 6 (p. 115).

Ebert says (3. 48) : 'Diese Betrachtungen gründen sich bei Gregor auf einzelne Stellen des Alten Testaments die auf Christi Himmelfahrt bezogen werden '; but it is not easy to discover the original in Gregory's Homily.

587. hydercyme. Advent; cf. (I) 142, 367; 250. — **hāls.** Cosijn would emend to *hālor*.

591 ff. Note the rime, perfect and imperfect, and cf. 757, 1320, 1481-2, 1496, 1570-1, 1646. In Anglian, we should have *hĕnþu, mĕrþu, leht, nœht.* Brooke renders:

> As of Hell the scornful story,   so of Heaven the noble glory;
> As the lightsome light,   so the loathly night;
> Glory's rush of gladness,   or of gloomy souls the sadness;
> As with devils all discord,   so delight with God the Lord;
> Torment grievous with the grim,   glory with the seraphim,
> Either life or death!

592. lēohte lēoht. Pleonasm; so (I) 41, 118.

593. þrymmes þræce. Th. 'power of dignity'; Gr. (*D.*) 'Glanz der Glorie,' but (*Spr.*) *þrym* = 'majestas, magnificentia, pompa,' and *þracu* = 'impetus, tumultus, pugna'; Go. 'majestic state'; Br. 'Glory's rush of gladness'; B.-T. 'power of glory.'

þȳstra. So I believe we must read, and not *þrȳstra.* The reasons in favor of the latter are the more perfect alliteration, and the difficulty of ascribing personality to *þȳstro.* However, the poet here has his eye upon rime, rather than alliteration; and *ðȳstro* (*ðēostor*) seems sometimes to be used for 'hell,' 'hell-torments,' through some such evolution as this: darkness > spiritual darkness, privation of the Sun of Righteousness, banishment from God > the gloomy, eternal prison of hell > the punishment inflicted through this agency. As illustrations cf. 1247, 1385; *Gu.* 607, 668; *Jul.* 419, 554; etc. The joy in light, and dread of darkness, are very noticeable in this poem, and throughout the OE. Christian poetry; in fact, the sentiment is almost Zoroastrian in its character. For the most part the words must be taken figuratively, to denote spiritual illumination and the horror of thick darkness enveloping the soul: cf. 27, 106, 400, 504, 696, 900, 1463, 1643, and especially 585; 118, 257, etc. Add Gen. 15. 12; Job 3. 5; 10. 22; Joel 2. 2; Mt. 25. 30; 2 Pet. 2. 4; Jude 6, 13.

596. Cf. *El.* 606.

597. flǣsc ond gǣst. Cf. *Rid.* 2¹⁸.

599. Þrȳnysse þrym. Cf. *Jud.* 86; *Gu.* 618.

600-778. Conybeare directed attention to our poem in 1812, in vol. 17 of the *Archæologia.* On p. 181 he remarks concerning this section: 'It ... has been erroneously described by Wanley as two separate poems, "De Mundi Creatione," and "De Christi Incarnatione." It is evidently one hymn' (cf. above, p. 68).

600-612. See *Analysis,* 7 (p. 115). Conybeare's poetic paraphrase should be noted.

603. So *Gu.* 616.

604 ff. Perhaps from Ps. 65. 9 ff.

605. ofer wīdlond. Cf. (III) 1384. Br. tr. 605-9.

606. under swegles hlēo. Cf. *Ph.* 374; *An.* 834; *El.* 507. — **Sunne ond mōna.** Perhaps anticipatory of 694.

607. æþelast tungla. Applied to the sun in *Ph.* 93.

609. dēaw ond rēn. Cf. *Ps.* 64¹¹. Note the change of number in the verbs.

610. tō feorhnere. So 1596 (III).

613–632. See *Analysis*, 8 (p. 116). The original is Gregory, *Hom. in Evang.*
29. 10: 'Sed hoc nobis magnopere, fratres carissimi, in hac solemnitate pensan-
dum est quia deletum est hodierna die chirographum damnationis nostrae, mutata
est sententia corruptionis nostrae. Illa enim natura cui dictum est: *Terra es, et
in terram ibis* (Gen. 3. 19), hodie in caelum ivit.' Cf. Col. 2. 14.

617. Cf. *Beow.* 459.— **swǣsne.** Cf. the twofold sense of the Homeric φίλος.

618. ānboren. Lat. *unigenitus.* So *El.* 392 ; cf. *āncenned*, 464.

621–6. This is merely an extended paraphrase of the quotation from Genesis.
It is still further paraphrased by Conybeare in these lines :

> Lo I have set thee on earth's stubborn soil
> With grief and stern necessity to strive,
> To wear thy days in unavailing toil,
> The ceaseless sport of torturing fiends to live.
> Thence to thy dust to turn, the worm's repast,
> And dwell where penal flames through endless ages last.

621. of. So Cosijn would read.

625. wyrmum āweallen. Perhaps suggested by 2 Macc. 9. 9 : 'Ita ut de
corpore impii vermes scaturirent,' or possibly by Exod. 16. 20 : 'Scatere coepit
vermibus.' The radical notion of *scatere*, like that of *weallan*, is to boil up.
Cosijn compares Ælfric, *Hom.* 1. 86, 472, and ON. *vella.*

627. þis. The doom, curse.

629. monnes magutūdre. Th. 'for man's offspring'; Gr. 'eines Menschen-
kindes '; Go. 'from child of man.' I see in this an adaptation of Heb. 2. 16 :
'semen Abrahae apprehendit,' with the substitution of 'hominis' for 'Abrahae ' ;
magutūdre would thus be dat. after *onfēng*, and appositive with *līchoman.*

630. engla ēþel. So *An.* 525, 642.

631b–632. Th. 'for us the will him entered, in help to the humble, at that holy
tide '; Gr. 'dieser Wille kam zur Hilfe uns Gebeugten in der heiligen Zeit '; Go.[1]
'at that holy tide, the wish arose to help us, the forlorn '; Go.[2] 'upon that holy
tide, the wish arose to help us, wretched men.'

632. hēanum tō helpe. So 1471. Cf. also 427, 1173, and Rose, p. 29.

633–658. See *Analysis*, 9 (p. 116). Based upon Gregory, *Hom. in Evang.* 29
(following the above ; see on 613–632) : 'Pro hac ipsa namque carnis nostrae sub-
levatione per figuram beatus Job Dominum avem vocat. Quia enim Ascensionis
ejus mysterium Judaeam non intelligere conspexit, de infidelitate ejus sententiam
protulit, dicens : *Semitam ignoravit avis* (Job 28. 7). Avis enim recte appelatus
est Dominus, quia corpus carneum ad aethera libravit. Cujus avis semitam ignoravit quisquis eum ad caelum ascendisse non credidit. De hac solemnitate per
Psalmistam dicitur: *Elevata est magnificentia tua super caelos* (Ps. 8. 2). De hac
rursus ait: *Ascendit Deus in jubilatione, et Dominus in voce tubae* (Ps. 47. 5). De
hac iterum dicit: *Ascendens in altum captivam duxit captivitatem, dedit dona
hominibus* (Ps. 68. 18). Ascendens quippe in altum, captivam duxit captivitatem,
quia corruptionem nostram virtute suae incorruptionis absorbuit.'

633. Cf. *Beow.* 1724 : 'Ic þis gid be þē āwræc '; similarly *Beow.* 2108 ; *Mod.* 51.

634. Helm wera. So *El.* 475.

635. Sunu Wāldendes. Cf. *Sat.* 119: *Wāldendes Suna.*

636. frēonoman. Renders Lat. *cognomentum*, Bede, *Eccl. Hist.* 2. 5; 4. 2; 5. 11, 19 (Miller 110. 18; 258. 28; 422. 3; 452. 29).

fugel. Lauchert, *Gesch. des Physiologus*, p. 158, thinks this must be the phœnix, because in the OE. *Phoenix* (550 ff.) there is a reference to Job; but our passage refers to Job 28. 7, that in the *Phoenix* to 29. 18, as Lauchert himself points out.

638. Gǣstes strengðu. Cf. Rom. 15. 13, 19.

640. dyrne ond dēgol. Cf. *El.* 1093; *Gn. C.* 63.

641. heortan stǣnne. Cf. Ezek. 11. 19; 36. 26.

643. Frēobearn Godes. So 788; *Sat.* 289.

644. mislicu. The emendation according to Frucht (p. 78), who instances *heardlicu, Jul.* 263 ; Cosijn approves.

645. fǣla. See Grimm's *Andreas und Elene*, note on *El.* 88.

646. Cf. 630.

647. mǣran. This is evidently right; cf. *An.* 227.

648. gestylde. An artistic anticipation of 716, 720 ff., 745 ff.

649. þurh Gǣstes giefe. So 710; *Gu.* 1088; *El.* 199, 1058, 1157.

651–3. Dietrich compares Ps. 8. 1; 18. 10. See also what is said in the note on 494.

657. hīw. For *hīwe* ; so 721. Cf. *Gu.* 682.

659–690. See *Analysis*, 10 (p. 116). Based upon Gregory (following that under 633–658): ' Dedit vero dona hominibus, quia, misso desuper Spiritu, alii sermonem sapientiae, alii sermonem scientiae, alii gratiam virtutum, alii gratiam curationum, alii genera linguarum, alii interpretationem tribuit sermonum (1 Cor. 12. 8). Dedit ergo dona hominibus.' Conybeare's version (pp. 221–3), in the form of an ode, is praised by Körner, p. 263. W. Clarke Robinson, *Introd. to our Early Eng. Lit.*, p. 66, renders vv. 659–678a.

659. world. See note on 8.

660. Godes Gǣstsunu. So 860 ; *El.* 673.

661. uppe mid englum. Cf. 387 (I), 1467–8 (III); *Sat.* 123.

662. mōdes snyttru. So *El.* 554; cf. *Jul.* 366.

663. sēow. Plummer says (*St. Luke*, p. 218), commenting on Lk. 8. 5: ' The comparison of teaching with sowing is frequent in all literature.'

664–682. Translated by Brooke, p. 398; cf. p. 129.

664–685. Cf. Homer, *Il.* 4. 320–5: ' But the gods in no wise grant men all things at once. As I was then a youth, so doth old age now beset me. Yet even so will I abide among the horsemen and urge them by counsel and words ; for that is the right of elders. But the young men shall wield the spear, they that are more youthful than I and have confidence in their strength '; *Il.* 13. 726–734 : ' Hector, thou art hard to be persuaded by them that would counsel thee; for that God has given thee excellence in the works of war, therefore in council also thou art fain to excel other men in knowledge. But in nowise wilt thou be able to take everything on thyself. For to one man has God given for his portion the works of war, to another the dance, to another the lute and song, but in the heart of yet another hath far-seeing Zeus placed an excellent understanding, whereof many men get gain, yea he saveth many a one, and himself best knoweth it ';

Od. 8. 167-177 : ' So true it is that the gods do not give every gracious gift to all, neither shapeliness, nor wisdom, nor skilled speech. For one man is feebler than another in presence, yet the god crowns his words with beauty, and men behold him and rejoice, and his speech runs surely on his way with a sweet modesty, and he shines forth among the gathering of his people, and as he passes through the town men gaze on him as a god. Another again is like the deathless gods for beauty, but his words have no crown of grace about them ; even as thou art in comeliness pre-eminent, nor could a god himself fashion thee for the better, but in wit thou art a weakling ' ; *Od.* 1. 347-9 : ' It is not minstrels who are in fault, but Zeus, methinks, is in fault, who gives to men that live by bread, to each one as he will ' ; *Od.* 8. 62-4 : ' Then the henchmen drew near, leading with him the beloved minstrel, whom the muse loved dearly, and she gave him both good and evil ; of his sight she reft him, but granted him sweet song.' Cf. *Il.* 1. 280, 352 ff. ; 9. 37 ff. ; 18. 106 ; 23. 670 ; *Od.* 8. 481 ; 17. 518 ; 22. 347 ; 24. 198 ; Hesiod, *Theog.* 80 ff. ; Bergk. *Anal. Lyr. Gr.* Part 2 (Marburg, 1852), p. 4 ; *Poet. Lyr. Gr.*[3], p. 1324, No. 10 ; *Anthol. Gr.* 12. 96 ; Virgil, *Ecl.* 8. 63 (from Lucilius, *Sat.* 5. 21 (Gerlach)) ; Livy 22. 51 ; Macrobius 5. 16. 7 ; 6. 1. 35 ; A. Seneca, *Excerpta Controv.* 3, *Proaem.* 1. 3. 5 (paraphrased by Ben Jonson, *Timber*, ed. Schelling, p. 29). Professor Bright suggests Chaucer, *Wife of Bath's Prologue* 99-104, but this reposes rather on 1 Cor. 7. 7 than on 12. 8. Dietrich compares Eph. 4. 8.

Cf. Ælfric's version of 1 Cor. 12. 8-11 (*Hom.* 1. 322) : ' Sumum men hē forgifð wīsdōm and spræce, sumum gōd ingehȳd, sumum micelne gelēafan, sumum mihte tō gehǣlenne untruman, sumum wītegunge, sumum tōscēad gōdra gāsta and yfelra ; sumum hē forgifð mislice gereord, sumum gereccednysse mislicra spræca. Ealle ðās ðing dēð se Hālga Gāst, tōdǣlende ǣghwilcum be ðām ðe him gewyrð.' In the same Homily (1. 326 ; cf. 1. 328 ; 2. 14, 292, 398) Ælfric explains : ' We wurðiað þæs Hālgan Gāstes tōcyme mid lofsangum seofon dagas, forðam ðe hē onbryrt ūre mōd mid seofonfealdre gife, þæt is, mid wīsdōme and andgyte, mid geðeahte and strencðe, mid ingehȳde and ārfæstnysse, and hē ūs gefylð mid Godes ege. Se ðe ðurh gode geearnunga becymð tō ðissum seofonfealdum gifum þæs Hālgan Gāstes, hē hæfð þonne ealle geðincðe.'

In conjunction with this passage there should be read the whole of the two poems, *Gifts of Men* (*Bi Monna Cræftum*, Gr.), and *Fates of Men* (*Bi Manna Wyrdum*, Gr.). The most remarkable parallels will be quoted, but these alone will not suffice to disclose the similarity.

The subjects which are mentioned are, in succession : (1) eloquence (and social charm ?) ; (2) instrumental music ; (3) theology ; (4) astronomy ; (5) authorship ; (6) prowess in war ; (7) seamanship ; (8) athletics ; (9) armory ; (10) wayfaring.

664-668. Sumum . . . fērðe. Cf. *Gifts of Men* 41-43 :

> Sum in mæðle mæg mōdsnoterra
> folcrǣdenne forð gehycgan,
> þǣr witena biþ worn ætsomne.

Also 35-36 :

> Sum biþ wōðbora,
> giedda giffæst.

Also 52 :

> Sum lēoða glēaw.

664. wordlaþe. Cf. *An.* 635. Con. 'orationis vocem'; Th. 'eloquence'; Gr. (*Spr.*) 'sermocinatio,' 'loquela,' (*D.*) 'Wortbegabtheit'; R. 'invitatio verbi,' 'suadela'; K. 'Redegabe,' 'Rede,' 'Beredsamkeit'; Go.[1] 'eloquence'; Go.[2] 'charm of . . . words.'

665. his mūþes Gǣst. Con. 'per spiritum oris ejus'; Th. 'through his mouth's guest' (interpreting in a footnote as 'the tongue'); Gr. 'durch seines Mundes Geist'; Go. 'through (Go.[2] the) spirit of the mouth'; Br. 'through the spirit of his mouth.' Cf. Ps. 33. 6; 2 Thess. 2. 8. The former has: 'Verbo Domini caeli firmati sunt, et *spiritu oris ejus* omnis virtus eorum.' On this Neale and Littledale have: 'Here we have one of the most remarkable testimonials in the Old Testament to the doctrine of the Trinity. Almost all the Fathers have so applied it. . . . Some of these have gone further, and have attributed the creation of the heavens more especially to the Word, that of the stars and Angels more especially to the Holy Ghost.'

667. singan ond secgan. A formula; cf. *Wid.* 54; *Met.* 2[17]; and Lachmann, *Ueber Singen und Sagen* (*Kleinere Schriften* 1. 461–479).

668-670. Sum . . . grētan. Cf. *Gifts of Men* 49–50 :

> Sum mid hondum mæg hearpan grētan;
> āh hē glēobēames gearobrygda list.

So *Fates of Men* 80–84 :

> Sum sceal mid hearpan æt his hlāfordes
> fōtum sittan, feoh þicgan,
> and ā snellice snēre wræstan,
> lætan scralletan scearo se þe hlēapeð
> nægl nēomegende; bið him nēod micel.

669. glēobēam. Cf. *Beow.* 2263. Con. 'gaudii tubam' [!]; Th., Go.[2], Br. 'glee-beam'; Gr. (*D.*) 'Lusthol2'; R. 'Baum der Freude,' 'Harfe'; K. 'Freudenholz'; Go.[1] 'minstrel's joy' [!].

grētan. In this sense *Beow.* 2108; *Gn. Ex.* 171. Con. '*inflare*' [!].

On harp-playing among the Anglo-Saxons, cf., besides the quotations above, such as *Beow.* 89, 2105 ff., 2456; *Ph.* 135; *Gen.* 1079; *Seaf.* 44 ff.; Bede, *Eccl. Hist.* 4. 24; *Cura Past.* 175. 6; *Lchdm.* 3. 202. See especially Pseudo-Bede, *Comm. in Psalm.* 52 (Migne 93. 1110) : 'Sicut peritus citharoeda, chordas plures tendens in cithara, temperat eas acumine et gravitate tali, ut superiores inferioribus conveniant in melodia, quaedam semitonii, quaedam unius toni, quaedam duorum tonorum differentiam gerentes, aliae vero diatessaron, aliae autem diapente vel etiam diapason consonantiam reddentes,' etc. On the general subject of music and musical instruments among the Anglo-Saxons, Mr. F. M. Padelford, Fellow in English of Yale University, expects to publish a monograph which will tabulate practically all the Old English material (*Bonner Beiträge*, No. 4).

670b-671a. See note on 682-4, s. f.

671. ryhte ǣ. Cf. *An.* 1513, but especially *El.* 281; *ryhte* may possibly be adv., as Th., Go., Br. render. Cf. note on 682-684.

ryne tungla. So *Met.* 28. 1–5 (cf. *Jul.* 498) :

Hwā is on eorðan nū unlærdra,
þe ne wundrige wolcna færeldes,
rodres swifto, *ryne tungla,*
hū hȳ ælce dæge ūtan ymbhwerfað
eallne middangeard?

Cf. Cicero, *The Dream of Scipio,* in *Republic* 6. 17. 17: 'The Universe is composed of nine circles, or rather spheres, one of which is the heavenly one, and is exterior to the rest, which it embraces; being itself the Supreme God, and bounding and containing the whole. In it are fixed those *stars* which revolve with never varying *courses (stellarum cursus sempiterni).*' Cf. Judges 5. 20: '*Stellae* manentes in ordine et *cursu* suo.'

672. sīde gesceaft. So (III) 1087; cf. (I) 59, 239, 356.

672–673. Sum . . . wrītan. Cf. *Gifts of Men* 95–96:

Sum bið listhendig
tō āwrītanne wordgeryno.

673–676. Sumum . . . flāngeweorc. Cf. *Gifts of Men* 39–40:

Sum bið wīges heard,
beadocræftig beorn, þær bord stunað.

673. wīges spēd. Note the peculiar genitive.

674. gārgetrum. Con. 'exercitus'; Th. 'shaft-shower'; Gr. 'der Geere Schauer' (*D.*), 'telorum impetus' (*Spr.*); R. 'Kraft oder Menge der Geere'; Go., Br. 'storm of darts'; (p. 129) 'javelin shower.' Körner says (p. 264): 'Nach Grein "telorum *impetus,*" was mir falsch scheint; *getrum* heisst "Heer," "Schar," "Haufe," demnach *gārgetrum* "Speerhaufe," wie in meiner Uebersetzung steht, oder "Speerheer," "mit Speeren bewaffnete Schar," wie *gārhēap (Exod.* 321, *hæfdon ārēred in ðǣm gārhēape gyldenne lēon*), oder wie *scildtruma* "das schild-bewaffnete Heer," "die Schlachtreihe." Nimmt man das letztere an, was ich vorziehe, so wäre *gārgetrum* nom., mit ihm stände *scēotend* parallel, nach *sendað* wäre das Komma zu tilgen: "wenn das speertragende Heer, die Schützen, senden die im Zickzack dahin schwirrenden Pfeile."'

675. scildhrēadan. Cf. *Exod.* 113, 160, 236, 320; *Beow.* 2203; *An.* 128; *El.* 122. Con. 'clypeorum testudines'; Th. 'shield's defence'; Gr.[1] (*Spr.*) 'clypeus,' (*D.*) 'Schildes Rand'; R. 'Phalanx,' 'Schlachthaufe mit eng an einander geschlossenen Schilden' = *scildburh ;* K. 'Schildüberzug'; Go., Br. 'shield's defence'; (p. 129) 'shelter of the shield.' Körner comments: 'Sonst *scild-, bordhrēoðan; . . .* die Bedeutung des zweiten Teiles des Comp. ist noch nicht mit Sicherheit ermittelt; . . . jedenfalls ist zunächst an die gefärbte oder sonst verzierte Aussenseite des Schildes zu denken; dann allgemein: Schild.' Cf. *hrēodan (hroden),* 292, 330, and Brooke, pp. 123–4.

676. flacor flāngeweorc. Con. 'volucrem sagittae operam'; Th. 'flickering arrow-work'; Gr. 'das flüchtige Pfeilgeschoss'; K. 'flackerndes Pfeilwerk'; Go.[1] 'the wingèd javelin'; Go.[2] 'swift-flying arrow-work'; Br. 'winging-work of arrows'; (p. 129) 'flickering flight of arrows.' Cf. *Gu.* 1117.

flacor. So *Gu.* 1127. Cf. the verbs *flack* and *flacker* in the *N. E. D.*; the primary meaning of each is 'flap,' 'flutter,' 'throb'; of *flacker,* esp. of birds: 'flap the wings,' 'fly flutteringly.' One of the quotations is from the Coverdale Bible, Isa. 6. 2: 'From above *flakred* the Seraphins.' Murray thinks this verb may possibly represent an OE. **flacorian*, cognate with MDu. *flackeren*, ON. *flǫkra*, MnG. *flackern*.

flāngeweorc. Gr. (*Spr.*) 'apparatus jaculatorius,' comparing *Rid.* 37[12] (emended); R. 'Arbeit mit Pfeilen,' 'Pfeilschiessen'; K. 'Pfeilwerk'; Sweet (*Dict.*) 'arrows.'

676–678. Sum . . . holmþræce. Cf. *Gifts of Men* 53–57:

> Sum [on] fealone wǣg
> stefnan stēoreð, strēamrāde con
> weorudes wīsa ofer wīdne holm,
> þonne sǣrōfe snelle mǣgne
> ārum bregdað ȳðborde nēah.

677. sealtne sǣ. So *salsum mare*, Enn. ap. Macr. 6. 4 (Ann. v. 453 Vahl.); *id.* ap. Non. 183. 19 (Trag. v. 145 *ib.*); *salsum aequor*, Lucr. 3. 493, etc.; *salsa vada*, Virg. *Aen.* 5. 158; *salsus fluctus*, *Aen.* 5. 182. The epithet is common in OE. poetry in this application; see Grein, *Spr.*, s.v. *sealt*.

sundwudu. Cf. *flōdwudu*, 853, and the compounds under *wudu* in Grein, *Spr.*

678. hrēran. Cf. *Wand.* 4; *An.* 491. — **holmþræce.** Cf. *An.* 467; *El.* 728; *Ph.* 115.

678ᵇ–679ᵃ. Conybeare mistakes: 'Aliqui possunt altum telum chalybe praetentem attollere.'

679–680. Sum . . . gewyrcan. Cf. *Gifts of Men* 61–66.

> Sum mǣg wǣpenþrǣce wīge tō nytte
> mōdcræftig smið monige gefremman,
> þonne hē gewyrceð tō wera hilde
> helm oþþe hupseax oððe heaþubyrnan,
> scīrne mēce oððe scyldes rond,
> fǣste gefēgan wið flyge gāres.

679. stǣlgne. Perhaps miswritten for *stāglne*. If not, it is a case of metathesis (*Gr.* 183), for OHG. has *steigal*, and the OET. *stǣgil-*. Cosijn agrees, saying: 'Wenigstens dünkt mich die Metathese verdächtig, denn die volle Form ist *stǣgil*. Man erwartet *stēapne* = *hēanne*.'

stȳled. The bronze age was evidently past; cf. *stȳlecg*, *Beow.* 1553, and *Rid.* 41⁷⁹, 88¹⁴; *Beow.* 985; *Sal.* 299.

sweord. Cf. Bosworth-Toller, s.v., and Brooke, pp. 121–3, for interesting accounts of the sword among the Anglo-Saxons.

680–1. Sum . . . wīdgielle. Con. 'Aliqui possunt ora exercere . . . elata voce'; Th. 'One knoweth the course of the fields, the spacious ways'; Gr. 'Mancher kennt der Welt Länder, weitführende Wege'; K. 'Ein Anderer kennt das Gebiet der Fluren, die weithin sich erstreckenden Wege'; Go. 'One knoweth the plains' direction, the wide ways'; Br. 'One the spacious ways knows, and all the plains' outgoing.' Conybeare adds: 'I do not clearly perceive its construction, unless *wonga wegas* are to be taken together as "the way or passage of the mouth."'

680. wonga. *Wangas* may sometimes be taken as a poetical expression for 'earth.' Thus, *Met.* 20[77] : '*wangas* ymbe licgað, *eorðe* ælgrēno'; *Rid.* 13[2] : '*foldan* slīte, grēne *wongas*'; 67[5]; so even the singular, *Beqw.* 92 : '*eorðan* worhte, wlitebeorhtne *wang*, swā wæter bebūgeð'; *Rid.* 41[51, 83].

bīgong. Cf. *Az.* 129; *Beow.* 362, 860, 1497, 1773, 1826, 2367; *Jul.* 112; *An.* 195, 530; *Met.* 11[80].

681. wegas wīdgielle. *Weg*(*as*) is frequently used in composition with words denoting distance to express extent of space rather than of linear direction: thus *feorweg*(*as*), *Gu.* 228, *Beow.* 37, *An.* 930, etc.; *sīdwegas*, *El.* 282; *wīdwegas*, *Beow.* 840, 1704, *Ps.* 144[80], 105[36]. Cf. 482, and our expression 'wayfarer.'

682. giefe bryttað. Cf. *Gifts of Men* 105; *Wid.* 102; *An.* 755; and, for the sense, *Beow.* 1726.

682-684. From Gregory, *Hom. in Ezech.* lib. 1, hom. 10 (Migne 76. 899) : '*Non enim uni dantur omnia, ne in superbiam elatus cadat,* sed huic datur quod tibi non datur, et tibi datur quod illi denegatur, ut dum iste considerat bonum quod habes et ipse non habet, te sibi in cogitatione praeferat, . . . et fiat quod scriptum est : *Superiores sibi invicem arbitrantes* ' (Phil. 2. 3).

Gollancz calls attention to this passage in the following curiously oblique fashion : ' I am inclined to think that Gregory's *Commentary on Job*, xxxviii. 4–5, was the original of the poem [*Gifts of Men*]. Here we have the motive, which is not in the Homily. At the same time I should not be surprised to find a passage in Gregory's works even nearer to the Anglo-Saxon. The original of ll. 682–4 [683–5] should be words to this effect : —

"Non enim uni dantur omnia, ne in superbiam elatus cadat."

(Cp. Gregory, Lib. 1, Homilia x. sect. 32, on Ezekiel iii. 13, with marginal note, "cur divisiones gratiarum sint.")'

The passage from the *Commentary on Job* (Migne 76. 461–462) is indeed parallel. Referring to 1 Cor. 12. 8 ff., Gregory says : ' Sic itaque Creator noster atque Dispositor cuncta moderatur, ut qui extolli poterat ex dono quod habet humilietur ex virtute quam non habet.'

Again he says : ' Huic illa largitur quae alii denegat, alii haec denegat quae isti largitur '; and at the close of the same sentence : . . . ' ut si fortasse . . . is, quem supernae virtutis donum ad sola miracula roborat, etiam *divinae legis pandere* occulta contendat.' The italicized words may possibly have been in the poet's mind in writing 670[b]–671[a].

684. þȳ-læs him gielp sceþþe. Cf. *Gifts of Men* 24–26 :

> þy-læs hē for wlence wuldorgeofona ful
> mon mōde swīð of gemete hweorfe,
> and þonne forhycge hēanspēdigran.

Also 100–101 :

> þy-læs him gilp sceððe,
> oþþe fore þære mærðe mōd āstīge.

685. ofer ōþre forð. Cf. *Gifts of Men* 102 :

> Ofer ealle men.

And *Beow.* 1717.

The break here, though authorized by the manuscript, is evidently not structural; Grein (see p. 69) was right.

686. geofum unhnēawum. Cf. *geofum unhnēawne, Wid.* 139.

687–690. Note the correspondence between earth and heaven.

Cyning alwihta. So *Gen.* 978 (*eall-*) ; *Exod.* 420 ; *Sat.* 616, 671.

688. eorþan tuddor. So *Gen.* 1402 ; *Sat.* 659, etc. Gr. interprets as 'Erdenkinder' (D.), 'homines' (*Spr.*).

689ᵇ–690. Cf. 581ᵇ–582, and note on 11.

691–711. See *Analysis*, 11 (p. 116).

Based upon Greg. *Hom. in Evang.* 29. 10 (following the above ; see on 659–690) : 'De hac Ascensionis ejus gloria etiam Habacuc ait : *Elevatus est sol, et luna stetit in ordine suo* [Hab. 3. 11, sec. LXX ; the Vulgate is quite different : ' Sol et luna steterunt in habitaculo suo]. Quis enim solis nomine nisi Dominus, et quae lunae nomine nisi Ecclesia designatur ? Quousque enim Dominus ascendit ad caelos, sancta ejus Ecclesia adversa mundi omnimodo formidavit ; at postquam ejus Ascensione roborata est, aperte praedicavit quod occulte credidit. Elevatus est ergo sol, et luna stetit in ordine suo, quia cum Dominus caelum petiit, sancta ejus Ecclesia in auctoritate praedicationis excrevit.'

692. gimmas. Cf. Sylvester's *Du Bartas*, p. 84 : 'Heaven's richest *gemm*.'

693. hædre heofontungol. Cf. *Met.* 22²⁴, *hādor heofontungol* (the sun). *Hādor* also appears *El.* 748 : *hādrum stefnum* ; elsewhere *hādor*, but adv. *hādre*.

694. sunne ond mōna. Cf. note on 606. Brooke says (p. 483) : 'It is worth while to compare Gregory's phrase . . . with Cynewulf's expansion of it into a simile. . . . How much tenderness, how much delight, in the nature of the sun and moon themselves is added to the Latin !' He tr. 692–701ᵃ.

695. gimmas. Not properly both ; cf. the Latin.

696. An echo of 106 (I). Cf. Mal. 4. ᴢ.

697. Cf. 690 ; *Gu.* 579.

699. circe. So often by mystical interpretation of Cant. 6. 10, though this is often applied to the Virgin Mary. Thus Augustine, *Ep.* 55. 10 ; Mone 1. 325 (Hymn 316, vv. 29–32) :

> Pulcra, potens, partu mirabilis,
> ut luna sol fulget spectabilis,
> plus acie multa terribilis
> ordinata.

700. gesomninga. Th., Br. 'congregations' [!].

sōðes ond ryhtes. For the association of these two words in different cases, cf. *Sat.* 207 ; *Beow.* 1700 ; *El.* 390, 662 ; *Gu.* 782 ; *Hy.* 7⁷⁶ ; *Ps.* 95¹⁸, 111⁶ ; *Gen.* 21. For the association of *justus* and *verus*, see Rev. 15. 3 ; 16. 7 ; 19. 2.

701. bōcum. *Bēc* = ' Biblia,' Bible. So 453, 785, 793, 1630.

701ᵇ–704. Th. · As it saith in books, when from earth the Child divine ascended, King of all purity, then the Church here of the faithful awaited persecution '; Go. 'As it saith in books, that when the Child divine, the King all pure, had risen (Go.² ascended) from the earth, then the Church here of the faithful ones endured oppression." Gr. as in our text. So Dietrich : 'Nachdem das Gotteskind vom Erdengrund *aufgestiegen*, hatte die Kirche heidnische Verfolgung zu leiden; doch gedieh durch des Geistes Gabe der Segen der Gottesmänner *nach der* Himmelfahrt.'

Against this view is to be adduced : (1) it contradicts the Latin, which Dietrich and Gollancz themselves cite ; (2) *sibban* and *þā* are not usually correlative ; (3) it destroys the parallelism of *āstāg*, 702, and *ūpstige*, 711.

703. clǣnra. So *Jul.* 420 ; *El.* 96. Th. and Go. both mistake.

þā. Must refer to the period antedating the Ascension.

704. ǣfyllendra. Cosijn says : '*ǣfyllendra* fasse ich als gen. subj., also *fyllan* = *fellan* ; vgl. *El.* 1040 : *gedwolan fylde, unrihte ǣ* ; vgl. auch unten v. 709, wo *blōdgyte worhtan* (708) einzuklammern ist.'

eahtnysse. Cf. *Jul.* 4.

706. þǣr. Gr. connects with the preceding: 'als sich die wilden Sünder,' etc. ; this is correlating *þā* and *þǣr*, which is hardly admissible.

sōþes ne gīemdon. Cf. *rihtes ne gīemdon, An.* 139.

707. gǣstes þearfe. So 816 (III), 1057; *Gifts of Men* 86. — **tempel.** In this sense *Gu.* 461.

709. fēodan ond fyldon. Note the echo from 486, with new application.

forð bicwōm. In Lind. Jn. 5. 29, *forðcuma* translates *procedere*.

710. þurh Gǣstes giefe. So 649.

712–743. See *Analysis*, 12 (p. 116).

Based upon Greg. *Hom. in Evang.* 29. 10 (following the above ; see on 691–711) : 'Hinc ejusdem Ecclesiae voce per Salomonem dicitur: *Ecce iste venit saliens in montibus, et transiliens colles* (Cant. 2. 8). Consideravit namque tantorum operum culmina, et ait : *Ecce iste venit saliens in montibus.* Veniendo quippe ad redemptionem nostram, quosdam, ut ita dixerim, saltus dedit. Vultis, fratres carissimi, ipsos ejus saltus agnoscere ? De caelo venit in uterum, de utero venit in praesepe, de praesepe venit in crucem, de cruce venit in sepulcrum, de sepulcro rediit in caelum. . . .'

712. Dāuīþes. But *Dāuīdes*, 96, 165, 191. Such wavering between the original *d* of foreign proper names and OE. *ð* is frequent, e.g. in Anglian, cf. the *Dāuīdes* of Lind. Mt. 1. 1, 20; Jn. 7. 42, etc. with the *Dāuīðes* of Mt. 9. 27 ; 21. 9 ; Mk. 10. 47 ; Lk. 1. 32, etc. ; the *Dāuīd* of Rush. Mk. 2. 25 ; 12. 36 with the *Dāuīð* of Mk. 12. 37, etc. ; in Rush.² always *Dāuīðes*.

713. giedda gearosnottor. So *El.* 418 ; cf. *El.* 586 ; *Wīd.* 139.

713. gǣstgerȳnum. So 440; *An.* 860; *El.* 189, 1148; *Gu.* 1086; cf. *Gu.* 219.

716. Meotud, meahtum swīð. So *An.* 1209; *Sat.* 262 ; *Gifts of Men* 4; cf. *Az.* 5; *Dan.* 284.

717. gehlēapeð. In *By.* 189: 'hē gehlēop þone eoh.' — **hēadūne.** Cf., in Grein, the numerous compounds in *hēa(h)-: hēahburg, hēahclif,* etc.

718. woruld ālȳseð. Cf. Jn. 1. 29 ; 3. 17 ; 4. 42 ; 1 Jn. 2. 2 ; 4. 14.

719. ealle eorðbūend. Note the exegesis of *woruld*. Br. tr. 715–9 (p. 209).

720 ff. Cf. 1418 ff. (III).

720. se forma hlȳp. The ultimate source of this mystical interpretation of Cant. 2. 8 is to be found (as I wrote on Apr. 4, 1895, for the *Festgabe für Eduard Sievers*) in two passages of Ambrose. I subjoin that note : 'The first is (*De Isaac et Anima* 4. 31 ; Migne 14. 513) : "*Saliens super montes, et transiliens super* *colles* (Cant. 2. 8). Super majoris gratiae animas salit, inferioris transilit. Vel sic: saliens quomodo venit? Saltu quodam venit in hunc mundum. Apud Patrem erat, in Virginem venit, et ex Virgine in praesepe transilivit. In praesepi erat, et fulgebat in caelo, descendit in Jordanem, ascendit in crucem, descendit in tumulum, surrexit e tumulo, et sedet ad Patris dexteram." The second is (*In Psalmum 113 Expositio, Sermo* 6. 6; Migne 15. 1269-70): "Videamus salientem. Salit de caelo in Virginem, de utero in praesepe, de praesepio [*sic*] in Jordanem, de Jordane in crucem, de cruce in tumulum, in caelum de sepulcro." Ambrose is followed by (Pseudo-) Cassiodorus, in his commentary on the Canticles (Migne 70. 1064): "Potest etiam hoc ad incarnationem Christi referre, qui veniens quosdam saltus dedit: quia de caelo venit in uterum Virginis, de utero Virginis in praesepe, de praesepi in baptismum, de baptismo in crucem, de cruce ad sepulcrum, de sepulcro ad caelum." [Then followed the quotation from Gregory.] Finally, Alcuin has the same thought, and in almost the same words as Gregory (*Compendium in Canticum Canticorum* 2. 8; Migne 100. 646-7): "Tales enim saltus fecit dilectus meus: de caelo venit in uterum, de utero in praesepe, de praesepi in crucem, de cruce in sepulcrum, de sepulcro rediit in caelum." Cf. Pseudo-Jerome (Migne 30. 379).

'It will be remarked that Cynewulf omits the leap into Jordan (baptism), like Gregory and Alcuin. In this respect, and in adding the descent into hell, there is an agreement between the *Christ* and the Middle English homily on the Ascension, now printed in *Old English Homilies of the Twelfth Century*, Second Series, pp. 111-3 (cf. Conybeare's note in his *Illustrations*, p. 202): "*ecce uenit saliens in montibus et transiliens colles*. Here he cumeð stridende fro dune to dune, and ouer strit þe cnolles. *Septem igitur ut ita dicam saltus dedit: e celo in uirginis uterum; inde in presepium; inde in crucem; inde in sepulcrum; inde in infernum; inde in mundum; et hinc in celum*.' 'Seuen strides he makede: on of heuene into þe maidenes inneðe; oðer þenne in to þe stalle; ðridde in to þe holi rode; feorðe þanne in to þe sepulcre; fifte into helle; sixte into þis middenerd; þe seueðe eft into heuene." Here the "*ut ita dicam*" suggests Gregory as the source of the passage in general. Bede, in his commentary on the Canticles, has nothing about the leaps. It might be suspected that the thought would occur in Origen, but I have not found it there.'

The suggestion for this interpretation may have come from Wisd. 18. 14, 15: 'Cum enim quietum silentium contineret omnia, et nox in suo cursu medium iter haberet, omnipotens *sermo tuus de caelo* a regalibus sedibus, durus debellator in mediam exterminii terram *prosilivit*.' This is rendered in the English Apocrypha: 'For while all things were in quiet silence, and that night was in the midst of her swift course, thine Almighty word leaped down from heaven out of thy royal throne as a fierce man of war into the midst of a land of destruction.' The Latin has been adapted in the Antiphon for the Magnificat for the Sunday before the Octave of Christmas: 'Dum medium silentium tenerent omnia, et nox in suo cursu medium iter perageret, omnipotens sermo tuus, Domine, a regalibus sedibus venit. Alleluia.'

721. hīw. Cf. 657.

722. onfēng. Cf. 418 (I), 628. — tō frōfre. Cf. 65 (I), 1421 (III).

723. stiell. Note the order: *gestyllan*, 648, 716; *gehlēapan*, 717; *stiell*, 719;

hlȳp, 720 ; *stiell*, 723 ; *hlȳp*, 726 ; *stiell*, 728 ; *hlȳp*, 730, 736 ; *styllan*, *hlȳp*, 745 ; *styllan*, *hlȳp*, 747. In other words, after preluding with *-styll-*, the poet employs the two stems, in verb and noun, in almost absolute alternation, and ends with two phrases in which both stems occur ; yet even here the two phrases are not identical. This is hardly to be ascribed to chance (see note on 729).

724. binne. Not 'bin' (Th.). The regular word for Lat. *praesepe;* cf. my *Bibl. Quot.* 118. 1 ; 187. 5, 14, 23 ; 188. 10, 29 ; so in the Gospel of Luke. The etymology is uncertain ; see *NED.* Unlike *crybb* (1425), it retains this specific sense no later than 1425 (*Leg. Rood* 211 : 'God was borne with beest in bynne'). The chief modern sense appears with Chaucer, *Prol.* 593.

725. hīw. Trautmann, *Kynewulf* 80, regards this and the other instances as acc. — **clāþum bewunden.** Cf. *biwundenne mid wonnum clāþum*, 1423 (III). Cf. Lk. 2. 7 (Corp.) : 'Hine mid cildclāþum bewand, and hine on binne ālēde'; Ælfric, *Hom.* 1. 30 (*Bibl. Quot.*, p. 187) : 'Mid cildclāðum bewand, and ālēde þæt cild on heora assena binne'; (Lind.) : 'Mid cildclāðum bewand, and eftgebēg hine in binnæ'; (Rush.): 'Mið clāðum hine biwand, and efnegibēg hine in binne.'

726. ealra þrymma þrym. So *Ph.* 628; *Gu.* 1076; *El.* 483.

727. Rodorcyninges. So *Jul.* 447; *El.* 624 (*Rādor-*), 887. — **ræs.** Not 'career' (Go.).

728. Fæder, frōfre Gæst. So *Jul.* 724; *El.* 1106. For the suggestion of the Trinity, cf. *Jud.* 83 ; *An.* 1686. — **Fæder.** Not 'Father's' (Th.), 'des Vaters' (Gr.).

729. in byrgenne. So 1467. Gr. inclines to think this dat.

bēam. The two words for 'cross' are thus distributed in the poem : *rōd*, 727 ; *bēam*, 729 ; (III) *rōd*, 1064, 1084 ; *bēam*, 1089, 1093 ; *rōd*, 1101, 1114 ; *bēam*, 1446 ; *rōd*, 1447, 1487, 1489.

In the *Elene*, besides compounds, we have a third synonym, *trēow.* The manner of their distribution is again significant for Cynewulf's art. Disregarding compounds, we have : *trēow*, 89 ; *bēam*, 91 ; *rōd*, 103 ; *trēow*, 107, 128 ; *rōd*, *trēow*, 147 ; *trēow*, 165 ; *rōd*, *trēow*, 206 ; *trēow*, 214 ; *bēam*, 217 ; *rōd*, 219 ; *bēam*, 421 ; *trēow*, 429, 442 ; *rōd*, 482 ; *trēow*, 534 ; *rōd*, 601 ; *trēow*, 624 ; *rōd*, 631 ; *trēow*, 664, 701, 706 ; *rōd*, 720, 774 ; *trēow*, 828 ; *rōd*, 834 ; *trēow*, 841 ; *bēam*, 851 ; *rōd*, *trēow*, 856 ; *bēam*, 865 ; *trēow*, 867 ; *rōd*, 869, 880 ; *bēam*, *rōd*, 887 ; *rōd*, 919, 1012 ; *bēam*, 1013 ; *rōd*, 1023 ; *trēow*, 1027 ; *rōd*, 1067 ; *bēam*, 1074 ; *rōd*, 1075, 1224 ; *bēam*, 1225 ; *rōd*, 1235 ; *trēow*, 1252 ; *bēam*, 1255. That is, of 51 occurrences of the different words, 8 are of pairs of words in the same line, and 10 are of a repeated occurrence of the same word before another is employed ; with these exceptions, the expressions are alternated. Take the first three, for example : *trēow*, *bēam*, *rōd* ; and the last three : *rōd*, *trēow*, *bēam.* As bearing on the question of authorship, what conclusions might not be drawn from the fact that Cynewulf regularly employs in the *Elene* at least one synonym for 'cross' not found in the *Christ!*

730. foldærne. So *Gu.* 1004. — **fæst.** In the same construction *El.* 723, 883; *Beow.* 1007, 2901 ; *Gu.* 1005, etc.

732. cwicsūsle. Not 'quick sulphur' (Th.). Cf. *Whale* 38, and WW. *Voc.* 144. 14 : '*baratrum, uorago profunda*, cwicsūsl, *vel* hellelic dēopnes.' See also Bosworth-Toller, s.v.

733. fēonda foresprecan. Cf. *Gu.* 236. WW. has (140. 3) : '*causidicus, aduocatus,* forespeca.'

fȳrnum. Cf. *Panther* 60; *An.* 1380.

736. synnum gesǣled. Cf. 117 (I).

737. hyhtplega. Cf. *Rid.* 21²⁸. Not 'Triumph' (Gr.).

738. his ealdcȳ𝐝𝐝e. Cf. *Ph.* 351, 435.

739. blīþe. Cf. 519, 550ᵇ–551ᵃ.

741. æþelinga Ord. So 515, 845; *El.* 393; *Gen.* 1278.

742. beorhtra bolda. Not 'brighter dwellings' (Th.), nor ' Bau des Glanzes' (Gr.).

743. ēce gefēa. Cf. *ēcne gefēan,* 159 (I). — **plega.** Cf. 737. Not 'solace' (Th.), nor 'revel' (Go.).

744-755. See *Analysis,* 13 (p. 116).

Based upon Greg. *Hom. in Evang.* 29. 11 (following the above; see on 712–743) : 'Unde, fratres carissimi, oportet ut illuc sequamur corde, ubi eum corpore ascendisse credimus. Desideria terrena fugiamus, nihil nos jam delectet in infimis, qui Patrem habemus in caelis.' Cf. Bede, *Hom. in Ascensione* (Migne 94. 181) : 'Et ipsi quoque ut ejus vestigia sequi, atque ad caelos mereamur ascendere. . . . Ad hujus ergo patriae perpetuam felicitatem omni studio festinemus. In hac quia necdum corpore possumus, desiderio semper et mente versemur.' There is a translation of the close of this homily in Mayor and Lumby's *Bede,* p. 404.

745. hēahhleoþu. Cf. *Gen.* 1439.

748. of mægne in mægen. So in Bede's *Eccl. Hist.* (*Bibl. Quot.,* p. 71) : 'Hālige gonga𝐝 of mægene in mægen,' as tr. of Ps. 84. 7, where Ælfric (*ib.* 113) has : 'Đā hālgan fara𝐝 fram mihte tō mihte.' Th., Go., Br. 'from virtue (un)to virtue'; Diet. 'von Tugend zu Tugend'; Gr. 'von Thaten zu Thaten'; Hammerich, 'von That zu That.'

749. hrōfe. The word sometimes translates *cacumen, culmen.* Cf. Tennyson's (*Lotos-Eaters* 69)

> Why should we only toil, the *roof* and crown of things?

750. hyht ond blis. Cf. 529ᵃ–530ᵃ.

751ᵇ. So 847ᵇ.

753. þǣr. Not 'that' (Th.). — **gelȳfa𝐝.** Not 'repose' (Go.¹).

754. þæt þæt. Not 'so that' (Go.).

755. mid ūsse līchoman. Not 'with our *bodies*' (Th., Go.); cf. *corpore,* above : 'our human body.'

756-783ᵃ. See *Analysis,* 14 (p. 116).

757. sēllran. This looks like ' contamination' of *sellan* and *sēlran.*

synwunde. Artistic anticipation of *wunde,* 763.

Note the rime.

758. Fæder on roderum. Mt. 6. 9.

759. āras. In this sense 493, 503; *Gen.* 2424; *An.* 831; etc.

760. hālig of hēahðu. So 789; *El.* 1087 (*hīehðo*); *Jul.* 263; *An.* 1146 (*hēhðo*); cf. *Gu.* 910, 1061.

761. Gesctldaþ. With general reference to such passages as Ps. 34. 7; 91 10, 11 (Mt. 4. 6; Lk. 4. 10, 11); Heb. 1. 14.

sceþþendra. So *Gu.* 375.

762. **earhfarum.** For the word in this sense, cf. *Jul.* 404; *Sal.* 129. Not 'quivers' (Th.), nor 'arrow-shafts' (Go.[1]).

763. **wunde gewyrcen.** Cf. *Beow.* 2906. — **wrŏhtbora.** *Wrŏht* means, according to Grein, (*a*) accusation; (*b*) crime, offense; (*c*) strife; (*d*) injury, harm. He renders *wrŏhtbora* by 'scelerum auctor,' and in *D.* by 'Wutkampf-bringer'; Th., Go.[1], Br. by 'accuser.' The last word would best translate *diabolus* in its primary signification.

763[b]–771[a]. Tr. by Brooke.

764. **folc Godes.** Cf. Heb. 4. 9; 11. 25; 1 Pet. 2. 10; also Lk. 1. 68; 7. 16; etc.

765. **brægdbogan.** Perhaps this is the 'deceitful bow,' *arcus pravus, dolosus*, of Ps. 78. 57; Hos. 7. 16. Th., Go., 'drawn bow'; D. (*Haupt's Zs.* 9. 208) 'Trugbogen'; Gr. (*Spr.*) 'arcus fraudulentus,' (*D.*) 'des Bogens Sehne'; Br. 'bended bow.' 'Drawn sword' I understand, but not 'drawn bow.' 'Bend' is OE. (*ge*)*bendan*, or (once) *teon*, not *bregdan*.

Representations of the Old English bow and arrow (from MSS. Cott. Claudius B. IV and Tiberius C. VI) are to be found in Strutt, *Sports and Pastimes*, Bk. 2, chap. 1, and *Horda Angelcynnan*, Pl. 17, Fig. 2 (Claud. B. IV); Pl. 22, Figs. 23, 24, 25; and in Green's *Short History of the English People*, illustrated edition, pp. 100, 152, from MSS. Cott. Galba A. VIII and Claudius B. IV.

Hewitt, *Ancient Armor and Weapons in Europe* 1. 55, remarks: 'According to the testimony of Henry of Huntingdon [6. 29], William the Conqueror re-proached the English with their want of this weapon. The Bayeux tapestry, however, seems to authorize the belief that they were not entirely without it. (See the first group of Anglo-Saxons in Stothard's XIVth plate.) The proba-bility seems to be that, while the Normans employed archers in large bodies, the English merely interspersed them in small numbers among their men-at-arms. The bow, at all events, was in use among the Anglo-Saxons; it is frequently represented in manuscript illuminations, and arrow-heads have been found in the graves. Figs. 1, 2, 3, and 4 in our Plate are from Kentish interments; the others, figured in the *Nenia Britannica*, were found on Chatham Lines. The whole are of iron. Pictorial examples of the Anglo-Saxon bow, arrows, and quiver may be seen in Cotton MSS. Cleop. C. VIII, Claudius B. IV, Tiberius C. VI, and in the fine Prudentius of the Tenison Library.'

Henry of Huntingdon's (d. 1155) supposed testimony is worthless, since it is contained in a speech of William the Conqueror to his troops before the battle of Hastings, which, according to his editor in the Rolls Series (p. 201), is 'a rhetorical flight of Henry's own invention; no contemporary author mentions anything of the kind.' Besides, William's alleged words, 'gentem nec etiam sagittas habentem,' need only mean that the ammunition of the English soldiery was momentarily deficient.

De Baye, *Industrial Arts of the Anglo-Saxons*, pp. 30–31, is of little value.

Oman, in Traill's *Social England* 1. 411, evidently thinks these to have been short bows : 'Whence the English got their long-bow is not quite easy to decide; the Normans at Hastings — as the Bayeux Tapestry clearly shows — still used the short four-foot bow, not the great six-foot weapon with its cloth-yard arrow.'

Elsewhere he says (1. 179): 'The bow, though not uncommon, was never a typical nor a very effective weapon with the Old English.'

The bow was sometimes known as *flānboga, Beow.* 1432-5:

> Sumne Gēata lēod
> of *flānbogan* fēores getwǣfde
> ȳðgewinnes, þæt him on āldre stōd
> herestrǣl hearda.

Sometimes as *hornboga, Beow.* 2437-40:

> Syððan hine Hæðcyn of *hornbogan*,
> his frēawine, flāne geswencte,
> miste mercelses ond his mǣg ofscēt,
> brōðor ōðerne blōdigan gāre.

Jud. 220–223:

> Hīe ðā fromlīce
> lēton forð flēogan flāna scūras,
> hildenǣdran of *hornbogan*,
> strǣlas stedehearde.

See also *Rid.* 24, and Brooke, pp. 125, 128, 129, 131.

biterne strǣl. Cf. Eph. 6. 16. Referring to the sin of pride, *Beow.* 1743-6 has:

> Bona swiðe nēah
> se þe of flānbogan fyrenum scēoteð;
> þonne bið on hreþre under helm drepen
> *biteran strǣle.*

So of a sword, *Beow.* 2704. The Gr. πικρός originally meant 'pointed,' 'sharp,' 'keen'; cf. πικρὸς ὀϊστός, *Il.* 4. 118. So Tennyson, *Oriana* 37:

> The *bitter arrow* went aside.

Biter probably stands in ablaut relation with *bītan.*

767. wearde healdan. Cf. *Beow.* 305, 319; *Jul.* 664; *Jud.* 142.

768. ǣttres ord. So *Jul.* 471; cf. *ǣtres drync, An.* 53.

On the construction, cf. Buttmann, *Gram. N. T. Greek,* tr. Thayer, p. 161: 'The use of a substantive in the genitive as a periphrasis for an adjective, which is mentioned as a poetic peculiarity among the Greeks, is found not infrequently in the N. T.; at any rate, there are numerous genitives that can hardly be reproduced by us otherwise than by means of their corresponding adjectives. In this peculiarity the influence of the genius of the Oriental tongues is unmistakable, for they were especially addicted to this more poetic mode of expression.' See, in the Greek, Lk. 4. 22; 16. 8; 18. 6; Rom. 1. 26; 12. 20; Heb. 12. 15; Matt. 24. 31. Winen, ed. Thayer, p. 237, adds Col. 1. 13; Rev. 13. 3; 2 Pet. 2. 10; Jas. 1. 25; Heb. 1. 3, and says: 'This, in prose, is a Hebraistic mode of expression, and is to be attributed not merely to the want of adjectives in Hebrew, Ewald 572, but to the peculiar vividness of the Oriental languages. In the more elevated style, however, there are instances of the same construction even in Greek authors; see Erfurdt, Soph. *Oed. R.* 826.' Of the above instances, the Vulgate imitates this idiom in all except Matt. 24. 31 and Jas. 1. 25. The OE.

omits the genitive in Lk. 4. 22, renders it by a genitive in Lk. 16. 8, and changes it to the adjective in Lk. 18. 6 (but North. has genitive).

Poisoned arrows are elsewhere mentioned in OE.: *Jul.* 471; *An.* 1333; *Rid.* 18⁹, 24⁴,⁹; *By.* 47, 146; WW. 143⁷ has: *scorpius*, 'geættrad flaa.' In the *Life of St. Neot* (Cockayne, *Shrine*, p. 13) occurs: 'Ongann þā sænden his ǣttrige wǣpnen, þæt synd costnungen, tōgēanes þān hālgen were.' Cf. *Bl. Hom.* 199. 17–19: 'Þā genam hē his bogan, and hine gebende, and ðā mid geǣttredum strǣle ongan scēotan.'

Alfred's translation of Orosius relates of the attempt to capture the city ruled over by Ambira: 'Þǣr forwearþ micel Alexandres heres for geǣtredum gescotum (*sagittis veneno illitis*).' However, a number are saved by an herb which is shown to Alexander in a dream.

In *Beowulf* we are told of the sword Hrunting (1459):

> ecg wæs īren ātertānum fāh,

where some scholars read 'ātertēarum.' Arrows (and darts?) are called *hildenǣdre* (cf. Æsch. *Eum.* 181), perhaps with reference to their venom, as well as to their biting and hissing: *Jud.* 222; *El.* 119, 141.

Interesting for its parallelism to our passage is an extract from the *Life of St. Guthlac*, ed. Goodwin, pp. 26, 28: 'Þā gelamp hit sume dæge mid [þȳ hē] þān gewunnelican þēawe his sealm sang, and his gebedum befēal, þā se ealda fēond mancynnes (efne swā grymetigende lēo, þæt hē his costunga āttor wīde tōdǣleð), mid þȳ hē þā his yfelnysse mægen and grymnysse āttor [tōdǣlde], þæt hē mid þān þā menniscan heortan wundode, þā semninga swā hē of gebendum bogan his costunge strēale on þām mōde gefæstnode þæs Crīstes cempan.¹ Ðā hē þā, se ēadiga wer, mid þǣre geǣttredan strēale gewundod wæs þæs āwerigedan gāstes, ðā wæs his mōd, þæs ēadigan weres, swīðe gedrēfed on him. . . Ðā hæfde hine sēo dēofollice strǣl mid ormōdnysse gewundodne; wæs se ēadiga wer, Gūðlāc, mid þǣre ormōdnysse þrī dagas gewundod.'

The poisoning of arrows is mentioned in the *Odyssey* (1. 261–3): 'For even thither [to Ephyra] had Odysseus gone on his swift ship to seek a deadly drug, that he might have wherewithal to smear his bronze-shod arrows; but Ilus would in nowise give it him, for he had·in awe the everliving gods.'

Ovid thus speaks of the Sauromatae, Bessi, and Getae (*Ex Ponto* 1. 2. 17–23): 'These foes, that they may effect a twofold cause for death in the cruel wound, dip all their darts in the venom of the viper. Provided with these, the horseman surveys the fortifications, just like a wolf prowling round the sheep in their fold. Their light bow, when once stretched with the horse-hair cord (*nervo equino*), always remains with its string unrelaxed. The houses bristle as though palisaded with the arrows fixed there.' Cf. *Trist.* 3. 10. 63, 64; *Ex Ponto* 4. 7. 11, 12.

Pliny says of the Scythians (*H. N.* 11. 53): 'The Scythians dip their arrows in the poison of serpents and human blood; against this frightful composition

---

¹ Goodwin (p. 111) gives the Latin from the Life by Felix of Croyland: 'Dum enim omnis nequitiae suae vires versuta mente tentaret, tum veluti ab extenso arcu venenifluam desperationis sagittam totis viribus jaculavit, quousque in Christe militis mente umbone defixa pependit.'

there is no remedy, for with the slightest touch it is productive of instant death.' *Ib.* 25. 25: 'The people of Gaul, when hunting, tip their arrows with hellebore, taking care to cut away the parts about the wound in the animal so slain ; the flesh, they say, is all the more tender for it.' Again (27. 11. 76): 'Limeum is the name given by the Gauls to a plant, in a preparation of which, known by them as "deer's poison," they dip their arrows when hunting.' Strabo asserts (4. 4. 6) : 'The following is also credible : that a tree grows in Keltica similar to a fig, which produces a fruit resembling a Corinthian capital, and which, being cut, exudes a poisonous juice, which they use for poisoning their arrows.' On the poisoned arrows of the Moors, cf. Hor. *Od.* 1. 22. 3; of the Arabs, Pollux 1. 138; Seneca, *Medea* 693–5. Add Plin. 16. 10. 20, Caecil. and Afran. ap. Fest. p. 355 Müller; Dioscor. 6. 20. Ambrose has *sagitta toxicata* (Tob. 7. 26). The etymology of *toxicum* is significant of this custom.

in gebūge. Similarly 1504 (III).

769. bordgelāc. Gr. (*Spr.*) 'clypeorum impugnatio ?', (*D.*) 'Geschoss'; Th. 'shield-play '; Go. 'dart '; Br. 'bitter piercing dart, stormer of the shield '; Hall (Dict.) '(sport of shields) dart'; Sweet (*Dict.*) 'weapon.' There is a *lindgelāc*, *Ap.* 76, which Grein renders 'pugna scutiferorum.' Cosijn says: '*bordgelāc*, *lindgelāc*, *lindplega* bedeuten einfach "streit," eigentlich *gelāc* (*plega*) *borde-*, *lind-hæbbendra*. Ich verwerfe Grein's deutung "clypeorum impugnatio." '

771. blātast. Cf. *An.* 1090; *Gen.* 981 ; *Met.* 8[64]; 20[llb].

773. Cf. *Beow.* 188; *Dan.* 222. See Grein, *tō* (3).

774. Note the Trinity.

þone blīðan gæst. Cf. *Gu.* 306.

775. Cf. 761. The thought occurs in the Advent **Hymn,** 'Conditor alme siderum ' (*Surtees Hymns*, p. 34), in the lines:

> Conserva nos in tempore
> Hostis a telis perfidi.

The last line is glossed : 'fēondes fram flānum gelēaflēase' (*sic*).

sceaþan wǣpnum. So *An.* 1293.

776. līf forgeaf. So *Gen.* 2843.

777ᵃ. leomu, līc, ond gæst. Cf. *Ph.* 513; *Gu.* 810, 1149.

777ᵇ–778. Cf. *Ph.* 661ᵇ–662 :

> Sȳ him lof symle
> þurh woruld worulda and wuldres blǣd.

779–782ᵃ. This is certainly transitional. Since it echoes the preceding lines, it ought perhaps to be reckoned with them: cf. *strǣl*, 765: *strǣlas*, 779; *on eorðan*, 772, 780; *earhfarum*, 762 : *gārfare*, 781 ; *gescildaþ*, 761, *gescilde*, 775 : *scildeþ*, 781. Against it is the doxology just preceding, which suggests the close of a division.

779. dēofla strǣlas. Cf. *dēofles strǣl*, *An.* 1191, and note on *ǣttres ord*, 768.

780. ǣlda cynnes. So *Ph.* 546; *Gu.* 727, 793, 948; cf. *Ph.* 198 ; *Jul.* 727.

781. gārfare. Only *Exod.* 343, and there in another sense.

782. duguða Dryhten. So *Ph.* 494; *El.* 81.

Is þām dōme nēah. Impersonal construction. Cf. the two following passages from Bede (quoted by Wülfing, I. 61): *Bd.* 598. 37: 'Ne ðīnre forðfōre swā nēah is'; 599. 3: 'Hū nēah ðǣre tīde wǣre þætte ...' See Jas. 5. 8.

782ᵇ-796. See *Analysis*, 15 (p. 116). Based upon Gregory, *Hom. in Evang.* 29. 11 (following the above; see on 744–755): 'Et hoc nobis est magnopere perpendendum, quia is qui placidus ascendit terribilis redibit, et quidquid nobis cum mansuetudine praecepit, hoc a nobis cum districtione exiget. Nemo ergo indulta poenitentiae tempora parvipendat, nemo curam sui, dum valet, agere negligat, quia Redemptor noster tanto tunc in judicium districtior veniet, quanto nobis ante judicium magnam patientiam praerogavit. Haec itaque vobiscum, fratres, agite, haec in mente sedula cogitatione versate.' Cf. Bede, *Hom. in Ascensione* (Migne 94. 181): 'Cum *ipse qui placidus ascendit terribilis redierit*, nos paratos inveniat.'

783. þæt. Perhaps we should read *þǣr.* — **lēanum hlēotan.** Cf. *lēana hlēotan, Jul.* 622. Cynewulf changed the construction, then.

784. Cosijn inserts *ūs* after *wē*, to provide an object for *hlōdun.* — **weorcum.** Cf. Mt. 16. 27; Rom. 2. 6; 2 Cor. 5. 10; Rev. 20. 12; 22. 12. — **hlōdun.** Cf. 1034; *Hel.* 2469, 3785, 4255.

785. geond sīdne grund. So *Gen.* 134, 1388, 1429; *Jul.* 332; *Hy.* 3¹¹.

786. ēadmōd. Echoing 255 (I).

787. Goldhord. Cf. *Bl. Hom.* 9. 28: 'þā wæs gesended þæt *Goldhord* þæs mægenþrymmes on þone bend þæs clǣnan innoðes'; 11. 29: 'On þissum dæge āstāg *þæt heofonlice Goldhord* on þisne ymbhwyrft fram þǣm hēahsetle ūre[s] Gescyppendes, *þæt wæs Crīst*, þæs lifgendan Godes Sunu.'

788. Frēobearn. Cf. 223 (1).

789. Hūru. So (I) 22, 82, 337; (II) 613. On account of the metre, Frucht (p. 30) would either cancel *mē*, place it before *wēne*, or prefix it to the next line.

790. dōm ðȳ rēþran. Th., Go.² 'a doom the sterner'; Gr. 'das furchtbare Gericht'; Go.¹ 'a sterner doom.' — **ðȳ rōþran ... þe.** Cf. *Gen.* 1325: 'symble bið ðȳ heardra þe hit hrēoh wæter swīðor bēata'ð.' See Wülfing I. 378–9; Grein, *Sprachschatz*, s. v. *þæt*, pron. (2). For the line, see *Doomsday* (Bede) 15.

791-808ᵃ. Printed in Hickes' *Thesaurus*, vol. 1, after p. 4 of the *Grammatica Islandica*, following Table 4 of Runes. It is headed: 'Specimen e Cod. MS. Exoniensi C.' On p. 5 says: 'In Tab. C describitur conclusio seculi, et adventus Christi ad judicium.'

791. engla þēoden. So 332; *Exod.* 431; *An.* 290, 902; cf. *þēoden engla, Sat.* 388, 666; *Pa.* 63; *Men.* 85; *El.* 487, 777, 858.

794. As against Thorpe's note, cf. 1539; *Gu.* 832.
þæs þe ic sōð talge. So *An.* 1565; cf. *Beow.* 532.

795. monige. The verb evidently requires the emendation, as appears from *Ph.* 491. —on gemōt. So 832, (III) 942.

796. So 836; *Gu.* 755, 1161; *El.* 746; cf. *Ph.* 600; *An.* 721.

797-807ᵃ. See *Analysis*, 16 (p. 116).
On the runes, cf. Gollancz, *Christ*, pp. 173-4: 'The runes in this passage stand for the letters CYNWULF, and together form the name of the author. A similar artifice is found in three other poems — *Elene, Juliana,* and *The Fates of the Apostles. Christ* and *Juliana* are both in the Exeter Codex; *Elene* and *The*

Fates of the Apostles in the Vercelli Codex. . . . . The four runic passages may be divided into two divisions; the first, in which the runes stand merely for the letters of the poet's name; the second, in which the runes discharge a twofold function, representing not merely the letters of the poet's name, but also the words that the letters suggest, the names of the letters or homonyms. To the first class belongs the passage in *Juliana ;* to the second, the other three passages. The interpretation of the runes in these latter passages is one of difficulty.' Conybeare had already said (p. 119) that 'several runic characters are introduced, obviously as monogrammatic cyphers, each denoting an entire word, either the same with that which gave its name to the respective letters of the runic alphabet, or some one of similar sound.'

Any deeper consideration of one of these runic passages demands a comparison with the others, and I accordingly print them all here. In using the title, *Fates of the Apostles,* I leave out of account the question whether the lines so named are part of the *Andreas,* or independent. On the restoration of this passage, see especially Napier, *Haupt's Zeitschrift* 33. 66 ff. ; Sievers, *Anglia* 13. 1 ff.; Trautmann, *Kynewulf,* pp. 50–51.

The runes of the manuscripts are here represented by the corresponding letters of the alphabet.

JULIANA (695–710).

Is mē þearf micel
þæt sēo hālge mē helpe gefremme,
þonne mē gedǣla'ð dēorast ealra,
sibbe tōslīta'ð sinhīwan tū,
micle mōdlufan, mīn sceal of līce
sāwul on sī'ðfæt, nāt ic sylfa hwider,
eardes uncy'ðþu ; of sceal ic þissum,
sēcan ōþerne ærgewyrhtum,
gongan īndǣdum. Gēomor hweorfe'ð
· C · · Y · ond · N ·. Cyning biþ rēþe,
sigora Syllend, þonne synnum fāh
· E · · W · ond · U · ācle bīda'ð,
hwæt him æfter dǣdum dēman wille
līfes tō lēane. · L · · F · beofa'ð,
seoma'ð sorgcearig, sār eal gemon,
synna wunde, þe ic sī'ð o'ð'ðe ǣr
geworhte in worulde.

FATES OF THE APOSTLES (unrestored).

Her mæg findan for þances gleaw. se'ðe *h*ine lyste'ð leo'ð gid
dunga. Hwa þas fitte *fegde* · F · þær on ende standaþ
eorlas þæs oneor'ðan b(*r*) : ca*þ*. Nemoton hie awa æt
somne woruld wu*nigende* · (W) · sceal gedreosan · U ·
on e'ðle æfter to (*h*) : : : : : : : (*l*) : *e*ne lices frætewa efne
swa · L · to glide'ð. : (*swa*). (C) (Y?) cræftes neota'ð. nihtes
nearowe on him. : : : : : : : : : ninges þeo dōm. Nv 'ðu
cunnon miht .(*h*) : : : : : : : : (*r*)*d*um wæs werū on cy'ðig.

FATES OF THE APOSTLES (Napier's restoration).

Hēr mæg findan foreþances glēaw,
se ðe hine lysteð lēoðgiddunga,
hwā þās fitte fēgde. FEOH þǣr on ende
standeþ, eorlas þæs on eorðan brūcaþ.
Ne mōton hīe āwa *eardian* ætsomne,
woruldwunigende. WĒN sceal gedrēosan,
ŪR on ēðle; æfter tōh*rēosaþ*
lǣne līces frætewa, efne swā LAGO tōglīdeð.
. swa CĒN *ond* ȲR cræftes nēotað
nihtes nearowe on him . . . .
*c*yninges þēodōm. Nū ðū cunn*an* miht,
*hwā on þām w*ordum wæs werum oncȳðig.

FATES OF THE APOSTLES (Sievers' restoration).

Hēr mæg findan foreþances glēaw,
se ðe hine lysteð lēoðgiddunga,
hwā þās fitte fēgde. FEOH þǣr on ende stand*eð*;
eorlas þæs on eorðan br*ū*caþ; ne mōton hīe āwa ætsomne,
woruldwunigende; WYNN sceal gedrēosan,
ŪR on ēðle, æfter tōh*rēosan*
lǣne līces frætewa, efne swā LAGO tōglīdeð.
*þ*onne (?) CĒN *ond* ȲR cræftes nēo*s*að
nihtes nearowe; on him *nȳd lige*ჳ,
*c*yninges þēodōm. Nū ðū cunn*an* miht,
*hwā on þǣm w*ordum wæs werum oncȳðig.

ELENE (1257–1271).

Ā wæs secg[1] oð ðæt
cnyssed cearwelmum, · C · drūsende,
þēah hē in medohealle māðmas þēge,
æplede gold. · Y · gnornode,
· N · gefera nearusorge drēah,
enge rūne, þǣr him · E · fore
mīlpaðas mæt, mōdig þrægde
wīrum gewlenced. · W · is geswīðrad,
gomen æfter gēarum; geogoð is gecyrred,
āld onmēdla. · U · wæs gēara
geogoðhādes glǣm; nū synt gēardagas
æfter fyrstmearce forð gewitene,
līfwynne geliden, swā · L · tōglīdeð,
flōdas gefȳsde. · F · ǣghwām bið
lǣne under lyfte; landes frætwe
gewītaþ under wolcnum winde geliccost.

---

[1] MS. sæcc.

CHRIST (796–806).

þonne · C · cwacaᵹ, gehȳreᵹ Cyning mæᵹlan,
rodera Ryhtend, sprecan rēþe word
þām þe him ǣr in worulde wāce hȳrdon,
þendan · Y · and · N · ȳþast meahtan
frōfre findan. Þǣr sceal forht monig
on þam wongstede wērig bīdan
hwæt him æfter dǣdum dēman wille
wrāþra wīta, Biþ se · W · scæcen
eorþan frætwa. · U · wæs longe
· L · flōdum bilocen, līfwynna dǣl,
· F · on foldan.

The most important document for the interpretation of these passages is the
Runic Poem, first published by Hickes (*Thesaurus* 135) from MS. Cott. Otho B. X,
which was destroyed in the fire of 1731. Other editions are by W. Grimm (1821),
Ueber Deutsche Runen, pp. 217–225; Kemble (1840), in *Archæologia* 28. 339–345;
Ettmüller (1850), *Scopas and Boceras*, pp. 286–9; Zacher (1855), *Das Gotische
Alphabet;* Grein (1858), *Bibliothek* 2. 351–4; Rieger (1861), *Lesebuch*, pp. 136–9;
Botkine (1879), *La Chanson des Runes*, pp. 9–11; Wül(c)ker (1882), *Kleinere
Angelsächsische Dichtungen*, pp. 37–40; *Bibliothek* 1. 331–7. Translations: into
German by Grimm, 225–233; English, by Kemble, pp. 339–345; French, by Bot-
kine, pp. 12–14. Chief commentaries: Grimm and Zacher (as above); Kirchhoff
(1851, 1854), *Das Gothische Runen-Alphabet.*
  The Old English Runic alphabet is also found on the so-called Thames Knife,
and in several MSS. dating from the ninth to the eleventh century. These are
reproduced by Hickes, *Gram. Anglo-Sax.*, p. 136; *Gram. Isl.*, tabb. II and VI;
Grimm (as above), tables I–III, and *Zur Literatur der Runen* (Vienna, 1828),
pp. 1–2, 23, 25 (from the *Wiener Jahrbücher der Literatur*, vol. 43); Kemble
(as above), pl. XV–XVI; G. Stephens, *The Old-Northern Runic Monuments* 1.
100–114, cf. 829–832. On the whole subject, cf. the prime authority, Wimmer,
Die Runenschrift (Berlin, 1887); an accurate outline of the subject, based on
Wimmer, by Sievers, in Paul's *Grundriss*, vol. 1.
  The runic passages of the Cynewulfian poems have been discussed in the following works, which may be consulted in addition to those cited above:
  1840. Kemble, in *Archæologia* 28. 360–364.
  1840. Grimm, *Andreas und Elene*, pp. 169–170.
  1842. Thorpe, *Codex Exoniensis*, pp. 50, 284–5.
  1850. Ettmüller, *Scopas and Boceras*, pp. 161, 177–8, 239–240.
  1856. Kemble, Poetry of the *Codex Vercellensis*, pp. 74–75 (as in *Archæologia*).
  1857-8. Grein, *Bibliothek der Angelsächsischen Poesie* 1. 169–170; 2. 70, 135–
6; *Dichtungen der Angelsachsen* 1. 171; 2. 66, 138.
  1857. Leo, *Quæ de se ipso Cynevulfus Poeta Anglosaxonicus tradiderit*, pp. 6–
11, 16–19, 28–29.
  1859. Dietrich, in *Jahrbuch für Romanische und Englische Literatur* 1. 242–3.
  1869. Rieger, in *Zeitschrift für Deutsche Philologie* 1. 219–226.
  1879. Ten Brink, in *Anzeiger für Deutsches Alterthum* 5. 65–68.

1885. Wülker, *Grundriss*, pp. 158 ff.

1890. Cosijn, *Cynewulf's Runenverzen* (from *Verslagen en Mededeelingen der Koninklijke Akademie van Wetenschappen, Afdeeling Letterk.* III. 7).

1890 (1891). Sievers, *Anglia* 13. 1 ff.

1892. Gollancz, *Cynewulf's Christ*, pp. 173 ff.

1894. Wülker, *Bibliothek der Ags. Poesie* 2. 196 ff.

1895. Gollancz, *The Exeter Book*, pp. 51, 285.

1897. Wülker, *Bibliothek* 3. 27–28, 138.

1898. Trautmann, *Kynewulf*, pp. 43–70, containing a review of the whole subject.

From the *Runic Poem* and certain of the alphabets we derive the names of the runic letters, as given in the following table ; and from the *Runic Poem* the most that we know concerning the signification of these words, when they are other-wise unknown. The *Runic Poem* is, however, on all hands assumed to be late, and perhaps, in part at least, an adaptation of a Scandinavian original, so that too much reliance must not be placed upon its indications in the interpretation of a poem of the eighth century. The substitutions made by various scholars for the words of the *Runic Poem* are appended in the table for convenience of reference. For justification and explanation of these renderings, the works themselves should be consulted. Where blanks are left, Kemble's renderings are accepted, or the runes in question are not discussed.

RUNES IN THE CYNEWULFIAN POEMS.

LETTERS.	NAMES.	KEMBLE'S DEFINITIONS.	KEMBLE.	GRIMM.
ᚻ	cēn	'torch'	cēne, 'bold'	C
ᛇ	ȳr	'bow'	yrmðu, 'misery'	Y
ᛉ	nēd	'need'		'anxiety'
[M]	eoh	'horse'		
ᛈ	wēn (wynn)	['hope']		'presumption'
ᚾ	ūr	'bull'	ūr, 'of old'	U
ᚱ	lagu	'water,' 'sea'		
ᚡ	feoh	'money'		

NAMES.	THORPE.	ETTMÜLLER.	GREIN.
cēn	'bold'	cempa, 'pugnator'	cēne; cēn
ȳr	'misery'	yrming, 'pauper'	yrmðu; ȳr
nēd			
eoh			ege-, 'dread-'
wēn (wynn)	'wain'		wynn, 'joy'
ūr	'of old'	unne, 'favor'	'of old'
lagu			
feoh	'wealth'		

NAMES.	LEO.	DIETRICH.	RIEGER.
cēn			'pine-tree'
ȳr	ȳr, ēar, 'state of col-		ȳr, 'money,' or œ̄ðil,
nēd	lapse'		for wǣdl or ādl
eoh		Not treated, except u.	ēhlǣca, 'demon'
wēn (wynn)			
ūr	ōr (= ōra), 'money'	ufan, 'from above'	ūr, 'bison'
lagu		or, uppe, 'lascivia'	
feoh			'cattle'

NAMES.	TEN BRINK.	WÜLKER.	COSIJN.	SIEVERS.
cēn			C	
ȳr	œ̄ðil	ȳr, or yrmðu	Y	
nēd			N	
eoh				
wēn (wynn)			wyn, 'joy'	wyn, 'joy'
ūr			ūre, 'our,'	ūr, 'possession,'
lagu			or ūr, 'dampness'	'goods'
feoh				

NAMES.	GOLLANCZ.	TRAUTMANN.
cēn	cēne	cearu, 'care'; ceorl, 'man'; cyn, 'mankind'
ȳr	yfel (1) 'wretched,'	'ȳst,' 'passion'
nēd	(2) 'affliction'	nīed; nēod, 'desire'; nīð, 'ardor of battle'
eoh		
wēn (wynn)	wyn, 'joy'	wela, 'wealth'; wyn, or willa, 'joy'
ūr	ūr, 'our'	unne, 'possession'
lagu		lagu; lond; līc (in Jul.)
feoh		fæt (in Jul.)

The portions of the *Runic Poem* which bear on the interpretation of the runic passages in our poems are printed below. In the original, as given by Hickes, the runic letters have their names written near them, by whose hand or at what period is uncertain, because of the subsequent destruction of the manuscript. Here the names are substituted for the runes. Variations from the text of Hickes are recorded in foot-notes.

Cēn byþ cwicera gehwām cūþ on fȳre,
blāc and beorhtlīc, byrneþ oftust
ᚦ̇ǣr hī æþelingas inne restaþ.

Ȳr byþ æþelinga and eorla gehwæs
wyn and wyrþmynd, byþ on wicge fæger,
fæstlīc on færelde fyrdgeatewa [1] sum.

Nȳd byþ nearu on brēostan, weorþeþ hīo [2] ᚦ̇ēah oft niþa bearnum
tō helpe and tō hǣle gehwæþre, gif hī hire [3] hlystaþ ǣror.

[*Eh* byþ for eorlum æþelinga wyn,
hors hofum wlanc, ᚦ̇ǣr him hæleþ ymb
welege on wicgum wrixlaþ sprǣce,
and biþ unstillum ǣfre frōfur.]

*Wyn*ne [4] brūceþ ᚦ̇e can wēana lȳt,
sāres and sorge, and him sylfa hæfþ
blǣd and blysse and ēac byrga geniht.

Ūr byþ ānmōd and oferhyrned,
felafrēcne dēor; feohteþ mid hornum
mǣre mōrstapa; þæt is mōdig wuht.

Lagu byþ lēodum langsum geþūht,
gif hī sculun nēþan [5] on nacan tealtum,
and hī sǣȳþa swȳþe brēgaþ,
and se brimhengest brīdles ne gȳmeᚦ̇.[6]

Feoh byþ frōfur fīra gehwylcum;
sceal ᚦ̇ēah manna gehwylc miclun hyt dǣlan,
gif hē wile for Drihtne dōmes hlēotan.

Space will not permit of a full discussion of the difficulties presented by the runes in the Cynewulfian poems. For a conspectus of opinion on the subject, the student is referred to Trautmann's monograph. Only the more important considerations will be presented in the following notes.

Cēn. In Old English this is found only as the name of the runic letter. It is Mod. G. *Kien*, from MHG. *Kien*, OHG. *chien, kēn*. It had the double sense in these other dialects of 'pine' and 'pine-torch'; cf. the þwo meanings of Lat. *pinus*, e.g. (1) *Æn.* 9. 116; (2) *Æn.* 7. 397; 9. 72. The substitutions proposed have been: *C; cēne; cempa; cearu; ceorl; cyn.*

Ȳr. This is one of the most difficult. Variations of the name are (*Archæologia*, Pl. XV): *yur* (Fig. 4), *uyr* (Fig. 6), *huyri* (Fig. 1), and even *yn* (Fig. 2). Kemble translates the relevant lines of the *Runic Poem*: '*Bow* is of nobles and of every man joy and dignity; it is fair on the horse, firm in the expedition, part of warlike arms.'

Wimmer, the highest authority on runes, assumes (pp. 241 ff.) that this runic letter, represented by *ȳr*, at one time stood for the final *r* (*R*) corresponding to Goth. *s, z*; later, this *r* was designated by another sign, and this left the abandoned runic letter free to represent *ȳ*. He rejects (p. 243) the theory of Müllenhoff (*Zur Runenlehre*, pp. 60 ff.) according to which the *Scandinavian* name *ȳr* is

---

[1] MS. fyrdgeacewa.   [3] MS. his.   [5] MS. neþun.
[2] MS. hi.   [4] MS. wen.   [6] MS. gym.

identified with OHG. *īwa*, Mod. G. *Eibe*, OE. *ēoh* (*īh*) = *ēow* (*īw*), not because it is linguistically untenable, but because of considerations derived from the history of the runic alphabet. Further, the final *r* (*R*), which eventually came to be called *ȳr*, was originally called *elgr*, the name *ȳr* being borrowed from the OE. at a comparatively late period, and the OE. *yr* being derived from the OE. *ur* (*ūr*). Thus he says (p. 244):

'Als Erklärung dafür, dass das *ȳr* im jüngsten Nordischen Futhark *elgr* als Namen für die Rune ⋏ verdrängt hat, sehe ich nur eine Möglichkeit, (. . .) *dass die Nordleute erst in sehr später Zeit den Namen* ȳr *aus dem Altenglischen Runenalphabete aufgenommen haben.* Hier hatte man früh aus der alten *u*-Rune ein neues Zeichen für *y* gebildet, welches hinter die ursprüngliche Reihe gestellt wurde, und den Namen *yr* hatte. Die Form des Nordischen ⋏ *elgr* führte leicht zu der Annahme das es, wie Altengl. *yr*, eine Umbildung von ⋂ sei, und, als man ⋏ auf den letzten Platz im Futhark gestellt hatte, wurde die scheinbare Uebereinstimmung mit dem Altenglischen Zeichen noch grösser, was mit sich brachte dass auch der Altengl. Name auf die Nordische Rune übertragen wurde; dies konnte um so leichter geschehen, als man im Altengl. Namen *yr* das Nordische Wort *ȳr* zu finden glaubte. Wir haben hier dann denselben Vorgang wie wenn Altengl. *ōs* später das nordische *āss* verdrängt, und mit Altnord. *ōss* identificiert wird. Zwar scheint der Futhark in der Handschrift von St. Gallen zu beweisen, dass *ȳr* im Norden frühzeitig als Name für ⋏ gebraucht worden; aber ich kann dem Zeugnis dieser Handschrift bezüglich dieser Frage kein grosses Gewicht beimessen, da Einwirkung von dem Altenglischen Alphabete gerade hier so nahe lag, dass ich kein Bedenken hege anzunehmen, der Name *yr* im cod. Sangall. sei durch ein Missverständnis, unter Einfluss der *yr*-Rune des Altenglischen Alphabetes, in das Nordische gekommen, welche man natürlich mit dem Nordischen Zeichen identificierte. *Dessen wirklicher Name war damals und weit später*, nach meiner Meinung, elgR, *und* elgR *wurde erst dann von* ȳr *verdrängt, als man das Bedürfnis nach einem eigenen Zeichen für den y-Laut fühlte.*'

And a little later he adds: 'Eine befriedigende Erklärung der Thatsache, *dass die Rune* ⋏, *während sie noch in vollem Gebrauch als Zeichen für das "Schluss-R" war, und lange bevor sie mit der jüngeren Bedeutung y auftritt, zugleich als Bezeichnung für den e- und œ-Laut angewandt werden kann*, finde ich darin, dass sie noch zu der Zeit den alten Namen *elgR* gehabt hat; am Ende der Worte fuhr sie fort mit der ursprünglichen Bedeutung *R* gebraucht zu werden; aber man konnte auch, wie bei den andern Runenzeichen, ihre Bedeutung in dem Buchstaben suchen womit der Name begann, und sie konnte somit zugleich für *e* und *œ* angewandt werden. . . . Als ⋏ später wieder in die Runenschrift aufgenommen wurde, hatte es *die neue Bedeutung* y, *und den neuen Namen* ȳr. Wie ein punktiertes | (✝) Zeichen für *e* wurde, so bildete man das punktierte ⋂ (⋔) als Zeichen für *y*; aber auch das alte ⋏ wurde später als eine veränderte Form von ⋂ *aufgefasst*, und bekam daher dieselbe Bedeutung wie ⋔. Den Namen für diese Rune entlehnte man von der Altenglischen *y*-Rune, die weit früher von ⋂ gebildet war, und in der Form ziemlich genau mit dem Nordischen ⋏ übereinstimmte, weshalb bereits im *Abecedarium Nordmannicum* der Name *yr* auf ⋂ übertragen ist. Ich nehme deshalb an, dass man gleichzeitig Altengl. *ōs* und *yr*, die mit Nord. *ōss* und *ȳr* identificiert wurden, als Namen für die Runen aufgenommen hat, welche auf der *jüngsten* Entwicklungsstufe der Runenschrift Zeichen für *o* und *y* wurden. Wo früher die *áss-* und *elgr*-Rune gestanden hatten, dahin stellte man jetzt die *óss-* und *ȳr*-Rune' (pp. 249–255).

Relatively to the replacement of older *y* by later *ȳ* (see above), it is to be noted that the runic signs for short and long *u* are identical (pp. 191, 324, etc.).

We are now ready to summarize such statements by Wimmer, or inferences from them, as bear upon the problem of this rune:

1. The OE. rune for *y* was earlier than that in ON., and the ON. use was borrowed from the OE.

2. The use of a rune for the *y*-sound in ON. was late.

3. The *y*-rune in OE. did not originally designate a long *y*, or at least not exclusively.

Another conclusion, formulated by Müllenhoff, and accepted by Wimmer and other authorities (e.g. Kluge, *Etym. Wört.* s. v. *Eibe*) is this:

4. ON. *ȳr* = OE. *éoh*.

We are now ready to take another step: The OE. *éoh* occurs in the *Runic Poem* :

> Ēoh byþ ūtan unsmēþe trēow,
> heard, hrūsan fæst, hyrde fȳres,
> wyrtrumun underwreþyd, wyn [1] on ēþle.

This is universally interpreted as 'yew'; but, according to 4, above, this is the interpretation that we should expect to find for *ȳr* (on the supposition that *ȳr* = the ON. *ȳr*). Accordingly, we find *ȳr*, in the *Runic Poem*, interpreted as 'bow,' i.e. 'the bow made of yew-tree.' Cf. the Old Norwegian runic poem of the end of the twelfth or early part of the thirteenth century (Wimmer, p. 280) :

> Ȳr er vetrgrønstr viða ;
> vant er, er brennr, at svíða.

'Eibe ist der wintergrünste Baum ; es pflegt zu sengen wo (wenn) es brennt.' Also this from the Icelandic (p. 286) :

> Ȳr er bendr bogi
> ok brotgjarnt jārn
> ok fífu fārbauti.
> arcus. ynglingr.

' *Yr* ist gespannter Bogen, und sprödes Eisen, und des Pfeiles Riese ' [the bow]. And again (p. 288): 'Arcus er bogi, bogi er ȳr, ȳr er rūnastafr' [*Arcus* is bow, bow is *ȳr*, *ȳr* is rune].

To sum up: If *ȳr* is 'bow' in ON., and ON. *ȳr* is phonetically equivalent to OE. *éoh* ; if, moreover, ON. *ȳr*, as a runic name, is late, and borrowed from some OE. original ; then an OE. runic poem in which *ȳr* occurs in its Old Norse sense, side by side with *éoh* in practically the same sense, must be a decidedly late poem. Corroborative of this are Wimmer's remarks on the blunder made with regard to the rune *eolhx* (p. 132), and the statement of Kemble's (*Arch.* 28. 345) : 'The language, the introduction of Christian thoughts and words, and some gross blunders in the explanations given by the Anglo-Saxon poet himself, place the date of this composition at a late period.' Cf. p. 155.

---

[1] MS. wynan.

If, then, $\bar{y}r$, interpreted in a late poem as 'yew' or 'bow,' makes no sense in our eighth century poems; and if there was an earlier runic *yr* in OE., from which the ON. $\bar{y}r$, which is not etymologically explainable in OE. as anything but a borrowed word, is derived, it is clear that we have no right to press upon the Cynewulfian runic sign an interpretation of $\bar{y}r$ derived from the *Runic Poem ;* and it is also clear that the original OE. rune for *y* may have had quite a different meaning.

The substitutions proposed have been: *Y; yrmðu ; yrming; $\bar{y}r = \bar{e}ar$; $\bar{y}r$,* 'money'; *æðil* (for *wædl,* or *ādl*); *yfel ; $\bar{y}st.$*

Nēd (Nȳd). Concerning this there has been but little discussion. Besides unimportant variations in the rendering of it, the substitutions have been: *N; nēod ; nīð.* The rune occurs also *Rid.* 43[8].

Eoh. The rune is clear. Substitutions: *ege-; ēhlæca.*

Wyn. The earlier editors understood the rune as *wēn,* but Grein (*Spr.* s. v.) called *wēn* the 'Name der Rune V., deren Zeichen jedoch auch zum Teil im Text für *ven = vynn* steht: *El.* 1090, 1264; *Rä.* 87[7]; *Jul.* 706; *Cri.* 805; *Run.* 8'; in *D.* he translates our rune in *Christ* by 'Lust.' This view is well substantiated by Sievers, *Anglia* 13. 3–4: 'Zwar kann es wol keinem Zweifel unterliegen dass die *w*-Rune bei den Angelsachsen auch einmal *wēn* geheissen hat, denn dieser Name liegt in mehreren Ags. Runenalphabeten vor; aber der ältere Name war sicher *wyn,* dem Got. *uuinne* der Salzburger Handschrift näher entsprechend (Zacher, *Das Goth. Alphabet,* s. 9 f.). So bietet die Salzburger Handschrift in ihrem Ags. Alphabet selbst den Namen *uyn* (Wimmer, *Runenschrift,* s. 85), und auf diese Form gehen die vielfachen Entstellungen des Namens in den offenbar aus sehr alten Quellen geflossenen deutschen Umschriften der Ags. Runenalphabete zurück, wie bereits Kirchhoff, *Das Goth. Runenalphabet*[2], s. 40, angemerkt hat. Das Alphabet des Runenliedes (Wimmer a. a. o.) giebt freilich dem Zeichen P die Ueberschrift *wen,* aber das P *ne* des Contextes ist sicher mindestens dem Sinne nach in *wynne* aufzulösen (vgl. Grein, *Sprachsch.* 1. 145; 2. 658), wie der Zusammenhang zeigt. . . . Ausserdem findet sich *W.* in unseren poetischen Texten noch öfter, namentlich *Räts.* 87[7]. und sechsmal bei Cynewulf; doch kommt von den letzteren Stellen *Jul.* 706 nicht in Betracht, da das Zeichen hier bloss als Buchstabenname fungiert. *Alle anderen Stellen verlangen notwendig die Auflösung* wyn.'

Proposed substitutions have been: *wela ; willa.* Thorpe translated: 'wain.'

Ūr. Properly designating the aurochs or urus, an extinct species of wild ox. Cognate are MHG., OHG. *ūr,* ON. *ūrr ;* from the Germanic word come Lat. *urus* (Cæs. *B. G.* 6. 28; Plin. 8. 15. 15. § 38; Macr. *S.* 6. 4), Gr. οὖρος. In the Norwegian runic poem (Wimmer, p. 276) we have: 'ūr er af illu jarne' (Schlacke kommt von schlechtem Eisen); and in the Icelandic runic poem (p. 282): 'ūr er skȳja grätr, ok skara þverrir, ok hirðis hatr' ('Staubregen ("Wasser") ist der Wolken Weinen, und der Eisränder Auflöser, und (Gegenstand für) des Hirten Hass'). Cosijn calls attention to the OE. adj. *ūrig-,* 'dewy.'

Proposed substitutions: *U; ūr,* 'of old'; *unne ; ōr (ōra) ; ufan ; uppe ; ūr, ūre,* 'our'; *ūr,* 'dampness'; *ūr,* 'possession.'

Lagu. This has occasioned but little discussion. Proposed substitutions: *lond ; līc.*

Feoh. This is accepted as 'money,' 'wealth,' or 'cattle.' Trautmann substitutes *fæt* in *Juliana.*

I append the various translations of the runic passage in *Christ:*

Kemble, *Archæologia* 28. 362 : 'Then shall the *bold* quake; shall hear the king discourse, the Ruler of the Heavens speak stern words to them who him before that in the world weakly (ill) obeyed, while *misery* and *need* might most easily find consolation. There shall many a one in terror on that plain weary await what to him after his deeds [God] shall adjudge of angry penalties. *Hope* hath departed, the treasures of earth; long was it *of old* surrounded with the *sea*-streams, a portion of the joy of life, *money* on the earth.'

Thorpe, *Codex Exoniensis*, p. 50: 'Then the *bold* shall quake, shall hear the King harangue, the Ruler of the skies speak angry words to those who him ere in the world weakly obey'd; while *misery* and *need* might easiest comfort find. There many a fearful one shall on that plain weary await what he to him, according to his deeds, will judge of wrathful punishments. . . . The *wain* shall have departed of earth's treasures. *Of old* was long with *water*-floods enclos'd the region of life's joys, men's *wealth* on earth: so then shall their treasures burn on the pile,' etc.

Grein, *Dichtungen*, p. 171 :

> Der *Kühne* bebt alsdann, hört er den König sprechen
> den Richter der Himmel rauhe Worte
> zu denen die wenig ihm gehorchten in der Welt zuvor,
> solange sie noch Abhilfe leicht des *Elends* und der *Not*
> und Friede mochten finden. Da wird furchtsam dann
> gar mancher Sünder harren auf dem Siegesfelde,
> was ihm nach seinen Thaten da ertheilen wolle
> an dem angstreichen Tage der Engel König
> an leidvollen Strafen. Dann ist die *Lust* zergangen
> nach Erdenschätzen. *In Urzeiten* waren
> bedeckt mit *Wasser*fluten des Lebens Wonnegüter,
> die *Freudenschätze* lange.

Leo, *Quæ de se ipso*, etc., pp. 17, 19 :

> Dann erzittert der *Kühne;* er hört den König verhandeln,
> Den Himmelsrichter, (hört ihn) sprechen rauhe Worte
> Zu denen, die ihn früher nur nachlässig hörten,
> Während *Verfall* und *Noth* gar leicht konnten
> Trost erhalten.[1] Da wird mancher furchtsam
> Auf dem Versammlungsfelde gebrochenes Geistes harren,
> Was er ihm nach seinen Thaten gemäss zuertheilen werde
> Zorniger Strafurtheile. Der *Wahn* wird zerschüttert sein,
> Die Herrlichkeit der Erde. *Geld* war lange,
> Das durch *Meeres*wogen abgeschlossene, ein Theil der Lebenswonne
> Der *Reichthum* auf der Erde.[2]

---

[1] I.e. facillime tabescentes et miseros consolari potuissent, si non tam negligenter Dei praecepta audiissent.

[2] Pecunia, quae ab hac insula undis secluditur (in transmarinis partibus), divitiae terrae diu et avide a me adpetebantur. In hoc loco ubi ' divitiae terrae' uti ad positio ad litteram runicam ūr atque ad

Gollancz, *Cynewulf's Christ*, p. 69:

> The *Keenest* there shall quake, when he heareth the Lord,
> the heaven's Ruler, utter words of wrath
> to those who in the world obeyed Him ill,
> while they might solace find most easily
> for their *Yearning* and their *Need*.   Many afeard
> shall wearily await upon that plain
> what penalty He will adjudge to them
> for their deeds.   The *Winsomeness* of earthly gauds
> shall then be changed.   In days of yore *Unknown*,
> *Lake*-floods embraced the region of life's joy,
> and all earth's *Fortune*.

Cynewulf's Christ, p. 182:

> Then the *Keen* shall quake; he shall hear the Lord,
> the heaven's Ruler, utter words of wrath
> to those who in the world obeyed Him ill,
> while *Affliction* and *Distress* most easily
> might find solace.   There many afeared
> shall wearily await upon that plain
> what dire penalty He will adjudge to them,
> according to their deeds.   The *Winsomeness* of earthy gauds
> shall then be changed.   Long time ago *Our* portion of life's joys
> was all encompassed by *Water*-floods,
> yea, all our *Possessions* upon earth.

Exeter Book, p. 51:

> Then the *Keen* shall quake, when he heareth the king,
> heaven's ruler, speak and utter wrathful words
> to those who erewhile in the world obeyed him feebly,
> while *Yearning* and *Need* might most easily
> find solace: there many a one afeard
> shall wearily await upon that plain
> what fearful penalty He will adjudge to him
> after his deeds: then the *Winsomeness* of earthly gauds
> shall be all changed.   Longsince, the portion of life's joys
> allotted *Us*, by *Lake*-floods was enclosed,
> our *Fortune* on the earth.

Brooke, p. 379:

> Then the *Courage-hearted* quakes,[1] when the King he hears
> Speak the words of wrath — Him the wielder of the Heavens —
> Speak to those who once on earth but obeyed him weakly,
> While as yet their *Yearning pain* and their *Need* most easily
> Comfort might discover. . . . .
> . . . . Gone is then the *Winsomeness*
> Of the earth's adornments !   What to *Us* as men belonged
> Of the joys of life was locked, long ago, in *Lake-flood*(s),
> All the *Fee* on earth !

---

accuratius definiendum sensum nominis litterae runicae adhibentur, luce clarius est, hoc nomen *non*
ûr (urus) esse *posse*, sed synonymiam inter hoc nomen et feoh on foldum existere — nulla alia vero
vox, quam ōr, inveniri potest, qua sic uti potest poeta.   [1] Br.[2], cowers.

Trautmann, p. 61 :

> Dann bebt die *Menge;* sie hört den König reden,
> den Richter der Himmel, zornige Worte
> zu denen die ihm früher in der Welt schwach gehorchten,
> so lange *Leidenschaft* und *Begierde* auf leichteste Weise
> Befriedigung finden konnten. Da muss mancher in Furcht
> auf dem weiten Felde in Betrübnis harren,
> was ihm nach seinen Taten der Richter (zuerkennen)
> an herben Strafen will. Dahin geht die *Freude*
> an den Schätzen der Erde. Mein *Besitz* war lange
> ein fiutumschlossnes *Land,* ein Teil der Lebenswonnen,
> *Reichtum* auf der Erde. Hernach müssen die Schätze
> verbrennen im Feuer.

799. wāce hȳrdon. Cf. *Hy.* 4¹⁶ : ' þēah þe ic Scyppendum, Wuldorcyninge, *wācor hȳrde,* rīcum Dryhtne, þonne mīn rǣd wǣre.' Add Wulfstan 91¹³ : '. . . þæt wē tō *wāce hȳraƀ* ūrum Drihtne.'

800. Cosijn (*Cynewulf's Runenverzen*) takes C, Y, and N as forming the word *cyn = monna cyn.* In favor of this is the circumstance, which seems to have been overlooked by most of the commentators, that Old English does not speak of abstractions, like misery and need, but of persons, as finding help or consolation : thus *Gu.* 860, 895 ; cf. *Hy.* 4⁴⁷. People find relief *from* affliction (expressed by the genitive), as in *Beow.* 628 : ' þæt hēo on ǣnigne eorl gelȳfde *fyrena* frōfre.' Until parallels to the other construction are found, it may be just as well to abstain from seeking recondite meanings for the runes Y and N. According to the most natural rendering, Cynewulf's references to himself would end with 796, and the rune passage would refer to people in general.

ȳþast meahtan. Cf. *ȳþæst mæg,* 1283 (III).

801. forht monig. So *An.* 1087 ; cf. *An.* 1551, 1598.

802ª. on þām wongstede. So (*wang-*) *An.* 990 ; *El.* 1104.

802ᵇ–804. bīdan . . . wīta. Cf. *Jul.* 705-7 : ' bīdaƀ hwæt him æfter dǣdum dēman wille līfes tō lēane.'

802ᵇ. bīdan. Cf. 1020.

803ª. æfter dǣdum. Cf. *Hel.* 3319 ; ' adēlean aftar iro dādiun.'

803ᵇ. dēman wille. So *Sat.* 623. Cf. *Rood* 107-9 : ' þæt hē þonne wile dēman, se āh dōmes geweald, ānra gehwylcum swā hē him ǣrur hēr on þyssum lǣnum līfe geearnaƀ.' Cf. 2 Cor. 5. 10.

With reference to the loss of a line, as postulated by Thorpe and others (see Variants), Sievers remarks (*Anglia* 13. 11) : ' Dem gegenüber möchte ich betonen, dass der Zusammenhang hier ebenso wenig gestört ist wie in der fast wörtlich übereinstimmenden Stelle der *Juliana,* die doch das hier vermisste *E* enthält. . . Die beiden Stellen stützen sich gegenseitig. Entweder ist das Subject an beiden Stellen " Gott " (*Cyning, Jul.* 704 = *Crist* 797), oder es liegt eine unpersönliche Construction vor, wie sie im Nordischen so häufig sind (s. z. b. Grimm, *Gr.* 4. 54 ; vgl. auch das Alts. (*al*) *sō* (*it im*) *an ira ēuua gibōd, Hel.* 529, 975, und ähnlich 1419, 1476, 1528, 3267, 5197), und die man am bequemsten durch Umsetzung in's Passivum auflöst : " was ihnen nach ihren Taten beschert werden wird zum Lohn für ihr Leben," bezw. " an grimmigen Strafen." ' He adds : ' Als Resultat ergibt

sich also, dass Cynewulf seinen Namen im *Crist* und unsern Schlussversen |of
the *Fata Apostolorum*] als *Cynwulf*, in der *Juliane* und *Elene* aber als *Cynewulf*
gibt. Ob diese Doppelheit der Form für die Bestimmung der Zeitfolge der ein-
zelnen Dichtungen zu verwerten ist, lasse ich dahingestellt sein. . . . Dass die
Form *Cynwulf* gegenüber *Cynewulf* die relativ jüngere ist, steht ausser Zweifel.
. . . So schreibt Beda (Sweet, *O. E. T.* 132 ff.) *Cyniberd*, etc. . . . Nur spärlich
treten daneben verkürzte Formen auf. Der älteste Beleg dürfte *Cynuise reginam*,
Beda 196, sein. . . . Reichlicher sind die Zeugnisse in den *North. Genealogien*,
Sweet 167 : *Cynheard* 21, etc. . . . Ueberblickt man diese Beispiele : *Cynlāf;
Cynrēd, -rēou, -rūc ; Cynuis, -uulf ; Cynheard, -helm*, so sieht man leicht dass die
Verkürzung nur vor *l, r, w*, und *h* eingetreten ist, d. h. vor Lauten welche eine
Absorption des vorausgehenden unbetonten Vokals besonders begünstigten. . . .
Im Uebrigen stehen die *Cyni-, Cyne-* ohne Synkope für die ganze Dauer der Ags.
Sprachperiode fest. . . . Auf alle Fälle ist die Namensform *Cynwulf* als gut Ags.
für das 8. Jahrhundert bezeugt, und man braucht also auch von dieser Seite her
an dem Schwanken Cynewulf's in der Wiedergabe seines Namens keinen Anstoss
zu nehmen. Leider lässt sich weder die Entstehungszeit noch das Verbreitungs-
gebiet der Form *Cyn-* genauer bestimmen. Belegt ist sie für Northumbrien,
Mercia, und Kent; dem rein-Sächsischen scheint sie dagegen bis auf das stereo-
type *Cynric* fremd zu sein. . . .

'Nach einer andern Seite hin gibt die vollere Namensform *Cynewulf* Anlass
zu näherer Erörterung. . . . Der Uebergang von *i (æ)* zu *e* . . . ist im Süden und
Mittellande etwa um die Mitte des 8. Jahrhunderts eingetreten. Mit einer ein-
zigen, mir unerklärlichen Ausnahme . . . herrscht bis ca. 740 das *i*. . . . Aber mit
740 setzt *e* ein. . . . Im ganzen . . . darf man . . . behaupten dass in dem Urkunden-
gebiet der Uebergang zum *e* im Allgemeinen um 750 vollzogen gewesen ist. Für
Northumbrien versagen uns freilich die urkundlichen Hilfsmittel. Aber es liegt
doch kein dringender Grund vor, den Norden hier speciell auszuschliessen.'

804ᵃ. wrāðra wīta. Cf. *Jul.* 177.

804ᵇ. Cf. Sievers, *Anglia* 13. 5 : 'Mit dem zuletzt angeführten Citat [*Beow.*
1730 : 'seleð him on ēðle eorðan wynne tō healdanne, hlēoburh hæleða'] berührt
sich ganz nahe die Stelle in dem Akrostichon des *Crist*, . . . bei der man nur
zweifeln kann ob *wynn eorðan frætwa* mit "die Freude an irdischen Gütern,"
oder — was mir wahrscheinlicher ist — " die wonniglichen Erdengüter" zu über-
setzen sei; für die erstere Möglichkeit vgl. " þæt hē dæghwīla gedrogen hæfde,
eorðan wynne," *Beow.* 2727.'

On this masculine *se* Sievers remarks (*Anglia* 13. 5, note) : 'Das handschrift-
liche masc. *se* ist ganz richtig auf *W.* als Buchstabennamen bezogen, denn diese
Namen sind in Ags. — nach *stæf* — männlich ; vgl. *z. B. sē Grecisca, ylca y*, Ælfr.
Gr. 5. 14 f., *sē i*, 6. 16 f., *sē u*, 6. 17 f., *sē a*, 7. 5, etc. Dasselbe gilt schon von
den Runennamen ; vgl. namentlich *Räts.* 43. 8 ff.' To the same effect Cosijn
(*Cyn. Run.*, pp. 57–8). The two articles were written in the same month.

sceacen. Cf. *Beow.* 1124 ; *Doomsday* 45 ; *Fates of Men* 39.

805ᵃ. eorþan frætwa. Similarly *Pa.* 48 ; *Ps.* 101²² ; cf. *foldan frætuwe, Men.*
207 ; and see *El.* 1270 (above, p. 153). Perhaps from Gen. 2. 1 : 'Igitur perfecti
sunt caeli et terra, et omnis *ornatus* eorum' ; Ælfr. tr. : '. . . heofonas and eorðe,
and eall heora *frætewung*.'

805ᵇ ff.　The thought seems to be that of 2 Pet. 3. 5–7 : '. . . Caeli erant prius et terra de aqua et per aquam consistens Dei verbo, per quae ille tunc mundus aqua inundatus periit; caeli autem qui nunc sunt, et terra, eodem verbo repositi sunt,igni reservati in diem judicii et perditionis impiorum hominum.' Cf. Greg. *Hom. in Ezech.* I. 9 (Migne 76. 867) : 'Unde est in arcu eodem color aquae et ignis simul ostenditur, quia et ex parte est caeruleus, et ex parte rubicundus, ut utriusque judicii testis sit, unus videlicet faciendi, et alterius facti, sed quia mundus quidem judicii igne cremabitur, sed jam non ulterius faciendi, aqua jam diluvii non deletur.' The point is illustrated by *Ph.* 39ᵇ–49; cf. *Hel.* 4362–6, though this reposes rather on Mt. 24. 17 ff. *Chr.* 984 ff. is hardly a parallel. Cf. Th. p. 502.

805ᵇ–806ᵃ. Cf. *El.* 602, 793.

805ᵇ. **ūr.** Cf. note 2 on Leo's translation, above, p. 161. Sievers remarks on the corresponding line in the *Fata Apost.* (see above, p. 153) : 'Der Sinn ist untadlig, wenn man, ähnlich wie Leo, *ūr* als Synonymon von *feoh,* "Besitz, Güter," fasst. Im *Crist* 806 ff. wird *ūr* geradezu mit *feoh* variiert : "ūr wæs longe laguflōdum bilocen, lifwynna dæl, feoh on foldan "; und ähnlich heisst es in der *El.* 1266 ff.' (above, p. 153).

806. **laguflōdum.** Cf. *Hel.* 4363, *lagustrōmun.* — **lifwynna.** The word occurs *Beow.* 2097 ; *El.* 1269.

807ᵇ–849. See *Analysis,* 17 (p. 116).

807ᵇ–814. Tr. by Brooke (p. 400; Br.² p. 173).

807ᵇ. **frætwe.** No doubt as in 805.

808. **blāc.** Grein tr. (*D.*) by 'bleich,' contrary to *Spr.* See *An.* 1543 ; *Met.* 4⁸; *Alms* 7 ; etc.

rāsetteð. Grein says in a note: '*Rāsettan* ist abgeleitet von *rǣs,* 'impetus,' und findet sich ebenso in Alfr. *Metr.* 9¹⁴ : " þæt fȳr meahte rēad rāsettan," wo *rēadra settan* (Fox, Ettm.) sinnlos ist.' He defines (*Spr.*) as 'grassari cum impetu,' 'rasen,' and tr. (*D.*) by 'wütet.' But cf. *Doomsday* (Bede) 152, 165.

809. **recen.** Gr. (*Spr.*) 'fumosus'; but there is no other instance of *recen* in the poetry. In *D.* he renders *recen rēada* by *rauchrote,* following Th.'s 'smoke-red'; but smoke does not render flame red. The meaning of *recen* may be gathered from the adverb, and from the three examples: *Met.* 24¹⁷; *Wald.* 2²⁶; *Ps.* 105¹⁸. Cf., however, *Gen.* 44. — **rēþe.** Cf. *Fates of Men* 46.

810. **Wongas.** Cf. note on 680. — 'Sunken are the plains' (Brooke), following Thorpe's 'The plains shall sink down,' hardly renders *Wongas hrēosað.* Gr., 'Es wanken die Gefilde.'

811. **burgstede berstað.** Cf. *burgstede burston, Ruin* 2. See Rev. 16. 19. **Brond bið on tyhte.** Cf. *Ph.* 525: *fȳr bið on tihte.* Thorpe read *ontyhte,* 'kindled.' Brooke renders: 'See! the Burning on its way.'

812. **æleð.** Brooke: 'gorges.' — **unmurnlīce.** So *Beow.* 449, 1756.

813. **gǣsta gīfrast.** Cf. Grimm, *Teut. Myth.* 601 : 'Fire, like water, is regarded as a living being : corresponding to *quecprunno* we have a *quecfiur,* "daz quecke fiwer," *Parz.* 71. 13; . . . τὸ πῦρ θηρίον ἔμψυχον of the Egyptians, Herod. 3. 16; "ignis *animal,*" Cic. de *N. D.* 3. 14, i.e. a devouring, hungry, insatiable beast, vorax flamma ; *frekr* (" avidus "), *Sæm.* 50ᵇ; *bitar fiur, Hel.* 78. 22; *bitar logna,* 79. 20; *grādag logna* (" greedy lowe "), 130. 23 ; *grim endi grādag,* 133. 11 ; *eld unfuodi* (" insatiabilis "), 78. 23 ; it licks with its tongue, eats all round

it, *pastures*, νέμεται, *Il.* 23. 177; the land gets eaten clean by it, πυρὶ χθὼν νέμεται, 2. 780; lēztu eld *eta* iöfra bygdir,' *Sæm.* 142ᵃ; it is restless, ἀκάματον πῦρ, *Il.* 23. 52.' Cf. (III) 972; *Ph.* 507; *Beow.* 1123. Th., Go., Br. render: 'greediest of *guests*.'

gēo guman. One does not see why Grein renders: ' die Gaumänner '; not so in *Spr.*

814. þenden him on eorþan. Cf. 772ᵃ. — onmēdla. Cf. *El.* 1266.

815. Cf. *El.* 522. — gǣstes þearfe. So 1057; *Gifts of Men* 86..

817ᵃ. Cf. *Father's Maxims* 41 : *gēotende gielp ;* see also *Gu.* 1206: *on gēaðᵈ gutan.* Is not *gēotan* here intransitive = ' dissolve ' ?

819. Cf. 597ᵇ–598ᵃ, 1326, 1579–80; *Ph.* 584; *El.* 880.

820. gǣsthofe. So *gystsele, Exod.* 534, probably referring to the ' tabernacle ' = σκῆνος, of 2 Cor. 5. 1, 4; see also 1480. Cf. 1 Chr. 29. 15; Ps. 39. 12; 119. 19; Heb. 11. 13; 13. 14; 1 Pet. 2. 11; etc.

820ᵇ ff. Cf. Prudentius, *Cath.* 11. 97–108 :

> Hunc, quam latebra et obstetrix
> et virgo feta et cunulae
> et inbecilla infantia
> regem dederunt gentibus,
>
> peccator intueberis
> celsum coruscis nubibus,
> deiectus ipse et inritus
> plangens reatum fietibus.
>
> Non esca flammarum nigros
> volvamur inter turbines,
> vultu Dei sed compotes,
> caeli fruamur gaudiis.

820ᵇ. gumena gehwylc. Gr.: 'der Gaumänner [!] jeder.'

822. Cf. 627–632.

823. æt ǣrestan. The first time. — þurh þæs engles word. Cf. 201 ff., 335 ff.; 120.

824. eorneste. Not 'earnest' (Thorpe, Brother Azarias). Cf. 1100, unless we should there read *eornesse.*

825. rēðe. Cf. 1527 ; *Jul.* 704. — Rodor bið onhrēred. Cf. 932, and Mt. 24. 29.

826–827ᵃ. Cf. Isa. 41. 5; Ps. 67. 7 (?). So, in the Latin MS. quoted by Nölle (*PBB.* 6. 460) we read (v. 18): 'Colles vallesque timebunt.' Add 881, and *Doomsday* 112: 'wongas beofiað; cf. *Doomsday* 58.

827. beofiað. Cosijn condemns Wülker's reading, and adds: ' Hatte das Original *behofiaðᵈ,* wie *geholu* für *geolu, Erf.* 1064 u. s. w. ?'

As to Rieger's suggestion, the position of *þonne* is certainly unusual, but the sense seems to be better if it is construed with *beofiað.*

828–9ᵇ. eargum dǣdum lifdon. Cf. *Soul of Man* 75–6: *eargum dǣdum leofaðᵈ in leahtrum ;* for the inst. see also *Beow.* 2144: *þeawum lifde.*

829. leahtrum fā. So 1538 (III) ; *Whale* 66; cf. 1000, 1632.

830. fērðwērge. Cf. *Gu.* 1130. — **fȳrbaðe.** So 985 (III); *El.* 919; *Ph.* 437.

831. wælnuum. Cf. (III) 931, 965, 1006.

832-833ᵃ. Cf. 941-2 (III).

832. þonne. Gr., Go. translate as if there were a comma at the end of 831, and a semicolon at the middle of 833 ; but this seems inconsistent with *longe*, 829. — **mægua Cyning.** Cf. *Mægencyning*, 916, 942 (III). — **gemōt.** Not 'meeting' (Th.).

833. For the retention of *mǣste*, as against Go.², cf. 950; *Ph.* 167, 618 ; *An.* 1503 ; *Gu.* 882 ; *El.* 274.

834. bi. Go. 'amid'; Grein (*Spr.*) compares 998 (III), and designates the prep. as 'instrumental and causal.' — **heofonwōman.** Gr. (*D.*) 'Himmels-schrecken,' but (*Spr.*) 'fragor caelestis.'

835. cwānendra. Cosijn advocates this emendation. — **cearige.** Not 'sadly' (Th., Go.). — **rēotað.** Cf. 1229 (III). See note on 1454 ff. (3).

836. So 796.

837. wāce. Cf. 799.

838 ff. Cf. Joel 2. 2 ; Mt. 24. 21 ; Mk. 13. 19.

841. snūdan. Gr. (*D.*) 'schlimmen '; but Thorpe's 'sudden' is better.

842. lēofra. Cosijn thus argues for the retention of this form, instead of substituting *lēofre :* '(nsn.), wie *Guthlac* 1294 : *þǣr wæs ǣnlicra & wynsumra*, etc. Ebenso *sōþra*, *Guthl.* 1096, und Beispiele für die weibliche Endung *-a* sind *swǣrra*, *Crist* 1490 ; *heardra*, 1489 ; *lēohtra*, 1652 ; *sylfa*, *Guthl.* 964 ; *bāncoþa* 998 (?). Darf man dies alles ändern? Was die Bedeutung unsrer Stelle betrifft, vgl. *Sal.* 30 : 'þonne him bið lēofre þonne eall þēos lēohte gesceaft . . . gif hē ǣfre þæs organes ōwiht cūðe ' ; *Beow.* 2651 steht *þæt*, was aber mit *gif* synonym ist, wie mit *þǣr*, weshalb Ettmüller's Aenderung, v. 844 [843] unnötig ist.'

Gollancz makes this extraordinary comment: 'The change to the neuter is, perhaps, unnecessary, as the word probably anticipated a masculine noun, *þær* = *sum stede hwær*.'

þēos lǣne gesceaft. So *Beow.* 1622 ; *Hy.* 11¹².

843. þæt. See last note.

847ᵇ-866. Brooke translates twice (pp. 187-8, 400); the former version is repeated, with some changes, on p. 169 of his *English Lit. from the Beginning to the Norman Conquest* (Br.²).

847ᵇ. So 751ᵇ. Cf. *An.* 1168, 1607 ; *El.* 426 ; also *Bede's Death Hymn*, and *Hel.* 1585, 2376, 4275 ; see on 760.

848-9. gǣstes wlite . . . georne biþencen. Cf. (III) 1580-1 : *sāwle wlite . . . georne bigonge*.

848. wlite. Not 'Heil' (Gr.). Gollancz's (Brooke's) 'grace ' is ambiguous. — **gryrebrōgan.** Cf. *Beow.* 2228.

849ᵃ. Cf. (III) 1558ᵇ, 1585ᵇ.

850-866. See *Analysis*, 18 (p. 116).

Based upon Greg. *Hom. in Evang.* 29. 11 (following the above ; see on 782ᵇ-796) : 'Quamvis adhuc rerum perturbationibus animus fluctuet, jam tamen spei vestrae anchoram in aeternam patriam figite, intentionem mentis in vera luce solidate. Ecce ad caelum ascendisse Dominum audivimus. Hoc ergo servemus in meditatione quod credimus.'

850 ff. Brooke compares this with the Latin source, and remarks (p. 483): ' What a change; what an illústration it is of what a poet can do with a well-worn thought! How little of the Latin convention in it, how much of Northumbrian individuality and of Cynewulf's distinctive feeling!'

850ª. Cf. *An.* 501ª, *Dan.* 275.

850ᵇ. lagnflōde. Not 'liquid flood' (Thorpe, Brother Azarias), nor 'lake of ocean' (Br.). Cf. 806.

851. cēolum līðan. So *An.* 256.

852ᵇ-853ª. Th. 'on ocean-horses the flood-wood traverse'; Gr. 'mit Sundhengsten das Flutholz treiben' (Gr. s. v. *Sundhengest* defines: 'die das Schiff bewegende Kraft'); Go.¹ 'driving our vessels ... with horses of the deep'; Go.² 'drive the flood-wood ... with horses of the deep'; Br. 'with our stallions of the Sound forward drive the flood-wood'; (p. 400) 'driving the sea-wood on our sea-steeds'; Br.² 'with our stallions of the deep forward drove the Flood-wood.' But no doubt Ettmüller is right in his emendation, and *fergen* is intr., as in *Ps.* 67⁸; *Gen.* 2100; *By.* 179; *Rid.* 53¹.

853. flōdwudum. Not 'flood-wave' (Br. Az.). — **fergen.** Not 'traverse' (Th.).

854ª. yða ofermǣta. Not 'übermässiger Wogen' (Gr., *D.*), 'of boundless waves' (Th., Br. Az., Go.), ' of immeasurable surges,' ' of endless waves ' (Br.) ; cf. the parallel ' windge holmas.'

854ᵇ. ' On which here we are tossed ' (Br. Az.) ; ' where we ... swing to and fro ' (Br.). Th. reads *onlācað*, ' are tossed ' ; Go.'s ' toss ' is best.

855-6. Gr., Wü. print:

> geond Jás wácan woruld, windge holmas ;
> ofer dēop gelád wæs se drohtað strong,

which of course makes nonsense of *windge holmas*, as Cosijn sees.

855. wācan. Br. 'wavering,' 'swooning.'

856. dēop gelád. In the same sense *An.* 190, *Gu.* 1266. Br. 'upon the unfathomed road.' — **Wæs se drohtað strong.** Cf. *An.* 313.

857. Cf. *Jul.* 677 ; also *El.* 249.

858. hrycg. Like the Homeric νῶτον, νῶτος; cf. *Il.* 2. 159; *Od.* 3. 142. Perhaps this may be taken as one of the proofs of a familiarity with Homer on the part of OE. poets, since *tergum* is rarely used in Latin of the sea. Cf. *Beow.* 471 ; *Sal.* 19; *Ps.* 68²; also *Rid.* 4³³. Br.'s 'rough sea-ridges,' 'storm-ridged deep' miss the point.

859. hǣlo hȳþe. So *Ps.* 106²⁹; *Sal.* 245; cf. Ps. 107. 30. Br. 'That to hithe of Healing homeward led us on,' 'That led us to the hithe where Healing is' [!].

860. So 660.

861ᵇ. Br. 'Outlooking o'er the bulwarks of our keel' [!].

863. yðmēaras. So *Whale* 49. — **ancrum fæste.** So *El.* 252. Br. 'deeply set,' as if inst. On p. 187 he translates the line: ' Fast a-riding by their anchors — ancient horses of the waves!'

864. Utan. Cf. 771, 773. — **stapelian.** Cf. ' figite,' note on 850-866.

865. gerȳmde. Br. 'roomed' [!]. — **rodera Wāldend.** Ælfric has once *roderes Wealdend* in prose (*Hom.* 2. 256), in a translation of Lk. 23. 42. See my *Bibl. Quot.*, p. 208.

866ª. Cf. *Muspilli* 18: 'pidiu ist durft mihhil daz ze pidenchanne.' — **hālge.** Must agree with *ða*, referring to *hȳðe*, unless we emend to *hālig*, following the suggestion of 760, 789. Br. assumes that it agrees with *Wāldend.*

866ᵇ. Cosijn also inserts *tō*, saying: 'Lies mit Ettmüller "þā hē tō heofonum āstāg," wie v. 737 (vgl. auch *El.* 188) vorkommt.'

Hammerich, p. 85, remarks: 'Aus dieser Abtheilung der Kynewulfschen Dichtungen hat der Däne Grundtvig, welcher zur Wiederbelebung des Nordischen Alterthums in Sage und Literatur soviel geleistet hat, dabei als Dichter eine hervorragende Bedeutung hat, den Hauptgedanken zu mehreren seiner, zum Theil kirchlich recipirten geistlichen Lieder geschöpft. Seine Production als geistlicher Liederdichter lässt überhaupt in Bildern und Ausdrücken die Einwirkung der Angelsachsen überall erkennen.'

PART III.

It is difficult to make a satisfactory analysis of this Part. However, since a general survey is desirable, I present the following as an attempt (cf. pp. 70–71):

1. The great day of the Lord shall appear suddenly, like a thief in the night (867–874).

2. The dead shall be raised by the sound of trumpet. Both the righteous and the evil shall assemble; the wicked shall lament (875–898).

3. Christ shall come in great glory to Mount Zion, benign to his own, but forbidding to his enemies (899–920).

4. The righteous will have no occasion to fear when the Lord comes with the host of angels (921–929).

5. Fire shall go before the Lord; the moon and stars shall fall, and the sun shall be turned into blood (930–940).

6. The saints shall accompany their King. The trumpet shall sound, seven winds shall blow, and there shall be din immeasurable (941–955).

7. Fire shall consume the universe; the whole world shall break out into lamentation (956–1006).

8. God shall come with his angels, who will tremble at the Judgment. That will be a dreadful Day when the King of Glory summons the dead before his throne (1007–1026).

9. Every one shall rise with the good or evil which were in his soul on earth; deeds, words, and thoughts shall be manifest (1027–1038).

10. All mankind shall arise; fire shall ravage; all secrets shall be disclosed. Let him who will be justified in that day take heed in time (1039–1060).

11. Called by name, each shall appear before the Son of God. Well for him who shall be pleasing in the Lord's sight (1061–1080).

12. The Cross shall appear in the heavens. It shall drip with blood, yet shall shine like the sun (1081–1102).

13. They shall look on Him whom they pierced and mocked (1103–1127[a]).

14. The dumb creation trembled and mourned at the death of its Maker; only hard-hearted men were insensible (1127[b]–1198).

15. The sinful shall look with anguish upon the wounds of the Crucified, which were meant to purchase for them the joy of heaven (1199–1215).

16. The sheep shall be divided from the goats (1216–1233).

17. The three marks of the righteous (1234–1261).

18. The three marks of the ungodly (1262–1300).

19. Better had they confessed to God's ambassador (1301–1311).

20. Let us try to see our sins with the eye of the mind, since with the bodily eye it is impossible (1312–1333, with the parenthetical 1316–1326: Every one should try to live longer and grow continually better, that he may be unblamable among men!).

21. The welcome to the righteous (1334–1361).

22. Christ addresses the ungodly. They need hope for no mercy (1362–1383).

23. Christ recounts his benefits and sacrifices for mankind (1384–1468).

24. He asks why they have scorned his redemption, and made light of his sufferings (1469–1498).

25. They have not kept his commandments (1499–1514).

26. Christ pronounces the doom of the wicked (1515–1529).

27. With the sword of victory he smites the disobedient down to hell (1530–1548).

28. Beware in time ; Doomsday will be too late for repentance (1549–1590).

29. The horrors of hell (1591–1633).

30. The joys of heaven (1634–1664).

As I showed in *Modern Language Notes* for June, 1889, an important source for this Part is the alphabetic hymn quoted by Bede in his *De Arte Metrica* (translations by Neale, Calverley, and Mrs. Charles), which I here subjoin :

Apparebit repentina dies magna Domini,
fur obscura velut nocte improvisos occupans.

Brevis totus tum parebit prisci luxus saeculi,
totum simul cum clarebit praeterisse saeculum.

Clangor tubae per quaternas terrae plagas concinens,　　　　　5
vivos una mortuosque Christo ciet obviam.

De caelesti Judex arce, majestate fulgidus,
claris angelorum choris comitatus aderit.

Erubescet orbis lunae, sol et obscurabitur,
stellae cadent pallescentes, mundi tremet ambitus.　　　　　10

Flamma ignis anteibit justi vultum Judicis,
caelos, terras, et profundi fluctus ponti devorans.

Gloriosus in sublimi Rex sedebit solio ;
angelorum tremebunda circumstabunt agmina.

Hujus omnes ad electi colligentur dexteram ;　　　　　15
pravi pavent a sinistris, hoedi velut foetidi.

' Ite,' dixit Rex ad dextros, ' regnum caeli sumite,
Pater vobis quod paravit ante omne saeculum ;

Karitate[1] qui fraterna me juvistis pauperem,
karitatis[1] nunc mercedem reportate divites.'　　　　　20

Laeti dicent : ' Quando, Christe, pauperem te vidimus,
te, Rex magne, vel egentem miserati juvimus ? '

Magnus illus dicet Judex : ' Cum juvistis pauperes,
panem, domum, vestem dantes, me juvistis humiles.'

Nec tardabit et sinistris loqui justus Arbiter :　　　　　25
' in gehennae maledicti flammas hinc discedite ;

Obsecrantem me audire despexistis mendicum,
nudo vestem non dedistis, neglexistis languidum.'

---

[1] Daniel has an initial *c* in both cases.

Peccatores dicent : ' Christe, quando te vel pauperem,
te, Rex magne, vel infirmum contemnentes sprevimus.'   30

Quibus contra Judex altus: ' Mendicanti quamdiu
opem ferre despexistis, me sprevistis improbi.'

Retro ruent tum injusti ignes in perpetuos,
vermis quorum non morietur, flamma nec restinguitur,

Satan atro cum ministris quo tenetur carcere,   35
fletus ubi mugitusque, strident omnes dentibus.

Tunc fideles ad caelestem sustollentur patriam,
choros inter angelorum regni petent gaudia ;

Urbis summae Hierusalem introibunt gloriam,
vera lucis atque pacis in qua fulget visio,   40

XPM Regem jam paterna claritate splendidum
ubi celsa beatorum contemplantur agmina.

Ydri fraudes ergo cave, infirmantes subleva,
aurum temne, fuge luxus, si vis astra petere ;

Zona clara castitatis lumbos nunc praecingere,   45
in occursum magni Regis fer ardentes lampades.

Daniel, the celebrated hymnologist, says of this composition : ' Juvat carmen fere totum e Scriptura sacra depromptum comparare cum celebratissimo illo extremi judicii praeconio, *Dies iræ, dies illa*, quo majestate et terroribus, non sancta simplicitate et fide, superatur.' Ebert, *Gesch. Lit. des Mittelalters* (I. 530) thinks it may be as old as the sixth century.

In my article I endeavored to establish general parallels as follows (I designate the couplets of the Latin hymn by the letter with which they begin) :

(I) A : 867–873; (II) C : 878–889ᵃ; (III) D : 899–909, 927–9; (IV) E : 934–940; (V) F : 930–932ᵃ, 964–968ᵃ; (VI) G : 1007–1014, 1216–7; (VII) H : 1221–1231; (VIII) I, K, M : 1344–1361; (IX) N, O, Q, R, S : 1362–3, 1499–1514, 1519–1526; 1535, 1541–8; (X) T, U, X : 1634–5ᵃ, 1639, 1645, 1647ᵇ–1651, 1658–1660, 1662ᵇ–1664. I then added (pp. 173–6; I change Grein's numbering of the lines) :

' It will not escape observation :

' 1. That there is a considerable number of verbal resemblances between the Latin and the Old English, amounting in several instances to literal translations. Thus :

I.   a. repentina : *mid fēre, semninga.*
      b. dies magna : *se micla dæg.*
      c. Domini : *Dryhtnes.*
      d. fur : *þēof.*
      e. velut : *swā.*
      f. obscura nocte : *on sweartre niht.*
      g. improvisos : *sorglēase.*
      h. occupans : *forfēhð.*

II. a. clangor tubae: *bȳman on brehtme.*

 b. per quaternas terrae plagas : *from fēowerum foldan scēatum.*

 c. concinens: *singað and swinsiað.*

 d. ciet mortuos : *weccað of dēaðe dryhtgumena bearn.*

 e. obviam Christo : *tō meotudsceafte* (?).

III. a. majestate fulgidus: (loosely paraphrased in ll. 899-909, preserving, however, the thought of both, words) ; cf. *mægenþrymme,* l. 1008.

 b. comitatus: *on healfa gehwone.*

 c. angelorum choris: *heofonengla þrēat, hergas hāligra.*

 d. claris: *ælbeorhtra.*

IV. a. sol obscurabitur : *sunne sweart gewended.*

 b. erubescet: *gewended on blōdes hīw* (applied to the sun instead of the moon).

 c. stellae cadent: *steorran strēdað of heofone.*

V. a. ante vultum Judicis : *fore Dryhtne.*

 b. flamma ignis: *wælmfȳra mǣst, hāta lēg.*

 c. caelos: *ūpheofon.*

 d. terras: *eorðan.*

 e. fluctus ponti : *sǣs.*

VI. a. in sublimi solio : *on his cynestōle, on hēahsetle.*

 b. sedebit: *siteð.*

 c. gloriosus Rex : *heofonmægna God.*

 d. circum-: *ymbūtan.*

 e. angelorum agmina : *engla gedryht.*

 f. tremebunda : *forhte beofiað.*

VII. a. electi: *gecorene.*

 b. colligentur: *bēoð gesomnad.*

 c. ad dexteram : *on þā swiðran hond.*

 d. a sinistris : *on þā winstran hond.*

 e. pravi : *womsceaðan.*

 f. pavent: *beofiað fore Frēan forhte.*

 g. velut : *swā.*

 h. hoedi: *gǣt.*

 i. foetidi: *fūle, unsȳfre* (?).

VIII. a. sumite : *onfōð.*

 b. regnum : *rīce.*

 c. Pater : *Fæder.*

 d. quod paravit : *þæt . . . wæs . . . gearo.*

 e. ante omne saeculum : *ǣr woruldum.*

 f. mercedem : *lēan (gē þæs earnedon).*

 g. reportate : *gē . . . sceolon . . . brūcan.*

 h. pauperes : *earme men.*

 i. panem : *hlāf.*

 j. vestem : *hrægl.*

IX. a. sinistris : *yflum.*

 b. loqui : *wordum mæðlan.*

 c. nec tardabit : *onginneð.*

    d. obsecrantem me : *þurh minne noman . . . bǣdan.*

    e. nudo vestem : *hrægles nacedum.*

    f. neglexistis languidum : *sārge gē ne sōhton.*

    g. me sprevistis : *gē þæt mē dydon tō hȳnðum.*

    h. maledicti : *āwyrgde.*

    i. in flammas gehennae : *on ēce fīr.*

    j. discedite : *farað.*

    k. Satan cum ministris : *Sātāne and his gesīðum mid.*

    l. ruent : *gē hrēosan sceolon, sceolon raðe feallan.*

    m. carcere : *wītehūs.*

    n. in perpetuos : *sinnihte, tō wīdan fēore.*

    o. vermis : *wrāðum wyrmum.*

X. a. fideles : *þā gecorenan.*

    b. patriam : *ēðel.*

    c. inter choros angelorum : *engla gemānan, engla song.*

    d. paterna : *Fæder* (?).

    e. beatorum agmina : *ēadigra gedryht.*

    f. lucis visio : *Dryhtnes onsīen sunnan lēohtre.*

    g. pacis : *frið, sib.*

'2. That, in certain of these cases, the Old English word or phrase would not correspond to the Latin of the Vulgate texts on which the Latin hymn is based. Thus :

  I. f. obscura : *sweartre.*

  I. g. improvisos : *sorglēase.*

  I. h. occupans : *forfēhð.*

  II. c. concinens : *singað and swinsiað.*

  II. d. ciet : *weccað.*

  III. d. claris : *ælbeorhtra.*

  V. e. fluctus ponti : *sǣs.*

  VI. e. angelorum agmina : *engla gedryht.*

  VI. f. tremebunda : *forhte beofiað.*

  VII. f. pavent : *beofiað fore Frēan forhte.*

  VII. i. foetidi : *fūle.*

  VIII. f. mercedem : *lēan.*

  VIII. i. panem : *hlāf.*

  VIII. j. vestem : *hrægl.*

  IX. g. me sprevistis : *mē dydon tō hȳnðum.*

  IX. k. Satan cum ministris : *Sātāne and his gesīðum mid.*

  IX. l. ruent : *hrēosan, feallan.*

  X. b. patriam : *ēðel.*

  X. e. beatorum agmina : *ēadigra gedryht.*

  X. g. pacis : *frið, sib.*

Most of the foregoing seem to me conclusive with respect to Cynewulf's use of this hymn.

'3. That, as a rule, the order of events in the Latin hymn is followed by Cynewulf. So in I, II, III, IV, V, VI, VII, VIII, IX (in general), X (in general).

With respect to V, the Old English poem anticipates a portion, that referring to the flame of fire, placing it before the whole of IV.

'4. That certain distichs of the Latin hymn are not paraphrased by Cynewulf. These are the distichs beginning with B, L, P, Y, and Z. B interrupts the narrative, though not more than Cynewulf frequently does in other places; L and P introduce a dramatic element, which would be out of place here (Ebert, *op. cit.*, 3. 50–51); Y and Z are hortatory, and not epical. The omission of L and P is more intelligible than that of B, Y, and Z; Cynewulf is dramatic in the first part of the *Christ*, the Advent, and not in the second and third; but he is frequently hortatory and admonitive, perhaps so frequently as to leave no space for sermonizing at just these points. Another reason for the exclusion of the questions put by the righteous and the wicked respectively may be found in Cynewulf's probable unwillingness to interrupt these solemn and awful deliverances by anything in the nature of a retort.

'5. That the passages of *Christ* here quoted do not cover the whole of Dietrich's third division, and, in fact, that only a small proportion of these 916 lines is adduced in evidence. To meet this objection it will be necessary to examine these lines somewhat more carefully, but first to consider what subject-matter is furnished us by the stanzas of the Latin hymn, so far as made use of by Cynewulf. An analysis of these stanzas or distichs shows that we have ten stages in the development, ten *Leitmotive*, as they might be called.

I. The great day of the Lord shall appear suddenly, like a thief seizing the unwary in the dark night.

II. The sound of the trumpet shall summon quick and dead from the four corners of the earth.

III. The Judge shall approach, resplendent in majesty, attended by the angelic choirs.

IV. The sun shall be turned into darkness, and the moon into blood; the stars shall fall, and the earth be shaken.

V. Fire shall break out before the face of the Judge, and consume heaven, earth and sea.

VI. The King shall sit on the throne of his majesty, surrounded by trembling hosts of angels.

VII. The elect shall be gathered at the right, and the wicked, like fetid goats, at the left.

VIII. The righteous shall be welcomed to the kingdom, because of their pity for the poor.

IX. The wicked shall be cast into hell, because of their uncharitableness.

X. The faithful shall be admitted to the joys of Paradise.

'For the sake of brevity, these may be called respectively the Doomsday motive, the Trumpet motive, the Judge, Darkness, Fire, Throne, Assemblage, Welcome, Sentence, and Paradise motives. The object of this analysis is to exhibit the re-introduction and blending of these motives in various transitional passages. Other motives are occasionally found, and will be characterized as occasion requires.

'Grein's sixteenth Canto of the *Christ*, ll. 779–866, is a transitional passage; 779–782ᵃ, connective passage, referring to the close of the preceding division;

782ᵇ–785ᵃ, Doomsday motive; 785ᵇ–789ᵃ, Advent motive; 789ᵇ–796, Doomsday motive, personal fear; 797–807ᵃ, Doomsday motive, Rune passage; 807ᵇ–814, Fire motive; 815–825ᵃ, exhortation; 825ᵇ–827ᵃ, Darkness motive (cf. IV); 827ᵇ–831, Sentence motive; 832–847ᵃ, Judge motive, and terror of sinners; 847ᵇ–849, exhortation; 850–866, comparison of life to a voyage, with exhortation (864–866), ending in Ascension motive (*þā hě [tō] heofonum āstāg*). The whole passage forms a kind of interlude, while it is also a prelude to Part III, as is apparent from the repetition of the whole Judgment motive in various forms, while the Advent and Ascension motives occur only once each.

'A strong chord is struck at the opening of the Judgment Poem proper (Grein's Seventeenth Canto). This is the passage first quoted under I (ll. 867–873); 874 amplifies 872–873; 875–877 possibly renders the *vivos* of II; 878–889ᵃ is the passage given under II, the principal Trumpet motive; 889ᵇ–898 seems to be a variation on the Assemblage motive, anticipatory; 899–909, principal Judge motive; 910–920, paraphrase of *majestate fulgidus*; 921–924ᵃ, exhortation, passing into (924ᵇ–929) second part of principal Judge motive (the attending angels); 930–932ᵃ, first half of principal Fire motive, anticipatory of its place in the Latin hymn; 932–933, opening chord of Darkness motive; 934–940, principal Darkness motive; 941–943ᵃ, repetition of Judge motive, extended by mention of the accompanying multitude (943ᵇ–947ᵃ); 947ᵇ–955, repetition of Trumpet motive; 956–959, anticipation of Sentence motive (?); 960, Doomsday motive as terror, passing over into (964–968ᵃ) principal Fire motive, second part; 968ᵇ–988ᵃ, poetical amplification and variation of Fire motive; 988ᵇ–991ᵃ, repetition of Darkness motive, last part (*mundi tremet ambitus ?*); 991ᵇ–993, Doomsday motive, terror; 994–996, Fire motive repeated; 997–999ᵃ, Doomsday motive, terror and anguish, passing into (999ᵇ–1006) Fire motive repeated, which ends the canto with conflagration.

'In contrast with the close of the preceding, the Eighteenth Canto begins (1007–1014) with the coming of the King in glory (Throne motive blended to some extent with Judge motive); 1015–1021ᵃ, amplification of Throne motive (*tremebunda agmina*); 1021ᵇ–1042ᵃ, resumption of Trumpet motive (*Christo ciet obviam*); 1042ᵇ–1044ᵃ, Fire and Darkness motives; 1044ᵇ–1080, Throne motive (thoughts and intents of the heart revealed before a word is spoken), complicated by passing allusions to previous motives; anticipatory introduction of the Rood motive in 1064ᵇ–1065 (*and sēo hēa rōd, ryht ārǣred rīces tō bēacne*); 1081–1215, Rood motive, with extended reference to the Crucifixion, its import, and the accompanying signs.

'At the beginning of the Nineteenth Canto stands the principal Throne motive (1216–1217), which is extended in 1218–1220; the Assemblage motive follows immediately, 1221–1231; 1232–1233, the Welcome and Sentence motives are slightly anticipated, though only as a kind of extension of the Assemblage motive; 1234–1261, the three notes of the righteous, and, 1262–1300, those of the wicked; 1301–1333, the advantages of confession and self-knowledge, passing into the Throne motive (1334–1335). The whole of the Twentieth Canto (1336–1361) is occupied by the Welcome motive. The first lines of the Twenty-first Canto (1362–1364) introduce the Sentence motive; 1365–1376ᵃ, folly of expecting mercy, passing into (1376ᵇ–1498) an address by the Judge to the wicked, in which his loving-kindness is rehearsed, with introduction of the Advent motive (1418ᵇ–1425ᵃ) and the Passion motive (1433–1453); the Sentence motive then appears, justified by their uncharitableness (1499-1514), and culminating in the sentence itself (1515-1523); 1524-1548, fulfilment of the decree. In the Twenty-second Canto, general reflections and admonition (1549-1633), passing into the Paradise motive (1634-1664). . . .

'The proof that the Third Part of Cynewulf's poem is based on the Latin hymn will now, I think, appear conclusive. It has been shown that, in general, the order of events is that of the hymn, and that deviations from this order are either quite exceptional or only apparent, and are due in the latter case to the fondness for variations upon a theme, and for the interlacing of motives, both of which are almost inseparable from the peculiar constitution of Old English poetry. It has been shown that, in a large number of instances, the Old English words correspond to the Latin words of the hymn, and might often be regarded as literal translations of them, and that in many cases it would be vain to seek for their originals in corresponding portions of the Vulgate. It has further been shown that the omission of certain distichs of the Latin hymn from Cynewulf's scheme can be easily accounted for. No other production antecedent to Cynewulf's presents the incidents of the Last Judgment in the same order and at the same time in similar language, so far as is yet known. The principal motives frequently occur at the beginning of a canto, or are introduced by the adverb *þonne*. Finally, though episodes, reflective passages, and exhortations are interspersed, there is nothing, either in their frequency or character, to invalidate the theory which is here set forth.'

Some of the identifications under (5) are very likely fanciful, and I am quite ready to abandon them for cause shown, but the main contention of the article will, I presume, be admitted.

867-874. Tr. in Ten Brink, *Early Eng. Lit.*, p. 55. The *Heliand* has (4358-60):

> Mutspelli cumid
> an thiustria naht, al sô thiof farit
> darno mið is dâdiun, sô cumit thie dag mannun.

867. mid fêre. See (above) I. a. Th. 'with its coming' [!].

868. se micla dæg. See I. b. Cf. Joel 2. 11, 31; Zeph. 1. 14; Mal. 4. 5; Acts 2. 20; etc. — **meahtan.** For the form cf. *Ph.* 377; *Ps.* 118^{13}, and *ælmeaht-igne*, 759. Th. 'might.' — **Dryhtnes.** See I. c.

869. æt midre niht. Cf. Mt. 25. 6. — **mægne.** Cf. 382; *Gifts of Men* 56; *Rid.* 24^{13}. — **bihlæmmeð.** Cosijn rejects the MS. reading *bihlæmeð*, adding, 'denn das *mm* ist organisch; s. *Walfisch* 61 und 76, und vgl. weiter *hlimman*, *hlemm*, Gott. *hlamma*, u. s. w.'

870. scîre gesceafte. Similarly *Jul.* 728; *Hy.*10^2; *Met.* 20^8. — **swâ.** See I. e; Thorpe makes everything parenthetical from here to 874 inclusive. — **sceaða fæcne.** Not 'with robbers' guile ' (Th.).

871. þeof. See I. d; 1 Thess. 5. 2; 2 Pet. 3. 10.

872. on sweartre niht. See I. f. — **sorglêase.** See I. g.

873. forfêhð. See I. h.

874. yfles. *Genǣgan* again takes the gen. in *Gu.* 261; *Beow.* 2206 (?). Gollancz tr. *yfles* by 'barely' (Go.^{1}), 'evilly' (Go.^{2}), though he apparently understands the construction.

875–877. I do not understand Gollancz's comment: 'These lines do not paraphrase any words of the Latin hymn; they were, perhaps, vaguely suggested by
the second couplet, "brevis totus . . . saeculum."'

875. Sȳne beorg. Cf. 899, 1007. Properly the Mount of Olives; cf. note on
900, and Ezek. 11. 23.

Brooke says (p. 400): 'Then Cynewulf, as if suddenly smitten with a vision
(and he is the only Anglo-Saxon poet who has these poetic outbursts), breaks
into a noble description of the four summoning angels.' He then renders 878–
889a (slightly varied in Br.², p. 173).

878 ff. Cf. II. b, and *Bl. Hom.* 95. 13 ff.: 'þonne æfter þeossum þingum biþ
neh þæm seofoþan dæge; ond þonne hāteþ Sanctus Michahel se hēahengl blāwan
þā fēower bēman æt þissum *fēower endum middangeardes.*' Add *PBB.* 6. 470
(cf. note on 1634ᵇ–1635ᵃ); Wulfstan 183. 10. From Mt. 24. 31; Mk. 13. 27.

878. Þonne. Th. 'When'; so Gr. (*D.*).

880. englas. These angels are also four in number, and blow from the four
cardinal points, in Giotto's fresco in the Arena Chapel at Padua; there are likewise four in the Byzantine mosaic, executed about 1075 in the Church of St.
Angelo in Formis, near Capua, under the orders of a certain Desiderius (Crowe
and Cavalcaselle, Vol. 1); then, too, in the fine Roger van der Weyden at the
hospital of Beaune, in Burgundy. On the other hand, in the Memling at Dantzic
(see note on 1532) there are three; in the Orcagna (?) of the Campo Santo at Pisa,
the Fra Angelico of the Florentine Accademia and elsewhere, the Fra Bartolom-
meo of Santa Maria Nuova at Florence, and the Signorelli of the Cathedral of
Orvieto, there are two; while the Michael Angelo of the Sistine Chapel has seven,
no doubt in allusion to Rev. 8. 2 ff. The Tintoretto of Santa Maria del Orto, at
Venice, has a number that I have not ascertained.

Cf. *Debate between Body and Soul* (Böddeker, *Altengl. Dicht.* p. 240):

> þe seste day ayen þe dom
> shule four aungles stonde,
> blowe þat þis world shal quaque
> wiþ beme in here honde.

ælbeorhte. Br. 'a-glow.' One is reminded of Milton's (*Sol. Music* 10–11)

> Where the bright seraphim, in burning row
> Their loud, uplifted angel-trumpets blow.

Brooke is right in saying (p. 210): 'This trumpet-voice of the heart belongs to
the English nature, and the lofty music of Milton's praise came down to him in
legitimate descent from the earliest exultation of English psalm.' Cf. 548.

881. bȳman on brehtme. See II. a; Mt. 24. 31; 1 Cor. 15. 52; 1 Thess.
4. 16. —beofa∂ middangeard. Cf. Jer. 10. 10; Ps. 60. 2; 114. 7; also Joel 2.
10; Rev. 6. 12; 16. 18. Br. 'Trembles Middle-Garth.' See *Doomsday* (Bede) 99.

882. Th. makes *hrūse* the subject of *hlȳda∂*, and *trume* and *torhte* substantive
adjectives.

883. trume ond torhte. Cf. 933. Go.¹ 'gloriously and long'; Go.² 'boldly
and gloriously'; Grein recognizes no such adverbs, and how could *trume* mean
either 'boldly' or 'long'? As adjectives they are admirable.

wið tungla gong. Toward the region of the stars, i.e. toward the heavens. Cf. *ryne tungla*, 671, and note. With *tungla gong* might be compared the *gyrus stellarum* of Sap. 13. 2, translated 'the circle of the stars.' So light is thrown upon the *swegles gong* (*gang*) of *An.* 208, 455, 871 by such expressions as *gyrus caeli*, 'the circuit of heaven,' Ecclus. 24. 8; *meatus caeli*, 'the paths of heaven,' Virgil, *Æn.* 6. 849; *vias caeli*, 'the paths of heaven,' *Georg.* 2. 477. So also Cosijn: 'wie *sprecan wið* — construiert: = *wið gongende tungl*, i.e. *wið heofones weard.*' So already Th.: 'towards the stars' course,' but Gr. 'über der Sterne Gang.'

884ᵃ. singað ond swinsiaþ. See II. c; cf. *Ph.* 124, 140.

884ᵇ-885ᵃ. See Job 37. 17; Cant. 4. 16; Ezek. 17. 10; Exod. 10. 19. Cf. *Gen.* 807.

886. See II. d. Br. renders 886ᵇ by 'bairns of doughty men' [!]. One does n't quite understand Gollancz's 'sons of (warrior-) men *and* all mankind'; surely the two phrases are synonymous.

887ᵇ. See II. e. Th. 'to the Godhead.'

888ᵃ. egeslīc. Cosijn would read *egeslīce*, but without assigning a reason; Th. 'terrific'; Gr. (*D.*) 'mit Angstgraus.' — of . . . moldan. Cf. *Sat.* 604. Brooke's 'all aghast from the grey mould' is better than usual.

888ᵇ-889ᵃ. Cf. *An.* 793, 796ᵃ.

890. gefȳsed. Grein, *Spr.*, suggests *conturbatus;* but *D.*, 'erschüttert.' Neither can easily be reconciled with the etymology, nor with 475. Th. 'urged on'; Go. 'bestead.'

891. cearum cwīþende. Cf. 1130, 1285; *Gu.* 194; *Wand.* 9. — cwicra gewyrhtu. The deeds which they performed when alive; so already Thorpe and Grein.

892. forhte. Professor Bright prefers to regard it as an adverb; so Go., 'sorely'; Gr. (*D.*) renders *forhte āfǣred* 'von Furcht überfallen.' Cf. *An.* 1342; *Ph.* 525.

foretācna mǣst. See the parallel expressions, 550, 931, 954, 1069, 1624, 1626. The *XV Signa ante Judicium*, so well known in the Middle English period, do not seem to have been in Cynewulf's mind, though the earliest distinct formulation of them is attributed to Bede (Nölle, in *PBB.* 6. 460). Jerome is constantly cited as an authority deriving his information from the Hebrew Annals, but no such passage is found in his works. Cf. *Bl. Hom.* 91. 28: 'Ond syx dagum ǣr þissum dæge gelimpeþ syllice tācn æghwylce āne dæge'; and see notes on 878 ff., 1174–1176ᵃ.

893ᵃ. A grammatical transgression found also in Greek and Latin, and so in Milton, e.g. *P. L.* 4. 324.

895. onhǣlo gelāc. Gollancz comments: '"the hidden hosts"; Gr. renders *onhǣle* = "entire"; no other instance occurs of *onhæle* in the sense of "whole"; the usual frequent usage is "secret," "hidden"; cp. *wid is þes wēsten, wræcsetla fela, eardas onhæle earmra gæsta*, *Guth.* 268. Th. renders, "an unsound assemblage"; Toller, "the entire hosts."'

Dietrich had said (p. 211): 'Es sind nicht "unheile" (an unsound assemblage), sondern ganze, sämmtliche Schaaren, die am Gerichtstage versammelt werden sollen'; as other instances of this sense he added *Gu.* 322. 505; *Gn. Ex.* 1; *Rid.* 16⁷.

engla ond dēofla. Shall we not rather understand 'saints and sinners?'

897[b]. Cf. *Gu.* 649[b].

898. **ungelīce.** Cf. 909.

899–909. See III. a.

899. **semninga.** This has already been twice effectively employed, 491, 873.
—on **Sȳne beorg.** So 875.

900. **sūþanēastan.** This is explained by Jerome, in his commentary on Zech.
14. 4, 5 (Migne 25. 1525): 'Cum mons Oliveti grandi voragine praeruptus fuerit,
ita ut una pars voraginis ad Orientem, altera ad Occidentem respiciat, repente
et in ipsa voragine excelsa ex utraque parte praerupto, alia vorago rumpetur ad
Aquilonem, alia ad Austrum, et praeruptum quadrangulum fiet, ut quadrifariam
in quatuor plagas Orientis et Occidentis, Aquilonis et Austri vorago tendatur.
Et fugietis, inquit, ad vallem quae est inter templum et Sion. Hi enim templi et
Sion duo montes, Dei montes appellantur; quia vallis illa montis Oliveti, quae
praeruptis hinc atque inde montibus cingitur, usque ad templi montem qui sanctus
est, suam voraginem trahet. . . . Transeamus ad intelligentiam spiritualem. Postquam mons Olivarum ad Orientem et Occidentem vocatione Gentium et abjectione
Judaeorum fuerit separatus, rursum alia scissura fiet Aquilonis et Austri. Aquilo
jungetur Occidenti, *Auster Orientali plagae;* ad sinistram stabit Circumcisio, ad
dextram populus Christianus. De his duobus ventis Ecclesia loquitur: *Surge,
Aquilo, et veni, Auster* (Cant. 4. 16), ut Aquilone vento frigidissimo recedente, qui
interpretatur diabolus, Auster calidus ventus adveniat, quem sponsa perquirens,
ait: *Ubi pascas, ubi cubas, in meridie* (ibid. 1. 16)? De quo et Abacuc mystice
loquitur: *Deus de Theman veniet* (Abac. 3. 3), pro quo in Hebraico scriptum est:
Deus ab Austro, id est, *a luce plenissima.* De qua alibi Psalmista conclamat:
Illuminans tu mirabiliter a montibus aeternis (Psal. 75. 5). Cum antem tanta
fuerit duorum populorum in toto orbe divisio, ut *alii ad Orientem et Austrum,* id
est, ad dextram: alii ad Aquilonem et Occidentem, ad sinistram videlicet sepa-
rentur, tunc quicumque sanctus est fugiet ad vallem montium Dei, de quibus
supra diximus, templi et Sion.'

This interpretation, as Jerome explains, rests upon the assumption that the
word which in English (Zech. 14. 5) is retained as 'Azal,' should, with Symmachus,
be interpreted as 'adjoining' (*proximum*), so that Jerome renders: 'Quoniam
conjungetur vallis montium ad proximum.' If, then, the valley cloven toward
the east and west is to be united with that which is next it, we must assume
that another valley is opened from north to south crossing the first at right
angles. The east is the direction whence comes the sun, but the south is the
quarter whence we look for heat; then, too, Habakkuk, in the Hebrew, speaks
of God as coming from the south; accordingly, if the assembled nations are to
be divided into faithful Christians and unbelieving Jews, the station of the
former must be assigned to the south and east, the two directions from which
their Lord is represented as coming. This, however, does not abrogate the
prevailing assumption, according to which he is to come from the east; see
note on 906.

Less to the point, though significant, is Gregory's comment, *Hom. in Ezech.* 2.
10 (Migne 76. 1062–3): 'Potest autem per Aquilonis portam gentilitas, per Austri
viam Judaea, per Orientis autem portam ipse Dominus designari. Per Aquilonem
quippe non immerito gentilitas figuratur, quam ille in torporis frigore possedit qui

dixit: *Sedebo in monte testamenti, in lateribus Aquilonis* (Isai. 14. 13). Per
Australem quoque portam recte Judaea accipitur, in qua spiritales patres caelesti
amore ferbuerunt. Quorum unus loquitur, dicens: *Convertc, Domine, captivitatem nostram, sicut torrens in Austro* (Psal. 125. 4). Quae etsi carnalem populum
habuit in quo velut Aquilonis frigora portavit, in sanctis tamen suis doctoribus ac
Prophetis ad Deum ac proximum calore charitatis arsit. Orientalis porta non
immerito ipsum signat, de quo scriptum est: *Ecce vir, Oriens nomen ejus* (Zach.
6. 12). Et de quo Zacharias ait: *Visitavit nos Oriens ex alto* (Luc. 1. 78).' Cf.
note on 104.

sunnan lēoma. Jerome on the same passage (Migne 92. 1524): 'Et ipse mons
Olivarum, in quo stant pedes Domini, contra Jerusalem est ad Orientem, unde
oritur sol justitiae.' Cf. also *Gen.* 666–8 (Satan's address):

> 'Ic mæg heonon gesēon
> hwǣr hē sylf siteð — *þæt is sūðēast* —
> welan bewunden, se þās woruld gescēop.'

So in the passing of Chad (Bede 4. 3; Miller 264[22]) the light appears in the southeast (*ēastsūðdǣl*: Lat. *ab euroaustro*). So after Drihthelm had been in the darkness of hell, his guide, who had disappeared, rejoined him (Bede, *Eccl. Hist.* 5. 12;
Miller, p. 428): 'þā cerde hē ðā sōna on ðā swiðran hond, and mec ongon lǣdan
sūðēast on þon rodor, swā-swā on wintre sunne ūpp gongeð. þā wǣre wit sōna
of ðām þēostrum ābrogdene, and hē mec lǣdde in fægernesse smoltes lēohtes.'
Auster is tr. by *sūþanēasterne* in *Ps. Lamb.* 77. 26. Among the *Ascetica Dubia*,
printed with the works of Bede, is an alphabetical one entitled *Hymnus de Die
Judicii*, in which, under D, we have: '*Deus ab austro apparebit*, terribilis adveniet
orbem ponere in desertum, et vindictam retribuere in tremendo die.'

·It should be noted that the passage commented by Jerome (Zech. 14. 4) is
among the Lessons for Thursday of the Third Week in Advent. The Respond
after the Third Lesson on Tuesday of the First Week in Advent is : 'Ecce ab
Austro venio ego Dominus Deus vester, visitare vos in pace.' After the Seventh
Lesson of the Second Sunday in Advent, the Respond begins : 'Egredietur
Dominus de Samaria ad portam quae respicit ad Orientem.'

902. Cf. 989.

904. heofona gehleodu. Cf. (II) 518. Cf. Ælfr. *Hom.* I. 170: '... seðe
gebīgde þone hēagan heofenlican *bīgels*' (from Ps. 18. 9; 144. 5?).

906. Cf. Ezek. 43. 2: 'Et ecce *gloria Dei* Israel ingrediebatur *per viam orien-
talem.*' See the quotations in the note on 900, and cf. Ps. 67. 34 (68. 33): 'Qui
ascendit super caelum caeli ad Orientem '; add from the *Apostolic Constitutions*
(quoted by Warren, *Liturgy of the Ante-Nicene Church*, p. 319): 'After this, let
all rise up with one consent, and looking eastward, ... pray in the eastward position to God who ascended up to the heaven of heavens.' Add the following from
John of Damascus, *De Fide Orthodoxa* IV. 12 (*Patr. Gr.* 94. 1135): 'Rursus cum
in caelum reciperetur, versus orientem ferebatur, sicque a discipulis adoratus fuit,
atque ita venturus est, sicut eum in caelum euntem conspexerunt. Quemadmodum ipse quoque Dominus dixit: *Sicut fulgur exit ab oriente, et paret usque in
occidentem, ita erit et adventus Filii hominis.* Quocirca quia ejus adventum
exspectamus, ad orientem adoramus. Est autem apostolorum haec traditio, in

sacras Litteras minime relata. Complura enim illi nobis tradiderunt quae scriptis consignata non fuere.'

907-8. Jerome (Migne 92. 1523) using for an illustration Isa. 42. 13: *Dominus virtutum egredietur*, remarks: 'Egredietur ergo Deus de loco suo quando quietem et mansuetudinem et clementiam suam pro emendatione peccantium rumpere cogitur; qui cum per naturam *dulcis* est, vitio nostro παραπικραίνεται, id est, *amarus* efficitur; non sibi, sed patientibus, quibus amara tormenta sunt.'

908. gebléod. Since Gollancz defines *gebléod* 'of different colors,' it is not surprising to find him commenting as follows: 'Cp. Ða *wyrta gréowon mid menig-fealdum blostmum mislice gebléode*, "the plants grew diversely coloured with manifold blossoms" (the Anglo-Saxon version of the *Hexameron of St. Basil*, ed. Norman, 10. 36).' However, he translates by 'visaged,' Th. 'colored,' Gr. (*D.*) 'zu erblicken'; Br. 'countenanced.'

910-920. There is probably a common source for this and the lines in Hampole's *Pr. Consc.* 5235-40 (cf. Julianus, in Migne 96. 501):

> Christ ful awsterne þan sal be
> Agayn synful me [n] þat him sal se;
> And dredful and hydus, als says þe boke,
> He sal be to þam when þai on hym loke,
> And ful delitable unto þe sight
> Of ryghtwyse men þat lyffed here ryght.

912. léoftǽl. Cf. *lufsum and léoftǽl*, *Pa.* 32; also *Sal.* 366.

913a. Cf. *Gen.* 468a.

914. Th. 'to behold the beauteous aspect'; Gr. '(liebsam und linde ist den lieben Menschen) da anzuschauen des Anblickes Glanz'; yet in *Spr.*, under *líðe*, he reads: 'Críst bið fréond and leoftǽl, lufsum and líþe léofum monnum'; Go.[1] appears to assume syncope of the copula: '(Sweet shall it be and pleasant for His beloved) to gaze upon that aspect all so fair'; similarly Go.[2]

915. mid willum. Th. 'with good-will'; Go. 'of will.' Cf. 1343, 1519; *Ph*, 149. Perhaps we might here take the phrase as an adv. = 'delightfully.'

917a. Cf. 1236a; also 1037.

920b. Th. 'ever fordone'; Gr. (*D.*) 'verwürkt hervor (kommen)'; Go.[1] 'damned eternally'; Go.[2] 'aye fordone.' Gr. (*Spr.*) classifies *forð* under 'hervor, herbei, in conspectum,' and interprets here: 'in conspectum Domini.'

921 ff. The sense, and even the construction, is somewhat uncertain. Th. renders: 'That may of punishment for a warning be to those [*sic*] who have wise thought that he entirely dread nothing: he before that countenance shall not with dread become fearful in soul, when,' etc. Gr. 'Das mag ein Wahrzeichen sein dem der hat weise Gedanken dass dem ganz und gar nicht zu grauen brauchet wer von dem Anblicke dann von Angst nicht wird von Furcht erfüllt, wenn,' etc. Go.[1] 'He that is wise of thought may well regard it as a sign that he need be nowise adread, if he, afore that Presence, becometh not dismayed with terror in his soul, when,' etc. Go.[2] 'It may be for a sign unto his mind who has wise thought, that he need dread him nought at all, who afore that presence becometh not afeard with terror in his soul, when,' etc.

The renderings of Grein and Gollancz may be dismissed as meaningless. If they signify anything, it is that he who is not afraid in the presence of the great Judge need not be afraid at all, — a sufficiently axiomatic proposition.

If we may trust the parallelism of *Gu.* 772, he 'who has wise thought' is the good man; there the saints 'beraᵒ̃ in brēostum bēorhtne gelēafan, . . . habbaᵒ̃ wīsne geþōht fūsne on forᵒ̃weg tō Fæder ēᵒ̃le.' If *wearninga* be regarded as equivalent to 'warning,' the opt. *ondrǣde* should replace *ondrǣdeᵒ̃* (cf. *Gen.* 527); if it be taken as 'sign,' this substitution is less necessary. In either case, *wītes*, with the sense usually attributed to it, seems superfluous or inappropriate; may we possibly have here a form of the root *wīt-* in *wītga*, just as we have *wītedōm* parallel with *wītigdōm?* Then *wītes tō wearninga* might signify 'warning of prophecy,' or 'prophetic intimation,' and *ondrǣdeᵒ̃* could stand as a future.

A slighter difficulty arises with respect to *egsan.* Is it to be construed, as a dative, with *for,* or as an instrumental, with *forht?* In favor of the former we have 1014; the latter is slightly supported by 1020, yet here, as elsewhere, *egsan* is dependent upon a past participle; nowhere do we find it with a mere adjective, like *forht.* Then, too, the position of *egsan* is hardly consistent with its dependence upon *forht.*

We may now attempt a paraphrastic rendering of 921 ff., though with hesitation: 'That [namely the statement that Christ will be gracious to those who have done his will] may be accepted as a prophetic intimation [or 'warning having reference to punishment,' though not to *his* punishment] by him who is wise of thought, that he will have no occasion whatever [note both the *eallunga* and the *ᵒ̃wiht*] to be afraid; he shall not be alarmed in soul because of the terror of the Presence, when he beholds the spectacle of the Lord of all creation approaching with mighty wonders to the doom of many.'

921. wītes tō wearninga. Go. comments: 'That may be for the soul's warning,' supplying *wesan.* Gr. (*Spr.*) enters *wītes* under *wit,* 'mens, intellectur'; but see Variants. On the omission of *wesan,* cf. Sievers, *Anglia* 13. 2.

923. sē. Cannot = 'who,' as in Go.[2]

926ª. Cf. Mt. 16. 27; 24. 30; Mk. 13. 26.

926ᵇ. þing. This suggests the Old Norse sense.

927. on healfa gehwone. See III. b. — **heofonengla þrēat.** See III. c; also Mt. 16. 27; 25. 31; Dan. 7. 10; *þrēat* seems to be a collective.

928. ælbeorhtra. See III. d. — **scolu.** Cf. Phineas Fletcher, *Purple Island,* s. f.: 'Heaven's winged *shoals.*' Gr. tr. the line: 'Aussen um den Edelen all-glänzend fahren' [!].

929. hergas hāligra. See III. c.

930-956. Tr. by Hammerich-Michelsen, p. 86.

930-940. Tr. by Brooke; 934-940; also on p. 483.

930ª. A reminiscence of Rom. 8. 22, or 2 Pet. 3. 10? Cf. *PBB.* 6. 469: 'Biᵒ̃ micel stefen gehȳred of þām heofones tungle.' Add *Bl. Hom.* 91. 29.

930ᵇ-932ª. Cf. Ps. 50. 3; 97. 3; Dan. 7. 10; Hab. 3. 5; 2 Thess. 1. 8; *Bl. Hom.* 93. 3: 'Blōdig regn ond fȳren fundiaþ þās eorþan tō forswylgenne ond tō forbær-nenne.' See V. a, b.

932. hlemmeᵒ̃. Th.; Go. 'shall roar'; Gr. (*D.*) 'rauscht'; Br. 'hurtle.' Cf. *Whale* 61; Grein defines in the latter instance (*Spr.*), 'Cum crepitu collidere,' which of course will not do here.

heofonas berstað. Cf. *Bl. Hom.* 93. 4: 'Sēo heofon biþ gefeallen æt þǣm fēower endum middangeardes.' Cf. Isa. 34. 4; Rev. 6. 14.

933 ff. Cf. Is. 13. 10; Ezek. 32. 7; Joel 2. 10, 31; 3. 15; Mt. 24. 29; Mk. 13. 24, 25; Rev. 6. 12, 13.

933. trume ond torhte. Cosijn would refer this to *heofonas*; but surely *torhte* must apply rather to *tungol*, notwithstanding 967–8: 'ūpheofon torhtne mid his tunglum,' for here the brightness is a brightness explicitly proceeding from the stars. Cf. 883. Except for 'planets,' Brooke's rendering of the line is good: 'All the firm-set flashing planets fall out of their places.' On p. 483 he has: 'Likewise the stars from heaven hurtle down.'

934. See IV. a.

935. on blōdes hīw. Should refer rather to the moon; cf. Joel 2. 31; Acts 2. 20. See IV. b.

936. Br. (p. 483): 'Above the Ere-world for the bairns of men.' — **ælda bearnum.** A common Hebrew idiom; cf. Gen. 11. 5; Ps. 4. 2; etc., etc. The OE. phrase occurs in Cædmon's Hymn; cf. my *The Bible and English Prose Style* (Boston, 1892), p. xi.

938ᵇ. 'Nither tumbles down,' as Brooke elegantly expresses it.

939. See IV. c, and note on 933 ff.

940. Cf. 990. Gollancz renders well: 'Tempest-driven through the stormy air.'

941ᵇ. Cf. 515ᵇ (II).

942ᵃ. Go.¹ rightly (not Go.²): 'The King of Kings.'

942ᵇ. Cf. 832ᵇ; *El.* 279.

943. þegna. Not angels, apparently; but cf. 927–9.

946ᵃ. So 1364ᵃ. Th. 'with dread of punishment'; Gr. 'mit angstlicher Drohung'; Go.¹ 'with direful penalty'; Go.² 'with dread punishment.'

946–7. eorðan mǣgðe sylfa gesēceð. Cf. 62 (I), but especially 523–4 (II).

947. geond sīdne grund. So 785 (II); cf. 1164. Go.¹ 'from pole to pole.'

948ᵇ. Cf. the references under 881. The trumpet is now but a single one, the poet adhering more closely to the Bible.

949. seofon. *Possibly* with allusion to Rev. 8. 2 ff. — **healfa.** Cf. 1267. — **swōgað.** Cf. *Rid.* 8⁷.

950. brecende. Cf. *gebrec*, 953, and *Rid.* 4⁴⁰, ⁴⁴. Grein relates the verb to ON. *braka.*

952. fēre. On this emendation I copy my note in *Jour. Germ. Philol.* 1. 336–7: 'Cynewulf, in describing the end of the world, mentions the voice of the celestial trumpet, and the winds that blow from seven quarters, rousing and devastating the world with tempest. These winds, then, according to the received text of the *Christ* (v. 952),

fyllað mid fēore foldan gesceafte.

Thorpe translates:

With their breath shall fell the earth's creation.

Grein translates (apparently after Ettmüller):

Und füllen all mit Feuer die Fluren dieser Erde.

Gollancz renders (*Christ*) :

　　　　　　　O'erthrowing all creation with their breath ;
(*Exeter Book*) :
　　　　　　　And with their breath o'erthrow the earth's creation.

Ettmüller (*Scopas and Boceras*) emends *fĕore* to *fȳre*.　Grein, apparently accepting this in his *Dichtungen* (see above), afterwards interprets *fĕore* as the abl.
" vita " (*Germania* 10. 420), comparing v. 974 :

　　　　　　　Fylleð on foldwong fȳres egsan.

'As against the rendering of Thorpe and Gollancz, " breath," it may be urged
that, though *feorh* is of frequent occurrence in the poetry, this meaning is nowhere
found.　As against Ettmüller's emendation, there is no suggestion of fire in this
context, but only of wind, uproar, and tempest.　As against Grein's later rendering, " life," the word has here no pertinence ; do these winds fill the creatures of
the earth with *life ?*　A mere glance at the passage will show the absurdity of such
a hypothesis.

'I would make the simplest sort of emendation, and read *fĕre* (Anglian for *fǣre*).
This involves only the suppression of a single letter, which, owing to the relative
frequency of *feorh* in this poem (*feorh* : *fĕr* :: 11 : 2 ; in all but one instance in an
oblique case, and so without *h*), might easily have intruded ; it is supported by
the *mid fĕre* of 867 ; and in the latter passage it is again *gesceafte*, appositional
with *foldbūende*, which is the object of the verb.　If this is accepted, *fyllað* means,
of course, ' fill.'

'As for the use of *fĕr* (*fǣr*) in the modern sense of "fear," we might compare
the use of *tremor* in the *Dies Iræ :*

　　　　　　　Quantus *tremor* est futurus
　　　　　　　Quando iudex est venturus,
　　　　　　　Cuncta stricte discussurus !

　　　　　　　Tuba, mirum spargens sonum, etc.

In the *Christ* (cf. 941 ff.), as in the *Dies Iræ*, the coming of the Judge (*Ælmihtig,
folca Weard*) inspires *terror*, expressed by *egsan þrēa*, 946 ; in both the mention
of the Lord, and of the effect of his appearance, is immediately followed by that
of the trumpet.'

956. **mægen.**　Cf. 1018.　See Variants ; Gr. ' mächtiggrosse.'

957. Go.[1] renders well : ' shall throng unto the all-embracing flame.

958. **cwice.**　Gr. (*D.*) seems to refer this to *fȳr ;* not so in *Spr.*

959. Th. ' a glut ' (reading *fylle*).　With *ǣldes fulle* cf. 1562ᵃ.

960. **untwēo.**　See Variants.　Gollancz comments : ' So Gr. ; MS. *untreo*, an
obvious scribal error, due, perhaps, to the rare use of *untweo ;* no other instance
of the word is recorded, but cp. *untweo-feald*, " *untwéo-fealde tréowa* " (Boethius,
Metre, 11. 95).

961. **cyn.**　Gr., Wü. place at end of 960, perhaps influenced by 1027.　Frucht
(p. 2) and Cosijn protest.　The latter remarks : ' *Cyn* gehört zum folgenden Verse,
wie auch die Hs. andeutet.　Welcher Metrik folgt Assmann ?'

cearena . . . cwīþeð.　Cf. 891, 1130, 1285.

962. Th. apparently construes *lȳtlum* with *lēode*.

963. mægenearfeþum. Cf. 1410.

964-9. Cf. *Muspilli* 51–54.

964. eall þrēo. See V. c, d, e; cf. Rev. 21. 1. Go.[1] 'all there' (no doubt misprint for 'three'). See 2 Pet. 3. 10, 12.

965[a]. Br. 'wan welter of fire.'

966. swearta līg. So 994; cf. 983, 1532; *Gen.* 1926, 2415, 2505, 2541, 2857. See note on 1532.

968[a]. Cf. 107, 235 (I); 1150.

968[b]. Tēonlēg. So *El.* 1279.

970. gesārgad. So 961.

971[b]. So *Jul.* 731[b]. — mǣran. Th. 'awful'; Gr. 'offènen'; Go. 'mighty.' Cf. 1054.

972–993. Tr. by Brooke, pp. 401–2 (Br.[2], p. 174).

972–984[a]. Tr. by Brother Azarias.

972[a]. gǣst. Not 'guest' (Th., Br. Az., Go.); cf. 813.

972[b]. Br. 'shall gang [!] searchingly through earth.'

973. hīþende. Cf. 1043, and *hūþa*, 568. — hēahgetimbro. Cf. 1181. Br. 'the high up-timbered houses.' Th., Go. have no point following.

974. fylleð. Th. 'shall fell'; Gr. (*D.*) 'füllet' (so *Spr.*); Br. Az. 'shall fill'; Go., Br. 'shall hurl.' I incline to Grein's opinion, though the acc. *foldwong* is against it. If Thorpe is followed, *hēahgetimbro* must be synonymous with *woruld*, 975, and the second sentence is somewhat overweighted. Th.'s 975–976[a] do not apparently form part of a sentence. — foldwong. Cf. *Gu.* 1300. — egsan. *egsa?*

975. woruld mid ealle. Cosijn : 'die ganze Welt,' comparing *Saints* 6. 285 : 'his weleras wæron āwlætte *mid ealle.*' Surely *mid ealle* must be an adverb; but perhaps Cosijn means this. Th. 'the whole world together'; Gr. 'die Welt auf einmal'; Go., Br. 'withal.' Translate, 'completely,' 'wholly.'

976. heorogīfre. Th., Br. Az. 'all-devouring'; Gr. 'gierig'; Go. 'fierce-devouring'; Br. 'hungry as a sword.' Cf. *Jul.* 567, 586. — geneahhe. Th. 'abundantly'; Gr. 'häufig.'

976[b]–981[a]. Tr. by Brooke (p. 182).

979. sceldun. I agree with Thorpe (see Variants). Th. 'shielded'; Gr. schützten'; Go. 'parted'; Br. 'kept apart.' The vowel finds no support in this text, and may be *i*; but cf. *Nar.* 337 (Baskervill) : 'Mid-þȳ ðā lēon þyder cwōman, þā rǣsdon hīe sōna on ūs, and wē ūs wið him *sceldan*.' Cosijn remarks : '*scehdun* ist ein Unding, *scehtun* (Kenticismus für *scyhtun*) sinnlos.' He therefore accepts Thorpe's emendation.

980. Gr. 'als starke standfeste Stützen gegen Wogen,' yet (*Spr.*) he refers the adjectives to *beorgas*; Go. 'stoutly and steadfastly.' But surely the adjectives must belong to *hēahcleofu.*

981. windendum. Th. 'encircling'; Gr. 'wälzende'; Go. 'circling'; Br. 'winding.'

984. weallende. Th. 'burning'; Gr. 'wallende'; Go., Br. 'raging.' — Swā. For this sense of 'where,' cf. *An.* 1451, 1584.

985. flōdas āfȳsde. Cf. *El.* 1270.

986. sundes getwǣfde. Th., Br. Az. 'cut off from ocean'; Gr. 'des Sundes

beraubt'; Go.¹ 'reft of their craft'; Go.² 'bereft of swimming-craft.'   Gó. compares *Beow.* 517.   Cf. Rev. 8. 9.

988. swā weax.   In the altar-candles, Cynewulf may be thinking.

989.   Cf. 902.

990. gestun.   Only *Rid.* 4⁵⁶.   Cf. Tennyson, *The Princess* 6. 319:

> The *roar* that breaks the Pharos from its base.

sēo stronge lyft.   Cf. 940ª.

992.   Cf. *An.* 59.

993ª.   So *El.* 1216; cf. *An.* 1089, 1559.

993ᵇ.   Cf. 1298ᵇ.

997. cwicra gewin.   Th. 'of the living strife'; Gr. 'aller Lebenden Tumult';
Go.¹ 'the anguish of the living'; Go.² 'the strife of those alive.'

998.   Cf. 834.   Cosijn suggests *ge hrēow*, with reference to 1147.

999–1001.   Cf. 1628–9ª.

999. gedreag.   The other instances are: *An.* 43 (*gedrӕg*), and esp. 1557;
Beow. 756 (*gedrӕg*); *Rid.* 7¹⁰; *Deor's Lament* 45.

1000–1003.   Tr. by Hammerich-Michelsen, p. 87.

1000. firendǣdum fāh.   Cf. 1632; *Beow.* 1001; *Jul.* 59.

1001. londes.   Similarly, *Husband's Message* 3; *Ps.* 58ᵇ; *Wife's Lament* 8;
Gen. 1003, 2705; *Rid.* 85¹⁸.

1002. gehwæt.   One would expect *gehwone.*

1003. āsēceð.   Cf. 972.

1005–1006.   Cf. *El.* 1312ᵇ–1314, and my comment in *Anglia* 15. 18.

1007 ff.   Cf. 899 ff.

1007. mǣran.   Not 'vast' (Th.).

1011. ymbūtan.   See VI. d. — æþelduguð.   Go. 'chivalry.'

1013. engla gedryht.   See VI. e.   Cf. 515 (II), 941. — ingeþoncum.   Gr.
'in den innersten Gedanken.'

1014. forhte beofiað.   See VI. f.   Cf., from the Ascension Hymn of the
Breviary, ' Æterne Rex altissime,' the lines :

> Tremunt videntes Angeli
> Versa vice mortalium.

See also Ephraem Syrus, *Opera Omnia* (Rome, 1743) 5. 215: 'Tunc intuebimur
innumerabiles angelorum virtutes circumstantes cum tremore'; *ib.* 5. 504: 'Con-
tremiscet omnis creatura, ipsaque sanctorum angelorum agmina ob majestatem
illam et gloriam adventus ejus expavescent.' So John of Damascus, *Or. adv.
Const. Cab.*; Pseudo-Augustine, *Sermo* 155 (Migne 39. 2052), quoting Mt. 24. 26;
Cursor Mundi 22597 ff.; Böddeker, *Altengl. Dicht.*, p. 241 ; Hampole, *Pr. Consc.*
5381, 5391.

1016. unclǣne.   Frucht (p. 96) notes that the stress is on the second syllable;
cf. 388, *unāþrēotendum.*

1018.   Br. 'the white host of archangels, bright as heaven.' — heofonbeorht.
So *Dan.* 341 ; *Az.* 56.

1025. foldgrafum.   Cf. *El.* 845.

1027. Ādāmes cynn.   So 960.

1028-9. weorþeð foldræste eardes æt ende. Th. 'shall be of their earth-rest, their dwelling at the end'; Gr. 'der Feldruhe kommet ein Ende an dem Tage'; Go. 'their earthly rest and sojourning shall then have end'; Go.[2] 'there shall be an end of their earthly rest and of their sojourn.' Grein (*Spr.*) uncertainly assigns to *eard* the meaning of 'dwelling,' 'domicile.' The phrase, *æt ende*, is idiomatically used for the nom. *ende;* cf. *Jud.* 272; *Doomsday* 2. See also *Hel.* 2201-2 ; *Musp.* 89.

1029-1031. Cf. *Musp.* 81-2.

1031-2. Cf. 1068, 1070.

1032. edgeong. So *Ph.* 435; cf. *Ph.* 373, 536, 581, 608, In the latter poem, their youth is renewed, not as the eagle's (Ps. 103. 5), but as the phenix's.

1035. gēara gongum. So *Jul.* 603 ; *El.* 648. Cf. the *anni cursus* of Sap. 7. 19, which the English version of the Apocrypha renders by 'the circuits of years.'

1036. līc ond sāwle. Cf. 819, 1326. — Sceal on leōht cuman. Cf. 1 Cor. 4. 5; also 3. 13; Matt. 10. 26; Rom. 2. 16; 14. 12.

1037-1038[a]. Br. 'the figure of their works, the memory of their words, and the thoughts of their heart.'

1041-2. dēaþes bend tōlēseð. Cf. Acts 2. 24.

1042. Līffruma. Cf. 504, 656 (II); also 15 (and note), 27 (I). — Lyft bið onbærned. Cf. 967[b].

1043. hrēosað heofonsteorran. Cf. 933, 939, and Rev. 6. 13.

1043[b]-1044[b]. hȳpað wīde gīfre glēde. Cf. 972-3.

1045[a]. Cosijn proposes to read *on ē(a)cne* (= *ēacenne*) *eard*, 'denn das *ē* beruht auf Palatalumlaut: vgl. *Beow.* 1621: *ēacne eardas.*' He might have added, as examples of the palatal umlaut, *ēcne, An.* 636, 881 ; but his interpretation does not seem mandatory, though perhaps admissible. Accepting it, *ēcne* would mean 'teeming.' Identical is *Gu.* 1155[a]; cf. *Gu.* 628; *Met.* 23[11].

1047 ff. Cf. Heb. 4. 12, 13; Ps. 90. 8; 139. 12. See also Ephraem Syrus, *Opera* 5. 50: 'Ibi manifesta erunt quae unusquisque in occulto et obscuro gesserit. ... In illa horribili die, quaecumque hominum corpora gesserint, sive bona, sive mala, palam proferent; et deferet secum unusquisque ante tremendum Christi tribunal proprias actiones tamquam fructus bonos et jucundos, locutiones autem ut folia. ... Horrendum ibi, fratres, erit judicium, in quo etiam absque testibus cuncta erunt manifesta, opera atque sermones, cogitationes et animorum sensa.' Add note on 1634[b]-1635[a].

1047-8. Cf. *Musp.* 90: 'sō dār manno nohhein uuiht pimīdan ni mak.'

1047. Cf. 1055. — hord. Cosijn remarks: '"Das verborgene," denn Schätze verbirgt man ; warum aber immer diese "Schätze" in den Uebersetzungen angebracht?' Against this view, cf. the equation, *hord* = *frætwe*, 1072-3, though 'secrets' will often be the best rendering. — weras. See Variants. One would like to see Gollancz's authority for using *bemīþan* intransitively.

1052. Cf. *Musp.* 70; 'daz der man ēr enti sīd upiles kifrumita.' — ǣr oþþe sīð. Cf. 893, 1067; also 602 (II).

1054[b]. se mǣra dæg. See note on 868.

1057. gǣstes þearfe. Cf. note on 707.

1058. beorhtne wlite. So 1076. — wlite. Cf. 848, 1580, 1587.

1059. **hāt, heorugīfre.** So 976.

1060. **Sigedēman.** Only *An.* 661.

1061 ff. See the much longer enumeration in Wulfstan, p. 186.

1061. **bȳman stefn.** So *Dan.* 179; *Ph.* 497. — **bȳman.** Cf. 948. — **stefen.** Cf. *Rev.* 1. 10; 4. 1; 8. 13.

se **beorhta segn.** Anticipatory of 1084; cf. Mt. 24. 30.

1062. **þæt hāte fȳr.** Cf. 974, 976. — **duguð.** Cf. 1011.

1063. **engla þrym.** Cf. 1013; *Sat.* 36; *Hy.* 7[II, 50]. — **egsan þrēa.** Cf. 946.

1064. Brother Azarias says (p. 145) : ' I consider the poem of the Last Judgment as belonging to Cynewulf. The previous poems are more rhapsodical, and seem to have been intended as Church hymns. The style of the Last Judgment is of an older flavor. Mythological allusions are more frequent. The imagery is more heathenish. The only artistic fault is the twofold digression on the Rood.'

1064. **dæg.** Cf. 868, 1054; also 1310. — **rōd.** Cf. 1101.

1065. **ryht.** Th., Go.[2] ' erect '; Gr. (*D.*) ' recht,' (*Spr.*) ' grade '; Go.[1] ' rightwise '; cf. *Gu.* 1286. — **rīces tō bēacne.** Th. ' in sign of sway ' ; Gr. ' als des Reiches Zeichen '; Go. ' in sign of mastery.'

1070[a]. So *Ph.* 608[a].

1071. **nēode ond nȳde.** Th. ' by force and need '; Gr. (*D.*) ' nachdrücklich und nötlich '; Go.[1] ' by dire compulsion forced '; Go.[2] ' by force and need.' But Grein is right in *Spr.* s. v. *nēod* : ' partim studio commoti, partim coacti,' i.e. ' eager or compelled.'

1072. **berað.** So 1300, 1634; cf. *bringað*, 1077, and note on 1047 ff. ; also *Gu.* 770. — **brēosta hord.** Cf. 1047, 1055; *brēostgehygd*, 262. Not ' breasts' recesses ' (Th.).

1073. **frætwe.** Cf. 1635. Cosijn refers to *Bl. Hom.* 95. 19 : ' Mid gōdum dǣdum ond hālgum wē sceolan bēon *gefrætwode*, gif wē þonne willaþ bēon on þā swiþran healfe Drihtnes.'

1074. **gesunde.** Agrees with *sāwle*.

1077. **meaht ond gefēa.** For the thought, cf. Milton's (*P. L.* I. 157)

Fallen cherub, to be weak is miserable.

Note the verb in the singular.

1079[a]. Cf. *Gu.* 1347.

1079[b]-1080. **Wel . . . līcian.** Cf. *Sat.* 365; *Wand.* 114; *Beow.* 186; *An.* 887; *Hy.* 7[17] ; *Alms* 1; but especially 1333; *Ph.* 516.

1080. **on þa grimman tīd.** So *Rid.* 4[30].

1081. Go. makes 1083[b] ff. explanatory of *sorga mǣste*.

1082. **sārigferðe.** So *Beow.* 2863; *Gu.* 1326, 1352.

1083. **ellþēodum.** Cosijn remarks : ' l. *eallþēodum*, wie 1337 [1336], = *yrmenþēodum* ; besser noch vergleicht sich *ealwihte*.' This is carrying a little further Grein's view, for he translates *omnes gentes*, without, however, proposing to emend.

1084 ff. Cf. Ephraem Syrus, *Opera* 5 (2). 213 : ' Quum videbimus signum Filii hominis in caelo lucens, pretiosam scilicet ac vivificam Crucem omnes fines terrae illustrantem ' ; *ib.* 5. 193 : ' Quomodo sustinebimus tunc, Christo dilecti, quum videbimus terribilem thronum praeparatum, et signum Crucis apparens, in quo affixus est Christus voluntarie pro nobis?' *ib.* 5. 250: 'Haec rursus pretiosa Crux in secundo adventu Christi prima in caelo apparebit, tamquam pretiosum, vivificum, et venerabile, et sanctum magni Regis Christi sceptrum, secundum verbum Domini dicentis, quod *apparebit signum Filii Hominis in caelo.* Haec igitur prima apparebit in caelo cum omni exercitu angelorum, universam terram illuminans. a finibus usque ad fines, super claritatem solis, et adventum Domini adnuncians'; *ib.* 5. 212: 'Haec sancta Crux rursus in consummatione saeculi, cum secundus illuxerit Domini adventus, prima cum gloria ingenti et angelicorum exercituum multitudine apparebit in caelo inimicos quidem terrens et vexans, fideles autem laetificans atque illuminans, adventumque magni Regis adnuncians.' Cf. *Musp.* 100 ff., Müllenhoff und Scherer, *Denkmäler*[8] 2. 39, and Ebert 3. 163.

I can not help thinking that the description here, and in the *Dream of the Rood*, may owe something to the vision of Constantine. As the original account by Eusebius, though frequently referred to, is but seldom quoted, I subjoin it here (*Life of Constantine*, Bk. 1, chaps. 28–31): 'Accordingly, he called on Him with earnest prayer and supplications that he would reveal to him who He was, and stretch forth His right hand to help him in his present difficulties. And while he was thus praying with fervent entreaty, a most marvelous sign appeared to him from heaven, the account of which it might have been difficult to receive with credit, had it been related by any other person. But since the victorious emperor himself, long afterwards, declared it to the writer of this history, when he was honored with his acquaintance and society, and confirmed his statement by an oath, who could hesitate to accredit the relation, especially since the testimony of after times has established its truth? He said that about midday, when the sun was beginning to decline, he saw with his own eyes the trophy of a cross of light in the heavens, above the sun, and bearing the inscription, "Conquer by this." At this sight, he himself was struck with amazement, and his whole army also, which happened to be following him on some expedition, and witnessed the miracle.

'He said, moreover, that he doubted within himself what the import of this apparition could be. And while he continued to ponder and reason on its meaning, night imperceptibly drew on; and, in his sleep, the Christ of God appeared to him with the same sign which he had seen in the heavens, and commanded him to procure a standard made in the likeness of that sign, and to use it as a safeguard in all engagements with his enemies.

'At dawn of day he arose, and communicated the secret to his friends; and then, calling together the workers in gold and precious stones, he sat in the midst of them, and described to them the figure of the sign he had seen, bidding them represent it in gold and precious stones. And this representation I myself have had an opportunity of seeing.

'Now it was made in the following manner. A long spear, overlaid with gold, formed the figure of the cross, by means of a piece laid transversely over it. On the top of the whole was fixed a crown, formed by the intertexture of gold and precious stones; and on this, two letters indicating the name of Christ symbolized the Saviour's title by means of its first characters —the letter P being intersected by X exactly in its centre; and these letters the emperor was in the habit of wearing on his helmet at a later period. From the transverse piece which crossed the spear was suspended a kind of streamer of purple cloth, covered with a profuse embroidery of most brilliant precious stones ; and which, being also richly interlaced with gold, presented an indescribable degree of beauty to the beholder. This banner was of a square form ; and the upright staff, which, in its full extent, was of great length, bore a golden half-length portrait of the pious emperor and his children, on its upper part, beneath the trophy of the cross, and immediately above the embroidered streamer.

'The emperor constantly made use of this salutary sign as a safeguard against every adverse and hostile power, and commanded that others similar to it should be carried at the head of all his armies.'

That Cynewulf was familiar with the story is evident from the passage in the *Elene* (69–104):

> þā wearð on slǣpe sylfum ætȳwed
> þām cāsere, þǣr hē on corðre swæf,
> sigerōfum gesegen swefnes wōma :
> þūhte him wlitescȳne on weres hāde,
> hwīt ond hīwbeorht, hæleða nāthwylc
> geȳwed, ǣnlicra þonne hē ǣr oððe sīð
> gesēge under swegle. Hē of slǣpe onbrægd,
> eoforcumble beþeaht ; him se ār hraðe,
> wlitig wuldres boda, wið þingode,
> ond be naman nemde (nihthelm tōglād) :
> 'Constantīnus ! hēht ⌐ē Cyning engla,
> wyrda Wealdend wǣre bēodan,
> duguða Dryhten. Ne ondrǣd þū ðē,
> ðēah ⌐ē elþēodige egesan hwōpan
> heardre hilde ; þū tō heofenum beseoh
> on wuldres Weard ; þǣr ðū wraðe findest
> sigores tācen.' Hē wæs sōna gearu
> þurh þæs hālgan hǣs, hreðerlocan onspēon,
> ūp lōcade, swā him se ār ābēad,
> fǣle friðowebba. Geseah hē frætwum beorht
> wlīti wuldres trēo ofer wolcna hrōf,
> golde geglenged ; gimmas līxtan ;
> wæs se blāca bēam bōcstafum āwriten
> beorhte ond lēohte : ' Mid þȳs bēacne ðū
> on þām frēcnan fǣre fēond oferswīðesð,
> geletest lāð werod.' þā þæt lēoht gewāt,
> ūp sīðode, ond se ār somed
> on clǣnra gemang. Cyning wæs þȳ blīðra
> ond þē sorglēasra, secga āldor,
> on fyrhðsefan þurh þā fægeran gesyhð.
> Hēht þā onlīce æðelinga hlēo,
> beornā bēaggifa, swā hē þæt bēacen geseah,
> heria hildfruma, þæt him on heofonum ǣr
> geīewed wearð, ofstum myclum
> Constantīnus Crīstes rōde,
> tīrēadig cyning tācen gewyrcan.

Ælfric derives his information on the subject from Rufinus' version of Euse-bius, ascribing the authorship, however, to Jerome. He says (*Hom.* z. 304) :

' þā fēɪde se cāsere swīðe carful mid fyrde, and gelōme behēold wið heofonas
weard, biddende georne godcundne fultum. Ðā geseah hē on swefne, on ðām
scīnendan ēastdǣle, Drihtnes rōdetācn dēorwurðlice scīnan; and him sǣdon ðā
tō gesewenlice englas: " þū cāsere Constantīne, mid ðisum tācne oferswīð ðīne
wiðerwinnan." And hē āwōc ðā blīðe for ðǣre gesihðe and for ðān behātenan
sige, and mearcode him on hēafde hālig rōdetācn, and on his gūðfanan, Gode tō
wurðmynte.'

Stories of the apparition of a cross in the heavens (see Brewer, *Dictionary of
Miracles*, pp. 72-73, 282, 314) were related by Cyril of Jerusalem (A. D. 386), by
Gregory Nazianzen concerning the Emperor Julian, by others concerning St.
Ouen (646), etc. Cf. Alban Butler, *Lives of the Saints*, Sept. 14, note.

One of the most recent occurrences of this sort is stated to have been in 1719.
It is related of Colonel James Gardiner by Doddridge, and from the latter is
excerpted by Sir Walter Scott in Note C to Waverley. On account of a significant correspondence with another passage of the *Christ* (see note on 1379-
1498) I quote a brief extract: ' Lifting up his eyes, he apprehended to his extreme
amazement that there was before him, as it were suspended in the air, a visible
representation of the Lord Jesus Christ upon the cross, surrounded on all sides
with a glory; and was impressed, as if a voice, or something equivalent to a voice,
had come to him, to this effect (for he was not confident as to the very words):
" O sinner, did I suffer this for thee, and are these the returns?" ' (*Works* 1. 248).

As affording indications that the Church recognized a connection between the
vision of Constantine and the Sign of the Son of Man, we may refer to the Feast of
the Invention of the Cross (3 May) and of the Exaltation of the Cross (14 September). At the First Vespers of these Feasts, the hymn is ' Vexilla Regis prodeunt,'
and the Antiphon of the Magnificat begins: ' O Crux splendidior cunctis astris.'
At the Second Nocturn of the Invention, the First (Fourth) Lesson begins:
' Post insignem victoriam quam Constantinus imperator, divinitus accepto signo
Dominicae crucis, ex Maxentio reportavit, Helena Constantini mater, in somnis
admonita, conquirendae crucis studio Jerosolymam venit.' At the end of the
Third Lesson occurs the Respond: ' Hoc signum crucis erit in caelo cum Dominus ad judicandum venerit; tunc manifesta erunt abscondita cordis nostri' (cf.
1036-8, 1045-1056). The beginning of this is likewise used at the First Vespers,
the Third Nocturn, Terce, and Nones of the Invention, and at First Vespers,
First, Second, and Third Nocturns, Terce, and Nones of the Exaltation.

May it not be that in the story by Eusebius we have the original suggestion
for the following lines in the *Dream of the Rood* (14-17)?

> Geseah ic wuldres trēow
> wǣdum geweorðode wynnum scīnan,
> gegyred mid golde; gimmas hæfdon
> bewrigene weorðlice Wealdes trēow.

We have seen that the Labarum was adorned with both gold and precious
stones (cf. *Dream of the Rood* 75-77, where there is apparently a reference to
the Invention). Perhaps the *wǣdum* of v. 15 might refer to the square banner
attached to the cross as made under Constantine's direction.

Note that *sigebēacen* is used in the *Elene*, *sigebēam* in both the *Elene* and the
Dream of the Rood, to denote the cross, and that *sigbecn* occurs in the runic inscrip-

tion on the Bewcastle Column (Sweet, *OET.*, p. 124). This points to the deep impression made by the Constantine story.

1085. blōde bistēmed. So *Brussels Cross* 2 (Grein-Wülker *Bibliothek* 2. 489). Cf. *Dream of the Rood* 47-8 : 'Eall ic wæs mid blōde bestēmed, begoten of þæs guman sīdan '; 23-24 : 'hwīlum hit wæs mid wǣtan bestēmed, beswyled mid swātes gange.'

This conception of the blood-stained cross is at least as early as Paulinus of Nola, who writes (*Epist.* 32. cap. 14) :

> Ardua floriferae crux cingitur orbe coronae,
> Et *Domini fuso tincta cruore* rubet.

And again (cap. 17) :

> Inter floriferi caeleste nemus Paradisi,
> Sub *cruce sanguinea* niveo stat Christus in agris.

Cf. Fortunatus, ' Vexilla Regis prodeunt ':

> Arbor decora et fulgida,
> Ornata Regis purpura.

1087. swāte. Not 'sweat' (Go.). Th. tr. the hemistich : 'shall see with sweating.'

1088ᵇ-1091ᵃ. Br. paraphrases : 'All shade is banished by its brilliancy. . . . The evil see it for their torment and their teen.'

1090 ff. Cf. (Pseudo-) Augustine, *Sermo* 155 (Migne 39. 2052) : 'Sed quare crux apparebit tunc ? . . . Ut agnoscant consilium iniquitatis suae, qui Dominum majestatis crucifixerunt ; per hoc enim signum impudens Judaearum redarguitur impietas. . . . Quid autem miraris si crucem afferens veniet ubi et ipsa vulnera ostendit. *Tunc videbunt*, inquit, *in quem compunxerunt* (Jn. 19. 27). . . . Tunc ostendet vulnera, et crucem manifestabit, ut ostendat quoniam ipse est qui crucifixus est.'

1090. getēod. This would mean 'made,' as, e.g., in *Dan.* 111.

1091. þrēa. Frucht (p. 82) demands a disyllabic form, referring to *PBB.* 10. 479.

1092ᵇ. Gollancz thus interprets : ' *wita ne cuþun*, "they did not know " ; *wita* = *witan* ; *cuþun* used as auxiliary ; Gr. construes *wita* as gen. plur. of *wite*, "punishment"; cp. l. 1212, *wita ne cuþun*, which Gr. treats similarly ; the omission of the *n* in the phrase is, probably, due to the northern archetype.' Grein renders *wita* ' für seine Schmerzen.'

'For *wihte* cf. 1048, 1556 ; Th. already saw the remedy.

1097ᵇ-1098ᵃ. Cf. 2 Cor. 5. 21. Th. 'whose body no crime committed, wicked sins '; Gr. 'dass keine Sünde that noch Lasters Frevel sein Leib auf Erden '; Go.¹ 'whose body wrought no sin, nor guilty was of any wicked deed '; Go.² ' He whose body wrought no crime, nor any wicked sin.' Professor Bright paraphrases : ' With this price, (namely) because (that) his body was sinless, with this he released us.' The passage may be corrupt.

1100. As suggested in the Variants, see *Bl. Hom.* 123. 8 : ' . . . þe ūre Drihten ǣr þurh eornesse tō þǣm ǣrestan men cwæð : *Terra es, et in terram ibis.*' — **gemonian.** Grein made the emendation, and no doubt correctly.

1101-2. Cf. (Pseudo-) Augustine, *Sermo* 155 (Migne 39. 2051) : 'Tanta enim

erit eminentia splendoris in Christo ut etiam clarissima caeli luminaria prae fulgore luminis divini abscondantur. . . . Considerasti quanta virtus sit signi, hoc
est, crucis: *Sol obscurabitur, et luna non dabit lumen suum ;* crux vero fulgebit,
et obscuratis luminaribus caeli delapsisque sideribus sola radiabit, ut discas quoniam crux et luna lucidior et sole erit praeclarior, quorum splendorem divini
luminis illustrata fulgore superabit. Quemadmodum enim ingredientem regem in
civitatem, exercitus antecedit, praeferens humeris signa atque vexilla regalia, . . .
ita Domino descendente de caelis praecedet exercitus angelorum, qui signum illud,
id est, triumphale vexillum sublimibus humeris praeferentes, divinum regis caelestis ingressum terris trementibus nuntiabunt.' This is adapted, with but slight
changes, by Julianus (Pomerius), Archbishop of Toledo from 680 to 690 (*Progno-
sticon* lib. 3. cap. 5; Migne 96. 500).

1101. **rēade.** With blood.

1102. **gyld.** In this sense *Gen.* 101, 1104, 1109. Br. paraphrases: ' The sun
is gone; it shines instead of the sun.'

1103. **firenum fordōne.** Cf. 994.

1105-6. Th. misunderstands: ' Shall see to their own harm, that it had best
become them, that they it to good purpose would have understood.' Gr. 'sie
sehen sich zum Harme, was zum Heile ihnen kam, wofern zum Guten sie's
begreifen wollten'; Go. 'the best thing in the world shall seem their bane, when
they would fain regard it as their bliss '; Go.[1] note: ' Lit. " They shall see as their
bane that which came to them best." '

The interpretation must begin with *þǣr* = 'if,' as in 1494; the *woldan* must
evidently be pluperfect, since their willingness at the Judgment Day could no
longer avail. It follows that *bicwōm* must be regarded as doing duty for a pret.
opt. (= *bicwōme*). In other words, the cross, which, had they regarded it as a
means of salvation, would have conduced to their greatest weal, is now the token
of their condemnation; cf. 1083, 1090-2.

1107 ff. Cf. Zech. 12. 10; Rev. 1. 7; Ps. 22. 16.

1107. **wunde.** Cf. (Pseudo-) Augustine, *Sermo* 181 (Migne 39. 2087): 'Vulnera portavit; ipsa iterum reportabit. Crucem retulit cum triumpho; signum Filii
hominis vobis parebit in caelo.' Cf. the sermon in MS. Bodl. Jun. 24 (see note
on 1634[b]) : ' Đonne ætȳweð Drihten þā rōde þe hē on þrōwade; and þēr scīneð lēoht
ofer eallne middangeard ; and hē ætȳweð þā wunda on his sīdan, and þǣra nægla
wunda swā þā on his handum and fōtum, þe hē mid wes on rōde gefæstnod, swā
blōdig swā hī wēron on þām forman dæge. Đonne cwið se ēca Cyning tō ānra
gehwylcum : " Men þā lēofestan, sege mē hwet geworhtest þū, oþþe hwet gecwēde
þū, oþþe hwet gedydest þū? Syle wedd be þissum eallum þe ic for þē dyde and
for þē þrōwade." Đonne andswaraþ se man ūrum Drihtne and cwið : " Nebbe ic
ǣnig wedd tō syllanne nimþe mīne." '

See also Böddeker, *Altengl. Dicht.*, p. 241 :

> þenne shal segge oure Louerd
> to Seinte Marie,
> bringinde þe rode opon ys bake
> þat stod on Caluarie,
> ant schowend vs hise fet
> ant honden al blody.

This is common in the representations of the Last Judgment on the rose windows of cathedrals, and elsewhere (Didron, *Christian Iconography* I. 256).

oud **þā openan dolg.** Cf. *Dream of Rood* 46-7 : 'þā dolg . . . , opene in widhlemmas.'

1109. **swā.** *Perhaps* as in 984 ; see note.

1110. Note the tenderness. Cf. 1455.

1111-12. From Jn. 19. 34 ; cf. 1447ᵇ-1449ᵃ, 1458.

1111. Cf. *An.* 970.

1112. Cf. *Jul.* 292.

1115. Cf. 1081.

1116. **open, orgete.** So *An.* 760.— **for ǣlda lufan.** Anticipatory of 1379 ff. ; cf. 1433, 1470 ; *Hel.* 5505 ; *Musp.* 103.

1120 ff. Cf. Mt. 27. 29-30; etc.

1120ᵃ. Cf. *An.* 671.

1121. **spātl.** Cf. 1435-6. *El.* 300 has *spāld ;* see Variants, and *Gram.* 196. z.

1123. Cf. Mt. 26. 67. — **helfūse.** Only *An.* 50.

1125-6. Cf. 1443ᵇ-1445.

1127. **dysige.** There is syncopation in Lind. Matt. 7. 26 ; Cosijn notes no instances in EWS. It is exceptional in the poetry, *Rid.* 12³ being the only other example.

1127ᵇ-1198. From Gregory *Hom. in Evang.* ɪ. 10, as pointed out by Dietrich (p. 212) : ' Omnia quippe elementa auctorem suum venisse testata sunt. Ut enim de eis quiddam usu humano loquar : Deum hunc caeli esse cognoverunt, quia protinus stellam miserunt. Mare cognovit, quia sub plantis ejus se calcabile praebuit. Terra cognovit, quia eo moriente contremuit. Sol cognovit, quia lucis suae radios abscondit. Saxa et parietes cognoverunt, quia tempore mortis ejus scissa sunt. Infernus agnovit, quia hos quos tenebat mortuos, reddidit. Et tamen hunc, quem Dominum omnia insensibilia elementa senserunt, adhuc infidelium Judaeorum corda Deum esse minime cognoscunt, et duriora saxis scindi ad poenitendum nolunt ; eumque confiteri abnegant, quem elementa, ut diximus, aut signis aut scissionibus Deum clamabant.' Go.¹ omits several words, and thus makes nonsense of the second sentence.

This was translated by Ælfric, *Hom.* I. 108 : ' Ealle gesceafta oncnēowon heora Scyppendes tōcyme, būton ꝺām ārlēasum Iūdēiscum ānum. Heofonas oncnēowon heora Scyppend, ꝺā-ꝺā hī on his ācennednysse nīwne steorran ætēowdon. Sǣ oncnēow, ꝺā-ꝺā Crīst mid drīum fōtwylmum ofer hyre ȳꝺa mihtelice ēode. Sunne oncnēow, þā-þā hēo on his ꝺrōwunge hire lēoman fram middæge oꝺ nōn behȳdde. Stānas oncnēowon, ꝺā-ꝺā hī on his forꝺsīꝺe sticmǣlum tōburston. Sēo eorꝺe oncnēow, ꝺā-ꝺā hēo on his ǣriste eall byfode. Hell oncnēow, ꝺā-ꝺā hēo hire hæftlingas unꝺances forlēt. And ꝺēah þā heardheortan Iūdēi noldon for eallum ꝺam tācnum þone sōꝺan Scyppend tōcnāwan, þe þā dumban gesceafta undergēaton, and mid gebīcnungum geswutolodon.'

Ælfric again renders it in a slightly different form, *Hom.* I. 228. Thorpe was misled, by finding the passage in Ælfric, into assuming that Cynewulf derived it from Ælfric. He thus comments (*Hom.* I. 622) : ' The passage is evidently the original of the lines in the Codex Exoniensis, p. 69, 30 sq., and contributes to strengthen the opinion that Cynewulf was the author of that work, as well as of the Vercelli poetry. To him Ælfric dedicated his *Life of S. Æthelwold.*' On this Dietrich remarks : 'Beide schöpften unabhängig aus derselben Quelle; somit kann diese Stelle auch nicht eine Stütze der Behauptung sein, Cynewulf sei ein Zeitgenosse Ælfric's gewesen, was mit der Sprachgeschichte geradezu unvereinbar ist.'

1127b-1132. Tr. by Bugge ; see note on 1130.

1128. Cf. *An.* 799.

1130. **cwiōdun.** Sievers' emendation is hardly necessary. For the change of construction, cf. Bede 595. 42 (as quoted by Wülfing 2. (86)) : 'Đā *geseah* hēo . . . mycel lēoht *cuman,* & eall þæt hūs *gefylde.*'

þēah hī cwice nǣron. A modern commentator on Luke, Godet, says : 'On ne peut méconnaître une relation profonde, d'un côté entre l'homme et la nature, de l'autre entre l'humanité et Christ.'

It has sometimes been maintained that this passage, and the similar one in *The Dream of the Rood,* merely echo the Old Norse account of the weeping for Balder, as contained in the *Gylfaginning* and elsewhere. Bugge (*Studien über die Entstehung der Nordischen Götter- und Heldensagen,* pp. 59–61) reverses the order: 'Dieses Motiv vom Weinen der gesammten Natur über Baldr stammt, nach meiner Meinung, aus der mittelalterlichen Schilderung von Christi Tod. . . . In dem oben erwähnten altenglischen Gedicht vom Kreuz heisst es : "Finsterniss hatte verhüllt mit Wolken des Herrschers Leichnam ; über das helle Licht fiel der Schatten schwer, dunkel unter den Wolken. *Die ganze Schöpfung weinte ;* sie jammerten über des Königs' Fall. Christus war am Kreuz." Stephens, der zuerst diese Stelle mit der Erzählung von Baldr zusammenstellte, hat gemeint, dieser Zug von dem Weinen der ganzen Kreatur im Gedicht vom Kreuz sei aus dem heidnischen Baldrmythus herübergenommen [*Runic Monuments* 1. 432]; doch diese Auffassung scheint mir unzulässig. Es ist nichts was bewiese dass die heidnischen Engländer je den Mythus von dem unschuldigen Gott Baldr kannten, von dem wir im Norden erst aus Quellen Kunde haben die wahrscheinlich jünger als das altenglische Kreuzgedicht sind. Sodann hat das Weinen im Kreuzgedicht, wo es in einer vollständig christlichen Umgebung erwähnt wird, auch nicht die Bedeutung wie im Baldrmythus, nämlich den Dahingeschiedenen aus dem Reiche des Todes zu erlösen.' Bugge then refers to our poem, translating vv. 1127b-1132, 1169-1176, 1182-1190, 1208-1213. He then adduces Dietrich's discovery of the source, ascribing the latter to about the year 592, and adds : 'Den Gedanken, dass die stumme Natur bei Christi Tod seine Gottheit bezeugt, hat Cynewulf von Gregor entlehnt. Cynewulf, der seine Quellen mit dichterischer Freiheit benützt, bezeichnet deutlicher als Gregor die Sprache der stummen Natur beim Tod des Erlösers als Jammer, aber dies hat seinen natürlichen Grund darin, dass Gregor die Zeugnisse der Natur für Jesu Gottheit bei seiner Geburt, während seines Lebens auf Erden, und bei seinem Tod zusammenfasst, während Cynewulf sich insbesondere mit seinem Tod beschäftigt.'

Bugge points out the occurrence of the same thought in the *Heliand,* v. 5674, and cites the earlier passage to the same general effect from a sermon of Leo the Great (440–461) on the Passion (*Serm. VI de Pass. Dom.,* cap. 4): 'Exaltatum autem Jesum ad se traxisse omnia, non solum nostrae substantiae passione, sed etiam totius mundi commutatione monstratum est. Pendente enim in patibulo

Creatore, *universa creatura congemuit*, et crucis clavos omnia simul elementa senserunt. Nihil ab illo supplicio liberum fuit. Hoc in communionem sui et terram traxit et caelum ; *hoc petras rupit*, monumenta aperuit, *inferna reseravit, et densarum horrore tenebrarum radios solis abscondit.* Debebat hoc testimonium suo mundus Auctori, ut in occasu Conditoris sui vellent universa finiri.' Other passages to the like effect are found, as Bugge notes, in other sermons by the same Pope. He also observes that the words, *In tua morte omnis contremuit creatura*, are found in the Gospel of Nicodemus (Tischendorf[2], p. 399). Finally, he cites as illustrations passages from the *Cursor Mundi* (p. 959), the *Disputatio inter Mariam et Crucem* (Morris, *Legends of the Holy Rood*, p. 145), the Cornish *Passion of our Lord* (ed. Stokes, pp. 64–5), Uhland's *Volkslieder*, No. 443, and the Breton *Grand Mystère de Jésus*, pp. 148 ff., appealing also to plastic art as described by Piper, *Mythologie und Symbolik der Christlichen Kunst* 2. 156, and Menzel, *Christliche Symbolik* 1. 526.

1133. The punctuation because of the close association in Lk. 23. 45. The Vulgate has : ' Et obscuratus est sol, et velum templi scissum est medium.' On this Bede's comment is (Migne 92. 619) : ' Volens [sc. Lucas] enim miraculum miraculo adjungere, cum dixisset *sol obscuratus est*, continuo subjungendum existimavit : *Et velum templi scissum est medium*.' — þrēam āþrysmed. Th. ' with sufferings obscured '; Gr. ' mit Finsternis befangen '; Go., Br. 'darkened with misery.'

1134. Gollancz notes : ' The alliteration is wanting; Gr. reads [*hu*] *in hierusalem*, etc. ; it is noteworthy that the chief initial letters in the line — *h, g, c* — approximate to alliterative effect (? cp. l. 23).' The editor might have compared 533; *Gu.* 785; *Sat.* 234, as other instances of ' alliteration wanting,' i.e. of *g* alliterating with the initial of *Hierusalem*.

Perhaps Grein's emendation should be adopted; it would certainly relieve the difficulty presented by *forbærst* as an independent verb.

godwebba cyst. On this curtain, cf. Plummer, *International Critical Commentary on Luke* 23. 45 : ' Between the Holy Place and the Holy of Holies (Exod. 26. 31 ; Lev. 21. 23 ; 24. 3 ; Heb. 6. 19 ; comp. Heb. 10. 20) there was a curtain called τὸ δεύτερον καταπέτασμα (Heb. 9. 3), to distinguish it from the curtain which separated the outer court from the Holy Place.'

1137. ufan. Matt. has (27. 51) 'a summo usque deorsum '; so Mk. (15. 38).

1138. on twām styccum. This from either Matthew or Mark. The former has (Mt. 27. 51) *in duas partes* (WS. *on twēgen dǣlas*) ; the latter (15. 38), *in duo* (WS. *on twā*). Lk., on the other hand (23. 45), has *medium* (WS. *on middan*).

temples segl. The *velum templi* of Mt., Mk., Lk. The MS. Gospels have, for *velum*, *wāhryft* (·*rift*) ; the North, *wāghrægl* ; the Rushworth Matt., *wāgryft* ; and the Rushworth Mk. and Lk., *wāghræ(g)l*. Is *segl* due to confusion with the commoner sense of Lat. *velum*, i.e. ' sail ' ?

1139. wundorblēom geworht. On embroidery among the Anglo-Saxons, cf. Turner, *Hist. Anglo-Saxons* 2. 250–1.

1140. seaxes ecg. So *Rid.* 27[6]. *Seax* here may = 'knife.' It is not easy to decide.

1142. mūras. ' Parietes.' — stānas. Cf. Mt. 27. 51.

1143. myrde. Cf. *An.* 747; *Jul.* 412. Cosijn comments: '*egsan myrred?* aber der Ausdruck is⁺ unbelegt.' Th. 'was mindful of that terror' (see Variants); Gr. 'von Angst erschüttert'; Go.[1] 'was troubled sore with fear'; Go.[2] 'was marred through fear'; Br. 'marred by fear.'

1144ᵇ–1150. Tr. by Brooke.

1144ᵇ–1146. This does not follow Gregory, but apparently the Fifteen Signs; cf. Pseudo-Bede, in *PBB.* 6. 460: 'Prima die eriget se mare in altum quadraginta cubitis super altitudinem montium, et erit quasi murus.' But cf. 1163ᵇ ff.

1145. cræftes mealht. So Lat. *potentia virtutis*, Gr. κράτος τῆς ἰσχύος, 'power afforded by strength'; see *hygecræftig*, and cf. *Eph.* 1. 19; 6. 10; *El.* 558; *An.* 585.

clomme. Th., Go.[2], 'durance'; Gr. 'den Klammern'; Go. 'its bonds'; Br. 'clasping marges.'

1146. fæðm. The translators render 'bosom' or 'breast.' Gr. (*Spr.*) suggests 'expanse, tract, surface,' comparing *Doomsday* 54, *An.* 336; etc. *Eorþan fæðm* occurs *Ph.* 487; *Beow.* 3049.

1147. stede. Cf. *Doomsday* (Bede) 107: 'stedelēase steorran hrēosað.'

1148. swǣsne. See note on 617.

On þā sylfan tīd. Gr. connects this with the first hemistich. The phrase precedes the verb, as *Gen.* 2391; otherwise *Men.* 231. The preceding sentences (except that in 1141, which begins boldly with an adverb of manner) are introduced by connectives, or have a note of time; in this sentence there would be neither, if our phrase were drawn to the preceding. Besides, without this note of time, the perception of the heaven would seem to relate wholly to the birth of Christ. It needs this indication to keep the connection sufficiently close, and, in any event, it is difficult to see what the heaven did on *this* occasion.

1149–1150. hēalīce torhtne. Br. 'so upsoaring and so sheen.'

1150. Cf. *Il.* 18. 485:

ἐν δὲ τὰ τείρεα πάντα, τάτ' οὐρανὸς ἐστεφάνωται.

And the signs every one wherewith the heavens are crowned,

or, as Pope has it:

The starry lights that heaven's high convex crowned.

Cf. Hes. *Theog.* 382.

tungolgimmum. So in Spenser, *Hymn of Heavenly Love* 58–60:

Not this round heaven, which we from hence behold,
Adorned with thousand lamps of burning light,
And with ten thousand *gemmes* of shining gold.

Cf. Shak. *Sonn.* 27:

Which, like a *jewel* hung in ghastly night,
Makes black night beauteous, and her old face new.

Perhaps also *R. and J.* I. v. 47–8:

It seems she hangs upon the cheek of night
Like a rich *jewel* in an Ethiope's ear.

Ben Jonson, *Underwoods* (ed. 1640, p. 241):

The stars that are the *jewels* of the night.

Milton, *P. L.* 4. 649 :

> And these the *gems* of heaven, her starry train.

Cf. *P. L.* 4. 604–5 :

> Now glowed the firmament
> With living *sapphires.*

Cf. also *Com.* 732–4 :

> The sea o'erfranght would swell, and the unsought *diamonds*
> Would so emblaze the forehead of the deep
> And so bestud with stars, etc.

Pope, *Odyssey* 15. 123 :

> Like radiant Hesper o'er the *gems* of night.

Shelley, *Calderon* 2. 116–7 :

> In his high palace roofed with brightest *gems*
> Of living light — call them the stars of Heaven.

And for the verb in this sense, cf. *Prol. Hellas* 18; *Hellas* 770; *Triumph of Life* 22 ; *Q. Mab.* 1. 99 ; 5. 144.

In the edition of 1830, Tennyson has (*Poems* 144) :

> The *diamonded* night.

1151. bodan. Singular in Grein, *D.*, though plural in *Spr.*, as well as in Thorpe and Gollancz. It is probably singular, referring to the star in the east. Cf. Ælfric, *Hom.* 1. 298 : 'þā-þā Crīst ācenned wæs, þā sende sēo heofen nīwne steorran, ðe bodade Godes ācennednysse.' So *Hom.* 1. 108 (note on 1127ᵇ– 1198), and *Hom.* 1. 228 : 'Heofonas oncnēowon Crīstes ācennednysse, forðan ðā-ðā hē ācenned wæs, þā wearð gesewen nīwe steorra.'

Cf. Giles Fletcher, *Christ's Victory and Triumph*, Triumph over Death :

> And at His birth, as all the stars heaven had
> Were not enough, but a new star was made,
> So now both new and old, and all away did fade.

1154ᵃ. Cosijn says : 'Man folge Grein' (see Variants). This is probably correct, though not absolutely necessary.

1154ᵇ. þēodwundor. *þēod-* is an intensive, deriving its signification from the notion of multitude.

1155 ff. Cf. Mt. 27. 51–53.

1155. āgeaf. Cf. Rev. 20. 13.

1157. bifēn. Gr. compares *gedēn*, 1265; add *fordēn*, 1206; see *Gram.* 429, N. 1.

1159ᵇ–1179. Condensed paraphrase by Brooke.

1161. þā hēo þæt weorud āgeaf. Cf. 30–32, 145 ff., 558 ff., 730 ff., and notes.

1165. tīrmeahtig Cyning. So *Ph.* 175.— **tredne.** The meaning must be inferred from the cognate verb.

1167–8. Cf. Mt. 14. 25, 26.

1169–1179. Brother Azarias slightly changes Thorpe's translation, and adds : 'Here is a remembrance of the myth of all nature weeping over the death of Baldr.'

1169–1176. Tr. by Bugge ; see note on 1130.

1169. blēdum. Th. 'branches'; Gr., Bugge 'blüten '; Go. 'blossoms'; Br. 'blossoming.' Gr. (*Spr.*) gives the various meanings, 'germen, frons, fructus, herba, flos.'

1170. monige, nāles fēa. Cf. 1194. This peculiar combination of direct statement with litotes is found, e.g. Herodotus 7. 40. 4 : στρατὸς παντοίων ἐθνέων ἀναμὶξ, οὐ διακεκριμένοι; 7. 46. 13 : πολλάκις, καὶ οὐκὶ ἅπαξ; 7. 226. 11 : ὑπὸ σκιῇ, . . . καὶ οὐκ ἐν ἡλίῳ; cf. 2. 172. 6 ; Hom. *Il.* 1. 416; for negative followed by positive, Herod. 7. 58. 12; 7. 119. 22 ; Plutarch, *De Is. et Osir.* 7. I owe this note to my friend, Mr. Charles G. Osgood, Jr., Fellow in English of Yale University.

1172–1173. Cf. 1423, 1441ᵇ–1442.

1174–1176ᵃ. Based upon the Apocryphal 2 Esdras (4 Esdras) 5. 5 : 'Et de ligno sanguis stillabit.' This eventually becomes one of the Fifteen Signs of the Judgment, attributed throughout the Middle Ages to Jerome, but not found in his works. Cf. Nölle, in *PBB.* 6. 413–476, and see *Anglia* 11. 369–371, where Assmann prints an extract from MS. Cott. Vesp. D. 14, fol. 102ᵃ, from which I extract : ' On þām fīften dæige ealle wyrte and ealle trēowwcs āgeafeð rēad swāt swā blōdes dropen ; þæt dōð þā wyrten for þȳ þæt þā synfulle rhæn hēo trǣden, and þā trēowen forþan þe þā synfulle hæfden freome of heom and of heora wǣstmen.'

1175. rēade ond þicce. Grein classifies as adverbs, comparing, for *rēade*, *Rid.* 70¹.

1177ᵇ. Cf. 1192ᵃ.

1179. þrōwinga. Br. 'travail.'

1182–1190. Tr. by Bugge; see note on 1130.

1183. forht āfongen. So *Jul.* 320; cf. *forht āfǣred, Ph.* 525.

1184. cūþen. Cosijn: '"haberent"; vgl. *Gen.* 357.'

1185. wēndon swā-þēah wundrum. Th. 'weened yet wondrously'; Gr. 'so wusten sie es durch ein Wunder doch '; Go.¹ 'yet wondrously they knew it'; Go.² 'yet wondrously had they knowledge.' Perhaps 'had a dim perception,' 'had an inkling,' might better express the force of *wēndon.*

1186–8ᵇ. Cf. *El.* 565, and esp. 808–9.

1187ᵃ. So *An.* 815ᵃ.

1188. flintum heardran. Cf. 6; *Rid.* 41⁷⁸. The expression is Biblical : cf. such passages as Ezek. 3. 9; Jer. 5. 3; Job 41. 24. However, the comparison of the heart to a stone is also Homeric : *Od.* 23. 103.

1194ᵇ. Note the artistic parallel, 1198ᵇ.

1195. earcnanstān. Cf. Isa. 28. 16 ; 1 Pet. 2. 6; or perhaps Dan. 2. 34, 35, 45. The two conceptions, as I have elsewhere said, seem to have coalesced as early as the second century; cf. Irenaeus, *Contr. Haer.,* quoted in Salzer, p. 113, and Mone's Hymn No. 507, str. 9. According to this view, the 'mountain' of Dan. 2. 45 represented the Virgin Mary ; cf. 1198ᵇ. The forms of the word are various : *eorcan-, eorcnan-, eorclanstān.* The ON. has *iarknasteinn.* Grein compares Goth. *airknis,* OHG. *erchan,* but refers to Bouterwek in *Haupt's Zs.* 11. 90.

1196. So *An.* 567 ; cf. *An.* 111.

1197. wuldres Āgend. So *An.* 210, 1717 ; *Jul.* 223.

1198. Ordfruma. Cf. 227. — **cwēnn.** Cf. 276. The form is peculiar.

1199. **Hwæs wēneð sē.** Th. 'What thinketh he'; Gr. 'Was wähnt der Mann doch'; Go. 'What hope hath he?' Rather our familiar, 'What is he thinking of?'

1201. **earfeðu.** Cf. 1171.

1203. **āgan mōsten.** Cf. 1246, 1402.

1204. **Swā þām bið grorne.** For the construction, with *grorne* as adv., cf. 1079. — **on þām grimman dæge.** Cf. 1080, 1333.

1205ᵇ-1206ᵃ. Th. 'whom the Lord's death shall for their crimes foredo'; Gr. 'wer durch Frevel verthan dann soll des Waltenden Tod (schauen).' In the *Spr.* Gr. connects *dēað* and *firenum*.

1206ᵇ. **dolg.** Cf. 1107.

1207. **wīte.** Th. 'punishment'; Gr. 'sein qualvoll Leiden'; Go. 'torments.' Th., Go. put the stop after *sefan.*

1208-1213. Tr. by Bugge.

1208. **hȳ.** There is a real difficulty here. *Hū* occurs elsewhere after *gesēon*, as, for example, *Exod.* 88; *Ps.* 65⁴; if this reading is retained, however, the clause explanatory of *sorga* (1212ᵇ ff.) occurs at a great distance from the *hū*, and the clause immediately following *hū* seems intrusive. Then, too, the retention of *hū*, without the provision of a direct object for *lȳsde*, requires one either to postulate for *lȳsde* some such meaning as *effected* (*through his redemption*) or else to suppose that the direct object is mentally to be supplied; and both of these are rather daring assumptions. On the other hand, *hȳ*, Grein's proposed reading, is supported by 1210, 1212, 1229, 1238, etc. (though the text also has *hī:* 1183, 1188, 1233, etc.), and it supplies an object for *lȳsde.* The epexegetical clause is still far from *sorga*, but this perhaps the poet could not help.

1210. **þurh milde mōd.** So *Part.* 9. — **mānweorca.** Only *Jul.* 439, 459, 505.

1211ᵃ. **tōme.** Adv. in Gr. Cf. OHG. *zōmi*, ON. *tōmr*, and OS. *tuomian.*

1211ᵇ-1212. Cf. *An.* 105-6.

1215. **gōdum.** The emendation according to 1234 (cf. 910).

1216-1231. Mt. 25. 31-33. Th., Go. continue the preceding sentence with a comma after *ungesǣlge.*

1216. See VI. a, b.

1219. **scrīfeð.** Cf. *Beow.* 979; *Jul.* 728; not found in the poetry in the sense of 'shrive.' — **bī gewyrhtum.** So 128, 1367.

1220. **rodera Wāldend.** This phrase is only found elsewhere in the *Christ* at the close of Part II, The Ascension (v. 865).

1221. See VII. b, c.

1223. **gecorene.** See VII. a. Cf. *Ps.* 64⁴.

1225. **womsceaþan.** See VII. e. Cf. 1569; *El.* 1299; *Jul.* 211.

1227ᵇ. See VII. d.

1228ᵃ. So *Gen.* 1797.

1229. **beofiað.** See VII. f.

1230ᵇ. See VII. g, h, i; contrast *ēowde*, 257 (I). The poet avoids the introduction of the word 'sheep'; so *Hel.* 4390; Otfrid 5. 20. 31.

1233ᵇ. Cf. 1219ᵇ.

1234. **ēðgesȳne.** So *Beow.* 1110, 1224; *El.* 256.

1235. **þrēo tācen.** Three signs (cf. note on 1267):

1. They (and their deeds) shall shine like the sun (1237–1241).

2. They shall be happy with the angels in heaven (1242–1246).

3. They shall be exempt from the misery of the wicked (1247–1259).

1239. burga gesetu. So *Sat.* 602. Th. 'the cities' dwellings'; Gr. 'die Sitze der Burgen'; Go. 'the homes on high,' 'the cities' dwelling.' Hardly satisfactory.

1240. ǣrgewyrhtu. Cf. *ǣr gedēnra*, 1265; *ǣrdǣdum, Doomsday* (Bede) 93, 96.

1241[b]. Cf. 1651[b]; *El.* 1110; *Gu.* 1287; esp. *Ph.* 601. See Mt. 13. 43.

1243. Th. 'that they for them in glory know the grace of the Supreme'; Gr. 'dass sie die Gaben des Waltenden sich in der Glorie wissen'; Go.[1] 'in glory shall they know their Sovran's grace'; Go.[2] 'that they shall know, for their glory, the Ruler's grace.' The reference of *in wuldre* is not clear; one would like to interpret: 'in the bestowal of glory (upon themselves).'

1246[a]. So *An.* 599[a].

1247–1259. Cf. Greg. *Hom. in Evang.* 40. 8 (Migne 76. 1308): 'Ut ergo peccatores in supplicio amplius puniantur, et eorum vident gloriam quos contempserunt, et .... Credendum vero est quod ante retributionem extremi judicii injusti in requie quosdam justos conspiciunt, ut eos videntes in gaudio non solum de suo supplicio, sed etiam de illorum bono crucientur. Justi vero in tormentis semper intuentur injustos, ut hinc eorum gaudium crescat, quia malum conspiciunt quod misericorditer evaserunt; tantoque majores ereptori suo gratias referunt, quanto vident in aliis quod ipsi perpeti, si essent relicti, potuerunt. Nec illam tantae beatitudinis claritatem apud justorum animum fuscat spectata poena reproborum, quia ubi jam compassio miseriae non erit, minuere procul dubio beatorum laetitiam non valebit. Quid autem mirum si dum justi injustorum tormenta conspiciunt, hoc eis veniat in obsequium gaudiorum, quando et in pictura niger color substernitur, ut albus vel rubeus clarior videatur? Nam sicut dictum est tanto bonis sua gaudia excrescunt, quanto eorum oculis damnatorum mala subterjacent quae evaserunt. Et quamvis eis sua gaudia ad perfruendum plene sufficiant, mala tamen reproborum absque dubio semper aspiciunt, quia qui Creatoris sui claritatem vident, nihil in creatura agitur quod videre non possint.' Adapted by Ælfric, *Hom.* 1. 334.

1247. þӯstra. Cf. note on 593.

1250. wyrma slite. The phrase is found in Wulfstan 209. 17; cf. *Dooms-day* (Bede) 168, 210. Go. 'luring [!] serpents' (reading *wlite*).

1251. byrnendra scole. Br. 'school [!] of burning creatures.'

1252. of þām. Not from the misery of the lost, but, as explained immediately after, that they are exempt from that misery.

1256. blǣdes ond blissa. Cf. 1346; *Gu.* 1348.

1260. sceal. For the omission of the infinitive, as frequently after *sculan*, see 233; *Beow.* 2816.

1265. gedēnra. Cosijn says: '*gedēnra* gehört zu *synne*, ist aber von *tō fela atolearfoða* attrahiert.'

1267. þroht. Cf. *Gu.* 1324. — **þēodbealu.** Only *An.* 1138.

þrēo healfa. The three are these (cf. note on 1235):

    1. They are to be wretched in hell (1268–1271; cf. 2, above).

    2. Their guilt is blazoned to the world (1272–1283; cf. 1, above).

    3. They have forfeited the bliss of heaven, which the righteous enjoy (1284–1300; cf. 3, above).

1272. earfeþu. Cosijn would read *earfeðe*, and is very likely right.

1279. mirce mægencræft. Power of darkness. Th. 'dark powerful craft'; Gr. 'ihre finstere Kraft'; Go. 'darksome craft.'

1280 ff. Cf. Gregory, *Moral.* lib. 18, cap. 48 (Migne 76. 84): 'Ibi quippe uniuscujusque mentem ab alterius oculis membrorum corpulentia non abscondet, sed patebit animus, patebit corporalibus oculis ipsa etiam corporis harmonia, sicque unusquisque tunc erit conspicabilis alteri, sicut nunc esse non potest conspicabilis sibi. Nunc autem corda nostra quandiu in hac vita sumus, quia ab altero in alterum videri non possunt, non intra vitrea, sed intra lutea vascula concluduntur. . . . In hac itaque terrestri domo quousque vivimus, ipsum, ut ita dicam, corruptionis nostrae parietem mentis oculis nullatenus penetramus, et vicissim in aliis videre occulta non possumus' (commenting Job 28. 17). For the general idea, cf. Mt. 10. 26; Lk. 12. 2; 1 Cor. 4. 5; (?) 1 Cor. 13. 12.

1282. scandum þurhwadene. Frucht remarks (p. 74): 'An den verkürzten Typ. A I darf für diesen Halbvers auch nicht gedacht werden, da ja der genannte Typus einen Nebenaccent in der ersten Senkung beansprucht.'

scīre glæs. Cf. *Bl. Hom.* 109. 36: 'Biþ þonne se flæschoma āscyred swā glæs; ne mæg ðæs unrihtes bēon āwiht bedīgled.'

So in Beaumont and Fletcher, *Philaster* III. ii :

> Make my breast
> Transparent as pure crystal, that the world,
> Jealous of me, may see the foulest thought
> My heart holds.

Cf. *ib.* I. i.: 'Every man in this age has not a soul of crystal, for all men to read their actions through.' More remote are *Two Noble Kinsmen* I. i. 111–3; Tennyson, *Princess* 2. 305–7.

1284–1300. Cf. note on 1247–1259.

1289. wepende sar. Th. 'sorely weeping'; Gr. 'wehevollen Schmerz'; Go. 'weeping sore' (part. and adv.). I make *sār* in some sense parallel to *sorg*, 1284; cf. *sār*, 1266.

1299. swīman. Cf. *Jud.* 30, 106.

1300. berað. See note on 1072. — **þæt.** Cosijn would emend to *þā*.

1301. Cosijn would read *bealodǣda*, gen. plur. But *unryhtes* is a sing.; why not *ǣlcere bealodǣde?* For the word, cf. *El.* 515; *Hy.* 4[19, 34].

1304. sægdon. Optative. — **tō gyrne.** So *Rid.* 80[7]. 'To their sorrow,' or, possibly, 'as an injury to themselves.' Th., Go. 'too well' (understanding *gyrne* as *georne*); Gr. 'zu grossem Kummer.'

1305. scrift. Cf. Ælfric, *Hom.* 1. 164: 'Cume forði gehwā crīstenra manna tō his *scrifte*, and his dīglan gyltas geandette.' So Wulfstan, p. 275: 'Godcunde bōte sēce man iorne tō his *scrifte*.' See especially Greg. *Moral.* lib. 8. cap. 20 (on Job 7. 11); Migne 75. 822: '*Iram Judicis in confessione praeveniunt electi*. Ori etenim suo parcit qui confiteri malum quod fecit erubescit. . . . Justus ori suo non parcit, quia iram Judicis districti praeveniens, verbis contra se propriae confessionis saevit. Hinc Psalmista ait: *Praeveniamus faciem ejus in confessione* (Psal. 94. 2). Hinc per Salomonem dicitur: *Qui abscondit scelera sua non dirigetur; qui autem confessus fuerit et dereliquerit ea misericordiam consequetur* (Prov. 28. 13).

Hinc rursum scriptum est: *Justus in principio accusator est sui* (Prov. 18. 17). Add Wulfstan 115. 12; 150. 2; 238. 11.

1307. bigǣð. Gollancz comments: ' I feel sure that here we have an instance of *bigān* in the sense of " to confess " (cp. MHG. *bigehan*), though no instance is recorded in Anglo-Saxon lexicons. The more usual usage of the word is "to commit"; Th. " when they commit sins "; similarly, Gr. Toller.' But Grein had already translated (*D.*) : ' Wenn man die Sünde *beichtet.*' Cosijn comments : ' *he*, i.e. *se scrift ; bigǣð*, "nachgeht," kommt sonst nur vor in *ðone æcer begān* (Toller), *plantan, impan begān, C. Past.* 381. 17.' The decision is difficult.

1308. gelācnigan. Cf. *Hy.* 1⁶.

1312. þǣr. ' If,' as 1106, 1494. ' If we only might see our sins with our bodily eyes ! ' Then, after a parenthetical reflection, the poet continues (1327–1333) : ' But we cannot see them with our bodily eyes; all the more necessary is it, therefore, that we scan the iniquity of the soul with the mind's eye ' (paraphrasing freely).

Cosijn remarks : ' Interpungiert man wie Assmann, dann bedeutet *þær* hier "utinam," wie *El.* 979, *Jul.* 570, und *Seel.* 141 (vgl. Got. *iþ wissedeis*, εἰ ἔγνως, Luc. 19. 42). Aber dann muss *wille*, v. 1318 [1317] in *scyle* geändert werden ; sonst wäre *þær* hypothetisch zu fassen, nach *ingeþoncas* Komma zu setzen, und würde v. 1317 [1316] in Prosa lauten : *þæt bið unasecgendlic.* Aber Assmann's Text bietet (mit Ausnahme von *wille*) wol hier das Richtige, wie auch *Ēalā* wahrscheinlich macht.' Cosijn's alternative suggestion would require the change of *magon* to *meahten*, of *wille* to *wolde*, and properly of the tense of the dependent verbs as well.

nū. Emphatic; cf. 1327.

1313ᵇ. So *El.* 514; *Jul.* 355, 710.

1314ᵇ. So *Jul.* 652ᵃ.

1316–1326. ' No one can express the eagerness with which every one will [we should expect ' ought to '] endeavor by all means to prolong and amend his life, so that he may pass his earthly career free from the reproach of men.' This reflection seems to me misplaced and inartistic — the most inartistic passage of the poem. The reference is not to the shame experienced at the Judgment Day in the presence of an assembled universe ; cf. *eorðbüendra, mid monnum,* and 1325ᵇ–1326. No, it is this life, and a bad name among men, that the poet is thinking of ; surely an anti-climax, as well as irrelevant. Even if we suppose that it originally belonged elsewhere, and has been misplaced by a copyist, the case is not much improved ; for it would be difficult to assign it a context into which it would fit. For a slighter infelicity in the *Elene*, cf. Kail, *Angl.* 12. 38.

1317. wille. ' Sceolde ' (?). Grein, s.v. *willan*, suggests ' wollen sollte,' and ; *D.*, ' sollen.' Cf. note on 1312.

1318. þurh ealle list. Frucht (p. 74) calls attention to the fact that the alliteration is, exceptionally, in the second foot. So in 241. — **lífes tiligan.** So *Sal.* 159.

1319. āðolian. Rieger (*Zs. f. d. Phil.* 1. 225) would derive the verb from *ādl*, and translate by ' deficere.' Th. ' endure '; Gr. (1317–9) ' mit welchem Eifer wir drum alle sollen hier fort und fort in Furcht unser Leben *adeln* immer mehr mit aller Kunst '; Go.¹ ' with how great zeal, by every artifice, each mortal striveth

(Go.[2] desireth) to attain life's goal, anxious to protract existence forth.' Gollancz comments: '*aðolian*, "to endure." I can see nothing against this straightforward way of rendering the word; Grein's view that it is OHG. *adaljan*, MHG. *edelen*, "nobilitare," is untenable; the sense of the whole passage has, I think, escaped both Th. and Gr. The rendering of the former is quite meaningless.'

Cosijn would emend *forð aðolian* to *fērð staðolian*. He says: '*forð aðolian*. Lächerlich: weder ein *āþolian* "to endure," noch ein Ahd. "*adaljan*" hilft uns hier aus der Not; *forð* ist *ferð* (vgl. v. 1361 [1360] und *Rä.* 74. 5), und *aðolian*, das manchen den Kopf irre machte, hat selbst den Kopf verloren, und ist verstümmelt aus *staðolian; ferð st.* ist bekannt genug. Aber vor *ferð* Komma.' This emendation deserves to be pondered, though it is rather bold.

Professor Bright would construe *fēores* with *tiligan*, and translate *forð aðolian* 'to endure patiently on,' or, to quote his words: '"to continue in patience"; a virtue that in prose might be expressed thus: *on geðyld ðurhwunian*.' But this notion, 'In your patience possess ye your souls' (cf. Lk. 21. 19) seems to me to have nothing to do with the context; I prefer to regard *aðolian* as virtually synonymous with *tiligan;* the notion seems to be 'to gain time for repentance and amendment (cf. 1322), so that he may come to live irreproachable.' We might, perhaps, extend the idea of finally living thus blameless among men into a resulting freedom from reproach at the Last Day, and thus connect it with 1272 ff.

1320. Note the rime. Cosijn remarks: '*þwēan* zweisylbig, *þrēan* einsylbig ist merkwürdig.'

synrūst. I thus commented on the word in *Mod. Lang. Notes* for May, 1889: 'The word *synrust* occurs once in poetry, *Chr.* 1321 [1320]; the simple *rust* apparently not at all. Grein translates "aerugo peccatorum, Sündenrost, Sündenschmutz." Whence did Cynewulf derive the word and the idea? He coined the word, I believe, as he did *synbyrðen, Chr.* 1300 [1299]; *synfā(h), Chr.* 1083 [1082]; *synlust, Chr.* 269; *synwracu, Chr.* 794, 1540 [1539]; *Gu.* 832; *synwund, Chr.* 757. The idea he found in Christian Latin writers. *Aerugo* is already used by Horace in the two senses of "envy, jealousy, illwill" and "avarice," and *ferrugo* appears to be once used in Latin in the sense of "envy." Such transferred senses of *rubigo* do not seem to occur in the classical literature; that is, this word seems never to indicate an evil passion, or sin in the abstract. Augustine, however (*Comment. on Ps.* 77 [78]: 46), assigns to the *rubigo* of his text the metaphorical signification of "superbia," though *rubigo* must here be taken to mean "blight, mildew." Prudentius seems to be the first to employ *rubigo* in the sense of "evil, sin." Cynewulf may very well have seen the *Cathemerinon* of this author, who was so popular during the whole Middle Ages, and an Old English gloss on whom has been published by Mone. If so, he probably knew the line, *Cath.* 7. 205 : 'quod limat aegram pectoris rubiginem.' Here *rubigo* is employed with a meaning different from that of Seneca's "*rubigo* animorum" (though a transitional sense may be found in *Epist.* 7. 7), and quite identical with that of Cynewulf's *synrust.* This theory is perhaps in a measure confirmed by an accessory fact. Dressel, the latest editor of Prudentius, seems to think that Prudentius may have composed two versions of some of his works, and that the glosses of Iso may represent various readings belonging to the alternative version :

'"Quos Prudentii vidi codd. vetustos, ii omnes et variis lectionibus et glossis aut interlinearibus aut ad marginem adpositis instructi erant, cum recentiores utrisque fere carerent. (Quae *Isonis* nomine feruntur, reliquis fere praestant.) Hinc collegerim aut Prudentium ipsum duas carminum recensiones confecisse, aut non multo*post eius obitum critici cuiusdam manum textum lectionum varietate suo sibi usui vel aliorum illustrasse" (Dressel, p. xxiv and note).

'It is significant that Iso's gloss upon *limat* is *purgat, mundat*, and that the phrase of *Chr.* 1321 [1320] is *synrust þwēan*. Now it would be a little more natural to translate *mundare, purgare* by *þwēan*, than *limare*. If, therefore, Cynewulf's copy of Prudentius substituted either of these synonyms for *limare*, the indebtedness of the Old English poet would be somewhat more evident. Should my association of the two passages be approved, it will be seen that we ought to translate *synrust* by "*rubigo* peccati" rather than by "aerugo peccatorum."'

1322. þone lȳtlan fyrst.   For the acc. as the measure of time, see Wülfing I. 266 (§ 119. 1. a).

þe hēr līfes sȳ.   Cosijn remarks: 'Vgl. Beda-Miller 462. 7 (v. 20): *þæt hē līfes wæs*. Später *be līfon bēon*, Thorpe, *An.*[2] 112; mehr Beispiele bei Toller.'

1326. līc ond sāwel.   See the Variants; also 1036. Grein adduces, as an occasional nom. *sāwle* (*sāule*): *Soul's Address* 10; *Ap.* 62; *Met.* 20[162]. As another *mōte* for *mōten* he cites *Ps. C.* 145; see also Wulfstan 10. 10; 25. 10, 20; 159. 8; 162. 14.   MS. has *sawle.*

1327–1333.   Cf. Greg. *Moral.* lib. 11. cap. 42 (Migne 75. 979): 'Per Psalmistam dicitur: *Delicta quis intelligit* (Psal. 18. 13)?   Quia videlicet peccata operis tanto citius cognoscuntur quanto exterius videntur, peccata vero cogitationis eo ad intelligendum difficilia sunt quo invisibiliter perpetrantur. Quisquis igitur aeternitatis desiderio anxius apparere venturo Judici desiderat mundus, tanto se subtilius nunc examinat quanto nimirum cogitat ut tunc terrori illius liber assistat, et ostendi sibi exorat ubi displicet, ut hoc in se per paenitentiam puniat, seque hic dijudicans injudicabilis fiat.'

1328. heortan ēagum.   'The eyes of the heart'; cf. Shakespeare's 'the mind's eye.'

1329. uncyste.   Cf. *Ph.* 526.

1330. hēafodgimmum.   So Shak. (?) *Pericles* III. ii. 99:

> Her eyelids, cases to those heavenly *jewels*
> Which Pericles hath lost.

Cf. *Lear* V. iii. 188–190 :

> And in this habit
> Met 1 my father with his bleeding rings,
> Their *precious stones* new lost.

See also *An.* 31; *Ex. Gn.* 44; esp. *Ph.* 301 ff.

1333.   Cf. 1080.

1334. wuldre scīneð.   Cf. 900 ff., 1009[b].   See Mt. 16. 27; 24. 30; 25. 31.

1335–1336.   The break is left only to indicate the historic division made at this point by Grein and Wülker; they substitute comma for period after *līcie*, as likewise do Thorpe and Gollancz.   The comparison with 1080 shows that 1333 may well end a paragraph, and 1334 as the beginning of a section may be compared

with 897, 1007, 1216 (the two latter recognized by Grein and Wülker).   Note,
too, how frequently divisions begin with *þonne.*

1335. hēahsetle. Cf. 1217 ; *Ph.* 515.

1342. Th. 'go unto the land of angels' joy '; Gr. 'hin zu des Engeljubels Erd-
sitz fahren '; Go. 'fare to the home of angels' harmony.'

1343. þæs. Possibly we should read *þǣr,* because of *An.* 811.—**willum
nēotan.** So *Gu.* 1347.

1344 ff. Cf. Mt. 25. 34 ff., and see VIII. a–j.

1345. gearo. Prepared.

1347. hwonne. In anticipation of the time when.   See note on 27.   Cosijn
says : ' gehört zu *gearo.*'

1348. swegldrēamas. Only *An.* 720 ; *Gu.* 1098.

1351. þurh mīnne noman. So 1506.

1352. For the construction, cf. *Ps.* 140.[1]

1353. hyra. For the case, cf. 1502.

1354. hrægl nacedum. Cf. 1505[b].

1355. lāgun. Perhaps we should read *lǣgun.*

1356. æfndon. Cf. 1429.— **unsōfte ādle gebundne.** So *Gu.* 858.

1357. hyge staþeladon. Cf. *An.* 1212 ff.; *El.* 1094 ; also 1 Thess. 3. 13; Jas.
5. 8.

1358. mid mōdes myne. Cf. *Jul.* 379, 657.   Th. 'with love of mind'; Gr.
'mit Gemütes Liebe ' (but *myne* = 'cogitatio ' in *Spr.*); Go.[1] 'with loving hearts ';
Go.[2] 'with the soul's affection.'   Perhaps we might think of Acts 11. 23, and
understand '*purpose* of heart.'

1360. Cosijn says : '*forð* ist *ferð* ; vgl. oben v. 1320 [1319].'   This is very
plausible.

1361. lēan. *Brūcan* takes the gen., except *Wand.* 44 (*Run.* 8 is no exception); cf. Wülfing 1. 175.

1362–3. See IX. a, b, c.

1364[a]. Th. 'through terror's pain '; Gr. 'mit angstlicher Drohung '; Go. 'with
fearful threatening.'   Cf. note on 946[a].

1366. līfes nē lissa. So *Gu.* 806 ; cf. *Ph.* 150.

1369[b]. Cf. 1516[b].

1373. frǣte folc. So *An.* 1508.— **stǣleð.** Cf. Frucht, p. 80.

1374. riht. For the sense, Grein compares *Soul's Address* (Ex.) 98 ; *Doomsday* 105.   Th. 'course' (note, *ratio*); Gr. 'Recht'; Go. 'account.'   See the
original in Caesarius, below, p. 210.

1377. Cf. Caesarius' *reos* and *te.*

1379–1498. Miss Rossetti's poem is a beautiful parallel:

> I bore with thee long weary days and nights,
>   Through many pangs of heart, through many tears ;
> I bore with thee, thy hardness, coldness, slights,
>   For three and thirty years.
>
> Who else had dared for thee what I have dared ?
>   I plunged the depth most deep from bliss above ;
> I not My flesh, I not My spirit spared ;
>   Give thou Me love for love.

For thee I thirsted in the daily drouth;
  For thee I trembled in the nightly frost;
Much sweeter thou than honey to My mouth;
  Why wilt thou still be lost?

I bore thee on My shoulders and rejoiced;
  Men only marked upon My shoulders borne
The branding cross; and shouted hungry-voiced,
  Or wagged their heads in scorn.

Thee did nails grave upon My hands; thy name
  Did thorns for frontlets stamp between Mine eyes:
I, Holy One, put on thy guilt and shame;
  I, God, Priest, Sacrifice.

A thief upon My right hand and My left;
  Six hours alone, athirst, in misery;
At length in death one smote My heart, and cleft
  A hiding-place for thee.

Nailed to the racking cross, than bed of down
  More dear, whereon to stretch Myself and sleep;
So did I win a kingdom, — share My crown;
  A harvest, — come and reap.

This I cited in *Mod. Lang. Notes* for May, 1892, together with vv. 17111–17270 of the *Cursor Mundi* (Cotton and Göttingen MSS.), calling attention also to somewhat similar passages in the York *Play of the Crucifixion* (p. 357), York *Harrowing of Hell* (p. 372), Towneley *Harrowing of Hell* (York Plays, p. 372), Towneley *Juditium* (pp. 315-6 of the Surtees Society edition); and Towneley *Resurrectio Domini* (pp. 259–261; cf. *Chester Plays*, ed. Wright, 2. 89–90), and suggesting Lam. 1. 12 as a possible source: 'O vos omnes qui transitis per viam, attendite et videte si est dolor sicut dolor meus.' On the use of this chapter as a Scripture Lesson in Passion Week, I referred to Mone, *Schauspiele des Mittelalters*, p. 204.

I would now add that, in the Sarum Use, the verse in question is variously employed: as Antiphon for Lauds in the Saturday of the Paschal Vigil; as Respond to the Ninth Lesson of the Third Nocturn of the same day; and as part of the First Lesson for the First Nocturn of Good Friday.

In Middle English, besides the places cited above, we find the theme of Christ's address to the sinner treated in Ryman's poems (see *Herrig's Archiv* 89. 218 ff.; cf. p. 337); in the *Testamentum Christi*, better *The Charter of Christ, Herrig's Archiv*, 79. 424-432 (with quotation of Lam. 1. 12); in *York Plays*, pp. 506–8 (XLVIII. 245–276); and in two poems of MS. Cambr. Dd. V. 64 (fol. 134–142), printed in Horstmann's *Richard Rolle of Hampole*, pp. 71, 118. Horstmann thinks the first of these furnished the theme for the *Testamentum Christi*. Here the Scripture referred to would seem to be rather 2 Cor. 8. 9. These poems, with their context, may profitably be consulted.

In Old English we have it in Assmann, *Ags. Hom.*, p. 168: 'þonne cwyð Drihten: "Ēalā man, ic þē geworhte, and ic for þē þrōwude, and ic wæs a rōde āhangen, and mid swipum geswungen. Ēalā man, hwār syndon þā lēan þe þū mē dydest for mīnre þrōwunge?"'

Then in Wulfstan, ed. Napier, p. 90 (cf. the variants on pp. 124, 189): 'And ou þām dōme þe ealle men tō sculan, ūre Drihten sylf ēowaδ ūs sōna his blōdigan sīdan, and his þȳrlan handa, and δā sylfan rōde þe hē for ūre nēode on āhangen wæs, and wile þonne ānrædlice witan hū wē him þæt gelēanedan.'

Again briefly in Wulfstan, p. 23: 'Witodice, witan wē mōton hū wē Crīste gelēanian eal þæt hē for ūs and for ūre lufan þafode and δolode.'

Then in *Bl. Hom.* 23. 29 ff.: 'Nū wē gehȳraδ þæt Drihten forseah þone welan þisse worlde, and hē æfter fæce æt þǣm unlædum Iūdēum manig bysmor geþrōwade; hīe hine swungon, and bundon, and spætledon on his onsȳne, and mid brādre hand slōgan, and mid heora fȳstum bēotan; and þā wundan bēag of þornum and him setton on hēafod for cynehelme, and hine þā on rōde āhēngon. Eal þis hē þrōwode for ūre lufan and hǣlo; þȳ hē wolde þæt wē þæt heofonlice rīce onfēngon, þæt þā ǣrestan men forworhtan þurh heora gīfernesse and oferhygde. Hwæt wille wē on dōmes dæg forþberan þæs wē for ūrum Drihtne ārefnedon, nū hē swā mycel for ūre lufan geþrōwode?' Cf. Gregory's *Post. Care*, ed. Sweet, p. 260.

Finally, the occurrence of an undramatic form in Basil's *Admonitio ad Filium Spiritualem* might lead us to suppose that in that Father the earliest sketch was to be found. The passage is (*Hexameron*, ed. Norman, pp. 42–44): 'Wē wǣron unδancwurδe, and wendon ūs fram Crīste, ac hē ūs gesōhte, swā δæt hē sylf nyδer āstāh of his heofenlican settle on swā mycelre ēaδmōdnysse, δæt hē man wearδ for ūs on middanearde ākenned, and læg on cildclāδum [cf. 1423]. Sē δe belȳcδ on his handa ealle δās eorδan, swā-swā Ælmihtig God, and sē δe heofenas gehealdeδ, næfde hāmas on worulde, nē hwider hē āhyllde his hēafod on līfe. And sē wæs hafenlēas for ūs se δe hæfδ ealle δing, δæt hē ūs gewelgode on his ēceum welum. And him wæs gedēmed fram unrihtwīsum dēmum, δām δe on wolcnum cymδ on δysre worulde ende eallum tō dēmenne δe ǣfre knce wǣron. And sē δe is līfes wylle, hē gewilnode wæteres æt δām Samaritaniscean wīfe, swā-swā ūs sægδ δæt godspell. And sē δe ealle δing āfēdeδ, sē gefrēdde hungor, δa-δā hē on δām wēstene wæs gecostnod fram dēofle, æfter-δām-δe hē fæste fēowertig daga on ān. And δām δe englas δēniaδ, hē sylf δēnode mannum, and δwōh his gingrena fēt mid his fægerum handum [cf. 1110]. And sē δe fela wundra geworhte mid his handum, sē geδafode for ūs δæt man gefæstnode his handa mid nægelum on rōde, and ēac his fōtwylmas. And δā-δā hē drincan bæd, δā dydon δā earman Jūdēiscean geallan tō his mūδe, of δām mannum becōm sēo godspellice lār mid his līflican bodunge. And sē δe mannum ne derede, him man dyde talu, and hē wæs beswungen unscyldig ēac for ūs. And sē δe δā dēadan δurh his drihtenlican mihte ārǣrde tō līfe, sē lēt hine āhōn on rōde gealgan be his āgenum willan, and swā δeaδ geδrōwode, and hē syδδan wæs bebyrged; ac hē ārās of dēaδe on δām δriddan dæge, and hē āstāh tō heofenum tō his hālgan Fæder. Eall δis hē geδrōwode for ūre ālȳsednysse, δæt hē forgēafe δæt ēce līf ūs mannum; and hē ne biddeδ ūs tō edlēane nānes ōδres δinges būton ūs sylfe him, and ūre sāwla clǣne, δæt hē on ūs wunige, and ūre willa mid him, and δæt hē ūs sylfe hæbbe tō δām heofenlican līfe.' The parallel with the lines in the *Christ* is the more striking because the foregoing extract is immediately followed

by words similar in purport to *Christ* 1498–1501[a] : 'Gif wē nū habbað on horde
gold oððe seolfor, ðæt hē hēt ūs dǣlan, for his lufan, ðearfum.' Cf. note on
1421[b].

I have discovered nothing more ultimate as a source, or clue to a source,
than a passage from Ephraem Syrus, *De Judicio et Compunctione* (*Opera* 5. 51) :
'Rationem etiam a nobis de tanta brevis hujusce vitae negligentia exquiret ; dicet-
que ad nos ipse : "Propter vos incarnatus sum, propter vos in terris palam incessi,
propter vos flagellatus sum, propter vos virgis caesus sum, propter vos crucifixus
sum, exaltatus in ligno ; propter vos terrenos aceto potatus sum, ut vos sanctos
atque caelestes redderem.   Regnum meum donavi vobis.   Omnes vos meos
vocavi fratres ; Patri vos obtuli ; Spiritum misi vobis.   Quid amplius his mihi
fuit agendum, quod non egerim, ut salvemini ?   Tantum liberam vestram volun-
tatem nolo cogere, ne saluti vestrae vis ac necessitas imponatur.   Jam dicite, peccatores et natura mortales, quid vos propter me Dominum vestrum perpessi estis,
quum ego pro vobis sum passus ?" .   . Venite omnes, procidamus coram ipso, et
ploremus coram Domino, qui fecit nos, dicentes : "O Domine, haec omnia tu Deus
propter nos sustinuisti ; at nos peccatores multarum miserationum tuarum
immemores sumus.   Quid igitur peccatorum genus tibi incomprehensibili,
benignissimo, et misericordi Deo retribuet ?" '

But the direct original of our passage is evidently Pseudo-Augustine, *Sermo*
249, or rather Caesarius of Arles (Migne 39. 2207) : 'Dominus ... rationem vitae
coeperit postulare, et plus jam justus quam misericors, severitate judicis con-
temptae misericordiae reos coeperit accusare, et dicere : "Ego te, O homo, de limo
manibus meis feci ; ego terrenis artubus infudi spiritum ; ego tibi imaginem
nostram similitudinemque conferre dignatus sum ; ego te inter paradisi delicias
collocavi ; tu vitalia mandata contemnens, deceptorem sequi quam Deum malui-
sti.   Cum expulsus de paradiso jure peccati mortis vinculis tenereris, virginalem
uterum sine dispendio virginitatis pariendus introivi ; in praesepio expositus et
pannis obvolutus jacui ; infantiae contumelias humanosque dolores, quibus tibi
similis fierem, ad hoc scilicet ut te mihi similem facerem, pertuli ; irridentium
palmas et sputa suscepi ; acetum cum felle bibi ; flagellis caesus, vepribus coro-
natus, cruci affixus, vulnere perfossus, ut tu eripereris morti, animam in tormentis
dimisi.   En clavorum vestigia, quibus affixus pependi ; en perfossum vulneribus
latus.   Suscepi dolores tuos, ut tibi gloriam darem ; suscepi mortem tuam, ut in
aeternum viveres.   Conditus jacui in sepulcro, ut tu regnares in caelo.   Cur quod
pro te pertuli perdidisti ? cur, ingrate, redemptionis tuae munera renuisti ?   Non
te ego de morte mea quaero ; redde mihi vitam tuam, pro qua meam dedi.   Redde
mihi vitam tuam, quam vulneribus peccatorum indesinenter occidis.   Cur habitaculum, quod mihi in te sacraveram, luxuriae sordibus polluisti ? cur corpus meum
illecebrarum turpitudine maculasti ?   Cur me graviore criminum tuorum cruce,
quam illa in qua quondam pependeram, affixisti ?   Gravior enim apud me peccatorum tuorum crux est, in qua invitus pendeo, quam illa in qua tui misertus
mortem tuam occisurus ascendi." ' Caesarius was very likely indebted to the Orient,
and perhaps directly to Ephraem : cf. his *rationem vitae* with the latter's λόγον ...
καιροῦ, and note that both are talking of the Judgment Day.

Among modern poets there is an echo in the *Brothers, and a Sermon* of Jean
Ingelow, especially of 1474 ff.   Miss Havergal's 'I gave my life for thee' is well

known. On this hymn Julian's *Dictionary of Hymnology* has (p. 555): 'Miss M. V. G. Havergal's MS. account of this hymn is: "In F. R. H.'s MS. copy, she gives this title, 'I did this for thee; what hast thou done for Me?' Motto placed under a picture of our Saviour in the study of a German divine. On Jan. 10, 1858, she had come in weary, and sitting down she read the motto, and the lines of her hymn flashed upon her. She wrote them in pencil on a scrap of paper."'

But the latest and most remarkable, because most unexpected, rendering of the idea is the beginning of a poem in Verlaine's *Sagesse* (in *Choix de Poésies*, p. 180):

> Mon Dieu m'a dit : ' Mon fils, il faut m'aimer. Tu vois
> Mon flanc percé, mon cœur qui rayonne et qui saigne,
> Et mes pieds offensés que Madeleine baigne
> De larmes, et mes bras douloureux sous le poids
>
> De tes péchés, et mes mains! Et tu vois la croix,
> Tu vois les clous, le fiel, l'éponge, et tout t'enseigne
> A n'aimer, en ce monde où la chair règne,
> Que ma Chair et mon Sang, ma parole et ma voix.
>
> Ne t'ai-je pas aimé jusqu'à la mort moi-même,
> O mon frère en mon Père, ô mon fils en l'Esprit,
> Et n'ai-je pas souffert, comme c'était écrit ?
>
> N'ai-je pas sangloté ton angoisse suprême
> Et n'ai-je pas sué la sueur de tes nuits,
> Lamentable ami qui me cherches où je suis ?'

1379 ff. Cf. 621 ff.

1379. hondum mīnum. So Ælfric, *Hom.* i. 16: 'And hē worhte ðā þone man *mid his handum.*' The transposition according to Frucht, p. 73, which see. Professor Bright suggests: 'Hwæt, mon, ic þec, mīnum hondum' ($\times \perp \times \perp \mid - \times \perp \times$). He compares 586, 627, 1152, 1423, etc., where *hwæt* does not alliterate. See also 162.

1381. Cf. 621; Gen. 2. 7: 'God gescēop eornostlice man of þære eorðan lāme, and onāblēow on his ansīne līfes orðunge'; also Ælfric, *Hom.* i. 12 (*Bibl. Quot.*, p. 76): 'And God þā geworhte ænne mannan of lāme, and him onāblēow gāst.'

1382. Cf. Gen. i. 27, 28.

1383^b–1384^a. See the remarkable parallel, 604^b–605^a (II).

1383^b. meahta spēd. Cf. note on 296.

1384. wīdlonda. Cf. *An.* 198; *Gen.* i 56, 1412, 1538.

1385^a. ōÿstra. Note the apposition with *wēan*, and cf. note on 593.

1385^b. Cf. 1472–3, 1497–8.

1386. scīenne gesceapen. Cf. *Gen.* 547–9: 'þær hē þæt wīf geseah ... *scēone gesceapene.*'

1388. Cf. Gen. i. 28. — **mōstes.** One would expect *mōste :* cf. 1426; on the other hand, see Wulfstan 259. 9: *fēddest.*

1390. neorxnawonges. On this word Mr. Henry Bradley has a note in *The Academy* for Oct. 19, 1889 (No. 911, p. 254): 'I venture to offer a suggestion that the primary application of the word may have been to the *celestial* paradise (which, indeed, is the sense in the great majority of instances) ; and that it is a contraction of a fuller form *neo-rōhsna wang*, the Gothic equivalent of which would be *nawi-rōhsnē waggs*, "field of the palaces of the dead." The stem *nawi-*, "dead person," is represented in Old English compounds by *neo-*, as in the words *neo-bed*, *neo-sīð*, etc.; and the disappearance of a long vowel in the unstressed second element of a compound occurs in many unquestioned instances: cf. *ǣlc*, *ǣfst*, *fylst*, *orð* (Sievers, *Ags. Gram.* § 43). The sense yielded by the proposed explanation may be compared with that of *wælheal*, "Valhalla." The Teutonic word *nawi-z* does not, any more than its probable cognate νέκυς, mean exclusively "corpse." The wider meaning of "dead person" is fully authenticated. It is true that the word *rōhsn* (*rēhsn*) = Gothic *rōhsns* (stem *rōhnsi-*), "palace," is not recorded in Old English; but I do not see that this constitutes a serious difficulty.' Mr. Bradley then refers to Kluge's conjecture (*Kuhn's Zs.* 26. 84) that the word may be a compound of *neo-* = *nawi-*. Another explanation has been offered by Reinius (*Angl.* 19. 554–6). He assumes an original *nerksana*, from *ne-werksana*. This would be from a Germ. past. part. *werkusan*, becoming a pres. part. in meaning, so that OE. *ne werksan* would mean 'not working' or 'not suffering.' The word for Paradise would accordingly mean 'the field of the idle.' Cf. Gen. 2. 15: 'God ... gelōgode hine on neorxena wange'; Ælfr. *Hom.* I. 12 (*Bibl. Quot.*, p. 77) : 'God þā hine gebrohte on neorxnawonge.'

1392–5. Cf. Genesis, chap. 3.

1393. bibod brǣce. Cf. *Ælfred's Laws* (*Bibl. Quot.*, p. 68): 'þæt hē ne cōme nō þās *bebodu tō brecanne.*'

1395ᵃ. Note the etymological alliteration, and cf. 592ᵃ, 980, 1121.

1400. lȳtel. The emendation according to Frucht, p. 30; cf. *PBB.* 10. 457.

1401. meahta spēd. Cf. 1383.

1404ᵃ. Cf. *Jud.* 296; *Ph.* 565.

1405–6. Gen. 3. 23, 24.

1405. nȳde. So 1071.

1407ᵇ–1408ᵃ. Cf. 563 (II), and *Gen.* 929ᵇ–930ᵃ: 'neorxnawonges *dugeðum bedǣled*'; *Beow.* 721 : *drēamum bedǣled*.

1408ᵃ. Cf. *Hy.* 11¹¹.

1409ᵇ–1413. Cf. (II) 621ᵇ–626.

1409ᵇ–1411. Gen. 3. 17–19.

1418ᵃ. sīþas. Th. 'fortunes' (so Gr., *Spr.*); Gr. 'Wege'; Go. 'vicissitudes.' **1418ᵇ–1419ᵃ.** Cf. 720ᵇ.

1420. ǣghwǣs. Not 'of every one' (Th.). — **onwǣlg.** Cf. (I) 207ᵃ, 211ᵃ. **1420ᵇ–1425ᵃ.** Tr. by Brooke.

1420ᵇ. Br. 'All alone I was begotten'; Gr. rightly: 'Ich allein ward geboren.' With *āna* cf. *āncenned*.

1421ᵇ ff. Cf. Ælfr. *Hom.* I. 34, 36: 'Hē wæs mid wācum cildclāðum bewǣfed, þæt hē ūs forgēafe ðā undēadlican tunecan þe wē forluron on ðæs frumsceapenan mannes forgǣgednysse. Se ælmihtiga Godes Sunu, ðe heofenas befōn ne mihton, wæs gelēd on nearuwre binne, tō ðī þæt hē ūs fram hellicum nyrwette ālȳsde. ... Se Godes Sunu wæs on his gesthūse genyrwed, þæt hē ūs rūme wununge on heofonan rīce forgife, gif wē his willan gehȳrsumiað. Ne bitt hē ūs nānes ðinges tō edlēane his geswinces būton ūre sāwle hǣlo.' Cf. Ælfric's Basil, p. 209.

1422ª. þearfan. Not 'thrifty' (Th.).

1423ª. Cf. 725, and note. Br. 'all bedight with dusky swathing.

1424. Lȳtel. Br. 'Of a little worth.'

1425. cildgeong on crybbe. Th. 'a young child in a crib'; Gr. 'kindjung in einer Krippe'; Go. 'a young child in its crib'; Br. 'young, a child within its crib.' — **cildgeong.** Cf. *An.* 685; *Gn. Ex.* 49.

crybbe. Properly, *cribbe*. This seems to be the only extant instance of the OE. word. It exists, however, in several of the cognate tongues: O Fris. *cribbe*, OS. *kribbja* (MDu. *cribbe*, Du. *krib, kribbe*), OHG. *chrippa* (MHG., MnG. *Krippe*). The OS. word occurs *Hel.* 382, translating Lk. 2. 7 (12, 16). In ME. the *NED.* quotes *Orm.* 3711; *Cursor Mundi* 11253 (Cott.); Hampole, *Pr. Consc.* 5200. The only other senses which go back to ME. are: 'The stall or cabin of an ox'; 'A wickerwork basket, pannier, or the like.' The sense of 'child's bed' does not occur till 1649. Cf. note on 724.

1427. wonn. For the sense, cf. *winnende*, 1271.

Cosijn remarks: 'Der Punkt hinter *wonn*, also *Næs* ('es war nicht') neuer Satz, macht den Vers fast unverständlich. Ändere den Punkt in Komma, und lies *næs mē for mōde*, "und nicht meinetwegen aus Uebermut"; vgl. v. 1442 [1441], *ic þæt sār for ðē ðurh ēaðmēdu eall geþolade*.'

1428. Næs mē for mōde. Th. 'It was not for pride' (so Go.); Gr. (*Spr.* s. v. *mōd*): 'Ich that es nicht aus Uebermut' (similarly *D.*). — **magugeoguðe.** This is probably one of the compounds referred to by Kail, *Angl.* 12. 37, under (b), in which the first element is due to alliteration, and is practically meaningless.

1429. līcsār. So *Beow.* 815.

1433 ff. Repeating the theme of 1107 ff.

1433. fore monna lufan. Cf. 1116; *Harr. Hell* 110 ff.; *Men.* 86; *El.* 564.

1434ᵇ-1435. Mt. 27. 30; Mk. 15. 19. It is somewhat difficult to decide whether 1434ᵇ should be construed with the foregoing or with the following.

1435. ondlata. Cosijn has: 'Ein *andwlāta* citiert Toller 1. 46 aus *Leechd.* 1. 356; es kann dem Zusammentrang nach nur n-loser acc. plur. sein. Einen nom. sing. *and(w)lata*, "Antlitz," nach dem *Liber Scint.* hier anzunehmen hilft nichts.'

Frucht says (p. 73): 'Herr Prof. Konrath hat mich darauf hingewiesen, dass vielleicht an *andwlata*, "Antlitz," als Apposition zu *hlēor* zu denken sei, die mir durchaus gerechtfertigt erscheint. Der Halbvers gehörte dann als X. ⌣̣ | ⌣̣ ⌣ x, eine Form die sich bei Cynewulf nicht selten findet, zum Typ. D I.'

1437-8. Mt. 27. 34. Cf. *An.* 33-34.

1438ᵇ. Cf. *Ps.* 68²².

1441ª. Mt. 27. 26; Mk. 15. 15.

1443ª. heardcwide. Cosijn: 'ändere man in *hearmcwide*.'

1443ᵇ-1445. Mt. 27. 29; Mk. 15. 17; Jn. 19. 2.

1443ᵇ. hwæsne. Cf. Goth. ON. *hwass*, OHG. (h)was, MHG. wa(h)s.

1445. þrēam biþrycton. Cf. *Jul.* 520; *Gu.* 1171; *El.* 1277. — **þrēam.** Th. 'with reproaches'; Gr. (*Spr.*) 'violenter (?),' (*D.*) 'drangsalvoll'; Go.¹ 'fiercely'; Go.² 'with cruelty.'

1447ᵇ-1449ª. Jn. 19. 34. With 1449 cf. *An.* 971.

1447ᵇ. mid spere. The wounding is represented as occurring before his death (cf. *oþþæt*, 1452). So Ælfric, *Hom.* I. 216 : ' And mid spere gewundedon. And ða embe nōntīd, þā-þā hē forðfērde,' etc.

As for the metre (see Variants), Frucht assigns the phrase to this line, and scans (p. 14) : x x ⌣x́ | x x ⌣x́.

1451. womma lēas. So 1464.— **wīte þolade.** Cf. *Gen.* 323[b].

1452[b]-1453. Mt. 27. 50; Mk. 15. 37; Lk. 23. 46; Jn. 19. 30. Cf. *El.* 479; *Jul.* 310.— **ānne . . . gāst.** Cf. [*Chr.* 1692], p. 64 : *ænne gāst.* · With *ānne . . . forlǣtan* cf. 1295, 1397, and Gr. *Spr.* s. v. *forlǣtan* (1).

1454 ff. Brooke says (p. 404) : ' Nor, indeed is the passage less effective when Christ, apparently turning to the gigantic rood, as a Catholic preacher to the crucifix, points to himself hanging there, and cries to all the vast host of the lost, " See now," ' etc. Against this picturesque conception there are only these objections :

1. The Cross in the sky has not been mentioned for over 350 lines, and is not mentioned again.

2. In the whole context, Christ is talking of himself, and not of an image.

3. The author is evidently thinking of Biblical passages like Zech. 12. 10: ' And they shall look upon me whom they have pierced, and they shall mourn for him '; Rev. 1. 7 : ' Behold, he cometh with clouds ; and every eye shall see him, and they also which pierced him ; and all kindreds of the earth shall wail because of him.'

Brooke translates or paraphrases various lines from here to 1532.

1454. Grein's note is : ' *gesēoð* von *gesēon* = *gesīhan* (vgl. *bisēon* v. 1088)' ; (*Spr.*) ' die Wunden fliessen noch (?) oder videte vulnera (?) '; (*D.*) ' Die Wunden triefen jetzt.' Cf. p. 210, above.— **feorhdolg.** Cf. *feorhben*, *Beow.* 2740; *feorhwund*, *Beow.* 2385.

1455. Lk. 24. 39; Jn. 20. 20. Cf. 1110; *Beow.* 745[a].

1457. orgete. So 1116.

1458. Jn. 20. 20. Cf. 1111.

1459. Th. ' How uneven an account was there to us in common !'; Gr. ' Wie ungleich war die Sache uns doch gemein !'; Go. ' How unequal (Go.[2] uneven) was the reckoning 'twixt (Go.[2] there between) us two !'

1461. eþelrīces. Cf. *An.* 120, 432; *Sal.* 106.

1462-3. gebohte . . . līf. Cf. 1095.

1466. niþre. Cf. *Pa.* 74.

1470. for lufan. Cf. 1433.

1471. hēanum tō helpe. So 632 (II).— **gecȳpte.** Cf. *gebohte*, 1462.

1472. gewitlēas. Cf. *Met.* 19[46].

1474-5. Cf. Caesarius, above : ' Non te ego de morte mea quaero.'

1476[b]-1477. Th. ' of which for thee I mine of yore, through worldly penalty, gave as price '; Gr. ' dass ich für dich das meine dahingegeben durch harte Qualen '; Go.[1] ' for which, in martyrdom, I gave thee formerly (Go.[2] once) Mine own as price.' Cf. Caesarius : ' pro qua meam dedi.' Probably *þæs þe* is not conj., but pron.; see 1478.

1480-1483. Cf. 1 Cor. 3. 16, 17; 6. 19; 2 Cor. 6. 16.

1480. selegescot. ' Habitaculum.' Eight times in *Ps.* Cf. note on 820.

1481-2. Note the rime.

1482. Cosijn: '*fûle synne* muss acc. plur. sein, regiert von *þurh;* also lese man *firenlusta.*' But why?

1485. fēondum of fǣðme. Cf. *Exod.* 294: *of fēonda fæðme.*

1487ᵃ. hefgor. Corresponding to *graviore* (*cruce*).

1487ᵇ. honda. Is this merely for the sake of alliteration? Cf. 'criminum,' p. 210, and *synna*, 1489.

1488. heardra. Irreg. for *-e*; so next line.

1489. mid. 'Apuḍ.'

1491. gestāg. Cf. *Rood* 34, 40.

1493. gehrēaw. Cf. 1414.

1494. þǣr. If.

1496. Rime.

1497-8. Cf. 1091-2; 1212-3; 1385ᵇ; 1472-3; contrast with 127 ff.; 209 ff.; 599-612.

1499-1514. Mt. 25. 40, 42, 43. See IX. d-g. Contrast with 1349 ff.

1502ᵇ. Contrast with 1224.

1505ᵇ. Cf. 1354ᵇ.

1506. metelēasum. Cf. *El.* 612, 698.

1506ᵇ-7. Cf. 1351-2.

1507. wonhāle. Cf. *An.* 580; *El.* 1030.

1508ᵇ. Cf. *Ph.* 454.

1509. geþegede. Gr. (*Spr.*) hesitates between this form and *geþēgede;* he compares also *þurste geþēwde, Ps.* 106³². Dietrich (p. 212) postulates an inf. *þegan* or *þēgan.* Gollancz remarks (p. 169): 'I take this word to be the weak past participle of *geþicgan,* "to take"; hence "taken by thirst"; similarly, *æþelinga bearn ecgum oþþegde, Gen.* 2002. . . . It does not seem to have occurred to lexicographers to bring the word in (*sic*) connection with *þicgan,* the past participle of which verb seems to be singularly rare.' Cf. Sweet, *Dict.* s. v. *ðecgan.*—**oftugon.** So 1504.

1511-2. þȳ frēoran hyge, mōde gefēngen. *Gefōn* seems here to govern the instrumental, in the sense of the Lat. *capio;* cf. expressions like 'patrium animum virtutemque capiamus,' Cic. *Phil.* 3. 11. 29. Hertel makes *gefōn* here govern the acc. and inst. (p. 38), which can only mean that he takes *þæt* as acc., and consequently has no means of accounting for the opt. *gefēngen.* Rose (p. 38) explains the inst. as signifying measure of difference or superiority, but does not account for the government of the verb; on p. 41 he suggests that it may be an original locative. Th. 'that they thereby a gladder spirit might in mind receive'; Gr. 'damit sie Trost im Herzen im Gemüt empfiengen'; Go.¹ 'that their hearts might win a cheerful spirit'; Go.² 'that they might gain within their hearts a spirit the more buoyant.'

1512ᵇ. So 1358ᵇ.

1513ᵇ-1514. Contrast with 1360ᵇ-1361.

1515. cwide. Cf. 618.

1516ᵇ. Cf. 1369ʰ.

1517ᵃ. Cf. 1373ᵃ; *El.* 117ᵃ.

1519-1526. Mt. 25. 41. See IX. h-o. Cf. *Sat.* 628 ff.

1519. willum biscyrede. Th., Go. 'wilfully cut off'; Gr. 'der Freude bar':

Br. 'cut off by your own will'; Gr. (*Spr.*) classes *willum* under *willa* (3): 'voluptas, gaudium, Wolgefallen.' Cf. 32, 1343, 1586; *Gu.* 1047.

1523. hāt ond heorogrim. So *Gu.* 952; cf. 1612, and note on 1428, s. f.

1526. on grimne grund. Professor J. M. Hart suggests *in ginne grund,* comparing *Beow.* 1551; but see *Sat.* 260: *grimme grundas.*

þā ǣr wið Gode wunnon. Cf. *Exod.* 514; *Beow.* 113; *Sat.* 327.

1527. rīces Weard. So *Beow.* 1390.

1528. yrre ond egesful. So *Exod.* 505.

1529. foldwege. In this sense *An.* 206; *Gu.* 1224; cf. note on 681. But Br. renders: 'path of earth.'

1530. Cf. Prudentius, *Cath.* 6. 85 ff., where the two-edged sword of Rev. 1. 16, proceeding out of the mouth of him who was like unto the Son of Man, is transferred to the hand of Christ the Judge:

> Hujus manum potentem
> gladius perarmat anceps,
> et fulgurans utrimque
> duplicem minatur ictum.
> Quaesitor ille solus
> animaeque corporisque,
> ensisque bis timendus
> prima ac secunda mors est.
>
> .   .   .   .   .   .
>
> Huic inclitus perenne
> tribuit Pater tribunal.

I recall nothing like this in pictures of the Last Judgment (see note on 880), though Didron (*Christian Iconography* 1. 257) describes a picture in the convent of St. Laura on Mount Athos, in which Christ holds in his left hand an open book, and in his right a naked sword. A red sword is suspended on the left of Christ's head in the fine Memling at Dantzic (Waagen, *Handbook of Painting,* p. 97), as a lily-branch on the right; and perhaps this is to be found in other pictures. Cf. *El.* 760 ff.

sigemēce. A notable compound. Cf. Shakespeare, *Lear* 5. 3. 132:

> Despite thy victor sword.

Ant. and Cleop. 1. 3. 99–100:

> Upon your sword
> Sit laurel victory.

Milton, *P. L.* 6. 250–253:

> Saw where the sword of Michael smote, and felled
> Squadrons at once; with huge two-handed sway
> Brandished aloft, the horrid edge came down
> Wide-wasting.

Shelley, *Ode to Liberty* xv. 7:

> Lift the victory-flashing sword.

1531–4. Note the parallelism in the successive lines.

1531. on þæt dēope dæl. Cf. *Gen.* 305, 421.

1532. in sweartne lēg. Cf. Bede, *Eccl. Hist.* 5. 12 (Miller, p. 426) : 'And mid ð̄y wit ða forðgongende wǣron under ðǣm scūan þǣre ðēostran nihte, ða ǣtēowdan sǣmninga beforan unc moniga hēapa *sweartra lēga*, ða wǣron ūp āstīgende swā-swā of miclum sēaðe, and eft wǣron fāllende and gewītende in ðone ilcan sēað.' See Ælfric's account, *Hom.* 2. 350. Milton's (*P. L.* 1. 62–63)

> Yet from those flames
> No light, but only darkness visible

is familiar. The spiritual interpretation is, according to Gregory (*Moral.* lib. 9, cap. 65; Migne 75. 912) that hell, by dividing the soul from God, shuts out its light and darkens its vision : 'Sicut mors exterior ab anima dividit carnem, ita mors interior a Deo separat animam. Umbra ergo mortis est obscuritas divisionis, quia damnatus quisque cum aeterno igne succenditur, ab interno lumine tenebratur. Natura vero ignis est ut ex se lucem exhibeat et concremationem, sed transactorum illa ultrix flamma vitiorum concremationem habet, et lumen non habet. . . . Si itaque ignis qui reprobos cruciat lumen habere potuisset, is qui repellitur nequaquam mitti in tenebras diceretur. Hinc etiam Psalmista ait : *Super eos cecidit ignis, et non viderunt solem* (Psal. 57. 9). Ignis enim super impios cadit, sed sol igne cadente non cernitur, quia quo illos gehennae flamma devorat, a visione veri luminis caecat, ut et foris eos dolor combustionis cruciet, et intus poena caecitatis obscuret.' Cf. notes on 106, 344, 1536ᵇ–1537ᵃ; *Sat.* 715; *Doomsday* (Bede) 241; and add Ælfr. *Hom.* 1. 532 : 'Witodlice þæt hellice fӯr hæfð unāsecgendlice hǣtan and nān lēoht, ac ēcelice byrnð on sweartum þēostrum.' In the Advent Hymn of the Breviary, 'Verbum supernum prodiens,' occur the lines, which are not, however, found in the earlier form of the hymn :

> Non esca flammarum nigros
> Volvamur inter turbines.

On *esca* cf. Isa. 9. 19.

1535. See IX. m. — **wītehūs.** So *Gen.* 93 ; *Sat.* 628.

1536ᵃ. dēaðsele. So *Gu.* 1048 ; *Whale* 30.

1536ᵇ–1537ᵃ. Th. 'Not the Lord's remembrance shall they seek afterwards' ; Gr. 'von wo sie nicht die Theilnahme Gottes seitdem wieder suchen' ; Go.[1] 'Ne'er shall they seek again remembrance of the Lord' ; Go.[2] 'They shall nowise thereafter seek remembrance of the Lord.' Better Gr. *Spr.* s. v. *gesēcan* (2) : 'non venient in memoriam ei' ; cf. e.g. Ecclus. 23. 19 (Vulg.) : 'ne forte obliviscatur te Deus' ; 35. 9 : 'memoriam ejus [justi] non obliviscetur Dominus.' Our passage is very likely from Pseudo-Augustine, *Sermo* 251, or rather Caesarius (Migne 39. 2210) : 'Ubi lux nunquam videbitur nisi tenebrae, et non venient unquam in memoriam apud Deum.' A parallel is *El.* 1302–4 : 'Gode nō sӯððan of þām morðorhofe in gemynd cumað, Wuldorcyninge.'

1538–9ᵇ. Cf. *Hel.* 2603–4 : 'thar sculun sia, gibundana bittra lōgna, thrāuuerc tholon.'

1539. synwracu. Cf. 794 (II) ; *Gu.* 832 ; and note on 1320.

1541–3. Contrast with *El.* 1308ᵇ ff.

1541. heoloðcynne. Cf. *heoloðhelm, Whale* 45.

1542. Matt. 8. 12. Cf. 117, 1631 ; *Gen.* 42 ; *Gu.* 650 ; *Sal.* 68.

1544. fēdeð. A remarkable metaphor (see *esca*, note on 1532, s. f.); perhaps with allusion to 1 Kings 22. 27; Ps. 80. 5; 42. 3; 102. 9.

1545. grundlēas. Rev. 9. 1; etc. Cf. *Gen.* 390; *Whale* 46; *Sat.* 721ᵇ ff.

1546. Cf. Milton, *P. L.* 2. 600–603:

> From beds of raging fire to starve in ice
> Their soft ethereal warmth, and there to pine
> Immovable, infixed, and frozen round
> Periods of time, — thence hurried back to fire.

And *Meas. for Meas.* 3, 1. 121–3:

> And the delighted spirit
> To bathe in fiery floods, or to reside
> In thrilling region of thick-ribbed ice.

Add Dante, *Inf.* 3. 86, and Bede, in the vision of Drihthelm (*Eccl. Hist.* 5. 12; Miller, p. 424): 'Ōðer dæl wæs wāllendum lǣgum full suiðe egesfullice, ōðer wæs nōhte þon lǣs unaarefndlice cele hægles and snāwes. . . . þonne hēo þæt mægn þǣre unmētan hǣttan aarefnan ne mehtan, þonne stǣldun heō eft earmlice in middel þæs unmǣtan ciles; and mid þȳ hēo ðǣr nǣnige reste gemētan mihtan, þonne stǣldon hēo eft in middan þæs byrnendan fȳres and ðæs unadwǣscedan lēges.' Add Bede, *Works*, ed. Giles, 1. 101–2 (*De Die Judicii*); 9. 179; 11. 191; also Wulfstan, p. 138: 'Ðǣr synd sorhlice tōsomne gemencged se þrosmiga līg and se þrece gycela, swiðe hāt and ceald helle tōmiddes; hwȳlon þǣr ēagan ungemetum wēpað for þæs ofnes bryne, hwȳlon ēac þā tēð for mycclum cyle manna þǣr gnyrrað.' Likewise Ælfr. *Hom.* 1. 132, 530; *Gen.* 43, 313 ff.; *Sat.* 132, 335, 637; *Doomsday* (Bede) 190 ff., 205; *Sal.* 466–8. All derive from Job 24. 19 (Vulg.): 'Ad nimium calorem transeat ab aquis nivium'; so explained, e.g., by Bede on Lk. 13. 28 (*Works* 11. 191).

ealdan. Perhaps with some suggestion of the sense of 'old' in familiar speech, and in Shakespeare (cf. Schmidt, *Shak. Lex.* s. v. (7)); so *M. W.* 1. 4. 5: 'Here will be an *old* abusing of God's patience.' — **egsan.** Gr. (*Spr.* s. v.) suggests that this may be an adj., a view one would be glad to accept.

1547. wyrmum. Cf. Isa. 66. 24; Mk. 9. 44; etc. Also *Doomsday* (Bede), 167, 210.

1548. Th. 'with rugged fatal gums afflicteth people'; Gr. 'mit furchtbarer Nahrung die Völker plagend'; Go. 'with sharp and deadly jaws it scatheth folk.' See Variants.

1549. on ān. Mod. Eng. *anon.* Here = 'with one consent.' In *Ps.* 54¹³, 82⁹, 132¹ used to render *in unum, unanimis, unanimiter.* The notion of unanimity passes into that of heartiness, and so into that of confidence or conviction. We might render 'with one accord,' 'with one voice,' 'one and all.'

1550. sāwle weard. The translators have rendered as if *weard* were the subject, and Grein (*Spr.*) explains the phrase by 'homo'; but it is better to regard it as the object. Wisdom may well be regarded as the keeper of the soul; he has lost such wisdom who does not provide for an eternity of future bliss or woe. This view seems to be substantiated by *Beow.* 1739–1744:

> Hē þæt wyrse ne con
> oð þæt him on innan oferhygda dǣl

weaxeð and wrīdað þonne *se weard swefeð*,
sāwele hyrde; bið se slǣp tō fæst,
bisgum gebunden, bona swīðe nēah,
se þe of flānbogan fyrenum scēoteð.

This surely does not mean that the man is asleep, but that the faculty that ought to be on guard (Gr. 'conscientia,' 'das Gewissen ') has relaxed its vigilance.

1552ᵇ-1554. Professor J. M. Hart suggests a comparison with *Bede's Death Song:* 'than him þarf sīe . . . ǣr his hiniongæ, hwæt his gāstæ gōdæs æththa yfles. . . .'

1553. earm þe ēadig. Cf. 909, 1496; *Doomsday* (Bede) 162.

1555. tō fremman. So *Jul.* 408 ; uninflected prepositional infinitives are also found *Dan.* 76; *Az.* 37; *Ph.* 275; *Scaf.* 37 ; *Beow.* 316, 2556; *Jul.* 557; *Gu.* 502; cf., on *Jul.* 569, *PBB.* 10. 482.

1557. Hālig Gǣst. Cf. 1623; Eph. 4. 30 ; 1 Thess. 5. 19. Not 'his holy spirit ' (Th., Go.).

1558ᵇ. So 1585ᵇ. Cf. *Gu.* 940, 1093.

1560. deorc. Th. 'sad '; Gr. 'der finstre '; Go. 'black.' Cf. Matt. 6. 23; Eph. 5. 8.

1561. wǣrloga. Implacable(?); cf. 2 Tim. 3. 3 ; Rom. 1. 31. Cf. 1604, 1613.

1562. fȳres āfylled. Cosijn: 'l. *fyrena* [*firena?*] *āfylled = firenfull.*' One would like to accept this ; but cf. Drihthelm's vision (Bede, *Eccl. Hist.* 5. 12; Miller, p. 428): 'Hæfdon hēo fȳrene ēagan, and *full fȳr* [Lat. *ignem putidum*] *of heora mūðe and of heora nasum wǣron ūt blāwende.*' Cf. 959.

fēores unwyrðe. Cf. Lk. 20. 35; Acts 13. 46; Rev. 3. 4. This is an unusual sense of *feorh* (= 'eternal life ').

1563. ēgsan geþrēad. Cf. 946, 1364; *Gen.* 1865, 2668.

1564. Cf. *An.* 1171 ; Joel 2. 6; Nah. 2. 10.

1565. fācentācen fēores. Th. 'a false sign of life '; Gr. 'des Lebens Falschheitszeichen '; Go. 'the token of a life of perfidy '; Gr. renders *fācentācen* by 'signum scelerum,' and *fācentācen fēores* by 'peccata.'

firena bearn. Gr. (*D.*) 'Frevelkinder '; (*Spr.*) 'peccatores.' See Variants, and 1598.

1566. tēaras. Cf. 172. So Th. suggests (p. 503). — tīd. Cf. *Jul.* 712.

1570. ealdgestrēon. So 812; *Beow.* 1381, 1458. Th. 'their works of old '; Gr. (*Spr.*) 'peccata olim commissa,' (*D.*) 'ihre alten Schätze ' ('d. i. ihre Werke '); Go. 'what erst they cherished.'

on þā openan tīd. Cf. *Ph.* 509. — openan. Th. 'public '; Gr. 'offenen '; Go. 'all-disclosing.'

1571ᵇ-1572ᵃ. Th. 'That shall not be a time for sorrows to nations granted '; Gr. 'Dann ist nicht Sorgens Zeit den Leuten da erlaubt '; Go. 'that time of sorrowing (Go.² sorrow) will not avail.' Cf. *Ps.* 118¹²⁶ : 'þis is wynne tīd þæt man ēac wel dō ' = *tempus faciendi.* In both cases the gen. is used quasi-adjectively to characterize *tīd*, but without emphasis, and in our sentence the *bið* is not to be regarded as a principal verb. Construe: 'That (sorrowful) time will not be granted to the peoples in order that he, who, etc., may there find,' etc. Note that *þæt* does not agree in gender with *tīd*, any more than *þis* in *Ps.* 118¹²⁶. Cf. 1566ᵇ.

1572. lǣcedōm. So *Sat.* 589.

1575. gnorn. So *Beow.* 2658.

1576. nē nǣngum. Cf. *nē nǣnig, Dan.* 437.

1576^b-1577. Th. 'but there each single deed present shall appear' (see Variants); Gr. 'der eine wie der andere trägt vor den Augen Gottes einfach das Verdiente'; Go. 'but there each one shall bear before God's sight his own desert.'

1579^b-1580^a. Th. 'while to him light and soul are together fast'; Go.[1] 'while light and life hold fast together.' Go.[1] says: 'cp. *lēoht and līf Widsith* 142.' See rather 597, and esp. 777, *Gu.* 940 ff.; *Jul.* 714.

1580. somodfæste. The emendation for metrical reasons. — **sīen.** The form *sēo(n)* is unknown in the *Christ.* — **sāwle wlite.** Cf. 848, 1058, 1076.

1583^a. Cf. *Gen.* 2413^a.

1583^b. Cosijn: 'Wie sonst *lēoht = woruld*, ist hier *woruld = lēoht;* darum steht *scīnan.*' Jansen (p. 123) makes *woruld* = 'Menschen.'

1584. sceadum scrīþende. Th. 'in shadows passing'; Gr. 'die in Schatten schreitende'; Go. 'speeding with mystic (Go.[2] its) shadows.' See Variants. Jansen (p. 117) makes *sceadu* = 'Irrthum.' Th. quotes Ps. 39. 6 in the Prayer Book version. Cf. 1409^a.

1586. his drēames blǣd. Th. 'his fruit of joy'; Gr. 'das theure Jubelglück'; Go. 'the blossom of his joy.'

1587. weorces wlite. Cf. 1037. — **wuldres lēan.** Th. 'reward of glory'; Gr. 'den Gnadenlohn'; Go.[1] 'glory's recompense; Go.[2] 'the reward of glory.' Cf. 1079.

1588. The type, *on þā ⏑ × tīd*, is found (II) 632, 739, 841, 849, (III) 971, 1080, 1148, 1558, 1570, 1585; cf. 1333.

1591-3. Cf. *Gen.* 319-320^a.

1592. weorþað. Cosijn approves this emendation.

1593. Grundas. Cf. note on 145.

1594. lācende lēg. So (*līg*) *Dan.* 476; *El.* 580, 1111. — **lāðwende.** Cf. *Gen.* 68, 448, 989, 2239.

1595. þeodsceaþan. Cf. *An.* 1117 ; *Beow.* 2278, 2688.

1597. Th. 'but the fire shall bind, shall bite the fast multitude'; Gr. 'sie bindet fest mit Brand die Schaaren'; Go.[1] 'the fire shall keep that (Go.[2] the) host immovable.' — **bīdfæstne.** Cf. *Rid.* 57[7].

1599. gǣstberend. Cf. *reordberend,* (I) 278, 381, (III) 1024, 1368.

1600. fremmað. Cosijn : '*hwæt* gehört zum folgenden Vers, und leitet den von *gīman* abhängigen indirecten Fragesatz ein ; auf *mān* muss ein Verbum wie *fremmað* (*dōað* ?) folgen.'

1602. līf ond dēað. For 'the abodes of life and death'; cf. 1591.

1603. swelgað. Here with inst., as in *Beow.* 3156; not acc., as 560, 1593. — **hūs.** Cf. 1535, 1624, 1627.

1604. Contrast with *Ph.* 11.

1605-6^b. Th. 'that shall fill sinful men with their swart souls'; Gr. 'das sollen füllen die Frevelsüchtigen mit ihren schwarzen Seelen'; Go.[1] 'sin-loving men, with swarthy souls, shall fill it'; Go.[2] 'sin-loving men shall fill it with their swart souls.'

1606. synna tō wrace. Cf. 1249, 1601, 1622. Cosijn approves.

1607^a. So *Gu.* 175^a.

1607^b. āscyred. So 1617 ; *El.* 1313.

1609 ff. Cf. 1 Cor. 6. 9, 10 ; 1 Tim. 1. 10.

1609–1611. Cf. Wulfstan, pp. 114–5, 204, 266, 309–310.

1613ᵃ. So *An.* 1071ᵃ.

1614ᵃ. fēondum in forwyrd. On account of the metre, Frucht (p. 74) suggests that the hemistich may possibly have belonged in the original to type A, with double alliteration, and thus we may either think of prefixal stress, or assume that *forwyrd* is a decidedly corrupt reading. See also Variants.

1614ᵇ–1615ᵃ. Th. 'hate they shall suffer, vital ill terrific'; Gr. 'die Frevler dulden angstvolles Uebel'; Go.¹ 'sinners shall endure dire racking agony'; Go.² 'the hostile foe shall suffer terrific racking pain.'—**ealdorbealu.** Gr., *Spr.*: '*malum vitam afficiens*, oder *malum sempiternum ?*' Cf. *Beow.* 1676.

1615ᵇ. wile. Frucht says (p. 31): 'Herr Prof. Konrath hat mich darauf aufmerksam gemacht, dass hier wohl *wille* zu setzen sei. Letzteres müsste dann als Opt. gefasst werden.'

1617ᵇ. Cf. 1607ᵇ.

1620ᵃ. Cf. *Jul.* 474ᵃ.

1621. Note that the verbs have a passive sense.

1622ᵇ. Cf. 1249ᵇ.

1623. bilūceð. Rev. 20. 3.

1625. fȳres fulle. Cf. 1562.—**herges.** Evidently required by the sense.

1626. worde. Cf. Lk. 5. 5.

1629ᵃ. Cf. *Seaf.* 10ᵃ.—**cāldan.** For *-um*. Cf. 1544ᵇ.

1630. beorht ... bibod. Cf. *Ps.* 118⁶⁹, ¹²⁷; *Gu.* 815.—**bōca.** Cf. note on 701 (II).

1631. sār endelēas. So *Jul.* 251.

1632ᵃ. Cf. 1000ᵃ.

1633. þrym. Perhaps personal, as in 423; cf. 83, 566, 740. See Jn. 12. 48; 1 Thess. 4. 8.

1634ᵃ. See X. a.

1634ᵇ–1635ᵃ. berað beorhte frætwe. Cf. 1058, 1076. I do not understand Gollancz's note: 'These words evidently render the Latin "regni petent gaudia"; perhaps the poet read "regni *ferent* gaudia."' Besides 1072–3, and note on 1047 ff., cf. an extract from the sermon from MS. Bodl. Jun. 24, printed by C. Hofmann in the Munich *Gelehrte Anzeigen*, vol. 50 (Kön. Bayer. Akad. der Wiss.): 'þonne sōþfeste and gecorene men forðberaþ heora wuruca hȳrsumnesse, and Drihtnes hālige martiras heora þrōwunga and þǣra carcerna nearownessa, and manige earfoðe þe hī ādrugon (MS. adrigon) for Drihtnes naman. Gehādode men beraþ heora hȳrsumnesse, and forwyrnednesse þyssa woruldlicra þinga, and heora þā singalan weccan, and þā drihtenlican bebodu, and hyra þā gāstlican þēowdōmas. Lǣwede men, þā þe hēr rihtlice hyra līf libbaþ, hī berað heora ǣlmesdǣda, and hlūttor līf and clēne on ansȳne þes hēhstan Scyppendes. ... Đonne þā ārlēasan and þā synfullan, hī berað nearowne wǣstm and sceandfulne on ansȳne þes hēahstan Scyppendes.'

beorhte frætwe. So *Beow.* 214, 896 (*-a*); cf. *El.* 88.

1635. blǣd. Perhaps we should associate this with *blēdum*, 1169, and understand 'fruit'; cf. note on 1047 ff. Th. 'fruit'; but Gr. 'Glück'; Go.¹ 'happiness'; Go.² 'bliss.' Very likely it means 'glory'; cf. Ps. 104. 31; *An.* 541, *ā þīn dōm lyfað*; similarly *Beow.* 954; *El.* 450.

1637. þæs þe. Relative, referring to *lifes;* cf. 1476, 1478.

1639-1664. Loosely paraphrased in riming couplets by W. Clarke Robinson, p. 68.

1639. ēþel. See X. b.

1642. lēohte biwundne. Cf. *El.* 734; *Rood* 5.

1643-4. Assonance.

1644. Th. 'by joys endeared, to the Lord faithful'; Gr. 'in Lust und Jubel die geliebten Schaaren'; Go. 'glorified by joy(s), endeared unto the Lord.'— **drēamum gedȳrde.** Cf. 686, and Prov. 3. 9.

1645. See X. c. — **engla gemānan.** So *Gu.* 642.

1646. Note the rime. So *Gen.* 2332; *Rim. Poem* 82; *Wond. Creat.* 100.

1647ᵇ-1648. Th. 'Father of all; power shall have and hold the host of holy'; Gr. 'es hat der Vater Aller Gewalt, und er hält und hütet der Heiligen Schaar': Go.[1] (Go.[2] the) 'Father of all, Sovran Preserver of the holy hosts (Go.[2] hosts of the holy).' But *geweald* requires a dependent gen. and a governing verb; if *hafað* (*healdeð*) is this governing verb, then the same verb can not govern *weorud*, which is accordingly outside of syntactical relations, unless we make of it the genitive which *geweald* requires. Gollancz remarks: 'I take l. 1647 [1648] as merely a poetical periphrasis for *þone wealdendne and healdendne haligra weoruda*,' which of course explains nothing.

1647ᵇ. Fæder. See X. d.

1649-1664. Tr. by Brooke (p. 405).

As the general source, cf. Greg. *In Septem Psalm. Poenit. Expositio* (Migne 79. 657-8): 'Ibi sancti sine fine laudabunt Deum, et in lumine claritatis ejus exsultabunt (Psal. 117), cives effecti illius civitatis, quae libera est, et aeterna in caelis. *Quam non obscurat tenebrae,* non obumbrat nox, *non consumit vetustas, non in ea rutilat lumen solis.* . . . *Claritas quippe divina eam illuminat, sol clarificat justitiae, lux vera illustrat,* lux, inquam, inaccessibilis, quae non clauditur loco, non finitur tempore, *non obumbratur tenebris,* non variatur nocte. . . . Canticum laetitiae sine fine in ea* [Jerusalem] *cantatur.* Ibi est lux sine defectu, *gaudium sine gemitu,* desiderium sine poena, *amor* sine tristitia, satietas sine fastidio, sospitas sine vitio, *vita sine morte, salus sine languore.* Ibi sancti et humiles corde; ibi spiritus et animae justorum; ibi cuncti caelestis patriae cives et beatorum spirituum ordines Regem in decore suo videntes, et in gloria virtutis ejus exsultatantes. *Perfecta viget in omnibus charitas, una omnium laetitia, una jucunditas.* . . . Ubi est certa securitas, et secura aeternitas, et aeterna tranquillitas, et tranquilla felicitas, et felix suavitas, et suavis jucunditas.' So already in Augustine, *Sermo ad Fratres in Eremo* 65 (Migne 40. 1351): 'Ibi vita sine fine, juventus sine senectute, lux sine tenebris, gaudium sine tristitia, voluntas sine molestia, requies sine labore, satietas sine fastidio, claritas sine nube.' Cf. *Sermo* 67 (Migne 40. 1353) and Pseudo-Augustine, *Sermo* 250, or rather Caesarius (Migne 39. 2210): 'Ut mereamur pervenire ad regna caelestia, ubi est satietas sine fame, ubi est lux sine tenebris, juventus sine senectute, requies sine labore, gaudium sine fine.'

Note the reminiscence in *Bl. Hom.* 65. 16-20: 'þær is þæt ēce lēoht būton þēostrum; þær is geogoþ būton ylde; þær is þæt æþele līf būton geendunge; þær is gefēa būton unrōtnesse. Ne biþ þær hungor nē þurst, nē wind nē gewenn ne wætres swēg, nē þær ne biðō lēofra gedāl nē lāþra gesamnung; ac þær biþ sēo ēce ræste, and hāligra symbelnes þǣr þurhwunaþ.' And so 103, end: 'þǣr biþ ā ēce gefēa būton unrōtnesse, and geogoþ būton yldo; ne biþ þǣr sār nē gewinn, nē nǣnig unēþnes, nē sorg nē wōp, nē hungor nē þurst, nē ēce yfel.'

Cf., too, the imitation by Wulfstan, pp. 139–140: 'þǣr niht ne genimð nǣfre þurh þȳstru þæs heofonlican lēohtes scīman; ne cymð] ǣr sorh nē sār, nē ǣnig geswinc, nē hungor nē ðurst nē hefelic slǣp; ne byð] ǣr fēfor nē ādl, nē fǣrlic cwyld, nē nānes līges gebrasll nē se lāðlica cyle. Nis ðǣr hryre nē caru nē hrēoge tintregu. Ne byð þǣr līget, nē lāðlic storm, nē winter, nē cyle, nē þunor. Ne byð] ǣr wǣdl, nē lyre, nē dēaðes gryre, nē yrmð, nē angsumnys, nē ǣnig gnornung.' In the foregoing, W. is reproducing *Doomsday* (Bede); see Wülker, *Bibl.* 2. 269. Add pp. 142–3: 'Ðǣr is ēce lēoht būton þȳstrum, . . . geogoð būtan ylde; . . . ne byð þǣr hungor nē þurst nē ǣnig gewinn, ac] ǣr byð se ēce rest.' And see Assmann, *Ags. Hom.* 166. 73.

Another is in Hampole's *Pricke of Conscience*, 7814–7:

> þare es ay lyfe withouten dede,
> þare es yhowthe ay withouten elde,
> . . . .
> þare es rest ay withouten travayle.

Cf. the numerous references to Otfrid, Notker, Bede, and others, in Müllenhoff und Scherer, *Denkmäler* [3] 2. 32. They trace this phraseology back to Homily 15 of (Pseudo-?)Boniface, and indicate Augustine or Caesarius of Arles as a more ultimate source. Piper, in his edition of Otfrid, commenting on 1. 18. 9, still thinks that the passage is not theological, but popular, and borrowed from the Muspilli:

> dārī ist līp āno tōd, lioht āno˙finstri,
> selida āno sorgūn,

where Otfrid has ˺

> Thār ist līb āna tōd, lioht āna finstrī,
> engillīchaz kunni ioh ēuuinīgo wunnī.

Cf. with the phraseology concerning the fate of the damned, Greg. *Moral.* lib. 9. cap. 66 (Migne 75. 915): 'Fit ergo miseris *mors sine morte*, finis sine fine, defectus *sine defectu*, quia et mors vivit, et finis semper incipit, et deficere defectus nescit.' After the same model is the following from Wulfstan (?), *Homilies:* 'Hellewītu sēcaþ, þǣr is dēað būtan līfe, and þēostru būton lēohte, and hrēow būton frōfre, and yrmþe būton ende.'

1649. Ðǣr is. For the anaphora cf. (II) 668–680. — **engla song.** See X. c.

1650–1651. See X. f. Cf. 900 ff.; Dante, *Par.* 30. 110–117; 31. 1–27, 107–109, 118–138.

1651. sunnan beorhtra. One is reminded of 26, 106, 114, etc. Cf. *Doomsday* (Bede) 117: 'sitt þonne sigelbeorht,' of Christ on the throne of judgment.

1652. lufu. Cf. 585; *Hy.* 9[46]. — **līf būtan dēaðe.** Cosijn: 'Entweder *ende*, oder mit Sievers (dem wol *Muspilli* 14, *līp āno tōd*, vorschwebte), *dēaðe*. *Līf būtan endedæge*, das einem sofort einfällt, ist metrisch verwerflich, und wird nicht gestützt durch die zweite Vershälfte in 1654, 1655, 1656, 1657, 1658, 1659' [reduce these by one]. The Latin decides it: '*vita sine morte*.' The scribe no doubt 'contaminated' *līf būtan ende* (cf. 271, 415, 439, 599) with *līf būtan dēaðe*, perhaps because he was familiar with the 'sine fine ' of Augustine as well as the 'sine morte ' of Gregory. Cf. *Gu.* 813.

1653. glæd gumena weorud. Br. ' Merry there man's multitude.'

1654ᵃ. þrym. 'Host,' or 'glory'? On the one hand, cf. 1063; on the other, *Gen.* 80. Th. 'glory'; Gr. (*D.*) ' Herrlichkeit,' but *Spr.* 'turma,' etc.; Go., Br. ' glory.'

1654ᵇ. hǣlu būtan sāre. Explained not only by Gregory's *salus sine languore*, but also by the occurrence, in a similar passage, of *salus sine aegritudine*, in a sermon of (Pseudo-?)Boniface (ed. Giles, 2. 106). Neale, in his translation of the Rhythm of Bernard of Morlaix, has the line

> The health that hath no sore,

though it does not seem to be suggested by anything in the original.

1655. ryhtfremmendum. Cf. *Jul.* 8; *Ph.* 632. Th. construes with all that precedes from 1652; Gr., Go. with *hǣlu būtan sāre;* Br. with *ræst būtan gewinne.*

ræst būtan gewinne. Cf. 1411 ; *An.* 890: 'nis þǣr ænigum gewinn.'

1656. dōm ēadigra. The phrase *dōmeādigra dæg* would be peculiar ; *dōm ēadigra* carries on the parallelism which is such a feature as well of the Latin original as of this passage; cf. 1649 ; *Beow.* 2820. The similar expression, *dōmfæstra drēam, Gu.* 1056, is almost decisive in its favor. Possibly, since the compound *dōmeādig* does occur (*Gen.* 1247 ; *Gu.* 699, 925 ; *Jul.* 288), we should read *dōmēadgum.* If we separate the words, it is somewhat doubtful whether *dōm =* ' glory ' or ' blessedness.' Th. construes : ' rest without toil of the blessed '; Gr. ' Ruhe ohne Kämpfe den Tugendhaften '; Go. ' and for souls sublime rest without (Go.² any) toil '; Br. ' rest for righteous doers, rest withouten strife, for the good and blessed.' Th. (p. 503) would render *dōmēadig,* ' blessed with,' or ' happy in, power ' or ' authority.'

1657. blǣdes full. Th. ' of enjoyment full '; Gr. ' mit Glückes Fülle '; Go.¹ ' gloriously ' [?] ; Go.² ' joyful '; Br. ' full of blossoming ' [?].

būtan sorgum. Cf. 1643ᵇ.

1658-9. See X. g.

1659. gesǣlgum on swegle. Th. construes with preceding and following ; Gr. with preceding ; Go., Br. with following. — **sib.** Cf. 50, 1643; *Gu.* 1055; *El.* 1315. — **nīþe.** Th. ' envy '; Gr. (*D.*) ' Neidkampf '; (*Spr.*) ' odium, zelus, invidia, inimicitia '; Go., Br. ' enmity.'

1660ᵇ-1662ᵃ. Cf. *Ph.* 50-59 :

> Nis þǣr on þām londe lāðgeniðla,
> nē wōp nē wracu, wēatācen nān,
> yldu nē yrmðu, nē se enga dēað,
> nē līfes lyre, nē lāþes cyme,
> nē synn nē sacu, nē sārwracu,
> nē wǣdle gewin, nē welan onsȳn,
> nē sorg nē *slǣp, nē swār leger,*
> nē wintergeweorp, nē wedra gebregd
> hrēoh under heofonum, nē se hearda forst
> cāldum *cyle*gicelum cnyseð ænigne.

For other descriptions of heaven in Old English poetry, see *An.* 102–6, 871–890; *Gu.* 783–790, 1054 ff.; *El.* 1319ᵇ–1321; *Hy.* 9⁴¹⁻⁴⁸; *Rood* 739 ff.; *Sat.* 233 ff., 507, 649; *Doomsday* (Bede) 255 ff., 271 ff.; *Ph.* 589–677, etc. Note, too, such passages in Wulfstan as that on p. 265.

For other descriptions of the Last Judgment in general, or references to it, see *Gen.* 2571; *Exod.* 539–547; *Sat.* 598 ff.; *Doomsday* (Exeter and Bede); *Soul and Body* (*passim*); *Ph.* 48, 491–545; *Beow.* 977–9, 3069; *An.* 1437 ff.; *Jul.* 723 ff.; *El.* 1277–1321; *Rood* 103–111, 116; *Ps.* 75⁸; *Hy.* 7⁸⁵; *Met.* 29⁸⁹; *Gn. C.* 60; *Sal.* 26, 272, 324, 335.

1660. hungor nē þurst. Rev. 7. 16, from Isa. 49. 10. Cf. note on 1649–1664. — **þurst.** Contrast with 1509.

1661ᵃ. swār leger. Th. 'grievous ail'; Gr. 'Siechenlager' (*Spr.* 'Kranken-lager'); Go. 'grievous sickness'; Br. 'heavy sickness.'

1662. cyle. See note on 1546. — **cearo.** Contrast with 997. — **giefe.** Cf. 660, 1243.

1663. āwo brūcað. Cf. 1645–6. — **āwo.** Sα 479 (II), 1276. — **ēadigra ge-dryht.** See X. e., and cf. 1013.

Gollancz (*Cynewulf's Christ*, p. 191), observes on the passage which follows: "In Appendix I I have printed fifty-eight [*sic*] lines hitherto regarded as part of the present poem, but most assuredly, if the original scribe may be credited, the opening lines of the *Legend of St. Guthlac*; there is absolutely no break in the MS. between these lines and the passage usually printed as the first section of the latter poem. I make bold to suggest that the whole section is a prelude to *St. Guthlac*, with motives derived from the concluding portion of the *Christ*. Thorpe, the first editor of the Exeter MS., is no doubt answerable for this error, which even the ingenuity of Dietrich and Grein did not detect."

Gollancz fails to remark, however, that he had been anticipated by Wanley (cf. above, p. 67, bottom). Upon his theory Thomas Arnold remarks (*Notes on Beowulf*, p. 122): 'There seems to be no verisimilitude in the view of Mr. Gollancz . . . that the last twenty-nine lines do not belong to that poem, but should be regarded as the opening of the poem which follows *Crist* in the Exeter MS., namely *Guthlac*. . . . This line of thought agrees in no way with that . . . which marks the opening of *Guthlac*.'

Cf. what Cosijn says: 'Hier endet der *dōmdæges* Abschnitt, der v. 779 einge-leitet, mit v. 868 [867] anhebt. Was folgt ist ein selbständiges Stück über das Schicksal der frommen Seele, welche die irdische Herrlichkeit, *þās eorþan wynne*, verlässt; dass dieser Ausdruck nach dem Weltbrande sinnlos ist, leuchtet ein: die Begnadigten am letzten Tage werden *en masse* selig (v. 1635 [1634]); hier wird nur eine fromme Seele von ihrem Schutzengel himmelwärts geführt. In der Schilderung der himmlischen Wonne stimmen beide Stücke überein: vgl. v. 1640 [1639], *þæt is se ēþel*, und v. 1683 [1682], *ðæt sind þā getimbru*. Lächerlich scheint es mir, ein umfangreiches Gedicht Cynewulfs v. 1694 [1693] mit einem Fragezeichen endigen zu lassen; ganz verwerflich ist Gollancz' Meinung dass der *Guthlac* v. 1666 [1665] anfängt, statt mit dem feierlichen *Manige sindon*, wie der *Heleand* mit *Manega wāron*, und der *Panther* mit demselben Verse.'

GLOSSARY.

[The vowels *a* and *æ* have the same position; initial ð follows *t*; otherwise the order is strictly alphabetic. Arabic numerals indicate the classes of the ablaut verbs; W1., etc., those of the weak verbs; R., the reduplicating; PP., the preteritive present verbs. The double dagger, ‡, is used to designate words not elsewhere found in the poetry, according to Grein. When the designations of mood and tense are omitted, 'ind. pres.' is to be understood; when of mood only, supply 'ind.' if no other has immediately preceded, otherwise the latter. Definitions are classed in groups, which are separated by semicolons. ME. signifies Middle English; MnE., Modern English; Sc., Scotch; NED., New. Eng. Dict.]

A.

ā, adv., *ever, for evermore, for ever and ever*: 101, 230, 271, 300, 387, 405, 415, 582, 756. [Cogn. Mn E. *ay*.] Cf. āwo, ō.

ǣ, f., *law*: gs. 140; as. 671. [Ger. *Ehe*.]

‡ ābēatan, R. trans., *scourge, smite, buffet*: pp. npm. ābēatne, 940.

ābēodan, 2. trans., *announce, declare, utter*: pret. 3 sg. ābēad, 229.

ābīdan, 1. intrans., *abide, remain, dwell*: inf. 1630.

ābūgan, 2. trans., *avoid, shun*: 3 sg. ābūgeð, 56. [MnE. *bow*.]

ac, conj., *but*: 56 etc. (23).

ācennan, W1. trans., *beget; bear*: pp. ācenned, 109, 218, 444, 452.

ācweðan, 5. trans., *speak, utter, pronounce*: pret. 3 sg. ācwæð, 316, 474, 714.

Ādām, pr.n., gs. Ādāmes, 960, 1027.

ādl, fn., *disease, sickness*: is. ādle, 1356. [Cogn. ād, 'fire,' Gr. αἶθος, 'fire,' 'burning heat'; hence orig. 'fever,' 'inflammation.']

ādrēogan, 2. trans., *endure, suffer, bear*: pret. 1 sg. ādrēag 1475; 3 sg. ādrēag, 1201; inf. 1513. [Sc. *dree*, 'suffer.']

ādwǣscan, W1. trans., *extinguish, put out, darken*: pp. ādwǣsced, 1132.

āfǣran, W1. trans., *affright, terrify*: pp. apm. āfǣrde, 892. [MnE. *fear*.]

æfest, fn., *dissension, disagreement, bickering*: dp. æfestum, 1658. [æf+ēst (Goth. *ansts*), 'favor.']

æfnan, W 1. trans., *endure, suffer, bear*: pret. 3 pl. æf[n]don, 1356. See geæfnan.

āfōn, R. trans, *seize*: pp. āfǫngen, 1183. [Cogn. MnE. *fang*.]

ǣfre, adv., *at any time; as yet; in any way; ever; always*: 73, 75, 79, 111, 178, 238, 311, 325, 479, 840, 893.

āfrēfran, W1. trans., *console, comfort*: opt. 3 sg. āfrēfre, 368; inf. 175. [frōfor.]

æfter, prep. w. dat., *after; according to; in; throughout, along, over*: 77, [153], 235, 322, 332, 573, 711, 746, 803, 846, 983, 1142, 1220, 1412, 1554.

æfter, adv., *afterward, later*: 473.

āfyllan, W1. trans., *fill*: pp. āfylled, 1562.

‡ ǣfyllend, m., *fulfiller of the law*: gpm. ǣfyllendra, 704.

āfyrhtan, W1. trans., *affright, dismay, appal*: pp. npm. āfyrhte, 1019.

āfyrran, W1. trans., *remove, take away, put away*: inf. 1425; pp. āfyrred, 1370. [feorr, 'far.']

āfȳsan, W1. intrans., *hurry on, drive*

on: pp. npm. āfȳsde (= *hurrying,
rushing*), 985. [**fūs**, 'ready.']

āgǣlan, Wı. trans., *neglect*: opt. 3 sg.
āgǣle, 816.

āgan, PP. trans., *have, possess*: 3 pl.
āgan, 1636; opt. 3 sg. āge, 598; inf.
159, 1203, 1212, 1246, 1402, 1578.
[MnE. *owe, own.*]

āgen, adj., *own*: nsn. 112, 572; dsm.
āgnum, 465, 532. [**āgan**; MnE. *own,*
Ger. *eigen.*]

āgend, m., *Lord*: ns. 420, 543, 1197;
as. 471, 513. [**āgan.**]

ǣghwā, pron., *every one*, neut. *everything*: gsn. ǣghwǣs, 1504.

ǣghwæðer, pron., *every one*: nsm.
ǣghwæþer, 1576. [MnE. *either.*]

ǣghwylc, pron., *every one*: nsm. 1317;
dsm. ǣghwylcum, 840.

āgiefan, 5. trans., *forego, resign; give
up, yield up; surrender, give, bestow*:
pret. 3 sg. āgeaf, 1155, 1161; inf.
1406; pp. āgiefen, 1259.

āhebban, 6. trans., *raise, strike up; lift
up, uplift*: pret. 3 pl. āhōfun, 502; pp.
āhafen, 658; āhæfen, 692. [MnE.
heave.]

† **āhladan**, 6. trans., *draw forth, lead
out, deliver*: pret. 3 sg. āhlōd, 568.
[MnE. *lade;* cf. *ladle.*]

āhōn, R. trans., *crucify, suspend*: pret.
2 sg. āhēnge, 1487; pp. āhongen,
1093, 1446. [Cf. MnE. *hang.*]

āhreddan, Wı. trans., *rescue, deliver,
save*: 3 sg. āhredde, 34; opt. pres. 2
sg. āhredde, 374; inf. 16. [MnE. *rid.*]

ǣht, f., *wealth, possessions, goods, substance*: gp. ǣhta, 604; dp. ǣhtum,
1501. [**āgan.**]

āhycgan, W3. trans., *conceive, imagine*:
inf. 902.

ǣlan, Wı. trans., *burn up, consume;
burn, scorch*: 3 sg. ǣleð, 812, 1546.
[Cf. *ǣled.*]

ālǣtan, R. trans., *forsake, cast off*: inf.
167.

ælbeorht, adj., *shining, radiant, re-*

splendent: nsn. wk. ællbeorhte, 1276;
npm. ælbeorhte, 548, 880; gpm. ælbeorhtra, 928; apm. ælbeorhte, 506.
[As if MnE. *albright.*]

ǣlc, pron. *every*: gsn. ǣlces, 333, 1302;
asf. ǣlce, 406. [MnE. *each.*]

ǣlde, mpl. *men*: gp. ǣlda, 780, 936, 999,
1116; ǣlda, 311; dp. ǣldum, 406,
582, 620, 955, 1201. [WS. *ielde.*]

ālecgan, Wı. trans., *lay*: pret. 3 sg.
ālegde, 1422.

ǣled, m., *fire*: gs. ǣldes, 959, 1005.
[**ǣlan.**]

ælmihtig, adj., *almighty*: nsm. 320,
331, 941, 1218, 1378; nsm. wk. ælmihtga, 443; gsm. ælmihtges, 395;
gsm. wk. ælmihtgan, 1372; dsm.
ælmihtgum, 121; asm. ælmeahtigne,
759; vsm. 215.

alwālda, m. and adj. (wk.), *almighty*:
nsm. 1190, 1364; gsm. alwāldan, 140.
[**wāldan**, wealdan, MnE. *wield.*]

alwiht, npl., *all creatures, all things*:
gp. alwihta, 274, 410, 687. [MnE.
wight, whit.]

ālȳfan, Wı. trans., *grant, vouchsafe*:
pp. ālȳfed, 1572, 1637. [Cf. Ger.
erlauben, MnE. *leave* in 'give me
leave.']

ālȳsan, Wı. trans., *redeem, release*: 3 sg.
ālȳseð, 718; pret. 1 sg. ālȳsde, 1484;
3 sg. ālȳsde, 1099. [Ger. *erlösen.*]

† **ālȳsnes**, f., *redemption*: gs. ālȳsnesse,
1473. [**ālȳsan.**]

amen, *amen*: 439. [Heb.]

ān, num., *one; alone*: nsm. wk. āna,
1420; nsf. 1268, 1292; nsn. 1237;
gsm. ānes, 567, 685; dsm. ānum,
153, 366, 683, 1303, 1309, 1377; asm.
ānne, 1171, 1452; ænne, 1369; asn.
ān, 969; npf. āne, 52; gp. ānra, see
ānra gehwylc; dpf. ānum, 1182. Cf.
on ān, ðæt āna. [MnE. *one, an, a.*]

ānboren, pp., *only begotten*: nsm. 618.

āncenned, pp., *only begotten*: nsm. 464.

ancor, m., *anchor*: dp. ancrum, 863
[Lat. *ancora*, Gr. ἄγκυρα.]

and, *see* ǫnd.

ǣne, adv., *once*: 329, 1194. [ān.]

ānfeald, adj., *single, individual*: asf.
　ānfealde, 1577. [fealdan, 'fold.']

ānforlǣtan, R. trans., *pass by, pass
　over; forsake, abandon*: 1 sg. ānfor-
　lǣte, 1396; pret. 3 pl. ānforlētun,
　1295. [Ger. *verlassen*.]

ǣnge ðinga, adv., *in any way*: 1331.

anginn, n., *beginning*: ds. anginne, 111.

ǣnig, adj., pron., *any*: nsm. 219, 241,
　311, 351, 780, 989, 999, 1316, 1628;
　nsf. 291; nsn. 1015; gsm. ǣnges,
　200; dsm. ǣngum, 683, 1575; asm.
　ǣnigne, 178, 1384, 1497; asf. ǣnge,
　184; asn. 1184: isn. ǣnge, 1331.
　[ān.]　*See* ǣnge ðinga, nǣnig.

ǣnlīc, adj., *incomparable, excellent*:
　apm. ǣnlīce, 1295. [ān.]

ānmōdlīce, adv., *with one accord*: 340.

ānra gehwylc, pron., *each one*: nsm.
　1029; nsn. 1025.

ār, m., *messenger, angel*: np. āras, 493,
　503; dp. ārum, 595; ap. āras, 759.
　[Goth. *airus*; cf. ǣrende, 'errand.']

ār. f., *mercy; grace; advantage; honor*:
　gs. āre, 70; ds. āre, 1083; as. āre,
　335; gp. ārna, 255, 1231, 1352.
　[ME. *ore, Cant. T.* A. 3726; Ger.
　Ehre.]

ǣr, adj., comp. gsf. wk. ǣrran, 1321;
　sup. dsn. wk. ǣrestan (in phrase æt
　ǣrestan, 'at first, in the beginning.'),
　786,823,1190,1397. [Cf.MnE. *early*.]

ǣr, adv., *before*: 39, 45, 63, 115, 161,
　252, 258, 269, 436, 466, 468, 602, 615,
　619, 799, 893, 916, 937, 978, 984,
　1051, 1052, 1056, 1067, 1135, 1157,
　1223, 1233, 1260, 1265, 1287, 1290,
　1302, 1375, 1454, 1491, 1526; sup.
　ǣrest, *first, at first*: 133, 225, 355,
　1151, 1237, 1337, 1380. [Cf. MnE.
　erst.]

ǣr, prep., *before*: w. dat. 216, 848, 1345.
　[MnE. *ere*.]

ǣr, conj., *before*, 315.

ārǣran, W1. trans., *uplift, raise up*:

pp. ārǣred, 1065. [MnE. *rear*;
　rīsan.]

ārāsian, W2. trans., *expose, detect, catch*:
　pp. npm. ārāsade, 1229.

ǣrdæg, m., *former day, past time*: dp.
　ǣrdagum, 79.

āręccan, W1. trans., *expound, explain*;
　expand, outstretch: imp. 2 sg. āręce,
　74; inf. 222, 247; pp. dpf. āreahtum,
　1124.

ǣrest, *see* ǣr.

ārētan, wv., *cherish*: opt. pret. 2 pl.
　ārētten, 1500. [rōt, 'cheerful.']

ārfæst, adj., *merciful, gracious*: nsm.
　245. [ār, 'mercy.']

ǣrgestrēon, n., *ancient treasure*: as.
　996. [Cf. MnE. *strain*, 'race, stock.']

ǣrgewyrht, n., *former deed*: np. ǣrge-
　wyrhtu, 1240. [wyrcean.]

ārian, W2. trans., *honor; have mercy
　upon, be gracious to*: pret. 1 sg. ārode,
　1382; imp. 2 sg. āra, 370. [ār,
　'mercy, honor.']

ārīsan, 1 intrans., *arise, rise (from
　death)*: 3 sg. ārīseð, 1040; pret. 3 sg.
　ārās, 467; inf. 267, 1024, 1030.

ārlēas, adj., *ungodly, impious*: asn.
　1429; gpm. ārlēasra, 1435. [ār,
　'grace' + lēas, '-less.']

ǣrn, *see* foldærn.

ǣrra, *see* ǣr.

ǣrðon, conj., *before, ere*: ǣrþon, 238,
　464, 544, 857.

‡ ǣrworuld, f., *ancient world*: as. 936.

āscian, W2. trans., *ask, inquire*: 1 sg.
　āscige, 1474.

‡ āscǫmian, W2. intrans., *be ashamed,
　be confounded*: pp. npm. āscamode,
　1298. [MnE. *shame*.]

āscyrian, W2. trans., *divide, separate,
　part*: pp. āscyred, 1607, 1617. [Cf.
　MnE. *share, ploughshare; shard,
　potsherd*.]

āsēcan, W1. trans., *seek out, explore,
　ransack*: 3 sg. āsēceð, 1003.

āsęcgan, W3. trans., *explain, unriddle*:
　inf. 221, 1176.

āspringan, 3. trans., *escape from* : 3 pl.
 āspringaðֹ, 1537.

āstandan, 6. intrans., *arise, rise* : pret. 3
pl. āstōdan, 1156; inf. 888.

āstīgan, 1. trans., *mount, ascend ; descend, come down* : pret. 3 sg. āstāg,
702, 720, 727, 737, 786, 866. [Cogn.
MnE. *sty* (*on the eye*), *stile, stair*.]

‡ āstyrfan, W1. trans., *slay, kill* : pp.
nsf. āstyrfed, 19ֹ. [Cogn. Ger. *ster-
ben*, Chaucerian *sterve*, MnE. *starve*.]

æt, prep. w. dat., *at ; in ; with ; from ;
to* : 153, 223, 225, 273, 366, 418, 500,
539, 615, 674, 786, 823, 869, 1029,
1190, 1397, 1493, 1579, 1618, 1636.

æt, n. (?), *food* : as. 604. [etan, 'eat.']

āteon, 2. trans., *draw forth* : pret. 1 sg.
āteah, 1493. [Cf. Ger. *ziehen*, MnE.
tow.]

ætgædre, adv., *together* : 1035. [Paral-
lel with tōgædre.]

æðelcyning, m., *noble king* : gs. æþelcyninges, 906.

‡ æðelduguð, f., *noble band* : ns. æþelduguð, 1011.

æðele, adj., *noble, .excellent, glorious,
splendid* : nsm. æþele, 697; dsm. wk.
æþelan, 350; dsn. wk. æþelan, 268;
asm. æþelne, 402; wk. æþelan, 719;
asf. wk. 455, 1198; asn. æþele, 666,
1193; sup. pred. æþelast, 1180; asn.
wk. æþeleste, 521; npn. æþelast, 607.
[Ger. *edel ;* cf. MnE. *Ethel*.]

æðelīc, adj., *noble, splendid* : nsm.
æþelīc, 308.

æðeling, m., *prince* : ns. æþeling, 448,
627; gs. æþelinges, 743; as. 503;
vs. 158; gp. æþelinga, 515, 741, 845.

æðelu, f., *nature* : dp. æþelum, ˙1184.

āðֶncan, W1. trans., *conceive, imagine* :
inf. āþֶncan, 989.

āðloga, m., *perjurer* : dp. āðlogum,
1604. [Cf. āð, 'oath,' and lēogan,
Sc. *lee*, MnE. *lie*.]

‡ āðolian, W2. trans., *seek after, aim at* :
inf. 1319. [MnE. *thole*, 'suffer' ; cf.
Ger. *dulden*.]

āðrēotan, *see* unāðrēotende.

‡ āðrysman, W1. trans.,*obscure, conceal,
becloud* : pp. āþrysmed, 1133. [ðrosm.]

atol, adj., *fell, malignant, merciless,
ferocious* : nsm. 1278. [Cogn. Lat.
odisse, 'hate.']

‡ atolearfoð, 11., *iniquity ;* gp. atolearfoða, 1265. [Cogn. Ger. *Arbeit*.]

ætsֹomne, adv., *together, at once* : 583,
1112.ֹ [Parallel with tōsֹomne, Ger.
zusammen.]

āttor, n., *poison, venom* : gs. āttres, 768.
[For ātor, Ger. *Eiter*.]

ætwist, f., *presence* : gs. ætwiste, 392.
[wesan.]

ætȳwan, W1. trans., *reveal, make
known, show* : 3 sg. ætȳweð, 1056;
pp. ætȳwed, 1575. [Goth. *ataugyan ;*
with *aug-* cf. ēage, 'eye.'] *See* ēawan, ēowan ; oðēawan, -ēowan,
-ȳwan ; ȳwan.

‡ āwæcnan, W1. intrans., *be born* : pp.
āwæcned, 67. [Cf. MnE. *awake*.]

āweallan, R. intrans., *swarm, teem,
abound in, be full of* : pp. āweallen,
625. [MnE. *well* (*up*); cf. Ger.
wallen, Welle.]

āweaxan, 6. intrans., *spring up, flow,
proceed* : 3 sg. āweaxeð, 1252. [MnE.
wax, 'grow.']

āweorpan, 3. trans., *remove, take off ;
cast out* : pp. āworpen, 98, 1404. [Cf.
MnE. *warp*, Ger. *werfen, Wurf*.]

āwo, adv., *for ever* : 479, 1270, 1645,
1663. *See* ā, ō.

āwrecan, 5. trans., *compose* : pret. 3 sg.
āwræc, 633.

āwyrged, pp., *accursed, cursed* : 1561 ;
nsm. wk. āwyrgda, 256; apm.
āwyrgde, 158; vpm. āwyrgde, 1519.

B.

bæl, 11., *fire, flame, conflagration* : ds.
bæle, 808. ֹ [Cogn. Gr. φαλός, 'shining,' 'bright'; cf. *bale-fire*, and Scott,
Lay of the Last Minstrel, III. xxvii;
Wm. Morris, *Sigurd*, III. 305.]

bǣm, *see* bēgen.

bānloca, m., *body* : as. bānlocan, 769.
[bān, 'bone'; cf. lūcan, ' lock.']

bærnan, W1. trans., *burn* : 3 sg. bærneð,
969; pret. 3 pl. bærndon, 708; ger.
tō bærnenne, 1621. *See* for-, onbærnan; beornan, byrnan.

bæð, *see* fȳrbæð.

be(-), *see* bi(-).

bēacen, n., *sign ; standard* : ds. bēacne,
1065; gp. bēacna, 1085.

bēag, m., *crown, ring* (?) : as. 1126,
1443; gp. bēaga, 292. [Cf. MnE. *bee*
as nautical term.]

beald, adj., *confident, of good courage* :
npm. bealde, 1076. [MnE. *bold* <
Angl. bāld.]

bealodǣd, f., *evil deed* : gs. bealodǣde,
1301.

bealofull, adj., *wicked* : nsm. wk. sb.
bealofulla, 259; dp. bealofullum, 908.

‡ bealorāp, m., *grievous cord* : dp.
bealorāpum, 365.

bealu, n., *misfortune, affliction, misery* :
ds. bealwe, 1105; as. bealo, 1247; gp.
bealwa, 182. [MnE. *bale*, 'evil.'] *See*
ealdor-, firen-, helle-, ðīodbealu.

bēam, m., *tree ; cross* : ns. 1089, 1174;
as. 678, 729, 1093, 1446 ; np.
bēamas, 1169. [MnE. *hornbeam*,
Ger. *Baum*.]

bearhtm, m., *crash, uproar* : ds. bearhtme, 1144; gp. bearhtma, 950. *See*
brehtm.

bearn, n., *child, son* : ns. 66, 147, 465,
572, 903; gs. bearnes, 38, 76, 724;
as. 205, 341, 774, 788, 1072, 1194; vs.
164; np. 85, 1118, 1277, 1565; dp.
bearnum, 242, 936, 1424, 1591; ap.
1598. [Dial. *barn, bairn*.] *See* frēo-,
frum-, God-, hǣlo-, sigebearn.

bēatan, *see* ābēatan.

bēgen, adj., *both* : npn. bū, 1325; npn.
būtū (from bēgen twēgen), 1112;
gpm. bēga, 896; dpm. bǣm, 100, 357 ;
apn. bū, 1035, 1256.

bend, mfn., *bond, bondoge, captivity* :

as. 1041; dp. bendum, 147; apf.
benda, 68. [Cf. MnE. *bend* as a
nautical term.]

benn, f., *wound* : gp. benna, 771.

bēodan, 2. trans., *proclaim* : 3 sg.
bēodeð, 1340. [MnE. *bid* combines
this with OE. biddan.] *See* ā-,
bi-, for-, onbēodan.

beofian, W2. intrans., *tremble, quake* :
3 sg. beofað, 881; 3 pl. beofiað, 827,
1014, 1229; pret. 3 sg. beofode, 1144;
ptc. npm. beofiende, 1020. [Ger.
beben.]

bēon, *see* wesan.

beorg, m., *mount, mountain* : as. 875,
899, 1007; np. beorgas, 977; dp. beorgum, 967. [MnE. *barrow*, 'mound,'
and dial. *bargh, barf, bar*.]

beorgan, 3. trans., *guard* (*ourselves*) (?),
beware of, guard against (*the wounds*,
with refl. dat.) (?) : inf. 771. [Ger.
bergen.]

beorht, adj., *beaming, glittering, radiant,
resplendent, effulgent ; illustrious,
glorious ; excellent, sublime ; fair ;
clear, ringing* : nsm. wk. beorhta, 827, 1346, 1657 ,
nsm. wk. beorhta, 1061 ; nsn. 412; 877 ;
dsf. wk. beorhtan, 519; asm. beorhtne.
205, 483, 1058, 1076, 1391 ; asf. wk,
beorhtan, 113, 292; asn. 1630; isf. wk.
beorhtan, 510; npm. beorhte, 1646;
npf. beorhte, 1020; gpm. beorhtra,
896; gpn. beorhtfa, 742; apf. beorhte,
1635; comp. npn. wk. beorhtran,
1241 ; sup. nsf. beorhtast, 1085; vsm.
beorhtast, 104. [MnE. *bright*.] *See*
æl-, heofon-, sigorbeorht.

beorhte, adv., *shiningly, radiantly,
dazzlingly* : 552, 701, 903, 935, 1467.

beorn, m., *man; hero; prince* : ns. 449;
gs. beornes, 530; np. beornas, 991 ;
dp. beornum, 412.

beornan, 3. intrans., *burn* : pret. 3 sg.
beorn, 540. [Cf. bærnan, byrnan.]

beran, 4. trans., *bear, carry* : 3 pl. berað,
1072, 1300, 1634. *See* geberan;
gǣst-, reordberend ; ānboren.

berstan, 3. intrans., *burst asunder, topple, tumble, crash, melt away* : 3 pl. bersta ð, 811, 932 ; pret. 3 pl. burstan, 1141. *See* **forberstan**.

betast, *see* **gōd**.

bētan, *see* **gebētan; unbēted**.

Bēthania, pr. ii., *Bethany*: ds. 456.

Bētlem, pr. n., *Bethlehem* : ds. Bētleme, 453 ; as. 449.

betlīc, adj., *excellent*: sup. vsf. betlīcast, 66.

betra, betst, *see* **gōd**.

bi, prep., *by ; by means of ; according to ; concerning ; because of ; for ; in exchange for* : w. dat. 128, 134, 212, 301, 1071, 1219, 1223, 1367, 1474 ; be, 1289, 1393 ; w. inst. 633, 650, 691, 712, 834, 998.

bibēodan, 2. trans., *command, enjoin* : pret. 1 sg. bibēad, 1499 ; 3 sg. bibēad, 543, 793.

bibod, n., *commandment, precept, behest*: as. 1158, 1393, 1524, 1630.

bibyrgan, W1. trans., *bury* : pp. npm. bibyrgde, 1158.

‡ **biclȳsan**, W1. trans., *shut, close*: pp. beclȳsed, 323. [From late Latin *clūsa*, for *clausa*.]

bicuman, 4. intrans., *come ; come to ; happen to ; arise*: pret. 3 sg. bicwōm, 631, 709, 822, 858, 1105 ; 3 pl. bicwōman, 1113.

bidǣlan, W1. trans., *deprive, bereave ; deliver, free*: pp. bidǣled, 563, 1407, 1432. [Cf. MnE. *deal*.]

bīdan, 1. trans., *await, expect, endure*: 2 pl. bīda ð, 510 ; 3 pl. bīda ð, 1020; pret. 3 sg. bād, 704 ; 3 pl. bidon, 147, 540; inf. 802. *See* **ā-, gebīdan**.

biddan, 5. trans., *beseech, implore, entreat*: 3 sg. bide ð, 113 ; 1 pl. bidda ð, 262, 337, 359; pret. 3 pl. bǣdan, 1507; bǣdun, 1352; inf. 774. [MnE. *bid* from this verb and **bēodan**.]

bīdfæst, adj., *irremovable, fixed*, asm. bīdfæstne, 1597. [**bīdan**.]

bidrīfan, 1. trans., *drive, thrust*: pp. bidrifen, 1408.

bidyrnan, W1. trans., *dispel, put to flight* (lit. *conceal*): pp. bidyrned, 1088. [Cf. dial., esp. Sc., *dern, darn, derned*.]

bifealdan, R. trans., *envelop, wrap*: pp. npm. bifealdne, 117.

bifēolan, 3. trans., *commit, entrust*: pp. bifolen, 668.

bifōn, R. trans., *receive ; confine, encompass, begird*: pret. 2 sg. befēnge, 80; pp. bifēn, 1157 ; bifǫngen, 527.

biforan, adv., *before, in time past ; to the presence*: 468, 1066.

biforan, prep. w. dat., *in the presence of*: beforan, 643.

bigān, PP. trans., *confess* (?) : 3 sg. bīgǣ ð, 1307. Cf. **bigǫngan**.

bigǫng, m., *extent, compass ; lapse*: ds. (is ?) 235; as. 680.

bigǫngan, R. trans., *foster, cultivate*: opt. 3 sg. bīgǫnge, 1581. Cf. **bigān**.

bigrafan, 6. trans., *bury*: pp. bigrafen, 1465.

bihelan, 4. trans., *mask, dissemble, cloak, hide*: inf. 1310 ; pp. biholen, 45. [Ger. *hehlen*.]

bihindan, prep., *behind*: behindan, 155.

‡ **bihlæmman**, W1. trans., *fall upon, surprise*: 3 sg. bihlæm[m]e ð, 869.

bihȳdan, W1. trans., *ensconce, shelter*: inf. behȳdan, 844.

bilūcan, 2. trans., *lock; encompass, shut in*: 3 sg. bilūce ð, 1623; pret. 3 sg. bilēac, 334; pp. bilocen, 252, 806, 1259.

bimī ð an, 1. intrans., *hide, dissemble*: inf. bemī þan, 1048.

bimurnan, 3. trans., *bewail, grieve over*: 2 sg. bemurnest, 176. [MnE. *mourn*.]

bindan, 3. trans., *enthrall, confine, fetter*: 3 sg. binde ð, 1597; ger. tō bindenne, 1621. *See* **gebindan**.

‡ **binn**, f., *manger*: ds. binne, 724. [MnE. *bin*.]

birēafian, W2. trans., *despoil, bereave*: pp. birēafod, 558 ; berēafod, 168.

birēofan, ʐ. trans., *deprive, bereave* : pp. npm. birofene, 1525.

‡ birinnan, 3. intrans., *suffuse*: pp. birunnen, 1175.

biscyrian, W2. trans., *deprive, dispossess*: pp. npm. bescyrede, 32 ; vpm. biscyrede, 1519.

bisencan, W1. trans., *overflow, submerge*: inf. 1168. [sincan.]

bisēon, 1. trans., *moisten, drench*: pp. 1087.

bismītan, 1. trans., *defile, pollute*: pret. 2 sg. bismite, 1483. [Prov. Eng. *smit.*]

bisorgian, W2. trans., *fear, be concerned about*: 3 sg. bisorgað, 1555. [Cf. MnE. *sorrow.*]

bistēman, W1. trans., *bedew*: pp. bistēmed, 1085. [MnE. *steam.*]

biswēðlan, W2. trans., *enfold*: pp. npm. biswēðede, 1643. [Cf. MnE. *swathe.*]

biteldan, 3. trans., *plunge, drown, overwhelm* : pp. bitolden, 538. [Cf. Ger. *Zelt.*]

biter, adj., *grievous, afflictive, wounding, painful, bitter*: nsm. 908 ; nsn. 769; dsm. wk. bitran, 1474; asm. biterne, 765; dpm. bitrum, 152, 1251. [bītan.]

biðeccan, W1. trans., *clothe, cover*: pret. 3 sg. biþeahte, 1422; pp. npm. beþeahte, 116. [Ger. *bedecken.*]

biðencan, W1. trans., *ponder, reflect upon, keep in mind*: opt. 1 pl. biþencen, 849; inf. biþencan, 821. [MnE. *bethink.*]

‡ biðryccan, W1. trans., *press on*: pret. 3 pl. biþrycton, 1445. [Ger. *drücken.*]

bittre, adv., *bitterly*: 1437. [biter.]

bitwēon, prep. w. dat., *among*: 1658.

biwerian, W2. trans., *shield, protect*: pp. npm. biwerede, 1643. [Ger. *wehren.*]

biwindan, 3. trans., *wrap, swaddle,*

(en)*swathe; encompass*: pret. 3 sg. biwond, 1421 ; opt. 3 sg. bewinde, 29; pp. bewunden, 725; asm. biwundenne, 1423; npm. biwundne, 1642.

biwitian, W2. trans., *watch over, perform* : 3 pl. biwitigað, 353.

biwrecen, pp., *surrounded*: npm. biwrecene, 831.

‡ biwrīðan, 1. trans., *encompass; garnish*: 3 sg. bewrīð, 718; pp. bewriþen, 310.

blāc, adj., *bright*: nsm. 808. [Ger. *bleich;* cf. MnE. *bleach;* blīcan.]

blæc, adj., *black*: gpm. blacra, 896.

blæd, m., *abundance; blessedness; glory; prosperity; reward*: ns. 710, 877, 1635; gs. blædes, 1256, 1657 ; as. 688, 1211, 1346, 1586 ; is. blæde, 1239, 1291. [Cogn. Lat. *flatus;* from blāwan, as *flatus* from *flare.*]

‡ blædwela, m., *wealth of vegetation, profusion of plants* : as. blædwelan, 1391.

blæst, m., *flame* : ns. 975.

blāt, adj., *livid, wan*: sup. ns. str. blātast, 771.   ˝

blāwan, R. trans., *blow*: 3 pl. blāwað, 880, 950.

blēd, f., *branch* (?), *fruit* (?), *blossom* (?) : dp. blēdum, 1169.

blendan, *see* geblendan.

blēo, n., *color, hue; complexion*: as. 1564; ip. blēom, 1391. [MnE. *blee.*] *See* wundorblēo; geblēod.

blētsian, *see* geblētsian.

blētsung, f., *blessing*: ns. 100.

blīcan, 1. intrans., *shine, glitter, glow* : 3 sg. blīceð, 701 ; 3 pl. blīcað, 1012; blīcaþ, 1238; inf. 507, 522, 903. [Gr. φλέγειν, 'burn,' and blāc.]

blind, adj., *(spiritually) blind, undiscerning, senseless* : npm. blinde, 1126. *See* mōdblind.

blis, f., *bliss, joy, happiness*: ns. 530, 750, 1649, 1657 ; ds. blisse, 552, 1646; as. blisse, 68; gp. blissa, 1256; dp. blissum, 1346. [For blīðs < blīðe.]

blissian, W2. intrans., *rejoice, gladden, cheer, make glad*: 3 pl. blissiað, 1286; pp. blissad, 1162. *See* **geblissian.**

blīðe, adj., *joyful, joyous, blithesome; kindly, compassionate, merciful*: nsm. blīþe, 739; nsn. blīþe, 877; asm. wk. blīðan, 774; asf. wk. blīðan, 519; ism. blīþe, 280.

blōd, n., *blood*: ns. 1112; gs. blōdes, 935; is. blōde, 259, 1085.

blōdgyte, m., *bloodshed, havoc*: as. 708. [gēotan, 'pour.']

blōdig, adj., *bloody, gory*: dpm. blōdgum, 1174.

bōc, f., *book*: np. bēc, 785; gp. bōca, 1630; dp. bōcum, 453, 701, 793.

bod, *see* **bibod.**

boda, m., *herald, messenger, ambassador*: ds. bodan, 1304; as. bodan, 1151; np. bodan, 449. [bēodan.] *See* **hēah-, spelboda.**

bodian, W2. trans., *preach*: imp. pl. bodiað, 483. [MnE. *bode.*] *See* **gebodian.**

boga, *see* **brægdboga.**

bold, n., *building, dwelling, habitation*: gp. bolda, 742. [For orig. boþl, botl.]

bona, m., *destroyer*: ns. 264; gs. bonan, 1393. [MnE. *bane.*]

bonnan, R. trans., *summon, cite*: 3 pl. bonnað, 1066.

-bora, *see* **mund-, wōð-, wrōhtbora.**

bord, n., *side (of a vessel;* cf. 'overboard,' 'go by the board'): as. 861.

‡ bordgelāc, n., *missile, dart*: ns. 769. [bord, 'shield.']

boren, *see* **ānboren.**

bōsm, m., *bosom*, poet. for *womb*: is. bōsme, 84.

bōt, f., *relief, succor*: ns. 152, 365. [MnE. *boot,* Ger. *Busse.*]

brād, adj., *broad, wide, ample*: nsm. wk. brāda, 1144; asf. brāde, 991; apm. brāde, 357.

brāde, adv., *far and wide, everywhere*: 380.

brǣce, *see* **unbrǣce.**

‡ brægdboga, m., *bended bow (?), deceitful bow (?)*: ds. brægdbogan, 765.

-brec, *see* **gebrec.**

brecan, 4. trans., *break down; shatter, rend; violate, transgress; burst forth*: 3 pl. brecað, 991; pret. 2 sg. brǣce, 1393; 3 sg. brǣc, 1145; 3 pl. brǣcon, 1629; brǣcan, 708. *See* **tōbrecan.**

brecan, W1. intrans., *roar*: ptc. npm. brecende, 950.

brego, m., *Lord, Prince*: ns. 403; brega, 456.

brehtm, m., *crash, clangor*: ds. brehtme, 881. *See* **bearhtm.**

brēman, W1. trans., *praise; proclaim*: imp. pl. brēmað, 483; ptc. npm. brēmende, 387.

brēost, n., *breast*: fig. *heart, spirit*: gp. brēosta, 1072; dp. brēostum, 341.

brēostgehygd, fn., *thought of the heart*: dp. brēostgehygdum, 262. [hycgan.]

brēostsefa, m., *heart, soul*: ns. 540.

brēotan, 2. trans., *dash to pieces, cut down*: imp. pl. brēotaþ, 485. [Cf. **brytta,** and MnE. *brittle.*]

bringan, W1. trans., *bring; offer, present*: 3 sg. bringeð, 68; 3 pl. bringað, 1077; pret. 2 sg. brōhtes, 289; 3 sg. brōhte, 336; opt. 3 pl. bringen, 1074; imp. sg. bring, 150; inf. 1058; pp. (str.) brungen, 120.

bringend, m., *bringer, giver*: ns. 140.

brōga, m., *terror, that which strikes terror, inspires dread*: as. brōgan, 793. *See* **gryrebrōga.**

brond, m., *fire, conflagration*: ns. 811. [MnE. *brand.*]

brosnian, *see* **gebrosnian.**

brōðor, m., *brother*: ap. brōþor, 1499.

brūcan, 2. trans., *enjoy, delight in*: 3 pl. 1646, 1663; inf. 392, 1325, 1361. [Ger. *brauchen,* MnE. *brook.*]

brȳd, f., *bride, spouse*: ns. 38, 280, 292. [Ger. *Braut.*]

bryne, m., *fire; burning*: ns. 1058,

1597, 1661. [Cf. **byrnan.**] *See* **lēgbryne.**

‡ **brynetēar,** m., *burning tear, scalding tear*: dp. brynetēarum, 152.

‡ **brytengrund,** m., *spacious land*: ap. brytengrundas, 357.

brytenwǫng, m., *spacious plain*: ap. brytenwǫngas, 380.

brytta, m., *Dispenser, Distributor, Lord*: ns. 334, 462; gs. bryttan, 281. [brēotan.]

bryttian, W2. trans., *dispense, distribute, apportion*: 3 sg. bryttað, 682. [brytta.]

bū, *see* **bēgen.**

būend, *see* **eorð-, fold-, sund-, ðēod-būend.**

būgan, *see* **ā-, gebūgan.**

burg, f., *city; fortress, stronghold, citadel*: ds. byrg, 461, 519; byrig, 542, 569; as. 534, 553; gp. burga, 66, 1239; dp. burgum, 530. [MnE. *borough, -bury.*] *See* **corðburg.**

‡ **burglǫnd,** n., *(site of a city), city*: vs. 51.

burgsittende, mpl., *citizens, burghers*: np. 337.

burgstęde, m., *(site of a castle), citadel, stronghold, castle*: np. 811.

burgware, mpl., *citizens, burghers*: dp. burgwarum, 742.

burgweall, m., *city wall*: np. burgweallas, 977.

būtan, prep. w. dat., *without*: 37, 111, 125, 207, 271, 290, 415, 439, 599, 722, 1652, 1653, 1654, 1655, 1656, 1657, 1658, 1659.

būtan, conj., *unless, except, but*: 272; būton, 695.

būtū, *see* **bēgen.**

bycgan, *see* **gebycgan.**

bȳgan, *see* **for-, gebȳgan.**

‡ **byldo,** f., *boldness, confidence, assurance*: as. 113. [beald.]

bȳme, f., *trumpet*: gs. bȳman, 1061; ap. bȳman, 881. [Dial. *beme.*] *See* **heofonbȳme.**

-byrd, *see* **gebyrd.**

‡ **byrdscipe,** m., *child-bearing*: gs. byrdscypes, 182. [beran.]

byrgan, *see* **blbyrgan.**

byrgen, f., *tomb, sepulchre*: ds. byrgenne, 1467; as. byrgenne, 729. [beorgan.]

byrhtan, W1. intrans., *shine, give light*: 3 sg. byrhteð, 1089. [beorht.]

byrhto, f., *brightness, splendor, effulgence*: is. byrhte, 1239. [beorht.]

byrnan, 3. trans. and intrans., *consume; be on fire*: 3 sg. byrneþ, 988; inf. 808; ptc. gpn. byrnendra, 1251. Cf. **bærnan, beornan; bryne.**

byrðen, *see* **synbyrðen.**

‡ **bysmerlēas,** adj., *blameless, unblamable*: nsm. 1325. [Cf. ME. *busemare.*]

C.

cǣge, *see* **lloðucǣge.**

cǣld, adj., *cold*: asn. 851; dp. cǣldan, 1629.

carcern, n., *prison, dungeon*: ds. carcerne, 25, 735. [Lat. *carcer*, under influence of OE. ærn, ęrn.]

ceafl, m., *jaw*: ip. ceaflum, 1251. [ME. *chaul*, MnE. *jowl.*]

cēapian, W2. trans. (w. gen.), *purchase*: pret. 3 sg. cēapode, 1095. [Eliz. *cheap.*]

cearful, adj., *sorrowful, melancholy*: gp. cearfulra, 25. [MnE. *careful.*]

cearian, W2. intrans., *be concerned, be disquieted*: ptc. nsm. cearigende, 177. [MnE. *care.*]

cearig, adj., *sorrowful, sad, joyless*: npm. ce[a]r[i]ge, 835; dp. cearigum, 148. [MnE. *chary.*] *See* **hrēowcearig.**

cearn, f., *sorrow, woe, distress, anguish, dole, grief; lament, wailing*: ns. 997; cearo, 1285, 1662; gp. cearena, 961; dip. cearum, 891, 1016, 1130. [MnE. *care.*] *See* **sorgcearn.**

ceaster, f., *city*: as. ceastre, 578. [MnE. *Chester, -caster, -cester;* Lat. *castra.*]

‡ ceasterhlid, n., *city gate*: gs. ceasterhlides, 314. [MnE. *lid*.]

cęmpa, m., *soldier*: np. cęmpan, 563.
[OE. *camp* < Lat. *campus*; cf. Ger.
kämpfen, MnE. *champion*.]

cęnnan, W1. trans., *bring forth, bear;
fashion, contrive, strike out*: 3 pl.
cęnnað, 87; pret. 3 sg. cęnde, 636;
inf. 298; pp. npm. cęnde, 232. *See*
ācęnnan, āncęnned.

cēol, m., *vessel, ship*: gs. cēoles, 861;
ip. cēolum 851. [Cf. Gr. γαῦλος,
MnE. *keel*.]

cēosan, *see* gecēosan.

cild, n., *child*: ns. 218; gs. cildes, 725.

cildgeong, adj., *of infant age, infantine*:
ns. 1425.

cinn, *see* cynn.

circe, wf., *church*: ns. 699, 703. [Gr.
κυριακόν, 'of the Lord.']

cirm, m., *outcry, clamor, din*: ns. 835,
997. [Dial. MnE. *chirm*; cf. Milton's
'*charm* of earliest birds.']

clǣne, adj., *pure, unsullied, spotless,
undefiled, immaculate, unblemished*:
asm. clǣnne, 444; asm. wk. clǣnan,
136; asf. 187, 298, 331; gp. clǣnra,
703; apm. wk. clǣnan, 1285; apn.
wk. clǣnan, 1222; sup. nsf. wk.
clǣneste, 276. [Ger. *klein*.] *See*
unclǣne.

clāð, m., *garment;* plur. *clothes*: ip.
clāþum, 725, 1423.

cleopian, W2. intrans., *exclaim, call
aloud*: 2 sg. cleopast, 177; pret. 3
pl. cleopedon, 508. [Arch. and dial.
clepe, yclept.]

clif, *see* bēahclif.

clīfan, *see* oðclīfan.

clǫmm, m., *fetter, chain, bond;* fig.
bound, confine: ds. clǫmme, 1145; dp.
clǫmmum, 1629; ip. clǫmmum, 735.
[MnE. *clam*.] *See* wundorclǫm.

clūstor, n., *lock, fastening*: as. 314.
[Lat. *clūstrum, claustrum*.]

clȳsan, *see* biclȳsan.

cnāwan, *see* ge-, oncnāwan.

cnēoris, f., *generation; tribe*: dp.
cnēorissum, 232, 1233. [cnēo, in
the sense of 'knee, joint, degree of
relationship.']

‡ cnoll, m., *peak*: ap. cnollas, 717.
[MnE. *knoll*.]

cofa, *see* hreðercofa.

cǫndel, *see* heofoncǫndel.

corðor, n., *multitude, legion, host*: ds.
corðre, 494; is. corðre, 578.

costian, W2. trans., *try, test*: 3 sg.
costað, 1058. [Cf. Lat. *gustare*.]

cræft, m., *power;* (*physical*) *strength;
ability; endowment; excellence;
marvel, prodigy*: ns. 421, 667; gs.
cræftes, 1145; as. 218, 685; ip. cræftum, 687. [MnE. *craft*, Ger. *Kraft*.]
See mægen-, mōd-, searocræft.

cræftga, m., *artificer, craftsman*: ns.
12. *See* hygecræftig.

Crīst, pr.n., *Christ*: ns. 95, 331, 391,
1216; gs. Crīstes, 51, 65, 283, 905,
1030; ds. Crīste, 1222; as. 1634; vs.
157, 215, 250, 358.

‡ crybb, f., *manger*: ds. crybbe, 1425.
[MnE. *crib*, Ger. *Krippe*; cf. Fr.
crèche.]

‡ culpa, m. (?), *fault, misdeed*: as. culpan, 177. [Lat.]

-cuma, *see* wilcuma.

cuman, 4. intrans., *come*: 3 sg. cymeð,
62, 791, 824, 832, 875, 901, 905,
1008; 3 pl. cumað, 920, 1366; pret. 2
sg. cwōme, 413; 3 sg. cwōm, 46, 74,
290, 420, 436, 448, 1160; 3 pl.
cwōman, 545, 549, 553; cwōmun,
494; opt. 2 sg. cyme, 114; 3 sg. cume,
12; opt. pret. 3 sg. cwōme, 148;
imp. sg. cum, 149, 243; cym, 372;
inf. 267, 942, 1026, 1036; pp. cymen,
66. *See* bi-, forcuman.

-cund, *see* God-, heofon-, ufan-, ūp-,
woruldcund.

cunnan, PP. trans., *know, comprehend,
be aware of; know, be acquainted
with, be familiar with; have* (*carnal*)
knowledge of; can, be able. Fērð-

gewit cunnan, *have intelligence;* þonc cunnan, *give thanks:* 1 sg. cǫnn (w. gen.), 198; 3 sg. cǫnn, 69; cǫn, 680; 2 pl. cunnon, 573; pret. 2 sg. cūðes, 77; 3 sg. cūþe, 419; cūðe, 633; 3 pl. cūþun, 1092; cūþon, 1213; cūþan, 1186; opt. pret. 3 pl. cūþan, 422; cūþen, 1184. [MnE. *con, can.*] *See* bicunnau.

cunnian, W2. trans., *essay, attempt; experience, put up with:* pret. 3 sg. cunnode, 645; inf. 1417.

cūð, adj., *known:* nsn. 95, 185, 715, 1049. [cunnan.] *See* uncūð.

cwacian, W2. intrans., *tremble:* 3 sg. cwacað, 797. [MnE. *quake.*]

cwalu, *see* hearm-, hęll-, nīðewalu.

cwānian, W2. trans., *bewail, lament:* ptc. gp. cwānendra, 835.

cwealm, m., *death; torment, agony:* ns. 1540; ds. cwealme, 87; as. 1425; gp. cwealma, 1626. [MnE. *qualm;* cf. cwęllan, 'kill.'] *See* māncwealm.

cwelman, W2. trans., *destroy:* ptc. nsn. cwelmende, 958. [cwealm.]

cwēman, *see* gecwēman.

cwēn, f., *woman, lady; queen* (?): as. cwēnn, 1198; vs. 276.

cweðan, 5. trans., *say, speak:* 3 sg. cwið, 453, 1518; cwiþ, 701; 3 pl. cweþað, 283, 401; pret. 3 sg. cwæð, 87, 691; 3 pl. cwædon, 65, 148; inf. 1376; cweþan, 1549; pp. cweden, 211, 547. [Cf. MnE. *quoth.*] *See* ā-, gecweðan.

cwic, adj., *alive, living:* nsm. 590, 1030; npm. cwice, 1130; gp. cwicra, 891, 997; apm. cwice, 958. [Cf. MnE. '*quick and dead,*' '*cut to the quick,*' *quitch-grass.*]

cwicsūsl, n., *(living torment), hell-torment, pit of hell:* ds. cwicsūsle, 561, 732.

cwide, m., *decree, sentence, commandment:* as. 618, 1223, 1515. [cweðan.]

See heard-, hearm-, hlēoðor-, sār-, wordcwide.

cwīðan, W1. trans., *bewail, bemoan, lament:* 3 sg. cwīþeð, 961; 3 pl. cwīþað, 1567; pret. 3 pl. cwīðdun, 1130; ptc. nsf. cwīþende, 1285; asn. cwīþende, 891.

cyle, ns., *cold:* 1662.

cyme, m., *coming, advent:* ns. 896; as. 530, 915, 1030. [cuman.] *See* hēr-, hidercyme.

-cynd, *see* gecynd.

‡ **cynelīce,** adv., *royally:* 157.

cynestōl, m., *throne; royal seat, royal dwelling:* ds. cynestōle, 1216; gp. cynestōla, 51. [MnE. *stool.*]

cyning, m., *king:* ns. 12, 61, 494, 528, 565, 578, 618, 687, 703, 715, 827, 832, 1009, 1152, 1165, 1208, 1588; gs. cyninges, 165, 1626, 1629, 1662; ds. cyninge, 1, 391; as. 136, 732, 797, 1038; vs. 18, 215, 372; gp. cyninga, 136, 215, 508. *See* æðel-, ēðel-, hēah-, heofon-, mægen-, rodor-, scīr-, sōð-, wuldorcyning.

cynn, n., *race, -kind:* ns. 224, 386, 1027; syn. 961; gs. cynnes, 780, 956; ds. cynne, 425, 610, 1196; as. 887; cinn, 1619. [MnE. *kin.*] *See* fædren-, frǫm-, frum-, heoloð-, mēdren-, mǫncyn(n).

cȳpan, *see* gecȳpan.

cyrran, W1. intrans., *return:* opt. 2 sg. cyrre, 155. [Cf. MnE. *ajar; chare, chore.*] *See* oncyrran.

cyst, m., *(what is chosen), best, choicest; election:* as. 391, 1134; vs. 51; dp. cystum, 1223. [cēosan.] *See* uncyst.

cȳðan, W1. trans., *announce, make known, reveal, proclaim, show forth, declare:* pret. 3 sg. cȳðde, 1145, 1163; 3 pl. cȳðdon, 65, 450; opt. 2 sg. cȳðe, 338; imp. pl. cȳðað, 482; inf. 297. [cūð.] *See* gecȳðan.

cȳððu, *see* ealdcȳððu.

D.

dǣd, f., _deed, act_: np. dǣde, 1046;
dǣda, 1049; gp. dǣda, 525, 1367,
1582; dp. dǣdum, 803; ip. dǣdum,
429, 828. _See_ **bealo-, firen-, gōddǣd.**

dǣdhwæt, adj., _untiring, indefatigable,
diligent, assiduous_: npm. dǣdhwæte,
385.

dæg, m., _day_: ns. 868, 1054, 1064, 1656;
ds. dæge, 1050, 1096, 1204, 1310,
1371; is. dæge, 1153; np. dagas,
1288; gp. daga, 1021; dagena (with
rīm), 467, 1586. _See_ **ǣr-, dōm-,
eald-, fyrn-, gear-, līf-, wildæg.**

dæl, n., _gulf, pit, abyss_: ns. 1541; as.
1531. [MnE. _dale,_ Ger. _Thal._]

dǣl, m., _share, allotted portion; division,
side; bit, jot, whit_: ns. 806; as.
1225, 1384. [MnE. _deal,_ Ger. _Theil._]

dǣlan, W1. trans., _impart, confer, be-
stow_: 3 sg. dǣleð, 428. [MnE. _deal,_
Ger. _theilen._] _See_ **bi-, gedǣlan.**

dafenian, _see_ **gedafenian.**

Dāuīd, pr. n, _David_: gs. Dāuīdes,
96, 165, 191; Dāuīþes, 712.

dēad, adj., _deceased; inanimate, lifeless_:
npf. dēade, 1179; apm. dēade, 1158.

dēað, m., _death_: ns. 1602; gs. dēaþes,
118, 1041; ds. dēaðe, 467, 886, 1475,
1618; as. 596, 1173, 1411; is. dēaðe,
1462, 1560. _See_ **ęndedēað.**

dēaðdęnu, f., _valley of death_: ds.
dēaðdęne, 344. [MnE. _dean, dene;_ cf.
Deepdene, Taunton Dean, Marden.]

‡ **dēaðfiren,** f., _deadly sin, mortal sin_:
dp. dēaðfirenum, 1206.

‡ **dēaðlēg,** m., _death flame_: ns. 982.

dēaðscūa, m., _death-shadow, shadow of
death_: ns. 257.

dēaðsęle, m., _death-hall_: as. 1536.

dēaw, m., _dew_: ns. 609. [Cf. Ger.
Thau.]

dēgol, adj., _hidden, unintelligible, enig-
matical_: ns. (pred.), 41, 640.

dēma, m., _judge_: gs. dēman, 796, 836.
[dōm.] _See_ **sigedēma.**

dēman, W1. trans., _adjudge_: 3 sg.
dēmeð, 845; inf. 803. [dōm.] _See_
gedēman.

dęnu, _see_ **dēaðdęnu.**

dēofol, n., _Satan; devil, demon_: ns.
1278; gs. dēofles, 1449, 1536; ds.
dēofle, 1522; np. 1531; gp. dēofla,
563, 779, 895, 1627; dp. dēoflum,
580, 594, 898, 1514. [Lat. _diabolus._]

dēop, adj., _deep; vast_: nsm. wk. dēopa,
1544; nsf. 930; asn. 856; wk. dēope,
1531.

dēope, adv., _profoundly_: 167.

dēor, n., _beast_: gp. dēora, 982. [Cf.
Ger. _Thier;_ Shak. 'small _deer._']
See **wǣgdēor.**

deorc, adj., _dark, murky, black; benight-
ed_: nsm. 257, 1560; dsf. wk. deorcan,
1522; asf. 118; asn. 640.

dēore, adj., _precious_: isn. wk. dēoran,
309. Cf. **dȳre.**

dēore, adv., _dearly, at a great price_:
1462.

dōgor, mn., _day_: gp. dōgra, 428.

dohtor, f., _daughter:—female descendant; female inhabitant_: ns. 191; vp.
91.

dolg, n., _wound_ (?), _scar_ (?): ap. 1107,
1206. _See_ **feorhdolg.**

dōm, m., _sentence; (Last) Judgment;
decision; condemnation; fate; glory;
reputation_: ns. 405, 1232, 1656; gs.
dōmes, 228, 1021, 1205; ds. dōme,
782, 1041, 1560; as. 790, 1368; is.
dōme, 168, 385. [MnE. _doom._] _See_
lǣce-, wīs-, wītedōm.

dōmdæg, m., _Doomsday, Day of Judg-
ment_: ds. dōmdæge, 1618, 1636.

dōmēadig, adj., _abounding in glory,
renowned, illustrious_: gp. dōmēad-
igra, 1656. [But see text.]

‡ **dōmhwæt,** adj., _eager for renown,
striving after glory_: npm. dōmhwate,
429.

dōn, anv. trans., _perform; commit, per-_

petrate; procure, compass, gain; do (supplying the place of another verb): 3 pl. dōð, 1567; pret. 3 sg. dyde, 17, 1097; 2 pl. dydon, 1358; dydan, 1512; 3 pl. dydon, 455; ger. tō dōnne, 1288. *See* for-, gedōn.

dor, *see* wealldor.

drǣdan, *see* ondrǣdan.

-dreag, *see* gedreag.

drēam, m., *joy, felicity, rapture, blessedness, beatitude; song, concert, minstrelsy, music*: gs. drēames, 1342, 1520, 1586; ds. drēame, 102; as. 580, 594, 1636, 1641; gp. drēama, 580; ap. drēamas, 1245, 1258; ip. drēamum, 1408, 1644. *See* swegldrēam.

drēamlēas, adj., *joyless, dismal, dolorous*: nsn. 1627.

drᵉccan, *see* gedrᵉccan.

drēfan, *see* gedrēfan.

drēogan, 2. trans., *endure, suffer, undergo, bear*: 3 pl. drēogað, 1274; pret. 1 pl. drugon, 615; inf. 118, 271, 622, 1253, 1271. [Sc. *dree*, 'suffer.'] *See* ādrēogan.

drēor, m., *blood, gore*: as. 1449; is. drēore, 1086. [drēosan.]

drēorig, adj., *mournful, disconsolate, rueful*: apm. drēorge, 1544.

‡ drēorigfērð, adj., *dejected, sad (at heart), downcast (in soul)*: npm. drēorigfērðe, 1108.

drēosan, 2. intrans., *distil, drop*: 3 sg. drēoseð, 609. [Cf. MnE. *dross*.] *See* gedrēosan.

drīfan, 1. trans., *impel, propel, urge forward*: inf. 677. *See* bi-, ðurhdrīfan.

drohtað, m., *experience, (mode of) life*: ns. 856. [drēogan.]

dryht, *see* folc-, gedryht.

dryhten, m., *Lord*: ns. 428, 782, 1274; gs. dryhtnes, 41, 186, 297, 396, 413, 711, 868, 1021, 1084, 1108, 1158, 1179, 1192, 1205, 1536, 1650; ds.

dryhtne, 601, 930, 1049, 1108, 1644; as. 512, 594, 1641, 1664; vs. 257, 272, 348, 366, 405; gp. dryhtna, 405. [dryht.] *See* slgedryhten.

dryhtfolc, n., *multitude, army*: ns. 1041.

dryhtguma, m., *(warrior), man*: gp. dryhtgumena, 886.

dryhtlīce, adv., *in lordly wise*: 228.

drync, m., *drink*: gs. drynces, 1508; as. 1438.

dugan, PP. intrans., *avail, profit, be good for something*: 3 sg. dēag, 21, 189. [Cf. Ger. *taugen*, MnE. *doughty*.]

duguð, f., *(that which avails); benefit, blessing, bounty; plenty, abundance; glory; host; people, men*: ns. 1062; gp. duguða, 601, 782; duguþa, 1508; dp. dugeþum, 413; ap. duguðe, 609; ip. duguþum, 563; dugeþum, 1408. [Ger. *Tugend;* cf. dugan.] *See* æðel-, heofonduguð.

dumb, adj., *mute, voiceless*: asf. wk. dumban, 1127.

dūn, *see* hēadūn.

durran, PP. trans., *dare*: pret. 3 sg. dorste, 1167.

duru, f., *gate*: ns. 309.

dwǣscan, W1. trans., *extinguish, abolish, annul*: imp. pl. dwǣscað, 486. *See* ādwǣscan.

dwellan, *see* gedwellan.

-dwola, *see* gedwola.

dyn(n), *see* swēgdyn(n).

dynnan, W1. intrans., *resound*: 3 sg. dyneð, 930. [Cf. MnE. *din*.]

dȳran, *see* gedȳran.

dȳre, adj., *dear, beloved*: nsf. 1650; dsf. dȳrre, 96. Cf. dēore.

dyrnan, *see* bidyrnan.

dyrne, adj., *concealed; incomprehensible, inscrutable, unfathomable*: nsm. (pred.), 640; npf. 1049. *See* undyrne.

dysig, adj., *foolish*: npm. dys[i]ge, 1127. [MnE. *dizzy*.]

E.

ēac, adv., *also, too, likewise, besides, more-over; at the same time; yet; even*: 93, 115, 136, 145, 156, 282, 301, 662, 790, 943, 1107, 1124, 1143, 1152, 1159, 1163, 1169, 1181, 1258, 1276, 1383, 1457. [MnE. *eke*, Ger. *auch*.]

ēacen, adj., *great, pregnant; exalted*: nsf. (pred.) 38; asn. 205. *See* **tōēacan**.

ēacnung, f., *conception, pregnancy*: as. ēacnunge, 75.

ēad, n., *happiness, felicity, blessedness*: ns. 1293; gs. ēades, 1198, 1400.

ēaden, pp. *granted, vouchsafed*: ns. (pred.) 200.

ēadfruma, m., *source of happiness, giver of joy*: ns. 532.

‡ **ēadgian**, W2. trans., *bless, gladden*: imp. sg. ēadga, 20.

ēadgiefa, m., *giver of happiness*: ds. ēadgiefan, 546.

ēadig, adj., *blessed; blissful, happy*: nsm. 1427, 1461, 1496, 1553; nsf. 1013; nsf. wk. ēadge, 87; asm. wk. ēadgan, 1122; npm. ēadge, 1246; gp. ēadigra, 1649, 1656, 1663; dp. ēadgum, 688, 743, 909, 1234; sup. dp. ēadgestum, 1327. [Goth. *au-dags*.] *See* **dōm-, hrēðēadig**.

ēadmōd, *see* **ēaðmōd**.

ēage, n., *eye*: gp. ēagna, 7, 1113; dp. ēagum, 1244, 1323; ip. ēagum, 327, 392, 536, 1315, 1328, 1331.

ēahstrēam, m., *water-flood*: ns. 1167.

eahtan, W1. trans., *perceive, observe, remark, take note*: inf. 1073, 1549. [Ger. *achten*.]

ēahtnes, f., *persecution*: gs. ēahtnysse, 704. [ēhtan, 'persecute.']

ēalā, int., *O; oh, lo; alas*: 18, 50, 71, 104, 130, 164, 175, 214, 275, 348, 378, 416, 1312.

eald, adj., *old, time-honored, ancient, olden, pristine*: asf. wk. ealdan, 1396;

ism. wk. ealdan, 1546; apm. ealde, 863; apf. wk. ealdan, 1107.

ealdcȳ̄ðu, f., *former dwelling, pristine home*: as. ealdcȳ̄ðe, 738. [MnE. *kith*.]

‡ **ealddæg**, m., *day of old, former time*: dp. ealddagum, 303.

ealdfēond, m., *inveterate enemy, ancient foe*: dp. ealdfēondum, 567.

ealdgestrēon, n., *ancient treasure, what was formerly cherished or prized*: ap. 812, 1570.

ealdor, m., *King, Lord*: ns. 229; as. 8.

ealdor, n., ds. ealdre (in phrases **tō ealdre, tō wīdan ealdre,** *for ever, always*): 479, 690, 1514, 1645.

ealdorbealu, n., *vital evil, mortal agony*: as. 1615. [MnE. *bale*.]

ealgrēne, adj., *entirely green, verdant*: asf. 1128.

eall, adj., *all, the whole of*: nsf. 842; eal, 42, 971; nsn. 1052; gsn. ealles, 544, 556, 559, 577, 585, 611, 1100, 1497; asm. ealne, 72, 439, 481; asf. ealle, 208, 240, 683, 885, 1318; asn. 887, 1032, 1115, 1358, 1442, 1512; isn. ealle, 382, 975; npm. ealle, 278, 340, 359, 422, 540, 1278; npn. 7, 1182(?); eal, 85; gp. ealra, 136, 215, 287, 402, 516, 520, 726, 925, 1647; dp. eallum, 216, 245, 607, 723, 845, 1195, 1400, 1651; apm. ealle, 291, 719, 1056, 1101, 1377, 1515; apf. ealle, 1382; apn. 964, 996, 1220 (adv.?); eal, 1201; ip. eallum, 1407. In phrase: mid ealle, 975.

eall, adv., *wholly, entirely, completely; full, very*: 366, 1005, 1027, 1137, 1220 (adj.?), 1283; eal, 97, 153, 305, 308, 666, 969.

eallunga, adv., *at all*: 922.

earcnanstāu, m., *precious stone*: nsm. 1195.

eard, m., *dwelling, home, abode, habitation; abiding, sojourn*: gs. eardes, 1029; as. 63, 514, 646, 772, 1045, 1202, 1417.

eardgeard, m., *dwelling-place* : ds. eardgearde, 55.

eardian, W2. intrans., *dwell, abide, sojourn* : 3 sg. eardaŏ, 438 ; pret. 3 pl. eardedon, 125. [eard.] *See* geeardian ; efeneardigende.

‡ ēarendel, *rising sun* : vs. 104.

earfeŏe, u., *tribulation, affliction, pain, hardship* : as. earfeþe, 1427 ; ap. earfeŏu, 1201 ; earfeþu, 1171, 1452. [Ger. *Arbeit.*] *See* mægenearfeŏe.

earfeŏu, f., *misery, affliction* : ns. earfeþu, 1272.

earfoŏ, *see* atolearfoŏ.

earg, adj., *wicked, vile, evil, sinful* : nsm. 1407 ; gsm. earges, 1297 ; gp. eargra, 1303 ; ip. eargum, 828. [Ger. *arg.*]

earge, adv., *ill* : 1502. [earg.]

earhfaru, f., *arrow-flight* : dp. earh-farum, 762. [Cf. Lat. *arcus, for arquus.*]

earm, adj., *wretched, forlorn ; poor, needy* : nsm. 1496, 1553, 1615 ; wk. earma, 70 ; · npm. earme, 382 ; gp. earmra, 1502 ; dp. earmum, 909 ; apm. earme, 17, 1349. [Ger. *arm.*]

earmlīc, *sorry, pitiful, lamentable* : nsm. 999.

earnian, W2. trans., *deserve, merit* : pret. 3 sg. earnode, 1051 ; 3 pl. earnedon, 1349. [MnE. *earn.*]

ēastan, adv., *from the east* : 885, 906. *See* sūŏanēastan.

ēaŏe, adj., *mild, easy* : comp. asn. ȳŏre, 627.

ēaŏe, adv., *easily* : 173 ; sup. ȳþast, 800 ; ȳþæst, 1283. Cf. ēŏgesȳne.

ēaŏmēdu, f., *humility, lowliness, meekness, humbleness* : as. 359, 1442.

ēaŏmōd, adj., *humble* : nsm. ēadmōd, 786 ; vsm. 255.

ēaŏmōde, adv., *humbly, meekly* : 1352.

ēawan, W1. trans., *disclose, manifest* : pp. ēawed, 55, 955. [Cf. Goth. *augjan,* and Ger. *Auge.*] *See* oŏēawan ; ēowan, oŏēowan ; ȳwan, ætȳwan, oŏȳwan.

Ebrēas, pr. npl., *Hebrews* : gp. Ebrēa, 67. [Lat. *Hebræus.*]

Ebrēsc, adj., *Hebrew* : asn. 133.

ēce, adj., *eternal, everliving, everlasting, endless, perennial, ceaseless, unending* : nsm. 532, 743, 1540 ; nsf. 411, 415 ; nsn. 744, 1070 ; gsm. ēces, 140, 796, 836 ; wk. ēcan, 396, 711 ; gsn. ēces, 1051 ; dsn. wk. ēcan, 305, 1427 ; asm. ēcne, 159, 209, 1045 (?), 1212 ; wk. ēcan, 355 ; asf. 690 (adv. ?) ; asn. 1520 ; vsm. 272, 366 ; apm. 661, 1258. *See* efenēce.

ēce, adv., *eternally, for ever* : 322, 690 (adj. ?), 1553.

eced, u., *vinegar* : gs. ecedes, 1438. [Lat. *acetum.*]

ecg, f., *edge* : ns. 1140.

ēcnes, f., *eternity* : as. ēcnesse, 313, 1203.

edgeong, adj., *rejuvenated, restored to youth, made young again* : nsm. 1032 ; nsn. 1070. [geong, 'young.']

ednīwian, *see* geednīwian.

edwīt, n., *abuse, railing, insult* : as. 1121. [Cf. MnE. *twit.*]

efen, *see* on efen, unefen.

‡ efeneardigende, ptc., *co-dwelling* : nsm. 237. [eardian.]

‡ efenēce, adj., *coeternal* : nsn. 122, 465.

‡ efenlīc, adj., *like, equal* : nsf. 39.

‡ efenmicel, adj., *equally great* : asf. efenmicle, 1402.

‡ efenwesende, ptc., *coexistent* : nsm. 350.

efne, adv., *just, even, very ; nevertheless, notwithstanding* : 300, 330, 436.

eft, adv., *again ; afterward(s), thereafter, subsequently ; on the other hand ; still* : 86, 122, 133, 325, 333, 455, 523, 587, 614, 618, 624, 626, 648, 791, 824. [Cf. MnE. *eftsoons.*]

‡ eftlēan, n., *reimbursement, compensation* : as. 1099. [Ger. *Lohn.*]

eftlifgende, ptc., *revivified, reanimated, resuscitated* : npm. 1156.

ęgesfull, adj., *terrible* : nsm. ęgesful,
1528.

ęgeslīc, adj., *terrible, awful, dreadful,
terrific ; terrified, aghast, horror-
struck* : nsm. 918; nsn. 955; asm.
ęgeslīcne, 1515; asn. 888, 1615;
sup. nsm. ęgeslīcast, 1021. [ęge;
cogn. ON. agi > MnE. *awe.*]

ęgle, adj., *grievous, deadly, pitiless, insupportable* : dp. ęglum, 762.

ęgsa, m., *terror, fear, dread, dismay* : ns.
838; gs. ęgsan, 946, 1063, 1364,
1546; ds. ęgsan, 17, 1014; is. ęgsan,
923 (?), 974, 1019, 1143, 1369, 1563.
[ęge.] *See* ōēodęgsa.

ēlde, *see* ǣlde.

ęllen, n., *exertion, effort* : is. ęlne, 1317.
[Goth. *aljan.*]

ęlōēoda, fpl. *all peoples, all nations* :
dp. ęlþēodum, 1336; ęllþēodum,1083.
[Cf. Lat. *alienus.*]

Emmānūhēl, pr. n., *Emmanuel* : ns.
132. [Heb.]

ęnde, m., *end* : ds. 271, 415, 439, 599,
1029.

‡ ęndedēaō, *death, annihilation* : ds.
ęndedēaōe, 1652. But see text.

ęndelēas, adj., *endless, never-ending* :
asn. 1631.

ęndian, *see* geęndian.

ēnga, adj., *only, sole* : asm. ēngan, 237.
[ān.]

ęnge, adj., *narrow, straitened* : asn. 32.
[Ger. *eng.*]

ęngel, m., *angel* : ns. 132, 315, 335,
351; gs. ęngles, 823; np. ęnglas,
448, 546, 548, 880; gp. ęngla, 52,
102, 104, 332, 474, 515, 630, 646,
651, 690, 715, 738, 791, 895, 941,
1013,1063,1342,1520,1645,1649; dp.
ęnglum, 387, 582, 661, 697, 898, 1246,
1336, 1468; ap. ęnglas, 506. [Lat.
angelus.] *See* hēah-, heofonęngel.

eorl, m. (*hero*), *man* : ns. 219; gp. eorla,
546; ap. eorlas, 874. [MnE. *earl.*]

‡ eornest, f., *rigor, severity, sternness* :
as. eorneste, 1100. [MnE. *earnest.*]

‡ eorneste, adj., *rigorous, severe, stern* :
nsm. 824.

eorōbūend, m., *dweller on earth, in-
habitant of the world* : np. 422, 1278;
gp. eorōbūendra, 1323; ap. 719.

‡ eorōburg, *earth-fortification* : ap.
eorōbyrig (but doubtful), 7.

eorōe, f., *earth, globe* : ns. 1143, 1155;
gs. eorōan, 523, 946, 1004, 1180;
eorþan, 688, 805, 879; ds. eorōan,
200, 608, 621, 626, 772, 780, 840,
1501; eorþan, 255, 411, 639, 648, 814,
828, 1137, 1146; as. eorōan, 329,
1128; eorþan, 276, 967. [Ger. *erde.*]

eorōlīc, adj., *on earth* : nsm. 406.

eorōware, mpl., *dwellers on earth, inhabitants of the world* : np. 382; dp.
eorōwarum, 697, 723.

eorōwela, m., *mundane riches* : as.
eorōwelan, 611.

ēowan, W2. *show, manifest* : inp. sg.
īowa, 335. *See* oōēowan; ēawan,
oōēawan; ȳwan, ǣtȳwan, oō-
ȳwan.

ēowde, n., *flock* : as. 257.

ēower, poss. pron., *your* : dsn. ēowerum, 1503.

ermōu, *see* yrmōu.

Esaias, pr. n., *Isaiah* (properly *Ezekiel*):
ns. 303.

-ēsc, *see* Ebr-, Gālīlēsc.

ēōel, m., *fatherland, native land ; home,
country ; land, realm, domain ; heri-
tage* : ns. ēþel, 1639; gs. ēōles, 1212,
1324, 1346; ēþles, 741; ds. ēōle, 436,
1075, 1496; as. ēþel, 630, 1342, 1406;
is. ēōle, 32. [Cf. MnE. *allodial.*]

ēōelcyning, m., *king of the land* : gp.
ēþelcyninga, 996.

ēōelrīce, n., *native realm* : gs. ēþelrīces,
1461.

ēōelstōl, m., *royal seat, metropolis* : as.
ēþelstōll, 516; vs. ēþelstōl, 52.

ēōgesȳne, adj., *visible, easy to be discerned* : npn. 1234.

Ēva, pr. n., *Eve* : gs. Ēuan, 97.

F.

fā, *see* **fāh**.

fācen, n., *misconduct, criminality, guilt*: ds. fācne, 207.

fācentācen, n., *sign of guilt*: as. 1565.

fǣcne, adj., *wily, stealthy; perfidious*: nsm. 870; dsm. fǣcnum, 1394.

fæder, m., *father*: ns. 211, 320, 728, 1073, 1218; gs. 110, 345, 475, 516, 1014, 1344; ds. 121, 465, 532, 773; as. 163, 349, 472, 617, 758, 1647. *See* **sōð-, wuldorfæder**.

‡ **fædrencynn**, n., *paternal descent*: as. 248.

fǣge, adj., *doomed, devoted, condemned*: asn. 1517; npm. 1533. [Sc. *fey*.]

fæger, adj., *beautiful; lovely, winsome*: nsm. 912; asf. wk. fægran, 1389; apm. fægre, 1294. [MnE. *fair*.]

fægre, adv., *sweetly, nobly, kindly, gently, gloriously*: 390, 472, 507, 1340, 1360.

fāh, adj., *discolored, pale (as death)*: nsm. 1560.

fāh, adj., *guilty; damned*: nsm. 1000, 1616; npm. fā, 829, 1538, 1614, 1632. [**gefā**, 'foe.']

fǣhðu, f., *hostility; feud*: gs. fǣhþe, 1440; as. fǣhþo, 368; gp. fǣhþa, 617. [**fāh**; cf. Ger. *Fehde*.]

fǣle, adj., *dear* (?): nsm. wk. fǣla, 645.

fǣlsian, *see* **gefǣlsian**.

fǣmne, f., *maiden, maid, virgin*: ns. 35, 123, 195, 211; gs. fǣmnan, 788; ds. fǣmnan, 418; as. fǣmnan, 187, 720; vs. 72, 175.

fǣmnanhād, m., *virginity, maidenhood*: as. 92.

fǣr, m., *fear, alarm, terror; suddenness*: is. fēre, 867, 952. [MnE. *fear*.]

faran, 6. intrans., *go, depart; ascend; come; prowl; sweep*: 3 sg. fareð, 871; færeð, 930, 983; 3 pl. fara`ð`, 928, 945; pret. 3 sg. fōr, 1185; imp. pl. fara`ð`, 481, 1519; inf. 513, 925, 1342, 1596. [MnE. *fare*.]

fǣran, *see* **āfǣran**.

fǣrscyte, m., *sudden shot*: ds. 766.

‡ **fǣrsearo**, sn., *sudden device, contrivance*, or *enginery*: ns. 770.

faru, *see* **earh-, gārfaru**.

fæst, adj., *firm, steadfast; fixed, infixed, immovable; deep, profound* (of sleep); *firm, secure; secured, fastened*: nsm. 730; asf. fæste, 166; ism. wk. fæstan, 889; isn. fæste, 6; apm. fæste, 864; apn. wk. fæstan, 321. *See* **ār-, bīd-, hām-, hlēo-, sǫmod-, sōð-, stæð-, staðol-, ðrym-, wǣr-, wīsfæst**.

fæste, adv., *fast; staunchly, stoutly*: 766, 979, 1157.

fæstlīc, adj., *firmly fixed*: apm. fæstlīce, 312.

fæstnian, *see* **gefæstnian**.

fæðm, m., *embrace (arms); bosom; womb; power (hands)*: ds. fæðme, 1485; as. 788, 1146; ip. fæðmum, 651.

fēa, adj., *few*: npm. 1170; gp. fēara (fēara sum == 'a few'), 1275.

-feald, *see* **ān-, mǫnigfeald**.

fealdan, *see* **bifealdan**.

feallan, R. intrans., *fall*: inf. 1525. *See* **gefeallan**.

fēasceaft, adj., *miserable, wretched, disconsolate*: asm. fēasceaftne, 175; apm. fēasceafte, 368.

fēdan, W1. trans., *feed, nourish, sustain, maintain*: 3 sg. fēdeð, 1544.

fela, indecl. n., *many*: 43, 172, 181, 462, 666, 1117, 1178, 1263, 1268, 1399, 1547.

fēlan, *see* **gefēlan**.

fēogan, W3. trans., *hate; vex, trouble; destroy* (?): 3 sg. fēoð, 1598; pret. 3 pl. fēodan, 708; imp. pl. fēoga.ð, 486.

fēolan, *see* **bifēolan**.

-fēon, *see* **gefēon**.

fēond, m., *foe, enemy, adversary; fiend, devil*: ns. 1529; ds. fēonde, 1394; gp. fēonda, 569, 733, 770, 1415, 1439, 1625; dp. fēondum, 623, 639, 1404.

1485, 1614. [MnE. *fiend;* **fēogan.**
See **ealdfēond.**

fēondscipe, m., *hatred, enmity*: as.
fēondscype, 486.

feor, adv., *far*: 56, 390, 1404; comp.
fier, 248.

feorh, m., *life; soul*: gs. fēores, 1073,
1319, 1562, 1565; ds. fēore, 1573
(tō wīdan fēore, *ever; for ever,
eternally*: 230, 277, 1343, 1543);
asm. 439; ip. fēorum, 1592. *See*
wīdeferh.

‡ **feorhdolg,** n., *deadly wound, mortal
wound, fatal wound*: ap. 1454.

feorhgiefa, m., *giver of life*: as. feorhgiefan, 556.

‡ **feorhgōma,** m., *deadly jaw*: ip. feorhgōmum, 1548.

feorhnęru, f., *nourishment, sustenance,
food; salvation, security, safety*: ds.
feorhnęre, 610, 1596.

fēorða, num. adj., *fourth*: nsm. 728.

fēower, num. adj., *four*: dp. fēowerum,
878.

fēowertig, num. sb., *forty*: a. 466.

fēr, *see* **fǣr.**

fēran, Wl. intrans., *go, pass*: inf. 1415.

fęrgan, Wl. trans., *bring, conduct; sail,
journey*: opt. 1 pl. fęrgen, 853; inf.
518. [MnE. *ferry.*] *See* **gefęrian.**

fērð, mn., *mind, spirit, heart, soul*: ds.
fērðe, 476, 668, 924; as. 1330. *See*
drēorig-, sārigfērð.

‡ **fērðgewit,** n., *understanding*: as.
1183.

fērðwērig, adj., *weary in soul, full of
sadness*: npm. fērðwērge, 830.

fēða, m., *band, throng, host*: ds. fēþan,
1518. *See* **hęrefēða.**

fier, *see* **feor.**

fīfta, num. adj., *fifth*: nsm. 730.

findan, 3. trans., *find*: inf. 184, 801,
1573. *See* **onfindan.**

finger, m., *finger*: ip. fingrum, 668.

fīr, *see* **fȳr.**

fīras, mpl., *men*: gp. fīra, 35, 242, 610,
1592.

firen, f., *sin, transgression, iniquity;
violence, outrage*: gp. firena, 123,
181, 369, 1565, 1598; firina, 56; dp.
firenum, 722, 920, 1209; ap. firene,
1280, 1312, 1373, 1485; firena, 1098;
ip. firenum, 1103, 1440, 1616. *See*
dēaðfiren.

‡ **firenhealu,** n., *sin, iniquity*: as. 1275.

firendǣd, f., *crime, evil deed*: ap.
firendǣda, 1305; ip. firendǣdum,
1000, 1632.

‡ **firenfręmmend,** m., *sinner*: gp. firen-
fręmmendra, 1117.

‡ **firengeorn,** adj., *sinful, sin-loving*:
npm. firengeorne, 1605.

firenlust, m., *sinful lust, sinful desire*:
ap. firenlustas, 1482.

‡ **firensynnig,** adj., *sinful, sinning,
wicked*: asn. 1378.

‡ **firenweorc,** n., *evil deed, transgression, crime*: ap. 1300; ip. firenweorc-
um, 1398.

fisc, m., *fish*: dp. fiscum, 966. *See*
sǣfisc.

fiðere, n., *wing*: ip. fiþrum, 395.
[feðer, 'feather'; cf. Ger. *Gefieder.*]

flacor, adj., *flying* (of arrows): asn. 676.

flāngeweorc, n., *arrows*: as. 676.

flǣsc, n., *flesh; body*: ns. 123, 597; ds.
flǣsce, 1028; as. 418, 1305; np. 1281.

flǣschoma, m., *body, flesh*: ns. 1465;
gs. flǣschoman, 1297.

flēogan, *see* **geflēogan.**

fliht, *see* **flyht.**

flint, m., *flint*: as. 6; dp. flintum, 1188.

flōd, m., *flood, wave, tide, water*: is.
flōde, 1168; np. flōdas, 985; dp.
flōdum, 979; ip. flōdum, 806. *See*
laguflōd.

‡ **flōdwudu,** m., *ship, vessel, bark*: ip.
flōdwudu[m], 853.

flōwan, R. intrans., *flow*: pret. 3 pl.
f)ēowan, 984.

flyge, m., *flight*: gs. flyges, 645.

flyht, m., *flight*: ns. 639; as. 654; is.
flihte, 399.

-fōg, *see* **gefōg.**

folc, u., *people, folk, mankind, men;*
band, multitude, host; race, nation:
ns. 1231 ; gs. folces, 569, 1647; ds.
folce, 907, 1439; as. 484, 579, 588,
764, 889, 1025, 1373, 1517 ; np. 526,
1222, 1300 ; gp. folca, 426, 516, 556,
945, 1218; dp. folcum, 195, 225,
338, 1421, 1548; ap. 1378. *See*
dryht-, mægenfolc.

‡ folcdryht, f., *multitude, host, throng:*
as. 1066.

foldærn, u., *tomb, grave, sepulchre:* is.
foldærne, 730.

foldbüend, m., *man, dweller on the*
earth: np. foldbüende, 1177 ; ap.
foldbüende, 867.

folde, f., *earth, world; (dry) land;*
earth, ground, soil; district, region:
gs. foldan, 72, 144, 878, 952, 1533 ;
ds. foldan, 466, 807, 983, 1033, 1142,
1449, 1465; as. foldan, 279, 321,
408, 979, 1002, 1389.

foldgræf, n., *grave:* dp. foldgrafum,
1025.

‡ foldræst, f., *rest in the earth:* gs.
foldræste, 1028.

foldweg, m., *earth:* ds. foldwege, 1529.

foldwong, m., *earth, ground:* as. 974.

folgoð, m., *service, office, ministry:* gp.
folgoþa, 390. [folgian, 'follow.]'

folm, f., *hand; palm of the hand:* dp.
folmum, 1455; ip. folmum, 1124,
1421. [Cf. Lat. *palma.*]

fōn, *see* ā-, bi-, for-, ge-, onfōn.

for, prep. w. dat., *for, for the sake of;*
for, on account of, because of; before,
in the presence of: 22, 112, 169, 923,
1019, 1116, 1423, 1428, 1441, 1470.

‡ foran, prep. w. dat., *upon:* 341. *See*
biforan.

forbærnan, W1. trans., *consume, purge*
away: inf. 1542; pp. forbærned,
1006.

forbēodan, 2. trans., *forbid:* pret. 1 sg.
forbēad, 1485.

forberstan, 3. intrans., *be torn asunder:*
pret. 3 sg. forbærst, 1137.

forbȳgan, W1. trans., *cast down, bring*
low: pret. 3 sg. forbȳgde, 731.

forcuman, 4. trans., *vanquish, over-*
whelm; wear out, exhaust : pp. npm.
forcumene, 561 ; dpm. forcymenum,
151.

fordōn, anv. trans., pp. *undone, lost;*
polluted, defiled: pp. nsm. fordēn,
1206; asn. wk. fordōne, 1248; npm.
fordōne, 1103, 1274 ; dpm. fordōn-
um, 994.

fore, prep., *before, in the presence of,*
into, the presence of, in; before (temporal); *because of, on account of; for,*
for the sake of: w. dat. 669, 836, 930,
962, 963, 1014, 1030, 1048, 1060,
1069, 1083, 1114, 1172, 1182, 1201,
1226, 1230, 1232, 1238, 1286, 1303,
1323, 1336 (2), 1433, 1439, 1475,
1559; w. acc. 796, 1038, 1072, 1094,
1113, 1634.

‡ forescyttels, m., *bolt, bar :* ap. forescyttelsas, 312. [scēotan, ' shoot.']

forespreca, m., *spokesman:* as. foresprecan, 733.

‡ foretācen, n., *sign, portent:* gp. foretācna, 892.

‡ foreðoncol, adj., *wise, far-seeing:*
npm. foreþoncle, 1191.

forfōn, R. trans., *surprise, take by sur-*
prise, come upon suddenly: 3 sg.
forfēhð, 873.

forgiefan, 5. trans., *give, grant, vouch-*
safe: pret. 3 sg. forgeaf, 391, 587,
613, 776, 1258, 1375; pp. forgiefen,
1399; forgyfen, 1387.

forgiefnes, f., *bounty, largess:* as. for-
gifnesse, 427.

forgieldan, 3. trans., *give in return ;*
give, bestow: 3 sg. forgildeð, 434;
imp. sg. forgield, 1476.

forhelan, 4. trans., *hide, conceal, cover:*
pp. forholen, 1053.

forht, adj., *afraid, fearful; timid,*
trembling: nsm. 801, 924, 1559 ;
nsn. 1183; asf. 1129; npm. forhte,
1014, 1230; apm. forhte, 892.

forhtlíc, adj., *fearful, anxious* : npm.
forhtlíce, 1103.

forhtlíce, adv., *fearfully, anxiously* :
1319.

forhwan, adv., *why, for what reason* :
1480; forhwon, 1469, 1487.

forhwyrfan, W1. trans., *pervert;* pp.
froward, perverse: pp. forhwyrfed, 34.

forhycgan, W3. trans., *despise, disdain,
scorn; neglect:* pret. 3 pl. forhogdun,
1287 ; [for]hogdun, 1633.

forlǽtan, R. trans., *leave; forsake, re-
nounce; send forth, issue; loose, release, let out; lose; send away, dismiss; admit:* sg. forlǽteð, 15 7;
pret. 1 sg. forlēt, 1452 ; 2 sg. forlēte,
1469; 3 sg. forlēt, 30; 3 pl. forlēton,
1147; forlētan, 1111; imp. sg. forlǽt,
10, 208. *See* ānforlǽtan.

forlegen, pp. *adulterer, fornicator :* npm.
forlegene, 1610.

forlēosan, 2. trans., *lose; squander;
ruin, destroy:* pret. 2 sg. forlure,
1398; opt. 3 sg. forlēose, 1585; pp.
forloren, 1551.

forma, adj., *first :* nsm. 720.

‡ forpyndan, W1. trans., *take away,
do away with, blot out:* pp. forpynded,
97.

forsēon, 5. trans., *scorn, despise:* inf. 757.

forst, m., *frost, cold:* is. forste, 1546.

forswelgan, 3. trans., *consume, devour:*
3 pl. forswelgað, 995. [Cf. Ger.
schwelgen, MnE. *swallow.*]

fortēon, 2. trans., *lead astray, mislead,
beguile :* pret. 3 sg. fortēah, 270.

forð, adv., *forth, on ; henceforth, thenceforth, still, yet ; high, far:* 101, 211,
299, 375, 426, 489, 582, 685, 709,
764, 920, 1319, 1360, 1517, 1632,
1640, 1658 ; forþ, 230.

forðon, conj., *therefore, wherefore ; for,
because:* forþon, 33, 148, 241, 261,
287, 385, 408, 429, 756, 766, 815,
1015, 1151, 1165, 1202, 1214, 1630;
forðon, 169, 294, 1427, 1578 ; forþan,
94.

fortyhtan, W1. trans., *mislead, beguile:*
pret. 3 sg. forty[ht]e, 270.

forwyrcan, W1. trans., *ruin, undo:*
pp. npm. forworhte, 920.

forwyrd, mfn., *destruction, ruin, perdition:* ds. forwyrde, 1535; as. 1614.
[forweorðan.]

forwyrht, *see* mānforwyrht.

forwyrnan, W1. intrans., *forbid, refuse,
deny:* pret. 2 pl. forwyrndon, 1503;
pp. forwyrned, 20.

fōt, m., *foot:* dp. fōtum, 1455; ap. fēt,
1110, 1168.

fracoð, adj., *dishonored, despised:* nsm.
195. [*fra-cūð.]

frǽt, adj., *proud, perverse, stubborn:*
asn. wk. frǽte, 1373.

frǽtwe, fpl., *treasures; garniture:* np.
frǽtwe, 807 ; gp. frǽtwa, 805 ; ap.
frǽtwe, 1073, ˙ 1635; ip. frǽtwum,
507, 522, 556. [*fra-tāwe.] *See*
goldfrǽtwe.

frēa, m., *lord, king, master; the Lord:*
ns. 328, 404, 475, 1188, 1378; gs.
frēan, 395, 1129, 1168; ds. frēan,
945, 1230 ; as. frēan, 237, 355, 924.
See hēah–, līffrēa.

frēcne, adj., *dangerous, perilous; fearful, terrible; foolhardy:* nsf. 770;
nsn. 853, 1598; dpm. frēcnum, 1548.
[Cf. MnE. *freak.*]

frēfran, W1. trans., *cheer, comfort, console:* 3 sg. frēfreð, 1340. [frōfor.]
See āfrēfran.

fremde, adj., *alien, estranged:* nsm.
1403. [Ger. *fremd.*]

fremman, W1. trans., *do, make, commit:* pret. 3 sg. fremede, 643; pret.
3 pl. fremedon, 655, 1290; inf. 1555.
[Cf. Ger. *fromm.*] *See* gefremman;
firen–, mān–, ryhtfremmend.

fremu, f., *advantage, benefit:* dp. frem-
um, 1398.

frēo, adj., *buoyant:* comp. asm. frēoran,
1511. [MnE. *free.*]

frēobearn, n., *noble child, glorious son:*
ns. 643, 788; ds. frēobearne, 223.

frēod, f., *affection, troth*: as. frēode, 166.

frēogan, W3. trans., *adore, worship*: 3 pl. frēogaƌ, 1647.

frēolīc, adj., *fair, beautiful, noble*: sup. nsf. frēolīcast, 72.

frēolīce, adv., *gladly ; freely*: 187, 1290.

frēon, *see* gefrēon.

frēond, m., *friend*: dp. frēondum, 575, 1344, 1658.

frēond, adj., *friendly, loving*: nsm. 912.

frēonọma, m., *surname*: as. frēonọman, 636.

freoƌian, *see* gefreoƌian.

fricgan, 5. intrans., *ask*: 2 pl. fricgaƌ, 92. [Cf. Ger. *fragen*.]

frignan, *see* gefrignan.

frīgu, f., *embrace*: gp. frīga, 419; dp. frīgum, 37.

friƌ, n., *peace ; protection ; refuge ; friendship*: ns. 1658; as. 1000; friþ, 1340; is. friƌe, 489; gp. freoþa, 773. [Cf. Ger. *Friede*, Eng. *Frederick*.]

friƌgeard, n., *court of peace*: dp. friƌgeardum, 399.

frōd, adj., *wise ; deep, profound*: nsm. wk. frōda, 326; asn. 1177.

frōfor, f., *comfort, consolation ; help ; joy*: gs. frōfre, 207, 728; ds. frōfre, 65, 489, 522, 722, 758, 1360, 1421; as. frōfre, 338, 801, 1511.

frọm, prep. w. dat., *from ; since*: 17, 467, 658, 839, 878, 1191, 1257, 1493, 1608, 1617; fram, 906, 1189.

frọm, adv., *away*: 476.

frọmcyn, n., *origin, parentage*: as. 242.

frọmlīce, adv., *confidently*: 575, 676.

fruma, m., *beginning ; creator, author ; ruler, Lord*: ns. 294, 516, 579, 844; ds. fruman, 225, 1191; as. fruman, 44. *See* ēad-, līf-, ord-, tīrfruma.

frumbearn, n., *first-born child*: as. 507.

frumcyn, n., *race*: ns. 35.

frumgesceap, n., *beginning, creation*: ds. frumgesceape, 839.

frumsceaft, f., *creature, created thing, creation*: gp. frumsceafta, 472.

frymƌu, f., *beginning*: ds. frymƌe, 121, 223. [**fruma**.]

fugel, m., *bird*: ns. 645; gs. fugles, 639, 654; as. 636; gp. fugla, 982. [MnE. *fowl*, Ger. *Vogel*.]

ful, adv., *full, very*: 252, 389.

fūl, adj., *foul, unclean, vile*: asf. fūle, 1482; npm. fūle, 1230.

full, adj., *full ; overwhelmed, smitten*: nsm. 1657; nsf. 57, 88, 378; nsn. 961; asm. fulne, 1369, 1516; asf. fulle, 1625; npm. fulle, 959. *See* bealo-, cear-, ẹges-, hyht-, syn-, ƌrym-, wọmful(l).

‡ fulwian, W2. trans., *baptize*: imp. 2 pl. fulwiaƌ, 484. [full + wīh, 'sacred'; cf. Ger. *weihen*.]

furƌor, adv., *rather, in preference to*: furþor, 1394. [**fore**.]

fūs, *see* hẹllfūs.

fūslēoƌ, n., *death-song*: as. 623.

fylgan, W1. trans., *follow, pursue, afflict, persecute*: pret. 3 pl. fylgdon, 1440.

fyllan, W1. trans, *fill*: 3 sg. fylleƌ, 974; 3 pl. fyllaƌ, 952; inf. 1605; pp. npm. fylde, 1592. [**full**.] *See* ā-, gefyllan; æfyllend.

fyllan, W1. trans. *cast down, overthrow, destroy*: pret. 3 pl. fyldon, 709; imp. 2 pl. fyllaƌ, 486. [**feallan**.]

fȳr, n., *fire*: ns. 958, 1002, 1062; gs. fȳres, 965, 974, 1562, 1625; as. 625, 1619; fȳr, 1520. *See* hẹlle-, wǣlnfȳr.

fȳrbæƌ, n., *bath of fire, sea of fire, hell-fire*: ds. fȳrbaƌe, 830, 985.

fȳren, adj., *fiery, burning, glowing*: dpf. fȳrnum, 733.

fyrhtan, *see* āfyrhtan.

fyrn, *see* gefyrn.

fyrndagas, mpl., *former days, bygone days*: dp. fyrndagum, 1033, 1294. [Ger. *firn*.]

fyrnweorc, n., *creation, created things*: gp. fyrnweorca, 579.

fyrran, *see* āfyrran.

fyrst, m., *term, span*: as. 1322. [Ger. *Frist*.]

‡ **fyrsweart**, adj., *smoky*: nsm. wk. fyrswearta, 983. [MnE. *swart, swarthy*.]

fyrwet, n., *curiosity, inquisitiveness*: as. 92. [Ger. *Fürwitz*.]

fȳsan, *see* āfȳsan; getȳsed.

fȳst, f., *fist, clenched hand*: dp. fȳstum, 1124.

G.

Gabriēl, pr. n., Gabriēl, ns. 336; Gabrihēl, 201.

-gædre, *see* æt-, tōgædre.

gafol, n., *tribute*: gs. ğafoles, 559. [Celtic; cf. MnE. *gavelkind*.]

gāl, n., *evil*: gs. gāles, 1034.

galan, 6. trans., *sing, chant*: inf. 623. [Cf. MnE. *nightingale*.]

gǣlan, *see* āgǣlan.

Galilēsc, adj., *Galilean*: vpm. Galilēsce, 511.

gān, anv. intrans., *go, walk*: 3 sg. gǣð, 1070; inf. 1167. *See* bi-, gegān; gongan.

gārfaru, *spear-flight*: as. gārfare, 781. [Cf. MnE. *garlic*.]

‡ **gārgetrum**, n., *storm of darts, shower of missiles*: as. 674.

gǣsne, adj., *barren, unfruitful*: asf. wk. gǣsnan, 849. [MnE. dial. *geason*.]

gǣst, m., *spirit; soul; (holy or evil) spirit*: ns. 203, 207, 269, 597, 728, 972, 1552, 1557, 1579, 1623; gs. gǣstes, 145, 319, 638, 649, 684, 707, 710, 816, 848, 1057; ds. gǣste, 139, 753, 1034; as. 665, 774, 777, 1381, 1453; np. gǣstas, 363, 1044, 1533; gp. gǣsta, 130, 198, 572, 813, 1232, 1406, 1545; dp. gǣstum, 1568, 1590. *See* hēahgǣst.

gǣstberend, m., *possessor of a soul, being endowed with spirit*: np. 1599.

gǣstgerȳne, n., *meditation, reflection, thought*: ip. gǣstgerȳnum, 440, 713. [rūn, 'secret.']

gǣsthālig, adj., *holy, sacred*: nsn. 584.

‡ **gǣsthof**, n., *lodging place, tenement*: ds. gǣsthofe, 820. [Ger. *Gasthof*.]

gǣstlīc, adj., *spiritual*: nsf. 42; nsn. 699.

gǣstsunu, m., *spirit-son, spiritual son*: ns. 660, 860.

gāt, f., *goat*: np. gǣt, 1230. [Ger. *Geiss*.]

ge, conj., *and; moreover, also*: 846, 1147, 1169, 1484.

geæfnan, W1. intrans., *suffer, endure*: pret. 1 sg. geæfnde, 1429; inf. 1369.

gealla, m., *gall*: gs. geallan, 1438. [Ger. *Galle*; cf. Gr. χολή, χόλος.]

gēar, n., *year*: gp. gēara, 1035. [Ger. *Jahr*.]

geard, n., *dwelling, home*: dp. geardum, 201. [MnE. *yard*.] *See* eard-, frið-, middangeard.

gēardagas, mpl., *former days, old times; lifetime*: dp. gēardagum, 251, 559, 821. [Cf. MnE. *yore*.]

geare, adv., *well, certainly*: 573. [Shak. *yare(ly)*.]

gearo, adj., *ready, prepared; close by*: nsn. 1345; asn. 1269; npm. gearwe, 449, 460. [Shak. *yare*; Ger. *gar*.] *See* ungearu.

gearo, adv., *truly, verily*: 109.

gearosnottor, adj., *proficient, versed*: nsm. 713.

gearwian, *see* gegearwian.

geat, n., *gate*: vp. geatu, 576; ap. gatu, 318; geatu, 251.

gebędscipe, m., *carnal intercourse*: as. 76. [bědd.]

geberan, 4. trans., *bear; give birth to*: pret. 2 sg. gebǣre, 84; pret. 3 sg. gebær, 123; inf. 205; pp. geboren, 1151, 1420.

gebētan, W1. trans., *restore, repair*: opt. 3 sg. gebēte, 13. [bōt; MnE. *boot, recompense*.]

gebīdau, 1. trans. and intrans., *remain; wait for*: inf. 70, 1529.

gebígan, *see* gebȳgan.

gebindan, 3. trans., *bind, fasten, tie;*
wrap, encircle; overcome, prostrate;
overlay, incrust: pret. 3 sg. gebǫnd,
732; pp. gebunden, 308, 365; npm.
gebundne, 1356, 1538; apm. gebundne, 873.

geblęndan, W1. trans., *mingle, mix*:
pret. 3 pl. geblęndon, 1437. [MnE.
blend.]

geblēod, pp.,*varied*: nsm. 908. [MnE.
arch. *blee.*]

geblētsian, W2. trans., *bless*: pp.
geblētsad, 412. [**blōd.**]

geblissian, W2. trans., *gladden; bless*:
imp. sg. geblissa, 249; pp. geblissad,
380. [**blīðe.**]

gebodian, W2. trans., *announce, make*
known, bid: pret. 3 sg. gebodade, 202.

gebrec, n., *noise, crash*: ns. 953.
[**brecan.**]

gebrosnian, W2. trans., *ruin: dilapi-*
date; corrupt: pp. gebrosnad, 13, 84.

gebūgan, 2. intrans., *bend, turn;* with
in: *enter, penetrate*: opt. 3 sg. gebūge, 768; inf. 1504.

gebycgan, W1. trans., *purchase; re-*
deem: pret. 1 sg. gebohte, 1462;
pret. 2 sg. gebohtes, 259.

gebȳgan, W1. trans., *entwine, wreathe*:
pret. 3 pl. gebȳgdon, 1444; gebīgdon,
1125.

gebyrd, fn., *birth, child-bearing; con-*
ception: as. 38, 65, 298. [**beran.**]

gebyrdu, f., *birth; conception*: as. gebyrde, 76; np. gebyrda, 724.

gecēosan, 2. trans., *choose, elect*: pret.
3 sg. gecēas, 36, 446; inf. 590; pp.
asf. gecorene, 331; npm. gecorene,
497, 1223; npm. wk. gecorenan, 1634.

gecnāwan, R. trans.,*recognize*: inf. 654.

gecwēman, 1. trans., *please, satisfy*:
pret. 3 pl. gecwēmdun, 917. [Cf.
Ger. *bequem.*]

gecweðan, 5. trans., *proclaim, an-*
nounce: pret. 3 sg. gecwæð, 132.

gecynd, f., *race, species*: ns. 1016, 1017;
gp. gecynda, 1180. [MnE. *kind.*]

gecȳpan, W1. trans., *purchase*: pret. 1
sg. gecȳpte, 1471. [Cf. Ger. *kaufen,*
MnE. *cheapen.*]

gecȳðan, W1. trans., *manifest, show*
forth: imp. sg. gecȳð, 157. [**cūð** <
cunnan.]

gedafenian, W2. intrans., *be fitting, be*
proper: 3 sg. gedafenað, 551. [Cf.
MnE. *daft, deft.*]

gedǣlan, W1. trans., *divide; break off*:
pret. 3 sg. gedǣlde, 228; inf. 166.
[MnE. *deal.*]

gedēman, W1. trans.,*judge, pass judg-*
ment upon: inf. 525. [**dōm.**]

gedōn, anv. trans., *do; make; cause*:
pret. 1 sg. gedyde, 1382; imp. sg.
gedō, 30; pp. gpn. gedēnra, 1265.

gedreag, 11.,*plaint*: ns. 999.

gedręccan, W1. trans., *distress, trouble,*
torment: pp. npm. gedreahte, 993,
1298, 1508.

gedrēfan, W1. trans., *trouble, distress,*
grieve: pp. gedrēfed, 168. [Ger.
trüben.]

gedrēosan, 2. intrans.,*fall*: opt. 3 sg.
gedrēose, 265.

gedryht, f., *band, host, company*: ns.
1013, 1663; as. 457, 515, 519, 941.
[Cf. **dryhten.**]

gedwellan, W1. trans., *lead astray,*
deceive, beguile: pp. npm. gedwealde,
1127. [Cf. MnE. *dull.*]

gedwola, m., *error, godlessness*: as. gedwolan, 344. [Cf. **gedwęllan.**]

‡ gedȳran, W1. trans., *honor*: pp. npm.
gedȳrde, 1644. [**dēore, dȳre.**]

geēacnung, f., *conception*: ns. ge[ē]a[c]-
nung, 40.

geeardian, W2. intrans., *dwell, abide*:
pret. 3 sg. geeardode, 208.

geednīwian, W2. trans., *renew*: pp.
geednīwad, 1039. [**nīwe.**]

geęndian, W2. intrans., *end, bring to*
an end: pp. geęndad, 1639.

gefǣlsian, W2. trans., *purify; pass*
through: inf. 144, 320.

gefæstnian, W2. trans., *fasten, make*

fast: pp. gefæstnad, 735, 1447, 1456, 1490.

gefēa, m., *joy, gladness*: ns. 231, 585, 743, 1077, 1252; ds. gefēan, 912, 1403, 1596; as. gefēan, 159, 451; ap. gefē[a]n, 1294.

gefeallan, R. intrans., *fall*: 3 sg. gefeallað, 1531.

gefēlan, W1. trans., *feel; sympathize with*: inf. 1129, 1178. [Ger. *fühlen*.]

gefēon, 5. intrans., *rejoice, be joyful, be glad*: pret. 3 pl. gefēgun, 504; imp. pl. gefēoð, 476; inf. 757.

gefergan, W1. trans., *lead, conduct*: opt. 3 sg. geferge, 345. [MnE. *ferry*.]

geflēogan, 2. intrans., *fly*: inf. 295.

‡ **gefōg**, n., *union, compacture, compagination*: is. gefōge, 6. [Ger. *Gefüge*; cf. *Fug, fügen*.]

gefōn, R. trans., *call into action, summon, pluck up*: opt. pret. 3 pl. gefēngen, 1512. [Cf. MnE. *fang*.]

gefremman, W1. trans., *do; make; inflict; confer; wage, engage in*: pret. 3 sg. gefremede, 424, 566, 602, 627; pret. 3 pl. gefremedon, 526; gefremedun, 1454; opt. 2 sg. gefremme, 263; ger. gefremmanne, 597; pp. gefremed, 207, 369.

gefrēon, W3. trans., *free, liberate, set free*: pret. 3 sg. gefrēode, 588.

gefreoðian, W2. trans., *watch over, care for, protect*: pret. 3 sg. gefreoþade, 588. [**frið.**]

gefrignan, 3. trans., *find out, learn, hear*: pret. 1 pl. gefrugnon, 301; gefrugnan, 78; opt. 3 pl. gefrugnen, 225; pp. gefrægen, 839. [Cf. Ger. *fragen*.]

gefyllan, W1. trans., *fill; fulfill, accomplish*: pret. 2 sg. gefyldest, 408; pp. gefylled, 181, 213, 326, 468. [**full.**]

gefyrn, adv., *long ago, of old, in times past*: 63, 135, 301, 349. [Ger. *firn*.]

gefȳsed, pp. *ready to set out, setting out; disquieted*: nsm. gefȳsed, 475; asn. 890. [**fūs.**]

gegān, anv. intrans., *happen, come to pass*: pret. 3 sg. geēode, 443.

gegearwian, W2. trans., *prepare, make ready*: pp. gegearwad, 1522. [**gearo.**]

gehæftan, W1. trans., *bind, confine, imprison*: pp. npm. gehæfte, 562.

gehǣlan, W1. trans., *heal*: inf. 174. [Cf. **hālig, Hǣlend.**]

gehālgian, W2. trans., *hallow, sanctify, consecrate*: pret. 1 sg. gehālgode, 1481; pp. nsm. wk. gehālgoda, 435. [**hālig.**]

gehāt, n., *promise*: gp. gehāta, 541.

gehātan, R. trans., *promise; summon; call, name*: 3 sg. gehāteð, 1338; pp. gehāten, 58, 142; npm. gehātne, 1071. [Ger. *heissen*; cf. MnE. arch. *hight*.]

gehealdan, R. trans., *keep; preserve; restrain*: pret. 1 sg. 93; inf. 300, 1494; pp. npf. gehealdne, 1059. [MnE. *hold*.]

gehladan, 6. trans., *garner*: pret. 3 sg. gehlōd, 1034. [MnE. *lade*.]

gehlēapan, R. trans., *leap upon*: 3 sg. gehlēapeð, 717.

gehlidu, npl., *arch, vault, canopy*: ap. gehlidu, 518; gehleodu, 904. [MnE. *lid*.]

gehrēodan, 2. trans., *endow, adorn*: pp. asf. gehrodene, 330.

gehrēosan, 2. intrans., *fall*: 3 sg. gehrēoseð, 938.

‡ **gehrēow**, n., *lamentation, lament*: ns. 998. [**gehrēowan.**]

gehrēowan, 2. trans., *grieve, make sorry*: pret. 3 sg. gehrēaw, 1493. [MnE. *rue*; cf. *ruth*.]

gehðu, f., *grief, sorrow*: ip. gehþum, 90.

gehwā, pron., *each* (with gen.; and often best translated *all, every*); *each thing, everything*: gsm. gehwæs, 703; gsn. gehwæs, 47; dsm. gehwām, 194, 231, 428?, 1241, 1638; dsf. gehwām, 490; asm. gehwone, 61, 815, 1026, 1279; asf. gehwone, 927; gehwane, 107; asn. gehwæt, 1002.

gehwylc, pron., *each, all, every (one)*:
nsm. 56, 589, 820, 1050 (add **ānra**
gehwylc, 1025, 1029); nsn. 987,
1334; gsf. gehwylcre, 180, 601 (?);
dsm. gehwylcum, 431; dsn. gehwylcum, 1218; dsf. gehwylcre, 847; asm.
gehwylcne, 1308; asf. gehwylce, 525,
981, 1023, 1067; asn. 1384.

gehwyrfan, W1. trans., *change*: pp.
gehwyrfed, 188.

gehycgan, W3. trans., *think, devise*:
pret. 2 sg. gehogdes, 1397.

gehȳdan, W1. trans., *hide, conceal*: pp.
gehȳded, 1466.

gehygd, fn., *thought, meditation*: ns.
1038; gp. gehygda, 1054; ap.
gehygdu, 1314; ip. gehygdum, 747.
[gehycgan.] *See* brēostgehygd.

gehyld, n., *secret recesses, hidden
regions*: as. (ap.?) 545.

gehȳnan, W1. trans., *humble, afflict,
lay low; scorn, disregard*: inf. 1524;
pp. npm. gehȳnde, 562. [hēan.]

gehȳran, W1. trans. and intrans., *hear;
hear, hearken to, give heed to; hear,
learn*: 3 sg. gehȳreð, 797; pret. 1
pl. gehȳrdan, 586; opt. 2 sg. gehȳre
360; inf. 890; pp. gehȳred, 171,
492, 834, 948.

gehyrstan, W1. trans., *adorn, array*:
pp. npm. gehyrste, 393.

gehyrwan, W1. trans., *disregard, be
indifferent to*: pret. 3 pl. gehyrwdon,
459.

gelāc, n., *host, throng*: np. 895. [Cf.
MnE. *lark*, 'play.'] *See* bordgelāc.

gelācnian, W2. trans., *heal*: inf. gelācnigan, 1308. [Cf. MnE. *leech, leech-
craft*.]

gelād, n., *road, path, way* (== *sea*): as. 856.

gelǣdan, W1. trans., *lead, conduct,
bring, pilot*: pret. 3 sg. gelǣdde,
859; inf. 579; pp. gelǣded, 304.
[gelād.]

‡ gelaðian, W2. trans., *summon, call*:
pret. 3 sg. gelaðade, 458. [Cf. Ger.
einladen.]

gelēafa, m., *belief, faith*: as. gelēafan,
483. [Ger. *Glaube*, MnE. *(be)lief*.]

gelīc, adj., *like (unto), similar (to),
resembling*: nsm. 1430, 1432; asm.
gelīcne, 1383; sup. nsn. gelīcost, 850.

gelīce, adv., *in like manner, according*
(w. correlative **swā**): 783. *See*
ungelīce.

gelimpan, 3. intrans., *happen, come to
pass*: pret. 3 sg. gelomp, 233; inf.
79.

gelīðan, 1. intrans., *come, sail*: pp.
geliden, 857.

gelong, adj., *dependent (on), owing (to)*:
nsf. 152, 365. [MnE. *along*.]

gelȳfan, W1. trans., *believe, trust*: 1 pl.
gelȳfað, 119, 753; pret. 3 pl. gelȳfdon, 656. [gelēafa.]

‡ gelȳfan, W1. trans., *endear*: pp. npm.
gelȳfde, 1644. [lēof.]

‡ gemǣcscipe, m., *cohabitation, wedlock*: as. 199. [Cf. MnE. *mate*,
'companion.']

gemāna, m., *fellowship, companionship*:
gs. gemānan, 1645. [Cf. MnE. gemǣne.]

gemǣne, adj., *common*: nsm. 357; nsf.
100, 581, 1459. [Ger. *gemein*; cf.
MnE. *mean*.]

gemeltan, 3. intrans., *melt away, be consumed, dissolve*: 3 pl. gemeltað, 977.

gemengan, W1. trans., *mingle*: pp.
npn. gemengde, 894. [gemong.]

gemet, n., *end*: np. gemetu, 826.

gemētan, W1. trans., *find*: pret. 3 sg.
gemētte, 330. [< gemōt; MnE.
meet.]

gemiclian, W2. trans., *enlarge, extend,
magnify*: 3 sg. gemiclað, 47. [micel.]

gemong, n., *company, congregation*: ds.
gemonge, 1660. [Cf. MnE. *among*.]

gemonian, W2. trans., *exact*: inf.
1100.

gemōt, n., *assembly, concourse*: ds.
gemōte, 1026; as. 795, 832, 942.
[Cf. MnE. *moot*.]

gemunan, PP. trans., *remember, be
mindful of*: inf. 1200.

gemynd, fn., *memory, recollection;
mind, thought*: ns. 1037; as. 431,
665, 1536. [**gemunan**.]

gēn, adv., *yet, still*: 192, 198, 734, 1457.
See ðā **gēn**.

genǣgan, W1. trans., *fall upon, assail*:
3 sg. genǣgeð, 874.

geneahhe, adv., *abundantly; zealously;
wholly*: 48, 929, 976.

genęrgan, W1. trans., *save, redeem,
deliver*: pret. 3 sg. genęrede, 1257;
pp. genęred, 1450.

 genesan, 5. trans., *be preserved from,
escape from*: pret. 3 pl. genǣson,
1254.

genēðan, W1. intrans., (very doubtful)
venture, strive: pret. 3 sg. (pp. apf.?)
genēðde, 69.

geniman, 4. trans., *take; take away*:
pret. 3 sg. genōm, 223, 580. [Cf.
MnE. *numb*, and Shak. *Nym*.]

genīðla, m., *hatred, cruelty*: ds. genīðlan, 1439. [**nīð**, 'hate.']

genīwian, W2. trans., *renew, restore*:
pp. genīwad, 529. [**nīwe**.]

genōg, adj., *enough, abundant*: apf.
genōge, 1264. . [Ger. *genug*.]

‡ genyrwian, W2. trans., *confine, fetter*:
pp. genyrwad, 364. [**nearu**.]

gēo, adv., *once, of old, formerly*: 813.
See īu.

gēoc, f., *help, succor*: ds. gēoce, 124.

gēocend, m., *savior, preserver*: as. 198.
[**gēoc**.]

geofu, see **giefu**.

geoguð, f., *youth*: ns. gioguð, 1653.
See **magugeoguð**.

gēomor, adj., *sad, sorrowful, troubled,
afflicted*: nsm. 499; npf. gēomre,
962; dpm. gēomrum, 124. [Ger.
Jammer.] *See* **hygegēomor**.

gēomormōd, adj., *sad at heart, sorrowful*: nsm. 173, 1406; npm. gēomormōde, 535.

gēomrian, W2. intrans., *grieve, sorrow*: ptc. npm. gēomrende, 90.
[**gēomor**.]

geond, prep. w. acc., *throughout,
through, along; in, on, upon*: 7, 59,
71, 279, 306, 380, 469, 481, 482, 644,
663, 785, 810, 852, 855, 947. [MnE.
(*be*)*yond*.]

‡ geondsēcan, W1. trans., *overrun*: 3
sg. geondsēceð, 972.

‡ geondsprūtan, 2. trans., *overspread,
fill*: pret. 3 sg. geondsprēot, 42.

geondwlītan, 1. intrans., *survey*: inf.
60. [Cf. **ondwlita**.]

geong, adj., *young*: nsf. 35, 175; nsn.
1425; dsf. geongre, 201. *See*
edgeong.

georn, *see* **firengeorn**.

georne, adv., *eagerly; gladly; earnestly;
carefully, well*: 397, 753, 821, 849,
1003, 1223, 1327, 1581, 1590; comp.
geornor, 1255. [Cf. MnE. *yearn*.]

geornlīce, adv., *zealously, earnestly,
diligently*: 262, 440; sup. geornlī-
cost, 433.

gēotan, 2. trans., *pour out, shed, dissi-
pate*: 3 pl. gēotað, 1566; pret. 3 pl.
g[u]tun, 1448; opt. 3 sg. gēote,
817; inf. 173.

geręccan, W1. trans., *interpret*: pp.
geręht, 133.

geręstan, W1. intrans., *rest, repose*: 3
pl. geręstað, 53.

gerīsan, 1. trans., *befit, become, beseem*:
3 sg. gerīseð, 3.

gerȳman, W1. trans., *open, prepare*:
pret. 3 sg. gerȳmde, 865. [<**rūm**;
Ger. *räumen*.]

gerȳne, n., *mystery; inner meaning,
hidden purpose, secret counsel*: ns.
41, 95; as. 74, 423; dp. gerȳnum,
134; ap. gerȳno, 603. [**rūn**.] *See*
gǣst-, ryht-, wordgerȳne.

gesǣlan, W1. trans., *bind, shackle*: pp.
gesǣled, 736. [Cf. Ger. *Seil*.]

gesǣlig, adj., *happy, blessed*: nsm. 438,
1460; nsn. wk. gesǣlge, 1248; dpm.
gesǣlgum, 1651, 1659. [Ger. *selig*,
MnE. *silly* (*e.g.* sheep).] *See* **ungesǣlig**.

gesæliglīc, adj., *affluent*, *plenteous*: nsm. 1078.

gesārgian, W2. trans., *afflict*, *trouble*, *distress*: pp. gesārgad, 961, 970. [sārig, 'sorry.']

gesceaft, f., *creation*; *creature*, *created thing*, *thing*: ns. 842, 930; as. 59, 239, 356, 672, 885, 991, 1087, 1127; np. gesceafte, 1020, 1179; gp. gesceafta, 402, 925, 1152; dp. gesceaftum, 1388; ap. gesceafte, 870, 952, 1382. [gescyppan.]

gesceap, *see* frumgesceap.

gescildan, W1. trans., *shield*, *protect*, *defend*: 3 pl. gescildaþ, 761; opt. 3 sg. gescilde, 775.

gescōmian, W2. intrans., *be ashamed*, *feel shame*: pret. opt. 3 pl. gescōmeden, 1302. [scōmu.]

gescot, *see* selegescot.

gescyppan, 6. trans., *create*, *make*, *form*: pret. 3 sg. gescōp, 14, 23, 659; pp. gesceapen, 1386.

gesēcan, W1. trans., *seek*; *visit*: 3 sg. gesēceð, 62, 947; 3 pl. gesēcað, 1537; pret. 3 sg. gesōhte, 646; imp. sg. gesēce, [154], 254; inf. 146, 524, 571, 626.

gesecgan, W3. trans., *tell*; *confess*: 3 sg. gesegð, 1309; inf. 1316.

gesēnian, W2. trans., *bless*: pp. apm. gesēnade,1341. [segn; Lat. *signare*.]

gesēon, 5. trans. and intrans., *see*; *behold*; *perceive*, *find*: 3 sg. gesihð, 924, 1248, 1274; 2 pl. gesēoð, 512, 522; 3 pl. gesēoð, 1081, 1105, 1108, 1208, 1214, 1253, 1256, 1291, 1311; pret. 3 sg. geseah, 1133; pret. 3 pl. gesāwan, 740; gesēgon, 498, 506, 554, 1153; gesēgun, 1127; imp. 2 pl. gesēoð, 1454; inf. 502, 794, 1115, 1264, 1281, 1306, 1313, 1348, 1457; ger. gesēonne, 919; pp. gesewen, 125.

geset, n., *dwelling*, *habitation*, *house*: ap. gesetu, 1239.

gesēðan, W1. trans., *show*, *declare*: inf. 243. [sōð.]

gesettan, W1. trans., *set*, *place*; *impose*; *make*, *create*, *form*: pret. 1 sg. gesette, 1381, 1389; pret. 3 sg. gesette, 1164, 1601.

gesihð, f., *sight*; *vision*; (?) *aspect*, *appearance*: vs. 50; ds. gesihþe, 910; as. gesyhð, 1113; is. (?) gesihþe, 7. [gesēon.]

gesīð, m., *comrade*, *companion*: dp. gesīþum, 473, 1521. [sīð; cf. Ger. *Gesinde*.]

gesittan, 5. intrans., *sit*: pret. 3 sg. gesæt, 531.

geslēccan, W1. trans., *unnerve*, *prostrate*: pp. npm. geslæhte, 149. [Cf. MnE. *slacken*.]

gesomnian, W2. trans., *assemble, gather together*; *join*, *unite*: opt. 2 sg. gesomnige, 5; pp. gesomnad, 1221. [Cf. Ger. *zusammen*.]

gesomning, f., *union*, *association*: ap. gesomninga, 700.

gesprecan, 5. trans., *speak*: pret. 2 pl. gespræcon, 1511.

‡ gestarian, W2. intrans., *gaze*, *fix one's eyes*: pret. 3 sg. gestarode, 307. [MnE. *stare*.]

gestaðelian, W2. trans., *establish, erect*: pp. gestaþelad, 307.

gesteald, n., *dwelling-place*, *abode*: as. 304. *See* ōryðgesteald.

gestīgan, 1. trans. and intrans., *ascend*; *rise, ascend to*; *descend*; *climb*: pret. 1 sg. gestāg, 1418, 1491; pret. 3 sg. gestāg, 1171; opt. 1 pl. 749; inf. 514, 630, 679. [Cf. MnE. *sty* (on the eye), *stile*, *stair*.]

gestrēon, *see* ǣr-, ealdgestrēon.

gestun, n., *din, roar* (?): ns. 990. [MnE. *stun*.]

‡ gestyllan, W1. trans. and intrans., *ascend*, *mount*; *descend*: 3 sg. gestylleð, 716; pret. 3 sg. gestylde, 648.

gesund, adj., *safe*, *unmarred*: apf. gesunde, 1074; apm. gesunde, 1341. [Ger. *gesund*, MnE. *sound*.]

geswęncan, W1. trans., *torment, afflict, harass*: pp. npm. geswęncte, 362.

gesweotulian, W2. trans., *manifest, exhibit, display*: imp. sg. gesweotula, 9. [sweotol.]

geswīðan, W1. trans., *signalize, crown*: pp. npm. geswīðde, 385. [swīð.]

gesyllan, W1. trans., *give*: pret. 1 sg. gesealde, 1477: inf. 683.

gesȳne, *see* ēðgesȳne.

geðęcgan, W1. trans., *parch, consume*: pp. npm. geþęgede, 1509.

geðęncan, W1. trans. and intrans., *think of, consider; intend, resolve*: pret. 2 sg. geþōhtest, 288; imp. sg. geþęnc, 370; inf. geþęncan, 1056.

geðēon, 1. trans., *perfect*: pp. geðungen (*excellent*), 751.

geðēon, W1. trans., *do, perform*: inf. geþēon, 377.

geðīngian, W2. trans. and intrans., *intercede, plead; compound, settle*: pret. 3 sg. geþingade, 616; imp. sg. geþinga, 342.

geðōht, m., *thought, meditation; mind*: as. 921; ap. geþōhtas, 1047, 1055.

geðolian, W2. trans., *bear, endure, suffer*: pret. 1 sg. geþolade, 1423, 1442; pret. 3 sg. geþolade, 1172, 1434; inf. geþolian, 1514. [Sc. *thole*.]

geðǫnc, m., *thought; mind*: as. geþǫnc, 315; gp. geþǫnca, 1583; dp. geþǫncum, 1126; geþǫncum, 1119. [Cf. ðęncan, 'think.'] *See* ungeðǫnc.

geðrēan, W3. trans., *overwhelm*: pp. geþrēad, 1563.

geðungen, *see* geðēon.

geðwǣre, adj., *harmonious, in unison*: npm. geþwǣre, 127.

getimbro, *see* hēahgetimbro.

getremman, W1. trans., *array*: pret. 3 sg. getremede, 1150.

getrum, *see* gārgetrum.

getrȳwe, adj., *faithful*: nsm. 876. [Cf. MnE. *true, troth*.]

getwǣfan, W1. trans., *deprive, cut off*: pp. npm. getwǣfde, 986.

geweald, n., *power; dominion, rule*: ns. geweald, 228; as. geweald, 1415, 1647; dp. gewealdum, 705. [Ger. *Gewalt*.] *See* nȳdgeweald.

gewęmman, W1. trans., *pollute, defile, stain*: pret. 2 sg. gewęmdest, 1486. [wǫm.]

gewēnan, W1. trans., *hope for, expect*: inf. 1365. [MnE. *ween;* Ger. *wähnen*.]

gewęndan, W1. trans., *turn*: pp. gewęnded, 934. [MnE. *wend, went*.]

geweorc, *see* flān-, hǫndgeweorc.

geweorðan, 3. intrans., *become, be turned; happen, come to pass; be created, arise*: 3 sg. geweorðeð, 715; pret. 1 sg. gewearð, 93, 210, 722, 1182; 3 sg. gewearð, 40, 122, 317; opt. pret. 3 sg. gewurde, 238, 277, 893; inf. geweorþan, 624; pp. geworden, 37, 216, 226, 230, 351, 551, 740, 1263.

geweorðian, W2. trans., *honor; reverence, adore*: pret. 3 sg. geweorðade, 659; pp. geweorðad, 407. [Cf. MnE. *worth, worship*.]

gewęrian, W1. trans., *clothe, array*: pp. npm. gewęrede, 447, 552.

gewill, n., *will*: as. 362.

gewin, n., *strife, conflict; toil, tribulation*: ns. 997; gs. gewinnes, 57; ds. gewinne, 622, 1655; as. 1411.

gewinnan, 3. trans., *win, gain, secure*: inf. 1000.

gewit, n., *mind, understanding*: ds. gewitte, 1199; as. 640, 1177, 1192; gewitt, 29. [MnE. *wit;* cf. witan, 'know.'] *See* ferðgewit.

gewitan, 1. intrans., *go, depart; set out*: pret. 3 sg. gewāt, 494; pret. 3 pl. gewitan, 533; inf. 1227.

gewitlēas, adj., *foolish, void of understanding*: nsm. 1472. [MnE. *witless*.]

gewitt, *see* gewit.

gewrit, n., *Scripture*: np. gewritu, 547.

gewrixlan, W1. trans., *give reward, make recompense*: pp. gewrixled, 1260. [Cf. Ger. *wechseln*.]

gewuldrian, W2. trans., *glorify, magnify, exalt*: pp. gewuldrad, 98. [wuldor.]

gewyrcan, W1. trans. and intrans., *create, make, weave; do, commit; inflict; deserve*: pret. 1 sg. geworhte, 621, 1380; pret. 2 sg. geworhtes, 161; pret. 3 pl. geworhtun, 1233; opt. 3 pl. gewyrcen, 763; inf. 680, 1616; pp. geworht, 1139, 1387, 1445; pp. gp. geworhtra, 179.

gewyrht, n., *deed, work; reward, desert*: as. 1577; dp. gewyrhtum, 128, 1219, 1367; ap. gewyrhtu, 891. *See* ǣrgewyrht.

geȳcan, W1. trans., *increase, multiply*: pp. geȳced, 1039. [ēac; cf. Lat. *augere*.]

giedd, n., *parable; poem*: as. 633; gp. giedda, 713.

giefa, *see* ēad-, feorh-, sine-, wilgicfa.

giefan, 5. trans. *give; bestow, grant; deliver*: 1 sg. giefe, 478; 3 sg. giefeð, 604, 674, 1613; pret. 1 sg. geaf, 1381, 1383, 1501; pret. 3 sg. geaf, 473; pret. 3 pl. gēfon, 1353; pp. gifen, 877. *See* ā-, for-, ofgiefan.

giefstōl, m., *throne of grace*: as. 572. [Ger. *Stuhl*, MnE. *stool*.]

giefu, f., *gift; grace, favor*: ns. giofu, 42; as. giefe, 649, 660, 682, 710, 860, 1243; gief[e], 1662; gife, 480; ip. geofum, 686. *See* hǣlo-, sundurgiefu.

gield, n., *recompense, reward; place, stead*: ds. gielde, 1078; as. gyld, 1102. [MnE. *yield*.]

gieldan, *see* forgieldan.

-giell, *see* wīdgiell.

gielp, mn., *pride; boasting*: ns. 684; as. gylp, 817. [MnE. *yelp*.]

gīeman, W1. trans. and intrans., *take notice of, take heed to, be heedful, regard; keep*: 3 sg. gīemeð, 1545,

1552; pret. 3 pl. gīemdon, 706; inf. gīman, 1568, 1599.

gīet, adv., *yet*: 318. *See* ðā gīet.

gietan, *see* ongietan.

gif, conj., *if*: 21, 190, 781, 1309, 1401.

gif-, *see* gief-.

gīfre, adj., *greedy, ravenous, insatiable, destructive*: nsm. wk. gīfra, 972; np. 1044; sup. nsm. gīfrast, 813. *See* heorogīfre.

gīman, *see* gīeman.

gimm, m., *gem, jewel (i.e. heavenly body)*: np. gimmas, 692, 695. [Lat. *gemma*.] *See* hēafod-, tungolgimm.

-ginn, *see* anginn.

ginnan, *see* onginnan.

giofu, *see* giefu.

gioguð, *see* geoguð.

glæd, adj., *glad, joyful; kind, amiable, loving*: nsn. 1653; asm. glædne, 315; npm. glade, 1286.

glædmōd, adj., *glad, joyful (in spirit or at heart)*: nsm. 910; npn. glædmōde, 576.

glæs, n., *glass*: ns. 1282.

glēaw, adj., *wise, shrewd, acute, foreseeing*: nsm. 139, 220. *See* hygeglēaw.

glēawlīce, adv., *shrewdly, keenly; well, aptly*: 130, 1327.

glēd, f., *fire, flame*: np. glēda, 995; glēde, 1044. [MnE. dial. *gleed*; cf. *glow*.]

glēobēam, m., *harp*: as. 670. [MnE. *glee*.]

glīdan, *see* tōglīdan.

gnorn, m., *sadness, sorrow, grief*: ns. 1575.

God, m., *God*: n. 109, 124, 135, 173, 226, 319, 324, 383, 407, 631, 686, 695, 755, 781, 817, 1007, 1010, 1161, 1166, 1170, 1190, 1217, 1364; v. 130, 273, 361; g. Godes, 120, 147, 205, 315, 336, 480, 572, 584, 643, 660, 699, 707, 710, 744, 764, 774, 788, 860, 903, 1072, 1304, 1581, 1593,

1624; d. Gode, 109, 1057, 1080, 1091, 1232, 1255, 1333, 1402, 1526, 1563, 1636; a. 122, 347, 433, 535. [Sanskrit *hutá*, 'the invoked.']

gōd, n., *good; gain; benefit*: ns. 1332; gs. gōdes, 1034; ds. gōde, 1106; gp. gōda, 1399.

gōd, adj., *good; righteous*: dp. gōdum, 910, 1215; comp. nsn. bętre, 1301; apm. bętran, 1291; gsn. sēllran, 757; apn. sēllan, 376; sup. nsn. bętst, 1105; nsf. bętast, 1011; nsn. sēleste, 520; gsn. sēlestan, 281.

Godbearn, m., *Son of God*: ns. 499, 682, 702.

godcund, adj., *divine*: asf. godcunde, 670; dsf. wk. godcundan, 638.

gōddǣd, f., *good deed*: dp. gōddǣdum, 1286.

‡ **godðrym**, m., *divine majesty*: as. godþrym, 139.

godwębb, n., *tapestry, precious cloth*: gp. godwębba, 1134.

‡ **goldfrætwe**, fpl., *golden ornaments*: ap. 995.

goldhord, nm., *treasury, storehouse, repository*: ns. 787.

gōma, *see* feorhgōma.

gomel, adj. as sb., *man of old time, ancient*: npm. gomele, 135. [ON. *gamall*.]

gong, m., *coming; course, circuit, revolution; pathway, circuit* (i.e. *region*): as. 254, 883; ip. gongum, 1035. *See* bī-, hin-, ingong.

gongan, anv. intrans., *go; continue*: imp. 2 pl. gongað, 576; inf. 533; pres. p. gongende, 426. *See* bigongan.

græf, *see* foldgræf.

grafan, 6. trans., *mine, burrow*: 3 sg. græfeð, 1003. *See* bigrafan.

grēne, *see* ealgrēne.

grētan, W1. trans. and intrans., *wail; bewail, lament, deplore*: 3 pl. grētað, 991; opt. 3 pl. grēten, 1571. [Sc. *greet.*]

grētan, W1. trans., *touch, play*: inf. grētan, 670. [Ger. *grüssen.*]

grim, adj., *dreadful, awful, terrible, horrid*: nsn. 1269; dsm. wk. grimman, 1204; asm. grimne, 1526; asf. wk. grimman, 1080, 1333. [MnE. *grim.*] *See* heorogrim.

grimne, adv., *fiercely*: 970.

grimlīc, adj., *fearful, terrible*: nsm. 918.

grimlīce, adv., *fiercely, savagely*: 1003.

grom, adj. as sb., *enemy, devil, fiend*: gp. gromra, 781.

gromhȳdig, adj., *hostile, fierce*: asm. gromhȳdigne, 734.

‡ **grorne**, adv., *sad(ly), wretched(ly), dismal(ly)*: grorne, 1204.

grornian, W2. intrans., *mourn, lament*: 3 sg. grornað, 970.

grund, m., *abyss, pit, hell; earth, world; bed (of sea)*: as. 265, 481, 562, 785, 931, 947, 1164, 1526; np. grundas, 1593; dp. grundum, 499, 682, 702, 744; ap. grundas, 145, 972. [Cf. Ger. *Abgrund.*] *See* brytengrund.

grundlēas, adj., *bottomless*: nsm. 1545.

‡ **grundscēat**, m., *precincts of earth*: as. 42, 649. [Cf. Ger. *Schoss.*]

gryrebrōga, m., *horror*: ds. gryrebrōgan, 848.

guma, m., *man*: np. guman, 813; gp. gumena, 820, 1653; dp. gumum, 427; vp. guman, 511. [Cf. MnE. *bridegroom.*] *See* dryhtguma.

gūð, f., *battle, fight*: ds. gūþe, 674. [Cf. Ger. *Hildegund, etc.*]

gūðplega, m., *contest, struggle*: ds. gūðplegan, 573.

gyld, *see* gield.

gylden, adj., *golden*: apn. wk. gyldnan, 251, 318. [gold.]

gylp, *see* gielp.

gyrn, n. (?), *sorrow*: ds. gyrne, 1304.

gyrwan, W1. trans., *render, make*: pret. 3 sg. gyrede, 1166. [gearo.]

gyte, *see* blōdgyte.

H.

habban, W3. trans., *have* (auxiliary); *have, possess, hold* : 1 sg. hæbbe, 169, 181 ; 2 sg. hafast, 1478; 3 sg. hafað, 256, 431, 558, 921, 1005, 1032, 1035, 1556, 1564, 1648 ; 1 pl. habbað, 758; 3 pl. habbað, 363, 390; pret. 1 sg. hæfde, 1386, 1399 ; 2 sg. hæfdest, 1382; 3 sg. hæfde, 468, 1157 ; 1 pl. hæfdon, 857; 3 pl. hæfdon, 641 ; opt. 3 sg. hæbbe, 1551 ; 1 pl. hæbben, 369. [Cf. Ger. *haben*, Lat. *habere*.]

hād, m., *sex ; rank, order; manner* : ns. 99; as. 49, 444 ; gp. hāda, 286. [MnE.*-hood*.] *See* **fǣmnan-, mægden-, mægðhād**.

hædor, adj., *bright, brilliant, radiant* : npn. hædre, 693. [Ger. *heiter*.]

hæft, m., *captive, prisoner ; captivity, bondage* : ds. hæfte, 568; as. 260; gp. hæfta, 360; ap. hæftas, 154.

hæftan, *see* **gehæftan**.

hāl, *see* **wonhāl**.

hǣlan, W1. trans., *heal, remove* : inf. 1321; pres. p. hǣlende, 250. *See* **gehǣlan**.

hǣle, *see* **onhǣle**.

hǣlend, m., *Savior, Jesus* : ns. 383, 435, 792 ; gs. hǣlendes, 505 ; as. 634; vs. 358. [**hǣlan**.]

hǣleð, m., *man ; hero, warrior* : np. 279, 461, 534; gp. hæleþa, 266, 372, 1196, 1277, 1591 ; dp. hæleþum, 608, 669, 882, 1193; ap. 872. [Ger. *Held*.]

hālgian, *see* **gehālgian**.

hālig, adj., *holy* : nsm. 403(2), 404, 653, 658, 760, 789, 1009, 1426, 1557, 1623; nsm. wk. hālga, 558; nsf. 379; nsf. wk. hālge, 1017 ; gsm. hālges, 737 ; gsm. wk. hālgan, 58; dsf. wk. hālgan, 461 ; dsn. wk. hālgan, 911, 1135; asm. wk. hālgan, 1093; asf. hālge, 866; asf. wk. hālgan, 534, 549, 632, 739, 1588;

vsm. wk. hālga, 348; isf. wk. hālgan, 1339 ; npm. hālge, 692, 1012, 1193 ; npf. hālge, 944; gpm. hāligra, 529, 929, 1638, 1648; dpm. hālgum, 284, 750, 1189, 1608, 1660 ; apm. wk. hālgan, 1110. *See* **gǣsthālig**.

hǣlo, f., *health ; salvation, deliverance, safety ; greeting, hail, hosanna, glory* : ns. 411; hǣlu, 1654; gs. 613, 859; as. 119, 752, 1574; hǣlu, 202.

‡ **hǣlobearn**, n., *Christ-child* : ns. 754 ; hǣlubearn, 586.

‡ **hǣlogiefu**, f., *saving grace* : as. hǣlogiefe, 374.

‡ **hǣlolīf**, n., *salvation* : as. 150.

‡ **hāls**, f., *salvation, redemption* : as. 587. Cf. **mundheals**.

hǣlu, *see* **hǣlo**.

hām, m., *home, dwelling* : ns. 897 ; ds. 305, 350; as. 647. [Ger. *Heim*.] *See* **heofonhām**.

‡ **hāmfæst**, adj., *resident, established* : nsm. 1554.

hand, *see* **hond**.

hāt, adj., *hot, fiery, eager, glowing* : nsm. 500, 539, 976, 1059, 1426; nsm. wk. hāta, 932; nsn. 1523; nsn. wk. hāte, 1062, 1541 ; dsm. wk. hātan, 1162 ; asn. wk. hāte, 1619. [Ger. *heiss*.]

hātan, R. trans. and intrans., *bid, command; name* : 3 sg. hāteð, 1024, 1227, 1341, 1374; 3 pl. hātað, 279, 888; pret. 3 sg. heht, 294; imp. sg. hāt, 253. [Ger. *heissen*.] *See* **gehātan**.

hǣðen, adj., *heathen* : gpm. hǣþenra, 705.

hē, pron., *he* : nsm. 14, *etc.* (76 times); nsf. hēo, 1157, 1161; nsn. hit, 233, 701, 1137; gsmn. his, 21, *etc.* (49 times); gsf. hyre, 1419; hire, 967 ; dsmn. him, 36, *etc.* (29 times); dsf. hyre, 1155; asm. hine, 129, *etc.* (13 times); asn. hit, 63, *etc.* (10 times); np. hī, 498, 501, 642, 707, 829, 1052, 1075, 1130, 1183, 1233, 1235, 1245, 1253, 1255, 1270, 1273, 1286, 1290,

1291, 1298, 1304, 1365, 1437, 1443,
1447, 1503, 1524, 1538; hȳ, 385, 392,
454, 458, 495, 506, 535, 1106, 1210,
1212, 1229, 1238, 1243, 1254, 1256,
1268, 1285, 1287, 1294, 1301, 1351,
1506, 1511, 1567, 1620, 1629, 1630;
hīe, 146, 455; hīo, 322; gp. hyra,
395, 398, 460, 537, 837, 945, 966,
1077, 1108, 1121, 1131, 1148, 1184,
1185, 1213, 1224, 1235, 1289, 1292,
1353, 1359, 1374, 1570, 1635; hira,
1171; dp. him, 142, etc. (43 times);
ap. hī, 559, 1188, 1613; hȳ, 325,
828, 888, 1169, [1208], 1257, 1341,
1359, 1546.

hēa, see **hēah.**

hēadūn, see **hēahdūn.** [MnE. *down.*]

heafela, m., *head*: ds. heafelan, 505.

hēafod, n., *head; head (of the corner)*:
ns. 4; as. 1125, 1434, 1444. [Ger.
Haupt; cf. Lat. *caput.*]

hēafodgimm, m., (*jewel of the head*),
eye: ip. hēafodgimmum, 1330.

hēagengel, see **hēahengel.**

hēah, adj., *high; lofty; exalted*: nsm.
653; nsf. 379; hēa, 1062, 1064; asm.
hēanne, 678, 1446; sup. dsm. hȳhstan, 749; npm. hȳhstan, 282. [Ger.
hoch.]

‡ **hēahboda,** m., *archangel*: as. hēahbodan, 295. [**bodian.**]

‡ **hēahclif,** n., *high cliff*: np. hēahcleofu,
978. [Ger. *Klippe.*]

hēahcyning, m., *arch-king,* (*most*) *high
king, supreme king*: ns. 150, 1339.
[Cf. Ger. *Hohepriester,* MnE. *high
priest.*]

‡ **hēahdūn,** f., *high down*: ap. hēadūne,
717.

hēahengel, m., *archangel*: ns. hēagengel, 202; gp. hēahengla, 403, 528;
hēagengla, 1018.

‡ **hēahfrēa,** m., *arch-lord, supreme lord*:
ns. 424; vs. 253.

‡ **hēahgǣst,** m., *supreme Spirit, Holy
Ghost*: ns. 358.

hēahgetimbro, n., *lofty edifice*: np.

1181; ap. 973.   [Cf. Tennyson's
'high-built.']

hēahhlið, n., *lofty hill*: ap. hēahhleoðu,
745.

hēahsetl, n., (*high*) *throne, judgment
seat*: ds. hēahsetle, 555; 1217, 1335.

hēahðu, f., *height, on high, heaven*: ds.
760; hēahþu, 508, 789, 866; as.
hēahþu, 498; dp. hēahþum, 414.
[Like the Biblical ὕψος, *altum.*]

healdan, R. trans., *hold, possess, preserve, keep*: 1 sg. healde, 489; 3 sg.
healdeð, 19, 1648; pret. 1 sg. hēold,
792; pret. 3 pl. hēoldon, 1159, 1236,
1260; hēoldan, 813; inf. 767. [Ger.
halten.]   See **gehealdan.**

healf, f., *side, direction; way*: gp. healfa,
61, 927; ap. healfa, 949, 1267. [Ger.
halb.]

hēalic, adj., *excellent*: nsm. 430.

hēalīce, adv., *highly, exceedingly; on
high*: 383, 389, 693, 1149.

heall, f., *hall, temple*: gs. healle, 4.
[Ger. *Halle.*]

heals, see **mundheals.**

hēan, adj., *downcast, disheartened, de-
sponding, wretched; lowly, weak;
worthless, abject, despised; headlong*:
nsm. 265, 1413; npm. hēane, 993,
1608; dpm. hēanum, 414, 632, 1471;
comp. nsm. hēanra, 99. [Goth.
hauns; cf. **hȳnan, hȳnðu,** and Ger.
Hohn.]

hēanlīce, adv., *miserably, ignominious-
ly*: 31, 372. [**hēan.**]

hēannes, f., (with prep. **in**: *on high, in
the highest* [*in excelsis*]): dp. hēannessum, 410; hēannissum, 162. [For
hēahnes.]

hēap, m., *multitude, host, band, legion,
company; crew, horde*: as. 16, 731,
944; ip. hēapum, 549, 929. [Ger.
Haufe.]

heard, adj., *hard; insupportable; un-
feeling, rigorous, severe; loud, violent*:
nsm. wk. hearda, 1064; nsn. 953;
dsm. heardum, 1424; dsm. wk. hear-

dan, 1310; asm. heardne, 1125, 1444, 1505; asn. 1612; comp. nsf. heardra, 1488; npm. heardran, 1188.

‡ heardcwide, m., *abuse, reviling*: as. 1443. [cweðan.]

hearde, adv., *cruelly, grievously; greatly, sorely*: 364, 890, 1017, 1456, 1513.

heardlīce, adv., *cruelly, sorely*: 260.

hearm, m., *contumely*: gs. hearmes, 171. [Ger. *Harm.*]

‡ hearmcwalu, f., *destruction*: as. hearmcwale, 1608.

hearmcwide, m., *blasphemy, insult*: ip. hearmcwidum, 1120. [cweðan.]

‡ hearmslege, m., *grievous blow, smiting*: as. 1434. [slēan.]

hearpe, f., *harp*: as. hearpan, 669. [Ger. *Harfe.*]

hebban, 6. trans., *carry up, bear aloft*: pp. hafen, 651. [Cf. MnE. *heave.*] *See* ā-, inhebban.

hefīge, adv., *painfully*: comp. hefgor, 1487.

helan, 4. trans., *conceal, cover*: opt. 1 sg. hele, 193. [Ger. *hehlen.*] *See* bi-, forhelan.

hell, f., *hell*: ns. 1159; hel, 1259, 1591, 1612; gs. helle, 265, 562, 591, 1619; ds. helle, 1493; as. helle, 558, 1413, 1623. [Cf. helan.]

‡ hellewalu, f., *hell-torment*: ds. hellcwale, 1189. [Cf. cwellan, and Ger. *Qual.*]

‡ hellebealu, m., *misery of hell*: as. 1426.

hellefȳr, n., *hell-fire*: as. 1269.

hellfūs, adj., *bound for hell, hell-destined*: npm. helfūse, 1123.

hellsceaða, m., *fiend, devil*: np. helsceaþa[n], 364.

hellwaran, mpl., *dwellers in hell*: gp. hellwarena, 731.

hellwaru, f., *dwellers in hell*: gp. helwara, 286.

helm, m., *protector, Lord*: ns. 463, 529, 566; as. 634; vs. 274, 410. [Cf. helan.]

help, f., *help, succor*: ns. 858; ds. helpe, 427, 632, 1173, 1471; as. helpe, 263, 424, 1568. [Cf. Ger. *Hilfe.*]

helpan, 3. trans. (w. gen. or dat.), *help, succor*: pret. 2 pl. hulpon, 1353; opt. pret. 2 pl. hulpen, 1502; imp. sg. help, 367. [Ger. *helfen.*]

helpend, m., *helper*: gp. helpendra, 1413.

hengest, *see* sundhengest.

heofon, m., *heaven; sky*: ns. 1149, 1591; gs. heofones, 61, 150, 202, 555, 591, 1181, 1588; ds. heofone, 939; np. heofonas, 932; gp. heofona, 253, 348, 424, 518, 545, 653, 904, 1038, 1339; dp. heofonum, 282, 286, 485, 737, 778, 866, 1495. *See* ūpheofon.

heofonbeorht, adj., *heavenly bright*: nsn. 1018.

‡ heofonbȳme, f., *heavenly trumpet*: gs. heofonbȳman, 948.

heofoncondel, f., *heaven's candle* (sun and moon): np. heofoncondelle, 608. [Lat. *candela < candere.*]

heofoncund, adj., *heavenly*: nsf. 379.

heofoneyning, m., *heavenly king*: gs. heofoncyninges, 1086, 1524; ds. heofoncyninge, 1513.

‡ heofonduguð, f., *heavenly host*: gp. heofonduguða, 1654.

heofonengel, m., *heavenly angel*: gp. heofonengla, 492, 927, 1009, 1277.

heofonhām, m., *heavenly home*: ds. heofonhāme, 293.

heofonmægen, n., *heavenly host*: gp. heofonmægna, 1217.

heofonrīce, n., *kingdom of heaven*: ns. 1259; gs. heofonrīces, 566, 1633; ds. 1638; as. 1245.

heofonsteorra, m., *star of heaven*: np. heofonsteorran, 1043.

heofontungol, n., *star of heaven*: np. 693.

‡ heofonwōma, m., *sound from heaven, thunder* (?): ds. heofonwōman, 834, 998.

‡ **heoloðcynn**, n., *dwellers in hell*: ds. heoloðcynne, 1541. [**helan.**]

heonan, adv., *hence, from hence*: 155, 514, 582, 754.

heorogīfre, adj., *devouring, consuming*: nsm. 976, 1059.

heorogrim, adj., *horrible, fierce*: nsn. 1523; asn. 1612. [heoro, 'sword.']

heorte, f., *heart*: gs. heortan, 174, 747, 1038, 1047, 1055, 1328; ds. heortan, 500, 539, 752, 1493; as. heortan, 641. [Ger. *Herz.*]

hēr, adv., *here*: 116, 224, 244, 521, 570, 590, 703, 744, 818, 854, 1322, 1457, 1574, 1633. [Ger. *hier.*]

‡ **hērcyme**, m., *advent*: as. 250.

here, m., *host, company, multitude*: ns. 1277, 1532; gs. her[*g*]e[*s*], 1625; as. 574, 1597; is. herge, 524; np. hergas, 929; gp. herga, 844. [Ger. *Heer*; cf. MnE. *heriot, harbor.*]

‡ **herefēða**, m. (*warrior*) *band, host*: np. herefēðan, 1012.

herenes, f., *praise*: ns. herenis, 415. [**herian.**]

herg, m., *idol*: ap. hergas, 485.

hergan, W1. trans., *praise, glorify*: opt. 1 pl. hergen, 430; pret. 3 sg. herede, 634; pret. 3 pl. heredon, 470; heredun, 503; inf. hergan, 49, 383.

‡ **hetol**, *hostile, malicious*: npm. het[*e*]-l[*a*]n, 364.

hider, adv., *hither*: 154, 295, 760, 904.

hidercyme, m., *advent*: ns. 367; as. 142; hydercyme, 587.

hīenðu, see **hȳnðu.**

Hierūsalēm, prn., *Jerusalem*: ds. 533, 1134; vs. 50.

higeglēaw, see **hygeglēaw.**

hild, f., *warfare, conflict*: as. hilde, 566. [Cf. Ger. *Kriemhild, Hildegund.*]

hindan, see **bihindan.**

hingong, m., *departure, decease*: as. hingonge, 1554; [h]ingonge, 1412.

‡ **hingran**, W2. intrans., *be hungry*: ptc. dpm. hingrendum, 1354. [For **hyngran** < **hungor.**]

hīðan, see **hȳðan.**

hīw, n., *form; color, hue*: ds. 657, 721, 725, 935.

hladan, 6. trans., *amass, lay up*: pret. 1 pl. hlōdun, 784. [MnE. *lade.*] See **ā-, gehladan.**

hlāf, m., *bread, food*: as. 1354. [MnE. *loaf,* Ger. *Laib,* 'bread'; cf. MnE. *Lammas.*]

hlǣfdige, f., *lady, queen*: ns. 284. [**hlāf.**]

hlāford, m., *Lord, Master*: ns. 574; as. 461, 498, 518. [**hlāfweard.*]

hlæmman, see **bihlæmman.**

hleahtor, m., *rapture*: is. hleahtre, 739. [Cf. Ger. *lachen*, MHG. *lahter.*]

hlēapan, see **gehlēapan.**

hlemman, W1. intrans., *hurtle*: 3 sg. hlemmeð, 932.

hlēo, m., *shelter; refuge, defense; protector*: ns. 409; ds. 606; as. 1196. [MnE. *lee.*]

‡ **hlēofæst**, adj., *protecting, comforting*: nsm. 358.

hlēor, n., *face*: ns. 1434; as. 1120. [MnE. *leer.*]

hlēotan, 2. *gain, obtain*: inf. 783. [Cf. MnE. *lot, lottery,* Ger. *Loos.*]

‡ **hlēoð**, f., *shelter, lodging place*: as. 1353. [**hlēo.**]

hlēoðorcwide, m., *speech, discourse*: as. hlēoþorcwide, 450. [Cf. **hlūd.**]

hlid, see **ceasterhlid; gehlidu.**

hlið, see **hēahhlið.**

hlōð, f., *host, multitude, horde*: as. hlōðe, 1162.

hlūd, adj., *loud*: nsm. 492, 834, 998; nsf. 948; nsn. 953; isf. hlūdan, 389. [Ger. *Laut;* cf. Lat. (*in*)*clutus, cluere.*]

hlūde, adv., *loudly*: 669.

hlūtor, adj., *bright; pure*: ism. hlūtre, 293; ism. wk. hlūtran, 1086, 1335; apm. hlūtre, 1245. [Ger. *lauter;* cf. Lat. *lautus,* Gr. κλύξειν, κλύδων.]

hlūtre, adv., *brightly, resplendently; clearly*: 1012; hluttre, 1149.

hlȳdan, W1. intrans., *sound*: 3 pl.
hlȳdaðð, 882. [**hlūd.**]

hlȳp, m., *leap*: ns. 720, 726, 730, 736;
ip. hlȳpum, 747 ; hlȳpum, 745. [Cf.
Ger. *Lauf.*]

hnēaw, *see* **unhnēaw.**

hof, *see* **gæsthof.**

hold, adj., *gracious, merciful*: nsm.
1471. [Ger. *hold.*] *See* **unholda.**

holdlīce, adv., *kindly ; devotedly, loyal-
ly*: 430, 1357.

holm, m., *billow ; sea*: ds. holme, 978;
np. holmas, 855.

holmðracu, f., *raging sea*: as. holmþræce, 678.

hōn, *see* **āhōn.**

hond, f., *hand*: ds. 1530; as. 1221,
1227, 1363; hand, 531 ;. gp. honda,
1487 ; ap. honda, 1110; ip. hondum,
162, 1123, 1132, 1379.

hondgeweorc, n., *handiwork*: ns. 266,
1414.

hongian, W2. intrans., *hang*: pret. 1
sg. hongade, 1456, 1488.

hord, n., *treasure, hoard; secret*: as.
(ap. ?) 1055, 1072; np. 1047. [Ger.
Hort, Goth. *huzd;* cf. Gr. κύσθος.]
See **goldhord.**

horsc, adj., *wise, discerning, enlightened*: nsm. 241; asm. ho[r]scne, 49.
[ON. *horskr.*]

hosp, m., *scorn, abuse, insult*: as. 171,
1443. [Cf. **hyspan.**]

hoðma, m., *darkness, shadow*: ds.
hoðman, 45.

hrā, ᵤ., *(living) body*: as. 14. [Goth.
hraiw.]

hrædlīce, adv., *quickly, speedily*: 263.
[Cf. **hraðe.**]

hrægl, n., *robe, raiment*: gs. hrægles,
1505; as. 1354; dp. hræglum, 447,
454. [MnE. obs. *nightrail.*]

hraðe, adv., *quickly, forthwith, soon*:
1027; raþe, 1525. [Cf. **hrædlīce.**]

hrēada, *see* **scildhrēada.**

hrēam, m., *clamor, uproar*: ns. 594.
[Cf. **hrēmig.**]

hreddan, W1. trans., *deliver, save*: inf.
274. [MnE. *rid,* Ger. *retten.*] *See*
āhreddan.

hrēmig, adj., *exulting, rejoicing*: npf.
hrēmge, 54. [Cf. **hrēam.**] *See*
sigehrēmig.

hrēo, adj., *stormy, tempestuous, rough*:
asm. hrēone, 858.

hrēodan, 2. trans., *adorn, deck out*: pp.
nsf. hroden, 292. *See* **gehrēodan.**

hrēosan, ᵤ. intrans., *fall ; perish*: 3 pl.
hrēosaðð, 810, 976, 1043; inf. 1412,
1523. *See* **ge-, ofhrēosan.**

hrēow, f., *sorrow, regret*: as. hrēowe,
1557; dp. hrēowum, 993. *See* **gehrēow.**

hrēowan, 2. intrans., *repent*: 1414.
[MnE. *rue;* cf. **hrēow.**] *See* **gehrēowan.**

hrēowcearig, adj., *sorrowful, troubled*:
dpm. hrēowcearigum, 367.

hrēran, W1. trans., *stir*: inf. 678.
[Ger. *rühren.*] *See* **onhrēran.**

‡ hrēðēadig, adj., *exultant*: nsm. 944.

hreðer, m., *breast, bosom ; mind, heart,
spirit*: ns. hre[ð]er, 539; ds. hreþre,
641, 1159, 1162.

‡ hreðercofa, m., *case of the soul, breast*:
ap. hreþercofan, 1328.

hreðerloca, m., *soul-casket, breast*: gp.
hreþerlocena, 1055. [**lūcan.**]

hrif, n., *womb*: as. 425. [MnE. *(mid)riff.*]

hring, m., *ring, i.e.* (?) *string, rosary*:
ns. 537.

hrōf, m., *roof; vault, arch ; summit,
height*: ds. hrōfe, 14, 749; as. 60,
495; ap. hrōfas, 528.

hrōðor, ᵤ., *pleasure, delight ; comfort;
help*: ds. hrōþre, 414; as. 623;
hrōðer, 1196.

hrūse, f., *earth, ground*: ns. 882 ; ds.
hrūsan, 658.

hrycg, m., *elevated surface* (lit. *back*) *of
the ocean*: as. 858. [MnE. *ridge,*
Ger. *Rücken.*]

hū, adv., *how*: 61, 70, 75, 92, 130, 183,
216, 222, 277, 362, 371, 423, 443,

586, 786, 990, 1015, 1050, 1059, 1074, 1119, 1178, 1208 (?), 1247, 1286, 1317, 1397, 1459, 1569. [From the pronominal stem of hwā.]

hungor, m., *hunger*: ns. 1660. [Ger. *Hunger.*]

hūru, adv., *verily, indeed; especially*: 22, 82, 337, 613, 789.

hūs, n., *house; home*: ns. 1603, 1627; gs. hūses, 1139; ds. hūse, 1135; as. 14, 1481. *See* morðor-, wītehūs.

hūð, f., *spoil*: gp. hūþa, 568.

hwā, pron., *who, any; neut. what, of what sort*: nsm. 1149, 1164, 1169; gsn. hwæs, 1199; nsn. hwæt, 89, 574, 694; asn. hwæt, 176, 510, 803, 1601. *See* ǣg-, gehwā.

hwǣr, adv., *where*: 862. *See* ōwēr.

hwæs, adj., *sharp, prickly*: asm. hwæsne, 1443.

hwæt, interj., *what*: 416, 586, 627, 1152, 1163, 1379, 1423, 1488.

hwæt, *see* dǣd-, dōmhwæt.

hwæðer, conj., *whether*: 1332; hwæþer, 1306, 1552. *See* ǣghwæðer.

hwæðre, conj., *however, yet*: hwæþre, 453, 709, 1377.

hwearfian, W2. intrans., *wander, go astray*: 1 pl. hwearfiað, 372.

hwearft, m., *circle*: ds. hwearfte, 511. [hweorfan.]

hweorfan, 3. trans. and intrans., *turn; depart; flock, throng; go*: 1 sg. hweorfe, 476; 3 pl. hweorfað, 957, 1044; imp. 2 pl. hweorfað, 485; inf. 31. *See* onhweorfan.

hwīlum, adv. (**hwīlum ... hwīlum,** *now ... now*): 646, 648. [hwīl, 'while'; cf. MnE. *whilom.*]

hwīt, adj., *white; shining*: nsn. 1018; npm. hwīte, 545; gpm. hwītra, 897; dpn. hwītum, 447, 454; apf. wk. hwītan, 1110. [Ger. *weiss.*]

hwon, *see* forhwon.

hwonne, conj., *until*: 27, 147, 1347.

hwylc, pron., *which* (*one*): nsm. 398. *See* ǣg-, ge-, nāthwylc.

hwyrfan, *see* for-, gehwyrfan.

hȳ, *see* hē.

hycgan, *see* ā-, for-, gehycgan; nīð-, ōrīsthycgende.

hȳdan, *see* bi-, gehȳdan.

hydercyme, *see* hidercyme.

hygd, *see* brēostge-, gehygd; cf. grom-, wonhȳdig.

hyge, m., *heart, spirit, soul; mood*: ns. 500, 1162; as. 620, 1357, 1505, 1511. [Cf. hycgan.]

hygecræftig, adj., *wise*: nsm. 241.

hygegēomor, adj., *sad, mournful, sorrowful*: asn. 890; npm. hygegēomre, 993; apm. hygegēomre, 154.

hygeglēaw, adj., *wise*: nsm. higeglēawe, 1193.

hygerōf, adj., *stout-hearted, valiant*: nþm. hygerōfe, 534.

hygesorg, f., *sorrow*: as. hygesorge, 174.

hygeðonc, m., *thought*: gs. hygeþonces, 1330.

hȳhst, *see* hēah.

hyht, m., *hope; joy*: ns. 99, 529, 585, 750; gs. hyhtes, 58; ds. hyhte, 613; as. 864.

hyhtan, W1. trans. and intrans., *hope for, expect; rejoice*: pret. 3 pl. 142; inf. 340.

hyhtfull, adj., *joyful*: npm. hyhtfulle, 119.

hyhtplega, m., *gambol, frolic*: ns. 737. [plega, 'play.']

hyld, *see* gehyld.

hyll, f., *hill*: ap. hyllas, 717.

hȳnan, W1. trans., *oppress*: 3 sg. hȳneð, 260. [hēan.] *See* gehȳnan.

hȳnðu, f., *ignominy; scorn, contempt*: as. hīenþu, 591; dp. hȳnþum, 1513. [hēan.]

hyra, hyre, *see* hē.

hȳran, W1. trans. and intrans., *hear, harken; obey, be obedient*: 3 pl. hȳrað, 360, 1590; pret. 2 sg. hȳrdes, 1394; pret. 3 pl. hȳrdon, 73, 799; inf. 344. *See* gehȳran.

byrde, m., *shepherd*: gp. hyrda, 705;
dp. hyrdum, 450. [Ger. *Hirte*.]
hyrstan, *see* gehyrstan.
hyrwan, *see* gehyrwan.
hyspan, Wl. trans., *mock, revile*: pret.
3 pl. hysptun, 1120. [hosp.]
bȳð, f., *harbor, haven, port*: ds. hȳðe,
864; hȳþe, 859. [Cf. *Hythe, Rother-
hithe*.]
hȳðan, Wl. intrans., *ravage, consume*:
3 pl. hȳþað, 1043; ptc. hīþende, 973.
[hūð.]

I.

Iācōb, pr. n., *Jacob*: gs. Iācōbes, 164.
ic, pron., *I*: ns. 92, *etc.* (65 times); ds.
mē, 171, *etc.* (17 times); as. mec,
1414, 1421, 1422, 1487, 1489, 1492;
mē, 203, 789; dd. unc, 1459; np. wē,
22, *etc.* (47 times); gp. ūre, 362, 494;
dp. ūs, 20, 27, 74, *etc.* (34 times); ap.
ūs, 156 (dat.?), 158, 374, 659, 761,
771, 773, 775, 859, 864; ūsic, 30,
254, 272, 345, 1099.
īdel, adj., *vain, idle, unprofitable*: asm.
īdelne, 1297; apm. īdle, 756. [Ger.
eitel.]
īecan, Wl. trans., *increase, add to*: 3
pl. īecað, 611. [ēac.] *See* gēycan.
ilca, pron., *same*: dsf. ilcan, 624; asm.
ilcan, 570.
in, adv., *in*: 577, 768, 1504.
in, prep. w. dat. and occasionally w.
acc., *in, within, on, upon, amid,
among, during, at, by ;* w. acc., *into,
unto, to, against*: w. dat. 25, 40, 52,
55, 63, 79, 80, 82 (2), 96, 110, 110,
116, 139, 147, 162, 177, 195, 201,
207, 213, 232, 251, 303, 305, 344,
347, 350, 353, 399, 400, 410, 411,
413, 414, 416, 436, 437, 447, 453 (2),
454, 522, 530, 542, 551, 561, 598,
622, 638, 724, 732, 735, 799, 818,
819, 820, 830, 1022, 1033, 1053, 1134,
1197, 1243, 1465, 1467, 1495, 1500,
1542, 1631; w. acc. 265, 345, 406,

449, 452, 455, 534, 549, 553, 560,
562, 580, 652, 657, 725, 729, 748,
764, 787, 788, 1203(?), 1413, 1419,
1532, 1614, 1619.
inc, *see* ðū.
inca, m., *cause of complaint, ground of
suspicion*: as. incan, 178.
ingeðonc, m. *inmost thought, imagination*: dp. ingeþoncum, 1013; ap.
ingeþoncas, 1315.
ingong, m., *entrance, portal, doorway*:
ns. 308. [Ger. *Eingang*.]
inhebban, 6. trans., *undo, unfasten*: inf.
313.
inlēohtan, Wl. trans., *enlighten*: opt.
2 sg. inlēohte, 115.
inlīce, adv., *sincerely, heartily*: sup.
inlocast, 432.
inlȳhtan, Wl. trans., *enlighten; clear
up, explain*: 2 sg. inlīhtes, 108; pp.
inlīhted, 43.
innan, adv., *within*: 539, 1004, 1329.
innan, prep., *within, in* (?): 469.
inne, adv., *within*: 732.
Iōb, pr. n., *Job*: ns. 633.
Iōsēph, pr. n., *Joseph*: vs. 164.
īowan, *see* ēowan.
īu, adv., *once, long ago*: ᴢ, 138, 1476,
1488. *See* gēo.
Iūdēas, pr. n., *Jews*: np. 637.

L.

lāc, f., *gift, sacrifice*: ap. 292. [Cf.
MnE. *wedlock*.] *See* bordge-, gelāc.
lācan, R. intrans., *toss ; disport ; flicker*:
1 pl. lācað, 854; inf. 399; ptc.
lācende, 1594.
lǣcedōm, m., *salvation*: as. 1572.
[MnE. *leech*.]
lācnian, *see* gelācnian.
lād, *see* gelād.
lǣdan, Wl. trans., *lead, conduct, bring*:
3 sg. lǣdeð, 574; pp. lǣded, 795.
See gelǣdan.
lǣdend, m., *bringer, giver*: ns. 111,
141.

264 GLOSSARY. [lādian-lēof

lādian, W2. intrans., *confute, rebut*: inf.
lādigan, 183.
lǣfan, W1. trans., *leave* : imp. sg. lǣf,
159.
laguflōd, m., *sea, ocean*: ds. laguflōde,
850.
lām, m., *clay, earth, dust*: ds. lāme,
1381. [Ger. *Lehm*, MnE. *loam*.]
lange, *see* lọnge.
lǣmen, adj., *of clay, of earth, of dust*:
apn. lǣmena, 15. [lām.]
lǣne, adj., *transitory, fleeting*: nsf.
842; asf. wk. lǣnan, 1558, 1585.
[Cf. lǣn, 'loan.']
lange, *see* lọnge.
lār, f., *teaching, doctrine, precept*: as.
lāre, 1200; np. lāre, 44; gp. lāra,
141. [Ger. *Lehre*, MnE. *lore*.]
lǣran, W1. trans., *instruct, teach*: inf.
815. [Ger.*lehren*; cf. lāst, lǣstan.]
lārēow, m., *teacher, master*: gs. lārēowes, 458. [*lārðēow.]
lǣs, *see* ðȳ-lǣs.
lāst, m., *track, course*: as. 496. [Ger.
Leisten, MnE. (*shoemaker's*) *last*.]
lǣstan, trans. and intrans., *do, perform, fulfill; continue*: 1 sg. lǣste,
477; pret. 2 pl. lǣstun, 1502; pret.
3 pl. lǣstun, 1224, 1288; inf. 1392.
[Ger. *leisten*, MnE. *last*.]
lǣtan, R. trans., *leave; let, allow, suffer*:
3 sg. lǣteð, 1595; opt. 2 sg. lǣte,
343; imp. sg. lǣt, 158; [lǣt], 155.
See ā-, ānfor-, forlǣtan.
lāð, adj., *hostile; hateful, evil, grievous;*
as sb., *foe*: nsm. 194; asf. wk. lāðan,
183, 592; gpm. lāðra, 776 (sb.);
dpm. lāðum, 846 (sb.); dpf. lāþum,
1602; ipn. lāþum, 1374. [Ger. *leid*.]
laðian, *see* gelaðian.
lāðlīc, adj., *loathsome; horrible*: asm.
lāðlīcne, 1173; asn. 1275.
laðu, *see* wordlaðu.
lāðwẹnde, adj., *evil, wicked*: apm.
1594.
latian, W2. intrans., *tarry*: imp. sg.
lata, 373. [læt, 'late.']

lēafa, *see* gelēafa.
leahtor, m., *sin, crime, transgression,
vice, wickedness* : gp. leahtra, 1098,
1280, 1308, 1314; dp. leahtrum, 1478;
ap. leahtras, 1558; ip. leahtrum,
829, 1538. [lēan, 'blame.']
lēan, n., *recompense, reward, retribution*:
as. 434, 473, 846, 1361, 1587; np.
1366; ip. lēanum, 783. [Ger. *Lohn*.]
See and-, ẹft-, morðor-, sigor-,
wuldorlēan.
lēanian, W2. intrans., *recompense, re-
quite*: 3 sg. lēanað, 827.
lēas, adj., *without; void of, free from*:
nsm. 1413, 1451, 1464; nsf. 36; nsn.
123; asf. lēase, 188; npm. lēase, 1508,
1640. [Ger. *los*.] *See* ār-, bysmer-,
drēam-, ẹnde-, gewit-, grund-,
mẹte-, sorg-, wǣr-, wlitelēas.
lēas, adj., *false, lying*: npm. lēase, 1119,
1610. [Archaic Eng. *leasing*.]
lēaslīc, adj., *vain, deceitful*: asf. lēaslīce,
1296.
lẹcgan, *see* ālẹcgan.
lēg, m., *flame, fire*: ns. 809, 932, 973,
983, 994, 1594; līg, 966; gs. līges,
1620; as. 957, 1532; līg, 1250; is.
lēge, 1335, 1538; līge, 1546. [Ger.
Lohe; cf. Lat. *lux*.] *See* dēað-,
tēonlēg.
lēgbryne, m., *fire, conflagration*: ds.
1001.
leger, n., *sickness, disease*: ns. 1661.
lẹng, *see* lọnge.
lēode, fpl., *men, mankind, people, nation*:
np. lēode, 962, 1186; gp. lēoda, 194,
234, 1118, 1424; dp. lēodum, 1089,
1173, 1238, 1572, 1602. [Ger. *Leute*.]
lēodsceaða, m., *public enemy, common
enemy, (Satan)*: ds. lēodsceaþan, 273.
[Cf. Ger. *Schaden*, MnE. *scathe*.]
lēof, adj., *dear, beloved; pleasing, pleasant;* as substantive, *loved one, friend*:
gsm. lēofes, 496; asm. lēofne, 501,
1642; asn. 458; gpm. lēofra, 815, 1652;
dpm. lēofum, 473, 846, 913, 1361;
comp. nsn. lēofre, 596; lēofra, 842;

sup. dpm. lēof[s]tum, 1347. [Ger.
lieb, MnE. *lief*.]
lēoflīc, adj., *loved, beloved, dear* : asm.
lēoflīcne, 400.
lēoflīce, adv., *lovingly* : 1095.
lēoftǣl, adj., *kind, loving, gracious* :
nsm. 912.
lēofwęndum, adv., *gratefully* : 471 (ip.
of adj. lēofwęnde).
lēoht, n., *light, brightness, day* : ns. 231,
gs. lēohtes, 585; ds. lēohte, 400,
1463; as. 27, 227, 592, 1036; is.
lēohte, 504, 1238, 1642.
lēoht, adj., *bright, shining, resplendent* :
nsm. wk. lēohta, 1089; asn. lēohte,
592; nsf. comp. lēohtra, 1651.
lēohte, adv., *brightly, brilliantly ; clearly* : 1118; comp. lēohtor, 901.
‡ lēohtian, W2. intrans., *give light,
shine* : pret. 3 sg. lēohtáde, 234.
See lȳhtan; inlēohtan; in-, onlȳhtan.
lēoma, m., *ray, beam ; light, brightness,
splendor, effulgence ; glow* : ns. 106,
234, 696, 900, 1005; is. lēoman, 204.
lēosan, *see* forlēosan.
lēoð, *see* fūslēoð.
līc, n., *body* : ns. 1326, [1579]; gs. līces,
1296; ds. līce, 819; as. 777, 1036.
licgan, 5. intrans., *lie* : 3 sg. ligeð, 734;
pret. 1 sg. læg, 1424; 3 sg. læg,
1137, 1465; 3 pl. lǣgon, 45; lǣgun,
1155; lāgun, 1355. *See* forlegen.
līchǫma, m., *body, flesh* : ns. 1098 ; gs.
līchǫman, 1314; ds. līchǫman, 628,
755, 1031, 1186, 1453; as. līchǫman,
1068(?), 1484; is. līchǫman, 1209,
1470; np. līchǫman, 1280. [Cf.
Ger. *Leichnam*.]
līcian, W2. intrans., *please, be pleasing* :
opt. 3 sg. līcie, 1333; inf. 1080.
[MnE. *like*.]
līcsār, n., *pain of body, suffering* : as.
1429.
līf, n., *life* : ns. 1602, 1652 ; gs. līfes,
44, 204, 227, 304, 334, 471, 585,
1051, 1095, 1318, 1322, 1366, 1374,

1392, 1478, 1551, 1610, 1637, 1642;
ds. life, 416, 1427; as. 19, 596, 776,
1463, 1469, 1476, 1579. [Ger. *Leib*.]
See hǣlolīf.
līfdæg, m., *day of life* : dp. līfdagum,
1224.
līffrēa, m., *Lord of life* : ns. 15, 27.
līffruma, m., *Source of life, Author of
life* : ns. 656, 1042; as. līffruman, 504.
lifgan, W3. intrans., *live ; exist ; abide,
endure* : 3 sg. leofað, 1574, 1635;
pret. 3 pl. lifdon, 829, 1075; imp.
sg. leofa, 412; inf. lifgan, 194, 621,
1211, 1326; ptc. nsm. lifgende, 755;
asm. lifgendne, 1381, 1453; vsm. lifgende, 273; gpm. lifgendra, 231, 437.
līfwela, m., *riches of life eternal* : ap.
līfwelan, 1347.
līfwynn, f., *joy of life* : līfwynna, 806.
līg, *see* lēg.
līhtan, *see* lȳhtan.
lim, n., *limb, member* : ap. leoma, 777 ;
leomu, 1620; leomo, 15 ; dp. leomum,
628.
limpan, *see* gelimpan.
‡ lioðucǣge, f., *key of a member* or
organ : is. lioðucǣgan, 334. [Cf.
MnE. *key*.]
liss, f., *mercy, favor, grace ; love* : gs.
lisse, 434; is. lisse, 1646; gp. lissa,
373, 1366. [līðe.]
list, f., *art, artifice* : as. 1318. [Ger.
List.]
līð, n., *limb, member* : dp. leoðum, 1031,
1068; ap. leoð[o], 1381. [Cf. Ger.
Glied < *Gelied*.]
līðan, 1. intrans., *sail* : opt. 1 pl. 851.
See gelīðan.
līðe, adj., *mild, calm, serene ; pleasant,
sweet* : nsn. 913; gsn. līðes, 1637;
asn. 605. [Ger. (*ge*)*lind*, MnE.
lithe ; cf. liss < *līðs*.]
līxan, W1. intrans., *shine, gleam, be
bright* : 3 sg. līxeð, 698 ; pret. 3 sg.
līxte, 505; ptc. nsn. līxende, 231.
loc, n., *barrier, bar* : ap. locu, 321.
loca, m., *pale, barrier ; key* : as.

locan, 19, 1620. *See* bān-, hreðerloca.

lof, mn., *praise, glory*: ns. 411, 777;
as. 612. [Ger. *Lob*.]

lofian, W2. trans., *praise*: 3 pl. lofiað,
400, 1641; pret. 3 sg. lofede, 634;
pret. 3 pl. lofedun, 504.

lond, n., *land; dry land; country,
region*: gs. londes, 437, 1001; ds.
londe, 857; as. 32. *See* burg-,
ðeod-, wīdlond.

long, adj., *long*: asn. wk. longe, 1463.
See gelong.

longe, adv., *long, a long time*: 115, 141,
252, 805, 829; lange, 373, 1361;
comp. leng, 343, 501.

longsum, adj., *abiding, enduring*: npf.
longsume, 44.

losian, W2. trans. (w. dat.), *depart
from; escape*: opt. 3 sg. losige, 1558;
inf. 1001, 1628. [MnE. *lose*.]

lūcan, *see* bi-, onlūcan.

lufian, W2. trans., *show love to, worship,
adore*: pret. 3 pl. lufedun, 471.

lufsum, adj., *sweet, pleasant*: nsn. 913.

lufu, f., *love*: ns. 585, 1652; ds. lufan,
1116, 1433, 1470; as. lufan, 167, 477.
See mōd-, sib-, trēowlufu.

lungre, adv., *thoroughly, completely,
entirely*: 167.

lust, m., *desire, longing; lust*: as. 261,
369, 1297; ap. lustas, 756; ip.
lustum, 1224. [Ger. *Lust*.] *See*
firen-, synlust.

lȳfan, *see* ā-, gelȳfan.

lyft, f., *air; wind, blast; sky, heaven*:
ns. 990, 1042; ds. lyfte, 219, 491;
as. 940. [Ger. *Luft*.]

lyge, m., *lie, falsehood*: as. 1306.
[lēogan, 'lie.']

lygesearo, n., *wile*: dp. lygesearwum,
776.

lȳgnian, W2. trans., *deny*: pret. 3 pl.
lȳgnedon, 1119. [lēogan, 'lie.']

lȳhtan, W1. intrans., *shine, give light*:
pret. 3 sg. lȳhte, 938. [lēoht.] *See*
lēohtian; in-, onlȳhtan.

lȳsan, W1. trans., *ransom, redeem*: pret.
3 sg. lȳsde, 1209. *See* ā-, on-, tō-
lȳsan.

lȳtel, n., *little*: ns. lȳt[*el*], 1400.

lȳtel, adj., *little, small*: nsm. 1424;
asm. wk. lȳtlan, 1322; is. lȳtle, 578;
dpn. lȳtlum, 962.

M.

mā, n., *more*: ns. 988. [Archaic MnE.
moe.]

mā, adv., *again, hereafter*: 325.

mæcg, *see* wrǣcmæcg.

mæg, m., *descendant, son*: vs. 165.

mæg, f., *virgin, maiden*: ns. 87.

māga, m., *son*: ns. 1419.

magan, PP. trans., *can; be able to,
have the power to; may*: 1 sg. mæg,
183, 317; 2 sg. meaht, 1457; 3 sg.
mæg, 33, 173, 666, 668, 670, 671,
672, 676, 678, 679, 889, 921, 999,
1283, 1305, 1308, 1310, 1316, 1528,
1541, 1628; 1 pl. magon, 127, 1549;
mægon, 247; magun, 861, 1329;
3 pl. magon, 1115, 1263, 1280, 1524;
magun, 1047, 1118, 1176, 1178; pret.
3 pl. meahtan, 564, 637, 654, 800;
opt. 3 sg. mæge, 221, 242, 398, 844,
989, 1323; 3 pl. mægen, 902; magon,
1312; pret. 2 sg. meahte, 1401, 1431,
1467; 3 sg. meahte, 311.

mægdenhād, m., *maidenhood, virginity*:
ns. 1419.

mǣge, f., *descendant, daughter, kins-
woman*: ds. mǣgan, 96.

mægen, n., *strength, might, power; host,
throng, multitude*: as. 748; ds. mægne, 748; is. mægene, 382; mægne,
145, 319, 869; np. 956, 1018; gp.
mægna, 603, 657, 787, 832. [MnE.
main.] *See* heofonmægen.

mægencræft, m., *power*: as. 1279.

mægencyning, m., *mighty king; Lord
of hosts*: gs. mægencyninges, 916;
gp. mægencyninga, 942.

‡ mægenearfeðe, n., *misery, great hard-*

ship: as. mægenearfeþu, 1410; dp. mægenearfeþum, 963.

‡ **mægenfolc**, n., *host, (great) multitude*: ns. 876.

mægenðrym, m., *majesty; glory, heaven; heavenly host, angelic host*: gs. mægenþrymmes, 352, 557; ds. mægenþrymme, 296; is. mægenþrymme, 1008.

‡ **mægenwundor**, n., *mighty wonder*: ip. mægenwundrum, 926.

mægð, f., *virgin, maiden*: ns. 36; vs. 176; as. mægeð, 721; gp. mægða, 445. [Ger. *Magd.*]

mægð, f., *race, nation, tribe, people*: dp. mægþum, 234; ap. mægðe, 144, 523, 946.

mægðhād, m., *maidenhood, virginity*: ns. 85; as. 289.

‡ **magugeoguð**, f., *(period of) youth*: ds. magugeoguðe, 1428.

magutūdor, n., *offspring, progeny*: ds. magutūdre, 629.

mægwlite, m., *appearance, form, aspect*: ds. 1432; as. 1383.

mæle, *see* unmæle.

man, *see* mon.

mān, n., *sin, wickedness; evil*: gs. mānes, 36; ds. māne, 1432; as. 1600. [Cf. Ger. *Meineid.*]

mænan, W1. trans., *bemoan, lament*: 2 pl. mænað, 90.

mænan, W1. trans., *mean*: 3 sg. mæneð, 1377.

‡ **māncwealm**, m., *destruction*: as. 1416.

mānforwyrht, n., *sin*: ap. mānforwyrhtu, 1094.

mānfremmend, m., *sinner, worker of iniquity*: gp. mānfremmendra, 1436.

manian, W2. trans. (w. gen.), *claim, demand*: 1 sg. manige, 1478. *See* gemonian.

manigfeald, *see* monigfeald.

mænigo, f., *multitude, throng*: as. 156. *See* mengu.

mānsceaða, m., *sinner*: ns. 1559.

‡ **mānswara**, m., *perjured (person), for-*

sworn (person): ns. 193; np. mānsworan, 1611. [Cf. Ger. *Meineid.*]

mānweorc, n., *iniquity, transgression*: gp. mānweorca, 1210.

‡ **mānwomm**, m., *blot, sin*: gp. mānwomma, 1279.

māra, *see* micel.

mære, adj., *glorious; great, renowned, illustrious; dread; awful*: nsm. 138, 589; nsm. wk. māra, 441, 456, 1054; gsm. wk. māran, 94, 165; gsf. mærre, 4, 446; dsm. mærum, 210; asm. wk. māran, 647, 1007; asf. wk. māran, 971; vsf. māra, 275. [Cf. Ger. *Märchen.*] *See* wīdmære.

mærsian, *see* gemærsian.

Maria, pr. n., *Mary*: ns. 88; gs. Marīan, 445; vs. 176, 299.

mærðu, f., *glory; glorious deed*: as. mærþu, 591; dp. mærþum, 748.

mæte, *see* ofer-, or-, unmæte.

mæðlan, W1. intrans., *speak*: 3 sg. mæðleð, 1337; inf. 797, 1363. [**mæðel**, 'speech,' 'conference.']

meaht, f., *might, power; virtue, authority*: ns. 1077; as. 218, 478, 1145, 1624; gp. meahta, 296, 488, 652, 822, 1383, [1401]; ip. meahtum, 284, 330, 567, 647, 716, 1189. [Ger. *Macht*]

meaht, adj., *mighty*: gsm. wk. meahtan, 868.

meahtig, adj., *mighty*: nsm. 686, 1527; mihtig, 126, 475, 1007, 1170. *See* ælmihtig, tīrmeahtig.

mearh, *see* yðmearh.

mēce, *see* sigemēce.

‡ **mēdrencynn**, n., *maternal descent*: as. 246. [mōdor.]

Melchisēdech, pr. n., *Melchisedec*: ns. 138.

meltan, *see* gemeltan.

mengan, *see* gemengan.

mengu, f., *throng, multitude*: as. 509. [Ger. *Menge.*] *See* mænigo.

mennisc, adj., *human*: asn. 721. [Cf. Ger. *Mensch.*]

meotud, m., *God, Lord; Maker, Cre-*

ator; Father: ns. 716; gs. meotudes, 94, 126, 143, 197, 452, 589, 629, 1200, 1254, 1261; meotodes, 210; ds. meotude, 289, 876, 1077, 1365, 1559, 1579; as. 1040, 1187; vs. meotod, 244. [**metan**, 'measure.']

meotudsceaft, f., *judgment*: ds. meotudsceafte, 887.

mēowle, f., *maiden, virgin, damsel*: gs. mēowlan, 446.

mētan, W1. trans., *find, encounter*: 3 sg. mēteð, 958. [**mōt**.] *See* **gemētan**.

mętelēas, adj., *hungry, without food*: dpm. mętelēasum, 1506. [Cf. MnE. *meat*.]

micel, adj., *great; much; long; numerous; mighty; dread, awful;* inst. w. comp. as av. *much, far*: nsm. wk. micla, 85, 868; nsf. 751, 847; micle, 156; nsf. wk. micle, 1370; nsn. 876, 1040; gsm. wk. miclan, 352; dsm. wk. miclan, 1050, 1205; asf. micle, 1410; asn. 1154; isn. micle, 842, 1317; npn. wk. miclan, 826; apf. wk. miclan, 652; comp. nsm. māra, 421 (MS. mā), 838; sup. nsm. mǣst, 954, 1626; nsn. mǣst, 550, 892, 931, 1069, 1624; asf. mǣste, 568, 617, 1081, 1208, 1273; ism. mǣste, 833, 950; ism. wk. mǣstan, 1008; dpn. mǣstan, 963. [MnE. *much*, Sc. *muckle*.] *See* **efenmicel**.

miclian, *see* **gemiclian**.

mid, adj., *mid, middle*: dsf. midre, 869.

mid, adv., *also, besides; with*: 478, 488, 1521.

mid, prep., *with, together with; by means of; because of*: w. dat. 222, 225, 235, 278, 327, 381, 387, 391, 395, 406, 412, 594 (2), 595 (2), 661, 718, 753, 915, 920, 926, 952, 966, 967, 968, 1087, 1109, 1130, 1169, 1199, 1246, 1324, 1329, 1344, 1346, 1347, 1359, 1361, 1422, 1423, 1440, 1441, 1468, 1478, 1514, 1530, 1636; w. acc. 122, 163, 217, 237, 347, 349, 355, 461, 515, 519, 941, 1489, 1664;

w. inst. 240, 517, 755, 951, 975, 1008, 1097, 1099, 1209, 1317, 1425, 1470, 1546 (2); doubtful: 103, 124, 131, 135, 478, 488, 635, 752, 867, 945, 1314, 1358, 1447, 1470, 1547, 1646 (2).

middangeard, m., *earth, world*: ns. 881, 971; gs. middangeardes, 275, 557, 826; as. 105, 249, 452, 644, 698, 787, 1046.

mihtig, *see* **meahtig**.

milde, adj., *merciful, gracious; gentle, mild; charitable*: nsm. 417, 822; dsm. mildum, 1351; asm. 1210; apf. wk. mildan, 1200.

milde, adv., *graciously*: 249.

milts, f., *mercy, compassion*: ns. 1370; ds. miltse, 299; as. miltse, 156, 244, 1254, 1365. [**milde**.]

mīn, pron., *my*: nsm. 792, 1465; vsm. 164; nsn. 1414, 1433; gsm. mīnes, 1344; gsf. mīnre, 174; gsn. mīnes, 1460; dsm. mīnum, 1431, 1453, 1475, 1496; dsf. mīnre, 1448, 1458; asm. mīnne, 93, 1351, 1506; asf. mīne, 167, 480; asn. 1393, 1444, 1476; ism. mīne, 1462, 1470; dpf. mīnum, 1455; apm. mīne, 1499; ipm. mīnum, 1492; ipf. mīnum, 1379.

mirce, adj., *black, wicked*: asm. mircne, 1279. [MnE. *murk*.]

mislīc, adj., *manifold, various*: apn. 644.

mīðan, *see* **bimīðan**.

mōd, n., *mind; heart; soul, spirit; pride*: gs. mōdes, 662, 665, 1358; ds. mōde, 28, 916, 989, 1401, 1428, 1498, 1557, 1600; as. 1210; is. mōde, 280, 293, 371, 1512; ip. mōdum, 902. [Ger. *Mut*.] *See* **eað-, glædmōd**.

mōdblind, adj., *blind* (metaphorically), *undiscerning*: nsm. mōdblinde, 1187.

mōdcræft, m., *acuteness, shrewdness*: is. mōdcræfte, 441.

mōdig, adj., *courageous, bold*: nsm. 647, 746. [Ger. *mutig*.]

mōdlufu, f., *love*: as. mōdlufan, 126ᵛ.

mōdor, f., *mother*: ns. 93, 210; gs. 425; ds. mēder, 36; as, 1419.

molde, n., *earth*: ds. moldan, 888; as. moldan, 421.

mǫn, m., *man; human being; one, they; pl. mankind; men*: ns. 889, 1283, 1306, 1308, 1421, 1556; gs. mǫnnes, 126, 199, 421, 629, 657; ds. męn, 1303; as. 23; vs. 441, 1379; np. męn, 746, 902, 1082, 1123, 1152, 1187, 1191, 1600, 1605; gp. mǫnna, 287, 425, 431, 584, 589, 663, 690, 887, 956, 1046, 1050, 1054, 1433, 1627; manna, 85, 487; dp. mǫnnum, 94, 105, 299, 894, 913, 919, 1324; ap. męn, 291, 1349, 1594.

mōna, m., *moon*: ns. 606, 694, 698, 937.

mǫncyn, u., *mankind, men*: ns. 1040; gs. mǫncynnes, 244, 417, 1026, 1094, 1416; ds. mǫncynne, 937, 1096.

mǫnian, *see* gemǫnian.

mǫnig, adj., *many, many a (one)*: nsm. 801, 1174; npm. mǫnig[*e*], 795; mǫn[*i*]ge, 1142, 1170; dpm. mǫn[*i*]-gum, 926, 1162; apn. 644.

mǫnigfeald, adj., *manifold*: asf. mǫnig-fealde, 662; gpm. mǫnigfealdra, 603.

mǫnwīse, f., *manner of men, human fashion, custom*: ds. mǫnwīsan, 77.

morðor, nm., *crime, sin*: as. morþor, 193.

‡ **morðorhūs**, n., *house of torment*: gp. morþerhūsa, 1624.

‡ **morðorlēan**, u., *retribution for sin, reward of sin*: as. morþorlēan, 1611.

mōs, u., *food, meat, bread*: gs. mōses, 1506. [Ger. *Mus.*]

mot, u., *mote, atom*: as. 77. [mot ne = 'not an atom, not at all.']

mōt, *see* gemōt.

mōtan, PP. intrans., *may; must*: 3 sg. mōt, 100, 590; 1 pl. mōtan, 246, 339, 346, 384; 3 pl. mōtun, 1079, 1246; mōtan, 392; pret. 2 sg. mōstes, 1388; pret. 3 pl. mōstun, 501; opt. 3 sg. mōte, 267, 818, 1326, 1573,

1584; opt. 1 pl. mōten, 376; pret. 2 sg. mōste, 1402, 1426, 1460, 1464; 1 pl. mōsten, 1203; 2 pl. mōsten, 1348; 3 pl. mōsten, 1503; mōstun, 1210.

munan, *see* gemunan.

‡ **mund**, m., *continence, chastity*: as. 93.

mundbora, m., *protector, guardian*: ds. mundboran, 28.

‡ **mundheals**, f., *protection*: as. 446.

munt, m., *mountain*: as. 716; dp. muntum, 746. [Lat.]

‡ **mūr**, m., *wall*: np. mūras, 1142. [Lat.]

murnan, 3 intrans., *grieve, sorrow*: ptc. murnende, 500. *See* bimurnan.

murnlīce, *see* unmurnlīce.

mūð, m., *mouth*: gs. mūþes, 665; ds. mūðe, 1436.

myne, m., *love*: is. 1358.

myntan, W1. intrans., *intend, purpose*: 3 sg. mynteð, 1057.

myrran, W1. intrans., *disturb (?)*: pp. nsf. (?) myrde, 1143. [Cf. MnE. *mar.*]

N.

nacod, adj., *naked*: dpm. nacedum, 1354, 1505.

næfre, adv., *never*: 54, 476.

nǣgan, *see* genǣgan.

nægl, m., *nail*: ip. næglum, 1109.

nǣnig, pron., *no, no one, none*: nsm. 324, 1310; nsf. 39; dsm. nǣngum, 1466; dp. nǣngum, 1576. [*See* ǣnig.]

næs, *see* wesan.

nāles, adv., *no, by no means, not*: 962, 1170, 1194, 1275, 1536. [ne+ealles.]

nān, pron., *none, no*: nsm. 352; nsf. 290.

nāthwylc, pron., *some one*: gsm. nath-wylces, 189.

nāwðer, pron., *neither*: nsn. 189. [ne+āhwæðer.]

ne, adv., *not*: 21, etc. (67).

nē, conj., *nor*: 39, 81, 190, 241, 352, 420, 817, 1366, 1510, 1556, 1576, 1660, 1661 (2), 1662 (2).

nēah, adj., *near, nigh*: nsn. 782.

nēah, adv., *near; lately, recently*: 390; sup. nȳhst, 535; nēhst, 398.

nearoðearf, f., (*pressing*) *need, necessity*: as. nearoþearfe, 69.

nēhst, *see* nēah.

nellan, *see* willan.

nemnan, W1. trans., *name, call*: pret. 3 sg. nemde, 636; pp. nemned, 131.

nēod, f., *desire*: ns. 245; is. nēode, 1071; gp. nīoda, 261.

neorxnawong, m., *Paradise*: gs. neorxnawonges, 1390, 1405. [*nēorōhsna?]

nēosan, W1. trans., *visit, come to*: inf. 321, 741.

nēotan, 2. intrans., *enjoy*: 1343, 1461; ger. nēotenne, 1390. [Ger. *geniessen*.]

nergan, W1. trans., *save, deliver*: pret. 3 sg. nerede, 1188; pres. p. nergende, 157, 361. *See* genergan.

nergend, m., *Savior*: ns. 324, 426, 571; ds. nergende, 398, 1498; vs. 261.

nesan, *see* genesan.

nēðan, *see* genēðan.

nīedðīow, *see* nȳdðēow.

niht, f., *night; darkness; day* (with numerals): ds. 869, 872; as. 592; ap. 542. *See* sinniht.

nihtes, adv., *by night, at night*: 938.

niman, 4. trans., *take; seize; receive*: 3 sg. nimeð, 63, 260, 964, 982, 1002, 1612. *See* geniman.

nīod, *see* nēod.

nis, *see* wesan.

nīð, m., *enmity*: ds. nīþe, 1659. [Ger. *Neid*.]

nīðas, mpl., *men, mankind*: dp. niþum, 69.

nīðcwalu, f., *perdition*: ds. nīðcwale, 1257.

nīðer, adv., *down; beneath, below*:

niþer, 938, 959, 1618. [Ger. *nieder*, MnE. *nether*.]

nīðhycgende, ptc. as sb., (*plotter of enmity*), *hostile man, enemy, foe*: npn. 1109.

nīðre, adv., *below, beneath*: 1466.

nīwian, *see* geed-, genīwian.

nō, adv., *not; never*: 84, 1097, 1595, 1639. [ne + ō.]

noldes, etc., *see* willan.

noma, m., *name*: ds. noman, 413; as. noman, 48, 1351, 1506; is. noman, 131, 1071. *See* frēonoma.

norðan, adv., *from the north*: norþan, 884.

nū, adv, *now; then*: 9, 11, 15, 59, 66, 100, 112, 119, 122, 134, 146, 149, 166, 188, 206, 208, 219, 230, 243, 326, 335, 342, 370, 372, 440, 481, 512, 558, 561, 571, 573 (?), 575, 586, 589, 824, 850, 1312, 1327, 1344, 1396, 1454, 1457, 1474, 1489, 1519, 1552, 1573.

nū, conj., *now that, inasmuch as, since, because*: 13, 83, 247, 341, 383, 573 (?).

nȳd, f., *necessity*: is. nȳde, 1071, 1405. [Ger. *Noth*.]

‡ nȳdgewāld, m., *tyranny, oppression*: ds. nȳdgewālde, 1450.

‡ nȳdðēow, m., *servant*: gp. nīedþīowa, 361.

nȳhst, *see* nēah.

nyle, *see* willan.

nymðe, conj., *except, save, but*: nymþe, 324.

nyrwian, *see* genyrwian.

nysses, *see* witan.

O.

ō, adv., *ever*: 313. Cf. ā, āwo; nō.

of, prep. w. dat., *from; out of; of; by; to*: 74, 108, 109, 186, 296, 466, 499, 505, 508, 568, 569, 621, 626, 702, 748, 760; 765, 789, 886, 888, 889, 901, 939, 1025, 1075, 1111, 1145, 1162, 1184, 1186, 1209, 1252, 1335, 1381,

1403, 1436, 1445, 1448, 1449, 1453,
1485, 1501, 1541, 1543.

ofer, prep. w. acc., *over; above; more
than, beyond; on, upon; throughout,
among; to; across, through; contrary
to, in spite of*: 72, 105, 107, 158, 261,
276, 291, 421, 509, 518, 528, 605, 653,
657, 675, 677, 685, 698, 745, 851, 856,
858, 861, 885, 931, 936, 1010, 1046,
1087, 1101, 1167, 1239, 1334, 1382,
1384, 1515, 1517.

‡ ofermǣte, adj., *innumerable, illimitable, without end*: npf. ofermǣta,
854.

‡ oferðearfa, m., *one in dire need, one
in extreme distress*: dp. oferþearfum,
153.

ofgiefan, 5. trans., *leave, come down
from*: pret. 3 sg. ofgeaf, 729.

‡ ofhrēosan, 2. intrans., *fall down*: 3
pl. ofhrēosað, 933.

ofostlīce, adv., *quickly, speedily*: comp.
ofostlīcor, 272. [of + ēst; cf. æfest.]

ofslēan, 6. trans., *destroy, ruin*: pp.
ofslegen, 1479.

oft, adv., *often, oft*: 17, 870, 1194, 1435;
sup. oftost, 432.

oftēon, 2. trans., *withhold, deny*: pret.
2 pl. oftugon, 1504, 1509.

ōht, *see* ōwiht.

on, adv., *on, upon*: 327, 521, 570, 1240,
1244.

on, prep., *in, within; on, upon; into;
to, unto; among; at; according to*:
w. dat. or inst. 121, 282, 377, 459,
476, 489, 490, 491, 494, 497, 511,
550, 555, 578, 580, 608, 621, 639, 641,
668, 682, 689, 701, 727, 738, 744, 758,
772, 778, 780, 793, 802, 807, 808, 811,
814, 828, 840, 843, 850, 871, 872, 881,
907, 910, 916, 924, 989, 994, 1033,
1034, 1050, 1075, 1096, 1102, 1108,
1114, 1119, 1126, 1137, 1138, 1144,
1146, 1147, 1154, 1155, 1159, 1204,
1207, 1215, 1216, 1217, 1224, 1234,
1241, 1245, 1264, 1274, 1281, 1294,
1299, 1305, 1306, 1310, 1313, 1351,

1355, 1360, 1371, 1400, 1422, 1424,
1425, 1427, 1428, 1455 (2), 1458, 1463,
1468, 1480, 1490, 1495, 1496 (2), 1498,
1501, 1529, 1545, 1557, 1560, 1590,
1596, 1600, 1638, 1659, 1660;

w. acc. 127, 133, 156, 260, 267,
313, 329, 341, 498, 513, 531, 545, 632,
665, 720, 739, 795, 817, 832, 841, 849,
866, 875, 899, 927, 935, 942, 949, 957,
971, 974, 985, 1007, 1032, 1036, 1045,
1068, 1080, 1093, 1103, 1120, 1122,
1140, 1148, 1164, 1171, 1221, 1225,
1227, 1247, 1267, 1270, 1285, 1300,
1307, 1333, 1342, 1363, 1373, 1389,
1409, 1415, 1446, 1487, 1520, 1523,
1526, 1531, 1534, 1535, 1558, 1570,
1585, 1588, 1608.

Doubtful, 487, 854, 912, 1581.

on ān, adv., *at once, forthwith*: 969,
1549. [MnE. *anon*.]

onbærnan, W1. trans., *set on fire, en-
kindle*: pp. onbærned, 1042.

onbeht, m., *servant*: dp. onbehtum,
370. [ambiht, perhaps from Gallic
ambactus (cf. Cæs. *B.G.* 6.15); cf.
Ger. *Amt*, and MnE. *embassy*.]

‡ onbēodan, 2. trans., *make known,
proclaim*: pret. 3 pl. onbudon, 1169.

oncnāwan, R. trans., *recognize; understand, know; observe; confess, ac-
knowledge*: inf. 642, 861, 1118, 1187.

oncyrran, W1. trans. (*reverse*), *abolish,
terminate, put an end to*: pret. 3 sg.
oncyrde, 614.

ond, conj., *and; but*: 927, 1011, 1225;
other instances, including the prefix,
are represented in MS. by the abbre-
viation.

ond- (and-), in prefixes, is cognate
with the Gr. ἀντί, Ger. *ent-* = *against,
in return, opposite, fronting, toward*.

ondgete, adj., *manifest, obvious*: nsn.
1242. [gete < gietan, MnE. *get*.]

ondgiet, n., *understanding, intellect,
reason*: as. 666, 1380.

ondlata, m., *face, visage, countenance*:
ondlata, 1435. [Cf. ondwlita.]

ọndlēan, n., *retribution* : as. 831. [Cf.
  Ger. *Lohn.*]
ondrǣdan, R. trans. and intrans., *fear,*
  be afraid (of) : 1 sg. ondrǣde, 790 ;
  3 sg. ondrǣdeठ, 922 ; opt. pret. 3 sg.
  ondrēde, 1017 ; inf. 779.
ọndsǣc, m., *denial* : as. 655.
ọndsaca, m., *adversary, enemy.* ap.
  ọndsacan, 1593. [**sacan**, 'contend';
  cf. Ger. *Sache,* MnE. *sake.*]
ọndswaru, f., *answer, rejoinder* : as.
  ọndsware, 184. [**swẹrian**, 'swear.']
ọndweard, adj., *present, in presence,*
  in (one's) sight, before one's face : nsm.
  1528, 1577 ; nsf. 1084, 1540 ; nsn.
  1052, 1070 ; asm. ọndweardne, 925 ;
  asn. 1270, 1375.
ọndweard, prep. w. dat., *before, in the*
  presence of : 1563.
ọndwlita, m., *countenance, visage* : as.
  ọndwlitan, 1122. [Cf. ọndlata, and
  Ger. *Antlitz.*]
on efen, adv., *together, at once* : 880,
  964.
ōnettan, W1. intrans., *bestir oneself* :
  inf. 1578. [*on-hatjan.]
onfindan, 3. trans., *find, perceive ; be*
  sensible of : pret. 1 sg. onfunde, 178 ;
  pret. 3 pl. onfundun, 1178.
onfōn, R. trans., *take ; take on, assume ;*
  seize ; receive ; entertain ; inherit ;
  hear, learn ; bear, endure : 3 sg.
  onfēhठ, 1028 ; pret. 1 sg. onfēng,
  187, 1439, 1460 ; pret. 3 sg. onfēng,
  418, 628, 722, 1436 ; pret. 2 pl. on-
  fēngun, 1350 ; pret. 3 pl. onfēngon,
  1131 ; opt. 2 sg. onfēnge, 75 ; opt. 3
  pl. onfēngen, 1068 ; imp. 2 pl. onfōठ,
  1344 ; inf. 830, 1031 ; pp. onfọngen,
  182 ; onfangen, 99.
ongēan, prep. w. dat., *before, to, for* :
  1166, 1604.
ongietan, 5. trans., *understand ; per-*
  ceive, learn ; consider, regard : pret.
  3 sg. ongeat, 1149, 1159 ; inf. 637,
  1106.
onginnan, 3. intrans., *begin* : 3 sg. on-

ginneठ, 1362, 1376 ; pret. 3 sg. ongọn,
  1414.
‡ onhǣle, adj., *entire* : npn. onhǣlo,
  895. [**hāl**, 'whole.']
onhrēran, W1. trans., *shake, disturb* :
  pp. onhrēred, 825.
onhweorfan, 3. trans. *(reverse), annul,*
  rescind, cancel, abrogate : pret. 3 sg.
  onhwearf, 618.
onlūcan, W2. trans., *unlock, open* : 3
  sg. onlūceठ, 325 ; inf. 314.
onlȳhtan, W1. trans., *enlighten* : opt. 3
  sg. onlȳhte, 204.
onlȳsan, W1. trans., *loosen* : 3 sg.
  onlȳseठ, 68.
onmēdla, m., *pride* : ns. 814. [**mōd**,
  'pride.']
onsẹndan, W1. trans., *send* : 3 sg. on-
  sẹndeठ, 760, 764 ; opt. 2 sg. onsẹnde,
  114.
onsȳn, f., *presence ; face ; appearance,*
  aspect : ns. 905 ; onsīen, 1650 ; ds.
  onsȳne, 796, 836, 923, 1019 ; as.
  1382 ; onsȳne, 396.
onsȳn, f., *want, need* : ns. onsīen, 480.
ontȳnan, W1. trans. and intrans., *re-*
  veal ; open : 3 sg. ontȳneठ, 19 ; opt.
  3 sg. ontȳne, 27 ; imp. 3 pl. ontȳnaठ,
  576 ; inf. 253.
onwāld, mn., *power, dominion* : as. 159.
  [**wealdan.**]
‡ onwālg, adj., *inviolate* : nsm. 1420.
  [OHG. *anawalh,* 'absolute.']
onwrēon, 1. trans., *reveal, disclose,*
  make known, divulge ; expound, in-
  terpret : pret. 3 sg. onwrāh, 95, 139,
  195, 316, 384, 463.
open, adj., *open ; gaping ; manifest,*
  uncovered, exposed ; all-revealing :
  nsn. 1604 ; asf. wk. openan, 1570 ;
  asn. 1116 ; npf. opene, 1045 ; apn.
  wk. openan, 1107.
ord, m., *point ; chief, prince* : ns. 515,
  741, 768, 845. [Cf. MnE. '*odds*
  (ON. *oddr*) and ends.']
ordfruma, m., *creator, author, source* :
  ns. 227, 1198 ; as. ordfruman, 402.

orgete, adj., *manifest, plainly visible*:
nsn. orgeate, 1237; asf. 1457; asn.
1116; apn. orgeatu, 1215.

orlege, n., *place of strife*: as. 560.

ormǣte, adj., *huge, colossal*: nsf. 309.

oðclīfan, 1. intrans., *cleave to, cling to*:
3 sg. oðclīfeð, 1266.

oðēawan, W1. trans., *disclose*: pp.
oðēawed, 1604. Cf. oðēowan, oðȳwan.

oðēowan, W1. intrans., *appear*: pret. 3
pl. oðēowdun, 448. Cf. oðēawan,
oðȳwan.

ōðer, pron., *other; another; second*:
nsm. 324, 723; nsf. 291, 1272, 1491;
nsn. 1242; dsm. ōðrum, 20, 1316;
gpm. ōðerra, 1293; dpm. ōðrum,
1262, 1329; apm. ōðre, 685, 1253.

oððæt, conj., *until*: oþþæt, 307, 1005,
1452.

oððe, conj., *or*: oþþe, 184, 314, 893,
1034, 1052, 1067.

oðȳwan, W1. trans. and intrans., *appear, be shown, be seen*: 3 sg. oðȳweð,
904; opt. pret. 3 pl. oðȳwden, 454;
pp. oðȳwed, 838, 894. Cf. oðēawan,
oðēowan.

ōwer, adv., *anywhere; ever*: 199, 1001;
ō[w]ēr, 1628. [**āhwǣr.**]

ōwiht, pron., *anything, aught* (adverbi-
ally) *at all*: ns. ōht, 238; as. 922,
1474; is. ōwihte, 248, 343. [ā +
wiht, 'whit.']

P.

plega, m., *gymnastic, gymnastic feat,
exploit*: ns. 743. [MnE. *play.*] *See*
gūð-, hyhtplega.

pyndan, *see* forpyndan.

R.

racu, f., *story, narrative; account,
reckoning*: ns. 1459; as. race, 1396.
[Cf. reccan.]

rǣcan, W1. trans., *yield, stretch forth*:
3 pl. rǣcað, 1620. [MnE. *reach.*]

rǣd, m., *resource; wisdom*: ns. 430;
dp. rǣdum, 1525. [Ger. *Rath;* arch.
MnE. *rede.*]

rāp, *see* bealorāp.

rǣran, W1. trans., *ordain, establish*: 3
sg. rǣreþ, 689. [MnE. *rear.*] *See*
ārǣran.

rǣs, m., *bound, spring*: ns. 727. [ME.
rees.]

rāsettan, W1. intrans., *rage*: 3 sg.
rāsetteð, 808.

rāsian, *see* ārāsian.

rǣst, f., *rest*: ns. 1655. *See* foldrǣst.

raðe, *see* hraðe.

rēad, adj., *red*: nsm. wk. rēada, 809;
nsf. rēade, 1101.

rēade, adv., *red(ly), ruddily*: 1175.

rēcan, W1. intrans., *be averse to, shrink
from*: pret. 3 pl. rōhtun, 1440.
[MnE. *reck.*]

reccan, W1. trans., *set forth, expound*:
inf. 671. *See* ā-, gereccan. [Cf.
racu.]

reccend, m., *ruler, Lord*: vs. 18.

recen, adj., *swift*: nsm. 809.

rēn, m., *rain*: ns. 609.

rēofan, *see* birēofan.

reord, fn., *voice; word*: is. reorde, 510,
1339; gp. reorda, 47.

reordberend, m., *creature endowed with
speech, man*: np. 278; reordberende,
381; dp. reordberendum, 1368; ap.
reordberende, 1024.

reordian, W2. intrans., *speak*: pret. 3
sg. reordade, 196.

rēotan, 2. intrans., *lament, mourn, wail*:
3 pl. rēotað, 835, 1229.

restan, *see* gerestan.

rētau, *see* ārētan.

rēðe, adj., *severe, stern, austere, rigorous; fierce, raging*: nsm. rēþe, 809,
1527; rēðe, 825; apn. rēþe, 798;
comp. asm. rēþran, 790.

rīce, n., *kingdom, realm, domain;
mastery, sovereignty, authority*: gs.
rīces, 879, 1065, 1527; ds. 268, 475;
as. 345, 353, 1344. [Ger. *Reich;* cf.

MnE. *bishopric.*] *See* ēðel-, heofon-,
　woruldrīce.

rīce, adj., *exalted, mighty*: nsm. 1468.

ricene, adv., *quickly, forthwith*: 1447.
　[*See* recen.]

riht, *see* ryht.

rīm, nm., *number*: gs. rīmes, 467; as.
　1586. [MnE. *rime.*]

rinc, m., *man*: dp. rincum, 1114.

rind, f., *bark*: dp. rindum, 1175.

rinnan, 3. intrans., *run, gush*: inf. 1114.
　See birinnan.

rīpan, 1. trans., *reap*: 3 pl. rīpað, 86.

rīsan, *see* ā-, gerīsan.

rōd, f., *cross*: ns. 1064, 1084, 1101, 1489;
　ds. rōde, 1114, 1447 ; as. rōde, 727,
　1487 (?). [Ger. *Ruthe ;* MnE. *rood,*
　rod.]

rodor, m., *heaven, sky*: ns. 825; gs.
　rodores, 60; gp. rodera, 134, 222,
　423, 798, 865, 1220; dp. roderum,
　74, 353, 484, 526, 758, 906, 1468; ap,
　rodoras, 408. *See* ūprodor.

rodorcyning, m., *heavenly king*: gs.
　rodorcyninges, 727.

rōf, *see* hygerōf.

rōt, *see* unrōt.

rūm, *see* unrūm.

rūme, adv., *round about ; plainly, fully*:
　60, 134. [Cf. MnE. *room.*]

rūst, *see* synrūst.

ryht, n., *right, justice ; righteousness ;*
　truth, exactness ; account, reckoning:
　gs. ryhtes, 700; ds. ryhte, 222, 278,
　381, 846, 1220; as. 267; riht, 1374.

ryht, adj., *erect; just, righteous*: nsf.
　1065; asm. wk. ryhtan, 1368; asf.
　ryhte,671(?); vsm. riht,18. *See* unryht.

ryhte, adv., *rightly, aright*: 131, 671 (?).
　‡ ryhtend, m., *ruler*: as. 798.

ryhtfremmend, m., *worker of righteous-*
　ness: dp. ryhtfremmendum, 1655.

ryhtgerȳne, n., *mystery*: ap. ryht-
　gerȳno, 196, 247.

ryhtwīs, adj., *just*: nsm. 825. [MnE.
　righteous.]

rȳman, *see* gerȳman.

ryne, n., *course*: as. 47, 671.

rȳne, *see* ge-, ryhtge-, wordgerȳne.

S.

sǣ, m., *sea*: ns. 1144, 1163; as. 677,
　852; ap. sǣs, 966.

sǣc, *see* andsǣc.

saca, *see* andsaca.

sācerd, m., *priest*: as. 137. [Lat.
　sacerdos.]

sǣd, n., *seed, semen*: as. 420. [sāwan.]

sǣfisc, m., *fish of the sea*: np. sǣfiscas,
　986.

sǣl, nif., *weal*: dp. sǣlum, 1376. .[Cf.
　sǣlig.]

sǣlan, Wl. trans., *moor*: inf. 862. [Cf.
　Ger. *Seil.*] *See* gesǣlan.

sǣlig, *see* ge-, unge-, unsǣlig.

sǣliglīc, *see* gesǣliglīc.

sǣlignes, *see* gesǣlignes.

Salomon, pr. n., *Solomon*: ns. 712.

sancta, adj., *holy*: nsf. 88; vsf. 50.
　[Lat.]

‡ sǣp, m., *sap*: 1176.

sār, n., *pain, distress, suffering ; tribu-*
　lation: ns. 1266, 1289; gs. sāres,
　1516; ds. sāre, 1355, 1654; as. 1249,
　1411, 1441, 1460, 1631.

sār, adj., *sore, grievous*: asf. sāre, 209;
　apm. sāre, 1418.

sārcwide, m., *taunt, reproach*: gp.
　sārcwida, 170.

sāre, adv., *deeply, greatly*: 1571. [Ger.
　sehr.]

sārgian, *see* gesārgian.

sārig, adj., *sorrowful*: apm. sārge,
　1510. [MnE. *sorry.*]

sārigferð, adj., *sad at heart, sad, sor-*
　rowful: npm. sārigferðe, 1082.

Sātān, pr. n., *Satan*: ds. Sātāne, 1521.
　[Lat.]

sāwan, R. trans. and intrans., *sow ;*
　disseminate, diffuse: 3 pl. sāwað, 86,
　487; pret. 3 sg. sēow, 663.

sāwel, f., *soul*: ns. 819, 1326; gs.
　sāwle, 1550, 1580; ds. sāwle, 1306

1543; as. sāwle, 1036; np. sāwle,
944, 1060; sāule, 53; gp. sāwla, 571,
1067, 1518; dp. sāwlum, 1078, 1163,
1281, 1313, 1603; sāulum, 619; ap.
sāwle, 1074; ip. sāwlum, 1606.

scand, *see* scǫnd.

sceacan, 6. intrans., *depart, flee*: pp.
scæcen, 804. [MnE. *shake.*]

scēadan, R. trans., *decide, determine*.
pp. scēaden, 1232. [Ger. *scheiden.*]

sceadu, f., *shadow; darkness*: as. 118;
np. 1088; ip. sceadum, 1584.

scearp, adj., *sharp, keen*: nsf. 1141.
[scieran, 'cut.']

scēat, m., *corner; region, quarter;
surface*: as. 72, 1533; dp. scēatum,
878; ap. scēatas, 1004. [scēotan,
'shoot'; Ger. *Schoss.*] *See* grundscēat.

sceaða, m., *wicked man; robber; enemy,
foe, adversary; devil, fiend*: ns. 870;
ds. sceaðan, 1395; np. sceaðan, 1131;
gp. sceaðan, 775. *See* hel-, lēod-,
mān-, syn-, ðēod-, wǫmsceaða.

scēawian, W2. trans., *see, behold, look
upon*: 3 pl. scēawiað, 1276; pret. 3
sg. scēawode, 305; inf. 1136, 1206;
ger. scēawianne, 914.

scēotend, m., *bowman, archer* (or *hurler
of the javelin*): np. 675.

sceððan, 6. trans. (w. dat.), *do harm,
do mischief, injure*: 3 sg. sce[ðð]eð,
1548; pret. 3 sg. scōd, 1466; opt. 3
sg. sceþþe, 684; ptc. dsm. sceþþendum, 1395; gpm. sceþþendra, 761.
[sceaða.]

scīene, *see* scȳne.

scieppan, *see* scyppan.

scildan, W1. trans., *protect, defend,
shield*: 3 sg. scildeþ, 781; pret. 3 pl.
sceldun, 979. *See* gescildan.

scildhrēada, m., *shield*: as. scildhrēadan, 675.

scīma, m., *light, radiance*: ns. 697.

scīnan, 1. intrans., *shine, be bright, be
resplendent*: 3 sg. scīneð, 1009, 1088,
1102, 1334; 3 pl. scīnað, 607, 1240;

pret. 3 sg. scān, 935; inf. 1291, 1426,
1584; scȳnan, 901; ptc. scīnende,
1219, 1391..

scīr, adj., *bright; clear, transparent,
translucent*: nsm. 1152; nsn. wk.
scīre, 1282; apfn. scīre, 870. [MnE.
sheer.]

scīre, adv., *brightly; entirely, completely*: 1088, 1141.

scirian, *see* scyrian.

scolu, f., *multitude, throng, host; crew*:
ns. 928, 1534, 1607; ds. scole, 1522;
as. scole, 1251. [Lat. *schola.*]

scǫmian, *see* ā-, gescǫmian; unscǫm-
iende.

scǫmu, f., *shame, disgrace*: gp. scǫma,
1273.

scǫnd, f., *shame, disgrace, ignominy;
pollution, abomination*: ds. scǫnde,
1273, 1479; dp. scǫndum, 1486; ip.
scǫndum, 1298; scandum, 1282.
[Ger. *Schande.*]

scrīfan, 1. intrans., *allot, assign, adjudge*:
3 sg. scrīfeð, 1219. [Lat. *scribere.*]

‡ scrift, m., *confessor*: ns. 1305.

scrīðan, 1. intrans., *rush, dart, speed;
pass, glide*: 3 sg. scrīþeð, 809; ptc.
scrīþende, 1584. [Ger. *schreiten.*]

scūa, *see* dēaðscūa.

sculan, PP. transitive and auxiliary,
*must, shall, have to, be obliged to,
must needs; shall; will; ought,
should; be accustomed*: 1 sg. sceal,
172, 793; 2 sg. scealt, 166, 621,
624, 626; 3 sg. sceal, 1 5, 70, 191,
581, 801, 1029, 1036, 1056, 1205,
1260, 1553, 1578; 1 pl. sculon, 271,
611, 746, 756, 766; sceolon, 783,
862, 1327; 2 pl. sceolon, 1360, 1513;
sceolan, 1523; 3 pl. sculon, 381, 807,
829, 1270; sceolon, 1368, 1525, 1605,
1630; sceolan, 1609; pret. 1 sg.
sceolde, 204; pret. 2 sg. sceoldes,
1405, 1412; pret. 3 sg. sceolde, 212,
233, 1135, 1195; pret. 1 pl. sceoldan,
31; pret. 3 pl. sceoldan, 118; opt. 1
sg. scyle, 193; 3 sg. scyle, 820, 1616;

pret. 2 sg. sceolde, 298, 1385;
(?) pret. 3 sg. sceolde, 1415, 1417.

scyld, f., *guilt, sin*: ns. 97. [sculan;
Ger. *Schuld*.]

scyldig, adj., *guilty, sinful*: npm.
scyldge, 1152; gpm. scyldigra, 1607;
dpm. scyldgum, 1273.

scyldwręccende, ptc., *sin-avenging*:
nsf. 1160.

scyldwyrcende, ptc., *sinning, evil-
doing*: nsm. 1486.

scȳnan, *see* scīnan.

scȳne, adj., *bright, shining; fair,
beauteous*: asm. scīenne, 1386; asm.
wk. scȳnan, 914; asn. scȳne, 1469;
npm. scȳne, 695; dsm. scȳnum,
1147. [Ger. *schön*.] *See* wlitescȳne.

scyppan, 6. trans., *create, make; prepare, destine*: pret. 3 sg. scēop, 1169;
pp. sceapen, 897. [Cf. MnE. *shape*.]
See gescyppan.

scyppend, m., *Creator, Maker*: ns. 417,
1160, 1219; gs. scyppendes, 48; ds.
scyppende, 901, 1226, 1395, 1617;
as. 1131; vs. 266.

scyrian, W1. trans., *relegate*: pp. npm.
scyrede, 1226. [scieran, 'cut.'] *See*
ā-, biscyrian.

scyte, *see* fǣrscyte.

scyttels, *see* forescyttels.

sē, se, adj. pron., *the; he, etc.; who;
that, this*: nsm. 2, *etc.* (74 times); nsf.
sēo, 35, 123, 152, 195, 239, 276, 365,
378, 538, 699, 703, 990, 1016, 1062,
1064, 1143, 1370, 1491, 1650; sīo,
87, 419, 1017, 1061, 1101, 1133; nsn.
ðæt, 547, 600, 1639; þæt, 37, *etc.* (44
times); gsmn. ðæs, 314, 1478; þæs,
30, 146, 182, 220, 281, 337, 352, 458,
495, 505, 530, 553, 559, 600 (?), 611,
639, 654, 655, 757, 823, 1033, 1099,
1138, 1139, 1205, 1212, 1343, 1349,
1372, 1385, 1497, 1566, 1568, 1637;
gsf. þǣre, 434, 1102; dsmn. ðām,
1135; þām, 11, *etc.* (34 times); þān,
1403; dsf. ðǣre, 638, 923, 1019;
þǣre, 81, 461, 519, 542, 552, 613,

621, 624, 626, 864, 888, 1306, 1522,
1530, 1543; asm. þone, 16, *etc.* (18
times); asf. ðā, 534, 592, 865, 940,
1396; þā, 229, *etc.* (27 times); asn.
ðæt, 1605; þæt, 14, *etc.* (58 times);
ismn. ðȳ, 790; þȳ, 889, 1008, 1097,
1099, 1153, 1255, 1425, 1511, 1546 (2);
þī, 240 (*see* ðȳ, ðī lǣs); þon, 235,
272, 633, 650, 691, 712, 850;
np. ðā, 2, 706, 1633; þā, 52,
etc. (22 times) ; gp. ðāra, 48; þāra,
224, 277, 526, 893, 1067, 1268,
1293, 1518; dp. þām, 141, *etc.* (25
times); ap. ðā, 1201; þā, 115, *etc.*
(25 times). *See* se ðe; ðæs; ðæs
ðe.

sealt, adj., *salt*: asm. sealtne, 677.

searo, *see* fǣr-, lygesearo.

searocræft, m., *skill*: as. 9.

searolīce, adv., *skilfully*: 672.

searoðǫncol, adj., *shrewd, wise, clever,
sagacious*: ns. searoþǫncol, 220.

sēað, m., *pit*: ns. 1544.

seax, n., *sword*: gs. seaxes, 1140.

sēcan, W1. trans., *seek, inquire; visit*:
pret. 3 sg. sōhte, 649; pret. 2 pl.
sōhton, 1510; sōhtun, 1359; opt. 1
pl. sēcen, 752; imp. sg. sēc, 441.
See ā-, geond-, gesēcan.

sęcg, m., *man*: ns. 220.

sęcgan, W3. trans., *speak, say, tell, declare; mention; give (thanks)*: 1 sg.
sęcge, 197; 3 sg. sagað, 1307; 3 pl.
sęcgað, 279, 547, 785; pret. 3 sg.
sægde, 203, 302; pret. 3 pl. sægdon,
64, 137, 451, 1193; opt. 3 pl. sęcgen,
601; pret. 3 pl. sægdon, 1304; imp. sg.
saga, 209; inf. 33, 73, 128, 317, 612,
667, 672, 1550. *See* ā-, gesęcgan.

sęcge, f., *speech*: ns. 190.

sefa, m., *mind, heart, soul, spirit; mood,
disposition*: ns. 499; gs. sefan, 442;
ds. sefan, 907, 1207, 1351; ap. sefan,
487, 663, 1359. *See* brēostsefa.

segl, mn., *veil*: ns. 1138.

segn, m., *banner, standard*: ns. 1061.
[Lat. *signum*; cf. gesēnian.]

sęle, *see* dēaðsęle.

sęlegescot, n., *tabernacle* : as. 1480.

sēlest, sēll(r)a, *see* gōd.

self, *see* sylf.

sęllan, *see* syllan.

sęmninga, adv., *suddenly* : 491, 873, 899.

sęncan, *see* bisęncan.

sęndan, W1. trans., *send; let fly* : 3 sg. sęndeð, 664; 3 pl. sęndað, 675; pret. 3 sg. sęnde, 294, 1151; inf. 129; pp. sęnded, 105. *See* onsęndan.

sēnian, *see* gesēnian.

sēoc, adj., *sick* : npm. sēoce, 1355.

seofon, num. adj., *seven* : 949.

sēon, 5. trans., *see, behold; look; gaze upon, survey; experience* : 3 pl. sēoð, 1244, 1270, 1285, 1300; pret. 3 pl. sēgun, 495, 536; imp. sg. sioh, 59; inf. 1416, 1611. *See* for-, ge-, ðurhsēon.

sēon (*exude*), *see* bisēon.

sēoðan, z. intrans., *flame, blaze* : 3 sg. sēoþeð, 994. [Ger. *sieden*; MnE. *seethe*.]

seraphin, *seraphim* : gs. seraphinnes, 386. [Lat.]

sēðan, *see* gesēðan.

se ðe, pron., *who, he who* : nsm. 1466; se þe, 19, 47, 619, 1552; nsf. sēo ðe, 935; np. ðā þe, 1633; þā þe, 496. *See* se; ðe.

sē-ðēah, *see* swā-ðēah.

setl, *see* hēahsetl.

sęttan, W1. trans. *found, establish; ordain; plant* : pret. 3 sg. sętte, 236, 663; ptc. sęttende, 356. [sittan.] *See* gesęttan.

sib, f., *peace; love, friendliness* : ns. 581, 1659; gs. sibbe, 50; ds. sibbe, 619; as. sibbe, 487, 689, 1338; dp. sibbum, 1359; ip. sibbum, 1643. [Ger. *Sippe*; cf. MnE. *gossip*.]

siblufu, f., *love* : dis. siblufan, 635.

‡ sibsum, adj., *peaceful* : nsm. wk. sibsuma, 214.

sīd, adj., *wide, spacious, ample, illimitable, boundless, vast* : asm. sīdne, 785, 852, 947, 1164; asf. sīde, 672, 1087; wk. sīdan, 59, 239, 356; ism. sīde, 524; gpf. sīdra, 170; apm. sīde, 5. [MnE. *side*.]

sīde, f., *side* : ds. sīdan, 1111, 1448, 1458.

sīde, adv., *far, wide* : 394.

siexta, num. adj., *sixth* : nsm. 736.

sīgan, 1. intrans., *descend* : inf. 550.

sige, m., *victory* : gs. siges, 20. [Ger. *Sieg.*]

sigebearn, n., *son of victory* : gp. sigebearna, 520.

sigedēma, m., *victorious Judge* : ds. sigedēman, 1060.

sigedryhten, m., *Lord of victory* : ds. sigedryhtne, 128.

sigehrēmig, adj., *triumphant, exultant* : nsm. 531.

‡ sigemēce, m., *sword of victory* : as. 1530.

‡ sigeðrēat, m., *victorious host* : ds. sigeþrēate, 843.

sigor, m., *victory, triumph* : gs. sigores, 88, 243, 294, 404, 420, 513; as. sygor, 581; gp. sigora, 1228, 1516.

‡ sigorbeorht, adj., *triumphant, radiant with victory* : nsm. 10.

sigorlēan, n., *reward of victory* : dp. sigorlēanum, 1589. [Ger. *Lohn.*]

simle, *see* symle.

sīn, pron., *his, its* : dsn. sīnum, 907; asm. sīnne, 1223; asf. sīne, 1167; ism. sīne, 1209; gpn. sīnra, 1037. [Ger. *sein.*]

sinc, n., *metal, gold* : is. since, 309.

sincgiefa, m., (*giver of treasure*), *King, Lord* : gs. sincgiefan, 460.

singāles, adv., *always, continually* : 323, 393.

singan, 3. trans. and intrans., *sing; utter, pronounce* : 3 pl. singað, 283, 388, 884; pret. 3 sg. sǫng, 650, 712; pret. 3 pl. sungon, 468; inf. 667; pp. sungen, 619.

sinniht, f., *eternal night*: ds. sinnehte,
1542, 1631.

sinnihtes, adv., *in eternal night*: sinneahtes, 117.

sīᵟ, m., *course; trial, vicissitude; time*:
is. sīᵟe, 62; sīþe, 146, 318; ap. sīþas,
1418. [sęndan.] *See* ge-, wilsīᵟ.

sīᵟ, adv., *late*: 602, 893, 1052, 1067,
1567. [Ger. *seit.*]

sīᵟian, W2. intrans., *journey*: pret. 3 sg.
sīᵟade, 329; inf. sīþian, 819. [sīᵟ.]

sīᵟᵟan, adv., *afterwards, after, since;
henceforth, hereafter; thereafter,
thenceforth; again*: siþþan, 39, 194,
294, 339, 346, 375, 438, 1409, 1463,
1494, 1537. [*sīᵟ-ᵟām; Ger.
seitdem; MnE. since < sithence.*]

sīᵟᵟan, conj. *after (that); when (that)*:
siþþan, 445, 565, 629, 702, 1041.

sittan, 5. intrans., *sit; dwell*: 3 sg.
siteᵟ, 1216; 3 pl. sittaᵟ, 26; pret. 3
pl. sǣton, 117. *See* gesittan.

slǣp, m., *sleep*: ns. 1661; is. slǣpe,
889; is. slǣpe, 873.

slēan, 6. trans., *strike; beat, whip,
scourge*: pret. 3 pl. slōgun, 1123,
1441. [Ger. *schlagen.*] *See* ofslēan.

slęccan, *see* geslęccan.

slęge, *see* hearmslęge.

slītan, 1. intrans., *tear, be rent*: pret. 3
sg. slāt, 1140.

‡ slite, m., *gnawing*: as. 1250.

smītan, *see* bismītan.

snēome, adv., *immediately, straightway*:
889.

snottor, *see* gearosnottor.

snūd, adj., *coming soon* or *suddenly*:
asf. wk. snūdan, 841.

snūde, adv., *straightway*: 297.

snyttru, f., *wisdom, understanding*: ns.
snyttro, 239; gs. 667; as. 662, 684;
snyttro, 442. [snottor.]

sōfte, adv., *quietly, patiently*: 146.
[Ger. *sanft.*] *See* unsōfte.

Sōlima, pr. n., *Salem*: gs. Sōlimæ, 91.
[Lat.]

sǫme, adv. (always in the combination

swā sǫme: *also, too, besides, as
well; likewise, similarly; moreover,
furthermore*): 939, 1111, 1122, 1242,
1272, 1455.

sǫmne, *see* æt-, tōsǫmne.

sǫmnian, *see* gesǫmnian.

sǫmning, *see* gesǫmning.

sǫmod, adv., *together; at once; also,
and*: 91, 125, 875, 968, 1120, 1235,
1325; sǫmed, 819. [Ger. *sam(m)t.*]

‡ sǫmodfæst, adj., *joined together*: np.
sǫmodfæst[e], 1580.

sōna, adv., *soon, straightway*: 10, 233,
460.

sǫng, m., *song*: ns. 1649; as. 502.
[singan.] *See* wōᵟsǫng.

sorg, f. (pl. often with same meaning
as sg.), *sorrow, grief, trouble; anxiety*:
ns. 1284; ds. sorge, 620; np. sorge,
1163; gp. sorga, 170, 1081, 1208,
1571; dp. sorgum, 1293, 1643, 1657;
ip. sorgum, 86, 1104. [Ger. *Sorge,
MnE. sorrow.*] *See* hygesorg.

sorgcearu, f., *sorrow, care, anxiety*:
as. sorgceare, 209.

sorgian, W2. intrans. and trans., *sorrow, grieve, lament*: ptc. nsf. sorgende, 1016; asn. sorgende, 889;
npm. sorgende, 26; dpm. sorgendum,
1266. [sorg.] *See* bisorgian.

sorglēas, adj., *free from sorrow; care-
less, unmindful*: npm. sorglēase,
346; apm. sorglēase, 872.

sōᵟ, n., *truth; righteousness*: gs. sōᵟes,
700; sōþes, 706; ds. sōᵟe, 1153; as.
33, 190, 197, 1306.

sōᵟ, adj., *true; genuine* (?); *just, righteous*: nsm. 404; nsm. wk. sōᵟa, 214;
gsm. wk. sōþan, 110; asm. sōᵟne,
451, 512.

sōᵟ, adv., *truly, surely, well*: 317, 442,
794.

sōᵟcyning, m., *king of truth* or *righteousness*: ns. 1228.

sōᵟe, adv., *truly; actually*: 213, 1550.

‡ sōᵟfæder, m., *father of truth* or
righteousness: ds. 103.

söðfæst, adj., *true, just, righteous;
  truthful, veracious*: nsm. 10, 302,
  375, 1589; wk. söðfæsta, 106, 696;
  nsn. wk. söðfæste, 386; gpm. söð-
  fæstra, 53·
söðlice, adv., *truly*: 78, 137, 203.
‡ spätl, m., *spittle*: as. 1121, 1435·
spēd, f., *success; abundance, riches, fulness*: as. 296, 488, 604, 673, 1383, 1401;
  ap. (ds.?) spēde, 652. [spōwan.]
spelboda, m., *messenger*: 336.
spēowan, W1. trans., *spit*: pret. 3 pl.
  spēowdon, 1121. [Ger. *speien*; MnE.
  spew; cf. *spit*.]
spere, n., *spear*: is. (?) 1447·
spōwan, R. intrans., *succeed*: inf. 564.
spræc, f., *talk*: as. spræce, 183.
spreca, *see* forespreca.
sprecan, 5. trans. and intrans., *say,
  speak, tell, utter*: 1 sg. sprece, 190;
  2 sg. spricest, 179; 3 sg. spriceð,
  33; 3 pl. sprecað, 22, 171; pret.
  3 pl. spræcon, 1121; opt. 3 sg.
  sprece, 1377; inf. 24, 798. *See* gesprecan.
springan, *see* āspringan.
sprūtan, *see* geondsprūtan.
stælan, W1. trans., *charge, accuse*: 3
  sg. stæleð, 1373·
‡ stælg, adj., *steep*: asm. stælgne, 679.
  [For stægel = Ger. *steil*; stīgan.]
stān, m., *stone; rock*: ds. stāne, 1424;
  np. stānas, 1142; ip. stānum, 192.
  See weallstān.
standan, 6. intrans., *stand; remain*:
  3 sg. standeð, 1560; stondeð, 1084;
  3 pl. stondað, 322; pret. 3 pl. stōdan,
  252. *See* āstandan.
stænen, adj., *stony*: asf. stænne, 641.
  [stān.]
starian, W2. intrans., *look, gaze*: 1 pl.
  stariað, 341; 2 pl. stariað, 521, 570.
  [MnE. *stare.*] *See* gestarian.
staðelian, W2. trans., *settle, fix, stablish,
  confirm, strengthen*: 2 pl. staþeladon,
  1357; inf. staþelian, 864. *See* gestaðelian.

staðfæst, adj., *firm on the shore*:
  npm. 980.
staðol, m., *seat, habitation; bulwark,
  barrier*: np. staþelas, 980; ap. 661.
staðolfæst, adj., *steadfast, abiding, un-
  shaken*: disf. staþolfæstre, 490.
stęde, m., *place, station*: ds. 1147. *See*
  burg-, ðing-, wongstędc.
stefn, f., *voice; sound, blast*: ns. 948;
  stefen, 1061; as. stefne, 360; is.
  stefne, 389; ip. stefnum, 992. [Ger.
  Stimme.]
stēman, *see* bistēman.
stęncan, *see* tōstęncan.
steorra, m., *star*: np. steorran, 939,
  1147. *See* heofonsteorra.
stiell, *see* styll.
stīgan, 1. trans., *ascend*: opt. 3 sg.
  stīge, 754; pret. 3 sg. stige, 464,
  544; inf. 498; ptc. stīgende, 536.
  See ā-, gestīgan.
stige, *see* ūpstige.
stirgan, W2. trans., *touch, play*: inf.
  669. [MnE. *stir.*]
stīð, adj., *firm, immovable*: npm. 980.
stōl, *see* cyne-, ēðel-, gief-, ðeodenstōl.
stondan, *see* standan.
storm, m., *storm, tempest*: ns. 990; is.
  storme, 951; ip. stormum, 940.
stōw, f., *place*: gp. stōwa, 490. [MnE.
  stow.]
stræl, m., *arrow, shaft; dart*: as. 765;
  ap. strælas, 779. [Ger. *Strahl*.]
strang, *see* strong.
strēam, m., *stream, flood*: ns. 853.
  See ēahstrēam.
strēdan, W1 (?). intrans., *scatter, disappear*: 3 pl. strēdað, 939.
strengðu, f., *strength, power, might*:
  ds. 638; dis. 490. [strong.]
strēon, *see* ærge-, ealdge-, gestrēon;
  strynan.
strong, adj., *strong, powerful, mighty;
  violent, fierce, raging, furious: hard,
  severe*: nsm. 856; strang, 647; nsf.
  wk. stronge, 990; asf. wk. strongan,
  940; comp. nsn. strengre, 192.

strȳnan, Wl. trans., *gain, win, obtain,*
secure: inf. 1574. [streōn.]

stund, f., *time, while*: as. stunde, 1410.
[Ger. *Stunde.*]

stycce, u., *piece*: dp. styccum, 1138.
[Ger. *Stück.*]

‡ stȳlan, Wl. trans., *temper, harden*:
pp. stȳled, 679. [MnE. *steel.*]

‡ styll, m., *leap*: ns. stiell, 723, 728; as.
719.

styllan, Wl. intrans., *leap, spring,*
jump: pret. 3 sg. stylde, 745; inf.
747. *See* gestyllan.

styrfan, *see* āstyrfan.

sum, pron., *some, the, a, a certain, one*:
nsm. 302, 668, 670, 671, 672, 676,
678, 679, 680; dsm. sumum, 664,
673; asn. 1275; ism. sume, 318;
npm. sume, 959 (2).

sund, n., *ocean, water*: gs. sundes, 986.
[swimman.]

sundbūend, mpl. (*those who dwell near*
the sea), *men*: npm. 73; dpm. sund-
būendum, 221.

‡ sundhengest, m., (*sea-steed*), *ship,*
vessel, bark: apm. sundhengestas,
862; ipm. sundhengestum, 852.
[Ger. *Hengst.*]

sundurgiefu, f., *special grace*: ds.
sundurgiefe, 80.

sundwudu, m., *boat, ship*: as. 677.

sunne, f., *sun*: 606, 694, 934, 1132; gs.
sunnan, 26, 106, 696, 900, 1102,
1661; ds. sunnan, 1241, 1651; as.
sunnan, 114.

sunu, m., *son*: ns. 126, 143, 236, 297,
451, 464, 589, 629, 712; gs. suna, 94;
ds. 210, 635; as. 197, 205, 339; vs.
110; np. suna, 1074; vp. 91. *See*
gæstsunu.

sūsl, u., *affliction, suffering, torment*:
gp. sūsla, 1603; ip. sūslum, 149.
See cwicsūsl.

sūðan, adv., *from the south*: sūþan,
884.

‡ sūðanēastan, adv., *from the south-*
east: sūþanēastan, 900.

swā, adv., *so, thus, in this way; to such*
an extent; such; in like manner;
very; where; (swā some, *see* some;
swā ... swā, *as* ... *so*): 135, 138,
148, 233, 306, 312, 323, 330, 332,
426, 501, 645, 681, 695, 699, 746, 875,
939, 972, 984, 1111, 1122, 1204, 1242,
1260, 1272, 1294, 1295, 1386, 1399,
1455. [The adv. and the conj. cannot always be discriminated with
certainty.] *See* swā-ðēah.

swā, conj., *as, even as; as if; like;-*
according as, just as; since, because,
for; whether, or: 17, 58, 63, 85,
86, 109, 112, 135, 142, 180, 455,
468, 543, 547, 591 (2), 592 (2),
593 (2), 594 (2), 595 (2), 596 (3), 633,
701, 784, 850, 870, 897, 988, 1109,
1230 (2), 1233, 1282, 1377. *See*
swā-ðēah.

swāpan, R. trans., *sweep, swing*: 3 sg.
swāpeð, 1530.

swār, adj., *heavy; grievous, severe,*
hard; loud, deafening: nsm. 954,
1411, 1661; comp. nsf. swǣrra, 1489.
[Ger. *schweer.*]

swǣs, adj., *dear, beloved; own; sweet*:
asm. swǣsne, 617, 1148; asn. 1480;
apm. swǣse, 1348.

‡ swǣslīc, adj., *kindly*: asn. 1510.

swǣslīce, adv., *graciously, lovingly*:
adv. 1338.

swāt, n., *blood*: ds. swāte, 1176; as.
1111, 1448; dis. swāte, 1087. [Ger.
Schweiss; MnE. *sweat.*]

swātig, adj., *bloody*: apf. swātge, 1458.

swā-ðeah, adv. and conj., *however,*
nevertheless, yet: swā-þēah, 523, 1185,
1308; sē-þēah, 211.

sweart, adj., *black, dark, darkened,*
gloomy; dim, dusky; sinister, ma-
lignant: nsm. wk. swearta, 269, 966,
994; nsf. 934; dsf. sweartre, 872;
asm. sweartne, 1411, 1532; npm.
swearte, 1104; gpm. sweartra, 897;
ipf. sweartum, 1606. [Ger. *schwarz*;
MnE. *swart.*] *See* fȳrsweart.

swēg, m., *sound*: ns. 491. [swōgan.]

‡ swēgdynn, m., *crash, crack, violent noise*: gp. swēgdynna, 954.

swegl, n., *heaven, sky*: gs. swegles, 110, 203, 281, 543, 606; ds. swegle, 502, 550, 689, 1659; as. 513.

swegle, adv., *brilliantly, brightly; celestially*: 393, 1102.

swegldrēam, m., *joy of heaven*: ap. swegldrēamas, 1348.

swelan, 4. intrans., *burn, be consumed*: 3 pl. swelaðð, 986.

swelgan, 3. trans., *swallow, take in; engulf, swallow up*: 3 pl. swelgaðð, 1593, 1603; pret. 3 sg. swealg, 560. [Ger. *schwelgen*.] See **forswelgan**.

sweltan, 3. intrans., *die*: 3 sg. swelteðð, 987; inf. 191.

swęncan, see **geswęncan**.

sweopu, f., *whip, scourge*: ip. sweopum, 1441.

sweord, n., *sword*: as. 679.

sweotule, adv., *plainly, clearly*: 243, 512.

sweotulian, see **gesweotulian**.

swęðian, see **biswęðian**.

swēte, adj., *sweet, pleasant*: nsm. 907. See **unswēte**.

swīcian, W2. intrans., *wander, go astray*: 3 pl. swiciaðð, 1299.

swīge, f., *silence*: ns. 190. [Cf. Ger. *schweigen*.]

swīma, m., *giddiness, dizziness*: ds. swiman, 1299.

swingan, 3. trans., *scourge, beat*: ger. swingenne, 1622. [MnE. *swing, swinge*.]

swinsian, W2. intrans., *make melody*: 3 pl. swinsiaþ, 884.

swīðð, adj., *strong; comp. right (hand)*: nsm. 716; comp. dsf. swī[þ]ran, 1530; asf. swiþran, 531, 1221. [Ger. *geschwind*.]　.

swīðan, see **geswīðan**.

swīðe, adv., *deeply; very, exceedingly*, (tō þæs swīðe, *so*): 220, 310, 1078; supl. swiþast, 1492.

swīðlic, adj., *tremendous, violent*: nsn. 954.

swōgan, R. intrans., *roar, howl*: 3 pl. swōgaðð, 949.

swylc, pron., *such; such a thing, the like*: nsf. 290; asf. swylce, 80; asn. 78.

swylce, adv., *also, too, moreover*: 60, 145, 282, 688, 1437.

swylce, conj., *as if*: 1140.

swylt, m., *death, perdition*: as. 1539. [sweltan.]

sȳfre, see **unsȳfre**.

sygor, see **sigor**.

sylf, pron., *self, thyself, himself, itself; same; one's own* (with gen. usually *own* in a different construction): nsm. 62, 114, 319, 356, 543, 1140, 1376, 1418, 1516; nsm. wk. sylfa, 12, 135, 143, 149, 180, 236, 435, 524, 695, 947, 1208, 1494; nsf. sylfa, 59; gsm. sylfes, 9, 254, 581, 1483; gsf. sylfre, 339; dsm. sylfum, 108, 213, 1222, 1479; dsm. wk. sylfan, 1153; asm. sylfne, 129, 843, 1307, 1320; asf. wk. sylfan, 1148; npn. sylfe, 1081, 1115; gpm. sylfra, 362, 1241; dpm. selfum, 1264. See **ðæt sylfe**.

syllan, W1. trans., *give; grant*: 3 sg. syleðð, 1589; sęleðð, 689; opt. 2 sg. sylle, 375; pret. 1 sg. sealde, 1380, 1398; 2 sg. sealdes, 290; 3 sg. sealde, 660, 860. See **gesyllan**.

symbel, n., *rejoicing, revel, jubilee*: gp. symbla, 550.

symle, adv., *ever, always; for ever, eternally; continually*: 88, 103, 108, 128, 376, 432, 477, 767, 777, 1640; simle, 53, 323, 393, 404, 602.

syn, f., *sin, crime; guilt*: ds. synne, 1537; as. synne, 1482, 1542, 1555, 1567; is. synne, 994; gp. synna, 180, 1249, 1313, 1489, 1606, 1622, 1640; dp. synnum, 125, 290, 1060; ap. synne, 1264, 1307; ip. synnum 117, 736. [Ger. *Sünde*.]

Sȳn, pr. ıı., *Sion*: gs. Sȳne, 875, 899.
[Lat. *Sion.*]

‡ synbyrðen, f., *burden of sin*: as.
synbyrðenne, 1299.

‡ synfāh, adj., *guilty, sinful, wicked*:
npm. synfā, 1082.

synfull, adj., *sinful, wicked*: gpm.
synfulra, 1228, 1518, 1532.

synlīce, adv., *sinfully, wickedly*: 1479.

‡ synlust, m., *sinful desire* (?); *love of
sin* (?): as. 269.

synnig, adj., *guilty, sinful, wicked*:
npn. wk. syngan, 1281; dpm. syngum, 919, 1376; ipf. syngum, 1132.
See firensynnig.

‡ synrūst, m., *rust* or *stain of sin*: as.
1320.

synsceaða, m., *malefactor, evil-doer*:
np. synsceaðan, 706.

synwracu, f., *punishment* (*of sin*): ns.
1539; as. synwræce, 794.

‡ synwund, f., *wound of sin*: ap.
synwunde, 757.

synwyrcend, m., *worker of iniquity;
evil-doer*: npm. 1104; gpm. synwyrcendra, 841.

T.

tācen, n., *sign, token; trace; miracle;
mystery*: ns. tācn, 54; np. 1235;
gp. tācna, 462; ap. 642, 1214. *See*
fācen-, foretācen.

talgan, W2. intrans., *think, believe*: 1
sg. talge, 794.

tēag, f., *bond, chain, fetter*: ip.
tēagum, 733.

teala, adv., *well*: 792.

‡ tealtrian, W2. intrans., *stagger,
stumble*: 1 pl. tealtrigað, 371.

tēar, m., *tear; drop*: ap. tēaras, 172;
tēar[*as*], 1566; ip. tēarum, 1174. *See*
brynetēar.

teldan, *see* biteldan.

tempel, n., *temple*: ns 206; gs. temples,
495, 1138; ds. temple, 186; as. 707.

tēon, *see* ā-, for-, oftēon.

tēona, m., *calamity, affliction*: dp.
tēonum, 1090, 1214.

tēonlēg, m., *destroying flame*: ns. 968.

tīd, f., *time, tide, season; opportunity*:
ns. 1566, 1571 (n.?); ds. tīde, 82;
as. 406, 455, 549, 632, 739, 841, 849,
971, 1080, 1148, 1333, 1558, 1570,
1585, 1588; gp. tīda, 107, 235.

tilgan, W2. trans. (w. gen.), *strive, endeavor; seek after*: inf. 748; tiligan,
1318.

tīr, m.,*glory, honor; splendor*: gs. tīres,
270, 462, 1211; is. tīre, 29.

‡ tīrfruma, m., *King of glory*: as.
tīrfruma[n], 206.

tīrmeahtig, adj.,*almighty*: nsm. 1165.

tō, adv., *too; at*: 181, 373, 495, 1263,
1268, 1304, 1400, 1567.

tō, prep., *to, towards, unto, into, upon;
in, on; for; from, of; for, as*; (tō
ðæs, *so*): w. gen. 220; w. dat. 3, 8,
28, 30, 36, 57, 65, 67, 87, 101, 124,
148, 223, 230, 255, 268, 277, 293,
299, 414, 427, 456, 461, 475, 479,
485, 519, 533, 552, 577, 610, 613,
619, 620,. 624, 632, 648, 650, 690,
722, 737, 749, 758, 773, 857, 859,
864, 887, 921, 926, 1026, 1041, 1065,
1078, 1083, 1090, 1091, 1105, 1106,
1136, 1139, 1153, 1173, 1176, 1214,
1244, 1249, 1269, 1273, 1292, 1293,
1337, 1343, 1352, 1357, 1362, 1365,
1376, 1377, 1398, 1404, 1421, 1449,
1471, 1479, 1481, 1513, 1514, 1518,
1535, 1543, 1589, 1596, 1601, 1618,
1622, 1645; w. acc. 32, 623, 1196 (2);
[*tō*], 866; w. inf. 1555; w. ger. 597,
914, 919, 1288, 1390, 1621 (2), 1622.

tōbrecan, 4. trans., *break in pieces,
shatter*: pp. npm. tōbrocene, 977.

tōēacan, adv., *also, moreover*: 1242.

tōgædre, adv., *together*: 970. [Paral-
lel with ætgædre.]

tōgēanes, prep., *towards, to meet*: w.
dat. 546, 548, 575.

tōglīdan, 1. intrans.,*vanish, disappear*:
pp. npf. tōglidene, 1163.

tōlӯsan, W1. trans., *loose, undo, dissolve*: 3 sg. tōlēseð, 1042.

‡ tōm, adj., *free from, without*: npm. tōme, 1211.

torht, adj., *bright, resplendent, radiant; glorious*: nsm. 107, 235; gsm. torhtes, 206; dsf. wk. torhtan, 542; dsn. wk. torhtan, 186; asm. torhtne, 968, 1150; npm. torhte, 883; npn. torhte, 933; apn. wk. torhtan, 642.

torn, m., *sorrow, grief*: is. torne, 538.

‡ tornword, n., *insulting word, word of reproach*: gp. tornworda, 172.

tōsǫmne, adv., *together, at once*: 882, 965, 1437. [Ger. *zusammen;* parallel with ætsǫmne.]

tōstęncan, W1. trans., *scatter, disperse*: pp. tōstęnced, 256.

tōweard, adj., *future, to come*: asm. 137; asn. 82.

tōwiðere, prep. w. dat., *to, against*: 185.

tōwrecan, 5. trans., *scatter, disperse*: pp. asf. tōwrecene, 258.

‡ trede, adj., *passable*: asm. tredne, 1165. [tredan, 'tread.']

tremman, *see* getremman; trymian.

trēow, f., *faith; agreement*: 82, 584.

trēowlufu, f., *constant love*: 538.

trum, adj., *constant, steadfast*: npm. trume, 883; npn. trume, 933.

trūwian, W2. intrans., *have confidence in, rely on*: 3 pl. trūwiað, 837.

trymian, W1. trans., *sustain, cheer*: pret. 2 pl. trymedon, 1359. *See* getremman.

trӯwe, *see* getrӯwe.

tū, *see* twēgen.

tuddor, n., *offspring, progeny*: ns. 1416; as. 688. *See* magutūdor.

tungol, nm., *star*: ns. 699; np. 933; gp. tungla, 607, 671; 883; dp. tunglum, 235, 968; ap. tunglas, 107. *See* heofontungol.

‡ tungolgimm, m. *(starry gem), star*: ip. tungolgimmum, 1150.

twā, *see* twēgen.

twǣfan, *see* getwǣfan.

twēgen, num., *two*: dn. twām, 1138; am. 506; an. tū, 1140. *See* bēgen.

twēo, *see* untwēo.

twēon, *see* bitwēon.

tӯdre, adj., *weak, feeble*: asn. wk. 29; isn. wk. tӯdran, 371.

tyht, m., *motion*: ds. tyhte, 811.

tyllan, *see* fortyllan.

tӯn, num. adj., *ten*: 542.

tӯnan, *see* ontӯnan.

D.

ðā, adv., *then*: 491, 527, 659, 1174, 1392, 1403, 1414, 1446, 1447, 1451; þā, 195, 233, 307, 326, 468, 533, 550, 703, 738, 742, 771, 858, 1133, 1178 (pron.?), 1389, 1408, 1418, 1422, 1443, 1485, 1497.

ðā, conj., *when*: 456, 614, 1170; þā, 31, 34, 46, 233, 355, 443, 448, 628, 720, 724, 727, 729, 731, 737, 866, 1114, 1131, 1151, 1161, 1185, 1349, 1386, 1399, 1492, 1493.

ðæc, n., *roof*: þæce, 1503.

ðā-gēn, adv., *yet, still*: þā-gēn, 496, 542.

ðā-gīet, adv., *as yet*: þā-gīet, 351.

ðǣr, adv., *there, in that place; then*: 838, 997, 1311, 1609, 1628, 1649, 1652; þǣr, 43, 327, 447, 454, 462, 537, 540, 568, 706, 721, 801, 840, 889, 894, 920, 943, 956, 958, 960, 988, 1049, 1053, 1081, 1083, 1095, 1171, 1214, 1225, 1234, 1237, 1266, 1273, 1298, 1336, 1366, 1370, 1459, 1515, 1538, 1544, 1572, 1575, 1576, 1620, 1640, 1650, 1660, 1662.

ðǣr, conj., *where; whither; whence; if; when*: þǣr, 307, 346, 436, 438, 495, 734, 750, 753, 795, 1089, 1106, 1112, 1229, 1312, 1409, 1494, 1553; þǣ[r], 304.

ðæs, adv., *so*: þæs, 241 (2), 1472. *See* swīðe; tō.

ðæs, conj., *for this (reason), therefore; for which (reason), wherefore; for*

that, because; (þæs **ymb,** *after,*
466): þæs, 127, 466, 472, 598, 600 (?),
793, 829, 1093, 1360, 1513. [Some
of the foregoing are indistinguisha-
ble from the gen. of the dem. pron.]

ðæs ꝥe, conj., *for that, in that, because,*
for; so far as; as (794): þæs þe, 73,
129, 501, 794, 828, 1235, 1294, 1476.
See **ꝥe.**

ðæt, conj., *that; for that, because; in*
order that; so that; when (783):

in subject clauses: þæt, 4, 38, 186,
193, 201, 226, 246, 432, 447, 548, 552,
843, 858, 960, 1083, 1238, 1243, 1268,
1273, 1285, 1301, 1414, 1599;

in object clauses: 1195; þæt, 12,
24, 34, 80, 97, 100, 113, 198, 203,
210, 236, 263, 280, 284, 289, 297,
300, 304, 311, 318, 338, 343 (?),
345 (?), 360, 374, 392, 454, 692, 752,
754, 775, 816, 818, 822, 848, 861,
922, 1116, 1160, 1188, 1190, 1202,
1245, 1257, 1290, 1304, 1382, 1499,
1503, 1550, 1557, 1616 (?);

in final clauses: þæt, 7, 115, 160,
264, 367, 375, 442, 749, 1210, 1323,
1333, 1426, 1430, 1449, 1460, 1463,
1467, 1495, 1496, 1511, 1572, 1585;

in consecutive clauses: þæt, 270,
324, 384 (?), 479, 589, 1137, 1388,
1531;

in modal clause: 1472;

in temporal clause: þæt (þær ?),
783.

ðæt āna, adv., *alone:* þæt āna, 287.

ðæt sylfe, conj., *also, likewise:* 937.

ðætte, pron., *which:* þætte, 1588.

ðætte, conj., *that:* þætte, 143, 417, 451,
600, 656, 715, 1155.

ðe, pron., *who, which, that:* 353,
526, 580; þe, 2, 23, 25, 30, 33, 36, 45,
48, 89, 115, 121, 221, 224, 232, 239,
242, 251, 292, 335, 413, 431, 505,
521, 559, 570, 602, 613, 615, 640, 643,
655, 799, 837, 854, 871, 893, 916, 921,
937, 1033, 1057, 1067, 1075, 1076,
1079, 1091, 1097 (?), 1154, 1157, 1158,

1180, 1199, 1201, 1205, 1260, 1322,
1355, 1363, 1454, 1475, 1478, 1484,
1490, 1491, 1501, 1573, 1578, 1590,
1615, 1637, 1639; [þ]e, 277. *See se*
ðe.

ðe, conj., *or ; that, since; because:* þe,
466, 792, 1097 (?), 1256, 1306, 1332.
1553. *See* **forðon, ðæs ðe.**

ðēah, adv., *see* **swā-ðēah.**

ðēah, conj., *although; however, never-*
theless, yet: þēah, 368, 1090, 1130,
1183, 1419, 1506. *See* **swā-ðēah.**

ðearf, f., *need; necessity, distress; good,*
profit: ns. þearf, 11, 255, 373, 751,
847; gs. þearfe, 707, 1057; ds. þearfe,
22, 1172; as. þearfe, 816; dp. þearfum, 112. *See* **nearo-, oferðearf.**

ðearfa, m., *poor man, needy (person):*
gs. þearfan, 1422; dp. þearfum, 1503.

ðearfende, adj., *needy:* dpm. þearfendum, 1284. [Cf. Ger. *darben.*] *See*
woruldðearfende.

ðeaw, m., *conduct, behavior* (in pl.):
gp. þēawa, 1583.

ðeccan, *see* **biðeccan.**

ðecgan, *see* **geðecgan.**

ðegn, m., *follower, servant; disciple:*
np. þegnas, 283, 470, 497, 541, 553;
gp. þegna, 457, 710, 943. [Arch.
Ger. *Degen.*]

ðegnung, f., *service:* ap. ðegnunga, 354.

‡ **ðegnweorud,** n., *ministering band,*
host of retainers: ns. 751.

ðencan, *see* **ā-, bi-, geðencan.**

ðenden, conj., *while, as long as:* þenden,
597, 772, 814, 817, 1574, 1579, 1583;
þendan, 590, 800, 1325.

ðēod, f., *people ; men, mankind:* ns.
þēod, 1133; ds. þēode, 127, 377 ; gp.
þēoda, 224, 847, 1023; dp. þēodum,
1091. [Cf. Ger. *Deutsch.*] *See*
werðēod.

ðēodbealu, n., *great evil:* ns. þēodbealu,
1267.

‡ **ðēodbüende,** mpl., *men, people, man-*
kind, human race: gp. þēodbüendra,
1172; dp. þēodbüendum, 616, 1371

‡ ꝺēodĕgsa, m., *widespread terror*: ns.
þēodĕgsa, 833.

ꝺēoden, m., *lord, ruler, prince, king;*
always of *Christ* or *God*: ns. þēoden,
332, 457, 791, 943, 1096; gs. þēodnes,
354, 541, 553, 1235; ds. þēodne, 612.
[ꝺēod.]

ꝺēodenstōl, m., *throne*: as. þēodenstōl,
397.

ꝺēodland, n., *region, territory*: as.
þēodland, 306.

ꝺēodsceaꝺa, m., *arch-malefactor; robber*: np. þēodsceaþan, 1609; ap.
þēodsceaþan, 1595.

‡ ꝺēodwundor, n., *miracle, marvel*:
as. þēodwundor, 1154.

ꝺēof, m., *thief*: ns. þēof, 871; np.
þēofas, 1609.

ꝺēon, *see* geꝺēon.

ꝺēostor, n., *darkness, gloom*: ds. þēostre,
1422, 1545; dp. þēostrum, 116, 1656.
See ꝺȳstro.

ꝺēostre, adj., *dark, gloomy*: asf. wk.
ꝺēostran, 1409. [Ger. *düster*.]

ꝺēow, *see* nȳd-, wīteꝺēow.

ꝺēs, pron., *this*: nsf. þēos, 89, 842,
1488, 1583; gsn. þisses, 238; dsm.
þissum, 1529; dsf. þisse, 344; asm.
ꝺisne, 249, 570, 574; asf. þās, 59, 239,
329, 356, 515, 519, 659, 849, 855, 1409,
1558, 1585; asn. þis, 32, 627, 1115;
np. þās, 318, 826, 1599; apn. þās, 22.

ꝺicce, adv., *abundantly*: þicce, 1175.

ꝺīn, pron., *thy, thine*: nsm. þīn, 254 (?),
367, 405, 1492; nsn. þīn, 112, 257 (?);
gsmn. þīnes, 160, 409, 1393; gsf.
þīnre, 339; dsm. þīnum, 1395, 1496,
1498; dsf. þīnre, 1473; asm. ꝺīnne,
250; þīnne, 217, 237, 289, 349, 377;
asf. þīne, 244; asn. þīn, 9, 242, 246,
257, 266, 1460, 1476; gpmf. þīnra,
255, 361, 1487, 1489; dpf. þīnum,
162.

ꝺincan, *see* ꝺyncan.

ꝺing, n., *thing; doom, judgment;*
(ǣlces þinges, *entirely*): gs. þinges,
333; ds. þinge, 926; gp. þinga, 224;

ap. þing, 376 (?); þing, 25. *See*
ǣnge þinga.

ꝺingian, *see* geꝺingian.

ꝺingstĕde, m., *meeting-place*: ds. þing-
stĕde, 497.

ꝺōht, *see* geꝺōht.

ꝺolian, W2. trans., *bear, endure, suffer,
undergo*: pret. 1 sg. þolade, 1451;
pret. 2 sg. þolades, 1409; inf. þolian,
1385. *See* ā-, geꝺolian.

ꝺọnan, adv., *thence*: þọnan, 625, 759,
999, 1595.

ꝺọnan, conj., *whence*: þọnan, 269, 535.

ꝺọnc, m., *thanks, gratitude*: as. þonc,
127, 209, 599, 601, 612, 1091, 1212,
1385, 1473, 1497.

ꝺọnc, *see* ge-, hyge-, ingeꝺọnc.

ꝺọncian, W2. intrans., *give thanks*: 3
pl. þọnciaꝺ, 1255.

ꝺọncol, *see* fore-, searoꝺọncol.

ꝺonne, adv., *then, at that time, next*: 827,
867, 953, 1007, 1039, 1076, 1247, 1255,
1262, 1284, 1439, 1515, 1559, 1565,
1623; þonne, 13, 191, 254, 322, 525,
797, 807, 839, 878, 899, 934, 960,
981, 985, 1027, 1029, 1115, 1221,
1272, 1301, 1353, 1362, 1365, 1372,
1524, 1527, 1591, 1606, 1612, 1634.

ꝺonne, conj., *when; than*: 791, 964,
1017, 1061, 1069, 1101, 1232, 1351,
1359, 1568; þonne, 155, 422, 674,
763, 824, 832, 842, 844, 902, 903,
924, 945, 989, 1022, 1058, 1166, 1216,
1253, 1288, 1307, 1334, 1395, 1488,
1491, 1566, 1600, 1602.

ꝺorn, m., *thorn*: dp. þornum, 1445.

ꝺracu, f., *rush, burst*: as. þræce, 593.
See holmꝺracu.

ꝺrēa, f. (?), *misery, suffering; throe,
pang; punishment; threat, menace;
cruelty* (?), *violence* (?) (1445): ns.
þrēa, 1063; ds. þrēa, 1091; as. þrēa,
946, 1364; ip. þrēam, 1133, 1445.

ꝺrēan, W3. trans., *afflict, vex, harass;
chasten, discipline*: 3 sg. þrēaꝺ, 1023,
1595; inf. þrēan, 1320. *See* ge-
ꝺrēan.

ðrēat,n., *band, company, host, multitude*:
ns. þrēat, 492, 738; ds. þrēate, 517;
as. þrēat, 570; np. þrēat, 927. *See*
sigeðrēat.

ðrēo, num., *three*: þrēo, 964, 969, 1235,
1267.

ðrēotan, *see* unāðrēotende.

ðridda, num. adj., *third*: nsm. þridda,
726; nsn. þridde, 1247, 1284. [Ger.
dritte.]

ðringan, 3. intrans., *press, throng*: 3
pl. þringað, 397. [Ger. *dringen.*]

ðrīst, adj., *confident, assured, undoubt-
ing; shameless, impudent*: ipn.
þrīstum, 342. [Ger. *dreist.*]

ðrīste, adv., *insolently*: þrīste, 1509.

ðrīsthycgende, ptc., *courageous*: nsf.
þrīsthycgende, 288.

ðrīstlīce, adv., *boldly, daringly*: 871.

ðroht, adj., *grievous, dire*: nsn. þroht,
1267.

ðrosm, m., *fume, reek*: is. þrosme, 116.

ðrōwian, W2. trans. and intrans., *suffer; bear, endure*: 3 pl. þrōwiað,
1539, 1614; pret. 3 sg. þrōwade,
1117, 1154, 1433; inf. þrōwian, 1249,
1632.

ðrōwing, f., *suffering, passion*: ap.
þrōwinga, 470, 1129, 1179.

ðryccan, *see* biðryccan.

ðrym, m., *glory, majesty; power, might;
host, company, multitude*: ns. þrym,
599, 726, 1063, 1654; þrim, 423;
gs. þrymmes, 593; as. þrym, 71, 83,
204, 653, 657, 740, 1023, 1633; gp.
þrymma, 726, 833; dp. þrymmum,
217; ip. þrymmum, 388. *See* gōd-,
mægenðrym.

ðrymfæst, adj., *glorious*: nsm. þrymfæst, 457, 943.

ðrymfull, adj., *glorious*: npm. þrymfulle, 541.

ðrymlīce, adv., *magnanimously, nobly*:
þrymlīce, 288.

ðrȳnes, f., *Trinity*: ns. þrȳnes, 379;
gs. þrȳnysse, 599.

ðrysman, *see* āðrysman.

ðrȳst, *see* ðrīst.

ðrȳðum, adv. (ip. of ðrȳð, *strength*),
fiercely, furiously: þrȳþum, 969.

‡ ðrȳðgesteald, n., *glorious abode,
palace*: as. þrȳðgesteald, 354.

ðū, pron., *thou*: ns. 2, 80, 115, 176, 258,
338, 440, 1388, 1495, 1497; þū, 4,
18 (2), 58, 75, 83, 107, 109, 113, 130,
149, 155, 156, 161, 162, 166, 179, 180,
208, 211, 214 (2), 216, 236, 239, 249,
263, 272, 275, 280, 284, 287, 289, 297,
328, 348, 349, 355, 360, 374, 403, 404,
407, 408, 412, 442, 621, 1382, 1384,
1385 (2), 1392, 1397, 1401, 1403,
1409, 1426, 1431, 1449, 1460, 1463,
1467, 1469, 1472 (2), 1478, 1480,
1484, 1487, 1494, 1496; gs. þīn, 254;
ds. ðē, 1381, 1398, 1399, 1441; þē, 3,
52, 56, 63, 65, 68, 74, 82, 108, 114 (?),
153, 155, 169, 177, 261, 296, 301,
317, 335, 358, 366, 410, 414, 1380,
1381, 1382, 1383, 1387, 1400, 1425,
1430, 1462, 1470, 1475, 1476, 1480;
as. þec, 61, 112, 160, 278, 330, 368,
621, 1379, 1493; ð[*ec*], 381; ðē, 332,
1386; þē, 59 (?), 222, 299, 328, 1389;
dd. inc, 357; np. gē, 89, 476, 510,
512, 521, 570, 573, 575, 1347,
1349 (2), 1353, 1357, 1358, 1359,
1360, 1499, 1502, 1509, 1510, 1512,
1513, 1523; dp. ēow, 478, 479, 488,
489, 577, 1345, 1352, 1499, 1501; ap.
ēowic, 477.

ðurfan, PP., *need, have reason (to)*:
pres. 3 sg. þearf, 779; pres. 1 pl.
þurfon, 81; pres. 3 pl. þurfon, 1365.

ðurh, prep. w. acc., *through; throughout, on, in; during, for; with, by,
in, according to; on account of, in
consequence of, because of; by (means
of), through (the agency of); for the
sake of; in the name of, by* (in oaths):
þurh, 9, 38, 44, 49, 76, 92, 113, 120,
189, 197, 199, 218, 250, 254, 269,
298, 315, 321, 328, 359, 362, 369,
420, 423, 425, 442, 444, 450, 470,
480, 488, 495, 530, 581, 587, 603,

620, 649, 665, 685, 700, 710, 719,
778, 823, 904, 940, 946, 1002, 1023,
1040, 1100, 1177, 1192, 1198, 1210,
1254, 1261, 1280, 1296, 1305, 1318,
1351, 1364, 1430, 1442, 1449, 1456,
1477, 1482, 1505, 1506, 1558, 1624.

ðurhdrīfan, 1. trans., *pierce* : pret. 3
pl. þurhdrifan, 1109.

ðurhsēon, 5. trans., *look through, penetrate* : inf. þurhsēon, 1327.

ðurhwadan, 6. trans., *pass through ;
permeate* : opt. pret. 3 sg. þurhwōde,
1141; pp. þurhwaden, 1282.

‡ **ðurhwlītan**, 1. trans., *look through,
penetrate* : inf. þurhwlītan, 1283,
1331.

ðurst, m., *thirst* : ns. þurst, 1660; is.
þurste, 1509.

ðus, adv., *thus ; so* : 1686; þus, 156,
196, 744.

ðwēan, 6. trans., *wash away* : inf.
þwēan, 1320.

ðȳ-lǣs, conj., *lest* : þȳ-lǣs, 684, 768;
þī-lǣs, 762.

ðyncan, W1. intrans., *seem, appear* : 3
sg. þynceð, 1488 ; þinceð, 1598 ; pret.
3 sg. ðūhte, 1401, 1424.

ðyrnen, adj., *of thorns* : asm. þyrnenne,
1126.

ðyslīc, adj., *such a* : is. þyslīce, 517.

ðȳstro, fm., *darkness, gloom* : ds.
þȳstre, 871; as. þȳstro, 227; gp.
ðȳstra, 593, 1385 ; þȳstra, 1247. *See*
ðēostor.

U.

ufan, adv., *from the top* : 1137.

ufancund, adj., *heavenly, celestial, from
above* : npm. ufancunde, 503.

‡ **unāðrēotende**, ptc., *untiring, unwearied* : ipm. unāðrēotendum, 388.

‡ **unbēted**, ptc., *unatoned* : asn. 1311.

unbrǣce, adj., *unbreakable, infrangible,
adamantine* : asm. unbrǣcne, 6.

unclǣne, adj., *unclean, impure* : nsf.
1016; asn. 1309; apm. 1315.

uncūð, adj., *forbidding, inhospitable* :
asm. uncūðne, 1417.

uncyst, f., *vice, sin, wickedness* : ap.
uncyste, 1329.

under, adv., *under* : 1332.

under, prep., *under, beneath ; in subjec-
tion to ; in ; among* : w. dat. 14, 45,
219, 226, 286, 484, 502, 526, 588, 606,
705, 882, 1175, 1503; with acc. 769,
1533, 1619, 1620.

undyrne, adj., *manifest, clear* : nsf.
1540.

‡ **unefen**, adj., *unequal* : nsf. 1459.

‡ **ungearo**, adj., *unprepared, not expecting* : apm. ungearwe, 874.

ungelīce, adv., *differently, in a different
way, diversely* : 898, 909, 1262, 1362.

ungesǣlig, adj., *unhappy, wretched* :
npm. ungesǣlge, 1215.

unhnēaw, adj., *abundant, bounteous,
unstinted* : ipf. unhnēawum, 686.

‡ **unholda**, m., *devil, fiend* : np. unholdan, 762. [Ger. *Unhold*.]

‡ **unmǣle**, adj., *spotless, immaculate,
undefiled* · asf. 333, 721.

unmǣte, adj., *prodigious, stupendous* :
nsn. 953.

unmurnlīce, adv., *pitilessly, relentless-
ly* : 812.

uurīm, n., *countless number, great multitude* : as. 569.

unrōt, adj., *sad, sorrowful, joyless* :
nsm. 1407 ; nsn. 1182.

unryht, n., *wickedness ; unrighteous
deed, transgression* : gs. unryhtes,
1302 ; as. 1290.

unryhte, adv., *unjustly, wrongfully* :
560.

unsǣlig, adj., *unhappy, wretched* : npm.
unsǣlge, 1287.

‡ **unscomiende**, ptc., *unashamed* : nsm.
1324.

unsōfte, adv., *grievously* : 1356.

‡ **unswēte**, adj., *harsh, acrid* : asm. unswētne, 1438.

unsȳfre, adj., *unclean, impure* : ns.
1231.

‡ **unsȳfre,** adv., *filthily* : 1483.

‡ **untwēo,** adj., *certain, undoubted* : un-t[w]ēo, 960.

unwęmme, adj., *unspotted, undefiled* : asf. 300; asn. 418.

unwillum, adv., *unwillingly, reluctantly* : 1490.

‡ **unwyrðe,** adj., *unworthy, undeserving* : nsm. 1562.

ūp, adv., *up ; above, on high, overhead ; inland* (1146): 353, 464, 514, 536, 544, 630, 646, 754, 875, 959, 1146, 1156; upp, 528, 651, 693, 888.

ūpcund, adj., *heavenly, celestial* : dsn. wk. ūpcundan, 268.

ūpheofon, m., *heaven above, highest heaven* : as. 967.

ūplīc, adj., *heavenly, celestial* : dsm. wk. ūplīcan, 102.

upp, *see* **ūp.**

uppe, adv., *above, on high* : 387,661,1467.

ūprodor, m., *heaven above, high heaven* : as. 1128.

‡ **ūpstige,** m., *ascension* : gs. ūpstiges, 655; ds. 615, 711.

ūre, ūs, *see* **ic.**

ūser, pron., *our* : gsm. ūsses, 1084; dsm. ūssum, 28, 398, 612 ; ism. ūsse, 755; gpf. uss[a], 261 ; dpf. ūssum, 1313; apm. usse, 1328 ; apf. ūsse; 370.

ūsic, *see* **ic.**

ūt, adv., *out, forth* : 329, 1113, 1442.

utan, interj., *let us* : 771, 773, 864.

ūtan, adv., *without* : 1004.

W.

wāc, adj., *inconstant, changeful, fluctuating* : asf. wk. wācan, 855.

wāce, adv., *feebly, negligently* : 799, 837.

wæcnan, *see* **āwæcnan.**

wēd, f., *garment* : ip. wǣdum, 1422.

wadan, *see* **ðurhwadan.**

wǣdla, m., *poor man* : ns. 1495.

wāflan, W2. intrans., *wonder at* : 2 pl. wāfiað, 89.

wǣg, m., *wave* : ds. wǣge, 980.

‡ **wǣgdēor,** n., *sea-monster, sea-animal* : gp. wǣgdēora, 987.

wāldan, R. trans. (w. dat.), *rule* : ptc. nsm. wāldende, 1010, 1161 ; wāldend, 556; inf. wealdan, 1388.

wāldend, m., *ruler, sovereign, king, Lord (Christ, God)* : ns. 46, 258, 474, 544, 681, 714, 822, 865, 1185, 1220, 1569, 1601, 1613; gs. wāldendes, 635, 915, 1243; ds. wāldende, 1048, 1069, 1213, 1472 ; as. 163, 328, 394, 555, 577 ; is. wāldende, 240.

wǣlın, m. f., *tossing, surging* : ns. 965; is. wǣlme, 1006; dp. wǣlmum, 831. [weallan.]

‡ **wǣlmfȳr,** n., *raging fire* : gp. wǣlmfȳra, 931.

wanian, *see* **wǫnian.**

wānian, W2. intrans., *moan, lament* : ptc. npm. wānende, 992. [Ger. *weinen.*]

wǣpen, n., *weapon* : as. 680; gp. wǣpna, 565; dp. wǣpnum, 775.

wær, adj., *prudent, heedful* : nsm. [w]ær, 1582.

wǣr, f., *covenant, compact* : ns. 583.

waran, *see* **hęllwaran.**

wǣrfæst, adj., *faithful ; covenant-keeping* : nsm. 384.

wærgðu, f., *curse ; damnation* : ns. wærgðo, 98; gs. 57; as. wærgðu, 1271.

wǣrlēas, adj., *false, faithless* : gp. wǣrlēasra, 1613.

‡ **wærlīce,** adv., *warily, cautiously* : 767.

wǣrloga, m., *treacherous, faithless (one), covenant-breaker, transgressor* : ns. 1561. [lēogan, 'lie.']

waru, *see* **burg-, eorð-, hęllwaru.**

wǣta, m., *water (to drink)* : gs. wǣtan, 1507.

wæter, n., *water* : ns. 988, 1112 ; ds. wætre, 981 ; as. 851; np. 984.

wē, *see* **ic.**

wēa, m., *grief, misery, woe ; trouble, misfortune* : ns. 1492; gs. wēan, 1384 ; gp. wēana, 1263.

wealdan, *see* **wāldan.**

weall, m., *wall*: ds. wealle, 11; as. 11;
ap. weallas, 5. *See* burgweall.

weallan, R. intrans., *be stirred, be
moved, be agitated; rage*: pret. 3 sg.
wēoll, 539; ptc. nsm. weallende,
984; asm. weallendne, 1250.
See āweallan.

‡ wealldor, n., *door in the wall*: ns.
328.

weallstān, m., *corner-stone*: ns. 2.

weard, m., *guardian, preserver, protector, defender, Lord*: ns. 134, 222, 243,
527, 945, 1516, 1527, 1647; as. 1550.

weard, f., *watch, guard*: as. wearde,
767.

weardian, W2. trans., *guard, defend;
have, possess, keep to, hold;* (lāst
weardian, *remain behind*): 3 pl.
weardiað, 1641; wear[dia]ð, 396;
opt. 1 pl. weardigen, 772; pret. 3 pl.
weardedu[n], 496.

wearning, f., *warning*: ds. wearninga,
921.

weax, n., *wax*: ns. 988.

weaxan, *see* āweaxan.

wębb, *see* godwębb.

węccan, W1. trans., *awake, arouse;
summon, call forth*: 3 pl. węccað,
609, 886, 951.

weder, n., *weather*: as. 605.

weg, m., *way, path, road*: ap. wegas,
681. *See* fold-, wīdweg.

wegan, 5. trans., *bear, bring:* 3 sg.
wigeð, 1577.

wel, n. *weal*: 1576.

wel, adj., *as one would wish*: 1079.

wel, adv., *well, rightly; excellently; sat-
isfactorily; very, much*: 3, 547, 551,
668, 917, 1079, 1235, 1260, 1500.

wela, m., *wealth, riches; weal, prosperity*: as. welan, 605, 1384, 1387. *See*
blǣd-, eorð-, līfwela.

welig, adj., *rich*: nsm. 1495.

węmman, *see* gewęmman.

węmme, *see* unwęmme.

wēn, f., *belief, opinion*: ds. wēne, 212.

wēnan, W1. trans. and intrans., *hope;*

*expect; believe, think; perceive, be
conscious* (1185): 3 sg. wēneð, 1199;
3 pl. wēnað, 1231; 1 sg. wēne, 789;
pret. 3 sg. wēnde, 310; pret. 3 pl.
wēndon, 1185; inf. 81, 1610. *See*
gewēnan.

węndan, W1. intrans., *wend one's way,
come*: pret. 3 sg. węnde, 650. *See*
gewęndan.

‡ weolme, f., *flower, pick, pearl, para-
gon*: gs. weolman, 445.

weorc, n., *work; action, deed*: ns.
weorces, 1587; ds. weorce, 3, 11; as.
9, 691; gp. weorca, 1037, 1079, 1303;
dp. weorcum, 67, 837, 1289; ip.
weorcum, 750, 784, 917, 1236. *See*
firen-, flānge-, fyrn-, hǫndge-,
mānweorc.

weorpan, *see* ā-, wiðweorpan.

weorod, *see* weorud.

weorð, n., *ransom*: as. 1477; is.
weorðe, 1097.

weorðan, 3. intrans., *be, become; be
turned; happen, occur, come to pass*:
3 sg. weorþeð, 55, 877, 896, 923, 934,
947, 955, 1022, 1028, 1090, 1607,
1639; 3 pl. weor[þ]að, 1045, 1226,
1592; pret. 1 sg. wearð, 1420; 2 sg.
wurdeð, 1403, 1408, 1472; 3 sg.
wearð, 38, 43, 84, 200, 444, 491,
742, 1132, 1162, 1174, 1176; opt. 3
sg. weorðe, 28, 1582; 3 pl. weorðen,
232; pret. 2 sg. wurde, 1450, 1494,
1495; pret. 3 sg. wurde, 658, 839;
inf. 1197, 1617; weorþan, 1431. *See*
geweorðan.

weorðian, W2. trans., *honor; adore,
worship; enrich, endow*: 3 sg.
weorðaþ, 687; weorþað, 691; opt. 3
sg. weorþige, 433; opt. 3 pl. weorðien, 160; inf. 394. *See* geweorðian.

weorðlīc, adj., *exalted, admirable*:
nsn. weorðlīcu, 83.

weorðmynd, mfn., *honor, glory*: gp.
weorðmynda, 378.

‡ weorðung, f., *adornment*: ds. weorð-
unga, 1136.

weorud, n., *host, band, company, throng, multitude, people*: ns. 493, 554, 1136, 1248, 1653; ds. weorude, 911; as. 458, 1161, 1228, 1613; np. weorud, 1311; gp. weoruda, 1334, 1569, 1664; weorud[a], 1648; weoroda, 161, 229, 347, 407, 428, 631, 1069; dp. weorodum, 120; weoredum, 482; weredum, 1010. *See* ðegn-, wuldorweorud.

wēpan, R. intrans., *weep*: 3 pl. wēpað, 992; ptc. wēpende, 1289.

wer, m., *man*: gs. weres, 37, 419; gp. wera, 416, 509, 634, 1066, 1233; np. wera[s], 1047; dp. werum, 101, 1367. [Cf. Lat. *vir*.]

węrian, *see* bi-, gewęrian.

wērig, adj., *weary, exhausted; sad, sorrowful, dejected; miserable, wretched*: nsm. 802; nsn. 987; dsm. wērgum, 1207; asm. wk. wērgan, 16; npm. wērge, 1507; dpm. wērgum, 151; wērgum, 264; ipf. wērgum, 992. *See* fērðwērig.

wērig, adj., *accursed, damned*: gs. wērges, 1564; npm. wērgan, 363; npn. wērge, 956 (?), 1535.

werðēod, f., *nation*: np. werþēode, 600; gp. werþēoda, 714.

wesan, anv. intrans., *be; exist, dwell*: 1 sg. eam, 167, 206; bēom, 1490; 2 sg. eart, 2, 58, 239, 328, 403, 407; bist, 57, 404; 3 sg. is, 11, 13, 66, 89, 97, 98, 99, 133, 134, 152, 185, 188, 192, 245, 255, 326, 357, 365, 373, 416, 430, 547, 574, 583, 600, 696, 750, 751, 782, 847, 850, 853, 897, 1079, 1237, 1242, 1268, 1272, 1489, 1540, 1627, 1639, 1649, 1650, 1652; bið, 479, 596, 667, 770, 811, 824, 825, 833, 840, 892, 910, 918, 943, 960, 988, 997, 1042, 1049, 1053, 1077, 1083, 1204, 1232, 1234, 1247, 1259, 1262, 1284, 1292, 1363, 1370, 1527, 1539, 1561, 1575, 1603, 1615; biþ, 804, 838, 1039, 1566, 1626, 1637; 1 pl. sind, 362; 3 pl. sindon, 1049; sindan,

694; sind, 561, 1059, 1180; bēoð, 795, 894, 1019, 1076, 1088, 1221, 1281; pret. 1 sg. wæs, 1446, 1495, 1496; 2 sg. wǣre, 111, 131, 216, 236, 349, 355; 3 sg. wæs, 34, 35, 37, 41, 121, 124, 140, 142, 224, 228, 307, 308, 421, 499, 527, 529, 537, 538, 550, [619], 651, 720, 723, 724, 726, 728, 730, 736, 738, 805, 814, 856, 1093, 1114, 1151, 1345, 1419, 1445, 1459, 1491, 1521; pret. 3 pl. wǣron, 449, 460; opt. 2 sg. sīe, 4, 180, 280, 284; 3 sg. sīe, 230, 410, 414, 1552; sī, 777; sȳ, 1322; 3 pl. s[īe]n, 1580; opt. pret. 1 sg. wǣre, 1430; 3 sg. wǣre, 304, 451, 1301; 3 pl. wǣren, 692; inf. 583, 1032, 1468, 1554; bēon, 213;

negative, 3 sg. nis, 94, 219, 241, 1015, 1660; pret. 3 sg. næs, 351, 1428; 3 pl. nǣron, 1130. *See* efenwesende.

westan, adv., *from the west*: 885.

weðe, adj., *mild, benign, friendly*: asm. weðne, 915.

wīc, mfn., *abiding place, dwelling*: as. 1534.

wīd, adj., *ample, broad, spacious* (ealne **wīdan feorh, tō wīdan fēore, tō wīdan ealdre** = *ever, for ever*): ds. wk. wīdan, 230, 277, 1343, 1514, 1543; asm. wīdne, 931, 957; wk. wīdan, 439.

wīde, adv., *widely, extensively, far and wide*: 185, 258, 394, 407, 810, 965, 1043.

wīdeferh, adv., *for ever; during life*: 163, 583; wīdefeorh, 784. *See* feorh.

wīdgiel, adj., *far-reaching*: npm. wīdgielle, 681.

wīdl, *see* woruldwīdl.

wīdlǫnd, n., *spacious land; spacious earth*: as. 605; gp. wīdlǫnda, 1384.

wīdmǣre, adj., *far-famed*: nsm. 975.

wīdweg, m., *distant region*: ap. wīdwegas, 482.

wīf, n., *woman*: gs. wīfes, 40; gp. wīfa, 71; dp. wīfum, 101.

wīg, n., *battle, war*: gs. wīges, 673; ds. wīge, 564.

wiga, m., *warrior*: ns. 984.

wīgend, m., *warrior*: gp. wīgendra, 409.

wiht, fn., *creature; thing, anything;* inst. as av. *at all*: ns. 1053; as. [w]iht, 419; is. wihte, 1048, 1556; wi[*h*]t[*e*], 1092, 1213; gp. wihta, 981. *See* al-, ōwiht.

wilcuma, m., *welcome guest*: as. wilcuman, 554.

‡ wildæg, m., *joyful day*: ds. wildæge, 459.

wilgiefa, m., *king*: as. wilgifan, 537.

will, *see* gewill.

willa, m., *will; purpose, determination; wish, desire; joy, delight, pleasure;* (willum = *joyfully, willingly;* sylfes willum = *of one's own accord*): ns. 631, 1263; ds. willan, 1404, 1581; as. willan, 377, 1236, 1261; dp. willum, 915; ip. willum, 1343, 1350, 1483, 1492, 1519. *See* unwillum.

willan, anv., intrans., *will, be willing, wish, desire; will, shall*: 1 sg. wille, 815; 3 sg. wille, 803, 817, 1317; wile, 319, 514, 523, 571, 577, 941, 1073, 1099, 1578, 1615; 1 pl. willað, 517; 3 pl. willað, 49; pret. 1 sg. wolde, 1425; 3 sg. wolde, 129, 143, 631, 1166, 1202; 3 pl. woldan, 1106; opt. 2 sg. wille, 274; pret. 2 sg. wolde, 1494;

negative, 3 sg. nyle, 683, 1199, 1573; nele, 1568; 3 pl. nellað, 1599; pret. 2 sg. noldes, 1392; 3 pl. noldan, 642.

wilnian, W2. trans. (w. gen.), *beseech*: inf. 773.

wilsīð, m., *success; joyous journey* (or *longed-for journey* ?): gs. wilsīþes, 21; as. 26.

wind, m., *wind*: np. windas, 949.

windan, 3. intrans., *roll, heave*: ptc.

dsn. windendum, 981. *See* biwindan.

windig, adj., *windy*: npm. windge, 855.

winnan, 3. trans. and intrans., *fight, strive; bear, endure*: pret. 1 sg. wǫnn, 1427; 3 pl. wunnon, 1526; ptc. npm. winnende, 1271. *See* ge-, oferwinnan.

winster, adj., *left* (*hand*): asf. wk. winstran, 1227; wynstran, 1363.

wīs, adj., *wise, prudent*: asm. wīsne, 921; asf. wīse, 664; asn. 1192. *See* ryhtwīs.

wīsdōm, m., *wisdom*: as. 1551.

wīse, f., *condition, state of things, matter; hint, intimation; commandment*: as. wīsan, 229, 316; gp. wīsna, 43. *See* mǫnwīse.

wīsfæst, adj., *wise*: nsm. 306; npm. wīsfæste, 64.

wist, *see* ætwist.

wit, *see* gewit.

witan, PP. trans., *know, be conscious of, feel, experience;* (þǫne witan = *be thankful*): 3 pl. witon, 1243; pret. 2 sg. wisses, 1385, 1473; opt. 2 sg. wite, 442; 3 pl. wiston, 1304; inf. 384; negative, pret. 2 sg. nysses, 1384, 1498.

wītan, *see* gewītan.

wīte, n., *punishment, penalty; torment*: gs. wītes, 264, 625, 921; ds. wīte, 1249, 1269, 1292, 1622; as. 595, 1207, 1451, 1514; gp. wīta, 804, 1547. *See* woruldwīte.

wītedōm, m., *prophecy*: ns. 212.

wītehūs, n., *house of torment*: as. 1535.

‡ wīteðeow, m., *slave, convict*: dp. wīteþeowum, 151.

wītga, m., *prophet*: ns. 306, 650, 691; np. wītgan, 64, 1192; gp. wītgena, 46, 469.

witian, *see* biwitian.

wītig, adj., *wise*: nsm. 226.

witlēas, *see* gewitlēas.

wïð, prep., *with; against; from; towards; to*: w. dat. 11, 761, 766, 775, 978, 979, 980, 1060; wiþ, 567, 1526; w. acc. 368, 477, 617, 883.

wïðcrbreoca, m., *adversary*: np. wiþerbr[*eoc*]an, 564.

wïðweorpan, 3. trans., *reject*: pret. 3 pl. wiðwurpon, 3.

wlātian, W2. intrans., *gaze, look*: pret. 3 sg. wlātade, 327.

wlītan, 1. intrans., *look, gaze*: 3 pl. wlitað, 1104; pret. 3 sg. wlāt, 306. *See* ge-, ðurhwlītan.

wlite, m., *presence; appearance, aspect; beauty, splendor, glory; adornment*: ns. 906, 1037; ds. 1139; as. 848, 914, 1058, 1076, 1148, 1346, 1405, 1580, 1587. *See* mægwlite.

wlitelēas, adj., *unsightly, hideous*: nsm. 1564.

wlitescȳne, adj., *beauteous, splendid, glorious*: nsn. 493, 554; sup. nsn. wlitescȳnast, 1664.

wlïtig, adj., *glorious, radiant, bright, fair; propitious*: nsm. 911, 1464; gsm. wk. wlitigan, 21; vsf. wlitige, 378.

wolcen, nm., *cloud*: dp. wolcnum, 226, 588; ip. wolcnum, 527.

wọm, mn., *defilement, spot, stain, blemish; sin, evil, crime*: as. 1006, 1097, 1311, 1321, 1543; gs. wọmmes, 54; gp. wọmma, 179, 188, 1451, 1464; ip. wọmmum, 1561. *See* mānwọm.

wōma, *see* heofonwōma.

wọmful, adj., *depraved, corrupt*: gpm. wọmfulra, 1534.

wọmsceaða, m., *sinner, evil-doer*: np. wọmsceaðan, 1225, 1569.

wọmwyrcende, ptc., *working iniquity*: npm. 1092.

wọn, adj., *wan, ghastly; dark, dusky; lurid*: nsm. 1564; ns. 965; ipm. wọnnum, 1423.

‡ wọn, adj. (w. gen.), *without, void of*: npm. wọne, 270.

wọng, m., *field, plain*: np. wọngas, 810; gp. wọnga, 680. *See* brȳten-, fold-, neorxnawọng.

wọngstede, m., *place, spot*: ds. 802.

wọnhāl, adj., *languishing, ailing*: npm. wọnhāle, 1507.

wọnhȳdig, adj., *thoughtless, rash, foolish*: nsm..1556.

wọnian, W2. trans., *blast, blight, wither, shrivel*: 3 pl. wọniað, 951.

wōp, m., *weeping, lamenting*: ns. 998; gs. wōpes, 537; is. wōpe, 151.

word, n., *word; bidding, command, commandment*: ds. worde, 1393; as. 120, 316, 474, 714, 1392, 1510, 1629; is. worde, 1626; gp. worda, 1037, 1367, 1582; word[a], 169; ap. 22, 179, 401, 459, 469, 798, 823; ip. wordum, 64, 342, 429, 509, 917, 1236, 1363, 1374. *See* tornword.

wordcwide, m., *discourse, literary presentation of a subject*: as. 673.

wordgerȳne, n., *parable*: ip. wordgerȳnum, 463.

wordlaðu, f., *eloquence, persuasiveness*: as. wordlaþe, 664.

world, *see* woruld.

worn, m., *great number, multitude*: as. 169; ip. wornum, 957.

woruld, f., *world; mankind; age(s)*; tō worulde (twice), þurh woruld worulda = *for ever*: ns. 1583; gs. worulde, 217, 1191, 1388; ds. worulde, 101, 598, 650, 799, 818, 1022, 1053, 1197, 1423, 1495; worlde, 8, 40; as. 469, 718, 778, 810, 855, 951, 975, 1409; world, 659; gp. worulda, 778; dp. woruldum, 1345. *See* ærworuld.

‡ woruldcund, adj., *earthly, on earth*: nsm. 212; gpm. worl[d]cundra, 285.

woruldmọn, m., *man, human being*: gp. woruldmọnna, 1015.

woruldrīce, n., *world*: ds. 1500.

‡ woruldðearfende, ptc., *poor (in earthly things)*: apm. 1350.

‡ woruldwïdl, mn., *earthly corruption*: gs. woruldwīdles, 1006.

‡ **woruldwīte**, n., *martyrdom* : as. 1477.

wōðbora, m., *prophet* : ns. 302.

‡ **wōðsǫng**, f., *prediction* : ns. 46.

wræc, fn., *exile ; misery* : as. 1271, 1514.

wræclīc, adj., *wonderful, marvelous* : nsf. 416.

wræcmæcg, m., *exile, outcast* : ap. wræcmæcgas, 363.

wracu, f., *punishment, penalty* : ds. wrace, 1601, 1606 ; as. wræce, 593, 622. *See* synwracu.

wrǣtlīc, adj., *wondrous, strange* : ipn. wrǣtlīcum, 509.

wrāð, adj., *horrible ; enemy, foe* (16, 185) ; *adversary, fiend* (595, 1534) : gpn. wrāþra, 804, 1534 ; dpm. wrāþum, 16, 185, 595 ; apf. wrāþe, 1312 ; pm. wrāþum, 1547.

wrāðlīc, adj., *dire, grievous, horrible* : asn. wrāþlīc, 831.

wrecan, *see* ā-, bi-, tōwrecan.

wrecca, m., *wretch* : dp. wreccan, 264.

wreccan, *see* scyldwreccende.

wrēon, *see* onwrēon.

writ, *see* gewrit.

wrītan, 1. trans., *write* : inf. 673.

wrīðan, *see* biwrīðan.

wrixl, f., *innovation, novelty* : ns. 416.

wrixlan, *see* gewrixlan.

‡ **wrōhtbora**, m., *author of evil* : ns. 763.

wudu, *see* flōd-, sundwudu.

wuldor, n., *glory ; heaven* : ns. 598, 778 ; gs. wuldres, 8, 71, 83 ; 158, 160, 409, 463, 493, 527, 565, 740, 1197, 1202, 1587, 1664 ; ds. wuldre, 30, 57, 110, 347, 551, 718, 1243 ; as. 508, 595 ; is. wuldre, 1334 ; dp. wuldrum, 54.

wuldorcyning, m., *king of glory, Lord* : ns. 1022 ; as. 161.

wuldorfæder, m., *glorious father* : as. 217.

wuldorlēan, n., *glorious reward* : ns. 1079.

wuldorlīc, adj., *glorious, resplendent* : nsm. 1010.

‡ **wuldorweorud**, n., *heavenly host, host of glory* : gs. wuldorweorudes, 285.

wuldrian, W2. trans., *glorify, praise, magnify* : 3 pl. wuldriað, 401. *See* gewuldrian.

wulf, m., *wolf* : 256.

wund, f., *wound* : ns. 770 ; gs. wunde, 1321 ; as. wunde, 1458 ; ap. wunde, 763, 1107, 1207, 1313. *See* synwund.

wundor, n., *wonder, marvel ;* (ip. **wundrum** = *wondrously, in a wonderful way*) : ns. 1015 ; gp. wundra, 988 ; ip. wundrum, 908, 1185. *See* mægen-, ðēodwundor.

wundorblēo, n., *wondrous color* : ip. wundorblēom, 1139.

‡ **wundorclǫm**, n., *wonderful band* : ip. wundorclǫmmum, 310.

wundorlīc, adj., *wondrous* : nsf. 905.

wundrian, W2. trans., *wonder at, marvel at, be astonished at* : opt. 3 pl. wundrien, 8.

‡ **wundrung**, f., *astonishment, amazement* : ns. 89.

wunian, W2. intrans., *dwell, remain, abide ; continue, endure* : 1 sg. wunige, 478, 488 ; 2 sg. wunast, 163 ; 3 sg. wunað, 405, 439, 590 ; 3 pl. wuniað, 598 ; pret. 3 sg. wunade, 83 ; opt. 3 sg. wunige, 1332 ; inf. 103, 622, 818, 1464 ; wunigan, 347.

wynlīc, adj., *winsome* : asm. wynlīcne, 1387.

wynlīce, adv., *winsomely* : 1345.

wynn, f., *joy, gladness, delight* : ds. wynne, 437, 1244, 1481 ; as. wynne, 1296 ; vs. 71 ; ip. wynnum, 740. *See* līfwynn.

wynster, *see* winster.

wynsum, adj., *blissful* : nsm. 1252.

‡ **wynsumlīc**, adj., *pleasant, gracious, winsome* : nsm. 911.

wyrcan, W1. trans., *do ; make, create ;* (**blōdgyte wyrcan** = *shed blood*) : pret. 2 sg. worhtes, 240 ; 3 pl. worhtan, 708 ; worhtun, 1053. *See* for-, gewyrcan; scyld-, syn-, wǫmwyrcende.

wyrd, f., *event, occurrence*: gs. wyrde, 81. *See* forwyrd.

wyrgan, *see* āwyrged.

wyrhta, m., *workman, builder*: np. wyrhtan, 2.

wyrm, m., *serpent; worm*: gp. wyrma, 1250; ip. wyrmum, 625, 1547.

wyrnan, *see* forwyrnan.

wyrp, m., *casting, hurling*: ip. wyrpum, 565. [weorpan.]

wyrpe, m., *transformation*: ds. 67.

wyrs, *see* yfel.

wyrðe, adj., *worthy, deserving*: nsn. 600; apm. 30. *See* unwyrðe.

Y.

ȳcan, *see* geȳcan; īecan.

yfel, n., *harm, mischief; misery, suffering, punishment; sin, wickedness*: ns. 1332; gs. yfles, 874; as. 1253, 1309.

yfel, adj., *evil, wicked; sore*; comp. wyrsa = *left* (*hand*): dpm. yflum, 918, 1362, 1576; apn. 1452; comp. asm. wk. wyrsan, 1225.

yfle, adv., *evilly, wrongly, wickedly*: 1397.

yld, f., (*old*) *age*: ds. ylde, 1653.

ymb, prep., *round, about; on* (*every side*); *of, about*: w. acc. 61, 397, 507, 1125, 1194, 1444. [Cf. Ger. *um*.] *See also* ðæs, conj.

ymbūtan, adv., *round about*: 928.

ymbūtan, prep., *round, about*: w. acc. 1011.

yrmen, adj., *wide, spacious*: asm. yrmenne, 481.

yrmðu, f., *misery, distress, suffering, wretchedness*: ns. 1292; as. 614; yrmþu, 1429; ermþu, 271; gp. yrmþa, 1268; ap. yrmþa, 370; ip. yrmþum, 621. [earm.]

yrre, adj., *angry, wrathful*: nsm. 1528; asm. yrne, 620.

yrringa, adv., *wrathfully; fiercely, furiously*: 1146, 1372.

ȳtemest, adj., *uttermost*: dpm. ȳtemestum, 879.

ȳð, f., *wave, flood*: as. ȳðe, 1167; np. ȳða, 854. [Cf. Lat. *unda*.]

ȳðast, *see* ēaðe, adv.

ȳðmearh, m., *ocean-steed, ship*: ap. ȳðmēaras, 863.

ȳðre, *see* ēaðe, adj.

ȳwan, W1. trans., *show, reveal, disclose*: imp. sg. ȳwe, 245; inf. ȳ[w]an, 1375. *See* ætȳwan; ēawan, ēowan; oðēawan, -ēowan, -ȳwan.

APPENDIX I.

Bibliography of some more recent Works dealing with the *Christ*.

Abbetmeyer, C. *Old English Poetical Motives derived from the Doctrine of Sin.* New York, 1903.

Barnouw, A. J. *Textkritische Untersuchung nach dem Gebrauch des Bestimmten Artikels und des Schwachen Adjektivs in der Altenglischen Poesie.* Leiden, 1902.

Binz, G. *Untersuchungen zum Altenglischen Sogenannten Christ: Festschrift zur 49ten Versammlung Deutscher Philologen und Schulmänner* (Basel, 1907), pp. 181–197.

Brown, C. F. 'Cynewulf and Alcuin.' *Publ. Mod. Lang. Ass.* 18. 308–334.

Brown, C. F. 'The Autobiographical Element in the Cynewulfian Rune Passages.' *Engl. Stud.* 2. 196–233.

Holthausen, F. Review of this book, in *Literaturbl. für Germ. und Rom. Philol.* 21. 369–373.

Jansen, Karl. 'Die Cynewulf-Forschung von ihren Anfängen bis zur Gegenwart.' *Bonner Beiträge* 24. 1908.

Leiding, H. *Die Sprache der Cynewulfischen Dichtungen Crist, Juliana, und Elene.* Göttingen, 1887.

Sarrazın, G. 'Zur Chronologie und Verfasserfrage Altenglischer Dichtungen.' *Engl. Stud.* 38. 145–195.

Schwarz, F. *Cynewulf's Anteil am Crist: Eine Metrische Untersuchung.* Königsberg, 1905.

Simons, Richard. 'Cynewulf's Wortschatz.' *Bonner Beiträge* 3. 1899.

Trautmann, M. 'Berichtigungen, Erklärungen, und Vermutungen zu Cynewulf's Werken,' *Bonner Beiträge* 23. 85–139.

APPENDIX II.

Addenda and Corrigenda.

[The citations refer to pages of the Introduction and Glossary, and to lines in the Notes and Text.]

INTRODUCTION.

P. xxii. Add to the list of passages containing the motive of the Harrowing of Hell: *El.* 295–7 (?), 905–913; *Sat.* 379–521; *Rood* 148–152; *Credo* 30–32; *Pa.* 58–64 (?); *Ph.* 417–423; *Hy.* 10⁸⁰⁻⁸².

P. xxiii. To the list of instances at the foot of the page add: (*g*) 162ª : 621ª : 1380ª.

P. xxiv. I : III. Add: (*p*) 277 : 893.

295

P. xxv. II : III. Add: (*gg*) 491 : 873, 899; (*hh*) 786, 823 : 1190, 1397.

P. xlvii. *I*-umlaut of *a*. Cf. *fareð* (871) and *færeð* (930, 983).

P. xlvii. With *swǣr, swār*, cf. *fēre* (III), for *fǣre;* but *fǣrscyte* (II), *fǣrsearo* (II).

P. lxix. The views about the date of the *Elene* have been shown to be untenible by Professor Carleton F. Brown.

NOTES AND TEXT.

P. 71. For a discussion of 'the great O's,' with a bibliography of the subject, see Everard Green, *On the Words 'O Sapientia' in the Kalendar (Archæologia* 49. 219-242).

11ᵇ–14ᵇ. Cf. Henry Vaughan, *Burial,* first two stanzas.

50–70. See Eusebius, *Eccl. Hist.*, Bk. 10, ch. 4.

71–103. *Nec .. sequentem.* So in Sedulius, *Carm. Pasch.* 2. 68 (Migne 19. 600), and note.

72. Grammar requires *tōweardre;* see 137.

88, 176, etc. **Marīa.** Holthausen (*Literaturbl.* 21. 371) emends to *Māria.*

104. The conclusion of Donne's epitaph in St. Paul's is : 'Hic, licet in occiduo cinere, aspicit eum cujus nomen est Oriens.'

137. Grammar requires *tōweardne.*

168–174. Cf. Hemingway, *M. L. N.* 22. 623, for a different division of this dialogue.

261. MS. has *usse.*

320. Cf. Jerome, *Adv. Pelag.* 2. 4 (Migne 23. 538); Rab. Maur. *Comm. in Ezech.* 17. 44 (Migne 110. 1001–3); *Exp. in Apoc.* (Migne 17. 948).

485–6. On the source of the lines see Cook, *M. L. N.* 15. 506–7. Strunk (*M. L. N.* 17. 371 ff.) would emend *hweorfað* to *hǣðnum.*

523–4. Cf. *Dream of the Rood* 103–109.

558–585. For other references to the Harrowing of Hell in OE. poetry, see addendum to p. xxii. Cf. also *Martyr.*, p. 50; Wulfstan 23. 8–13, 145. 2; *Ben. Off.* (Feiler), pp. 56–7.

559. Read *hī*[o].

590. **þendan.** Cf. (II) 597, 772, 800, 814, 817; (III) 1325, 1574, 1579, 1583; the reference being always to the duration of life on earth, often with the notion of contrast with the enduring life of heaven.

591 ff. Cf. Wulfstan 136. 5 ff.

592. **lēohte lēoht.** Cf. *Ph.* 661: 'þæt lēohte līf.' But see Barnouw, p. 129. Strunk (*M. L. N.* 17. 371 ff.) proposes *þæt lēofe lēoht.*

593. **þȳstra.** Cf. Rab. Maur., *De Univers.* 10. 8 (Migne 111. 295).

595. Cf. *Soul and Body* 7ᵃ : 'swā wīte swā wuldor.'

701ᵇ–704. [Add to note:] But see *Anc. Laws*, p. 441; Ælfric *L. S.* 1. 350.

720. For the interpretation of Cant. 2. 8 see especially Ambrose, *Comm. in Cant.* ch. 2 (Migne 15. 1879). Cf. also Rab. Maur., *De Univers.* 1. 1 (Migne 111. 18).

768. **āttres ord.** For a proposed change in the reading see Hart, *M. L. N.* 17. 463; but cf. Ælfric, *Hom.* 2. 336.

842. Cf. Wulfstan 113. 14; 118. 9; 187. 5, 6; 209. 10.

875. Cf. Rev. 14. 1.

884. singaŏ. Cf. Wulfstan 183. 10.

900. [Add to note:] ˙ See also Gregory, *Hom. in Ezech.* 2. 8 (Migne 76. 1035).

907–926. Miss Mary W. Smyth calls my attention to a probable common source for this passage and Hampole, *Pr. Consc.* 5235–40 in Gregory the Great, 907–9 being related to *Moral.* 32 (on Job 40. 6: Migne, *Patr. Lat.* 76. 640), and 910–926 to *Hom. in Ezech.* 1. 22 (Migne 76. 850). She would then refer the *duct* of 921 to the statement in 918–920, which will thus be a warning to the good.

The twofold character, of mildness and sternness, is also noted in *Eng. Metr. Hom.* (ed. Small, p. 19, ll. 26 ff.) and is predicated of the Judgment Day, according to Miss Smyth, in *O.E. Misc.* 80. 261–4; *Engl. Stud.* 7. 341. 1095–8; of bishops, *Piers Plowman* C. 10. 15–16; and of Roland, *Das Altfr. Rolandslied*, ed. Stengel, 1163–4.

921. Holthausen (*Literaturbl.* 21. 372) would emend *wites* to *wilges.*

967–8ª. Cf. Wulfstan 183. 4, 5.

1007. Cf. Exod. 19. 16; 20. 18; 24. 16, 17; Heb. 12. 18 ff.

1090 ff. Cf. Marlowe, *Doctor Faustus:* 'See, see where Christ's blood streams in the firmament!'

1104. Read *synwyrcend*[e].

1170 ff. One might begin a new sentence with 1170b, and place comma after 1173b, beginning the next word with a small letter.

1170ª. For a similar combination of positive and negative statement cf. Mt. 13. 34; Mk. 4. 33, 34.

1239. Holthausen (*Literaturbl.* 21. 372), for metrical reasons, reads *burggesetu.*

1243. Krapp (*Mod. Phil.* 2. 407) regards *in wuldre* as parallel to *on heofonrīce*, 1245.

1326. Insert in the variant : *MS., Edd.* sawle.

1346. beorht. Does not agree with its noun ; *beorhtne čŏles wlite* would be metrically impossible.

1363. Insert in variants : *MS., Edd.* biŏ.

1391ª. Read *beorhtes blǣdwelan* (?), or *beorhtes boldwelan* (?).

1414–1420. Cf. *Sat.* 489 ff.

1487. Holthausen (*Literaturbl.* 21. 372) reads *hēnŏa* instead of *honda.*

1546. egsan. Holthausen (*Literaturbl.* 21. 372) suggests *eglan.*

1562. Holthausen (*Literaturbl.* 21. 372) would read *fēres* in place of *fȳres.*

1655. Cf. Rev. 14. 13; Heb. 4. 9.

GLOSSARY.

P. 228. **ǣghwæs,** adv., *in every respect:* 1420.

P. 254. Under **geweorc** insert : n., *handiwork:* ns. 112.

P. 267. Dele **mǣrsian,** *see* **gemǣrsian.**

P. 269. The **mōtan** of 246 is opt. ◦

P. 270. The **of** of 889 seems to govern the inst.

P. 284. Under **ŏæt,** conj., in object clauses, dele 246.

P. 290. Dele biŏ, 1363, and insert 3 pl. b[ēo]ŏ, 1363.

P. 293. Under **wuldor,** change 598 from ns. to as.

CPSIA information can be obtained
at www.ICGtesting.com
Printed in the USA
LVHW090151270621
691255LV00003B/136